SATURN

MARY

SOPHIA

# Saturn Mary Sophia

## Star Wisdom, Volume 2

### 2020

EDITOR
JOEL MATTHEW PARK

ADVISORY BOARD

Brian Gray ~ Claudia McLaren Lainson ~ Robert Powell, PhD
Lacquanna Paul ~ Robert Schiappacasse

Lindisfarne Books

Lindisfarne Books
an imprint of Steinerbooks/Anthroposophic Press, Inc.
402 Union Street, No. 58, Hudson, NY 12534
www.steinerbooks.org



With grateful acknowledgment to Peter Treadgold (1943–2005), who wrote the Astrofire program (available from the Sophia Foundation), with which the ephemeris pages in *Star Wisdom* are computed each year.

Disclaimer: The views expressed in the articles published in *Star Wisdom* are the sole responsibility of the authors of these articles and do not necessarily reflect those of the editorial board of *Star Wisdom*.

Design: Jens Jensen

ISBN: 978-1-58420-917-1 (Paperback)

ISBN: 978-1-58420-918-8 (eBook)

Printed in the United States of America

# CONTENTS

# ASTROSOPHY

The Sophia Foundation was founded and exists to help usher in the new Age of Sophia and the corresponding Sophianic culture, the Rose of the World, prophesied by Daniel Andreev and other spiritual teachers. Part of the work of the Sophia Foundation is the cultivation of a new star wisdom, *Astro-Sophia* (Astrosophy), now arising in our time in response to the descent of Sophia, who is the bearer of Divine Wisdom, just as Christ (the Logos, or the Lamb) is the bearer of Divine Love. Like the star wisdom of antiquity, astrosophy is sidereal, which means "of the stars." Astrosophy, inspired by Divine Sophia, descending from stellar heights, directs our consciousness toward the glory and majesty of the starry heavens, to encompass the entire celestial sphere of our cosmos and, beyond this, to the galactic realm—the realm that Daniel Andreev referred to as "the heights of our universe"—from which Sophia is descending on her path of approach into our cosmos. Sophia draws our attention not only to the star mysteries of the heights, but also to the cosmic mysteries connected with Christ's deeds of redemption wrought two thousand years ago. To penetrate these mysteries is the purpose of the annual volumes of *Star Wisdom*.

**Statue of Christ with the Milky Way**

*at La Cumbre, the peak of the high pass over the Andes, near La Paz, Bolivia*
*(photo © by James Brunker, Magical Andes Photography)*

# PREFACE

## *Robert Powell, PhD*

This is the second volume of the annual *Star Wisdom* (formerly *Journal for Star Wisdom*), intended to help all people interested in the new star wisdom of astrosophy and in the cosmic dimension of Christianity, which began with the star of the magi. The calendar comprises an ephemeris page for each month of the year, computed with the help of Peter Treadgold's *Astrofire* computer program, with a monthly commentary by Joel Park. The monthly commentary relates the geocentric and heliocentric planetary movements to events in the life of Jesus Christ.

Jesus Christ united the levels of the earthly personality (geocentric = Earth-centered) and the higher self (heliocentric = Sun-centered) insofar as he was the most highly evolved earthly personality (Jesus) embodying the higher self (Christ) of all existence, the Divine "I AM." To see the life of Jesus Christ in relation to the world of stars opens the door to a profound experience of the cosmos, giving rise to a new star wisdom (astrosophy) that is the Spiritual Science of Cosmic Christianity.

*Star Wisdom* is scientific, resting on a solid mathematical-astronomical foundation and also upon a secure chronology of the life of Jesus Christ, and at the same time it is spiritual, aspiring to the higher dimension of existence that is expressed outwardly in the world of stars. The scientific and the spiritual come together in the sidereal zodiac that originated with the Babylonians and was used by the three magi who beheld the star of Bethlehem and came to pay homage to Jesus a few months after his birth. In continuity of spirit with the origins of Cosmic Christianity with the three magi, the sidereal zodiac is the frame of reference used for the computation of the geocentric and heliocentric planetary movements that are commented upon in the light of the life of Jesus Christ in *Star Wisdom*.

Thus, all zodiacal longitudes indicated in the text and presented in the following calendar are in terms of the sidereal zodiac, which has to be distinguished from the tropical zodiac in widespread use in contemporary astrology in the West. The tropical zodiac was introduced into astrology in the middle of the second century AD by the Greek astronomer Claudius Ptolemy. Prior to this the sidereal zodiac was in use. Such was the influence of Ptolemy upon the Western astrological tradition that the tropical zodiac replaced the sidereal zodiac used by the Babylonians, Egyptians, and early Greek astrologers. Yet the astrological tradition in India was not influenced by Ptolemy, and so the sidereal zodiac is still used to this day by Hindu astrologers.

The sidereal zodiac originated with the Babylonians in the sixth to fifth centuries BC and was defined by them in relation to certain bright stars. For example, Aldebaran ("the Bull's Eye") is located in the middle of the sidereal sign–constellation of the Bull at 15° Taurus, and Antares ("the Scorpion's heart") is in the middle of the sidereal sign–constellation of the Scorpion at 15° Scorpio. The sidereal signs, each 30° long, coincide closely with the twelve astronomical zodiacal constellations of the same name, whereas the signs of the tropical zodiac, since they are defined in relation to the vernal point, now have little or no relationship to the corresponding zodiacal constellations. This is because the vernal point, the zodiacal location of the Sun on March 20–21, shifts slowly backward through the sidereal zodiac at a rate of 1° in seventy-two years ("the precession of the equinoxes"). When Ptolemy introduced the tropical zodiac into astrology, there was an almost exact coincidence between the tropical and the sidereal zodiac, as the vernal point, which is defined to be 0° Aries in the tropical zodiac, was at 1° Aries in the sidereal zodiac in the middle of the second century AD. Thus, there was only 1° difference between the two zodiacs. So, it made hardly any difference to Ptolemy or his contemporaries to use the tropical zodiac instead of the sidereal zodiac. But now—the vernal point, on account of precession, having shifted back from 1° Aries to 5° Pisces—there is a 25° difference and so there is virtually no correspondence between the two. Without going into further detail concerning the complex issue of the zodiac, as shown in the *Hermetic Astrology* trilogy, the sidereal zodiac is the zodiac used by the three magi, who were the last representatives of the true star wisdom of antiquity. For this reason the sidereal zodiac is used throughout *Star Wisdom.*

Readers interested in exploring the scientific (astronomical and chronological) foundations of Cosmic Christianity are referred to the works listed below under "Literature." The *Chronicle of the Living Christ: Foundations of Cosmic Christianity,* listed on the next page, is an indispensable source of reference (abbreviated *Chron.*) for *Star Wisdom.* The chronology of the life of Jesus Christ rests upon Robert Powell's research based on the description of Christ's daily life by Anne Catherine Emmerich in her three-volume work *The Visions of Anne Catherine Emmerich* (abbreviated *ACE*). Further details concerning *Star Wisdom* and how to work with it on a daily basis may be found in the general introduction to the *Christian Star Calendar.* The general introduction explains all the features of *Star Wisdom.* The new edition, published in 2003, includes sections on the megastars (stars of great luminosity) and on the 36 decans (10° subdivisions of the twelve signs of the zodiac) in relation to their planetary rulers and to the extra-zodiacal constellations, those constellations above or below the circle of the twelve constellations-signs of the zodiac. Further material on the decans,

including examples of historical personalities born in the various decans, and also a wealth of other material on the signs of the sidereal zodiac, is to be found in *Cosmic Dances of the Zodiac,* listed below. Also foundational is *History of the Zodiac,* published by Sophia Academic Press, listed below under "Works by Robert Powell."

## LITERATURE

*(See also "References" section)*

*General Introduction to the Christian Star Calendar: A Key to Understanding,* 2nd ed. Palo Alto, CA: Sophia Foundation, 2003.

Bento, William, Robert Schiappacasse, and David Tresemer, *Signs in the Heavens: A Message for our Time.* Boulder: StarHouse, 2000.

Emmerich, Anne Catherine, *The Visions of Anne Catherine Emmerich* (new edition, with material by Robert Powell). Kettering, OH: Angelico Press, 2015.

Paul, Lacquanna, and Robert Powell, *Cosmic Dances of the Planets.* San Rafael, CA: Sophia Foundation Press, 2007.

———, *Cosmic Dances of the Zodiac.* San Rafael, CA: Sophia Foundation Press, 2007.

Smith, Edward, *The Burning Bush: Rudolf Steiner, Anthroposophy, and the Holy Scriptures* (2nd ed.). Grt. Barrington, MA: SteinerBooks, 2001.

Steiner, Rudolf, *Astronomy and Astrology: Finding a Relationship to the Cosmos.* London: Rudolf Steiner Press, 2009.

Sucher, Willi, *Cosmic Christianity and the Changing Countenance of Cosmology.* Grt. Barrington, MA: SteinerBooks, 1993. *Isis Sophia* and other works by Willi Sucher are available from the Astrosophy Research Center, PO Box 13, Meadow Vista, CA 95722.

Tidball, Charles S., and Robert Powell, *Jesus, Lazarus, and the Messiah: Unveiling Three Christian Mysteries.* Grt. Barrington, MA: SteinerBooks, 2005. This book offers a penetrating study of the Christ mysteries against the background of *Chronicle of the Living Christ* and contains two chapters by Robert Powell on the Apostle John and John the Evangelist (Lazarus).

Tresemer, David (with Robert Schiappacasse), *Star Wisdom and Rudolf Steiner: A Life Seen Through the Oracle of the Solar Cross.* Grt. Barrington, MA: SteinerBooks, 2007.

## Astrosophical Works by Robert Powell, PhD

*Starcrafts (formerly Astro Communication Services, or ACS):*

*History of the Houses* (1997)
*History of the Planets* (1989)
*The Zodiac: A Historical Survey* (1984)
www.acspublications.com
www.astrocom.com
Business Address:
Starcrafts Publishing
334 Calef Hwy.
Epping, NH 03042
Phone: 603-734-4300
Fax: 603-734-4311
Contact maria@starcraftseast.com

### *SteinerBooks:*

Orders: (703) 661-1594; www.steinerbooks.org
PO Box 960, Herndon, VA 20172

*The Astrological Revolution: Unveiling the Science of the Stars as a Science of Reincarnation and Karma*, coauthor Kevin Dann (Grt. Barrington, MA: SteinerBooks, 2010). After reestablishing the sidereal zodiac as a basis for astrology that penetrates the mystery of the stars' relationship to human destiny, the reader is invited to discover the astrological significance of the totality of the vast sphere of stars surrounding the Earth. This book points to the astrological significance of the entire celestial sphere, including all the stars and constellations beyond the twelve zodiacal signs. This discovery is revealed by the study of megastars, illustrating how they show up in an extraordinary way in Christ's healing miracles by aligning with the Sun at the time of those events. This book offers a spiritual, yet scientific, path toward a new relationship to the stars.

*Christian Hermetic Astrology: The Star of the Magi and the Life of Christ* (Hudson, NY: Anthroposophic Press, 1998). Twenty-five discourses set in the "Temple of the Sun," where Hermes and his pupils gather to meditate on the Birth, the Miracles, and the Passion of Jesus Christ. The discourses offer a series of meditative contemplations on the deeds of Christ in relation to the mysteries of the cosmos. They are an expression of the age-old hermetic mystery wisdom of the ancient Egyptian sage, Hermes Trismegistus. This book offers a meditative approach to the cosmic correspondences between major events in the life of Christ and the heavenly configurations at that time 2,000 years ago.

*Chronicle of the Living Christ: Foundations of Cosmic Christianity* (Hudson, NY: Anthroposophic Press, 1996). An account of the life of Christ, day by day, throughout most of the 3½ years of his ministry, including the horoscopes of conception, birth, and death of Jesus, Mary, and John the Baptist, together with a wealth of material relating to a new star wisdom focused on the life of Christ. This work provides the chronological basis for *Christian Hermetic Astrology* and *Star Wisdom*.

*Elijah Come Again: A Prophet for our Time: A Scientific Approach to Reincarnation* (Grt. Barrington, MA: SteinerBooks, 2009). By way of horoscope comparisons from conception–birth–death in one incarnation to conception–birth–death in the next, this work establishes scientifically two basic astrosophical research findings. These are: the importance 1) of the sidereal zodiac and 2) of the heliocentric positions of the planets. Also, for the first time, the identity of the "saintly nun" is revealed, of whom Rudolf Steiner spoke in a conversation with Marie von Sivers about tracing Novalis's karmic background. The focus throughout the book is on the Elijah individuality in his various incarnations, and is based solidly on Rudolf Steiner's indications. It also can be read as a karmic biography by anyone who chooses to omit the astrosophical material.

*Journal for Star Wisdom* (Grt. Barrington, MA: Lindisfarne Books, 2010–2018), edited by Robert Powell and others engaged in astrosophic research. A guide to the correspondences of Christ in the stellar and etheric world. Includes articles of interest, a complete geocentric and heliocentric sidereal ephemeris, and an aspectarian. According to Rudolf Steiner, every step taken by Christ during his ministry between the baptism in the Jordan and the resurrection was in harmony with, and an expression of, the cosmos. The journal is concerned with these heavenly correspondences during the life of Christ. It is intended to help provide a foundation for Cosmic Christianity, the cosmic dimension of Christianity. It is this dimension that has been missing from Christianity in its 2,000-year history. A starting point is to contemplate the movements of the Sun, Moon, and planets against the background of the zodiacal constellations (sidereal signs) today in relation to corresponding stellar events during the life of Christ. This opens the possibility of attuning to the life of Christ in the etheric cosmos in a living way.

## *Sophia Foundation Press and Sophia Academic Press Publications*

Books available from Amazon.com
JamesWetmore@mac.com
www.logosophia.com

*History of the Zodiac* (San Rafael, CA: Sophia Academic Press, 2007). Book version of Robert Powell's PhD thesis on the *History of the Zodiac*. This penetrating study of the *History of the Zodiac* restores the sidereal zodiac to its rightful place as the original zodiac, tracing it back to fifth-century-BC Babylonians. Available in paperback and hard cover.

*Hermetic Astrology: Volume 1, Astrology and Reincarnation* (San Rafael, CA: Sophia Foundation Press, 2007). This book seeks to give the ancient science of the stars a scientific basis. This new foundation for astrology based on research into reincarnation and karma (destiny) is the primary focus. It includes numerous reincarnation examples, the study of which reveals the existence of certain astrological "laws" of reincarnation, on the basis of which it is evident that the ancient sidereal zodiac is the authentic astrological zodiac, and that the heliocentric movements of the planets are of great significance. Foundational for the new star wisdom of astrosophy.

*Hermetic Astrology: Volume 2, Astrological Biography* (San Rafael, CA: Sophia Foundation Press, 2007). Concerned with karmic relationships and the unfolding of destiny in seven-year periods through one's life. The seven-year rhythm underlies the human being's astrological biography, which can be studied in relation to the movements of the Sun, Moon, and planets around the sidereal zodiac between conception and birth. The "rule of Hermes" is used to determine the moment of conception.

*Sign of the Son of Man in the Heavens: Sophia and the New Star Wisdom* (San Rafael, CA: Sophia Foundation Press, 2008). Revised and expanded with new material, this edition deals with a new wisdom of stars in the light of Divine Sophia. It was intended as a help in our time, as we were called on to be extremely

wakeful up to the end of the Maya calendar in 2012.

*Cosmic Dances of the Zodiac* (San Rafael, CA: Sophia Foundation Press, 2007), coauthor Lacquanna Paul. Study material describing the twelve signs of the zodiac and their forms and gestures in cosmic dance, with diagrams. Includes a wealth of information on the twelve signs and the 36 decans (the subdivision of the signs into decans, or 10° sectors, corresponding to constellations above and below the zodiac).

*Cosmic Dances of the Planets* (San Rafael, CA: Sophia Foundation Press, 2007), coauthor Lacquanna Paul. Study material describing the seven classical planets and their forms and gestures in cosmic dance, with diagrams, including much information on the planets.

## *American Federation of Astrologers (AFA) Publications* (currently not in print)

www.astrologers.com

*The Sidereal Zodiac,* coauthor Peter Treadgold (Tempe, AZ: AFA, 1985). A *History of the Zodiac* (sidereal, tropical, Hindu, astronomical) and a formal definition of the sidereal zodiac with the star Aldebaran ("the Bull's Eye") at 15° Taurus. This is an abbreviated version of *History of the Zodiac.*

## *Rudolf Steiner College Press Publications*

9200 Fair Oaks Blvd., Fair Oaks, CA 95628

*The Christ Mystery: Reflections on the Second Coming* (Fair Oaks, CA: Rudolf Steiner College Press, 1999). The fruit of many years of reflecting on the Second Coming and its cosmological aspects. Looks at the approaching trial of humanity and the challenges of living in apocalyptic times, against the background of "great signs in the heavens."

## *The Sophia Foundation*

4500 19th Street, #369, Boulder, CO 80304; distributes many of the books listed here and other works by Robert Powell.
Tel: (303) 242-5388
sophia@sophiafoundation.org
www.sophiafoundation.org

Computer program for charts and ephemerides, with grateful acknowledgment to Peter Treadgold, who wrote the computer program

*Astrofire* (with research module, star catalog of over 4,000 stars, and database of birth and death charts of historical personalities), capable of printing geocentric and heliocentric–hermetic sidereal charts and ephemerides throughout history. The hermetic charts, based on the astronomical system of the Danish astronomer Tycho Brahe, are called "Tychonic" charts in the program. This program can:

- compute birth charts in a large variety of systems (tropical, sidereal, geocentric, heliocentric, hermetic);

- calculate conception charts using the hermetic rule, in turn applying it for correction of the birth time;

- produce charts for the period between conception and birth;

- print out an "astrological biography" for the whole of lifework with the geocentric, heliocentric (and even lemniscatory) planetary system;

- work with the sidereal zodiac according to the definition of your choice (Babylonian sidereal, Indian sidereal, unequal-division astronomical, etc.);

- work with planetary aspects with orbs of your choice.

The program includes eight house systems and a variety of chart formats. The program also includes an ephemeris program with a search facility. The geocentric–heliocentric sidereal ephemeris pages in the annual volumes of *Star Wisdom* are produced by the software program *Astrofire*, which is compatible with Microsoft Windows.

Those interested in obtaining the *Astrofire* program should contact:

**The Sophia Foundation**
4500 19th Street, #369
Boulder, CO 80304
Tel: (303) 242-5388
sophia@sophiafoundation.org
www.sophiafoundation.org

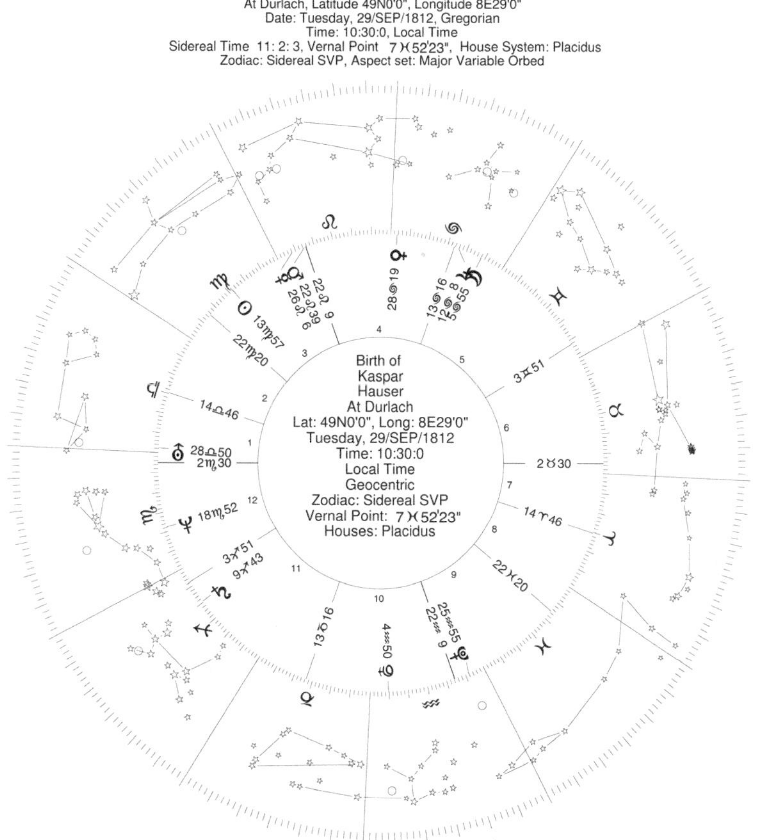


*A horoscope generated by the* Astrofire *program*

# THE SEVEN IDEALS OF THE ROSE OF THE WORLD

## Robert Powell, PhD

*In gratitude to Daniel Andreev (1906–1959), the Russian prophet of the Rose of the World as the coming world culture, inspired by Sophia—a culture based on Love and Wisdom.*

The Rose of the World is arising through the approach of Divine Sophia toward the Earth. Her approach is calling forth the following basic qualities or attributes of the new world culture that She is creating and inspiring:

1. First and foremost: interreligion. For Sophia all true religious and spiritual traditions are different layers of spiritual reality, which She seeks to weave together as petals of the Rose of the World. Sophia is not founding a new world religion as She approaches, descending from cosmic heights, and drawing ever closer to our solar system. On Her path of descent, approaching our planet to incarnate into the Earth's aura during the Age of Aquarius, She is bestowing insight concerning each religion and spiritual tradition, thus awaking interreligiosity, signifying a heartfelt interest in religious and spiritual traditions other than one's own. This signifies the blossoming and unfolding of the petals of the Rose of the World, creating brother–sisterhood between all peoples.

2. Sophia's approach toward our planet is bringing about an awaking of social conscience on a global scale, inspiring active compassion combined with unflagging practical efforts on behalf of social justice around the world.

3. Through Sophia a framework for understanding the higher dimension of historical processes is coming about: metahistory, illumining the meaning of historical processes of the past, present, and future in relation to humankind's spiritual evolution. This entails glimpses into the mystical consciousness of humanity such as may be found in the book of Revelation.

4. On the national sociopolitical level, Sophia's inspiration is working to transform the state into a community. The community of Italy, the community of France, etc., is the ideal for the future, rather than the political entity of the state representing (or misrepresenting) the people. And on the global scale Sophia is seeking to bring about the unification of the planet as a world community through bringing the different country communities into a harmonious relationship with one another on a religious, cultural, and economic level.

5. This world community, the Rose of the World, inspired by Sophia, will seek to establish the economic wellbeing of every man, woman, and child on the planet, to ensure that everyone has a roof over their heads and sufficient food to live on. Here it is a matter of ensuring a decent standard of living for all peoples of the Earth.

6. A high priority of the Rose of the World will be the ennobling of education. New methods of education are being inspired by Sophia to help bring out everyone's creative talents. To ennoble education so that each person's creativity can unfold is the goal here.

7. Finally, Sophia is working for the transformation of the planet into a garden and, moreover, for the spiritualization of Nature. Humanity and Nature are to live in cooperation and harmony, with human beings taking up their responsibility toward Nature, which is to work for the spiritualization and redemption of the kingdoms of Nature.

# EDITORIAL FOREWORD

## *Joel Matthew Park*

**W**arm greetings to you, dear reader, as we turn the page from 2019 to 2020: a year full of promise, as the articles and commentaries that lie ahead in the pages of this publication give testimony. This is the second volume of the *Star Wisdom* series, following upon last year's introductory volume, *Cosmology Reborn*. The series in general is a continuation and transformation of *Journal for Star Wisdom*, published from 2010 to 2018; the *Christian Star Calendar,* 1991 to 2009; the *Mercury Star Journal,* 1974 to 1980; and the *Monthly Star Journal,* 1965 to 1974.[1]

In the transition from *Christian Star Calendar* to *Journal for Star Wisdom* some ten years ago, the intention was to emphasize the fact that the publication was more than just astrosophical commentary and ephemerides; both the number and content of the articles indicated a striving for something more like an academic or scientific journal. The *Star Wisdom* series wishes to continue, even to broaden, the role of the publication as a vehicle for inspired articles, not just about astrosophy, but on a whole spectrum of topics relating to a variety of spiritual cosmologies. Part of the intention for removing the word "Journal" from the title was for the sake of aesthetics; another piece of the puzzle, however, is my view that the articles written and presented here do themselves a disservice by being categorized as strictly "academic" or "scientific" when there is much more at play under the surface.

The nuances involved here are best described in Valentin Tomberg's introduction to the collection of essays titled *Lazarus, Come Forth!* What he writes here is equally applicable to the *Star Wisdom* series:

> This book has no claim either to historical or to theological validity…this book is based on a different conception of truth than the conception of truth upon which theology and the science of history are based. The truth postulate underlying this book is that of *material insight* in contrast to *formal perspective…*i.e., a plunge from the realm of *formal knowledge* into that of *material knowledge.*

Henri Bergson designated such a faculty of knowledge as *intuition.* Thereby he means the kind of material knowledge that is yielded when intelligence, which is capable only of formal knowledge, unites itself with instinct, which is gifted with material certainty of knowledge—in that the former, with its illuminating light, allows the latter to take the reins. Thus, in Bergson's sense of the word, intuition is the faculty of knowledge that results from instinct that is illumined by reason. It is what brings two opposite poles in humans to a unity, or unites what is most deeply implanted in them, which works hidden in darkness in the depths of their beings, with the reflecting faculty of intelligence, which is most bright in human beings, lying uppermost within them.

Intuition, the highest ranking and surest kind of knowledge of the nature of being— i.e., material knowledge, or knowledge of the "what" (in contrast to knowledge of the "how" and of the mere interrelationships of things)—is spoken of also by Rudolf Steiner, the founder of the anthroposophic movement. For Rudolf Steiner, intuition is the aim and the result of the process of a stepwise convergence between the subject and the object of knowledge—it is their blending into a unity. Intuition is the knowledge that results from the unifying of subject and object after having passed through the stages of *objective consciousness, imaginative consciousness,* and *inspired consciousness.* In the first place, subject and object stand at a distance from one another; this is the stage of objective consciousness. In imaginative consciousness, the object of knowledge approaches nearer to

---

1   See the "Editorial Forward" in *Cosmology Reborn: Star Wisdom*, vol 1.

the subject insofar as it makes itself known to the subject in its "speech," i.e., it reaches out into the subject in the form of non-arbitrarily-arising symbolic pictures. In inspired consciousness the object draws still nearer to the subject in that it "speaks itself out," as it were, in the subject, i.e., it no longer makes itself known to him as a symbolic picture, but as a "word" (or "words") full of content and meaning. Intuition then follows the stage of inspired consciousness. Here object and subject become one, i.e., the most direct knowledge of the being of the object takes place through the being of the subject....

The way to intuition according to the various spiritual streams and authors may well be different, but all are in agreement that intuition is not attained through practical knowledge or intellectual consideration (reflection), but through direct experience of reality. This highest form of knowledge is "an evolving revelation from the inner being of man," as Goethe designated it, and "a direct grasping of the being of things," according to Spinoza.

For those who experience it, this form of knowledge counts as the highest because it is experienced by them as the result of the most profound contemplation and the greatest concentration, in comparison with which that of intellectual consideration and the practical knowledge gained by way of observation appears superficial. However, it does not count in the slightest way as knowledge (let alone as the highest form of knowledge) for the scientific disciplines—which, as such, lay claim to being of general validity. For the scientific approach is not to strive simply for the truth, but rather to strive for the brand of truth that is of general validity, or what can be comprehended fundamentally by everyone bestowed with healthy understanding and faculties of perception, and should thus be concurred with. A scientific discipline—whether a spiritual scientific or a natural scientific discipline—does not want to, and is not able to, address itself only to those people who are capable of the concentration and inner deepening necessary for intuition. Were it to do so, it would then not be scientific, i.e., generally comprehendible and provable. Rather, it

would be "esoteric," i.e., a matter for an elite group of special people...

On this account, when confronted with truth that appeals to intuition, the scientific disciplines cannot do anything other than to echo the words of Pontius Pilate, who, after hearing the words addressed to him by Jesus Christ: "Every one who is of the truth hears my voice," could only say: "What is truth?" (John 18: 37-38). For "to be of the truth" means direct knowledge of being. It is intuition of the truth, which is not of general validity, because it is not founded upon the experience and reasoning that is general and accessible to all—namely that of generally valid intelligence—but rather it demands and assumes a basis of "being of the truth and coming from the truth."

This is the deeper reason why this book does not pretend to advance any claim to being of scientific validity; nor has it the right to advance any such claim. It does not pretend to do so because it cannot be recognized by science as belonging to it. It is not allowed to do so because it would be hypocritical if it were to claim general validity, while in reality it is written—and could only be written—for those who have the capacity and disposition to make use of the faculty of intuition as the direct sense for truth. Thus, it is addressed to those "who have ears to hear and eyes to see."[2]

I could not express my sentiments any better than Tomberg has done so. I would add that it is my own striving, and as far as I can tell the striving of each of the contributors to this volume, to unite accuracy of perception (intelligence) with intuitive insight (wisdom). Only half of this is of "general validity," as Tomberg describes above—the accuracy of perception. As to the insights that each of these authors, myself included, come to in their research, none of these insights is "universally valid" in scientific terms. These conclusions are at the end of the day subjective—trans-subjective at best—and therefore can only be assessed by placing them on the "inner forum" of the conscience. And so this is the bargain assumed by you, dear reader, in picking up this book. You

---

2  Tomberg, *Lazarus, Come Forth!*, pp. 5–7.

will be confronted by points of view that arise out of another's "inner forum," their Holy of Holies, and can only assess such points of view in kind, through the exercise of your own conscience and capacity for intuitive insight.

This is, in truth, a meeting with the Self of another—and this demands an inner mood of *play*. Small children get to know each other in an intuitive sense through touch, through wrestling, tumbling, running and playing tag. This often entails a lot of laughter and tears! As we get older, we are no longer looking for Self-actualization and development in the other the way the child is; we become comfortable in our fixed identities, and don't wish to "play" anymore. Especially in the modern age, during which we can use hand-held devices to filter out opinions we don't wish to confront, we are increasingly rattled by the meeting with another Self—and a meeting that is meant to be playful is perceived as an attack.

I must confess and emphasize that this is my desire in reading any book—to be confronted, to some degree, with the intuitive insights of the one who wrote the book. And what this generally means is that, to some degree, I am made uncomfortable. I may be confounded, confused, and put off on the one hand, or I may be shocked, pleasantly surprised, or downright elated by some new insight of which I never could have previously conceived. This is the only way that I know of to continue to grow inwardly. And in editing this publication, I will strive to publish articles not based on whether I agree with the content—on the contrary, it may be articles with which I have strong disagreements!—but rather based on the intuitive perception I have had of the author. Fundamentally, I *trust* Kevin, Becca, Lucian, Robert, Julie, Yvan, Claudia, and Phillip to write *conscientiously* and *intuitively*, even if I don't agree 100% with the result.

I consider this an act of peacemaking, as described in the 16th Letter Meditation on the Tower of Destruction in *Meditations on the Tarot*. Peace is not the homogenizing of viewpoints; nor is it compromise. It is allowing two contrary points of view to sit side by side, until the emollient action of the Cross creates inevitable peace through proximity. This is the "alchemical wedding," the marriage of opposites—e.g., ideally a husband and wife do not lose their fundamental identities in getting married, rather should they be enhanced mutually. By placing differing points of view side by side in this publication, I engage in the Whitsun event; and you, dear reader, by picking up this publication and reading other people's perspectives, are also there with me. We become co-creators of the free cultural life.

I would like to invite readers to write to me with their reflections on and reactions to the articles published in these volumes. In the future, perhaps the contributions of readers could lead to the creation of a "Letters to the Editor" section in the series. My email is joelmpark77@gmail.com; I look forward to hearing from you!

Now, back to the matter at hand—introducing this year's volume! The title of the second volume, *Saturn – Mary – Sophia*, carries a twofold inspiration. On the one hand, 2020 celebrates 100 years since Rudolf Steiner gave his seminal lectures on "Isis, Mary, Sophia," in December, 1920, during which he planted the seeds and guiding images for the new Star Wisdom and Earth Wisdom that he hoped would arise out of Anthroposophy.[3] These lectures laid the basis for the "Astronomy Course" that would begin in January, 1921. We might say that, whereas the School of Michael has two main karmic streams of *research* (Aristotelians and Platonists), the School of Sophia has two main karmic streams of *revelation*: Kings and Shepherds. It is these two streams that Steiner characterizes in these lectures.[4] This publication considers itself to

---

3  See Steiner, *Universal Spirituality and Human Physicality*.

4  Both of these streams are approached from another point of view by the anonymous author in the 19th Letter Meditation of *Meditations on the Tarot* on The Sun (p. 530). For a deeper discussion of these various karmic streams, see my article series "Moving beyond Aristotle and Plato"; "Aristotle and Plato: Further Reflections"; and "The Fourth School (Aristotle and Plato Concluded)" at www.treehouse.live.

be an active part of the new Isis Mystery spoken of by Steiner in these lectures.

On the other hand, at the end of the 16th Letter Meditation on the Tower of Destruction, the Anonymous Author draws a connection between the classical spiritual identities of the planetary spheres (e.g. the Titan Chronos with the Saturn Sphere) and the leading spiritual beings of the Christian faith. He notes that rather than Chronos, it is the Virgin Mary who is now the ruler of the Saturn Sphere. This led to adapting the title of the Steiner lecture collection *Isis Mary Sophia,* which becomes *Saturn–Mary–Sophia.* We wish to emphasize this Saturnine aspect of the Divine Feminine in light of the two major conjunctions of this year: the year begins in January with a conjunction of Saturn and Pluto, which only occurs every 34 years on average, and it ends with a conjunction of Saturn and Jupiter in December, which occurs approximately every 20 years.

It is quite rare for both of these aspects to occur in the same year, and it portends to be a dynamic one because of that. Historically, the gesture of Saturn-Pluto conjunctions is rather dire, full of doom, constriction and restriction, death, and the deep shame that arises in the communal recognition of our failings as humanity. On the other hand, Saturn-Jupiter conjunctions tend to demarcate shifts in cultural consciousness, miniature cultural waves bringing in a new overall *Gestalt* of insights, experiments, discoveries, and creations.

In between these two is a Jupiter-Pluto conjunction, which takes place roughly every 13 years, and generally portends enthusiasm and positivity on both a cultural and individual level. So we are taken from the depths of despair and conflict at the beginning of the year, to the heights of flaming enthusiasm in the midst of the year, finally to be brought across the threshold of a new equilibrium at the end of the year—and the Virgin Mary, the Divine Mother, carries us with her abundance of grace through it all.

Looking back historically, we can see that the Jupiter-Pluto conjunctions have occurred during important moments in the evolution of our modern Grail Spirituality:

2007: Inauguration of the Grail Priesthood

1994: Founding of the Sophia Foundation

1981: *Meditations on the Tarot* is translated into English by Robert Powell (finished in 1982)

1968: The original manuscript of *Meditations on the Tarot* is completed in French (in 1967)

1956: The seed-idea for what will become *Meditations on the Tarot* is formed (in 1957)

1943: The end of the Valentin Tomberg's "Lord's Prayer Course" in Amsterdam

1931: The beginning of Tomberg's anthroposophical publications (in 1930)

1918: The first presentation of the Threefold Social Organism (in 1917)

1906: Start of Anthroposophical Christology in the form of "Theosophical Rosicrucianism"

1894: Publication of *The Philosophy of Freedom*

1882: Rudolf Steiner's first exposure of Goethe's *Fairy Tale*, and the start of a lifetime of writing and publication.

This continues back into the centuries, with Jupiter-Pluto conjunctions occurring around the birth of King Ludwig of Bavaria (1845), the deaths of Goethe and Kaspar Hauser (1832-3) and the death of the Count of St. Germain (1784). One might wonder what this year's conjunction in Sagittarius portends? The last time the conjunction occurred in Sagittarius was in 1771, around the birth of Novalis and the beginning of the public career of Goethe. This time period marked the beginning of the Romantic Movement, a cultural renaissance that swept Germany and England in particular. In France it saw the intersection of the careers of Louis Claude de St-Martin, Jean-Baptiste Willermoz, and Martinez de Pasqually, resulting in the creation of the Martinist stream of French Hermeticism. And it was just after this time period that the American and French Revolutions would begin. The Jupiter-Pluto conjunction in Sagittarius inaugurated a time of cultural revival in many parts of the world.

The previous Jupiter-Pluto conjunction in Sagittarius took place in the years 1521 to '22. Interestingly, the last time *Saturn* and Pluto were conjunct in Sagittarius was a few years prior, in 1518. This time period saw the end of the lives of Leonardo da Vinci and Raphael, the zenith of the artistic phase of the Renaissance. The years between 1518 and '22 were the very beginning of the Protestant Reformation, with Martin Luther's 95 theses and the resulting Diet of Worms. This time period also inaugurated the Age of Discovery, with Ferdinand Magellan accomplishing the first circumnavigation of the globe during exactly this time period. The years immediately following the 1520s would see the first major scientific revolution, hinging on the astronomical observations and deductions of Galileo, Copernicus, Brahe, and Kepler. Once again, Jupiter and Pluto in Sagittarius seemed to herald a brand new global culture, bolstered by the Saturn-Pluto conjunction in this same sign. Phillip Malone's "The Principle" is a review of a film that touches on the shifts in perspective that occurred during this time period, while Lucian Schloss's "The Saturn-Pluto Conjunction of 2020" emphasizes the inner, moral experience that may accompany this Saturn-Pluto conjunction. I have included selections from Yvan Rioux's *Mystery of Emerging Form* on Sagittarius in order to flesh out our picture of the cosmic realm in which the Jupiter-Pluto and Saturn-Pluto conjunctions will occur this year. I have also included his chapter on Capricorn, as this is the sign in which the Great Conjunction of Saturn and Jupiter will take place.

And what about this Great Conjunction? When were Saturn and Jupiter last conjunct in Capricorn, as they are this year? This is a tricky question. In the year 1961, something very unusual happened. Whereas Saturn and Jupiter were geocentrically conjunct in Capricorn, *heliocentrically* they were conjunct in Sagittarius. Therefore, in one sense one could say the last Capricorn conjunction was in 1961, but from another perspective it hasn't occurred for a much longer time period, nearly 800 years. Around the time of the 1961 conjunction, a spiritual battle manifested itself on the physical plane in the conflict between President

Kennedy and his strivings for peace, and the ever-looming threat of the intelligence agencies and their lust for war with Russia. It is difficult to say how consciously President Kennedy was operating as a public representative of the emerging Grail Culture; however, I can aver after a great deal of struggle in the "inner forum" of intuitive conscience that the intelligence agencies, both then and now, were conscious agents of the so-called "dark brotherhoods of the West" referred to many times by Rudolf Steiner.

At that time, there was a mismatch between the geocentric and the heliocentric; something attempted to manifest on Earth (geocentric) that wasn't actually ready in the spiritual world (heliocentric). President Kennedy took his stand: after the CIA failed to embroil him in war with Cuba in the Bay of Pigs debacle, he vowed that he would "splinter the CIA into a thousand pieces and scatter them to the winds." The intelligence agencies won in the end: their assassination of John F. Kennedy (with those of Martin Luther King, Jr., Malcolm X, and Bobby Kennedy soon to follow) stood as a warning to any future President and other influential public figures that they hold all of the power, and the consequences of making decisions independent of them are deadly.[5] We stand at a similar juncture at this time.[6] Perhaps with Saturn and Jupiter conjunct in Capricorn both geocentrically *and* heliocentrically, that which attempted to manifest in 1961 can make a second, successful attempt.[7] Robert Powell's articles in "Classics in Astrosophy" as well as Claudia McLaren Lainson's "Cultivating Light" address the significance of Saturn and Jupiter's conjunction in 1961.

We stand at a threshold: for 200 years, the Great Conjunctions occurred in Fire Signs (Leo, Aries, Sagittarius). Over the course of the

---

5   See, for example, James W. Douglass's excellent and comprehensive *JFK and the Unspeakable: Why He Died and Why It Matters.*

6   See for example Glenn Greenwald's work for *The Intercept* (https://theintercept.com).

7   One could make similar queries and comparisons in regard to the Catholic Church ca. 1961 vs the modern day—e.g., see the writings of Malachi Martin.

twentieth century, they transitioned from Fire to Earth Signs. As of this year's conjunction, this transition period will be over; the last Fire Sign conjunction was in the year 2000, in Aries. For the next 200 years or so, they will be in Capricorn, Virgo, and Taurus. Julie Humphrey's "Blessings of the Great Conjunction" magnificently surveys the last time period in history during which the Great Conjunction occurred in Capricorn and subsequently inaugurated a series of conjunctions solely in Earth Signs. This time period covers the twelfth to thirteenth centuries, the height of the Middle Ages, with its Gothic architecture, Knights Templars and Cathars, Saints Francis and Thomas Aquinas, the Troubadours and Minstrels.

Going further back, the previous change from Fire Sign conjunctions to Earth Sign conjunctions occurred in the third to fourth centuries AD. This was the time of the Prophet Mani, of the Neoplatonists, and of the great theologians of Alexandria. Emperor Constantine converted to Christianity, and Byzantium became the new center of the Roman Empire as Constantinople.

Prior to this was the sixth to fifth centuries BC, the heart of the Axial Age. Here we see the beginnings of Greek philosophy, architecture, sculpture, drama and social forms. It is the age of Buddha, Zarathustra, and Pythagoras. The Hebrew people were taken into captivity; Daniel and Ezekiel became pupils of Zarathustra at this time—at the origin of ancient astrology. Cyrus the Great set the Hebrews free, and they returned to their homeland, rebuilding the temple under Zerubbabel.

The Capricorn Great Conjunction that set off the sequence of Earth Sign conjunctions prior to this occured in October/November 1516 BC. According to the research of Paul Marx,[8] this coincides more or less with the birthdate of Moses—therefore, the life of Moses and the Exodus of the Hebrews out of Egypt and back to the Holy Land unfolds under the Earth Conjunctions of the 2nd millennium BC.

And prior to this, we have the 24th to 22nd centuries BC. This was the end of the Early Dynastic Period of ancient Mesopotamia, when Sargon of Akkad united the Akkadians and Sumerians into the first ancient empire of Mesopotamia. This was a culture dedicated to the Divine Feminine, Inanna. The first poet in history whose name is known comes from this culture and time period: the princess and priestess Enheduanna. This culture would later become Assyria and Babylonia, and Inanna would become Ishtar, the goddess of Love—known in Greece as Venus. This time period also saw the Sixth Dynasty of the Old Kingdom of ancient Egypt—the Dynasty that would transition out of the height of Egyptian culture that constructed the pyramids, sun temples, and the Sphinx, into the tumultuous and unstable Middle Kingdom.

In summary: the Jupiter-Pluto conjunction in Sagittarius heralds a time similar to the late eighteenth century and the early sixteenth century. Saturn and Pluto in Sagittarius also recalls the early sixteenth century. And a Great Conjunction in the early degrees of Capricorn recalls the Middle Ages, the Neoplatonists, Pythagoras, Moses, and ancient Egypt. We are entering into a massively propitious time period—one that reminds us of the words of the Anonymous author from the 11th Letter Meditation, on Force:

> The Virgin, the Force of our Arcanum, is the principle of springtime, i.e., that of creative spiritual élan and spiritual flourishing. The prodigious flourishing of philosophy and the arts in ancient Athens took place under the sign of the Virgin. Similarly, the flourishing of the Renaissance at Florence was under the vernal sign of the Virgin. Also, Weimar at the beginning of the nineteenth century was a place where the breath of the Virgin perceptibly moved hearts and minds.
>
> In ancient Egypt, the domain of the mysteries of death was attributed to Osiris, and that of life—including language, writing, law, and the arts—was attributed to Isis. Thus, Isis was the soul of the civilization of ancient Egypt, which we are still admiring after more than twenty centuries.[9]

---

8  Paul Marx, "Evolutionary Streams Accompanying Christ's Descent," *Journal for Star Wisdom 2014.*

9  Anon. *Meditations on the Tarot*, page 291.

Perhaps Saturn as Virgin—as Isis, Mary, Sophia—is the key to understanding "the sign of the Virgin" referred to above. We are entering a time that is also under this sign. Rudolf Steiner spoke (in the tradition of Trithemius of Sponheim) of 355-year time periods ruled over by seven archangels in succession. The time of 1524 through 1879 was under the rulership of Gabriel, the Lunar Archangel. This time saw the development of man's intellectual powers, the Scientific Revolution and Enlightenment that led to an exact perception of nature. Yet this time period led to the Cartesian split between the so-called "objective" outer world—a world that was considered "real"—and the "subjective" inner world—a world considered "arbitrary." This latter sphere became the realm of the Romantics and revolutionaries. Two spheres developed that had no relation to each other: romantics and revolutionaries on the one hand, and scientists and technocrats on the other; neither sphere any longer had a relationship to the sphere of morality, to the spiritual world.

Rudolf Steiner saw that this Cartesian experience of the world achieved full maturation in the mid-nineteenth century. Since then, it has been a backward, retarding force on human spiritual progress. Since 1879, we have been in the time of Archangel Michael, the *Solar* Archangel. We must discover a new fundamental paradigm, one that is a "Sun" to the "Moon" of the scientific, abstract intellect. It is this new paradigm that was experienced and described by Rudolf Steiner, Carl Jung, and the Anonymous author of *Meditations on the Tarot*—amongst many others. This is described in vivid detail in Richard Tarnas's *Cosmos and Psyche*—what is needed is a leap into the realm of the transpersonal, the archetypal, and the synchronous: a realm in which art, science, and morality find their mutual source.

Steiner emphasized that the opening of the window to make this leap was a relatively brief period of time—unlike prior developments in cultural evolution, this would not be a step that would happen unconsciously and automatically; it would require the conscious choice of participatory human beings. Perhaps the year 2020 heralds a *kairos*, a "now or never" moment. The first 140 years of the 355-year Age of Michael have been a struggle to relinquish the past, to tear ourselves away from the claws of the Dragon. Perhaps this struggle has been directly tied to the vacillation of Great Conjunctions between Fire Signs and Earth Signs. Perhaps only now can we truly take our shared destiny in hand, and move forward into a time under the "vernal sign of the Virgin."

It is this new paradigm that is being cultivated in my own article, "Saturn in Cancer," in "Everlasting Concrescence" by Becca Tarnas, Kevin Dann's "Into the Vortex II," and "The Galactic Horoscope" by David Bowden and Robert Powell. I want to extend my deepest gratitude and respect to each of this year's contributors, as well as to Jens Jensen, Stephan O'Reilly, John Scott Legg, and Kathy Donchak at SteinerBooks for making this publication possible.

And most of all, a warm *thank you* to you, dear reader. I hope you are nourished by what lies ahead, both in these pages and in the coming year!

*Pax et Bonum,*
*Joel Matthew Park*

# BLESSINGS OF THE GREAT CONJUNCTION

## *Julie Humphreys*

Planetary rhythms create both the foundation of our earthly experience as well as the impulses that move it forward. Great cultural impulses respond to planetary relationships as an orchestra does to its conductor. On an individual level, when the planets move across the zodiacal points which hold the memory of our astrological conception and natal charts, they shower us with opportunity, suffering, initiative, and restriction, each one offering us the chance to reach a bit nearer to the perfection of our "I," the eternal, divine spark within each of us.

The effects of these movements are not preordained, as a fatalistic worldview might assume; instead, they can be understood as humanity's striving toward its future and toward the divine. Our responses to these influences are far from perfect: in fact, only one human being—Jesus Christ—can be said to have lived fully in harmony with the heavens. As the Representative of Humanity, each step he took during his ministry of 1,290 days will be with us always, guiding us unto the end of the world.

Responding consciously to planetary influences gives us the resolve to carry out our tasks here on Earth. The more consciously one walks in harmony with the rhythms of the planets, the more peace and harmony are felt in the soul. This in no way protects one completely from suffering, nor should it: the gift that suffering brings to us is the opportunity to unite in community with our fellow men and women, each of whom bears this burden. The pain of suffering can, however, be softened by an understanding of the righteousness of karma and planetary rhythms. Materialism is useless here, for without the experience of the divine life that is behind these rhythms, humanity is seen to be merely responding to measurable physical forces. Materialism can never answer the question of what is directing these movements.

An enormously significant planetary rhythm that will be experienced this year is known as the Great Conjunction: the conjunction between Jupiter and Saturn, which will occur on December 21, 2020. This means that on this day, despite being more than 400 million miles apart, Jupiter and Saturn will reach the same zodiacal longitude: 5° Capricorn.

Saturn and Jupiter are the two outermost classical planets—that is, those that can be seen with the naked eye. Through the mighty Seraphim and Cherubim who dwell within the spheres of their orbits, we receive the higher faculties of conscience and reason, the faculties that enable us to think, feel, and perform deeds that are in the service of others. When conscience and reason are not our true guides, we are servants instead to our subjective thoughts, changing feelings, and subconscious will impulses.

As we descend toward incarnation from the land of pure spirit, we first encounter the sphere of Saturn, where we are given the spiritual resolves to be brought to bear during the coming life on Earth, through which we might best align ourselves to the higher moral demands of our troubled earthly existence. When we attempt to know the Blessed Virgin as the representative of Saturn, as described by the unknown author of *Meditations on the Tarot*,[1] a beautiful and clear picture can then form before our eyes: the restraint and delay often associated with Saturn become the Virgin lovingly holding us back, intending to keep us from straying too far from our true paths. It is the Virgin who holds the memory of each true Self; she walks with us through all the stations of our lives, so that all may be inscribed for future

---

1 See the end of the 16th Letter Meditation, "The Tower of Destruction."

understanding. As Saturn embraces the rest of the classical solar system, so does the Virgin forever hold us all within the folds of her deep-blue mantle.

*Mary in wood (Italian, 1448)*

The Holy Virgin protects us and reminds us always that our true home is in the spirit land.

Saturn is our conscience, the means through which the Guardian Angel of each of us most commonly communicates. When one fails to heed its call, one is quite literally turning one's back on one's Guardian Angel. The sorrow this engenders in our Angels is entirely on our behalf, as they know that in doing so, it will be that much harder for us to dig ourselves out of our karmic pits.

Jupiter has long been associated with wisdom and morality (or lack thereof) and authority (or abuse thereof). What supports our moral development? Jupiter will tell us. Through Jupiter we can encounter the true Emperor, whose timeless post requires the renunciation of personal thoughts, feelings, and action—in order that the Emperor may cede to divine, or true, authority. It might also be said that for each of us there is a bit (or a great deal, depending on the individuality) of true authority that might be achieved in a lifetime. One can identify true authority through its lack of control over others: to true authority, compulsion is superfluous.

While Mercury informs us as to our intellectual disposition, Jupiter stands for higher, reasoned thinking that is illumined by conscience; indeed, Jupiter was known by the ancients as the great cosmic thinker. When in right relationship to Jupiter, one knows that one's own thoughts are a mere shadow of great cosmic intelligence. As one ascends through this sphere after earthly life, one learns of the discrepancy between wisdom and its lack in the prior incarnation; as we then descend through it toward a new incarnation from the life of pure spirit, we breathe in an understanding of the wisdom of the spiritual resolves that we received from the Holy Virgin within the sphere of Saturn.

We also know that under Jupiter's influence we experience community. The eurythmic gesture for the sound "O," which, through spiritual hearing, can be heard within the sphere of the orbit of Jupiter, conveys this touchingly: the arms embrace all creation as the fingertips move toward each other.

Jupiter and Saturn find each other at the same zodiacal longitude every twenty years or so. Usually, the retrograde movement of the faster-moving planet, Jupiter, causes three consecutive conjunctions: Jupiter passes Saturn, stations retrograde, passes Saturn again, stations direct, then passes Saturn a third time. In 2020, Jupiter's seasonal retrograde movement will be over before the two planets meet, meaning that there will be only one conjunction; this will occur on Monday, December 21.

Before we can begin to understand the importance of this event, we need to briefly discuss the pattern traced by the sequential Great Conjunctions as they move through the zodiac.

Between conjunctions, Saturn advances about 240°, or two-thirds of the zodiacal circle, while Jupiter circles the entire zodiac *in addition to* the 240° traveled by Saturn. So, as an example, if a given conjunction falls in Aries, the following event, roughly twenty years later, will fall in Sagittarius, followed by the next in Leo, followed by another in Aries. As most readers will know, these signs form a triplicity of the element of *fire*. (The others are *earth*: Taurus, Virgo, and Capricorn; *air*: Gemini, Libra, and Aquarius; and *water*: Cancer, Scorpio, and Pisces.) If these conjunctions never advanced beyond 240° past their prior position, they would all occur in a single triplicity across time.

Fortunately for us all, the wisdom of Sophia has directed that the conjunctions progress through the zodiac; in other words, a cluster of conjunctions in the fire signs is followed by a cluster in the earth signs, by another in the air signs, and, finally, by one in the water signs, before returning to the fire signs again. In this way humanity is able to experience an ideal balance of all four elements—though one lifetime is not sufficient to experience the great conjunctions in more than two elements.

One other matter to note at this time is that there is always a period of blending as the conjunctions move from one element to the next. For example, the last "fire only" assemblage of conjunctions began in 1782 (in Sagittarius) and ended in 1901 (also in Sagittarius). The years 1921 to 2000 were a period of conjunctions in both fire and earth signs. The Capricorn conjunction of 2020 marks the start of the period of "exclusively earth" conjunctions, which will last until 2159, at which time humanity will experience its first "air" conjunction since the year 1583! The short earth–air blending period will end in 2179.

What can the conjunctions mean for humanity? Certainly they can denote spiritual events of great importance. Notably, it is now certain that the star followed by the Magi to the infant Solomon Jesus was really a Great Conjunction at 25° Pisces.[2] The conjunction at 27° Pisces that will take place in the year 4443 will herald the ascent of the Maitreya to Buddhahood.[3] (There will be only one intervening conjunction in the last 5° of Pisces, and that will take place in 2675).

So, too, can the conjunctions usher in periods of renaissance, as well as new forms of community. While Saturn is the planet of memory, the events of the past she bears can be illumined by the wisdom of the Cherubim of the Jupiter sphere, giving us moral perspective on our lives.

When there is a fiery assemblage of conjunctions, one could say that intensity, warmth of feeling, and creativity ray out upon the world. Human endeavor inspired by the spirit can move in harmony with world evolution; alternatively, the worst among us can fill with passionate intensity and do great damage. The midpoint of the last grouping of fire conjunctions occurred in 1861. Many readers will recall that this was the birth year of Rudolf Steiner, and that it was his birth that was the *cosmic indication* of the descent of the Christ "I" from the Sun.[4] That is, in 1861, the fiery "I" of Christ, source of the divine nature of all of humanity, began its descent toward Earth in concert with the birth of the one who would bring to us a true understanding of the Christ impulse. Furthermore, the 1861 conjunction occurred at 25° Leo, the zodiacal location of Steiner's natal Moon! Did he not pursue his karmic mission with fiery and tireless intensity? Additionally, 1861 marked the start of the American Civil War, which resulted in the preservation of the Union and the end of slavery (the opposite of freedom and compassion).

For further deepening into fire conjunctions, we might also look to the time of the life of Jesus. The year AD 14 marked the beginning of the fire grouping of that period, which would last for over two centuries. At this time the Nathan Jesus had already, through the preparation and sacrifice of many spiritual beings, received the "I" of Zarathustra. The subsequent fire conjunction occurred at 19° Leo, just a year after the Mystery of Golgotha: the Lion of Judah, the noblest of kings, raying compassion and courage to us so

---

2  Powell, *Chronicle of the Living Christ.*

3  Powell, *Hermetic Astrology*, vol 1.

4  Powell, "The Descent of Christ: Opening the Path to Shambhala," *Journal for Star Wisdom 2017.*

that we might find new life. (This same degree of Leo was graced with a conjunction of Venus and Uranus at the Raising of Lazarus, who had descended into a darkness from which only Christ could rescue him).

What does the earth element bestow upon humanity? It bestows purity, innocence, and devotion to the Earth, her creatures, and the Mother of us all who dwells within it; and knowing when to be a "rock," to stand one's ground, and when to bend in order to move forward. Should humanity ignore these blessings, we will devolve further into the drowning of innocence, through which purity becomes debauchery, and reverence for Mother Nature and all her creatures makes way for assault. Without the influence of the earth element, "the center cannot hold, and anarchy is loosed upon the world."[5]

As the 2020 conjunction in Capricorn marks the start of the "earth only" period of conjunctions (following a century of blending with fire conjunctions), let's endeavor to read the starry script by turning our gaze backward in time, to the last earth cluster. An "earth only" period began in the year 1107 (in Capricorn) and reached its end (in Capricorn) in 1226. The "earth–air" blending period of conjunctions that followed began in 1246, ending in 1285, with a final conjunction in Capricorn. The focus of this article will be the period of time from the first conjunction of the prior "earth only" period (in 1107) to the last earth conjunction of the "earth–air" period (in 1285).

From these years of the twelfth and thirteenth centuries resound the mysteries of the great School of Chartres and the Order of the Knights Templar. This was also the period that marked the emergence of the major Grail stories by Chrétien de Troyes (c.1118), Robert de Boron (c.1200), and Wolfram von Eschenbach (in 1213). The final 72 years of Hildegard of Bingen's life took place during the 1107–1285 period, as did the whole of the life of St. Francis. The golden notes of these centuries wove a radiant song of devotion to Mary,

to the Earth and her creatures, and to the Mother herself. As this year's conjunction in Capricorn heralds the sounding of these impulses from the past, we might attune ourselves to their chorus—a chorus of healing for our times, called forth by Sophia. We are now experiencing the emergence of the Sophianic stream of Christianity—accompanied by her descent from the stars.

## Chartres

Fifty-six miles southwest of Paris stands the Cathedral of Our Lady of Chartres, a structure which became, in the words of René Querido, a garment for Mary-Sophia.[6] Millenia before the cathedral was built, the land on which it stands was identified by the Druids, or Celtic priests, as a place of great importance; indeed, the Celtic origin of its name means "place of the altar." Similar to the druidic sites of Stonehenge and Glastonbury, the land beneath the cathedral is a meeting and an interplay between granite and limestone. Granite, rich in silicon, seems to reach toward Heaven, while limestone, which always strives to absorb water, exerts a pull toward the Earth. Clearly the Druids were sensitive to the spiritual forces of nature and chose Chartres for the properties they found there.

Within the granite at Chartres, the Druids found a grotto, in which they dug a well. For many centuries, until its desecration by French Revolutionaries, people would flock to its waters for healing. The Druids were deeply sensitive to the spirit behind nature, and through this spiritual hearing they established the ritual of the Black Madonna, through which they celebrated her nourishing and life-giving properties, and her sharing of their sorrows. For, long before the Blessed Virgin's heart was pierced with the suffering of her Son, the Black Madonna tended the collective heartbreak of humanity. Though the wooden figure used in ritual by the Druids was destroyed in the French Revolution, we know that on her lap sat a child—a child that represented the promise of birth and new life. The pear wood out of which she was carved was intentionally blackened, perhaps as a

---

5  Yeats, "The Second Coming," 1919.

6  Querido, *The Golden Age of Chartres*, p. 37.

symbol of the wounds that she bore, or as a reference to her yearly sojourn below ground. For during the ritual of the Black Madonna, the druidic statue followed the yearly path of the Sun: as winter's darkness approached, it is thought that she was taken by procession into the grotto, where she would remain until the spring, at which time she was brought out into the daylight again. Through imagining this procession, we can see before the minds' eyes the seasonal turning inward of the soul during the dark months of winter, as well as the triumph of the light over the darkness that occurs each spring. Each year Persephone enters into the darkness, but after she has done so, she is reunited in the daylight with her mother, Demeter. Death, rebirth. Darkness, light. Earth, Heaven. The Black Madonna brought the promise of new life.

The Black Madonna that can be seen at Chartres today is a copy of the druidic form and was made in the late nineteenth century. She is seated in the crypt, the underground structure that was built around the grotto under the direction of the founder of the great School of Chartres, Fulbertus, between the years 1020 and 1024. After entering the quiet darkness of the crypt, one can sit before the contemporary figure of the seated Black Madonna. Still holding a small child in her lap, she invites us to contemplate the mysteries of birth—both that of the Holy Child and the birth of what we might become.

Near the time of the Mystery of Golgotha, the worship of the Black Madonna was already in its twilight.[7] Could it be that the Black Madonna and her child gave way to another mother and child? Or that once the Christ Self descended to the Mother through the subearthly spheres on Holy Saturday, she was released from her confinement following the murder of Abel?[8]

It is said that Joseph of Arimathea, traveling to Chartres in the first century after Christ, was deeply moved by the beauty of the site and of the worship of the Black Madonna. He and his companions then sent a message to the Blessed Virgin in Ephesus (where she lived until her death), asking her permission to dedicate the place to her. According to the Grail account by Robert de Boron (*c.* 1200), during this visit to Chartres, Joseph carried with him the Holy Grail, the cup used by Jesus Christ during the Last Supper. Chartres, then, had become a protectorate of the mysteries of birth as well as those of the Holy Grail.[9]

The cathedral's elevated stature in the heart of humanity has been sustained, in part, by its special relic. In the ninth century, after the Vikings destroyed an earlier form of the cathedral, Our Lady of Chartres received the *Sancta camisa,* the veil Mary is said to have worn at the birth of the Redeemer. This veil, its age verified by carbon dating, miraculously survived the conflagration of the cathedral in 1194 and remains an enduring symbol of the birth mystery. Typically, church relics are reminders of Christ's death, or of the martyrdom of a saint, one example being the Crown of Thorns, which, until the horrific fire of April, 2019, was harbored in Notre Dame de Paris. The *Sancta camisa,* on the other hand, joyfully enkindles the hope and joy that accompanies all new birth—both infant birth and that within the human soul. It celebrates human potential.

It was from this fertile soil that the great School of Chartres bloomed. Lasting roughly throughout the eleventh and twelfth centuries, pupils came to the masters at Chartres to embark on a path of learning and initiation, a path which followed the steps of the ancient Greeks through the seven liberal arts, but did so in a way that was fully Christianized. This is quite amazing in and of itself. In the Middle Ages, Greek philosophers (who were considered pagan to the Catholic Church) "were not deemed an appropriate subject for study by good Catholics."[10]

The Cathedral itself, in stone and glass, supported this endeavor, as its reliefs, statues, and stained glass tell the stories of the ancient world, the Bible, and even of the cosmos. Indeed, these

---

7 Ibid., p. 30.

8 Estelle Isaacson, "The Mother in Shambhala," *Journal for Star Wisdom 2017.*

9 Querido, *The Golden Age of Chartres,* p. 29.

10 Ibid., p. 43.

stories live side by side, in harmony, at Chartres, and seem to foreshadow the understanding of the astrological significance of the life of Jesus Christ that would be illuminated by Robert Powell a millennium thence.

The individual who brought the remarkable School of Chartres to life was Fulbertus (c.960–1028), a kind and gentle man renowned for his musicality and healing ability. His pupils, who came from nearly half of Europe's countries, referred to him as "the venerable Socrates."[11] It was Fulbertus who determined the unusual orientation of the cathedral. Querido reminds us that churches up to that time were always aligned with the (more or less) east-west path of the Sun—though this is precisely so only at the vernal and fall equinoxes. Chartres is the exception, as it instead echoes the northeast-southwest orientation of many pre-Christian centers like Stonehenge:

> Its central nave is oriented to the northeast. By this design, the rays of the Sun at midsummer's solstice fall upon the altar and light up the cathedral's line of symmetry along the axis of its nave.
>
> We know that at the summer solstice…the Sun is at its greatest distance from the equator, rising near the northeast and culminating highest in the sky before beginning its descent. We can imagine a time of outbreathing for the Earth. With its flowers in bloom, and its trees fully in leaf, the Earth's forces of growth are most fully expanded.[12]

Thus, through the orientation of the cathedral, we are given a sense of the connection that must have been felt by Fulbertus between Nature and Spirit, and, in particular, our Mother.

Fulbertus's devotion to Mary is revealed in a fragment of one of his sermons; in it, he names Stella Maris, or "the star of the sea." Querido writes:

> In [this sermon], Fulbertus painted a picture of life. Life is like an ocean, he said, and we are like sailors crossing it…. But at night, he said, we can orientate ourselves because we can behold

Stella Maris, the star of the sea. Through this star that is Mary herself we receive her wisdom that shines brightly enough to guide our ship toward the right haven.[13]

Though the masters of the great School of Chartres drew inspiration from the ancient world, they also understood that man could not receive these teachings in the same way. In the seven liberal arts, the Greeks beheld seven spiritual beings; the masters of Chartres knew that something else was needed if their students were to experience a living connection to the Arts. The great work on the seven liberal arts by Martianus Capella, born in the fourth century in Carthage (now Tunisia), surely inspired them. *The Marriage of Philology and Mercury*, well known in the Middle Ages, became the basis for the Chartres curriculum.

The earliest sculptural representations at Chartres of the seven liberal arts can be found at the Royal (or West) Portal, which was completed in 1145. In Querido's words:

> In the center is a replica in stone of the Black Madonna, enthroned and carrying a standing male child…. She is the Virgin Mary. Beneath is depicted the birth of the Jesus Child and the adoration of the shepherds, obviously scenes from the New Testament. Surrounding these central figures are the seven female figures of the seven liberal arts, below each the representation of a historical personality who achieved mastery in that art: Donatus under Grammatica; Aristotle under Dialectica; Cicero under Rhetorica; Pythagoras under Musica and Arithmetica; Euclid under Geometrica; and Ptolemy under Astronomica.[14]

Through the proximity of these scenes and figures of the Royal Portal, we can begin to see the Liberal Arts through Christian eyes, as the Chartres masters saw them: study and mastery of the seven liberal arts was a path of spiritual development, inner discipline, and self-awakening that brought forth a new birth in the human soul. This purification, or new capacity, then drew one

---

11 Ibid., p. 41.
12 Ibid., p. 39.

13 Ibid., pp. 45-6.
14 Ibid., p. 73.

nearer to one's eternal self, the "I." It is Mary who makes this purification possible.

Querido says further:

This inner birth was what the Chartres masters attempted to attain in connection with the Mary mysteries. The esoteric side of the mysteries of birth revealed that one could so reorganize, harmonize, and purify one's soul forces that a higher, eternal being, the true self, became accessible to conscious experience.[15]

In the School of Chartres, one was taught that the seven female guardians of the Arts had their place in the spiritual world in the seven planetary spheres of the classical planets. Thus, in learning the Arts, one ascended in consciousness through these spheres.

In Grammatica, which led to Moon consciousness, one studied how the living Word is reflected in grammar, and how parts of speech and laws concerning speech affect our ability to communicate effectively. As the Moon mirrors the Sun's brilliance, so was the Logos reflected through grammar's working in language.

The study of Dialectica brought the student to logical thinking, the domain of the sphere of Mercury. As Mercury is the winged messenger between the earthly and the divine, so does mastery of Dialectica make one's thinking clear and mobile. Once achieved, one could then attune to both the ideas of men and those of the spiritual world. Dialectica reveals the truth—through it, truth is sought by two or more who come together in friendship to share ideas.

Mastery of Rhetorica brings beauty and persuasion to speech through the influence of the sphere of Venus. The Chartres masters believed that beautiful speech best expressed the creative goodness and morality of the archetypal Word that created Heaven and Earth.[16] Through Rhetorica we are drawn to moral communication that is intended to benefit another.

Rising through the Arts to the level of the Sun, the student encountered Musica. As the Sun is the center of the human rhythmic system, so the study of Musica encompassed rhythm, as well as harmony and composition. The importance of Musica to the Greeks and the masters of Chartres is represented both by the eternal appeal of the Sun's associated metal—gold—and its central position (as mediator) between the three planetary spheres above and below it. The study of Musica allowed the student entry to the joyous, open-hearted, and moral nature of the Sun.

The study of Arithmetica was the gateway to understanding the order of nature: the growth of plants, animals, and the human body follow the numerical laws of the cosmos. The connection of Arithmetica to the Mars sphere can be seen in the powerful, forward progression that is the Mars impulse.[17] Through the mighty Thrones that inhabit this sphere, we are able to manifest in the material world. Arithmetica, then, led the student to an understanding of the cosmic laws through which nature manifests on Earth.

In Geometrica, the student learned that Jupiter imbued number with form. In studying geometry, students at Chartres learned that the number one can be a circle, two a lemniscate, three a triangle, four a square, five a pentagram. Plato said, "God geometrizes," and through Geometrica students came to know the wisdom of the formative principle.[18]

The final and highest Liberal Art, related to Saturn consciousness, was Astronomica. After death, Saturn is the last sphere we pass through before ascending through the zodiac to Cosmic Midnight; before birth, we first encounter the Saturn sphere, where we meet the Holy Virgin and receive our spiritual commission for the coming lifetime on Earth. Through Astronomica, the student learned of the motions of the planets, the architecture of the universe, and the true meaning of the "circle of animals"—the zodiac—around us. The numerous zodiacal representations in the cathedral were intended to be understood in the light of the spirit. After more than four centuries of a progressively materialistic interpretation of the stars and planets, it is time again, through the

---

15 Ibid., p. 74.
16 Ibid., pp. 78-9.

17 Ibid., p. 80.
18 Ibid.

guidance of the Great Conjunction of 2020 and the new astrosophy, to endeavor to bring new life to the wisdom of the School of Chartres.

After Fulbertus, the School of Chartres passed into the care of other great men; Bernardus Silvestris was one of these. Little is known about him except that he was likely born in France and that he is the author of a great work of the twelfth century, *Cosmographia*, which described no less than the creation of the world. In *Cosmographia*, Bernardus begins with the ideas of the spiritual beings, before the creation of our world. This in itself is a Platonic concept—that ideas precede manifestation. It is almost certain, according to Querido, that Bernardus was a Cistercian (as were the next two masters of Chartres, who will be discussed below), an order that had its beginnings in the twelfth century. (It was the highly influential Cistercian, St. Bernard of Clairvaux, who gave the Knights Templar their Rule in 1128, and granted them the right to wear their distinctive white tunics, to which the red cross would be added in 1147).[19] The Cistercian way of life as healers of both the body and of the Earth was an expression of their understanding of the Earth as a living being, and this theme permeates *Cosmographia*. Querido explains:

> To [the Cistercians] the Earth was ill because it had not been sufficiently penetrated by the Christ impulse through the activity of human beings. They felt it their task to make the Earth worthy of the Christ.[20]

Our understanding of the gravity of the illness of the Earth continues to grow as we are faced with the obvious and tragic degradation of Nature. The Great Conjunction of 2020 is seeking to herald a time when more of humanity understands this to be the result of our fallen natures. As our spiritual health improves, through living into the Christ impulse and the emerging stream of Sophianic Christianity, so shall the condition of the Earth.

John of Salisbury (c.1120–1180) was a student at Chartres by the time he was seventeen. Born near the site of Stonehenge, he became a major figure of his time: advisor to archbishops, and friend of popes and kings. Querido recounts an event from his early youth in which John, who had obvious gifts of clairvoyance, was sent to a priest for instruction. The priest desired to use John's talents in service of black magic, but his efforts came to nothing, for the young boy was able to identify and resist what was happening.[21]

The three years that John spent as a student in Chartres informed the rest of his life. Following this course of study, he worked with some of the most significant personalities of the time.

> As a student, teacher, adviser, and friend, he carried the Chartres "spirit" with him…he remained out of the limelight, working, as he preferred, behind the scenes…. [John] felt that, if Platonism were fused with Christianity, then the Christian man could find his way into the spiritual world through inner development.[22]

In his 1159 work, *Policraticus*, or *The Statesman's Manual*, in which he explores the characteristics of an ideal ruler, John of Salisbury identified six keys that he deemed essential to finding one's way, and attributed them to Bernardus, whom he admired greatly. They were: humility of mind, zeal in the quest, a serene life, silence in the inner search, poverty, and homelessness, or the ability to be a citizen of the world, unanchored to any particular spot. John illuminates the meaning of each key, and adds a seventh: love for one's teachers. Interestingly, *Policraticus* also explores the theme of the health of the social organism, suggesting that this depends on both our interest in one another and the willingness of those with greater responsibility to serve those with less.

John's career was crowned with the bishopric of Chartres, a position he filled in July of 1176. He taught there until his death in 1180.

---

19 Steiner, *The Knights Templar*. p. 2.
20 Querido, *The Golden Age of Chartres*. p. 85.

21 Ibid., p. 111.
22 Ibid., p. 113.

Alanus ab Insulis (Alain de Lille, c.1128–1203) is known as an influential poet and is thought to have been the last master of Chartres. (Steiner referred to him directly as such.) Little but his published works is known about him. During one phase of his life he was revered in Paris as "Doctor Universalis," one who knew all there was to know about the arts, science, the macrocosm, and the microcosm.[23] René Querido shares an anecdote which begins with Alanus on a solitary walk, thinking of what he will teach his students regarding the Holy Trinity. A chance encounter with a child causes him to question his ability to speak meaningfully on the subject, after which Alanus abruptly departs from Paris to pursue a humble life as a Cistercian. Our attention is drawn to the union in Alanus of the wise, kingly nature he embodied in Paris with the humble, devoted, heart-filled life of service that he led among the Cistercians.

The first of Alanus's remarkable poems was *The Complaint of Nature*. In it he describes the intense grief of Nature over the inability of humanity to find communion with her cosmic forces. How man's alienation from Nature has grown since then! Early in the poem, which describes a series of mystic apparitions, a virginal woman glided down from the inner palace of the impassable heavens wearing a diadem with glittering stones representing the zodiac and the planets, and a gown that seemed to reveal all of nature.[24] She is Mary-Sophia, and she is lamenting the obtuseness of humanity:

> Alas…what blindness of ignorance, what delirium of mind, what failing of the senses, what infirmity of the reason has placed a cloud on thine understanding, has forced thy spirit into exile, has dulled the power of thy feeling, has made thy mind to sicken, so that…thine intellect is cheated out of its quick recognition of thy Nourisher…. Man alone rejects the music of my harp.[25]

Alanus's *Anticlaudianus* refutes the pessimism of a fourth century poem by Claudian. The subtitle of Alanus's work is *Saga about the Creation of the New Man and his Struggle for the Redemption of the Earth*; in it the beings of Nature convene with the seven liberal arts and the Virtues, showing humanity a way forward toward both spiritual rebirth and redemption of the Earth. As the book opens, Nature is weeping,

> …because she wants to create a new man and finds that her forces are inadequate to the task…. In this way, Alanus indicates that the forces of physical procreation cannot bear the man that is needed.[26]

The core teaching of the poem thus carries forth that of the School of Chartres—that this "new man" is created out of a collaboration between man and the hierarchies; in other words, one's higher nature, or "I," is not realized without personal effort. As the eternal individuality, or "higher eye," strives toward the earthly personality, or "lower eye," so must the lower eye strive toward the higher. Alanus argues that the healing of the Earth will occur only after humankind's return to a deeper understanding of his spiritual origin. *Anticlaudianus* ends with a lyric description of Nature responding to man's new capacities. The Earth is thus redeemed:

> Hope is surpassed by abundant fruition, the tree gives forth its fruit gratuitously, and the vine its clusters of grapes. The young tendril marvels at the bunches born without its help, and the rose, sprung from its own teguments…does not smell of the mother-thorn, but created of its own will buds forth, and without seed appears in new places.[27]

Yet, as Alanus felt the warmth of the fire of humanity's future, he seems to have sensed that experience of nature as a living being would soon be eclipsed by the oncoming influence of natural science, and that it would no longer be possible for man to receive the great teachings of Chartres in the same way. Upon his death in 1203, the School

---

23 Ibid., p. 119.
24 De Lille, *The Complaint of Nature*. p. 5.
25 Ibid., pp. 24, 36.

26 Querido, *The Golden Age of Chartres*. p. 125.
27 Ibid., pp. 130–131.

closed, retreating into a kind of hibernation. The reincarnation of many Platonists in the late twentieth century, as foretold by Rudolf Steiner, began to arouse Platonism from its sleep. This year's Great Conjunction is striving to bring it fully into the light.

One cannot speak of the Cathedral of Our Lady of Chartres without mention of the labyrinth. Built around the year 1220, the well-known mandala on the floor of the nave of the Cathedral measures about 40 feet in diameter. Walking the eleven concentric paths of turns that lead to its center has been the intention of many a pilgrim to Chartres. Simply entering the nave can easily enable a meditative state—such that stepping into the labyrinth with a question from the recesses of one's soul is almost second nature. One then seeks to bring this question—this seed—to the six-petaled center of the massive circle, so that it might be nourished and tended, to become (at the proper time) a new capacity or understanding.

The stone path in and out of the labyrinth brings many things to mind. One has the sensation of entering and leaving darkness, of going down and resurfacing, of death and rebirth, of emptying so that one may be filled with spiritual sustenance.

The stones on which one treads, which likely came from the quarry at nearby Berchères, are 273 in number—the average number of days of the gestational period of the human being! When on these stones, one is truly walking toward a new birth. As one approaches the center, one can experience the quickening of a higher capacity, worthy of each individuality; the egress can then be seen as the process of bringing this gift out to the world, where it can be used in service of humanity.

### The Order of the Knights Templar

Just eight years before the start of the "earth only" set of Great Conjunctions in 1107, the Crusaders captured Jerusalem from the Muslims. It was the goal of European Christians to protect the Holy Land and the memory of the Mystery of Golgotha, and to provide safe passage for its pilgrims.

From this intention there emerged a group of men with a fiery enthusiasm for their mission that never dimmed. The story of the Order of the Knights Templar, which began in 1119, is that of the blood of Christ and the Holy Grail. It is the story of treasure guarded. Those in the Order were, and remain, from spiritual realms, messengers of the Grail. It is important to examine the spiritual background of the Order of the Knights Templar as separate from the Crusades.

The seriousness for which the Knights were known is revealed in this passage from *The Rule of the Templars*:

> For with great difficulty will you ever do anything that you wish: for if you wish to be in the land this side of the sea, you will be sent the other side; or if you wish to be in Acre, you will be sent to the land of Tripoli or Antioch, or Armenia; or you will be sent to Apulia, or Sicily, or Lombardy, or France, or Burgundy, or England, or to several other lands where we have houses and possessions. And if you wish to sleep, you will be awoken; and if you sometimes wish to stay awake, you will be ordered to rest in your bed.[28]

### The Temple of Solomon

The term *Templar* refers to the Temple of Solomon. Following the capture of Jerusalem by King David, the First Temple was built by King Solomon (*c.* 1000 BC). In the sixth century before Christ, Jerusalem was destroyed utterly by the Babylonian King Nebuchadnezzar: thus began the Babylonian captivity of the Jews. As the Israelites were gradually allowed to return, the Second Temple was completed in the same century. In 37 BC, King Herod the Great—the King of Judea who would try to destroy the Solomon Jesus through the Slaughter of the Innocents—enlarged the Temple Mount and renovated the temple with the public's consent. Jerusalem was again destroyed in AD 70, this time by Titus. The Western (or Wailing) Wall, is a remnant of the second temple.

At their founding, the Knights were granted the Al-Aqsa mosque on the Temple Mount, which

---

28 Upton-Ward, *The Rule of the Templars*, p. 169.

was believed to be the site of the Temple of Solomon, so that "the holy wisdom from most ancient times and the wisdom of Solomon could work together for Christianity in this spot with all the feelings and sentiments that arose from the complete and holy devotion to the Mystery of Golgotha and its bearer."[29]

Rudolf Steiner was able to describe the Temple in glorious detail:

> We enter the Temple of Solomon. The [square] door itself is characteristic. The square used to function as an old symbol. Humankind has now progressed from the stage of fourfoldness to that of fivefoldness, as the five-membered human being who has become conscious of his own higher self. The inner divine temple is so formed as to enclose the fivefold human being. The square is holy. The door, the roof and the side pillars together form a pentagon. When the human being awakens from his fourfold state, that is, when he enters his inner being—the inner sanctuary is the most important part of the temple—he sees a kind of altar.... The whole inner sanctuary is covered in gold because gold has always been the symbol of wisdom.... We find palm leaves as the symbol of peace. That represents a particular epoch of humanity and is inserted here as something that only came to expression later in Christianity. The Temple leaders guarded this within themselves, in this way expressing something intended for later developments.[30]

Steiner said further:

> [The] God which is hidden in the human being's breast, in the deepest holiness of the human being's self, must be changed into a moral God. The human body is thus turned into a great symbol of the Inner Sanctuary [of the Temple of Solomon].... The human being...has to surround his higher self with a house created by his own spirit, by his own wisdom.[31]

In these descriptions, we can begin to delve into what it was that the Templars were guarding: the capacity for man's awakening and redemption through the experience of the Christ. For the Knights, the Temple was a template for the human being. They sought to revive the idea of Solomon's Temple by introducing temple thinking to the West, to make it a living reality in our hearts. In this way, the Templars were preparing for the future, with absolute certainty in their hearts that the future would find them.

As Christ gave up his spirit during his Passion, the veil that surrounded the Holy of Holies in the Temple of Solomon, the resting place of the Ark of the Covenant and former resting place of the Grail chalice, was rent from top to bottom, leaving no doubt as to the spiritual origin of the tear. Previously, this part of the Temple had been accessible only to the high priests, and then only once a year. The veil was symbolic of the separation of man from God through his sins; it was the sacrifice of Jesus that allowed, once the veil was torn, the so-called air of the world of the priests to circulate among humanity: from that point onward, it has been our task to find the altar of the temple within our own hearts, and to become, each and every one, priests.

### The Knights

The Order of the Knights Templar began as a group of nine, all of whom were well trained in warfare. These skills were essential to them, as they were forbidden to retreat from an enemy that was as much as three times as strong as they; should they be overcome, they were to await death calmly. To become a Knight, one had to surrender all of his earthly wealth to the Order. As the Knights were born into nobility, the order soon amassed a great deal of gold.

As mentioned earlier, it was the influential Cistercian, Bernard of Clairvaux, who gave the Order its Rule in 1128 and appointed to them their white habit (to which the well-known red cross would be added nineteen years later). Additionally, these capable men were known for putting all of their land holdings to effective use—either through farming or industry—thereby providing employment for many and rents for the Order. Though their primary mission was as servants of the Christ

---

29 Steiner, *The Knights Templar.* p. 49.

30 Ibid., pp. 119-120.

31 Ibid., pp. 118-119.

impulse, they also became excellent international bankers who were held in great trust. The Order's tremendous wealth drew forth much hostility and would eventually inspire an envy in the breast of France's Philip IV (also known as Philip the Fair) that would only be stilled by the complete destruction of the Order.

The Knights were, above all, devoted to the ideal of tending the fire of Golgotha for Christian pilgrims. This was the star that they followed. Steiner tells us:

> They had to live solely in what streams from the Mystery of Golgotha and fight for the continuance of the strongest impulses that are connected with the Mystery of Golgotha.
>
> The blood of the Templars belonged to Jesus Christ…. Every moment of their life was to be filled with the perpetual consciousness of how in their own soul there dwelt—in the word of St. Paul—"not I, but Christ in me!"[32]

To understand this, we need to turn our attention first toward the land of Palestine, which was prepared on many levels for the advent of the unique life and death of Christ; its description as the Holy Land can be traced back to this time. The Jewish people, for generations before Christ, were chosen to be those among whom he would live and die. One aspect of the preparation of Palestine for the Christ was the Yahweh current, which allowed the light of the spiritual world to funnel into the mineral stratum there; the result was an increased porosity of the mineral layer of the Earth. It was in this way that Palestine became a place where the higher world broke through the Earth's crust.[33] This current lived in the blood of the Hebrew people as love; thenceforth, the Hebrew bloodline bore the spiritual seed of the shining dodecahedron—the archetype of the spiritualized physical body of all of humanity, or *atma*. Thus the land of Palestine was prepared to provide substance for the mineral body of Jesus.

Another facet of this preparation was the horizontal flow of a revelation current from the spiritual world—"milk and honey": This "was experienced by humankind as astral and etheric blessings that hovered over the land like a breath of magic, and was felt as a breath of cosmic childhood and innocence."[34]

The blessings bestowed upon Palestine in expectation of the one who was to come were part of the pure, unfallen aspects of the soul of the Nathan Jesus (also known as the Sister Soul of Adam) that were held back at the time of the Fall. We can imagine these astral and etheric forces, in the beautiful words of Valentin Tomberg, stooping from Heaven to unite themselves ever more closely with the land that would give to the Nathan Jesus the mineral matter needed for his physical body.

As the Mother in the depths of the interior of the Earth is our planet's beating heart, so it can be imagined that Jerusalem is the beating heart, the center, of the surface of the Earth—where humanity dwells, and where the Son is met by willing human souls. In the words of Rudolf Steiner, "Jerusalem was to be the center [of Christianity], and from there the secret concerning the relationship of the human being to the Christ should stream out all over the world."[35] Indeed, Robert Powell and David Bowden, in their 2012 work, *Astrogeographia*, establish through spiritual, mathematical, and astronomical research, that Jerusalem is indeed the heart chakra and center of the Earth. The golden soil and golden sunlight well reflect this reality, as gold is the metal of the Sun. Honestly, where else could the Mystery of Golgotha have transpired?

It was the spiritual blessings of "milk and honey" that the Knights Templar sought and endeavored to protect. Since the Mystery of Golgotha, the "milk and honey" that once hovered over Palestine is now surrounding the entire globe. There they

---

32 Ibid., p. 75.
33 Tomberg, *Christ and Sophia*, p. 121.

34 Ibid., p. 122.
35 Steiner, *The Knights Templar.* p. 121.

wait, guarded by the Angel Jesus until souls are prepared to receive them, in expectation of a third blessing: the "bread of life."

The effects of this third blessing will permeate deep into one's physical body, transforming it, at the proper time far in the future, into its resurrection body. To understand it, we must look to the blood of Christ, to the Holy Grail, and to Shambhala, the dwelling place of the Mother within the heart of the Earth, from which her love for humanity and nature continuously flows.

The Grail vessel that would gather the blood of Christ is said to have been the same chalice used by Melchizedek, Abraham, and Moses. Following its subsequent safekeeping among the temple treasures, it was sold, through divine dispensation,[36] to a follower of Jesus.

According to Judith von Halle, before the crucifixion, blood flowed from the four nail wounds onto the golden soil of Jerusalem. Part of this spilled blood was etherized and taken up into the Earth's etheric field, transforming it forever.[37] Rudolf Steiner gives a lovely description of our perception of this substance after physical death: "This glistens and shines in the ether body, showing itself in such a way after death that one feels: this is new, germinating life; it makes the human being viable and takes him into the future."[38] It was precisely this preparation of the Earth's etheric field that enabled it to absorb Christ's resurrection body on Easter morning.

Following the Death of Deaths, the Roman Soldier Longinus was present as other soldiers sought to break Jesus's legs, as they routinely did to hasten the death of living victims of crucifixion. Why were the soldiers drawn to do this to Jesus? There was a sense, as Judith von Halle describes, that there was still life in him![39] With all his strength, Longinus then drove his spear into Jesus's right side, piercing lungs and heart. Now, if this were to happen to you or me, no blood would flow: blood does not flow

from an ordinary corpse. But, "the blood of the Redeemer gushed forth powerfully.... [It foamed and] shone like the Sun, [and] all were transformed. [Longinus], too—as if awakening from a deep sleep—appeared illumined, and fierily professed his faith in the living Son of God."[40]

The moment this blood touched the golden earth of Jerusalem, a sun seed was created at the center of the planet. Ptolemy called this the primeval Sun— and we know from Steiner's teachings that it will form the basis of the Vulcan planetary condition, the last of our evolution.

The same Grail vessel, of Melchizedek, Abraham, and Moses, was used by Joseph of Arimathea to collect the precious blood that flowed from Christ's side on Golgotha. Though Joseph was thenceforth imprisoned in Jerusalem for some years, it is said that the Grail chalice provided him sustaining nourishment throughout his confinement. Once released, Joseph was guided by Angels to take the Grail to the distant west. Later, it was borne by Angels to Titurel, with whom the origins of the Parzival story lie. The chalice forever retained the property of filling itself with the Christ's spirit.[41] The Holy Grail sustained life. Tomberg tells us that the mystery of the Holy Grail is the mystery of the members of the being of Jesus.... "The 'imprints'...of these members form...the sacred vessel that can receive the 'Holy Grail'—the 'I' imprint of Jesus Christ."[42] It represents communion with all aspects of the Christ impulse.

Now it is important to step back into time, to the moment that the Christ "I" left the body of the Nathan Jesus during the Passion. At the moment of Christ's physical death on the cross, a powerful earthquake shook Jerusalem, and the earth beneath the cross was opened. The Christ "I" then began its descent down through the subearthly layers, toward the Mother in Shambhala, bestowing blessings as he went:

36 Powell, *The Christ Mystery*, p. 12.
37 Von Halle, *Secrets of the Stations of the Cross and the Grail Blood.* p. 49.
38 Steiner, *The Fifth Gospel*, p. 186.
39 Von Halle, *Secrets of the Stations of the Cross and the Grail Blood.* p. 63.

40 Ibid., p. 65.
41 Tomberg, *Christ and Sophia*, p. 156.
42 Ibid.

**Mineral Earth:** *Blessed are the poor in spirit, for theirs is the Kingdom of Heaven.*

**Fluid Earth:** *Blessed are they that mourn, for they shall be comforted.*

**Air Earth:** *Blessed are the meek, for they shall inherit the Earth.*

**Form Earth:** *Blessed are those who hunger and thirst for righteousness, for they shall be satisfied.*

**Fruit Earth:** *Blessed are the merciful, for they shall receive mercy.*

**Fire Earth:** *Blessed are the pure in heart, for they shall see God.*

**Earth Mirror:** *Blessed are the peacemakers, for they shall be called the children of God.*

**Earth Severer:** *Blessed are those who are persecuted for righteousness' sake, for theirs is the Kingdom of Heaven.*

**Earth's Core:** *Blessed are you when men will revile you and persecute you and utter all manner of evil against you falsely on my account. Rejoice and be exceedingly glad, for great is your reward in the Kingdom of Heaven.*

These blessings can be imagined as nine tiny seeds of light that shone with the eternity of Divine Love, and must guide any who wander there.

At the Earth's Core, outside the boundary of Shambhala, lives pure hatred for all that is moral, good, and loving—in other words, a hatred that seeks to eradicate the Sacred Heart of Jesus from the hearts of men and women. Truly, it makes perfect sense that this layer surrounds Shambhala, when we recall that evil cannot create, but only imitate. Evil needs the pure, golden goodness of the dwelling place of the Mother (and humanity's future) from which to draw inspiration.

Following the passage of the Christ "I" through the Earth Core, he came to the Mother in Shambhala, where he received his immortal resurrection body. Imagine the joy they felt!

At this time it is appropriate to mention other forces that weave into this tapestry. One is the Second Coming of Christ in the etheric of the Earth, which began in 1933 and will continue throughout the upcoming Ages of Aquarius and Capricorn.

Steiner made it clear that the primary significance of this event is the opening of a path to Shambhala.[43] In other words, the Second Coming is making it possible for those who are not high initiates (a previous requirement) to penetrate the spiritual realms of the underworld. The perils of undertaking this journey are obvious, as one would encounter all the evil that has been deposited there, through humanity's misdeeds, since the Fall. However, Powell emphasizes that the journey is possible with the protection of Christ.

Though the Second Coming describes the presence of Christ's ether body (which moves in a 33-year rhythm) in the ether body of the Earth, all aspects of the Christ being are involved in the Second Coming, and can form the basis of communion with Christ. Another parallel rhythm is that of the astral body of Christ, which moves in accordance with the 29½-year orbit of Saturn and reveals the unfolding of the days of Christ's ministry on Earth. Many are familiar with the fact that we are now in the "day" of Christ's last day in the wilderness, when "temptation was overcome, the devil left him, and behold, angels came and ministered to him," (Matt. 4:11). This "day" began in February of 2018, and through it, humanity's experience of the angelic realm is being quickened. One of the Angels humanity is experiencing from this realm is the Angel Jesus.

There is yet another consideration of great importance: the 12-year rhythm of the "I" of Christ, explained in depth in many works by Robert Powell. This rhythm coincides with the Second Coming, and traces the descent of the Christ Self from spiritual realms into the layers of the Earth itself. Having traversed the Mineral Earth between 1933 and 1945, the "I" of the Risen One has now reached the eighth layer, the Earth Severer, in 2016, where it will remain until 2028. The forces of this layer work upon the human being so that he or she becomes wholly united with Ahriman. And it gets more challenging still. The ninth layer, that of pure hatred, will be traversed between 2028 and 2040, at which time the Christ "I" will again unite with

---

43 Powell, *Cultivating Inner Radiance and the Body of Immortality*, p. 39.

the Mother in Shambhala. These years on Earth are likely to be particularly challenging—perhaps full of war, hatred, further persecution of Christians, and cruelty—as the adversarial powers fight for their lives, scrambling for the Earth's surface as they cower from the light of Christ.

These contemporary considerations are breathing life into our understanding of the Grail Mystery, for as the Knights Templar sought communion with Christ through the Mystery of Golgotha, we must look elsewhere—to the ether body of Christ "in the clouds," to the being of Sophia, who is descending from the starry vault, and to the Christ "I" that is now beneath us, in the underworld. It is the communion with the Christ "I" that was the central motif of the Grail legend of Parzival.[44]

Across time, the search for the chalice has been associated with the longing for eternal life. Looked at from purely materialistic terms, this could be understood as being *preserved*, through methods such as genetic manipulation, surgery, drugs, and excessive exercise. From the spiritless worldview, death represents a nothingness that is to be avoided by all the means at one's disposal. In reality, eternal life can only be understood in spiritual terms. At the present stage of evolution, it is only the "I" of the human being that is eternal: the divine spark of the one immortal flame that accompanies us in each incarnation. Far into the future, our "lower bodies"—astral, etheric, and physical—will be spiritualized as well. It is only through the intervention of Christ that this can occur, as the three higher aspects of the human being—spirit self, life spirit, and spirit human—are now shining from the Sacred Heart of Jesus.

### The End of the Order

In 1187 Saladin recaptured Jerusalem, which remained in Muslim hands for 730 years. It was 1917 when General Edmund Allenby (under whom T. E. Lawrence served), victorious over the Turks, entered Jerusalem on foot through the stone portal of the west-facing Jaffa Gate of the Old City.

Following the loss of Jerusalem to Saladin, Acre (in modern Israel), too, fell to the Muslims in 1291, and the Order was forced to withdraw from the Holy Land. Still, it continued to function as protectors of pilgrims, supported by the Order's financial proficiency. It is estimated that by 1300, the Order was 15,000 strong, about a tenth of whom were Knights.

But it was not to last. One can hardly begin to comprehend the viciousness and fever with which Philip the Fair, abetted by the compliance of Pope Clement V (former Bishop of Bordeaux), pursued the wealth and power of the Knights Templar. On October 13, 1307, hundreds of Knights were arrested for heresy in one fell swoop, a technique which sadly persists to this day. On this day, Mercury, Saturn, Uranus and Neptune huddled in front of the final 3° of the Scales; above them shone *Unuk*, the star that marks the head of the Serpent. The imaginative vision of the Templars is revealed in the conjunction of Mercury and Uranus; in Mercury and Neptune, their desire to protect others and serve goodness; in the conjunction of Saturn and Neptune, their willingness to sacrifice (this aspect was present at the birth of Mary as well); and in the union of Saturn and Uranus, a foreshadowing of the "bushel" that would be set over their light for a time. While imprisoned, the Knights were tortured on "the rack" and forced to confess. The last Grand Master, Jacques de Molay, was burned at the stake in 1314.

The impulse of the Order was so consequential that it continues to arouse curiosity and inspire so many centuries later. This year's Great Conjunction in Capricorn draws us closer still to the treasure that they guarded, as the first Great Conjunction following the Crusaders' capture of Jerusalem occurred at 3° Capricorn, just 2° from the conjunction of 2020.

### Saints Hildegard of Bingen and Francis of Assisi

This study will conclude with a brief glance into the lives of two great individualities of the period 1107

---

44 Powell, "The Descent of Christ," *Journal for Star Wisdom 2017*, p. 33.

to 1285: Hildegard of Bingen and Francis of Assisi, whose deep devotion to Christ, Mary-Sophia, and the Earth guided all that they accomplished.

Saint Hildegard (1098–1179), as she is now known, began having visions at the age of three. Before reaching adulthood, she was offered by her parents to a Benedictine monastery. There she helped tend the herbal garden, eventually writing about her experiences with the healing properties of herbal tinctures; through this work, she became known as a great healer.

The visions continued; at the age of 42, she was guided to put into writing all that she had seen. From Pope Eugenius, she received the blessing and approval to do so, as he regarded her visions as true revelation from the Holy Spirit. The result appeared in three volumes, *Scivias* ("Know the Ways of the Lord") being the most recognized. In this work she refers to the Church as the Bride of Christ.

Saint Hildegard is also known for a large collection of musical compositions that are an expression of her devotion to Mary, whom she referred to in one piece as *auctrix vite*, or "source of life." She is also credited with what is thought to be the first opera. These compositions have been performed with increasing frequency in recent years, likely in relationship to her canonization in 2012 and the new 600-year cultural wave which began in 2014.[45] One can also sense a growing sensitivity to Sophia during this time. Through the exacting research of Robert Powell, we now know with certainty that the individuality of Hildegard of Bingen returned to Earth in the mid-nineteenth century as the Russian mystic Vladimir Solovyov.[46] His death in 1900 coincided with the birth year of Valentin Tomberg as well as the beginning of the period of integration of the Etheric Christ into the Angelic realm.

Solovyov, who experienced three different encounters with the being of Sophia, is known as the founder of the Russian stream of Sophianic Christianity that endeavored to bring Sophia

to the Christian tradition. It could be said that in the Russian Orthodox Church, there was and is the potential for greater receptivity to Sophia than there has been in the Roman Catholic Church. There's a reason it's called "Mother Russia!" This is in no way meant to diminish the importance of the Roman Catholic Church—in fact, Solovyov himself wrote of the three existing streams of Christianity, and how they must work together—but is instead being raised here to celebrate the work of the hierarchies that orchestrated this individuality's birth among the Russian people! There has been a quickening within this culture in anticipation of the coming Slavic cultural epoch—during which a culture of loving brother- and sisterhood will prevail. (The start of this cultural epoch in AD 3575 is 1,200 years behind the onset of the zodiacal Age of Aquarius in 2375, at which time the vernal point will move into the constellation of Aquarius. The cultural epoch, then, requires two 600-year cultural waves to "catch up" to the zodiacal reality. Solovyov was indeed ahead of his time, sensing the coming importance of the Slavic culture in the evolution of humanity).

One of the many indications Powell considers in comparing the death chart of Saint Hildegard to that of the birth of Solovyov is the position of Uranus at 11°37' Aries and 11°57' Aries, respectively—11°47' being the midpoint between them. This very year, Uranus, which takes an average of eighty-four years to circle the zodiac, will reach that exact position on April 30, the day on which the Sun will revisit its zodiacal longitude at the Resurrection. Hallelujah! After turning retrograde in August, Uranus will again reach 11°47' Aries on December 31st. Truly, this is a special year in which this great individuality is calling us from the stars. Tell a friend!

Hildegard of Bingen, according to Steiner,[47] was one of a great number of people who knew of the coming birth of St. Francis. Through visionary revelation, she knew that an important individual was about to be born—though she was taken back

---

45 Robert Powell, "2014 and the Coming of the Kalki Avatar," *Journal for Star Wisdom 2014.*
46 Powell, *Hermetic Astrology,* vol. 1.

47 Steiner, *The Spiritual Foundation of Morality.* p. 16.

to the spirit land two years before Francis's humble birth in a stable, on a bed of straw.

Saint Francis of Assisi (c.1181–1226) is especially beloved among saints, perhaps because he turned to his mission following what could be called a life of transgression; none among us ought to have difficulty relating to that. It is more difficult, I think, to relate personally to an individual who, as in the case of Saint Hildegard, appears to have been devoted and morally upright even as a toddler. Saint Francis is easier to take into our hearts.

He was born to a pious mother and a wealthy businessman. About to give birth while her husband was conducting business in France, his mother was visited by a pilgrim, or heavenly messenger, who told her to bring her child into the world in a stable lined with straw. She obeyed. Thus the Christ impulse embraced him at birth.

However, Steiner describes an energetic youth who was a spendthrift, and who readily engaged in physical conflicts resulting from feuds between Assisi and Perugia. Steiner tells us:

> As a youth…he was someone who conducted himself like a descendant of the ancient Germanic warriors…. He was brave and warlike, and filled with the weapons of war…. His comrades chose him to lead their youthful warlike expeditions.
>
> Later on…he had a dream vision. He saw a great palace, wherein were stored all kinds of weapons and shields…he said to himself, "This is a summons for me to become a soldier!"[48]

Then, as he prepared for a conflict with Naples, a voice commanded him to return to Assisi. It said:

> Do not seek your knighthood in external service. You are destined to transform all the forces at your disposal into powers of soul, into weapons to be used by your soul. The weapons you saw in the palace signify the spiritual weapons of mercy, compassion, and love.[49]

Francis was, to use Steiner's word, *reforged*: he returned to Assisi and dedicated his life to propagating these spiritual weapons, renouncing worldly goods, and adopting the familiar coarse tunic which was worn by only the poorest of his time. Inspired by a church reading of the story of the Commissioning of the Twelve (Matt. 10:1), Francis began the work of starting an Order, which had its official founding in 1210. Interestingly, the Franciscan Order has maintained a continuous presence in Jerusalem since 1217.

Saint Francis is well known for his ability to tame any wild creature—he is often depicted in the company of an obedient wolf—by virtue of his own moral development. As the mineral kingdom is related to our physical body, and the plant kingdom to our etheric, so does the animal kingdom represent our astral nature. It can be said that, by analogy, human deeds devoid of reason and conscience are carried out on an "animal" level.

Saint Francis's calming effect on animals is an expression of his communion with the purified astral body of Christ, which unfolds across time in a 29½-year rhythm known as the Apocalypse Code.[50]

Francis was also known for his open heart and healing abilities. Leprosy was a common affliction of his time, and, quite naturally, most sought to distance themselves from it, as Francis had as a boy. Following his conversion, though, he worked among the lepers, even kissing one on the lips as an expression of love and compassion. Steiner tells of his healing abilities, which were made possible by his communion with the Christ impulse:

> How did the Christ impulse work on further in Francis of Assisi? It acted in such a way that when he was placed in a population in which the old demons of disease were especially active, the Christ impulse approached the disease demons through him and absorbed their evil substance into itself, thereby removing it from the people.[51]

---

48 Ibid., pp. 17–18.
49 Ibid., p. 18.

50 Powell, "The Apocalypse Code," *Journal for Star Wisdom 2018.*
51 Steiner, *The Spiritual Foundation of Morality,* p. 35.

In 1224, at the age of 42, Francis received the stigmata. Likely during this same year, he composed *Cantico della Creature* ("Song of Nature"), the first piece of literature written in what is close to modern Italian. (This preceded Dante's *Divina Commedia*, published in 1320.) Before this time, all literature of the region had been written in Latin, and Francis's decision to use the local dialect is a reflection of his humility and his wish to connect with the common folk. In the *Cantico* he celebrates God, all of nature, and the Mother:

> Be praised, my Lord, through all your creatures, especially through my lord Brother Sun, who brings the day, and you give light through him. And he is beautiful and radiant in all his splendor! Of you, Most High, he bears the likeness.
>
> Be praised, my Lord, through Sister Moon and the stars; in the heavens you have made them, precious and beautiful.

Francis died in 1226, under a Great Conjunction in the middle decan of Capricorn.

The Great Conjunction of 2020 is being brought to us on the heels of another Saturn-Pluto conjunction, a meeting that represents the communion between love (*Phanes*) and holiness (Saturn).[52] These planets come into conjunction, on average, every 33 years; the prior cycle, which began in 1982, marked the start of the intensification of the horrific campaign against innocence and purity, largely targeting the most innocent among us: our children. Moral restraint began to loosen and give way; the debauchery that first appeared in popular music and art (Madonna's first recording was released in 1982) has now thoroughly saturated Western culture. To anyone who came of age before 1982, the culture is nearly unrecognizable. Before this time, it was still possible to dodge the cultural filth in order to protect our children and insulate ourselves from its effects. At present, though, this can only be accomplished by way of a recusal from society. As we now enter the "earth" period of great conjunctions, we are being called upon to step up our efforts to revere nature and protect innocence, and we will indeed receive the support of the heavenly beings if we do so. This means endeavoring to stop destructive technology. It means keeping children away from exposure to sexual topics in school, and from the schools themselves that insist on this grossly untimely exposure. It means harshly limiting access to television and films, which are of an increasingly debased nature. What has become of the culture, and what are the motivations behind these changes?

We must listen for the voice of the Divine Mother, Isis-Sophia. Peter Deunov said:

> When this Divine Mother has spoken, everyone should observe silence. Sometimes she forces us to remain silent. In this silence you have heard the voice of your Mother coming from the depths of the soul. This voice is calm and will speak to you as softly and gently as no other voice has spoken to you. But when will this voice speak to you? When one has gone through the greatest anguish and sufferings, having filled up ten pockets with tears. This voice provokes an instantaneous magical change in the human being. You may have been the most offended, the most bitter person on Earth, you may have been dying, but this voice has spoken to you; it is immediately a revival....
>
> Make an attempt to let your Mother talk to you. If you hold on to your views as you have them today, your Mother will not speak to you. I will give you some clarification: pay attention to the clouds, connect with them, and do not think that they are dead, but always consider them to be alive. In educating ourselves, we need to draw on Nature because in the various forms it has created lies a great purpose: to change the mood of our mind, heart, and will. Sometimes in the sky whole mountains of clouds are formed, aimed at north or south; watch these lively clouds in space, ponder why some are facing north and some southward.
>
> Modern people today are exhausted because they do not go out to observe the sky but turn only to...what they themselves have created [on Earth], and it is petty.

---

52 Claudia McLaren Lainson, "Communion of Love with Holiness: Saturn–Pluto Conjunctions," *Cosmology Reborn: Star Wisdom* vol. 1.

This is a task for you now…to come to the door of the Garden of Eden, to show you that you have taken a curved path. There was another: the Straight, Narrow Path, the great Path of Living Nature and you have to enter this Path.

You do not need great heroism, only Faith and obedience. Every good action is according to the Will of God. Every good thought, any good endeavor, as small as it is, is according to the Will of God. Know that every good endeavor breeds results though it takes a long time. The least good will, the smallest good urge, in time, will produce a good result. Every good thought and desire is due to the urge of your Divine Mother, who wants to lift you up to the full life she has in mind for you.[53]

The upcoming period of Great Conjunctions in Taurus, Virgo, and Capricorn will shower its blessings upon humanity until 2179, at which time Neptune will have made her way back to middle decan of Aquarius: the Orphean goddess Nyt, the divine feminine, leading us to our angelic future. The promise that this cycle holds for willing hearts is the renewal of the Sophianic impulses that were woven together in the twelfth and thirteenth centuries. Indeed, it is only with faithfulness and true reverence for nature (which are the teachings of Taurus), the purity and impulse to protect innocence (that are Virgo's wisdom), and the courage to move toward the future with proper reverence for the past (which shines from Capricorn) that we'll be able to find the door to Shambhala. Together, may we hear the music of Sophia's harp!

---

53 Peter Deunov, "The Great Mother," *Starlight*,
   vol. 18, no. 2, Advent 2018.

"Every earthly condition during a certain period of time is to be explained as a weaving and interplay of those forces that come into flower and those that die away, those that belong to the rising and those that belong to the falling line—sunrise and sunset—and in between, the zenith at noon, where the two forces unite and become one. Seen from one's horizon, a person beholds the stars in the sky, rising in the east and climbing ever higher until they reach their highest point in the south. From then onward, they sink until they set in the west. And though the stars disappear from sight in the west, one must nevertheless say to oneself: The real place of setting lies in the south and coincides with the zenith, just as the true place of rising is in the north and coincides with the nadir. The rising starts from the nadir. Through that, a circular motion is described that can be divided into two halves by a vertical line running south to north. In the part containing the eastern point, the rising forces are active. In the part containing the western point, the sinking forces are present. The eastern and western points cut the semicircle through the center. They are the two points in which, for our physical eye, vision of the forces begins and ends. They are one's horizon."

—RUDOLF STEINER, *"Freemasonry" and Ritual Work*, p. 387

# THE MYSTERY OF EMERGING FORM: CAPRICORN AND SAGITTARIUS

## *Yvan Rioux*

*The following is from chapters 7 and 8 of the author's magnificent work,* The Mystery of Emerging Form. *They describe the various qualities of the signs of Capricorn and Sagittarius, the two signs in which the three major conjunctions occur this year (Saturn–Pluto and Jupiter–Pluto in Sagittarius, Saturn–Jupiter in Capricorn). His template for these descriptions comes from the illustrations of the twelve signs of the zodiac made by Imma von Eckardstein for Rudolf Steiner's* Calendar of the Soul *in 1912. —J.M.P.*

### CAPRICORN

We are accustomed to qualify the vibrations of sound and the sub-world of the electromagnetic spectrum with frequencies. One vibration in a second is one hertz. The light in our home, because of the alternating current, flickers on and off 50 times per second, or 50 hertz. This is a low frequency compared with gamma and cosmic rays with their millions of vibrations per second. But what do we call a vibration or pattern of activity that occurs every two seconds, every minute or even every eight years like the dance of Venus around the Earth? Is it a pulsation, a recurring momentum, an oscillation? And, like any choreography, it must be an activity with a meaning. It represents a kind of intelligent activity.

Astronomers talk a lot about star movements, their electromagnetic activities and the tremendous speed of galaxies. From Earth we perceive the constellations as they come and go, turning around us as if we were inside a gigantic dynamic clock. Sometimes the Moon obscures their influences and sometimes the Sun amplifies their formative forces. We live inside constantly pulsing rhythms. Because of the Earth's motion within the solar system, we have days, seasons and geological periods. Nothing is static but everything has

an organized momentum. Our time scale is based on this movement. Our galaxy and solar system move at 500,000 km/hour toward the Hercules constellation. If we know now that matter is never at rest, why is it that most religions still imagine a spirit world as a frigidly unmoving realm eternally static?

In the rhythm of the natural world around us we perceive movements of contraction and expansion (night–day and winter–summer). The etheric nature of our being manifests in this way in order to create us. This is due to the constant increase and decrease of warmth and light.

Rhythms are not energy or matter but are essential for a spirit to manifest its threefold form in matter to create a vehicle that becomes, for a time, a creature in the kingdoms of nature. "Life is rhythm," said Steiner. What we perceive is the expression of life, not life itself. The twelve constellations are pulsing entities that contain intelligent intentions to direct nature toward particular directions. For Capricorn, that direction is to articulate various parts of the body.

*The Constellation of Capricorn (Goat/Fish)*

### *Content*

This text explores the imprint of the intelligent activity of Capricorn all around us in the constant forming of human and animal creation. What is the relation between the Capricorn sector of space, its glyph, the medieval image of this constellation, Imma's drawing, the element aluminum, the animal phylum Arthropoda, the sense of sight, the knee, Saturn as a ruling planet, the color peach-blossom and the consonant *L*? Based on Imma's drawings in the first edition of *The Calendar of the Soul* in 1912, we can try to find a golden thread linking the various ways Capricorn acts as a constant blueprint in nature.

### Description of the Glyph

No other sign of the zodiac has its glyph represented in so many different ways. In all the variations there is a common denominator: they express mobility or a tendency to establish a link between one part that is above and another below. It is often a cup shape with a line going down and another up, finishing with a loop. It suggests a connection between two things.

The traditional picture has an earthy aspect with a goat-like front body (hard and dry), as well as a watery whirly fish tail at the end. There is versatility in this symbolic picture. It is also seen as half animal with a human torso like the centaur. The goat fish, as well as the centaur, is a symbol of our physical and psychic animality.

### Description of the Drawing

Many whirly movements are present in this dark agitated drawing. Everything seems to whirl around a central sketchy creature. Its presence among the brouhaha shows three distinct parts: a head-like organization with prominent eyes, a suggested nose and a bushy mouth. Two swirls emerge from in-between the eyes and sit above the head like antennae.

Below the head, with its sensorial apparatus, there is a horizontal movement. If we start from the center of the left whirl, we see a clockwise movement that links with the right whirl. If we start from the center of the right we see a counterclockwise movement. This suggests a rhythmic oscillation.

From the left central oscillating whirl, we see a long wavy movement branching off at the end into a fish tail and surrounded by a bustle of activities on the right.

Finally, the bottom part stands like a dark watery pool with three strong vortical actions. Did this creature come out of the water? The whole dark background is peppered with vortical formative activities as if an invisible hand acts in the air behind the scene.

### *Aluminium: The Plasticity of Forms*

The numerous whirlwinds that seem so hurly-burly in this dark background, like the potter's work, remind us of the plasticity and water absorption of aluminum when associated with silica (to form clay). There is no fertile ground without it. "Clay is responsive to formative forces (fingers) working on it from outside. Just as a musical instrument responds to a musician, so plastic clay is the instrument for the music of forms composed by the sculptor."[1]

Aluminum, the most abundant metal in the Earth's crust, is not freestanding in nature but rather combines in manifold ways. Its main association is with silica in rocks (such as feldspar). It is also present in most precious stones. In fertile soil it brings plasticity (clay) and water absorption as well as retention.

In human ashes we find silica and aluminum, but physiologists don't fully understand why. Are they just pollutants that we store? It is only relatively recently (c.1880s), with the use of electricity, that we have been able to extract pure aluminum metal from bauxite. Our internal environment is more in touch with it through cooking in aluminum pots. The acidification of the soil can also release aluminum into fertile ground.

If silica (Aries) goes through us and lodges itself at the periphery of membranes and organisms as a transmitter of subtle influences, and if phosphorus (Cancer) gives surface sensibility to plants and animals, then aluminum introduces plasticity. We have aluminum in us in a very small quantity acting as an activity more than a substance.

---

1  See Hauschka, *The Nature of Substance.*

## Arthropoda: The Articulated One

*Arthropoda—insect, spider, scorpion, lobster...*: a million species. Imma's drawing of Capricorn shows a three-part being as a directional impulse. Centers for neural function, pulsating rhythm, and transformation of substance start to articulate and unify in one organism. Ninety percent of animal species on Earth are in these varied phyla—insect, spider, scorpion, lobster, crab. The head, thorax, and abdomen are serial articulated units (metamere structure).

The Arthropoda shows a segmented, mobile, chitinous exoskeleton with legs and wings ever adaptable and pliable. Like the glyph, all articulations have an element of concavity and convexity. The Arthropodes were the first to explore these new articulated possibilities. "It is difficult to say which of the two, the over-plastic or the over-rigid, appears the more weird to man."[2]

## Sense of Sight

The sensibility of plant cells to light is well known (heliotropism). Creatures that want to move more freely in space need to link light perception with movement because light reveals space. In the development of phyla the spirit in incarnation desires an apparatus. Very early on a primitive eye develops, even at an embryonic level. It reaches near perfection with the octopus. Arthropoda explored the eyes to an extravagant degree, from simple light receptors to complex compound eyes perceiving diverse aspects of the light phenomena, from infrared to ultraviolet rays.

What more is there to say about these huge eyes and aerials in Imma's drawing? The various species of Arthropoda will develop their capacity to perceive light in numerous ways. In this phylum, as in the drawing, the tactile antennae start around the eyes, opening these animals to specific aspects of the electromagnetic spectrum signals (infrared or ultraviolet). Each species has its specific antenna and there are hundreds of thousands of antenna types.

Entomologist Philip S. Callahan has put forth the controversial idea that insects have a generalized high sensitivity to the infrared energy spectrum perfectly designed to optimize the transmission and detection of free-floating scent molecules by "pumping" them into a coherent non-linear infrared emission phase through the use of sound. He states, "as long as sound is studied in one corner of the lab and scent in another, the mechanisms of these sound-modulated scent molecules will not be understood." Bees are one insect species well known to perceive and use ultraviolet.

*An insect's compound eyes*

What kind of consciousness accompanies compound eyes? "It must be a self-abandonment of the individual in a directionless multiplicity of all possible focal points or, as a mathematician might put it, facing the 'infinitely far plane' that surrounds our world."[3]
Their compound eyes see a decomposed space, or bits of information about space like serial linear units of pixels.

Self-abandonment is also there for us if we want to observe anything. If someone walks on a forest path but is busy in his mind sorting out a problem (e.g., anxiety), he won't see anything. The eyes are open, the visual information enters subliminally but doesn't reach the consciousness. Self-abandonment to sense the world is a heart decision to shut down the mental and observe. Then our inner light will meet the outer light. In this way, the eyes are formed in the embryo: an internal membrane movement comes to meet an external movement coming in.

In Imma's drawing, we can see a sort of tail branching off over the pool. It can be said that

2  Poppelbaum, *A New Zoology*, chap. 17.

3  Ibid.

the main function of a fish tail is propulsion. It seems that out of this whirling activity in the pool the creature in the drawing is propelled into gravity, into the air element. The nose of this threefold being is suggesting a passage from water to air. Of course, creatures of the air, like insects or spiders, are not breathing through a nose; their lung is in the abdomen. We can smell only in the air: animals can taste in water. The phylum insect represents the majority of all the animal species and they rely on smell for the running of their instinctual behavior.

Because of their lightness the pull of gravity is not so great for them. The insects invaded the air about the same time as the plant kingdom propagated on solid ground, establishing strong symbiotic links that last to this day. The insects also started to generate various sounds with their articulated body parts (such as crickets and cicadas still do today).

### Knee

In medieval pictures of the human being, Capricorn influences the knee, the mobile connection between our lower leg (Aquarius) and thigh (Sagittarius). As one of our biggest joints, and vital for our mobility in the outside world, the knee is a symbol of the whole articulated system animating our skeleton. Even the bones of the cranium have a kind of motion between them. This is what articulation is about. The constellation of Capricorn points to the knee as a symbol of the various ways the bones connect with one another to give us greater flexibility.

In the complex Capricorn glyph we sense a will to establish a link between two aspects. The cup shape at the top is a container that receives subtle energy. This energy enters and mingles with our own. "The knee is the area where the ether currents of the outer world (the Earth) enter into individual currents of the human being's own ether body" after going through the feet and legs that act as captors of Earth energy.[4]

### Saturn sphere rules Capricorn

The Saturn sphere invites the life of senses at the periphery of the body. Specialized organs of perception develop with the Arthropoda to have a better apprehension of the outside world.[5] The sense of sight already exists in more primitive creatures but with the articulated Arthropoda we reach a summit of variations.

It is the Saturn impact on animality that stimulates the opening of doors of perception (sense organs) to the multitudinous aspects of the outer world. Capricorn creates articulations between different parts to increase mobility. The sense of sight, omnipresent in Arthropoda, enormously favors flexible movements in space.

This Saturn sphere of activity tends to harmonize the outside and inside rhythms. It helps the integration of outside rhythmic stimuli inside an autonomous rhythmic organism. The subtle aspect of the spleen (the Saturn organ) does that in us.[6]

### The Consonant L

The consonant *L* "is a sound swinging in the element of life," or "a force relationship between human limbs and the Earth."[7] A sound between a vowel and a consonant "lifting us out of gravity."[8]

Imma's drawing shows a creature that is about to experience life outside water by being propelled into the air. In water, things have the same mass but weigh much less. For instance, our brain weighs 50 grams suspended in our brain fluid, whereas on a scale it weighs 1,500 grams. Arthropoda, out of water, are tiny (insects, spiders, etc.) and don't experience the full pull of gravity.

### Conclusion

The Capricorn impulse articulates three structural centers with limbs into a unity that serves the emergence of soul faculties. Saturn gives them, through multiple ways to use eyes, the chance to experience movement in space more fully. Percepts

---

4  McAllen, *The Listening Ear.*

5  Steiner, Cosmosophy, vol. 2, Oct. 29, 1921.

6  Steiner, *Occult Physiology.*

7  Steiner, quoted in McAllen, *The Listening Ear.*

8  Ibid.

and articulated movements come together more strongly with these varied groups of animals.

Some look clumsy and robotic with their instinctual drives (lobsters), whereas others have a more elegant fragile pliability—butterflies. Sometimes they dance in the air as a soul-group bringing a choreographic expression of their animal soul-group (a bee swarm).

The articulated external skeleton, made of chitin shields and rods with a ventral neural system, will reverse with the vertebrates into an internal articulated bone structure with dorsal neural system.

Through their many ways to sense the external world, Arthropoda harmonize their internal rhythms with the external ones—an aspect of the Saturn metabolic process.

## SAGITTARIUS

In the intimacy of our daily life we don't easily notice the vast pulsations of the dynamic cosmic clock we live by: that the Sun goes counterclockwise through the zodiac over a period of 25,920 years needs centuries of observation. That the planets seen from Earth trace a loopy pathway taking many years to complete would need long periods of careful observations. Nevertheless, ancient cultures were able to detect these pulsing rhythmic activities.

The main pulsing rhythms obvious to us are expressed in days and seasons. These pulses, owing to Earth's movements around itself and the Sun, accompany the threefold construction of plants (root, stem/leaves and flower/seed) and animals (head, thorax and abdomen). We notice that before this threefold nature can appear in space there is a need for a time process. This is simple observation.

The five Chinese HUA or movements (wood, fire, earth, metal, and water) express among other things this cyclical time process. These HUA have nothing at all to do with the four Greek elements and were incorrectly translated as five "elements" by the first translators of Chinese texts on physiology. These texts used ideograms that express more the idea of an activity and never a concept. That makes their translation difficult. It is like converting a poetic text on human physiology into a modern scientific language. The ideograms of the five HUA represent *a cyclical movement of metamorphosis through the constant increase and decrease of the light and warmth of the Sun on a daily and seasonal basis*. This time cycle has a profound impact on all the kingdoms of nature.

The plant emerges from a *point*—seed or bud. This is germination (*wood movement*), where *lines* of expression open in a vertical spiral gesture as roots and stems. Then the plant establishes itself in space with the rhythmic unfolding of *surfaces* with its leaves (*fire movement*). Maturity brings the growth of *volume* with flowers (*earth movement*). This last stage (fertilization) assures a future. In maturing, the seeds go into a desiccating process (*metal movement*) where the future germ is surrounded by compounds (oil and protein) essential for the next germination. Then the dry seeds disseminate and begin a period of dormancy in the ground (*water movement which is a return to the origin*). These five movements sum up the cycle of the plant. The basis of all geometry is here.

In animals, life starts with a germ (*contraction—water*) that expands into embryo/young (*opening into existence—wood*). Next we observe a full growth (*expansion in space—fire*). Like the flower stage, the animal reaches maturity and can reproduce (*contribution to the future of the species—earth*). The last stage we observe is old age (*a drying out process—metal*). With the animal expression again we have the five HUA.[9] We don't see life. We perceive its rhythms. What we see of life is its manifold manifestations. Life is never a mechanical rhythm but a dynamic one full of various pulses.

---

9   For more on the topic, see Jean Marc Eyssalet, *Dan l'Ocean des Saveurs, l'Intention du Corps—Les Cinq Chemins du Clair et de L'Obscur* (1988). Unfortunately I don't know of an English translation of these admirable books. A few decades ago a group of Chinese scholars in Paris decided to retranslate the old Chinese physiology books using the original roots of these ideograms. These old texts, written with pictograms, are not conceptual but represent images of activity. They look more like poetry books.

Earth's ecosystem rhythmically expands in spring-summer and contracts in autumn-winter. This is also the way the etheric world works outside and inside us. Plants and animals have various responses to this cycle (plants bloom and wither, animals hibernate and migrate, etc.).

Being smaller than nature, these five cycles reverberate much faster within human beings. To look at this cyclical movement within us we need to observe the only tissue that flows into the intimacy of each organ: the blood. Each organ influences the blood stream in a certain way many times a day.

For example: when the blood leaves the kidneys it loses heat, gases, liquids and various organic and mineral substances—this is urine. The kidneys, with their seed shape, constantly contract (water movement) the blood stream. No other organ reduces the blood like that to its essential mineral/organic content. Other organs are more involved in expanding the blood stream. This is the subject of another book.

*The Constellation of Sagittarius (Archer)*

### Content

This text explores the imprint of the intelligent activity of Sagittarius around us in the constant forming of human and animal creation. What is the relation between the Sagittarius sector of space, its glyph, the medieval image of this constellation, Imma's drawing, the element magnesium, the animal phylum fishes, the taste sense, the thigh, Jupiter as a ruling planet, the color rose–lilac and the consonants K and G? Based on Imma's drawings

in the first edition of *The Calendar of the Soul* in 1912, we can find a golden thread linking the various ways Sagittarius acts as a constant blueprint in nature.

### The Glyph and Traditional Picture

In the glyph we have an arrow pointing obliquely in a diagonal direction. The traditional picture shows a centaur with an arrow in tension on a bow pointing in one direction. The centaur is an image of the human being emerging slowly from its animal nature.

### The Drawing

The drawing shows a distinct vertical figure shooting out of the water where two whirls are seen on the surface.

On the shore of this patch of water behind the figure we see a rocky animal form resting like the Egyptian Sphinx.

From the water, like leaping arrows, two nearly vertical curves unite and give rise to two horizontal wings organizing the middle part of the drawing. The whole thing has a feeling of propulsion ending with flapping wings agitating the air below. These two vertical/horizontal central movements form an incomplete hollow at the center, where the human head of the Sphinx should be seen.

The human head of the Sphinx is not present in this drawing but instead a more animal-like mask is above suggesting a new direction of development toward more complex vertebrates. The word Sphinx comes from the Egyptian word *Shesepankh* meaning a living image. The Sphinx was created a long time before the pyramids, carved on the spot out of a single rock. Imma's drawing shows this rocky sculpture on a shore. It is known today that the basis of the Egyptian Sphinx was eroded by water. The centaur and the Sphinx are each half human half animal.

Then from this hollow between the wings a head form emerges and irradiates the top of the drawing with strong slanted eyes and a suggestion of a nose and mouth. In this hollow the glyph of Aries emerges suggesting a face.

## *Magnesium: A Lightning Element*

Magnesium is the substance used in nineteenth-century camera flashes. When it burns it has a dazzling, irradiating light that can overcome sunlight. The head mask in the drawing has this sort of irradiation. Magnesium itself has the role of a light propellant and is abundant in seeds to propel their new manifestation. It also sits at the center of the chlorophyll pigment essential to capture light in the vegetal kingdom. Magnesium propels light into the plant kingdom. In nature it often appears as magnesium silicate, as in the minerals serpentine and asbestos that tend to form a fibrous structure. In this drawing the head shows clearly this fibrous tendency to ray out. As magnesium oxide it is a solid that can hold a high temperature (2,000° C.). In association with sulfur, magnesium sulfate forms sixteen percent of ocean salts.[10]

In humans, in a very small quantity, it acts as a co-factor of enzymatic activities. Located inside cells it regulates the salt content (sodium pump) and acts on molecules that carry energy (ATP—ADP). The fulcrum point of magnesium in the blood is ruled by aldosterone from the adrenals acting on the kidneys.

## *Fishes: The Arrow-like Creatures*

*Fishes: 25,500 species:* The phylum fish is the first chordata group that has a vertebral column with a head. With his male/female head in meditation facing the sunrise, the Sphinx is an image of the animal on its way to the human. It is also an image of a listening heart.

The bottom part of this drawing with its whirly water is what is actually happening in the primitive ocean. One thing that is represented here is the beginning of the chordata venture (animal with a vertebral column/cranium). Sagittarius continues what has been started in Aries with the tunicata. We can see the Aries sign in the opening of the hollow formed by the wings.

With Aries we have the development of the phylum tunicata classified as pro-chordata because they don't form an inner skeleton. These are

among the first group of animals, during the Cambrian explosion to generate a notochord.[11] Some are still living embryos in the ocean today (lancelet). Human beings share this embryonic stage with a notochord with all the chordata, which is a kind of primitive cartilaginous backbone that synchronizes the formation of the neural tube in the embryo. The neural tube is the precursor of the central nervous system. The interior of our cartilaginous intervertebral discs is called the *nucleus pulposa* and is the remnant of the notochord.

With Sagittarius we see the emergence of the first real chordata, the multiple varieties of fishes. Some of them stay cartilaginous (sharks) but most of them develop bones. The two vertical movements in the drawing, uniting with the two horizontal flapping ones, may be seen as masses of muscles activating the wings. What is the shape of a fish? We can see it as a head-thigh moving like a directed arrow, as in the Sagittarius glyph.

Being practically weightless in water fishes don't need wings but only fins that help them to fly or glide in the liquid element and stabilize their position in connection with the light gravity they perceive. The whole fish form is an organ of propulsion not very different from our thighs. Both contain powerful muscles. These skeletal muscles are made of long, multinucleate cellular fibers giving them a structure like the two vertical fibrous movements in the drawing.

## *Sense of Taste*

Invertebrate animals have a diffuse nervous system, autonomous in nature, with several nervous ganglia ruling diverse basic functions. Added to that the chordata fishes initiate a central nervous system protected inside a flexible bony structure (vertebrae–cranium). Because of that, their sensorial and motor systems give rise to more complex instinctual behaviors. Creatures in the air can smell. Animals in the ocean can't; they taste, and the invertebrates develop it to various degrees. With fishes, we see the development of a very keen

---

10 See Hauschka, *The Nature of Substance.*

11 The Cambrian is the early Earth period where some representatives of most animal phyla first appear in the fossil record. The increase of free oxygen due to plant activity must have been a major factor.

sense of taste spread through their skin and gills. Salmon living in the ocean can find their way to the river where they were spawned just by tasting the river flowing into the ocean.

"The stripes down the side [lateral lines] exist to make them subtly sensitive to the light and warmth in their environment.... It is therefore a kind of nerve organ."[12]

### An Organ of Propulsion: Thigh

The thigh, with its powerful set of muscles, is designed to help us leap or spring forward. It is very useful for taking us in a particular direction. These muscles activate the leg (Aquarius) with the knee articulation (Capricorn).

### Jupiter Sphere Rules Sagittarius

With Jupiter, the life of nerves is essential to preserve the impressions received. The brain, which is made of nerves, increases its density and organization enormously with these first vertebrates.

The liver metabolic process is strongly involved in the organization of the inner territory (connective tissue) and defense (immunity). The liver helps the incarnated spirit to produce its unique set of proteins by juggling with organic matter.

### Consonants: K, G, NG, CH

In the center of the drawing there is a kind of tight hollow, a bit like a sphincter, where the flapping of the wings open and close. The word *sphincter* derives from the Greek verb *sphingo,* meaning to squeeze or tighten up. To make the consonants *K* and *G* we need to contract our abdominal muscles to increase air pressure, and at the same time block the air coming out by contracting the soft palate and tongue, the sudden opening of which

can generate the *K* or *G*. By doing so, we create a kind of sphincter link with air pressure.

In the drawing, at the meeting of the two wings, there is a sort of squeezing where the head suddenly pops out. The face in the drawing expresses an earthly animality in place of the listening human head facing the sunrise of the original Sphinx.

### Conclusion

The opposite of Sagittarius is Gemini. Gemini brings in the first multicellular creatures, a dual structure by initiating lateral bi-symmetry. With Sagittarius we tend toward a unity of direction within this symmetry. In water the fishes, as the first vertebrates, have the speed and versatility of an arrow while keeping the bilateral symmetry.

Fishes come with so many forms and colors. In general they are a concentration of strong muscles with a head—e.g. the salmon. They are designed to propel themselves forward. Their internal muscular-skeletal system is predominantly helping them to shoot ahead. The propulsion can be powerful, as with a shark, or when the soul-group inhabits the multitude they become one entity dancing in water like starlings in the air. This tendency to congregate together and act as one soul-group is present in all the phyla.

Experiencing slight gravity in water, fishes don't need wings but gentle fins to stay upright in water. Some of them, such as birds, develop wing-like structures (e.g. sting ray).

Speaking of wings, the constellation of Sagittarius is flanked by two bird constellations: Aquila, the eagle—symbol of immortality or of the spirit manifesting through the soul, and Cygnus the swan with its four stars in the form of a cross, symbolizing the soul crucified in matter.

---

12 Steiner, *From Elephants to Einstein...: Answers to Questions,* Feb. 20, 1924.

# INTO THE VORTEX, PART 2

## *Kevin Dann*

In my 2015 *Journal for Star Wisdom* article, "Into the Vortex," I offered a very limited survey of physical phenomena that have vortical form, concluding with the example of the "Polonaise" movements of cells anticipatory to the formation of the "primitive streak"—a formative movement by which the developing vertebrate embryo: establishes bilateral symmetry; determines the site of gastrulation; and initiates germ layer formation. Contemporary digital imaging techniques which make it possible to map the moment-to-moment migration of individual cells, their coalescence into tissues, and formation of organs, show that at almost every stage of embryogenesis, from initial cell division after fertilization to gastrulation to the full inventory of embryonic cell migration and organ formation, one observes "vortices all the way down."[1] Perhaps in no other arena of the physical world is it possible to find such overwhelming support for Rudolf Steiner's statement that "Everything real must be understood as a Vortex."[2]

Given that the vertebrate embryo is for the greater part of its lifespan a fluid, albuminous entity, it follows that it should obey the laws of fluid dynamics, and that the final ossified form should repeatedly display—from the skull's fontanel to the heart's musculature to the phalanges of our extremities—vortical form. Romanian artist Gabriel Kelemen's extraordinary drawings illustrate this ubiquity of the archetypal vortex form within the natural world (see Figure 1).

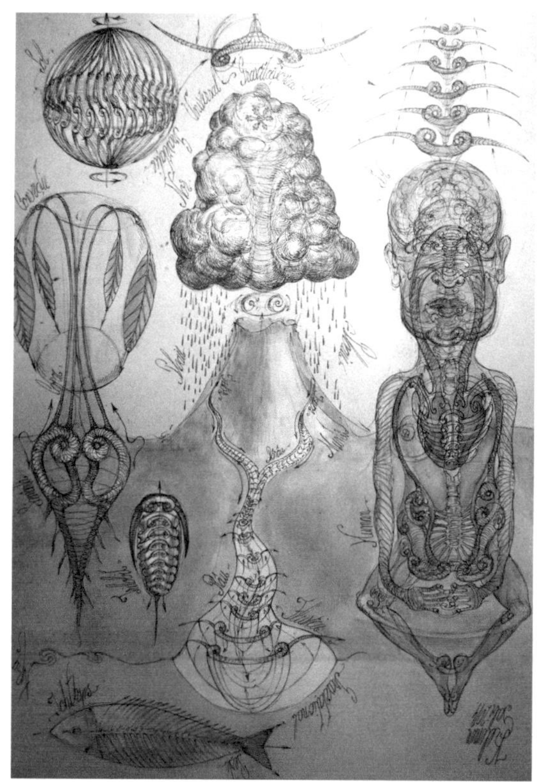

*Figure 1: "Drawing that renders the rheological structure of water flows from source to debouching into the sea, the relationship of similarity with solar equatorial cords, backbone and the rib network of the leaf" (Gabriel Kelemen,* Univeralitatea Arhetipuli Sfera: Vortex, *Romania, 2015)*

Translated as "vortex," rather than the more exact "vortex motion," Rudolf Steiner's term *Wirbelbewegung* loses the German word's emphasis on process, movement, becoming—qualities that

---

1   See for example the films made by Vincent Fleury's Materials and Systems Laboratory at Paris-Diderot University: http://www.msc.univ-paris-diderot.fr/~vfleury/portailembryonso.html. Fleury's *Les tourbillons de la vie: Une simple histoire de nos origins,* (Fayard: 2017) is perhaps the most radically "vorto-centric" of a suite of contemporary theories of vertebrate form that focus on the centrality of the toroid or vortex in morphogenesis. See also David B. Edelman, Mark McMenamin, Peter Sheesley, and Stuart Pivar, "Origin of the vertebrate body plan via mechanically biased conservation of regular geometrical patterns in the structure of the blastula," *Progress in Biophysics and Molecular Biology* (2016) pp. 212–244.

2   See Steiner, *Start Now!* p, 168.

characterize the dynamism of vortex action at any scale of nature. In German, *Wirbel* (vortex) is also the word for the *vertebra,* reminding us that the primary classificatory distinction we bring to the animal world is between all of those animals possessing a vertebra or backbone (*Wirbeltiere*) from all those which do not. *Wirbel* is deeply onomatopoeic in a way that our English *vortex* is not. Better to say "whorl" or "whirl." The bony vertebrae are indeed whirling, *wirbel*–ing whorls, Polonaise waltzes frozen in time. The spinal column and each of its graded forms from the Atlas to the Coccyx bone are vortex machines, etching into matter a stony frame upon which might be hung a glorious train of vortices arrested for the duration of every vertebrate's biography from birth to death as skull, brain, ears, nose, mouth, larynx, pharynx, shoulders, ribs, lungs, heart, liver, kidneys, pelvis, gonads, knees, ankles, and just about every tissue and organ and skeletal element in between.

In water or in air, at the scale of towering thundercloud or individual rain droplet, vortex movements continually reverse the inner and outer planes of their constituent forms, organs, organisms. Depending on the physical conditions of temperature, density, chemical composition, velocity, and so on, a vortex movement multiplies, ramifies, coalesces, disappears. It is simultaneously always a Time phenomenon as well as Space, whose true nature is better illustrated cinematically than merely via still photographs or drawings.

This characteristic of reversal, of turning outside in and inside out, seems to bear on the universality of Rudolf Steiner's three vortex axioms: The world is a vortex; the human being must become a vortex; everything performed as a vortex is magic.[3] In embryogenesis, vortices appear and disappear continuously, as new gestures, shapes, structures appear as if from nowhere, by "magic." Any honest examination of phylogenesis, of vertebrate evolution, finds this same *de novo* creation of physical form. Is the Vortex somehow implicated?

## Sea Cows, Sloths, and Speciation

In September 1922, in the first of three lectures to the Goetheanum workers describing "Early Conditions of the Earth," Rudolf Steiner characterized the pterosaurs—Earth's first flying vertebrate animals—as visual sense organs for the Cosmos, during the Lemurian period of Earth evolution:

These dragonbirds, they were in a way like eyes, which the Earth itself had.... [At that time] the Earth was like a giant fish, and these dragonbirds were the movable eyes with which the Earth perceived in the starry realm, in the realm of the Sun.

The Earth at one time was a giant animal, [which]…looked out into the universe through these dragonbirds, and with these movable eyes looked at everything.[4]

Always using the term *Drachenvogel,* rather than the scientific term "Pterosaur," Rudolf Steiner revealed out of his spiritual research a natural history that was totally unknown at that time or since. At a point when the "fire mist" atmosphere of the late Lemurian (Jurassic–Cretaceous, from 200 to 100 million years ago) had become to some extent purified of noxious sulfuric and nitric acid, the pterosaurs flew about on bat-like wings. "Acutely sensitive" to the Sun and Moon, the pterosaurs formed a luminous electromagnetic sheath around themselves, such that out of their own forces they would "shine and glimmer like fireflies."

Rudolf Steiner stressed the extreme sensitivity of these animals, particularly the eyes and their wings, which, when spread out under moonlight, gave them an extraordinary feeling of well-being. Just as a happy dog wags its tail, he said, the pterosaur's joy expressed itself in subtle waves of movement of its wings. The pterosaur also experienced the stars within its wings: "In the presence of the starry heavens they felt themselves blissfully within their wings. When the stars shone on them, these

---

3  Ibid., p. 169.

4  Steiner, "On Early Conditions (Lemuria)," *From Crystals to Crocodiles…: Answers to Questions,* Sep. 20, 1922. Translation here and throughout kindly provided by Richard Bloedon.

wings were speckled."[5] This seemingly poetic turn of phrase was meant literally by Rudolf Steiner, for he told his audience that close study of the fossil wing imprints of the pterosaur would show there to be "all kinds of stars" that had left impressions in the wings.

In 1921, a year before this lecture, Bernhard Hauff had published a monograph on the fossil fauna of the Holzmaden shale southeast of Stuttgart. Along with Jurassic ichthyosaurs and plesiosaurs, Hauff described two small pterosaurs—*Dorygnathus banthensis* (3-foot wingspan) and *Campylognathoides zitteli* (nearly 6-foot wingspan).[6] Though Steiner never specified a particular species of pterosaur (contemporary estimates give about 110 species in 85 genera), he explicitly says *"kleine Drachenvögel"* at one point in the lecture; this is consistent with both the Holzmaden animals and also *Rhamporhynchus muensteri* (4-foot wingspan) from the Solnhofen limestone—another German *Lagerstätte*—a place of exceptional fossil preservation. Like other Mesozoic reptiles—conspicuously, the dinosaurs—pterosaurs reached immense sizes. *Quetzalcoatlus northropi* fossils from Texas have wingspans ranging from 33 to 39 feet, the largest-known flying animal of all time.

Pterosaurs were not the only strange animals that moved about in the Jurassic; the late Mesozoic saw the proliferation of marine reptiles, including ichthyosaurs and plesiosaurs. While modern natural science has always conceived of these animals as swimming about in oceanic waters, Steiner's research showed that they inhabited a living, proteinaceous Life Sphere in between the upper fire mist, harboring the pterosaurs, and the slowly coagulating continental crust below.[7] Ichthyosaurs and plesiosaurs "half-swam, half-waded" in a muddy, greenish-brown "slurry" that encircled the Earth in the wake of

the Moon's separation from the Earth at the end of the Triassic (figure 2).

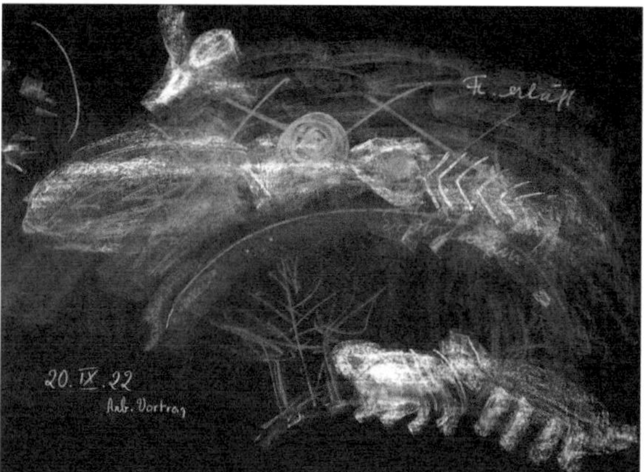


*Figure 2. Steiner's chalkboard drawing for the lecture of Sept. 20, 1922: pterosaur in "fire-mist" at upper left; ichthyosaur (left, with large pineal organ above head) and plesiosaur (right, with pronounced ribs) in the central "earth slurry" zone; and below, unidentified land mammals (on the right, perhaps the ground sloth?) on solid earth*

In that same 1922 lecture, Rudolf Steiner described the ichthyosaur as having gigantic, luminous eyes that attracted the pterosaurs like mosquitoes to a lamp. "Hypnotized" by the ichthyosaurs, the pterosaurs would fall to the surface of the half-water–half-earth habitat of the ichthyosaurs, which then ate them. Given that ichthyosaurs had by far the largest eyes of any terrestrial or aquatic vertebrates, including those larger in body size by orders of magnitude (like the great whales, or dinosaurs), Steiner combined astute, uncontestable natural history with simply astonishing statements. The luminous, mesmerizing ichthyosaur eye, however, is just the beginning: he also claimed that, because of their "electrical" nature, the pterosaurs caused the ichthyosaurs great abdominal pain. The pterosaurs, on the other hand, had a sense of wellbeing when they were in the throat of an ichthyosaur! "Just as the Turks wanted to go to Paradise, these birds regarded it as their salvation to go down the throat of an Ichthyosaurus."[8]

More astonishing still, the ichthyosaurs, in digesting the pterosaurs, took on new forms. This same process Steiner ascribed to the plesiosaurs:

---

5   Ibid.

6   Bernhard Hauff, *Untersuchung der Fossilfundstätten von Holzmaden im Posidonienschiefer des oberen Lias Württembergs. Palaeotographica, Beiträge zur Naturgeschichte der Vorzeit,* 1921.

7   See Bosse, *The Mutual Evolution of Earth and Humanity,* part 2.

8   Steiner, *From Crystals to Crocodiles…,* lect. 7.

"Due to the fact that the ichthyosaur and plesiosaur devoured dragon birds, their whole internal being was transformed."[9] From Rudolf Steiner's descriptions, this would seem to have been the late Jurassic or early Cretaceous periods; he notes the acceleration of the Earth's rotation at this time, as well as the appearance of gigantic cycads and tree ferns; the precipitation of sulfur and other elements out of the fire atmosphere; and an increasing hardening of the Earth's surface.

Without explicitly saying so, Rudolf Steiner was describing the transition from the Mesozoic to the Cenozoic—late Lemuria to early Atlantis. This was the time both of the extinction of the dinosaurs and the rise of mammals. Modern paleontology and evolutionary biology continue to put forward grand speculative explanations for this catastrophic event, during which 75 percent or more of all species vanished from the Earth. With the exception of some ectothermic species like sea turtles and crocodiles, no tetrapods weighing more than 55 pounds survived.

In describing this time period, Rudolf Steiner says not a word about extinction; instead, he speaks of how the ichthyosaur became the "*Seekuh*" (sea cow, or manatee, most likely *Prorastomus sirenoides*, a primitive sirenian from the Eocene, ca. 40 mya), and the plesiosaur became the "Megatherien" (the giant ground sloth, *Megatherium spp.*). "These animals have adopted the forms which were found in the air animals they ate. And the dragonbirds changed their shape because there were no more of certain substances in the air. They fell closer to Earth, and gradually emerged later as birds."[10] Elsewhere in this lecture, Rudolf Steiner seems to indicate a specific "reincarnation" of the pterosaurs as eagles and vultures, for he says that these birds "emerged from them later," preserving their acute eyesight.[11]

Each of these instances of radical transformation—pterosaur to birds of prey; ichthyosaur to manatees; plesiosaur to ground sloths—is not so much "speciation" as fantastic, unimaginable

metamorphosis, for in all three cases the shift is at the taxonomic level of *Class*—fully four ranks of biological classification above the species level. Reptiles (Class Reptilia) become birds (Class Aves) and mammals (Class Mammalia)! With this single lecture, and explicit attention to but three Lemurian–Mesozoic animals, Rudolf Steiner throws wide open the question of how, during Earth history, animal forms changed. This is, of course, the central question of evolutionary biology. Steiner left unanswered a vast array of fundamental questions about morphological change over time, despite his sustained critique of Darwinian theory, as well as his offering—throughout his books and lectures—a vastly elaborated view of evolution emphasizing: 1) the co-evolution of Earth and humanity; 2) the priority of spiritual involution in advance of physical evolution; and 3) the human being as the "stem" from which all animals originated.

### Turning Inside Out

Of all fossil animals, the ichthyosaur, plesiosaur, pterosaur, and *Archaeopteryx* are the only ones Steiner mentioned in his lectures. Perhaps it is unsurprising, then, that two of these ancient reptiles—the ichthyosaurs and plesiosaurs—are mentioned in a 1923 lecture that is the most explicit indication he ever gave about the manner by which dramatic changes occur in animal morphology:

> For example, let us assume that we were to go back a very long time in earthly evolution. We would then encounter completely different life forms, completely different earthly events. As you know, there have been epochs when huge animals lived on Earth that are now extinct. Entire species and orders of species have died out. Paleontologists and geologists now search for their fossilized remains in the formation of the Earth.
>
> Let us assume, then, that we have returned, roughly speaking, to this very early stage of evolution when ichthyosaurs, plesiosaurs, and other remarkable animals were living on Earth. These beings were not the products of the physical matter of the Earth. They were formed out of the cosmos, from the ether. And when the time

_______

9 Ibid.
10 Ibid.
11 Ibid.

came when these beasts gradually died out, all their etheric matter, if I may put it so, remained behind. The animals themselves were no longer there, of course. But the etheric matter from which they were formed stayed behind, just as our etheric body stays behind. And these etheric materials constituted the starting point or initiative from which later—after these etheric forms had passed through the cosmos—other beings were formed, until finally the world of animals as we know it today appeared.

Take for example the sequence of the three evolutionary periods leading up to the appearance of the human being. You find three successive animal forms following each other closely. We know that for one form to evolve out of the preceding form, a passage through the cosmos with the help of etheric forces is necessary, just as a similar passage through the cosmos between two human lives is necessary. Thus, when we come to the third form of animals, they too pass into the ether. And then, after a certain period of time, the human being—formed out of the ether—appears influenced, as always, by this detour through the cosmos.[12]

The story of our shared history with the animal kingdom is written into their spectacularly diversified forms, but in a much deeper and more meaningful way than neo-Darwinian theory offers us. Perhaps the deepest expression of that shared history is that just as our etheric bodies are turned inside out between incarnations; so, too, were the etheric bodies of our animal cousins, during the ancient time when the Earth Life Sphere was resonant with shimmering etheric forces. The starry group soul beings once transformed tissues, organs, and bodily structures of Earth's diverse creatures, on the human being's way through the long Lemurian afternoon.

Rudolf Steiner discovered that the most fundamental gesture at the heart of creation was that of turning outsides into insides, and insides into outsides. Finding this simple, elegant gesture as one of Creation's most constant leitmotifs, he often analogized it with placing one's hand in a glove and then turning the glove inside out. Speaking in 1908 of the evolution of fish, he dismissed the Darwinian view, saying that the fish's swim bladder, gills, and lateral line organs were transformed by turning them inside out, producing, respectively, the human being's eardrum, inner ear bones, and the three semi-circular canals. Some sense of the magical nature of this metamorphosis is given by Steiner's remark that "everything material vanishes" in this "marvelous astral work."[13]

Along with repeatedly drawing attention to the significance of Goethe's discovery of the skull as metamorphosed vertebral bone, Rudolf Steiner gave considerable weight to his own research into the polar and complementary relationship between the long bones and the skull—an example of "turning inside out," that opened out into the wider realm of the intertwined and intimate relationship between Embryology and Astronomy.[14] Speaking at another time of these skeletal transformations, he declared: "There is nothing in the realm of life that could not arise as a metamorphosis of a primary form."[15] When Rudolf Steiner speaks of the limbs of one incarnation transforming into the head organization of the next incarnation; the human countenance turned inward during the Old Saturn and Sun periods; the future human countenance bearing our inner moral qualities; the past and future transformations of the human being's primordial sense organ, the pineal gland (which bears the unmistakable form of the vortex); putting on the Resurrection Body; and the transformation of Earth into a Sun, in every instance he is speaking of "turning inside out," and each of these metamorphoses is accomplished through the effectual production of some manner of Vortex, at the center of which polarities come to rest, and spiritual beings—including the human being—and forces can work creatively, radically, metamorphically, *magically.*

---

12 Steiner, "What is Anthroposophy?" July 15, 1923. By "three successive periods," Rudolf Steiner I believe is speaking of Polarian, Hyperborean, and Lemurian, *not* Paleozoic, Mesozoic, and Cenozoic.

13 Steiner, "Some Characteristics of the Astral World," October 21. 1908.

14 Steiner, "Astronomy," January 1, 1921.

15 Steiner, "Working with Sculptural Architecture," Jan. 4, 1915.

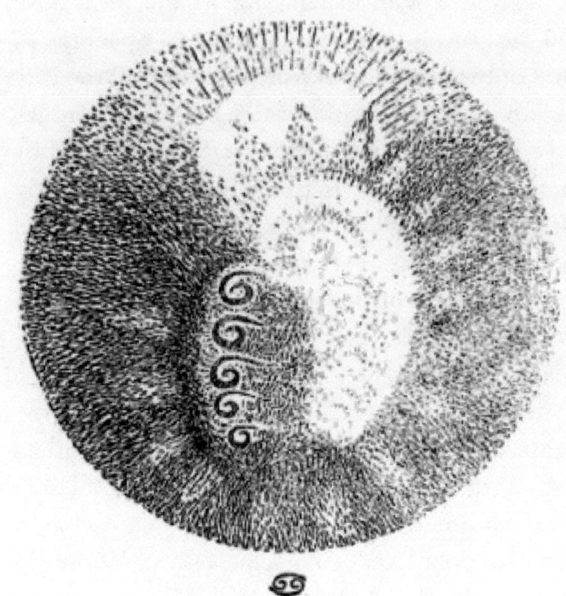

Figure 3: The Crab

## The Way of the Crab

Most importantly, Rudolf Steiner *performed* this gesture of the *Wirbelbewegung* throughout his own life, bringing to humanity the most extraordinary gifts. One sees this stamp of the Crab–Cancer (German=*Krebs*) everywhere in his biography. It runs like a red thread through his spiritual exercises (eg., the "basic exercises"; the *Rückschau;* the clay ball exercises and his indications about projective geometry); the structural form of his books, lectures, verses and meditations; his architectural and sculptural works (most spectacularly in the Goetheanum, both its fundamental form and its pictorial program; the Cancer–Vortex–Polonaise form is perhaps the most ubiquitous gesture throughout the interior and exterior of the building). Calling for the crafting of a spiritualized astronomy in his

introduction to the December 1920 "The Search for the New Isis, Divine Sophia" lecture series, Rudolf Steiner says "we must find the way of Cancer the Crab (*Krebsweg*); we must come to an astronomy inwardly, so that by the inner powers of vision we may awaken the course of the world that leads through the Saturn, Sun, Moon, Earth, Jupiter, Venus and Vulcan periods."[16] One could say that, in his pursuit of the Way of the Shepherds, to complement and metamorphose the Way of the Magi toward a spiritualized science of nature, Rudolf Steiner followed "the Way of the Crab."

From all directions, materialistic natural science, with its spectacular tools of digital visualization and demonstration, is once again bringing to us the image of the Vortex. As it came to be in the late nineteenth and early twentieth centuries, the Vortex looms as a kind of Arcanum, inviting exploration and discovery. Arcana, too, experience metamorphoses, and if we are to follow the Way of the Crab pioneered by Rudolf Steiner, we will find our way toward a higher, transformative meaning of the Vortex.[17]

---

16 Steiner, "The Search for the New Isis, Divine Sophia," December 23, 1920.

17 In their own pioneering work with the Minor Arcana of the Tarot, Joel Park and Phillip Malone have discerned a polarity between the "horizontal"/ Growth–Time/Water aspect of the 22 Major Arcana and the "vertical"/Eternity–Space/Fire aspect of the 10 Minor Arcana, that is bridged or mediated by four Minor "Court" Arcana that express the four planes of "magical influx from the Beyond." At the center of the Cancer/Vortex eternally lies the counterspatial realm of the Plane of Formation; the Plane of Creation; the Plane of Emanation; and the Ain Soph, the Plane of the Unlimited.

# SATURN IN CANCER:
## RETURNING TO THE ORIGIN OF THE HOUSES, PART 1

### *Joel Matthew Park*

### CANCER AND THE MIDHEAVEN

In my contribution to last year's edition of *Star Wisdom*, "First Steps Toward a Grail Timeline," I referred to a lecture given by Rudolf Steiner on January 2, 1914, in which he described Saturn and Sun in Cancer, approaching culmination, at the time of Parzival's first visit to the Grail Castle.[1] I noted that whereas I was advancing the hypothesis that Saturn and Sun were in *Libra* at the time of Parzival, Steiner seemed to be giving a picture at variance with that hypothesis (i.e., in *Cancer*). Is there any way of reconciling these two ideas? Is there a way that Saturn and Sun could be in *both* Libra *and* Cancer simultaneously?

This question is not as ludicrous as it might seem upon first reading. Steiner has left us a clue by the word "culmination." This word is used in an astrological and astronomical sense almost exclusively to refer to the Midheaven—i.e., the maximum northerly latitude approached by a given stellar body over the course of a *day* (as opposed to its moving exaltation, which is its maximum northerly latitude over the course of its movement through all twelve signs of the zodiac). In the story of *Parzival*, Eschenbach refers to the wounded King Anfortas experiencing maximum pain every time frosty Saturn reaches its zenith. If he were to mean moving exaltation by this, it would translate as: "Every 29.5 years, Anfortas experienced the greatest pain." This does not make sense in the greater context of the story, as Anfortas does not experience his wound for such a long period of time. If instead we understand Eschenbach to be referring to Saturn's *daily* zenith, its culmination in the heavens, this makes

much more sense: this implies he is referring to the time *each day* that Anfortas experiences the greatest amount of pain—the time that seems to determine when the Grail Rite is practiced in order to bring him some relief.

In the story, we know that it is around Michaelmas that Parzival first comes to the Grail Castle, and that there is "summer snow" on the ground (a reference to the first snowfalls that are sometimes experienced in late September in some regions north of the equator). If Sun and Saturn were conjunct in the *constellation* of Cancer, this would have been around July—which is nowhere near Michaelmastide, and a very unlikely time of year for snowfall in eastern France. Steiner's reference to Saturn and Sun together *at Michaelmas* does lead us to a very specific time in history, and therefore goes very far in helping us determine the *year* that these events occurred (see last year's article). But the reference to Cancer still remains a mystery—is there an astrological system that brings together the sign of Cancer and the Midheaven? Is Cancer related to the *diurnal* cycle in any way?

A further clue is contained in a lecture series that Rudolf Steiner gave only a few weeks later, on "Human and Cosmic Thought."[2] Over the course of the first two lectures, Rudolf Steiner laid out for the first time his teaching on the twelve points of view: Idealism, rationalism, mathematism, materialism, sensationalism, phenomenalism, realism, dynamism, monadism, spiritism, pneumatism, and psychism. In the third lecture, he explicitly placed these twelve points of view into relationship with the signs of the zodiac (see Figure 1, Zodiac of World Outlooks).

---

1   See the last lecture in Steiner, *Christ and the Spiritual World*.

2   See Steiner, *Human and Cosmic Thought*.

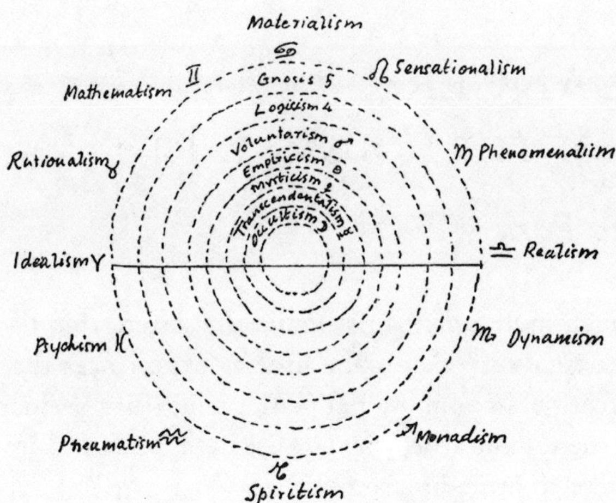



*Figure 1, Zodiac of Worldviews*

Notice that materialism, in relationship to Cancer, is in the Midheaven of this zodiacal wheel. Furthermore, notice the peculiar ordering of the constellations: they move from Aries at the Ascendent to Cancer at the Midheaven, down to Libra at the Descendent, then to Capricorn at the Nadir, and finally back to Aries. In other words, they are arranged *clockwise*. This is the opposite of how the constellations in the heavens would be arranged if Aries was rising: Capricorn would be directly overhead, and Cancer would be below us (see fig. 2).

By the way, these lectures give us a more enlivened picture of what "Saturn and Sun together in Cancer" would represent for Parzival. In the third lecture, Steiner brings Saturn into relationship with the soul-mood of Gnosis (that is, perception of fine details in a given domain), and the Sun with the soul-mood of Empiricism (acknowledging only what is within one's immediate surroundings and experience). With Cancer brought into connection with materialism, we see Parzival's dilemma: at that particular moment, he could only approach the wounded Anfortas with an empirical, materialistic gnosis; in layman's terms, he couldn't see past the end of his nose. All he could perceive were the mundane, material features of the situation; he had no insight into his own soul, nor the souls of others, let alone into the deeper spiritual realities at work underneath the bizarre procession of the Grail Rite. He was entirely lacking in depth of character or perception.

We come to a third development, a third clue in the eurythmy performance of Rudolf Steiner's "Twelve Moods" in 1915, only 19 months after the lectures on "Human and Cosmic Thought" and "Christ and the Spiritual World." Steiner crafted twelve verses, one for each sign of the zodiac; once again, they were presented in the order moving *clockwise* through the zodiac: Aries, Taurus, Gemini, Cancer, Leo, Virgo, Libra, Scorpio, Sagittarius, Capricorn, Aquarius, Pisces. Each of these verses had seven lines, one for each of the seven planets, in this order: Sun, Venus, Mercury, Mars, Jupiter, Saturn, and Moon. According to Ruth Pusch, Steiner "spoke of the whole poem as the journey of the Sun **through the day**: Aries at sunrise, Cancer at noon, Leo in the afternoon, etc. It could also denote, he said later, the changing course of humanity's life on Earth" (emphasis added).

And here we come to full clarity! We see clearly laid out: 1) the signs of the zodiac in a clockwise direction; 2) Aries representing the Ascendent, Cancer the Midheaven, Libra the Descendent, and Capricorn the Nadir; and 3) that this cycle shows us the diurnal movement of the Sun (and, by inference, the rest of the planets). Yet this still leaves us at a crossroads. We are presented with a spiritual crisis, an Arcanum—what does Steiner mean by the passage of the Sun or any other wandering star through all twelve signs of the zodiac in a single day? No planet moves that swiftly! And why, if the signs of the zodiac present themselves in one order in the sky does Steiner associate the movements of the planets diurnally with the opposite order?

When we look around us at the night sky, we see, for example, Aries to the East, then Pisces somewhat north of it, then Aquarius, then Capricorn at the Midheaven. This is the same order that the precession of the equinoxes takes, and therefore the change from one cultural age to the next: the Greco-Roman age of Aries, to the European age of Pisces, to the Russo-Slavic age of Aquarius, to the American age of Capricorn.

On the other hand, the cycle of the year moves through the signs of the zodiac in the opposite order. The Sun is in Aries from mid-April to mid-May, then Taurus, then Gemini, etc. And while

*Figure 2, Horoscope of the Resurrection*

the precession of the equinoxes moves the planets relatively slowly backward (i.e., counterclockwise) through the constellations, the daily apparent motion of the planets (and constellations, for that matter!) is forward (i.e., clockwise, rising in the east and setting in the west). We start to have the feeling of two simultaneous, oppositional yet complementary movements. This is akin to the two divergent ways of arranging the order of the planets: in terms of cosmic evolution (Saturn, Sun, Moon, Mars, Mercury, Jupiter, Venus) vs. in terms of biographical development (Moon, Mercury, Venus, Sun, Mars, Jupiter, Saturn).

In an email exchange with Robert Powell on this subject, he informed me that, as far as he knows, *everytime* Rudolf Steiner presented the zodiacal wheel, it was with the signs running clockwise![3] Why would he do such a thing? And what might be the value in learning to experience the movements of the seven planets over the course of the day? Is there any astrological tradition to which this unique astrological technique of Steiner's was related? Or did it emerge "ex nihilo," as a new creation all of his own, as so many of his innovations seem to be on first glance?

### The Problem of the Astrological Houses

What is reassuring about most of ancient astrology is its consistency. There seems to be, if not unanimous agreement, at the very least easily reconcilable and slight differences amongst the astrological traditions of ancient Babylonia, Egypt, India, Greece, etc., with most of these traditions originating in documented form in Babylon some 2,500 to 3,000 years ago.[4] The seven planets, the twelve signs, their archetypal representation and mythological significance were virtually universal. The signs were twelve, and 30° apiece; the stars upon which this order rested were found in Aldebaran at 15° Taurus and Antares at 15° Scorpio.

Then something happened. First of all, the tradition was lost: one particular codification of the sidereal zodiac (Ptolemy's *Tetrabiblios*) resulted in astrology getting "stuck." Rather than the Sun precessing through the signs of the zodiac, the Sun remained put: it would forever, it seemed, rise at 0° Aries on the first day of Spring—we would never enter the "Age of Pisces," let alone the longed-for "Age of Aquarius"! Perception began to separate from cognition (a phenomenon that would fully flower in Cartesianism and Copernicanism, a fundamental divide that insidiously underlies virtually every modern perspective, completely unnoticed!). Ancient astrology eventually divided into what we now know as astrology—which has nothing to do with the stars, retaining only the mytho-poetic and archetypal elements from the ancients—and what we now

call astronomy—which only addresses the outer garment of the stars, having sacrificed mythopoesis on the altar of so-called "objectivity." (The only culture to retain the original, sidereal astrology exists in the Vedic Astrology of India).

How did this happen? The destiny of Europe was to forget, to be cast into the wilderness culturally. While Europe suffered the "dark ages," with little advance in the way of either mythopoetic culture or technological achievement and scientific discovery, the advanced Islamic cultures of the Middle East both retained the treasures of past cultures (such as the writings of Ptolemy) as well as attempted to tap into the scientific revolution and discoveries that were only meant to begin to come about in the modern age. The School of Gondishapur effectively severed mythopoesis from science, and encouraged the former to remain stuck in a past "golden age," and the latter to advance as quickly as possible, drawing the technological future into the present in an increasingly destructive way.

Just prior to the beginning of this confusion (Ptolemy wrote in the second century AD) seems to coincide with the emergence of a new perspective in astrology: the so-called Astrological Houses. The first writing on the Houses come from the massive work *Astronomica,* written by Manilius in the first century AD. The earliest recorded horoscopes that were cast utilizing the Houses also come from this period, more or less contemporaneous with the life of Christ. However, almost since the beginning (unlike the original tenets of ancient, sidereal astrology) there has never been agreement as to the nature of the Houses.

We can briefly summarize the few features about which everyone seems to agree. First, regarding the matter of perspective, the movement of the planets through the twelve signs of the zodiac has to do with the way the planets appear to move through the *fixed* background of the zodiac from the point of view of the Earth. This movement is universal regardless of one's position on the Earth: when Sun is in Aries, this is true no matter where you live. When it comes to the Houses, on the other hand, this is not the

---

3   Another prime example was in his artistic representation of the eurythmy forms for the zodiac, placing them in a twelve-fold color wheel—once again, in a clockwise order (see fig. 3).

4   See, for example, Powell, *History of the Zodiac.*

case. Both the planets *and* the fixed stars—everything that is in the sky above us—dwell in different Houses based on the time of day and one's position (in the case of a horoscope, one's time and place of birth). This is due to the fact that, universally, the Ascendent (i.e., the degree of the zodiac that is rising in the east) determines the placement of the twelve houses. Generally speaking, there are somewhat different portions of the sky (and therefore planets and stars) in the Houses of each individual's horoscope. This fact is of key significance: that while the planets' movement against the background of fixed stars is universal, the firmament's relationship to the twelve Houses is *entirely individual,* it is determined by the subject's point of view.

This brings us to another point of agreement: there are twelve Houses, just like there are twelve signs of the zodiac. Finally, it is generally agreed that the placement of different planets (and to a lesser extent, fixed stars) in the different Houses gives some indication of specific destiny events in one's life. From there, the viewpoints splinter in every direction. For example, are the Houses of equal length, like the signs of the zodiac, or do they vary in length? How does one calculate the length if they do vary? Does the First House begin at the Ascendant, covering approximately the first 30° above the horizon, or is the Ascendent the midpoint of the First House? A brief perusal of astrological literature will quickly present at least a dozen different ways of divvying up the chart.[5]

And what do the different houses indicate in terms of one's destiny, what realms or stations of life do they rule over (e.g. birth, death, friendships, enemies, health, career, etc.)? There is little agreement here, either, but generally one finds the following categories: The 1st House deals with one's life and character. The 2nd House has to do with one's fortune and estate; the 3rd, with siblings. The 4th House is the realm of one's parents, and the 5th is the realm of children. The 6th House indicates health; the 7th, marriage. The 8th house

is that of death, and the 9th of journeys. The 10th house has to do with honors and preferments, and the 11th is the house of friendships. The 12th house is the house of enemies and misfortune.

This seems straightforward enough, except for the fact that (most) astrologers count the houses, starting from the Ascendent, in a counterclockwise motion, while others count them clockwise. This means that for many astrologers, the Midheaven indicates social status, while for others the Nadir is the proper realm for this aspect of life. This is perhaps the point of greatest divergence, and it hinges on a fundamental difference in perspective.

For those who arrange the houses counterclockwise, the justification is simple. The Ascendent (and the region of the sky trailing just behind it) is the first portion of sky to rise over the horizon at one's birth—for simplicity's sake, let's say 0° Taurus was the Ascendent at birth. That would make all 30° of Taurus the 1st House, as it proceeded to rise over the course of the next two hours (a little less, actually). Then Gemini would come over the horizon, becoming the region of the 2nd House; Cancer would follow as the 3rd House, and so on, all the way through the first day of life until Taurus was once again rising over the horizon. This then makes Taurus 1st, Gemini (which is now just below the horizon) 2nd, Cancer 3rd (even lower below the horizon), and Leo 4th (at the Nadir). The movement of the sky over the course of the first 24 hours of birth has determined the placement of the houses, in a counterclockwise order.

While there are other systems for building up the 12 houses counterclockwise (for example, Robert Powell's Hermetic House system from *Hermetic Astrology*, vol 2, a system he no longer uses), they basically all hinge on the idea that *the Houses are an epiphenomenon of the passage of time.* Whether it is the movement of the stars across the firmament over the course of the first day of life, or the movement of the Moon over the course of the gestational period (as in the Hermetic House system), the underlying assumption is that the Houses simply *do not exist* until these movements have created them over the course of time. From this

---

5   For a brief but informative summary, see Powell, *History of the Houses.*

point of view, they are not like the signs of the zodiac and the planets in having an independent existence—they exist only as a result of the activity of other independent phenomena.

The original system, as laid out by Manilius and rediscovered by Jacques Dorsan in the twentieth century,[6] is based on *space* rather than *time*. Manilius's twelve "temples," as he calls them, are based on a division of the starry heavens into four quadrants. This division emerges *from the Earth's relationship to the Sun*, based on East (the Ascendent), West (the Descendent), above (the Midheaven) and below (the Nadir). For Manilius, this is of the utmost importance; for him, the *entire universe* hangs together on this cross:

> Come now; prepare an attentive mind for learning the cardinal points: four in all, they have positions in the firmament permanently fixed and receive in succession the speeding signs. One looks out for the rising of the heavens as they are born into the world and has the first view of the Earth from the level horizon; the second faces it from the opposite edge of the sky, the point from which the starry sphere retires and hurtles headlong into Tartarus; a third marks the zenith of high Heaven, where wearied Phoebus halts with panting steeds and rests the day and determines the mid-point of shadows; the fourth occupies the nadir, and has the glory of forming the foundation of the sphere; in it the stars complete their descent and commence their return, and at equal distances it beholds their risings and settings. These points are charged with exceptional powers, and the influence they exert on fate is the greatest known to our science, because the celestial circle is totally held in position by them as by eternal supports; did they not receive the circle, sign after sign in succession, flying in its perpetual revolution, and clamp it with fetters at the two sides and lowest and highest extremities of its compass, Heaven would fly apart and its fabric disintegrate and perish.[7]

Manilius is unabashedly zealous and candid regarding his perspective: there may be manifold spheres of celestial entities circling perpetually around the Earth, but the foundation is the cross formed by the cardinal points of east, west, above, below: without them, all would disintegrate into chaos.

He then makes it clear in what order the story told through the four quadrants should be read. It is intuitive, and therefore simple and elegant:

> Nor must you rest content with observing each cardinal point; you must note with a retentive mind the spaces between them, which extend over a larger range and possess special powers. The curve which stretches from the orient to the topmost point of the circle claims the earliest age and infant years. The slope which sinks down from the summit of the sky till it reaches the Occident succeeds to the years of childhood and includes in its province control of tender youth. The portion which appropriates the setting Heaven and descends to the bottom of the circle rules the period of adult life, a period tested by incessant change and checkered fortunes. But the part by whose return to the orient Heaven's course is done and which with enfeebled strength slowly ascends the back-bent arc, this part embraces the final years, life's fading twilight, and palsied age.[8]

We can imagine the circle created by these twelve temples in relation to the light of the Sun: it emerges from the darkness below the horizon at dawn in the East, gives the greatest amount of light at midday directly overhead, then gradually the light dies as it sets in the West. At midnight, the darkness is greatest as the Sun is directly beneath us.

Rudolf Steiner created a twelve-fold color wheel in conjunction with his artistic representation of the eurythmy forms for the twelve signs of the zodiac. The seven so-called "constellations of light" were above the horizon, with Cancer at the Midheaven, while the five "constellations

---

6  Dorsan, *The Clockwise House System: A True Foundation for Sidereal and Tropical Astrology.*

7  Manilius. *Astronomica*, pp. 145, 147.

8  Ibid., p. 149.

of darkness" were below, with Capricorn at the Nadir (see fig. 3):

*Figure 3. Eurythmy Zodiac*

| Aries | = | Red |
| Taurus | = | Orange |
| Gemini | = | Yellow |
| Cancer | = | Green |
| Leo | = | Blue |
| Virgo | = | Indigo |
| Libra | = | Purple |
| Scorpio | = | Lilac |
| Sagittarius | = | Pale Lilac |
| Capricorn | = | Peach Blossom |
| Aquarius | = | Pale Rose |
| Pisces | = | Rose |

There are a number of astrologers who find a Hermetic "correspondence by analogy" between the twelve signs of the Zodiac and the twelve Houses. The First House is analogous to Aries, the second to Taurus, etc. In the counterclockwise system, this yields a wheel of Houses that would exactly mirror the signs were Aries rising in the east (see the order of the signs in fig. 2): Aries/1st House is in the East, Capricorn/10th House is above, Libra/7th House is in the West, and Cancer/4th House is below.

In the clockwise House systems, the analogy holds true (1st House = Aries, 2nd House = Taurus, etc.), but the order runs the other way. Aries as 1st House is still in the East, and Libra as 7th House still in the West, but Cancer as 4th House is above, and Capricorn as 10th House is below. This gives us exactly the picture formed by Steiner's various representations of the twelve signs (see fig. 1 and fig. 3).

Therefore, although he never *explicitly* named it as such, *implicitly* Rudolf Steiner seemed to use a clockwise House system throughout his career as spiritual researcher. It is this and, as far as this author can tell, only this, that makes sense of his statement that the Twelve Moods of the zodiac express the movement of the planets through the twelve signs of the zodiac *in the course of a day*, as none of them, even the rapidly moving Moon, moves through all twelve signs in one day. However, all of the planets and fixed stars, on a daily basis, move in a clockwise direction through all twelve Houses or "temples" of the firmament from the geocentric perspective.

This also solves the riddle of how Saturn and Sun could be in the sign of Libra at Michaelmas, while also being in the sign of Cancer. Steiner is merely pointing to the fact that both Saturn and Sun were more or less directly overhead, and that under this sign, Saturn exercised baneful effects on both Anfortas's health, as well as on Parzival's presence of mind. His lectures on "Human and Cosmic Thought" three weeks later throw more light on the importance of the placement of Saturn. Steiner argues that Saturn (as the soul-mood of Gnosis) is best placed in the "zodiac of world outlooks" in the sign of Capricorn (as the outlook of Spiritism), the sign at the Nadir, opposite to Cancer. Perhaps we can conclude that when Saturn is directly overhead (in "Cancer," i.e., the 4th House), it is in exile, and therefore has an unhealthy effect, whereas when it is directly below us (in "Capricorn," i.e., the 10th House), it is dignified and operates with a healing, life-giving effect.

Perhaps this gives us a secret as to Rudolf Steiner's seemingly miraculous effectiveness and productivity over the course of his life. Perhaps he knew not just the right *day,* in an astrological sense, for performing a certain activity or speaking on a certain topic; perhaps, by utilizing a combination of spiritual sensitivity and the clockwise House system, he knew the right *moment* to express certain teachings or perform certain actions. When we understand (as did Manilius) the twelve Houses emanating from the cross of the cardinal points formed on the Earth by the radiating light of the Sun, and that this cross is the very structure upon which the order of the universe hangs, we begin to feel the immense implications of keeping dutiful track of the position of the planets over the course of the day. This can become a part of our practice to remember "Our Mother in the darkness of the underworld"; this remembering may have been exactly the activity that Christ performed when every step taken by him was aligned with the cosmos—each moment of time used to its fullest potential.

> During the time that Jesus of Nazareth pursued his ministry and journeys as Jesus Christ in Palestine in the last three years of his life—from the age of thirty to thirty-three—the entire cosmic Christ-being continued to work in him. In other words, Christ always stood under the influence of the entire cosmos; he did not take a single step without cosmic forces working in him. The events of those three years in Jesus' life were a continuous realization of his horoscope, for in every moment during those years there occurred what usually happens only at birth. This was possible because the entire body of the Nathan Jesus had remained susceptible

to the influence of the totality of the forces of the cosmic–spiritual hierarchies that guide our Earth.[9]

It might be that Steiner's outpouring, as well, came from his ability to walk in Cosmic Time by aligning with the Father Sun above and the Mother Earth below.

However, this only leaves us with more questions: When were the astrological Houses first perceived and written about? Why at that time in particular? Why has there been confusion as to the particulars of their nature? Are each of the twelve Houses simply temples of mundane fortune such as health and marriage? Or do they carry a deeper significance? And what implications does a fuller understanding of the Houses bring in terms of cosmology as a whole? These questions will be addressed in the second part of this article in next year's edition of *Star Wisdom.* We will see if the Mystery of Golgotha has anything to do with the emergence of perception of the astrological Houses; what the implications of the Etheric or Elemental Christ have for their perception in our time; what connection this has to the Mother and the Tree of Life; and what the lives and activities of Christ and Rudolf Steiner might be able to indicate in terms of "walking in cosmic time"—i.e., what can come about when we access the full potential of the astrological Houses through deepening of awareness.

---

9 Steiner, *The Spiritual Guidance of the Individual and Humanity,* p. 65.

*A star is above my head.*
*Christ speaks from the star:*
*"Let your soul be borne*
*Through my strong force.*
*I am with you.*
*I am in you.*
*I am for you.*
*I am your I."*
—Rudolf Steiner

# FILM REVIEW:
## *THE PRINCIPLE*

### *Phillip Malone*

*"Even from a purely scientific point of view, what is called for at this moment in history is an enlarged and vastly deepened understanding of Nature: it is high time to... become philosophically literate once again."*
—WOLFGANG SMITH

*The Principle* was released in 2014 after several years of production. Named for the "Copernican Principle," the film poses a distinct challenge to this long-held idea (also known as the "cosmological principle"). Tracing its roots back to Copernicus, the Copernican Principle posits that reality, as portrayed through our senses, misrepresents the true state of affairs, specifically in that our sense of the physical orientation of the Solar System as geocentric is wrong. The philosophical and theological fallout of this perspective therefore undermined the sense that the Earth and human life on Earth are part of a unique and meaningful organization.

When generalized in the broadest way, this principle states: When the cosmos is viewed from a large enough scale, everything is homogeneous and no region or characteristic of the universe bears any unique or individually significant role.

The film begins by unpacking the Copernican Revolution, which highlights the flaws of the geocentric worldview that prevailed prior to the seventeenth century.

For example, Copernicus and other astrologers of the sixteenth and seventeenth centuries challenged geocentrism by asking: How does one arrive at "retrograde" motion if the planets are orbiting the Earth in perfect circles? Two systems, then, competed for a simple resolution to this question: 1) The Copernican heliocentric system, in which the Earth and all other planets orbit the Sun; and 2) the system of Tycho Brahe. This second system is a modified geocentric system; whereas Brahe maintained that both the Sun and Moon orbit the Earth, he also proposed that the planets orbit the Sun and not the Earth directly. This is a second possibility put forward to address the question of planetary retrograde motion as seen from the point of view of the Earth (see fig. 1).

Whereas it seems that the heliocentric cosmology has taken its rightful place at the forefront of human thought for hundreds of years and, along with it, the cosmological principle that the Earth and humanity are no more significant than anything else in the universe, *The Principle* pieces together a fascinating and surprisingly modern approach to revisiting this question, bringing directly to the fore the question of our Earth's place in the universe.

Modern astronomy has brought facts to light that threaten to upend the Copernican Principle. In 2005, Max Tegmark,

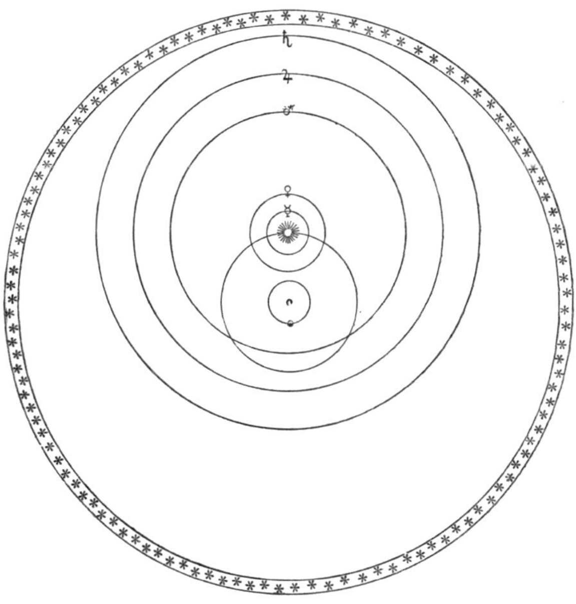

*Figure 1: The seventeenth-century Tychonic system of Tycho Brahe (1546–1601)*

a scientist at MIT, discovered an interesting anomaly while working on a program to map the Cosmic Microwave Background (CMB).

The CMB is considered the oldest remnant of energy from the Big Bang, a signature of hot and cold radiation that is more or less uniformly spread across the sky. Dr. Tegmark developed a program that could search for areas of organization within this apparently homogeneously dispersed field of hot and cold. To his surprise, he discovered that there is a faint but distinct structure to the CMB, so that one hemisphere of the sky is slightly warmer than the other. However, this is only the start; what has now come to be known as the "axis of evil" is the groundbreaking discovery that this plane, which divides the sphere of the surrounding CMB, also happens to be in alignment with the path of the Sun across the sky, our ecliptic.

While delivering no thunderclap from the heavens, the presence of this axis undermines the notion that all points of space are oriented equally toward the whole cosmos. The fact of this alignment points to a relationship between a structure in the farthest regions of the cosmos, this neatly cut "slice" in the sphere of the CMB and our own Sun–Earth relationship, the ecliptic. If there is indeed some kind of relationship between the two, then the cosmological principle may be due for some serious reexamination.

Taking their cue from this striking new discovery, the filmmakers present a variety of scientific viewpoints that (like the cosmological principle) rest unquestioned as parts of the foundational understanding of modern cosmology. Offering a survey of the highlights of modern cosmology, their foray goes far afield, from the Michelson–Morley experiment to the Geometry of Space–Time, Galaxy distribution as shown by the Sloan Digital Sky Survey, Dark Matter, and Quantum Theory.

When viewed critically, each of these areas of science, while broadly viewed as supporting the Cosmological Principle, begin to suggest significant cracks in the foundations of our modern Cosmological edifice, and perhaps—as the filmmakers propose—open the door to re-visioning our own cosmology.

For more information or to watch, visit the film's website: www.theprinciplemovie.com.

"When the Christ impulse entered the evolution of humanity in the way known to us, one result was that the chaotic forces of the sibyls were thrust back for a time, as when a stream disappears below ground and reappears later on. These forces were indeed to reappear in another form, a form purified by the Christ impulse.... Yes, a time is coming when the old astrology will live again in a new form, a Christ-filled form, and then, if one can practice it properly so that it will be permeated with the Christ impulse, one may venture to look up to the stars and question them about their spiritual script."

—RUDOLF STEINER (*Christ and the Spiritual World and the Search for the Holy Grail*, pp. 94, 122)

# THE GALACTIC HOROSCOPE AND THE CIRCLE OF THE GALACTIC CONSTELLATIONS

## David Bowden and Robert Powell, PhD

When the three Magi gazed up at the stars, did they have a wiser view than we usually imagine? When Hermes Trismegistos stated his famous "As above, so below," did he have a deeper understanding of this principle than we normally conceive? The following is an introduction to a new kind of horoscope, the galactic horoscope, as a contribution to our ongoing study of the stars.

### Zodiac and Galactic Constellations

*Sidereal horoscopes* used in astrosophy show a view of the planets against the background stars of the twelve *zodiac constellations*. These constellations form the Zodiac Circle: Aries, Taurus, Gemini, Cancer, Leo, Virgo, Libra, Scorpio, Sagittarius, Capricorn, Aquarius, and Pisces (fig. 1). The horizontal angle in the Zodiac Circle is the ecliptic longitude, measured from 0° Aries. Each constellation has an equal 30° longitude, within the total 360° of the full circle (fig. 2). The angle above and below the horizontal plane of the circle (ecliptic equator) measures ecliptic latitude. The zodiac constellations fit snugly within the zodiac belt, which covers the range 8° north to 8° south of the ecliptic equator.

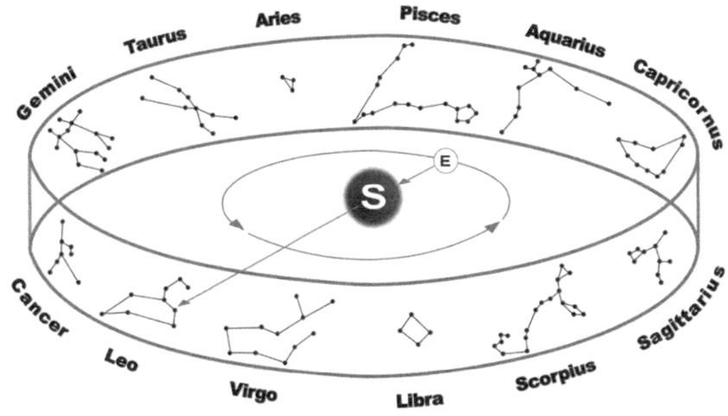


*Figure 1. The Zodiac Circle with its belt of twelve zodiac constellations encircling the Sun (S). As seen from the Earth (E), the Sun passes through each of the twelve constellations in turn, during the course of the year.*

| Sidereal longitude | Abbreviation | Zodiac constellation | Meaning |
| --- | --- | --- | --- |
| 0° – 30° | AR | Aries | The Ram |
| 30° – 60° | TA | Taurus | The Bull |
| 60° – 90° | GE | Gemini | The Twins |
| 90° – 120° | CN | Cancer | The Crab |
| 120° – 150° | LE | Leo | The Lion |
| 150° – 180° | VI | Virgo | The Virgin |
| 180° – 210° | LI | Libra | The Scales |
| 210° – 240° | SC | Scorpio | The Scorpion |
| 240° – 270° | SG | Sagittarius | The Archer |
| 270° – 300° | CP | Capricorn | The Goat or Sea-Goat |
| 300° – 330° | AQ | Aquarius | The Water Bearer |
| 330° – 360° | PI | Pisces | The Fishes |

*Figure 2. The zodiac constellations of the Zodiac Circle—the background stars of the sidereal horoscope.*

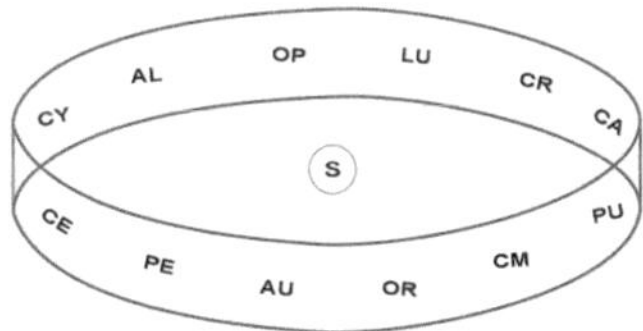


*Figure 3. The Galactic Circle with its twelve galactic constellations encircling the Sun: OP Ophiucus, AL Aquila, CY Cygnus, CE Cepheus, PE Perseus, AU Auriga, OR Orion, CM Canis Major, PU Puppis, CA Carina, CR Crux, LU Lupus*

In contrast, *galactic horoscopes*[1] show the planets against the background stars of the twelve *galactic constellations* (fig. 3). These constellations form the Galactic Circle: Ophiucus, Aquila, Cygnus, Cepheus, Perseus, Auriga, Orion, Canis Major, Puppis, Carina, Crux, and Lupus. The horizontal angle in the Galactic Circle is the galactic longitude, measured from 0° Ophiucus. Each constellation has an equal 30° longitude, within the total 360° of the full circle (figs. 4, 5). The angle above and below the horizontal plane of the circle (galactic equator) measures galactic latitude (fig. 6). It can be seen from all of the above that the sidereal and galactic constellations play analogous roles in the sidereal and galactic horoscopes.

---

1  The idea of a galactic horoscope first occurred to Robert Powell on Dec. 21, 2014, the winter solstice.

| Galactic longitude | Abbreviation | Galactic constellation | Meaning |
|---|---|---|---|
| 0° - 30° | OP | Ophiucus | The Serpent Holder |
| 30° - 60° | AL | Aquila | The Eagle |
| 60° - 90° | CY | Cygnus | The Swan |
| 90° - 120° | CE | Cepheus | The Crowned King |
| 120° - 150° | PE | Perseus | Hero in Greek mythology |
| 150° - 180° | AU | Auriga | The Charioteer |
| 180° - 210° | OR | Orion | Hunter in Greek mythology |
| 210° - 240° | CM | Canis Major | The Great Dog |
| 240° - 270° | PU | Puppis | Poop deck of the ship Argo |
| 270° - 300° | CA | Carina | Keel of the ship Argo |
| 300° - 330° | CR | Crux | The Southern Cross |
| 330° - 360° | LU | Lupus | The Wolf |

*Figure 4. The galactic constellations of the Galactic Circle, the background stars of the galactic horoscope*

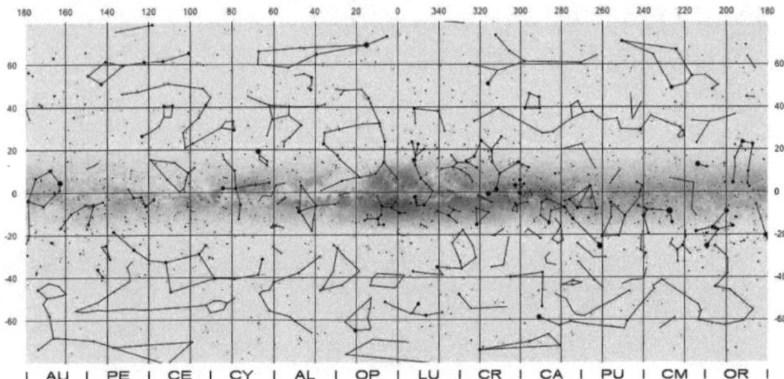


*Figure 5. Map of the galactic constellations of the Milky Way (scale: galactic longitude 0 to 360° vs. galactic latitude 80°S to 80°N)*

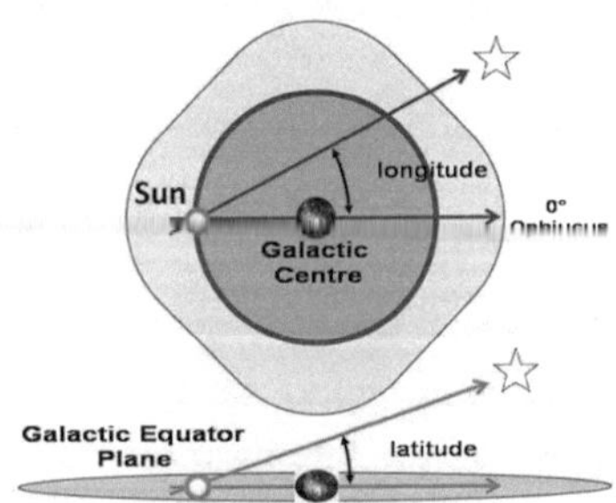


*Figure 6. Galactic longitude is measured from the Galactic Center,[2] which is aligned with 0° Ophiucus. Galactic latitude is measured above (north), or below (south), of the Galactic Equator Plane.*

## King Arthur and the Galactic Constellations

Astronomy recognizes eighty-eight constellations. Twelve of these are the zodiacal constellations. The remaining seventy-six are *extra-zodiacal* (outside the zodiac). Twelve of these seventy six are the galactic constellations. Intrinsic to the idea of horoscopes is that influences proceed from the greater cosmos toward the Earth. It is often thought that these influences come from the stars, or from the constellations of the zodiac. In introducing the galactic horoscope, the question arises whether there are influences proceeding not only from the zodiac constellations, but also from the galactic constellations. In his description below of King Arthur and the knights around him, Rudolf Steiner indicates in the affirmative:

> And the persons who expressed the transit of the cosmic forces through the signs of the Zodiac were those called "The Knights of King Arthur's Round Table." Twelve in number, they had around them a band of other men, but they were the principal Knights. The others represented the starry host; into them flowed the inspirations which were more distantly distributed in cosmic space; and into the twelve Knights flowed the inspirations from the twelve directions of the Zodiac. The inspirations, which came from the spiritual forces of the Sun and Moon, were represented by King Arthur and his wife Guinevere. Thus in King Arthur's Round Table we have the humanized Cosmos.[3]

Steiner describes here how it was the task of the Arthurian Knights to work with the inspirations received from the twelve directions of the zodiac constellations. A second band of men around them had the task to receive and work with the other kind of influences, those proceeding from the *directions* of "the starry host more distantly distributed in cosmic space." This statement implies that the second set of stars, for the second band of

---

2  The very center of our Milky Way galaxy, the Galactic Center, is actually discreetly hidden from telescope view by clouds of obscuring dust and gas.

3  Steiner, *Mysteries of the East and of Christianity*, Feb. 7, 1913, pp. 76–77.

men, is more distantly distributed than the zodiac constellations—in other words, they are extra-zodiacal constellations.

When we look up at a star, something of the star enters into us. Because of this, one can imagine that this "other band of men" around the principal Arthurian Knights worked with not only the inspirations flowing into them from the stars of the galactic constellations, but also actually observed those stars of the galactic constellations, in which are found many of the brightest stars in the sky. In fact, ten of the thirteen brightest stars belong to the galactic constellations (fig. 7).

| Sky brightness | Star | Constellation |
|---|---|---|
| 1 | *Sirius* | Canis Major |
| 2 | *Canopus* | Carina |
| 3 | *Alpha Centauri* | Centaurus |
| 4 | Arcturus | Boötes |
| 5 | Vega | Lyra |
| 6 | *Capella* | Auriga |
| 7 | *Rigel* | Orion |
| 8 | *Procyon* | Canis Minor |
| 9 | *Betelgeuse* | Orion |
| 10 | Achernar | Eridanus |
| 11 | *Hadar* | Centaurus |
| 12 | *Altair* | Aquila |
| 13 | *Acrux* | Crux |

Figure 7. *List of the thirteen brightest stars in the sky. Ten of these stars (shown in italics) are in the galactic constellations.*

Note that Rudolf Steiner describes the influences as proceeding from the *directions* of the constellations, not from the constellations themselves. This is an important distinction that can be further understood by studying Aristotle's View of the Universe (fig. 8). In this view, the outermost or tenth sphere is the Primum Mobile (first movement, or first cause), which *"cause"* passes through the crystal sphere, the Crystallinum (ninth sphere). From there, it passes to the firmament of the stars (eighth sphere). Continuing downward through the seven planetary spheres, and transformed by each sphere as it passes, it is finally received on Earth (the central sphere). In this view of the Universe, the origin of the influences is seen to be beyond the stars—that is, as coming from *every* direction of

the infinite periphery of space. The stars are seen as *markers* for the different directions of space. Relating this view of the universe to Rudolf Steiner's description above, if influences are proceeding from *every* direction of space, then they will be proceeding from the directions of every one of the eighty-eight constellations, including from the directions of the galactic constellations. This extended picture of the relationship of the macrocosm to the microcosm provides some basis for accepting the existence and validity of the galactic horoscope.

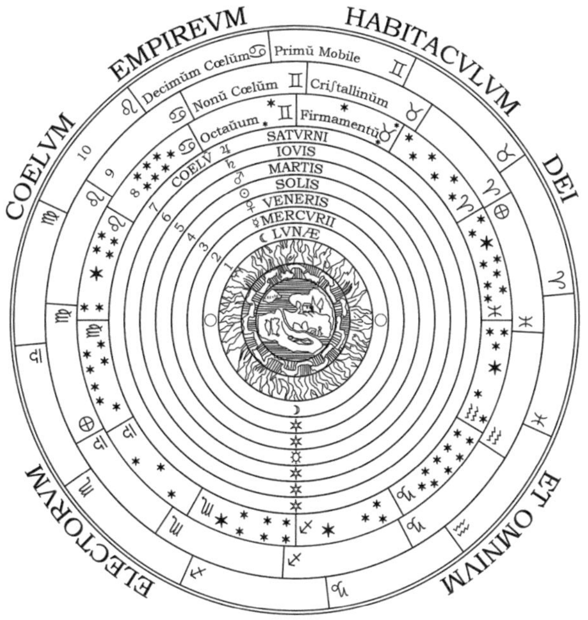

Figure 8. *Aristotle's view of the universe with its ten celestial spheres.*[4]

The galactic horoscope now needs some further astronomical introduction in order to understand how it can be calculated and constructed, including the question of how it relates to the Milky Way that we see in the night sky.

### The Human View of Galactic Constellations

In Hindu mythology, the Milky Way was called *"The Ganges of the Upper Sky;"* in Japanese mythology, *"Heaven's River."* Across many other cultures, it is called *"The Milky Way,"* which comes from the Greek *galaxias kyklos*, translated

---

4   Peter Apian, *Cosmographia*, p. 6.

as *"Milky Circle"*—"Milky" because the majority of its myriad of stars cannot be individually distinguished by the naked eye. *Circle*, because when viewed at night by human beings on Earth, it appears as a band of light encircling the Earth.

How can human beings come to any kind of comprehension of such vast macrocosmic realities as the Milky Way and the Galactic Circle? The answer is to start with the human-centered view, and then progress by analogy to wider perspective views of the Cosmos. The human-centered view is the Earth-centered (geocentric) view of the Cosmos. Beyond that are the Sun-centered (heliocentric) view, and the starry or Galaxy-centered (galactocentric) view of the Cosmos.

Figure 9. *The Milky Way is seen as a band of light stretched across the night sky.*[5] *The brightest region is the Galactic Center.*

The human view of the Milky Way is a band of light stretching in an arc across the night sky (fig. 8). The brightest region within this band is the Galactic Center, the heart of the Galaxy, and is located near 2° Sagittarius. In this direction, the band of light becomes especially bright as a result of the condensed light of trillions of stars concentrated in that region. Almost all of the individual stars (suns) that we see at night with our unaided eye belong to the Milky Way. We are actually *inside* the Milky Way, our Sun being located in the Orion Arm, one of its spiral arms (fig. 10). Thus,

---

5  Photograph taken at La Cumbre, the peak of the high pass over the Andes, near La Paz, Bolivia (photo © James Brunker, Magical Andes Photography).

when we look upward in a particular direction, we see only the stars in our neighboring spiral arms, and possibly in the arms behind those neighboring arms. For example, if we look in the direction of the stars of the Orion constellation, we are seeing stars belonging to the Orion Arm of the Milky Way, but also those in the Perseus Arm (behind the Orion Arm), and stars in the Outer-Cygnus Arm (behind the Perseus Arm).

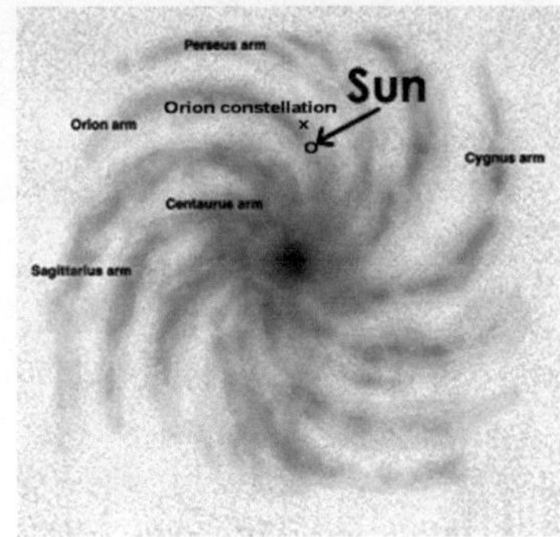


Figure 10. *Location of our Sun (o) and the Orion constellation (x) within the Orion Arm, one of the spiral arms of the Milky Way.*

### The Relationship between Mathematical Astronomy and the Search for the New Isis

We now need to look at some aspects of mathematical astronomy, keeping in mind that, in this process, we will be seeking to resurrect astronomy from its mathematics and geometry tomb, which seeking, Rudolf Steiner indicates, *is* the search for the new Isis–Sophia. As astrosophy, the new Isis–Sophia, develops, the key is to realize the necessity for it to remain always in complete agreement with the sense-perceptible (mathematical) observations of the stars and planets. If sometimes we feel that our seeking is becoming all too mathematical, then to balance this, we can draw guidance and inspiration from the words of Rudolf Steiner below, concerning the necessity for this seeking:

> The ancient astrology was transformed into the world we picture today in the sense of Copernicus, Galileo, Kepler, into the world of celestial mechanics, of mathematics.... What gave the Magi their knowledge of the world of stars draws inward, more backward toward the brain and becomes our mathematical, mechanistic world.... What today has

faded into the mathematical–mechanistic universe, what was once astrology contained such a power that the Christ was revealed to the Magi as a being of the heavens.... Astrology as it was to the Magi, heart vision as it was in the shepherds. With the knowledge that comes from Initiation Science through Imagination and Inspiration, modern human beings will rise to the spiritual realization of the living Christ. They must learn to understand how Isis, the living, divine Sophia, had to disappear when the time came for the development which has driven astrology into mathematics, into geometry, into the science of mechanics. But it will also be understood that when living Imagination resurrects from mathematics, kinematics, and geometry, this means the finding of Isis, of the new Isis, of the divine Sophia whom human beings must find if the Christ Power that is theirs since the Mystery of Golgotha is to become alive, completely alive, that is to say, filled with light within them.[6]

### The Three Great Centers and the Three Great Planes of the Cosmos

The three Great Centers of the Cosmos are the Earth, the Sun, and the Galactic Center. The first of the three Great Planes of the Cosmos is the galactic plane, the band of light across the sky that we know as the Milky Way. It is the only one of the three Great Planes that is directly sense-perceptible—we can actually see it in the night sky. The other two planes are more like ideas. Although mentally constructed from sensory observations, they are not *directly* sense-perceptible. The second plane is the ecliptic plane, the plane in which the Earth and Sun move. We construct it as a line (arc) in the sky, from our observation of the Sun, in its movement across the sky from its rising in the east, to its setting in the west. The third plane is the celestial equator plane. It is constructed by extending the Earth's equator plane out to meet the infinite sphere of the stars. It is the identical plane in space to the Earth's equator plane, only much larger in extent (fig. 11).

---

6 Steiner, *The Search for the New Isis*, pp. 68–71.

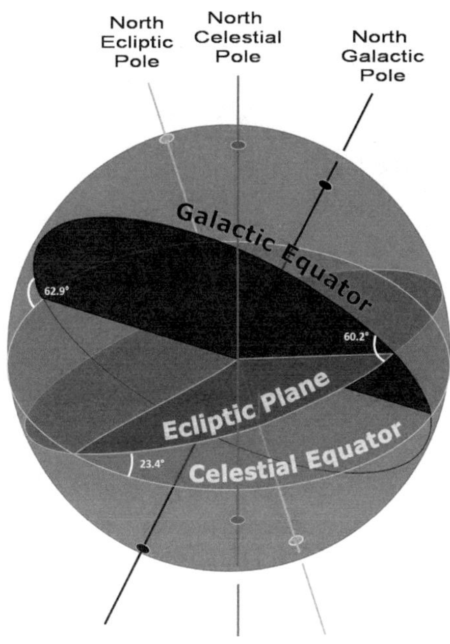



*Figure 11. The three Great Planes of the Cosmos. The galactic plane is tilted to the celestial equator at 63°. It is also tilted to the ecliptic plane at 60°. The celestial equator is tilted to the ecliptic plane at 23.5°, the obliquity angle of the Earth's north–south axis.*

Taken together, the unity of the three Great Planes reflects the Trinity of Space. The Father (as in "further") can be seen in the galactic plane, in which the stars of the Milky Way make a complete circular path around the Galactic Center during the course of 220 million years. The Son can be seen in the ecliptic plane, in which the Earth and the Sun orbit around each other during the course of a year. The Holy Spirit (active in the angelic hierarchies closest to the Earth: Angeloi, Archangeloi, Archai) can be seen in the celestial equator plane, in which plane the stars of the celestial equator (as well as locations on the Earth's equator) make a complete circular path around the Earth's Center during the course of a day.

Accurate observation of stars and planets in a modern sense was instituted by Tycho Brahe, from about 1570. For such observations, a precise longitude and latitude coordinate system is needed, to identify exactly where a star or planet is on the celestial sphere. All astronomical coordinate systems are based on the choice of a center, and a plane. The choice of center can be any of the three Great Centers of the Cosmos: the Earth,

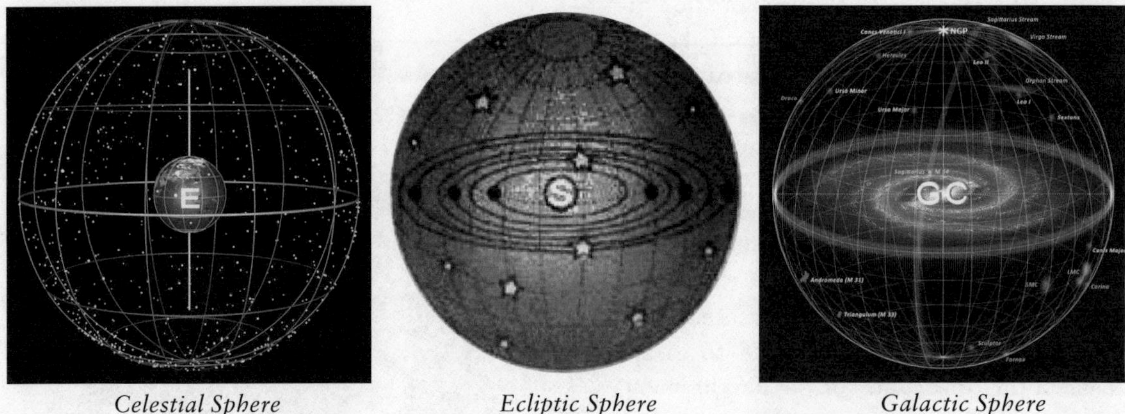

Celestial Sphere    Ecliptic Sphere    Galactic Sphere

*Figure 12. The three Great Centers and the three Great Planes of the Cosmos, with their astronomical coordinate systems.*

the Sun or the Galactic Center. The choice of plane can be any of the three Great Planes of the Cosmos: the celestial plane, the ecliptic plane, or the galactic plane. Every combination of center and plane defines a unique astronomical coordinate system (fig. 12).

### The Three Horoscopes of Astrosophy and their Astronomical Coordinate Systems

For a horoscope, the choice of center determines which perspective view is seen of the planets against their background stars: whether the view is from the Earth, from the Sun, or from the Galactic Center. The choice of plane determines which group of twelve constellations appears in the horoscope as the background stars of the planets: either the zodiac constellations for the choice of ecliptic plane, or the galactic constellations for the choice of galactic plane (fig. 13).

For the horoscopes used in astrosophy, the choices made for center and plane are: Earth center and ecliptic plane, Sun center and ecliptic plane, Sun center and galactic plane. In referring to these three horoscopes, the full names are usually abbreviated to: geocentric horoscope, heliocentric horoscope, and galactic horoscope. They are respectively the horoscopes of the earthly personality or self, the higher self, and the divine self (fig. 14).

### Galactic Research Work in Progress

To begin the new research of interpreting galactic horoscopes, fifty-five horoscopes (taken from *Chronicle of the Living Christ*, and *Hermetic Astrology*, volumes 1 and 2, by Robert Powell) have been converted to galactic coordinates, together with an analysis of aspects between their planets, as viewed from the galactic perspective. A report on the progress of this research will be given in the continuation of this article in the 2021 edition of *Star Wisdom*, including some examples of these galactic horoscopes.

### Addendum by Robert Powell

### Christ and the Galaxy

With regard to astrosophy, as the third level beyond astronomy and astrology, it is, above all, contemplation of the Christ Mystery in relation to the stars that occupies the central position here,[7] as is evident in the *Star Wisdom* series from perusing the monthly commentaries for the ongoing stellar events.[8] This new astrosophical star wisdom shares with Cosmic Christianity a focus upon the cosmos—a very different realm than that of traditional Christian theology.

As detailed in chapter 5 of *The Astrological Revolution*, it was precisely through empirical research

---

7   See Powell and Dann, *The Astrological Revolution*, chap. 5, "Christ and the Starry Heavens."

8   Heartfelt acknowledgment and appreciation to Claudia McLaren Lainson for her extraordinary contributions during the past ten years in laying the foundations with her monthly commentaries for true star wisdom (*astrosophy*).

|  | Center and Plane | Horizontal angle | Angle measured from |
|---|---|---|---|
| **Geocentric horoscope** | Earth center and ecliptic plane | sidereal longitude | 0° Aries |
| **Heliocentric horoscope** | Sun center and ecliptic plane | sidereal longitude | 0° Aries |
| **Galactic horoscope** | Sun center and galactic plane | galactic longitude | Galactic Center at 2° Sagittarius |

*Fig 13. The three kinds of horoscopes used in astrosophy, and their astronomical coordinate systems.*

| | | |
|---|---|---|
| Geocentric horoscope | Personal horoscope | Earthly personality or self |
| Heliocentric horoscope | Heliocentric or hermetic horoscope | Higher self |
| Galactic horoscope | Galactic horoscope | Divine self |

*Figure 14. The three kinds of horoscopes, and their significance for the human being*

into the cosmic dimension of Christ that one of the most significant astrosophical breakthroughs came with regard to research into the mysteries of the stars. This breakthrough demonstrates the truly cosmic nature of Christ in relation to the stars in the heavens. In connection with this far-reaching empirical discovery of Christ's connection with the starry realm, the intuition came that the cosmic dimension of Christ's life is of such a magnitude as to expand far beyond the sidereal zodiac to include the *entire celestial sphere of fixed stars*.

This signified a quantum leap with respect to the traditional astrological worldview. In this expansion of consciousness the nature of each sidereal sign—that is, each 30° division of the zodiacal belt—is perceived as a constellation or kind of "group effect" of each star belonging to that constellation and that, over and beyond the stars comprising each zodiacal sign–constellation, *all the stars* of the constellations above and below the zodiacal constellations also have an effect. In other words, the entire celestial sphere is the real domain not only of astronomy but also of astrology and astrosophy. Each and every star in the heavens is of significance to human beings and life here on the Earth.

It will take some time to assimilate the extraordinary consequences of this discovery. The following is an attempt to communicate the deeper implications of the expansion of consciousness to include the starry heavens in their entirety—this being a step into galactic consciousness. Specifically, it is through an understanding of the cosmic dimension of Christ that conclusive proof is offered of the *astrological significance of the*

*entire celestial sphere*, as elaborated upon with regard to several examples in chapter 5 of *The Astrological Revolution*.

In relation to the foregoing statement, these words of Rudolf Steiner need to be carefully considered:

> In Palestine during the time that Jesus of Nazareth walked on Earth as Jesus Christ—during the three years of his life, from his thirtieth to his thirty-third year—the entire being of the Cosmic Christ was acting uninterruptedly upon him, and was working into him. The Christ stood always under the influence of the entire cosmos; he made no step without this working of the cosmic forces into and in him.... It was always in accordance with the collective being of the whole universe with whom the Earth is in harmony, that all which Jesus Christ did took place.[9]

Here we need to remember that in 1911, when Rudolf Steiner gave voice to these words, there was no conception of galaxies beyond our own Milky Way galaxy. In other words, his listeners would have understood "the whole universe" as the entire Milky Way galaxy.

## The Galactic Equator and Center

Let us also recall that the term *Milky Way* originally meant the band of stars encircling the starry heavens at an angle of about 60° to the circle of the zodiacal constellations. These two great circles immediately catch the eye when gazing up to the starry heavens on a clear night—the Milky Way

---

9 Steiner, *Spiritual Guidance of the Individual and Humanity*, p. 28.

band of stars being most visible when the light of the Moon is diminished. In our time, now knowing the spiral structure of the Milky Way galaxy, it is generally known that the Milky Way band of stars comprises a vast conglomeration of stars—the band being about 16° wide—running through the center of the Milky Way galaxy. The central line though the Milky Way band of stars is called the *Galactic Equator*. The Milky Way band of stars extends approximately 8° above and 8° below the Galactic Equator.

For those who are practiced in stargazing and are familiar with the findings of the research summarized in *The Astrological Revolution*,[10] the most inspiring aspect about beholding the Milky Way band of stars extending approximately 8° above and 8° below the Galactic Equator is that through meditative stargazing, in due course, the possibility arises of coming to the experience that long ago Christ descended down from the galactic realm whence he came on his journey of incarnation. As Christ said: "I and the Father are one" (John 10:30). In terms of astrosophical research findings concerning Christ's relationship with the fixed stars, Christ was originally born from the Galactic Center, regarding which the Russian mystic Daniel Andreev said:

> I remember seeing a glowing mist of stunning majesty, as though the creative heart of our universe had revealed itself to me in visible form for the first time. It was Astrofire, the great center of our galaxy.[11]

In Christ's language, the "creative heart of our universe" can be considered as the *heart of the Father* or the *heart of the Creator*. Now, given that there are manifold galaxies, the heart of the Creator manifests mystically at the center of each galaxy, including the Milky Way galaxy.

Taking the center of the Milky Way galaxy as 0° on the Galactic Equator, a new twelvefold division of constellations around the Galactic Equator opens up, having to do with the Divine level of

existence, where Christ's words "I and the Father are one" hold good in the sense of this being the realm of the Creator, the realm from which Christ originated.

### *The Galactic Circle*

In the hitherto unpublished work of David Bowden relating to this realm—now published in this journal for the first time—we have chosen to call this new twelvefold division of constellations the *Galactic Circle*. It should be noted that the Galactic Circle is not galactocentric. In any case, we do not have names for most of the constellations as viewed from the Galactic Center. Rather, the framework of the Galactic Circle is heliocentric–galactic, utilizing the *galactic coordinate system* (fig. 15, in particular the second image showing the galactic coordinate system).

As David describes in his article, the Galactic Circle, like the zodiacal circle, comprises twelve constellations. Whereas the zodiacal constellations straddle or are close to the ecliptic, the constellations belonging to the Galactic Circle straddle or are close to the Galactic Equator, the central axis through the Milky Way galaxy as seen from the perspective of our solar system—hence the expression *heliocentric-galactic* (or simply *galactic*).

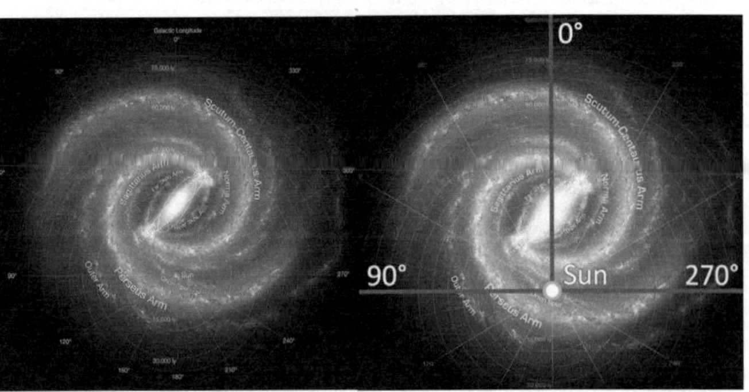


*Figure 15. Diagram of the Sun's location in the Milky Way, where the angles represent longitudes in the galactic coordinate system.*

The constellations—such as Canis Major (CMa), Orion (Ori), Auriga (Aur), Cassiopeia (Cas), Cepheus (Cep), Cygnus (Cyg), and so on—comprising the Galactic Circle, are mostly prominent constellations (fig. 16).[12]

---

10 Of particular importance here are the research findings summarized in *The Astrological Revolution*, chap. 5.

11 Andreev, *The Rose of the World*, p. 198.

12 This addendum is adapted from the last part of

These constellations are not reckoned to be equal-division (30°) constellations in terms of their visible appearance. And, clearly, they do not perfectly straddle the Galactic Equator. However, they are close enough to the Galactic Equator to be included in the list of constellations making up the Galactic Circle. Also they are big enough to occupy many degrees in the designated 30° divisions, without necessarily occupying their respective divisions completely.

In the case of the biggest constellation identified in antiquity, Argo Navis—the ship Argo of Jason and the Argonauts in search of the Golden Fleece—its stars stretch across much of two 30° divisions in the Galactic Circle. However, during the eighteenth and nineteenth centuries, Argo Navis was divided into three constellations (Puppis [Pup], Carina [Car], Vela [Vel]), first by the astronomer Nicolas Louis de Lacaille in 1763 and then again by the astronomer Sir John Herschel in 1841. These constellations relate to two of the 30° divisions of the Galactic Circle, designated Pup and Vel in the figure.

It needs to be taken into consideration that there is some overlap between various constellations by virtue of being positioned above each other in terms of the 30° divisions of the Galactic Circle straddling or close to the Galactic Equator—just as in the zodiacal circle, Ophiuchus, close to the ecliptic, is above the zodiacal constellation of Scorpio in terms of the 30° division of the ecliptic occupied by Scorpio. However, it is the more prominent Scorpio that is named as the zodiacal constellation representing the corresponding 30° division of the zodiacal circle. In the same way, the constellations tabulated in the Galactic Circle are generally the more prominent ones within their respective 30° divisions of the Galactic Circle, beginning with the Galactic Center at 0° galactic longitude. Proximity and prominence (and thus also size) are decisive factors in determining which constellation represents its particular 30° division

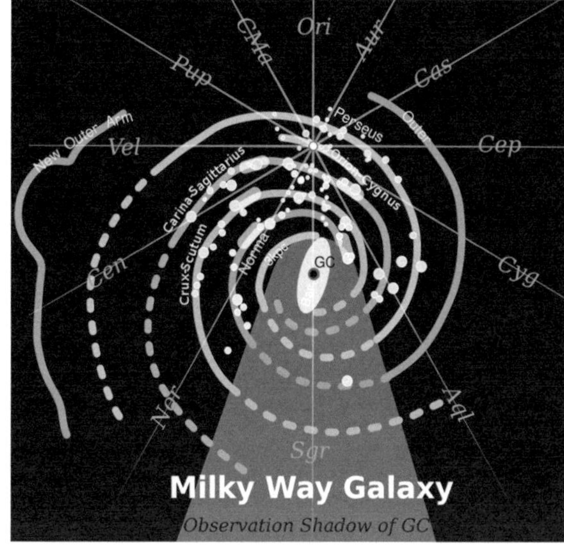



*Figure 16. A "God's view" map of the Milky Way as seen from far Galactic North (in Coma Berenices). The star-like lines center in a yellow dot representing the position of Sun. The spokes of that "star" are marked with constellation abbreviations, "Cas" for Cassiopeia, etc. The spiral arms are colored differently in order to highlight what structure belongs to which arm; Yenne and Krisciunas (The Pictorial Atlas of the Universe, p. 145)*

of the Galactic Circle, whereby in some cases the possibility arises that two overlapping constellations might be named.

In this issue of *Star Wisdom*, the Galactic Circle is precisely specified. One can see how it is possible, within the definition of the twelve 30° divisions comprising the Galactic Circle, to cast *galactic* (actually, *heliocentric–galactic*) horoscopes. This represents a new breakthrough in the domain of astrosophy explored by David Bowden and Robert Powell.[13] In *Star Wisdom*, vol. 3 we shall offer examples of galactic horoscopes.

---

"The Year 2019 and the New Star Wisdom," *Star Wisdom*, vol 1.

13  In *Astrogeographia,* Powell and Bowden bring forward their research into something indicated by Steiner in his *Astronomy Course*—that every place on the Earth corresponds to one or another star in the heavens. More recently they have begun exploring the galactic dimension of existence.

# EVERLASTING CONCRESCENCE:
# A PROCESS-RELATIONAL COSMOLOGY

*Becca S. Tarnas*

Substantial evidence has been put forward for the astrological perspective, demonstrating the multifaceted ways in which astrology works. Yet below the surface of this evidence lies other questions: *Why* does astrology work? What does the recognition of this highly precise, yet poetically subtle, correspondence between planetary movements and events on Earth indicate about the nature of the cosmos? The evidence for planetary correlations with human affairs can, in many ways, address the alienation from the rest of the cosmos felt by the human being in late modernity. Through the recognition of such symbolic patterns, we can feel the deep interconnection that has always been present between our world and us. We are our world. The cosmic web has not been cut, although part of our human journey has been to feel as though the threads of our existence have been severed.

In 1983, a conference was held at Claremont University, organized primarily by Catherine Keller and David Ray Griffin. The conference was called "Archetypal Process" and sought to bring into dialogue the process philosophy of Alfred North Whitehead and the archetypal psychology of Carl Gustav Jung and James Hillman. As Griffin observes, process philosophy and archetypal psychology are both postmodern movements, but postmodern in a sense different from the "relativistic, nihilistic, deconstructive postmodernism" that might better be called "*ultra*modernism or *most*modernism."[1]

Process philosophy and archetypal psychology, in Griffin's words, are examples of "a constructive, reconstructive, or revisionary postmodernism in which many of the presuppositions of modernity are challenged and revised."[2] They are postmodern movements that "want to return soul and divinity to the world."[3] In his talk at the conference, James Hillman spoke of the need for a metaphysics that can support archetypal psychology. Hillman had abandoned Jung's metaphysics to save his psychology. Yet this was not enough. Metaphysics is always operative whether one acknowledges it or not. What Hillman sought was a metaphysics of praxis, metaphysics that supports the practice of psychology, the practice of soul-making—an alchemical metaphysics. Whitehead can provide such a metaphysics, a cosmology in which soul can do its work.

Hillman focused particularly in his talk on the word *cosmology*: it both "refers to the astronomical order of the heavenly bodies, and it also has a metaphysical meaning, according to Whitehead's *Process and Reality*."[4] As Whitehead says, cosmology is a scheme "of general ideas in terms of which every element of our experience can be interpreted."[5] What if we do as Hillman suggested, and "keep together the two meanings, astronomical and metaphysical?"[6] Hillman elaborates on what it would mean to maintain the unity of the two meanings of the word cosmology:

> Let us say that the astronomical bodies (the planets) offer metaphysical bodies (the Gods [or one might say the archetypes]) by means of whom every element of experience can be interpreted. What is beyond in both meanings are the heavenly bodies. These afford some nouns and adjectives, some processes and some realities. The planetary persons fill the void of the beyond with the myths of their bodies and the bodies of their myths. This cosmology is a

---

1  Griffin, *Archetypal Process: Self and Divine in Whitehead, Jung, and Hillman*, p. 6.

2  Ibid., pp. 6–7.

3  Ibid., vii.

4  Ibid., p. 220.

5  Ibid., p. 3.

6  Ibid., p 220.

psychological field—a *field* because metaphysics is placed in imaginal locations; *psychological* because the planets are persons with traits, with behaviors, and in relation with one another.[7]

Hillman is offering here a vision of an archetypal cosmology, an archetypally-patterned, astronomically-grounded cosmology. In other words, Hillman is making the radical proposal that astrology can be the foundation for a metaphysics of practice. Astrology is a continuously ongoing, universally visible form of synchronicity, what Jung describes as a meaningful coincidence between an inner event and an outer event. Archetypal astrology is an empirically based, yet mythopoetically informed, practice—tracking the ongoing archetypal interconnection between psyche and cosmos, microcosm and macrocosm. But what is the philosophical basis for such a metaphysics of practice? To return to the opening question of this essay: why does astrology work? In dialogue with this question, Whitehead's process philosophy can, perhaps, offer a metaphysical foundation.

Before moving forward, I wish to say a word on the nature of archetypes. Perhaps this can best be conveyed by Jung himself, the great diviner of the archetypal patterning of the human psyche:

A kind of fluid interpenetration belongs to the very nature of all archetypes. They can only be roughly circumscribed at best. Their living meaning comes out more from their presentation as a whole than from a single formulation. Every attempt to focus them more sharply is immediately punished by the intangible core of meaning losing its luminosity. No archetype can be reduced to a simple formula. It is a vessel which we can never empty, and never fill. It has a potential existence only, and when it takes shape in matter it is no longer what it was. It persists throughout the ages and requires interpreting ever anew. The archetypes are the imperishable elements of the unconscious, but they change their shape continually.[8]

As this passage from Jung illustrates, it is the very nature of the archetypes not to be fully definable and describable, without misrepresenting and dulling their divine luminosity. Thus, I want to acknowledge the impossibility of capturing archetypal presence in a single metaphysical system that explains in totality how they operate in the world.

In his introduction to the book that emerged from the "Archetypal Process" conference, Griffin draws a parallel between Jung's concept of archetypes and Whitehead's concept of eternal objects, each being part of an explanation of formal causation. For Whitehead, an eternal object is "any entity whose conceptual recognition does not involve a necessary reference to any definite actual entities of the temporal world."[9] An eternal object is a potentiality relevant to some actual occasion, a possibility not yet defined by actuality. Eternal objects are like Platonic Forms in that they are real apart from any of their particular expressions, but unlike Plato's Forms, their reality is "deficient in actuality," according to Whitehead.[10] Because of this deficiency, eternal objects long to enter into actuality, to ingress into actual occasions. All the ways in which we describe this world—the adjectives— these are the eternal objects: the colors, shapes, feelings, smells, tastes, qualities. We come to understand archetypes through such qualities, but archetypes are the unifying fields or gravitational attractors that draw together a complex array of eternal objects into singular, though always fluid, form.

Grant Maxwell has also written about the relation between Whitehead's eternal objects and Jung's archetypes. He posits that planetary archetypes and eternal objects are both examples of formal causation, a mode of causality forbidden by modern materialism. He also suggests they should not be directly equated, with which I agree. I would speculate that planetary archetypes include both the potentiality of Whitehead's eternal objects and the incarnate experience of actual occasions. Archetypes are not just eternal objects or potentials, because they seem to have more agency and autonomy than Whitehead grants to eternal objects. Archetypes are

---

7  Ibid.

8  Jung, "The Psychology of the Child Archetype," in *The Archetypes and the Collective Unconscious*, p. 179.

9  Whitehead, *Process and Reality*, p. 44.

10 Ibid., p. 34.

complex personalities, "persons" even, to use Hillman's language, yet there is a metaphorical unity to their complexity. "All ways of speaking of archetypes," Hillman writes, "are translations from one metaphor to another."[11]

To explore metaphor more deeply, we can make a slight turn toward Owen Barfield, the anthroposophically informed philosopher who wrote such works as *Saving the Appearances* and *Poetic Diction*. Barfield posits an understanding of the evolution of consciousness in which the physical and psychical, material and spiritual, bodily and ensouled qualities of all entities in the world were once unified in the experience of ancient human consciousness.[12] Only over the slow course of history have these concepts been separated from each other—subjective from objective—so that even now my language describing this concept inherently reflects this split. I must speak of object *and* subject, body *and* spirit. To give an example Barfield uses to illustrate this: when we translate the Latin word *spiritus* into English, *spiritus* can mean "wind," "breath," or "spirit" depending on the context.[13] Yet for the ancient speakers of the word *spiritus* it meant all three of these words, and perhaps more, all at once—they were a unified whole in which the physical is utterly indistinguishable from its psychical, ensouled presence.

Yet these words are inherently related to one another at their source. They are examples of "true metaphor" in Barfield's understanding.[14] The way certain eternal objects complexify and ingress as archetypal beings is an example of such "true metaphor." As Hillman says: "All ways of speaking of archetypes are translations from one metaphor to another."[15] The infinite array of eternal objects that express the qualities of Saturn, or Venus, or Neptune, or any of the other planetary archetypes, are metaphorically related to one another, a relation that was much more apparent to ancient consciousness than to modern consciousness. This is how the ancients knew what names to give the planets, which physical planets belonged to which Gods, because the meaning of the celestial bodies was directly apparent to them. The world has changed because we have changed in our participation with it. Yet it still continues to change. The music of the spheres may have been silent for many in late modernity, yet now—at the turn of the tides—we are beginning to relearn the score.

For Whitehead the source of all things is creativity. Creativity is primary. Creativity is the realm of pure potential, of chaos. Griffin has referred to Whitehead's philosophy as "process theology," "especially when the chief focus is on God and other questions of 'ultimate concern' (Paul Tillich), such as ultimate origin, order, value, and meaning."[16] In Whitehead's scheme, God is not the ultimate, creativity is. God orders the chaos of pure potentiality into the hierarchy of eternal objects—and, I would posit, into the archetypes. God takes chaos and turns it into cosmos, but God is born of that chaos. God is the first concrescence, an everlasting concrescence, the first experiential achievement of chaos becoming cosmos.

An image that I find compelling to illustrate this—chaos becoming cosmos—is that of a prism refracting white light into an iridescent rainbow. The white light is that realm of pure potentiality, chaotic creativity. In Whitehead's scheme the prism itself is God, that which refracts the indefinite into the definite, that differentiates pure light into the colors of the rainbow. Each color is an archetype—red clearly different from blue, yellow distinct from purple. But within the band of light that is each color an infinity of shades is at play. Every shade of green could be seen as every possible eternal object that could ingress as an expression of Venus, or every shade of blue the endless possibilities of Neptune. They are still the same light as the white light, but the prism—which could be identified with God—has ordered them into colors.

What makes a rainbow so spectacular? Why do we stop to take note of them? Because we can *see* them. A rainbow makes light itself visible. The rainbow is a symbol of divine possibility entering

---

11 Hillman, *Re-Visioning Psychology*, xix.

12 Barfield, *Poetic Diction*, p. 71.

13 Ibid., p. 73.

14 Ibid., p. 84.

15 Ibid., xix.

16 Griffin, *Archetypal Process*, p. 3.

into the world, yearning for our participation in its beauty.

The moment a child takes her first breath can be seen as the first concrescence of that child independently of the mother's body. The child herself is a society of actual occasions, each of which are also concrescing in this moment, making up the experience of the newborn. This moment, the first inhalation, is when the birth chart of an individual is set. The archetypal energies expressed throughout the rest of an individual's life reflect the planetary configurations, the archetypal relationships or eternal potentialities of this particular moment. At the time of birth all of the actual occasions that have ever been, that have perished into objective immortality to use Whitehead's term, become one—are prehended by the actual occasion that is the newborn child in that moment—before also perishing. Every archetypal expression that has ever manifested is gifted to the child. Yet the past actual occasions that are most felt by the concrescing actual occasion are those that are immediately prior. Thus the positions of the planets and their correlated archetypal energies, that are being enacted everywhere upon the Earth, are what is most immediately inherited by the child in her first moment of independence. As the child continues to live and grow, her subjectivity—the crest of her concrescing wave—continues to inherit the archetypally-ordered actual occasions, as can be seen in the unfolding of astrological transits. Yet the birth chart is still effective, and can still be seen in the progression of the individual's life. How can this be so? How can a past actual occasion, from the moment of birth, be more archetypally influential than other past actual occasions?

Let us return to the image of God as an eternally concrescing actual occasion, never perishing but continuously feeling the procession of the cosmic community of finite actual occasions. Perhaps in this understanding of God we can glimpse what may be happening in relation to the actual occasion when the individual's birth chart is set. The actual occasion which concresced with the child's first intake of air can also be seen as an everlasting concrescence, one that continues from that moment of independence onward. Each preceding

concrescence takes place within the *gestalt* set by that first concrescence—which is how transits to the birth chart could be experienced by the individual. The birth chart is like the prism of that individual's life, refracting the archetypal potential into the archetypal particulars of this person. That moment when the birth chart is set concresces onward, even beyond the bodily death of the individual. One can see transits to the birth chart still being operative long after the person carrying that chart has died: for instance, when a renaissance of interest in someone's work occurs after their death.[17]

Like the dipolar nature of Whitehead's God, the archetypes too seem to have a primordial pole and a consequent pole. The primordial pole orders the realm of eternal objects so that they can ingress as relevant possibilities into the actual occasions of the cosmic community, while the consequent pole feels the experiences of this world community and continuously adjusts the ordering of the eternal objects. So too, I believe, it is with the archetypes. For as they ingress into living manifestation, we participate in their becoming, we co-creatively engage their archetypal qualities through our own lives. The archetypes also have a consequent nature, one that feels what we feel, and that forever reshapes the potentialities for the future ingression of the archetypes, in our own lives and in the lives of future generations. Our participation is enacting an evolution in the archetypes themselves.

We are being called upon to participate. By consciously engaging with the archetypes as we co-creatively manifest them, we are reshaping the potentialities with which they will manifest in the future. No future is yet set. But the past occasions that will inform it are here now. A rainbow makes white light visible. May we look forward with eyes open.[18]

---

17  As an example, at the time when this paper was presented at the conference on the philosophy of Alfred North Whitehead, Neptune in the sky was exactly crossing Whitehead's natal Mercury-Uranus square, bringing a revisioning and reimagining of worldview, which relates to Neptune–Uranus, to Whitehead's ingenious philosophical system, which relates to Mercury-Uranus.

18  Previously published in *Archai: The Journal of Archetypal Cosmology* 6 (2017).

# THE SATURN–PLUTO CONJUNCTION OF 2020

## *Lucian Schloss*

We are living in both exciting and trying times; we are collectively witnessing the corruption rampant in society and individuals, rising to the surface for all to see. In our personal lives, we are most likely confronting the darkness in those around us or ourselves. Many of my clients, friends, family members, and I have been faced with the results of unconscious shadow elements in others, the world at large, and ourselves. A helpful framework through which to observe the current state of life here on Earth is that there exists in the spiritual world not a dichotomy of good and evil but one of health and illness.

One of the gifts of paying attention to "above" is its help in making sense of our experience "below." The unfolding Saturn–Pluto Conjunction of 2020 is a transit of great intensity that all of us are experiencing both collectively and personally during this powerful time. This conjunction has special significance, as it will be happening on the South Nodes of the Moon, Saturn, and Pluto, acting as a catalyst to release the old story and step into a new one.

Saturn and Pluto are slower-moving planets that conjoin only approximately every 37 years. Richard Tarnas's book *Cosmos and Psyche* explores history through the archetypes of the outer planets and their correspondence to events on Earth.[1] Tarnas titles the historical cycles of Saturn and Pluto as times of "Crisis and Contraction." When these two planets come together they bring an overall zeitgeist of contraction, limitation, the gravity of incarnation, and the need to face the results of our actions and their moral substance.

Both World Wars began under hard aspects of Saturn with Pluto, as well as the first Gulf War and the terrorist attacks of September 11, 2001, which happened during an exact opposition between these two planets. These events define entire generations; they ripple out through history, reminding us that we are all capable of being overcome by darkness not just individually but as nations and as a collective (Pluto). The joining of Saturn and Pluto often marks the end of one era and the beginning of another. Europe was a very different place prior to the first and second world wars, whereas the US has had a vastly different identity since September 11.

Saint Augustine was born with this planetary duo. Augustine understood the importance of humility in our personal spiritual paths, that our fallenness is the foundation of the "Great Work" or apotheosis toward God. "God judged it better to bring good out of evil than to suffer no evil to exist."[2] We can imagine that part of the task brought to us by Saturn and Pluto, is to die and be reborn (Pluto) through soul and spiritual development (Saturn).

### The Nodes and Eclipses: Destiny Lines

The Nodes of the Moon[3] and the eclipse cycles are important rhythms in regard to the destiny of an individual. The Nodes mark the locations on the ecliptic at which the eclipses of the Sun and Moon will happen in a given year. The Nodes of the Moon take 18.6 years to return to their natal position for

---

1  Tarnas, *Cosmos and Psyche.*

2  Augustine, *Enchiridion*, viii, ca. AD 420.

3  A brief description of the Moon's Nodes from Wikipedia helps give a visual of the actual astronomy of the Nodes. "A lunar node is either of the two orbital nodes of the Moon, that is, the two points at which the orbit of the Moon intersects the ecliptic. The *ascending* (or *north*) node is where the Moon moves into the northern ecliptic hemisphere, while the *descending* (or *south*) node is where the Moon enters the southern ecliptic hemisphere." (https://en.wikipedia.org/wiki/Lunar_node). The ecliptic is the apparent path that the Sun makes around the Earth, or more accurately the path that the Earth makes around the Sun.

an individual and spend 18.6 months in each sign. In one minute the human being takes an average of 18 breaths; the nodal cycle, Steiner taught, represents one breath cycle of our star destiny.

> In our age, because the human has not yet been educated as he should be, he fails to pay attention to these special times. Could he but observe them properly, he would perceive that in fact something of greatest significance occurs within his soul. The nights lived through during these crucial moments are the most important nights of human life. As the macrocosm completes its 18 breaths, a minute has been completed; and there it happens that, in a certain way, man has opened a window into a totally different world. If we want to express this more exactly, then we should say: our world opens up anew to the astral sphere: astral streams flow in and out.[4]

The Theosophical Society, which was central in the development of modern astrology, may have influenced Steiner's thoughts on the Nodes. Likewise, the Theosophists had been influenced strongly by Vedic philosophy. In ancient Vedic Astrology the Nodes are imagined as the head of a dragon (North Node) and the tail of the dragon (South Node). The North Node is the place of inhalation and consumption, that which needs to be increased in our development. The South Node or dragon's tail is the place of exhalation, release and excretion. With the current planetary alignment, we can imagine Saturn and Pluto aligned with their own South Nodes and the South Node of the Moon, initiating the excretion of that which needs to collapse and the structures that must be released, so that something new from the North Node can enter into the collective or individual astral organism.

Dane Rudhyar emphasized the importance of the planetary Nodes because they don't represent a body in space, but the entire orbital movement and plane of the planet. Therefore, the Nodes represent the movement and evolution of a planet and not the form; i.e., they represent the supersensible part of the planet in question. The other important symbolic significance of the Nodes is that they exist in relationship to the Sun, Moon and Earth. With all the Nodes, they require an integration of body, soul and spirit.

The axis of the Nodes of the Moon, Saturn and Pluto is currently in tropical Cancer–Capricorn: the South Nodes are in Capricorn and the North Nodes are in Cancer. The Moon Nodes spend about 18 months in each sign, but the Nodes of Pluto and Saturn spend entire ages in one sign.

The evolutionary task of the Consciousness Soul Age is to reorient our will away from the externally motivated dictates of family, tribe, and nation (Capricorn), instead finding our inner fulcrum within our solar–lunar self: the inner spirit light, the drop of the divine ocean within the individual soul. Steiner's own personal Moon Nodes, the conjoined Nodes of Saturn and Pluto, signify that his personal destiny is strongly intertwined with this current developmental stage of humanity. We can think of the South Nodes in Capricorn as signifying the outward expression of power, as morality dictated from society or external ethical codes. Cancer represents the need to connect with the kernel of the divine within our own souls, and this is often what results from the crumbling of outer forms that no longer serve us.[5]

### Saturn: The Narrow Door

> *"We can now look upon Saturn in this way: the huge sphere of the Saturn of our solar system is the realm or region in which dwell the archetypes of all soul formations. Behind these*

---

4   Steiner, *Mystery of the Universe.*

5   Lucian offers a tropical perspective that might be of interest to our readers. Alternatively, from the sidereal standpoint, the North Node is in Gemini and the South Node in Sagittarius. We might consider the "tug-of-war" between these two in the light of the 19th Letter Meditation on The Sun from *Meditations on the Tarot*, in which the anonymous author brings the constellation Gemini into relationship with the Arcanum "The Sun" and the spiritual activity of cooperation and fraternity (pp. 528–529). This is in juxtaposition to the activity expressed by Sagittarius, which is Darwinian "survival of the fittest," the competition to survive and rise above our brothers and sisters at any cost. We must exhale the competition for power and breathe in friendship. —ED.

*archetypes is hidden the Will that came from the Spirits of Will. We can also call this the Will of the Father. This Will is the spiritual kernel of all soul life. It is the essence of human soul life when it strives toward perfection."*
—Willi Sucher, *Isis Sophia*)

Saturn is the last of the planets that can be seen with the naked eye. He marks the boundary between our personal experience of being incarnated in space and time and the transpersonal realm beyond. Our inner Saturn gives us the ability to bring the will of the spirit into psycho-physical form, to develop and work on ourselves and the world. Rudolf Steiner was born with a Sun-Saturn opposition, with the Sun in tropical Pisces and Saturn in tropical Virgo. Steiner's personal Saturnian task or initiation was to create a true science of the spirit. He needed the ability to think in the earthly, materialistic science of his time (Virgo), which allowed him to integrate his spiritual experience and understanding developed out of his personal connection with the spiritual world (Pisces).[6] Steiner frequently reminded his students that for each step one takes toward the spiritual or transpersonal world, one must take three in the realm of morality, that our moral imaginations must be grounded in the realm of space and time. To enter into the spiritual realm we must also have our worldly issues in order, we must work and participate in practical affairs. The challenge given to us by this current placement of Saturn is to cease subscribing to a set of arbitrary external rules to govern our morality (Capricorn), instead developing the inner spirit, within the soul, so that it is able to know the good, the true and the beautiful intuitively.

"Enter by the narrow gate; for wide is the gate and broad is the way that leads to destruction, and there are many who go in by it. Because *narrow is the gate* and difficult is the way which leads to life, and there are few who find it" (Matt. 7:13–14). The Saturnian path is not easy but the fruits of its trials birth crystals of wisdom.

Saturn has a deep, solemn and essential spiritual lesson for us; he reminds us that true spirituality must serve us and others in the darkest of circumstances. In our time much emphasis is placed on spiritual knowledge leading to a happier life instead of a more meaningful life, to a more productive and less reflective life, accumulating things and status rather than accumulating wisdom and the capacity to love. The materialistic use of sacred practices is a wolf disguised in sheep's clothing. We need a cosmology that brings out the spiritual meaning of our suffering, that offers us an imagination of our biography that allows us to integrate the realities of life's suffering into our soul's development.

"I will put aside the transitory effects of life; I will view my sufferings in such a way that I feel how they have attracted the wise man in me with a magic power. I realize that I have imposed upon myself certain experiences of pain without which I would not have overcome some of my shortcomings." A feeling of blissful wisdom will overcome us that makes us feel that, even if the world appears to be filled with suffering, it is nevertheless radiating pure wisdom.[7]

Saturn, the Moon and the Moon's South Node represent a sleep-like awareness that the soul gravitates toward: an awareness of our karmic past. This dim awareness indicates how and to what degree we have achieved mastery of an area of our evolution in the past, forming the circumstances of our birth in which we are offered the opportunity to develop something new (North Node). Saturn also sits at the other end of life, weighing on the scales (Saturn is exalted in Libra) the moral quality of our deeds, and encapsulating them for our next incarnation. We can imagine that in our present life we live with

---

6 At Steiner's birth the Sun was in sidereal Aquarius and Saturn in sidereal Leo (that is, if one were looking at the starry heavens on February 25, 1861, that is what one would have observed in the sky). One could see this as an image of the establishment of "heart-thinking" with the Sun (heart) in Aquarius (thinking) opposite Saturn (thinking) in Leo (heart). Steiner also had a close conjunction of Mercury and Neptune in sidereal Pisces, emphasizing the aspects of Steiner's mission and personality to which Lucian points here. Interestingly, in Steiner's previous incarnation he was Thomas Aquinas, and at Aquinas's death on March 7, 1274, the Sun was in sidereal Pisces and Saturn in sidereal Virgo. —Ed.

7 Steiner, *Anthroposophy in Everyday Life,* "Facing Karma," lect. Feb. 8, 1912, p. 54.

the results of previous actions while our current actions create the karmic seeds of our future reality. Saturn is both the star of birth and the star of death. He is our cosmic memory, inscribing our deeds into the memory body of the Earth. As this conjunction culminates we are seeing examples everywhere of people in power having the moral quality of their deeds exposed to the public. A new form must be developed between the gate of birth and death, a form that is worthy of the evolutionary beings overseeing the development of humanity.

### Pluto: The Spirit Seed

*"Christ has sown His spirit-seed in every human soul, and progress consists in the souls of men becoming conscious of this."*[8]

*"God grant me the Serenity to accept the things I cannot change, the Courage to change the things I can and the Wisdom to know the difference."*[9]

*"Pluto is the deep life of humankind operating in the unconscious of every individual; and this life is an aspect of divinity, for is it not said that man was created in the image of God? Surely by 'man' (or 'Adam') what was meant was not an individual, but a human prototype. Pluto is God alive in the common humanity of all men (and women), a mysterious, dark God. If it can be likened to the Eucharist, it is because, to the Christian mystic, the Christ—who is God incarnate—is also alive in all consecrated Hosts…"*[10]

Pluto was discovered in 1930, around the years that Rudolf Steiner predicted that the coming of Christ in the Etheric would begin (1935). Steiner characterizes the second coming of Christ in the Etheric realm as more and more individuals having the experience of "not I, but Christ in me," the birth of the Spiritual Sun within the soul. This transformation is a form of grace bestowed upon the individual not from an ecstatic state but in the middle of the desert, a dark night of the soul. The man who discovered Pluto was named Percival Lowell. *Percival,*

*Parzival* means "to pierce through the valley." With Pluto transits both personal and mundane, we must pierce through the valley of fallen ego consciousness, a deep emptiness and abyss, into the endless source of light and life.

Rudolf Steiner had his own personal experience of the Christ when he was in his late thirties, the age at which we all experience the waxing square of Pluto with Saturn and our nodal return (all elements in the current and 2020 mundane transits). Between thirty-seven and thirty-nine, we come fully to the point at which we must take full responsibility for our destiny; we can no longer rely at all on that which has been given to us from the stream of the past, the family, our origins, culture, etc. Steiner speaks of this time in his autobiography as particularly challenging and yet fruitful:

> During the period when my statements about Christianity seemed to contradict my later comments, a conscious knowledge of real Christianity began to dawn within me. Around the turn of the century, this seed of knowledge continued to develop. The soul test described here occurred shortly before the beginning of the twentieth century. It was decisive for my soul's development that I stood spiritually before the Mystery of Golgotha in a deep and solemn celebration of knowledge.[11]

In 1933, Bill Wilson, the founder of Alcoholics Anonymous (AA), was in his late thirties, a struggling alcoholic on the edge of death, when he had an overwhelming spiritual experience—an example of finding Christ at one's most vulnerable and darkest hour. He describes his experience as follows:

> My depression deepened unbearably and finally it seemed to me as though I were at the bottom of the pit. I still gagged badly on the notion of a Power greater than myself, but finally, just for the moment, the last vestige of my proud obstinacy was crushed. All at once I found my crying out, "If there be a God, will He show Himself!" The result was instant, electric beyond description. The place seemed to light up, blinding white. I knew only ecstasy and seemed on a mountain. A great wind blew, enveloping and penetrating me.

---

8  Steiner, *Life between Death and Rebirth.*

9  "The Serenity Prayer," recited at the opening of each Twelve-Step meeting.

10  Rudhyar, Dane. *The Magic of Astrological Relationship* (unknown).

11  Steiner, *Autobiography*, p. 188.

To me, it was not of air but of Spirit. Blazing, there came the tremendous thought, "you are a free man." Then the ecstasy subsided. Still on the bed, I now found myself in a new world of consciousness which was suffused by a Presence. One with the Universe, a great peace came over me.[12]

Wilson's spiritual experience was the seed that led to his developing, with a group of others, the Twelve Steps, one of the most transformative and significant spiritual paths of the twentieth century.

At the center of AA is the principle that one must "let go and let God," that our personality or ego is innately prone to egotism, and when we actively hand our will over to "The Will," we become more aligned with our spiritual soul. In the vision of the Twelve Steps a healthy community is based on service, inner work, personal responsibility, and making daily contact with one's higher power via the practice of prayer and meditation. In AA they talk about "progress, not perfection" as the foundation of inner work. Once one has found sobriety, one becomes a sponsor to others struggling in their addiction. Like Parzival at the end of his journey, one enters back into the Grail Castle and finally asks the most important question, "What ails thee, uncle?"

Bill Wilson, like Rudolf Steiner, had significant connections to the planetary Nodes of Saturn and Pluto. Both were not only spiritual teachers but have also laid out a path of personal and cultural transformation, bringing the spirit into the marketplace— a spiritual path that involves our transformation inside the "belly of the beast," not a mountain-top monastery. Bill Wilson has the axis of his MC–IC on the same degrees as these powerful collective points, and Steiner his personal Moon Nodes. The Midheaven represents one's gift to the world, or the space in which the self is most visible, whereas the Imum Coeli (lowest point) represents that which is most private or personal. Steiner's personal Moon Nodes show his destiny was powerfully connected with the evolution of humanity at this time.

_______________

12 Bill Wilson, quoted in Andrew Delbanco and Thomas Delbanco, "A.A. at the Crossroads," *The New Yorker*, March 20, 1995, p. 52.

### *Engaging with the Heavens*

The signature of the Saturn–Pluto–South Node conjunction of 2020 brings us into a confrontation with the unconscious shadow of both the world and the individual soul. At times many of us will be witnessing and facing personal and collective shadows, experiencing a stark awareness of the challenges of morality. There is a tremendous amount to learn during these times of exiting one era and entering another. We must consciously connect with the Inner Sun, the light that guides us through the dark, to see our way through at this time.

Saturn requires that we enter through the narrow door, that our will must develop a moral conscience in our spiritual development. Pluto brings us to a point of personal powerlessness: we can either sink into the resulting depression or, with a prayerful soul, seek spiritual illumination. A prayerful soul can receive the new seed, the spirit in the soul. When Pluto is in relationship with Saturn, changes of the basic structures, substances and states of soul are transmuted into a new form or state of being. This process is analogous to the alchemical transmutation of metals, with the goal of taking a metal from its fallen state and raising it into its spiritual or archetypal essence.

With Saturn and Pluto joining in the heavens, the consequence of our actions is placed on the cosmic scales. The need to take responsibility and release the unconscious will impulses to which we have succumbed until now becomes unavoidable. This process can be volatile, especially around the eclipses, which occur every six months. The next set of eclipses includes a solar eclipse (the soul darkening the spirit) on Christmas Day (2019) on the South Node, offering us a time to be aware of what can be released from the soul. The solar eclipse is followed two weeks later by the lunar eclipse (the spirit eclipsing the soul) on the North Node. This will be a time to plant seeds and receive inspiration and imaginations for the future.

This article is focusing on just one alignment amid several involving outer planets during the current time period. One must realize that no single alignment dominates for long, and a whole spectrum of archetypal dynamics are at play at any given time. I will mention in brief that Jupiter (in tropical Sagittarius) has been squaring Neptune (in tropical Pisces) for most of 2019. Using the sidereal zodiac, Jupiter is in Scorpio and Neptune is in Aquarius. This alignment reminds us that, the potential lies amid the trials of Saturn and Pluto to expand our understanding and imagination of the spiritual realm, to use the fallen nature, as Augustine taught, as the scaffolding for the new temple.

It is important to have a practice of meditation and/or prayer at this time. The importance of any meditation or prayer is that it is applicable to the karmic relationships and life circumstances in which you find yourself. Meditations help to address the anxiety we all experience daily, and to find equanimity of soul. In these challenging times we can find solace in the Serenity Prayer, the Lord's Prayer, or Steiner's different meditations (such as the Rose Cross Meditation described in chapter 5 of *An Outline of Esoteric Science*). I find the Rose Cross meditation particularly powerful when dealing with Saturn and Pluto: the dead matter of the cross and the purest roses blooming around and out of it. Rather than run from evil, we must participate in the transformation of it. Through the development of a thinking-heart, we can participate in the spiritual evolution of humanity, guided by the beings who are dedicated to this task. As Rudolf Steiner and Bill Wilson found their connection to the Christ in the midst of a true crisis, we must also find him, as inner spirit light in depths of soul.

## ADDENDUM BY ROBERT POWELL, PhD

The following indicates the historical truth concerning the zodiac, which offers a truthful point of departure as a basis for further considerations concerning the zodiac.

1. The original scientific definition of the zodiac, that of the Babylonians, originated about 500 BC.

2. The tropical zodiac was not originally a zodiac at all; it was originally a solar calendar, introduced in 432 BC by the Greek astronomer Euctemon, dividing the year into twelve solar months named after the twelve zodiacal constellations. Through the Greek astronomers Hipparchus (second century BC) and Ptolemy (second century AD), this solar calendar, relating to time (the cycle of the year) was transformed into a zodiac, relating to space as a coordinate system for locating astronomically the positions of the planets. Note that Euctemon's solar calendar is applicable in the Southern Hemisphere if one reverses the sequence of the months—for example, the month of Aries, denoting the start of spring, commences in the Southern Hemisphere when the month of Libra starts in the Northern Hemisphere, and so on.

3. The unequal–division astronomical zodiac used in modern astronomy goes back to Ptolemy's star catalogue compiled in AD 138. Whereas the Babylonians were clairvoyant—and this clairvoyance underlies their star catalog and their defining of the twelve 30° signs of the sidereal zodiac in relation to the stars of the like-named constellations—Ptolemy was not clairvoyant, so his specification of the constellations was solely from the perspective of physical observation of the stars.

4. Ptolemy was also responsible for introducing the tropical zodiac into astrology. If one studies the history of this, one has to say, "He was unwittingly responsible for introducing the tropical zodiac into astrology." Because, by reading his descriptions of the zodiacal signs in his astrological work *Tetrabiblos,* one sees that he is clearly describing the sidereal signs. However, because the vernal point at the time he was writing the *Tetrabiblos* (around AD 150) was at 1° Aries, he was accurate to within 1° in stating that the sign of Aries begins with the vernal point. Of course, there is much, much more to say about the zodiac question! See my *History of the Zodiac* for a relatively complete survey.

# CLASSICS IN ASTROSOPHY, PART III:
## THE GREAT CONJUNCTIONS

### Robert Powell, PhD

*For the past two years, I have been featuring classic and out of print articles written by Robert Powell in the late 1970s, when he was the editor of the* Mercury Star Journal, *the successor to Willi Sucher's quarterly publication. The* Mercury Star Journal *was also quarterly, until its final issue, released spring of 1980— that issue marked a change to the publication becoming annual rather than quarterly. Sadly, for a variety of reasons, the Journal ceased publication after that issue.*

*In concordance with this year's focus on the Saturn–Jupiter conjunction in Capricorn, I chose two of Robert's articles addressing different Great Conjunctions of these two planets. One of his earliest articles, "Astronomical Notes" (spring 1975) discusses the Great Conjunction of 1961 and the interesting stellium of the seven classical planets in Capricorn that occurred the following year (1962). Following this is Robert's editorial forward to the final edition of the* Mercury Star Journal *(spring 1980). Here he points to the Virgo triple conjunction of 1981. It is worth noting that Robert's work at the time (1974–1980) is bookended by references to Great Conjunctions, and, as we will see in next year's "Classics," he continued to focus on them in his articles on Grail Research at the Goetheanum. —*Ed.

### ASTRONOMICAL NOTES
(*Mercury Star Journal*, Easter 1975)

Ancient Sasanian astrology has a tradition that world history unfolds according to the influences of the periodically recurring conjunctions of Jupiter and Saturn.[1] This tradition seems to be associated with the Zoroastrian religion, having originated from the region of Iran. In fact, definite elements of Zoroastrian cosmology, although not explicitly attributed to Zarathustra, are to be found in the astrological history of Masha'allah (died c. AD 815) as preserved in Ibn Hibinta's *Kitab al-Mughni* (written in 941).[2] For example, Masha'allah divides time into millennia[3] in much the same way as in *The Bundahisn* (primordial creation).[4]

The periodicity of Saturn–Jupiter conjunctions supports the idea of millennial changes in history. A conjunction between Jupiter and Saturn takes place approximately every 20 years and each conjunction is roughly two-thirds of the zodiac ahead of the preceding one. For example, the most recent conjunction, in the constellation of Capricorn (as took place on Feb. 9, 1961), will be followed by one in the constellation of Virgo (as took place three times: Jan. 1, Mar. 8, and July 24, 1981). In this instance, the conjunctions remain in the same triplicity.[5] Roughly, the series of Saturn–Jupiter conjunctions occur in zodiacal constellations of

---

1 See David Pingree, "Astronomy and Astrology in India and Iran," *Isis*, 54 (1963), pp. 235–246.

2 Masha'allah was an eighth-century Jewish astrologer. Masha'allah's astrological world history, "Oh Conjunctions, Religions, and Peoples," is contained in the Arabic work *Kitab al-Mughni* (Munich Cod. Arab. 852, ff. 214v to 233v) written by Ibn Hibintā, a Christian astrologer who flourished in Baghdad in the ninth century. See Kennedy and Pingree, *The Astrological History of Masha'allah.*

3 For an account of the division of time into millennia, as in *The Bundahisn*, see Henry Corbin, "Cyclical Time in Mazdaism and Ismailism," *Man and Time* (papers from the Eranos Yearbooks), New York, 1957, pp. 115–125.

4 Anklesaria, *The Bundahisn*, the Pahlavi book of creation, as derived from Zoroastrian scriptures.

5 A triplicity consists of a set of three constellations, equally spaced on the zodiac at intervals of four constellations. There are four triplicities, each associated with one of the four elements as follows: *fire*, Aries, Leo, Sagittarius; *earth*, Taurus, Virgo, Capricorn; *air*, Gemini, Libra, Aquarius; and *water*, Cancer, Scorpio, Pisces

the same triplicity for about 240 years, or twelve conjunctions. Then the series moves into the next triplicity. Thus, the cycle of conjunctions through the four triplicities—*fire, earth, air, water*—takes about 960 years, or nearly one millennium.

According to the Sasanian tradition, changes of triplicity are indicative of significant historical occurrences (e.g., natural catastrophes, or the rise of a new nation), while the completion of a cycle, and therewith, approximately, the beginning of a new millennium, signals a major transition in historical evolution. (We stand at a turning point in the twentieth century, with the series passing over from the fiery to the earthy constellations.) A natural starting point for astrological history to begin the series is the mean conjunction of all the planets that took place at the first point of the constellation of Aries on February 17 and 18, 3102 BC. In Indian chronology this is the date of the commencement of the 5,000-year period known as Kali Yuga.

The transfer of triplicity during the twentieth century, the first century of the new yuga (following the termination of Kali Yuga in 1899) stands as the astronomical background to the historical events of this era. In addition, the Indian chronological perspective of history indicates that this century is a time of great significance. For the new yuga is termed "the age of Light," the reason being that the epoch following the end of Kali yuga ("the Dark age") will see the return of Christ. The renewed presence of Jesus Christ has been awaited down the centuries, but it has long been an open secret to be read from Indian chronology that the Parousia would commence only after the completion of Kali Yuga. Moreover, each yuga has a dawn and dusk period, each comprising approximately one-tenth of the yuga.[6] Theoretically, then, it is possible to calculate chronologically the exact date of the advent of the Parousia. As an approximation, since the age of Light is half the length of the Kali Yuga, it is clear that this date lies some 20 or 30 years after the start of the twentieth century. This is confirmed by the spiritual research of

Rudolf Steiner, whose investigations show that the beginning of the return of Jesus Christ to the etheric realm of the Earth (i.e., the Parousia, or coming "in the clouds") was in the 1930s.[7] Chronologically, then, we stand in a period of major transition, and the astronomical facts confirm this conclusion. It is enlightening to consider the astronomical events of this century in some detail.[8]

If attention is focused on the Saturn–Jupiter conjunctions from 1900 to 2000, in relation to the movements of the remaining planets, then the last conjunction (Feb. 19, 1961) appears in a most remarkable light. For, following this conjunction, there was a meeting of the seven visible planets (including the Sun and Moon) in the constellation of Capricorn.[9] (The mean conjunction occurred on Feb. 5, 1962, when there was a total eclipse of the Sun.) In view of the rare nature of such a gathering, the planetary synod of February 5, 1962 appears as the culminating point of all the astronomical events in the twentieth century.

Indeed, this meeting of the visible planets in the constellation of Capricorn prefigures a similar configuration that will occur in the eight millennium after Christ, an astronomical occurrence that is referred to by Berosus.[10]

---

6 Mircea Eliade, "Time and Eternity in Indian Thought," *Man and Time* (papers from the Eranos Yearbooks), New York, 1957, pp. 173–200.

7 Steiner, "The True Nature of the Second Coming"; also, Willi Sucher, *Cosmic Christianity* for an astronomical–chronological calculation that confirms Steiner's investigations.

8 NOTE: The length of the Satya Yuga, according to Rudolf Steiner and others, is 2,500 years, from 1899 through 4399. In terms of the dawn of the Yuga corresponding to one-tenth of the total length, this would result in a 250 year period, and not the "twenty to thirty years" to which Robert refers here. Perhaps he had used 1/100 for his calculation rather than 1/10. In any case, this makes our time of transition somewhat longer: all the way through to the year 2149. This is relatively close to the year 2133, a year Robert has discussed at length in other articles (see "The Descent of Christ" in *Journal for Star Wisdom*, 2017) —ED.

9 See "The Planetary Synod of Feb. 5, 1962," by Walter Buhler, MD, in *Mitteilungen*, Christmas 1961 (Stuttgart).

10 Berosus was a priest of Bel (c. 300–250 BC) who moved from Babylon to the island of Cos, where he had an observatory and a school for astronomy (Vitrivius, ix, 1).

Berosus, who thus interprets the Babylonian tradition, says that these events take place according to the course of the stars; and he affirms it so positively as to fix the time for the (general) conflagration of the world, and of the Deluge. He maintains that all terrestrial things will be consumed when the planets, which now are traversing their different courses, shall all coincide in the sign of Cancer, and be so placed that a straight line could pass directly through all their orbs. But the Flood will take place (he says) when the same conjunction of the planets shall take place in the constellation of Capricorn.[11]

Clearly, Seneca has confused the two occurrences, the Flood and the Conflagration, because it is affirmed by all interpreters of the conjunction theory of world history that the Deluge took place when there was a mean conjunction of all the planets at the vernal equinox in the constellation of Cancer (corresponding to the Ice Age). Similarly, from the indications of Rudolf Steiner[12] the apocalyptic event known as "the war of all against all" will take place in the Age of Capricorn (seventh and eight millennia AD). At present we stand a little over halfway between the two occurrences: The Flood in the Age of Cancer and the Conflagration predicted to take place when all the planets meet at the vernal equinox in the constellation of Capricorn.

In the light of the Sasanian tradition, the twentieth century as a whole is a time of shift of triplicity, while the outstanding astronomical event of this century is the planetary synod of February 5, 1962, which closely followed the Saturn–Jupiter conjunction of 1961. The tradition asserts that the historical events following a conjunction may be referred back to that conjunction. Thus, the period in which we are now (1961–1980) should be referred to the great conjunction in Capricorn. Similarly, new historical impulses will unfold during the interval from 1981 to 2000, following the triple Saturn–Jupiter conjunction in the constellation of Virgo. The conjunction of these two planets determines the general nature of the historical events throughout the following twenty-year period, but the events specific to each year within this period, so the tradition goes, are indicated by the planetary positions on the day of the vernal equinox (March 21).

## EDITORIAL FORWARD
### (*Mercury Star Journal,* Easter 1980–81)

"Two things fill the mind with ever new and increasing admiration and awe, the oftener and more steadily they are reflected on: The Starry Heavens Above Me and The Moral Law Within Me." This expression of Emmanuel Kant (*Critique of Practical Reason*, vol. 2) could well serve as an aphoristic definition of the spiritual axis about which the new wisdom of the stars revolves. The stars above in the firmament shine forth their steadfast illumination as a sign of the eternal Kingdom of Heaven, the divine realm from which humanity and all the kingdoms of nature have taken their origin. The moral law, as it comes to expression in terms of conscience, is a foundation within each human being for the Sun of Righteousness—indeed, conscience may be likened to a ray irradiated from the Sun of Righteousness that has taken up an independent existence within each morally conscious human being. The more that the light of conscience is allowed to shine, the more it can begin itself to become like a Sun, shining into the darkness of earthly existence as an inner lamp guiding human beings on their paths through life.

The quoted aphorism indicates a spiritual axis stretching from the inner human being upward into the realms of cosmic heights. This spiritual axis is none other than Jacob's ladder, upon which "the angels of God were ascending and descending" (Gen. 37:12). For it is the Angels who, ascending to behold the heavenly script wherein each individual destiny is inscribed, then descend to speak their inspiring words, within the clothing of moral consciousness, concerning that which is to be fulfilled. The coming to birth of a new wisdom of the stars in the twentieth century is a sign of the lifting of

11 From Seneca, Nat. Quaest., iii, 29, p. 70 in Cory's *Ancient Fragments*, London, 1876.

12 Steiner, *The Apocalypse of St. John.*

the veil surrounding the mystery of the work of the angels, whose activity as guides and helpers of human beings is one of helping those under their protection to find their way into and through earthly life, and then out of it again (expressing it rather prosaically).

A new wisdom of the stars is coming to birth in the twentieth century in order to help human beings to begin to find a more conscious relationship with the angelic beings, that—eventually—each individual may himself begin to assume this angelic activity. The glimpse that Jacob had of the divine mystery of angels ascending and descending is also a vision of one of humanity's future activities, when we will have attained to a certain degree of evolution or, correspondingly, a certain stage of initiation. For initiation is nothing other than a living out in advance of that which in the course of evolution will come to realization (the term *Grail initiation* in *Mercury Star Journal* is used to designate the initiation attained to by one who follows the esoteric Christian path).

The vision of angelic beings ascending and descending is thus also a prophetic vision of human beings ascending to behold the mysteries of destiny and descending in a spirit of loving service for the fulfillment on Earth of that which is inscribed above. An individual who, through initiation, advances to a level at which he is able to assume this angelic activity, can be designated—in the sense of Grail Christianity—an "astrologer," i.e., one who can read the mysteries of destiny from the stars. An astrologer—in this higher sense of the word—is a participant in a holy mystery, one that is known to angelic beings and to those who have advanced along the path of initiation. In this sense, an astrologer is one who can read *the writing on the Grail*. He can read the *scripta sacra* with, as it were, an "angel's-eye view" of the mysteries of God, an intimation of which can be gained from the following passage by Wolfram von Eschenbach:

> Of Thy depth and of Thy height
> And of Thy breadth the endless flight
> Was never measured, whose degrees
> Are lost in those Immensities.

> Within Thy hand's encircling hold
> The seven stars, by Thee controlled
> Speed on their courses, and embrace
> The whole of heaven's revolving space.[13]

Early in his search for the Grail, the hero of Wolfram von Eschenbach's *Parzifal* is granted a view of the Grail borne by a Queen, who is attended by twenty-four maidens.

> After them came the Queen. So radiant was her countenance that everyone thought that dawn was breaking. She was clothed in a dress of Arabian silk. Upon a deep green achmardi she bore the perfection of Paradise, both root and branch. That was a thing called the Grail, which surpasses all earthly perfection. Repanse de Schoye was the name of her whom the Grail permitted to be its bearer. Such was the nature of the Grail that she who watched over it had to preserve her purity and renounce all falsity.[14]

This scene beheld by Parzival is both real, i.e., it actually took place, and imaginative, i.e., it presents an "imagination" of a super-earthly reality. That is to say, there actually was a historical personality, given by Wolfram the name Repanse de Shoye, who fulfilled a role—as bearer of the Grail, surrounded by twenty-four maidens—which corresponds to a spiritual reality. This scene is a portrayal, in terms of earthly reality, of the "queen of the angels" surrounded and served by angelic beings. The "queen of the angels"—known in Christian occultism as the Archangel Sophia—bears the title *queen,* in the sense of being the "heart and center" of all the beings who guide and protect nations (just as angels guide and protect human beings). Sophia is thus "queen of all nations" and is able to inspire all angels, and hence all peoples, regardless of nationality.

In the imagination described by Wolfram von Eschenbach, Repanse de Schoye, the Grail queen, can be seen as a representative on Earth (at that time) of Sophia above in the spiritual world—in the same (analogous) way as he who lived on the Earth

---

13 *Willehalm* i, 33–40; Richey, *Studies of Wolfram von Eschenbach,* p. 217.
14 Eschenbach, *Parzival,* v, 235, 15–30, p. 129.

as Saint George acted as an earthly representative of the archangel Michael. And just as Michael has his sign in the zodiac—that of Libra, where Michael may be pictured with upraised sword, and holding the scales of justice—so has Sophia her sign in the zodiac, i.e., Virgo, where she may be pictured as the heavenly Grail queen, the essence of purity, bearing the Grail. This imagination of Sophia is the Christian metamorphosis of the Virgin holding the ear of corn—the latter symbolizing the bread of life, which is the power of the Grail, from which the knights of the Grail derive sustenance.

Repanse de Schoye fulfilled a similar role in the enactment of the Grail Mystery as did Mary in the events described in the Gospels. Thus Mary, like Repanse de Schoye, was a representative on Earth of Sophia above as indicated by the designation "Virgin Mary." The relationship between Mary and Sophia was grasped intuitively by Saint Bernard of Clairvaux in his *Homilies on the Blessed Virgin Mary*, where he ascribes to Mary the apocalyptic imagination of Sophia ("the Woman clothed with the Sun, having the Moon under her feet, and on her head a crown of twelve stars"—Rev. 12:1):

Thinkest thou is she the woman clothed with the Sun? For suppose even that the whole series of prophetic visions goes to prove that it is to be understood of the present Church; yet it does not seem improperly applied to Mary; for she it is who was, as it were, clothed with a new Sun...with every defect beneath her, even the least frailty or corruption, she surpasses and transcends all other creatures by a sublimity unapproachable, so that deservedly she is said to have the Moon under her feet. Otherwise it will appear nothing extraordinary to say that the Moon is under the feet of her who, we cannot doubt, is exalted above the choirs of angels, above the cherubim, also, and seraphim...For the "fool changes as the Moon, but the wise man continues in wisdom as the Sun" (Eccl. 27:12).... Justly then is Mary said to be clothed with the Sun, for she penetrated into the deep abyss of divine wisdom beyond all belief, so as to appear immersed in *light inaccessible*, as far as it is possible for a creature without personal union with the Deity.... All bright, indeed, and burning was the clothing of this woman,

everything in whom as we know sends forth such bright radiance, that we cannot suspect there was anything in her, not alone darksome but in the least obscure, or less bright, or even tepid—but all was glowing with light and love.[15]

In this contemplation of the Blessed Virgin Mary, St. Bernard of Clairvaux appears to ascend from Mary, who was the representative on Earth of the Archangel Sophia, to Sophia herself, who is portrayed in the Apocalypse as "the Woman clothed with the Sun, having the Moon under her feet, and on her head a crown of twelve stars" (Rev. 12:1). This apocalyptic vision is encapsulated in the Grail symbol on the cover of this publication (being a "Grail Symbol" insofar as Sophia is the heavenly queen of the Grail). The new wisdom of the stars (*Astro-Sophia*) is a child of the divine Sophia, as the symbol portrayed on the cover is intended to convey. It is Sophia who is humanity's guide into the deeper mysteries of the new star wisdom; it is she who shows the way of ascent of Jacob's ladder, which takes place in three stages— i.e., Astronomy, Astrology, and Astrosophy.

First, there is the stage of Astronomy. This is not to be confused with modern astronomy, which is, generally speaking, occupied with the physical and sub-physical universe. Astronomy, in the sense of the new star wisdom, is concerned with the relationships prevailing between the cosmos, the Earth and humanity, such as is outlined by Rudolf Steiner in the lecture "Man, Offspring of the World of Stars" as printed in the *Mercury Star Journal*.[16] An intensive study of this lecture may

---

15 *The Glories of the Virgin Mother*, pp. 137–139.

16 This lecture was intended for an audience familiar with the ideas of Spiritual Science as outlined by Steiner in his written works. The terms *physical body, etheric body, astral body,* and *"I"* relate to the present fourfold human constitution. In terms of Astrology, *etheric body* underlies" temperament," whereas the *astral body* is expressed as "character." *Cultural epoch* refer to distinct periods of civilization, the fourth of which corresponds to ancient Greek and Roman civilizations, when the intellectual life (or *mind soul*) developed culturally; the fifth epoch corresponds to modern civilization since the Renaissance, when self-awareness (*consciousness soul,* or *spiritual soul*) is being developed.

afford deeper insight into the new Astronomy, the first stage of the new star wisdom. Indeed, much of Rudolf Steiner's life work was concerned with the development of this new Astronomy, or spiritual–scientific cosmology, which forms the basis for the subsequent stages—Astrology and Astrosophy—of the new star wisdom. For example, his lecture course *Human and Cosmic Thought*, summarized by Elizabeth Vreede in part 1 of the "Astrological Studies" (reprinted in *Mercury Star Journal*) form the basis for Willi Sucher's contribution on the "spiritual nativity" (in "Astrological Studies" part 2), which is of central importance in the new Astrology. The "spiritual nativity"—i.e., the nativity of an individual's philosophical (world) outlook, is an altogether new discovery, belonging unequivocally to the new star wisdom. It is, according to Rudolf Steiner, "of much greater importance in the life of the person than...the external horoscope." In "Astrological Studies" part 2, Willie Sucher shows how the "spiritual nativity" may be found, with examples for several historical personalities. In this and in the later "Astrosophical Studies," the first steps toward a new Astrology are made—Astrology based on the foundation of the new Astronomy, which is none other than the spiritual–scientific cosmology described by Rudolf Steiner in *An Outline of Esoteric Science* and other cosmological works.

As to the third stage of the new star wisdom—Astrosophy—this belongs to the domain of Sophia herself. It is the Archangel Sophia—the queen of all nations—who holds the key to the innermost sanctuary of the divine mystery "Astro-Sophia." The development of Astrosophy consists not so much in external research, although this is certainly a valuable—and necessary—side of the new star wisdom, but lies rather in the unfolding of an inner activity, in devotion to Sophia—a beholding and contemplation of cosmic mysteries, of the mysteries connecting Heaven and Earth. The way has been prepared. And now we are entering into the time of Sophia, the "era of Sophia."

In the star calendar—referring to the period Easter 1980 to Easter 1981—printed in the following pages, reference is made to the threefold conjunction *in Virgo* between Jupiter and Saturn. The first of these conjunctions will occur on New Year's Eve at the end of this year, 1980. This conjunction signifies the start of the "era of Sophia"—a period of almost twenty years—leading up to the year 2000, when there will be a conjunction between Jupiter and Saturn in Aries (and, correspondingly, the start of a new cultural impulse, which will be under the sign of Aries). A conjunction between Saturn and Jupiter always signifies *the start of a new cultural impulse*, lasting just under twenty years, until the next conjunction occurs in a new (sidereal) sign of the zodiac. The last twenty years have stood under the sign of the Saturn–Jupiter conjunction in the sidereal sign of Capricorn, which occurred in 1961. The period from 1981 to 2000 will see the unfolding of the cultural impulse associated with the coming threefold conjunction between Saturn and Jupiter in the sidereal sign of Virgo. The "era of Sophia" (under the sign of the Virgin) is coming!

How will the "Queen of all nations" work during the era that stands under her sign? What form will the new cultural impulse of Sophia take?

A starting point for meditation can be taken from the twelfth chapter of the Apocalypse of Saint John, where Sophia is portrayed as being pursued by the dragon, where the dragon endeavors to sweep her away with a flood.[17] Thus, the "era of Sophia" (1981–2000) is a time during which the tide of cultural influence emanating from the dragon will swell to hitherto undreamt of proportions. The flood of "abomination" in our modern culture has as its aim the complete engulfment of all human beings in a current of influence that seeks to totally exclude the cultural impulse of Sophia from above. But if a sufficient number are able to find and remain true to Sophia, she will "stamp on the dragon's head" and bring the peace of the Holy Spirit to humankind. For Sophia is the

---

17 St. John uses the terms *serpent* and *dragon* interchangeably, and thus here *dragon* is not so much a designation for a specific being but a comprehensive expression for the combined influence of the powers that seek to oppose Sophia, although in other contexts the term *dragon* frequently refers specifically to Satan.

mediator between humanity and the Holy Spirit, just as at Pentecost she enabled the Holy Spirit to descend upon the apostles—in the midst of whom was Mary, who was overshadowed by Sophia.

World Pentecost! This is the positive aspect—or possibility—for the "era of Sophia" that is shortly to begin. The ushering in of the reign of the Holy Spirit is what may be accomplished through a community of human beings who find Sophia and unite together in her impulse. As to how this shall be accomplished, this depends upon Sophia herself. For no human being, no matter how evolved, can determine (or specify) how the Archangel Sophia will work in the spiritual fight that is to take place between now and the end of this century.

Nevertheless, three conditions can be enumerated that must be fulfilled by a community aspiring to be bearers of Sophia's impulse. The first is that such a community must have a worldview that is free from the hypnotizing *maya* of the materialistic–scientific outlook. Thinking must be purified of the illusion that the world is constituted solely from matter and energy, which *maya* excludes the reality of the Spirit. Secondly, peace must prevail between the members comprising such a community. All discord and strife excludes the possibility of the working of Sophia, who herself emanates nothing but grace and peace. Thus, feeling must be purified of those ignoble impulses that subvert brotherly love and which divide human beings into groups according to their sympathies and antipathies. Lastly, such a community must be free of motivation based predominantly on economic interests. The impulse of goodwill that characterizes Sophia's activity becomes corrupted wherever financial motives play the overriding role in deciding what is, or is not, to be done. Thus, the will must be purified of selfish economic interests in order to become united with the impulse of Sophia. These are three principal conditions to be fulfilled within a community aspiring to be the bearers of Sophia's activity. The fulfillment of these conditions creates a "space" within the flood pouring forth from the dragon, and this "space" in the world can be filled by the in-pouring of Sophia's impulse from above— the archetype of which is Pentecost.

The "era of Sophia" (1981–2000) is a time of the great fight against the Spirit, which, in the first place, is directed against Sophia, who is the mediator of the Holy Spirit to humanity. All events that will occur can be viewed in this context. The fight against the Spirit is the background to all occurrences taking place in this period of time leading up to the end of the century. There will be "no holds barred" in this fight, for the dragon has come "in great wrath, because he knows that his time is short!" He has come "to make war on the rest of her (i.e., Sophia's) offspring, on those who keep the commandments of God and bear testimony to Jesus" (Rev. 12:12, 17). Yet those who turn to Sophia, who keep the commandments of God, and who bear testimony to Jesus, shall prevail in the forthcoming spiritual fight. And thereby the descent of the Holy Spirit will be enabled.

The new star wisdom has a role to play in this fight, especially in the sense of helping firstly to create a consciousness of destiny and secondly to bring about its realization. The new wisdom of the stars can aid in bringing to consciousness, concerning destiny, what may otherwise remain slumbering in the depths of consciousness, and in this sense it does indeed work toward the raising of the veil that conceals the work of the angels in their ordering of destiny. It can thus be a real source of strength in the face of the chaoticizing currents sent forth by the dragon, which aim to sweep human beings off their feet, to disorient them, and thereby to bring disorder into the sphere of destiny. And if the question is raised: Where do I begin? How can I stand firm within the maelstrom of influences that threaten to overwhelm me? Then, the spiritual axis about which the new star wisdom revolves ever and again can be taken as a starting point and as a support amid the floods of chaos.

### The Starry Heavens above Me and the Moral Law within Me

Those who occupy themselves with both poles of this spiritual axis (Jacob's ladder) will also begin to find their way between the two poles— i.e., they will begin to learn to ascend and descend, to contemplate and to bring into action, to know the mysteries of Heaven and to act from the light of conscience, in the spirit of the Sun of Righteousness. And one day, if their efforts have sufficient purity (of aspiration), they might be blessed by Sophia herself, as is spoken of by David, King of Israel, to his son Solomon:

Let your heart hold fast my words:
keep my commandments and live;
do not forget, and do not turn away from
    the words of my mouth:

Find wisdom (*Sophia*)....
Do not forsake her, and she will keep you;
love her, and she will guard you....
Prize her highly, and she will exalt you;
she will honor you if you embrace her.
She will place on your head a fair garland;
she will bestow on you a beautiful crown.

(Prov. 4:4–9)

> *"The shadow intellect that is characteristic of all modern culture has fettered human beings to the Earth. They have eyes only for earthly things, particularly when they allow themselves to be influenced by the claims of modern science. In our age it never occurs to someone that their being belongs not to the Earth alone but to the cosmos beyond the Earth. Knowledge of our connection with the cosmos beyond the Earth—that is what we need above all to make our own.... When someone says 'I' to themselves, they experience a force that is working within, and the [ancient] Greek, in feeling the working of this inner force, related it to the Sun;...the Sun and the 'I' are the outer and inner aspects of one being. The Sun out there in space is the cosmic 'I.' What lives within me is the human 'I.'... Human beings are not primarily a creation of Earth. Human beings receive their shape and form from the cosmos. The human being is an offspring of the world of stars, above all of the Sun and Moon.... The Moon forces stream out from a center in the metabolic system.... [The] Moon stimulates reproduction.... Saturn works chiefly in the upper part of the astral body....Jupiter has to do with thinking...Mars [has] to do with speech.... The Mercury forces work in the part of the human organism that lies below the region of the heart...in the breathing and circulatory functions.... Venus works preeminently in the etheric body of the human being."*—RUDOLF STEINER, *Offspring of the World of Stars*, May 5, 1921

# CULTIVATING LIGHT:
# A MICHAELIC APPROACH TO LIVING
# IN THE SHADOW OF THE BEAST
### Contemplating the 2020 Jupiter–Saturn Conjunction

## Claudia McLaren Lainson

*"The ahrimanic incarnation cannot be averted; it is inevitable, for humanity must encounter Ahriman face to face."*[1]

*"Ahrimanic powers prepare the evolution of humankind in such a way that it can fall prey to Ahriman when he appears in human form within Western civilization."*[2]

In the book of Revelation, John witnesses the rising of two beasts (Rev. 13). Rising from the sea, the "first beast" has seven heads and ten horns. The Dragon gives it all his authority, his power, and his throne.[3] It thereby rules over all tribes, peoples, languages, and races. Moreover, it is given the power to unleash wars against all who are devoted to spirit. All the inhabitants of the Earth worship this beast—the one referred to in this essay as *the Antichrist–Ahriman*.[4]

John then sees the second beast rising out of the Earth. It has two horns ("like a lamb"), but its speech is that "of a dragon." Working magically in league with the authority of the first beast, it calls down fire from Heaven and delivers death to all who do not worship the first beast. It causes everyone—small and great, rich and poor, free or unfree—to become imprinted with a mark on the right hand or the forehead. There is no buying or selling without the mark. This beast—whose number in Hebrew is 666—is the one referred to in this essay as the Sun Demon–Sorath, the false prophet who represents the teachings of the beast.

Rudolf Steiner proclaimed that Ahriman would incarnate in the flesh before only a part of the third post-Christian millennium has elapsed.[5] In his karma lectures he makes it clear that a great crisis of civilization would come around 1998, and we can observe that this date marked only the beginning of this great crisis, which he prophesied would culminate with an incarnation of Ahriman into a human vessel.

In her book *The Descent into the Depths of the Earth*, Judith von Halle devotes considerable attention to Sorath. She describes how this being worked from the Sun until the time of Christ's descent into Hell, where Sorath followed on Christ's coattails, so to speak, and took up its abode in the Earth's ninth subearthly layer—a realm of pure evil. Thus John witnesses it rising from the Earth.

---

1   Steiner, *The Incarnation of Ahriman: The Embodiment of Evil on Earth*, lect. 5.

2   Ibid., lecture 2.

3   *Dragon*, as referred to here, can be thought of as a synonym for Ahriman, who breathes his life into the human vessel that rises from the *anti*-etheric world (i.e., the sea), into which he will incarnate. This individuality is the one to whom the Dragon gives his authority. This is the Dragon pictured in the sixth Seal of the Apocalypse, placed beneath the feet of Michael.

4   The word *Antichrist* is used throughout this essay, and there are at least two ways in which this word may be understood. The more general use of the word is found in the Bible and in Christian tradition, in which the Antichrist is understood to be the human being who bears the incarnated Satan–Ahriman, and who in Rev. 13 is called "The Beast." This is how the term is being used in this essay. Steiner's use of *Antichrist* refers to Sorath, the Sun Demon, who prepares the way for Ahriman's incarnation.

5   Steiner, *The Ahrimanic Deception*, Oct. 27, 1919: "Just as there was an incarnation of Lucifer at the beginning of the third pre-Christian millennium, as there was the Christ Incarnation at the time of the Mystery of Golgotha, *so there will be a Western incarnation of the Ahriman being some little time after our present earthly existence—in fact, in the third post-Christian millennium.*"

According to Daniel Andreev, in an unpublished section of *Rosa Mira (Rose of the World)*, there were two "leading souls" in the school of Ahriman, who were candidates to become the vessel into which Ahriman would incarnate later.[6] They had both been born during the latter part of the nineteenth century. "One of them incarnated in 1878 in Georgia and subsequently became the leader of the Soviet Union; the other incarnated in Austria in 1889 and became the leader of Nazi Germany."[7]

Exactly as predicted by Rudolf Steiner, the beast rose in 1933 and was the inspiring spirit working through both of Ahriman's disciples: the one in Russia and the other in Germany. Yet it would seem that these nineteenth-century incarnations were naught but preliminary saber rattling—for during the end of the twentieth century and the beginning of the twenty-first, we have witnessed an incredible intensification of what can only be called *evil*, indicating that something is indeed newly afoot.

While predicting the incarnation of Ahriman into a human being—whose path would have been prepared by the third rising of Sorath in 1998—Rudolf Steiner also prophesied 1933 as the date when the Etheric Christ would begin to manifest. He further saw that the coming of the Etheric Christ would be the beginning of an apocalyptic struggle: "Before the Etheric Christ can be comprehended by human beings in the right way, humanity must first cope with encountering the beast who will rise up in 1933."[8] With Hitler in power in Germany, and Stalin in power in Russia, humanity was directly encountering the beast and was thus distracted from recognizing the dawn of the Second Coming.

War and revolution ensued, and in the shadow of these world events, the beast most certainly lurked.

The two beasts (Sorath and Ahriman), as witnessed by John, have also emerged in modern prophecy, visions, and predictions. When a confluence of such prognostications presents itself, we are wise to be alert and vigilantly observe what is otherwise *hidden* behind events occurring on the world stage. Moreover, the precarious and often-disastrous global dilemmas of our time are evidence of a wide-ranging "crisis," the origins of which could only be spawned from the loins of evil.

The incarnation of Ahriman—the shadowy antithesis of the Etheric Christ—portends a tremendous escalation of evil in our time. We are called to seize the opportunity to awake and advance. *It all rests on our ability to recognize that an overshadowing matrix effectively conceals the activities of evil beings who are actually directing world events.*

The ahrimanic beast from the sea will turn many people into animal–humans; the sorathic beast from the Earth will then seize these animal–humans and cast them into its abyss. Under the influences of these two beasts, we abuse spiritual powers. Many of us do so unwittingly. *Such abuse is the origin of all black magic.* In contradistinction, the *right* use of spiritual powers is the origin of all white magic.

We are truly living in the shadow of these two beasts, for their impulses have converged—with the aim of sweeping away anything spiritual. The 2020 Great Conjunction, however, has the potential to begin a process of re-establishing all things spiritual.

Since the time of Christ, the Sun Demon has risen every 666 years: in 666, 1332, and 1998. His intention is to collaborate with Ahriman in order to destroy creation. Their common goal is to fabricate a world of their own making, one that is completely separate from Divine Worlds. Ahriman seeks to become the World Emperor, while Sorath seeks to become God.

By 1998, the Sun Demon had inspired the World Wide Web in preparation for the continued activity of Ahriman. Through this medium, the second

---

6  Steiner, *Karmic Relationships,* vol. 6: "While Michael above was teaching his hosts, there was founded—in the realm lying immediately below the surface of the Earth—a kind of sub-earthly, Ahrimanic school."

7  Powell, *Prophecy–Phenomena–Hope*, p. 19.

8  Steiner, *The Book of Revelation and the Work of the Priest*, p. 231. This subject is covered in depth in two of Robert Powell's books: *Prophecy–Phenomena–Hope* and (with Kevin Dann) *Christ and the Maya Calendar.*

beast can surely "work wonders," even bringing "fire down from Heaven." In league with the *authority* of the first beast, the Web propagates duplicity; it lures unsuspecting souls into domains of illusion, while moving them ever further from the Etheric Christ, Natura, and one another.

There is no question that this Web has gained a mesmerizing authority over the people of all nations. With its rise, moreover, the ground has been successfully established for the current onset of the reign of beasts. We are now experiencing an alarming increase, worldwide, in psychoses, random acts of violence, and mechanized assaults on nature. This increase is very much connected to all the various manifestations of the Internet and its Artificial Intelligence—for these phenomena steal the *god*-sense, replacing it with a *machine*-sense.

The prophecies of Daniel Andreev, Vladimir Soloviev, Judith von Halle, and Jeane Dixon (as well as significant others) lend credence to Steiner's proclamation of the Antichrist's incarnation. To completely ignore such insights would be folly. It would be equally foolish, however, to immediately accept and apply a given prophecy without deeply considering its message

Prophecy can appear at first as a somewhat nebulous cloud of potential, and the chaff must be carefully separated from any kernel of truth found therein. The vicissitudes of humanity's collective free will must also be taken into consideration. Indeed, prophecy is a draught best taken before bedtime, offered to spiritual worlds, and received anew as the Sun again crests the horizon. This should be repeated, night after night. Does the night not offer us intrigue, as well as clues and verification? How do we take in such prophecies as given by Steiner, Andreev, Soloviev, von Halle, and Dixon and *make them our own*?

We can include Willi Sucher as one who also found credence in an imminent appearance of Ahriman. In private conversation with Robert Powell, Willi indicated that he had done research into a vision by Jeane Dixon and had found it plausible, even identifying the place of birth as Tobruk, Libya. When he was asked about the significance of all seven planets aligned in Capricorn at the time of this birth, he replied:

> In antiquity, Capricorn was called the "gateway to the gods." And what better moment could the Antichrist choose to be born than when all the planets are aligned in front of Capricorn—blocking the gateway to the spiritual world—in order to establish his rulership in a world of materialism and thereby cut humanity off from all spirituality?[9]

## *Fear's Role in the Culmination*

In his karma lectures, Rudolf Steiner addressed the problem of fears among anthroposophists. It was clear to him that the initiative necessary to actually name evil caused a fear that repelled modern-day esotericists from doing what their karma had led them to do:

> This, too, is due to the fact that such people are predisposed to the unfolding of inner initiative. Their karma having placed them in the world with this quality, they are always in the position (forgive the comparison) of a bee that has a sting but is afraid to use it at the right moment. The sting is the initiative, but these people are afraid to use it. *They are afraid, above all, of stinging into the ahrimanic realm.* Not that they fear that they will thereby hurt what is ahrimanic. No, they are afraid that the sting will recoil into their own bodies. This, to some extent, is what this fear is like. Thus, through an undetermined fear of life, the initiative remains inactive.[10]

Judith von Halle was aware of why the "stingers" might be lamed. She experienced the grave danger of the ahrimanic deception owing to the literal presence of the beast within us:

> Intensive engagement with and study of the most incisive occult problems of our time is still largely suppressed and avoided in today's anthroposophical movement. Likewise, the

---

9  See article by Robert Powell, "Willi Sucher and Jeane Dixon's Prophecy," *Journal for Star Wisdom* 2010.

10  Steiner, *Karmic Relationships*, vol. 3, lecture 10. [My italics—CML.]

equally significant and striking utterances by Steiner about the mystery of the reappearance of the etheric Christ and the impulse of his adversary, the Antichrist, in the twentieth and twenty-first centuries, are only seldom examined, illumined, or cited; although the drastic nature of these comments, along with the radical form in which they were expressed, ought to place every student of Anthroposophy on the highest alert. In perception of and engagement with this highly topical phenomenon of our times, a scarcely explicable kind of paralysis seems to have taken hold of human spirits. There seems no other way to explain this paralysis than as the latent effect of the power of the Antichrist himself.[11]

We are indeed living in the time of a "great crisis." We recoil in fear from exactly that which we are supposed to do as students of Steiner: *name evil.* Thus, while sparing ourselves from seeing what is now taking place before our very eyes, we seek in vain to prove that the crisis still lies in the future.

The upcoming Great Conjunction between Jupiter and Saturn offers a remedy to our predicament, in that it will quicken our intuitions while also asking us to stand *in our time* as courageous knights, willing to serve Michael's ongoing battle with the dragon.[12] Furthermore, as this conjunction remembers the birth of a prophesied vessel, we are wise to find our "stinger" ready! We cannot ignore the significance of the third rising of the beast, in 1998, as the signature of evil's presence on a greatly magnified scale.

The period marking the influence of this year's Great Conjunction of Jupiter and Saturn spans twenty years. It will begin on December 21 at 5°27' Capricorn. This is the constellation to which Rudolf Steiner assigned the worldview of Spiritism—i.e.,

the removal of all egoistic resistance preventing us from receiving spiritual thoughts. *The influences inherent in this year's new conjunction bear the potential of opening spiritual gateways through which we can penetrate the barriers established by the beasts.* The next conjunction (at 22°37' Virgo) will not occur until October 31, 2040.[13] The year 2040 is nearly halfway through the TWENTY-first century, which may indicate a time that has moved past Steiner's indication of "some little time after our present earthly existence."

The most recent Great Conjunction in Capricorn occurred in February 1961; there was an amazing alignment of all planets in this same sign a year later, in February 1962. The return of Jupiter and Saturn to Capricorn might well activate what then occurred. The worldview that is Spiritism in its positive manifestation is, in its fallen manifestation, *anti*-spirit; it is Antichrist.

## *Platonists and Aristotelians*

A great *spiritual* crisis absolutely occurred when, despite heeding what Steiner admonished, the Platonists and Aristotelians failed to come together at the end of the twentieth century. In the void rendered as the two streams maintained their separateness, Ahriman gained an enormous advantage. Moreover, Michael's influence was tragically lamed, for the fruits such collaboration would have birthed did not manifest. Had the two united, a desperately needed third stream could have risen in the world as a result of this—through which Ahriman's insidious plan might have been revealed.

Anthroposophists should understand that they are called to prepare, already, that spirituality which must expand ever more and more until the culmination is reached at the end of the twentieth century—when true anthroposophists will be able to be here again, united with the others [Platonists].[14]

---

11 Von Halle, *Descent into the Depths of the Earth...*, p. 49.

12 Just as Jupiter–Holy Spirit represents *spiritual sight* (i.e., via the "third-eye"), so does Saturn–Holy Virgin represent our *spiritual uprightness* (i.e., our vertical alignment with Christ), through which we gain a "direct knowing": intuition.

13 See Powell, *The Christ Mystery.* The year 2040 marks the deepest descent of the Christ "I" into the subearthly layers of the inner Earth, after which his ascent begins.

14 Steiner, *Karmic Relationships*, vol. 3, p. 117.

Ahriman continues to be the powerful adversary of this culmination. He works into human minds and is thereby able to thwart such a tremendous spiritual potential. Steiner was quite specific in speaking about the *reincarnated* Aristotelians meeting the Platonists, who would by then also have reincarnated (likely beginning from the middle of the twentieth century). The key word here is *incarnated,* for the culmination could only take place as an event *on Earth*. This is what Michael needed—the *full* revelation that had been supersensibly prepared through the different streams.

This fullness would have forged a mighty counterforce to Ahriman. Steiner was so insistent on this recognition between the two streams that he referenced it in his "Last Address."[15] Therein he speaks of the lectures he had just given addressing "the karma of the Anthroposophical Society." He knew Spiritual beings had orchestrated the "timing" of this culmination, and thus was it destined to flow into time specifically at the century's end. Due to a lack of initiative, however, the fruits of this potential collaboration lay unclaimed. Ahriman could therefore steal it, invert it, and use it against us. This continues to stand as a tragedy.

### A Birth Prophecy

It was Jeane Dixon who prophesied the birth of one she called the "Middle Eastern child" (also referred to as the vessel for the Antichrist) on February 5, 1962.[16] This individual would therefore be fifty-eight years old this year. The Sun at the birth of this child was 21° Capricorn, just a few hours past a Capricorn New Moon. We can view a New Moon as a kind of "immaculate conception" (e.g., the woman clothed with the Sun, with the Moon under her feet, wearing a crown of twelve stars). In this case, however, we are speaking of a conception whose origin is not the virginal upper Worlds of light; rather it is the Antichrist conceived from *electromagnetic subearthly worlds* —thus fashioning an *anti*-immaculate conception. How fitting that this birth occurred only five hours after a total eclipse of the Sun!

Regardless of whether the Antichrist has incarnated or not, his signature is everywhere. And just as there is a source whence all goodness (the Son of God) streams into the world, is there not also a source whence all evil (the son of Ahriman) streams into the world? Furthermore, are we not seeing a kind of paralysis of humanity's moral sense for truth—a paralysis that tells of the "latent effects of the power of the Antichrist himself?"

> The aim of the ahrimanic powers…is to harden and freeze up the Earth, to shape it in such a way that, together with the Earth, the human being remains an earthbound creature—becoming hardened, as it were, within earthly substance *and continuing to live in the future ages of the world as a kind of statue of the past.*[17]

In fallen realms, Capricorn represents this hardening into the past. In its virtue, however, Capricorn showers stars of hope upon human beings who are courageous enough to face the trials of their own redemption. In order to make space for such redeeming thoughts, we must first restrain the momentum gained by "old" thinking—for Hope is a *new* force that eternally shines from the future. It promises us that if we overcome fear of our own darkness, we will reach new heights of evolution.

Thus a new force of hope is gained when we center ourselves in the heart, and from there perceive what is living at the periphery of our energy field. Then we become simultaneously aware of both point and periphery; we experience all the light that is now radiantly shining—from the fiery edge of the sense-world, as well as from the fiery center of our heart. *This radiant, peripheral-and-interior light is the presence of the Jesus-being, who is now offering to Christ his higher* (manas)

---

15 See appendix 6 in the author's book, *The Circle of Twelve, and the Legacy of Valentin Tomberg* (windroseacademypress.com).

16 See Powell, *Prophecy–Phenomena–Hope*. Jean Dixon gave this birthdate for the one she called the "Middle Eastern child." See also his article, "The Second Coming and the Approaching Trial of Humanity."

17 Steiner, *The Sun Mystery and the Mystery of Death and Resurrection*, June 11, 1922 (trans. rev. by Robert Powell; italics added—CML).

*consciousness as his fifth, and most recent, sacrifice.*[18] Through this sacrifice, we may now feel the "touch" of Christ approaching us from the encircling round. Our heart cognizes the rhythms that here live and breathe, for the intellect alone cannot perform this task.

We are left in no doubt that the third rising of the beast occurred sometime around 1998.[19] His rise, moreover, would necessitate the presence of human vessels (if not *the* human vessel) through whom his works are to be accomplished. Nick Fiorenza, an astrologer, speaks of the period of 2020 to 2030 as that of "The Great Transformation."[20] We can only wonder at how this may transpire. Are we to conservatively estimate that this great transformation will have something to do with the emergence of the Antichrist? According to Fiorenza: "In the year 2020, three major planetary cycles complete and begin anew, creating a societal reset and the start of 'The Great Transformation'—[which will unfold] throughout the next decade (2020-2030)."

The first 10 years of this twenty-year cycle represent its waxing phase, after which it begins its approximately ten-year waning phase. The waxing phase is the time for change and transformation; the waning phase is the time when the consequences of our collective human response will then rain down upon us.

All heavenly discourses have both virtue and vice. If the influences of this Great Conjunction fall into the hands of illicit powers, then what could have been the great transformation will instead become a woefully apocalyptic time of unrest—one that none of us would wish to experience.

In prudence, we must therefore seek to observe with an unprejudiced eye. Too much has been said—and too much is currently happening—for us to blithely disregard the signs of our times:

> This disregard of the weightiest truths is precisely what will build Ahriman the best bridge to the success of his incarnation. Moreover, except for an unprejudiced study of the forces through which Ahriman's influence works…nothing will help us to find the right position in regard to the part played by Ahriman in human evolution. For this reason, we will cast a brief glance today at various things that would foster support of Ahriman—and which ahrimanic powers, working out of supersensible worlds through human minds down here, will particularly employ in order to make his following as numerous as possible.[21]

Steiner goes on to speak about our separation from the cosmos, which resulted in the spiritless thinking of materialistic mathematics and science. He also speaks of the great discord felt by our modern souls—a discord that derives from the disharmony between what our souls experience in the night and what our waking-consciousness acknowledges in its world-conception. *Such discord has been prepared by Ahriman himself, as is evident from the intrusive nature of the materialistic worldview.*

Perhaps we have collectively created trolls. As in fairy stories, they lurk beneath the bridge that separates day from night. Sensitive souls, and especially the young among us, may perceive this threat, which has led to insomnia becoming a growing concern. Such people simply cannot release their souls. Evil souls, on the other hand, sleep like the dead, for they are nonplussed by the menace of their comrades skulking beneath this bridge; nor do they intend to enter the cosmic night.

Michael asks us to cultivate communion with the great School of the Night, wherein we are given experiences of moral truths that resonate into the morning. If we have accepted the *possibility* of an initiate from the school of Ahriman being present on the Earth, the night may offer a certain resonance with the moral integrity of this notion. If, in fact, we *do* feel such resonance, then the prophecy

---

18 *Manas* consciousness represents a state of purity in our astral bodies through which the thoughts of the gods flow directly into us, undisturbed by any egoism.

19 The Internet went "live" on Aug. 6, 1991, 58 years after 1933.

20 See https://www.lunarplanner.com/~lunarpla/2020/.

21 Steiner, *The Ahrimanic Deception,* Oct. 27, 1919.

in question can be experimentally applied to reality—without prejudice or personal opinion clouding its veracity. The night helps us to overcome what the ahrimanic master of deceit proffers as the most dangerous potion of all: half-truths and even quarter-truths. These cause the greatest devastation, for they are not readily apparent as such.

We must rise above fraudulence to commune with the night. We must verify truths by means of a process that is considerably more refined that the one to which we may already be accustomed. In light of the relevant prophecies, let us see what benefit we may discover by examining the stars of 2020.

### A Remarkable Alignment

On February 5, 1962, an amazing "grand alignment" of all seven classical planets occurred in Capricorn, from 8° through 25°. This marked the birth of the one here referred to as the Middle Eastern child (i.e., the one who would allegedly become the vessel for the Antichrist). The Sun on that day was 21°46' Capricorn. In the predawn hours, Mars rose shortly before the Sun, its red glow heralding the significance that warmongering would play in the destiny of this individuality. Thereafter, Saturn rose with the Sun. At this birth, therefore, three planets were situated above the horizon (Mars, Saturn, and Sun); the other four planets (Mercury, Jupiter, Venus, and Moon) lay below the horizon, in the 12th house: the region of secrets, occult capacities, and hidden agendas.

The Great Conjunction of 2020, in Capricorn, will activate the grand alignment of influences that took place at this person's birth—occurring just a few degrees from the above-mentioned astonishing congregation of birth influences. The God of the Underworld, Hades–Pluto, will be standing only a few degrees from this event. A great power may then be afforded to this individuality. His aim, of course, is to be a kind of World Emperor.

A passage from Revelation 17 might serve our collective awakening:

> Here is the mind that has wisdom. The seven heads are seven mountains on which the woman sits, and they are seven kings; five have fallen, one is [exists], and the other has not yet come; and when he comes, he must remain a little while. *The beast that was and is not, is himself an eighth, while also one of the seven; and he goes to destruction.*[22] The ten horns that you saw are ten kings who have not yet received a kingdom, but they receive authority as kings with the beast for one hour. These have one purpose, and they give their power and authority to the beast.

Where might an *eighth* king arise? Is he the re-emergence of one of the seven kings? Who is watching? Who will unmask his evil?

In our divided churches, Peter, Paul, and John embody three key tasks. Peter, as the shepherd of Catholicism, represents the continuity of the apostolic succession; Paul, as the keeper of the Damascus Gate, represents Protestantism; and John, as the revealer of the Sophia mysteries, represents the Orthodox Church. In Vladimir Solovyov's "Short Story of the Antichrist," it is John who initially unmasks him, whereupon Peter and Paul follow suit. This leads to the reunification of the three churches, establishing a force of familial love that leads their congregations into a future of peace. The Light of the World shines and overlights all religious streams. Those who see this Light are able, as was John, to expose and repudiate false prophets and their doctrines of deceit.

Regardless of whether we live in the actual time of the Antichrist, or whether we are still dolefully confined in the darkness that *prepares* for his arrival, we are faced with having to overcome malevolent forces in all aspects of life. We are not, however, to see ourselves as "sheep without a shepherd." Though the laborers may be few, we are tasked with using our "stingers" and revealing what may at first appear to be insurmountable. Naming the evil surrounding us invokes the power inherent in the "Word," wherein Christ becomes our inner experience:

> Because the great mass of antichristian and unchristian forces fills our entire life sphere, we must allow the power of thought, the life of the heart, and the feeling for truth to live in the word

---

22 Italics added—CML.

and to oppose the hostile world with the other World that can be experienced in the Word.[23]

The strength of faith stands, by analogy, as that of David standing before the temporal strength of the giant, Goliath. We must transform our perceptions of the physical world, raising them above what is conveyed strictly through materialistic sciences and fearful statistics. We are called instead to soar beyond the "measurable" as we take flight—through God's icons—into worlds of magic, mystery, and wonder. In these realms the Word lives eternal, benevolently streaming a "force" that opposes ahrimanic destructive technologies as well as all that ushers forth from the disciples of Ahriman himself.

During the remaining millennia of Earth evolution, our task as humans will be to set in motion *the truth of vertical causality*. This aligns us with the Logos, who assists us as we learn how to chain the Beasts beneath our feet. This is our protection against becoming "lost sheep" in the mass-flock of Ahriman.

### The Saturn Returns of the Antichrist

As the 2020 Great Conjunction of Jupiter and Saturn occurs on December 21, with the two planets standing at 5°27' Capricorn, we remember the Transfiguration of Christ.[24] For this conjunction is not only a mere 3° from the grand alignment of February 5th, 1962; it is also where the Moon stood in the heavens just before the Transfiguration. Furthermore, this conjunction falls fifty-eight years after the birth of this Middle Eastern child, marking his *second* Saturn return. The exact date of this Saturn return is January 26, 2021—a mere few weeks after the onset of this new twenty-year cycle.

Shortly thereafter, this individual will experience his fifth Jupiter return. Jupiter expands all it touches. If we are considering an *immoral* soul, Jupiter will expand tyranny; if we are considering a *moral* soul, it will expand kingliness. A wolf in sheep's clothing, however, may at first appear to be gentle.

In 1991, the child we are considering experienced his *first* Saturn return, during which his mission was laid upon him. If the prophecy is true—that an initiate from the School of Ahriman was born as this child—we must keep our eyes wide open. Between the first and second Saturn returns (i.e., between 1991 and 2021), preparation and "incarnation" would/will have occurred. Incarnation here means the point in time when the spirit of the Antichrist would/will have been incorporated into his sheaths. We know that Christ entered into the sheaths of Jesus at his Baptism in the Jordan River. In like manner, Ahriman would/will need to incarnate into the sheaths of the individual who had been so prepared by the powers of evil.

The electromagnetic grid was gathering force during this being's first Saturn return. Now, at this time of his approaching second Saturn return, we are on the verge of worldwide implementation of 5G (fifth-generation wireless technology).[25]

A further consideration is the fact that the second Saturn return of this being stands midway between the two Great American Solar Eclipses— the first one having occurred in 2017 (on August 21), and the next one due to take place in 2024 (on April 8). Indeed, to the extent that the prophecies are true, this being personifies *a total eclipse of the Christ–Sun*. Furthermore, we recall that this being was born only five hours after a total eclipse of the Sun in Capricorn.

Rudolf Steiner stated that this prepared human vessel would appear in the West. We can easily assume he meant America. Jeane Dixon, too, saw this. If this being were to rise to power in 2021 (just after his second Saturn return), his prophesied three-and-a-half-year reign would culminate

---

23 Tomberg, *Christ and Sophia*, p. 344.

24 At the event of the Transfiguration, Jesus Christ stood between Moses and Elijah. Whereas Moses represents *truth*, Elijah represents *life*: a directing force. The twentieth century situated humankind between these two, for Moses–Steiner's teachings began the century, and Elijah–Rachel (the reincarnated Elijah in our time) brought the century to its end.

25 The threatening nature of this momentous change in the very structure of our global electronic environment will be discussed later in this essay.

at the time of the next Great American Eclipse. Mere coincidence, or prophecy? This remains a question.

The second Saturn return (in January, 2021) would mark the fruition of his destiny task and his readiness to give humanity the crowning glory of the 29 years of his past efforts. As we are on the verge of launching 5G technologies, we can only wonder at the curious circumstance that links his second Saturn return with this event. Will his accomplishments be poured upon an unsuspecting humanity in a manner like unto the "vials of wrath" spoken of in Revelation?[26] Might such vials be an analogy for 5G technologies—which is a kind of "fire from Heaven"?

During his Passion, Christ received a "crown of thorns," representing his willingness to carry out deeds determined by the Father. The Antichrist also has a "crown of thorns," yet his crown does not pierce him with the weight of spiritual tasks; rather does it elevate him to a throne of his own making, *as his thorns pierce others*.

The manner of the Antichrist's appearance will doubtless be of a benevolent nature. Would a being this brilliant appear with horns and a red tail? *No, he would appear as a Christ-like figure!* His *initial* entrance into politics (or some other seat of authority) would most likely have accompanied the third rising of the Beast—i.e., around 1998. At the conclusion of his second Saturn return, he may indeed have a kind of "second coming," for he imitates the good prophecies of his time. Such a second coming would suggest that he may reappear, *as a kind of eighth king*, having already established people's trust through one of his past appointments.

If this occurs, what will be the nature of this crown? What power will be bestowed upon him? His new crowning will likely come in a form that allows him to rule with great power, for it is prophesied that he will unleash wars of even greater magnitude than those we have suffered continuously since the last Great Conjunction. And is it actually true that his reign will be naught but three-and-one-half years?

_______________

26 Divine wrath is the inversion of Divine love.

## Transfiguration in Light vs. Electrical Transmutation

Those who have the capacity to observe etheric worlds are able to gain perceptions not accessible to many of us:

The etheric forces are not empty rhythms or tones. The creative action of the cosmic Word, the Logos, is working through them. They are filled with meaning. Thus every species of plant not only has its characteristic form in space, which is in reality a pattern of movement called forth by the action of the etheric tones and rhythms working in time, but it also expresses a specific meaning. In older times, the "meaning" of a plant was also sometimes called its "virtue." Whoever can reach in actual perception from the form to the pattern of movements, and then from the movements to the cosmic rhythms or tones—and ultimately to the meaning expressing itself through them—begins to grasp the deeper sense of each living creature. When she beholds the trees and flowers of a landscape, these become for her like the worlds of a hidden language. She begins to read the book of nature.[27]

Initiates are particularly capable of following *human* etheric patterns. This is how they perceive individualities in their paths after death, as well as in their paths into birth. The information thus gained lends credence to what may later come forth as prophecy. Some of us are transfigured in life; others are *transmuted*. What does this mean? In a biological context, specific to the meaning here intended, it means the transformation of one species into another, from the human into the *machine–cyber* human—consequent to life forces transmuting into *anti*-life forces.[28] Such transmutation stands in opposition to the Transfiguration of Christ.

The day before the Transfiguration of Christ on Mt. Tabor, the Moon was at 5° Capricorn. As previously stated, this is exactly where the 2020

_______________

27 *Anthro-Tech News,* no. 13, winter 2011–2012. Anthro-Tech Research Institute, Switzerland.

28 Steiner, *The Apocalypse of St. John*: "Those who use the life in the body for anything more than an opportunity to gain ego-consciousness will descend into the abyss and form the evil race."

conjunction between Jupiter and Saturn is occurring. The Transfiguration occurred two years before the Crucifixion. Throughout the rest of his life, Christ's greatest enemy, the Antichrist, would work against him. It was Ahriman who tortured Christ in the Garden of Gethsemane, showing him all the deeds human beings would do in his name. And it is this same being who now tortures all of humanity. His aim is to strangle any possibility that the Second Coming may be recognized, as well as to destroy any possibility that human souls will become transfigured by a *manas* light. Steiner went so far as to say:

> The remainder of Earth evolution, with its machines and its mechanization, belongs to Ahriman. The Gods have given it over into his hands. This is a fact that, *like the explosion of a bomb*, should shake us to the very depths of our souls.[29]

The event of the Transfiguration marked the enlightenment of Jesus's astral body. It is the destiny of the next astrological age (Aquarius) that this will gradually occur within the astral bodies of many human beings.[30] Indeed, the seeds for this potential are quickening in our age of the consciousness soul. Moreover, in view of the fact that the enlightenment of Jesus Christ was bestowed upon him through beings indwelling the lunar realm of angels, the lunar memory accompanying this conjunction (i.e., memory of the Transfiguration) gives credence to the possibility that the 2020 Great Conjunction will bestow a wealth of new Imaginations from the realm of World Thoughts. These Imaginations may (or may *not*) affirm our considerations.[31]

The inversion of a Christological transfiguration would be an *electromagnetic* transmutation. We may imagine how the Antichrist would undergo his change: a cold and scintillating light would come over him; the light would be rigid, and the effects would be fantastical, perhaps even forcefully magnetizing for those bearing witness to it. Such a light as would come upon the Antichrist originates from underworldly depths. It consists of dead light and dead sound—i.e., *caricatures* of the living ethers. His transmutation would be more like living into the electro-magnetic "grid"; and by means of this very ahrimanically inspired connectivity, his body could expand throughout the globe.

Given that the anti-etheric forces have been passed from the gods into the hands of Ahriman, and due to the fact that the Internet came into being concurrently with the third rising of the Sun Demon in 1998, we have been warned regarding a possible inversion of the Transfiguration. *It would be a contraction of life and light into a mere caricature of the living field of life energies.*

Christ lives into the entire etheric aura of the Earth, continuously radiating forces of goodness from its realm of vital forces. And this is received by human souls who are cultivating light. The body of the Antichrist, in contrast, could easily live into the entirety of the deadening technological grid. Yet, in preservation of the lawfulness protecting human freedom, he would need to enter through a human host who is in his service. We can imagine the electrical light of such a host as being compelling, even attractive—in the same way that virtual and augmented reality is compelling, filled as it is with treachery. We can even imagine that the electrical light could actually masquerade as a *superficial warmth*; that is, until the time when goodness unmasks this being. Only then would his true nature be revealed. This is foretold in Vladimir Solovyov's "Short Tale of the Antichrist."[32]

---

29 Steiner, esoteric lesson of Nov. 19, 1913; Elizabeth Vreede Archives (italics added—CML).

30 The Aquarian astrological age begins in 2375.

31 According to the Apocalypse Code, humanity reached the end of the 39 days of temptation in 2018. Since then, we have been living in the 40th day, the day angels ministered to Jesus Christ. This enhances the possibility of angelic help as the influences of this conjunction unfold. The Apocalypse Code is described in Powell and Dann, *Christ and the Maya Calendar*, chap. 2.

32 In Solovyov's inspired work, "A Short Story of the Antichrist" (published Easter 1900, in Solovyov, *War, Progress, and the End of History*), we are told of the false Christ, who, in league with the *false prophet* (the magician Apollyon), becomes Emperor of the world and establishes his residence in Jerusalem.

## Social Disintegration

A resurrection of Capricorn's "Spiritism" will be actively opposed by beings promulgating destructive modern technologies. For, when black magic is not countered by white magic, it works against etheric perceptions. This can truly cripple our ability to develop spiritual faculties. The greater the ubiquity of mechanical–technological grids, the more is human nature programmed to resonate with the machine, which in turn leads to a state of world anxiety. Such anxiety contributes to the disintegration of the social organization of our entire global culture. When souls resonate with the *machine*—i.e., with electromagnetic cell towers and the like, they tend to isolate and contract into themselves. *This depletes the sap of life.* Thus is truth ultimately veiled from human beings whose life energies are drained. On the other hand, when souls resonate with spirit, they seek companionship. They know: *When soul meets soul, the universal sap of life flows.*

Just as transfiguration *expands* life forces, so do destructive technologies *contract* them. We can imagine that there is only one social fabric and that each of us is a part of this. Now, let us imagine this fabric shrinking in contraction, as life forces wither; we then become entombed in our personal opinions—which become increasingly "statue-like" (i.e., unbending). This inevitably causes lesions in the one social fabric. At first, it becomes brittle, and then it tears, leaving these lesions behind. Into these tears, into these lesions, *enters Ahriman* (the Antichrist).

Ahriman replaces what is culturally invigorating and socially harmonizing with video gaming, social medias, strip malls, banks, bars, gyms, and all manner of other material convenience and seductions. The loss of our town-centric community centers is analogous to the loss of the "center place" within us: our heart. In such vacuous environments, true social longing for one another rapidly dissipates. And as we lose touch with our sacred inner sanctuary, *moral conscience declines.* We become very busy, and this affects the way we move through the world. We rush and hurry, as if the very tempo of being human has sped up, while unconsciously matching the speed of the grid that interpenetrates us. Caught up as we are in this kind of frenetic culture, it is no surprise that we reach for Amazon's "one-click."

Perhaps the most harrowing aspect of our accelerated lifestyle is its effect on innocence. We briskly drag our children through their lives, whereby their souls are torn apart by the very power of the world. And we notice this not, for just as our culture has become tattered and torn, so, too, have our souls.[33] One consequence of this is that it has become increasingly difficult for us to protect the innate purity of our young. Children nowadays can rarely relax into the solace of timelessness, which once represented the very heart of childhood.

Addictions and suicides have also become ever more prevalent in our woefully troubled world. As we fall further from God, Truth, Nature, and even each other, "cheaper, faster, easier" continues to splinter the social organism. It is imperative that we recognize a pervasive presence behind all of this—one that is dark, sinister, and hungry. How the angels must pray that we stop feeding it! *Are we willing to acknowledge the enormous ground the Beast has gained over the past two decades?*

Resistance follows recognition:

It is no use harboring illusions today about these things. Ahriman will appear in human form, and the only question is: *How will he find humanity prepared?* Will his preparations have secured for him, as followers, the whole of humankind that today calls itself civilized; or will he find a humanity that can offer resistance? People nowadays flee from the truth, and one cannot give it to them in an unvarnished form—because they would pour scorn and ridicule upon it. The fact that people reject these things is just one of the means which ahrimanic powers can use and which will give Ahriman the greatest possible

---

33 In *The Search for the New Isis: Divine Sophia* (lectures of Dec. 1920), Steiner spoke auspiciously regarding the tearing apart of the human soul. It is perhaps also noteworthy that these lectures were given almost exactly 100 years before the current Jupiter–Saturn Great Conjunction.

following when he appears in human form on Earth.[34] (italics added)

Capricorn, by analogy, represents Mt. Tabor. This conjunction asks us to climb to the summit and re-establish our moral sensibility, which is otherwise known as our inner resonance with Truth. Such an ascent would bring forth the positive manifestation of a great transformation, whereby the eternal aims of gods would again resound through willing human vessels. Thus would our collective "inner resonance" find the antidote to destructive modern technology; for when we cultivate light, we attract light.[35]

Elemental beings must serve what human beings ask of them. And as more of these beings are asked to serve light, we will create rainbows of peace—which will serve to heal the disintegration of our one social fabric. *We will literally be lifting "neutral nature" closer to its virginal state.* By the end of time, Virgin Nature will manifest as the metamorphosed new Paradise, which is referred to in Revelation as the New Jerusalem.

The torrential agitations of the culture of death will surely continue to work against light-bearers—for when we see evil, evil sees us. Indeed, it will take enormous courage and conviction to shine light into the darkness. In communion with Christ and Sophia, however, we will endure the process of releasing darkness into light. *This is the blessed alchemy of transfiguring.* As Jupiter and Saturn commune in Capricorn, rivers of new ideas will flood the minds of those daring enough to take a leap into new possibilities.

---

34 Steiner, *The Incarnation of Ahriman*, lect. 2.

35 Whereas Moral Technology is positive, and destructive technology is negative, Resonance Technology is *neutral*. It can be used for both good and evil, as it represents the realm of human freedom. Morality lifts this neutral realm toward its virgin purity, whereas immorality causes this realm to descend into what is called "the second fall"—i.e., the fall of nature and human souls into subearthly realms. *Cultivating Inner Radiance*, written by Robert Powell, offers practices that create light, into which moral forces may then flow into human beings.

## The Revelation of John

The last Great Conjunction of Jupiter and Saturn occurred at 28° Aries on May 30, 2000. Venus, at the death of Novalis, was positioned at this same degree. Novalis was an incarnation of the same individuality who, at the time of Christ, was John the Baptist and later incarnated as the painter Raphael. Moreover, John and Lazarus were united at the time when Lazarus was raised from the dead.[36] As Lazarus–John is the author of both Revelation and the Gospel of John, we see that this conjunction at 28° Aries was pointing humanity toward the apocalypse ("the revealing of that which is hidden") as well as toward the central message of the John being—to *love* (Venus). The Great Conjunction in Aries indeed asked us to venerate the work of such a high initiate and to adhere to his one and only last teaching from Ephesus: *Love one another.* In this, however, we have miserably failed—as the past 20 years have amply informed us.

The conjunction that follows this year's meeting in Capricorn will occur in 2040 (at 22°37' Virgo). This will take place where the Sun was positioned at what is called the "Little Transfiguration." During this event, as light descended upon Jesus, Anne Catherine Emmerich witnessed the heavens opening. Above his luminous and transparent body, she bore witness to a radiantly shining city, lit in rainbow colors of light. She describes this as a vision of the Heavenly Jerusalem.

Just as the previous conjunction remembered Elijah–John, and the current conjunction remembers the position of the Moon on the eve of the Transfiguration, so will the succeeding conjunction in Virgo remember the "Little Transfiguration." We can imagine ourselves preparing, over the next twenty years, to stand before Capricorn's gateway of the gods. From there, we may be capable of perceiving the eternal Truths existing beyond what the sense-world obscures. This perspective invites us to sup from the upper waters of this constellation—from its Grail Waters.

---

36 See Powell, *The Mystery, Biography and Destiny of Mary Magdalene.*

### Twenty Years Past

When we look back twenty years to the onset of the previous conjunction, we can only feel astonished at how the world has changed. This was before events of 9/11 and the subsequent "War on Terror"—events that have completely, and forever, changed our world, including the very meaning of democracy. The speed of decline in the fabric of our global culture is stunning, and even frightening. Can we endure another twenty years of decline? Probably not; is it not time to open our eyes and see through the perspective of spirit?

Seeing through the eyes of Mammon has not served the wellbeing of either the Earth or humanity. The third-eye (also referred to as the *Jupiter* chakra) is the eye of spirit, through which the spirit "I" awakes. The crown chakra (also referred to as the *Saturn* chakra) is the means through which higher worlds anoint us if we have been so prepared. We will need the blessings of both Jupiter and Saturn if we are to meet what is coming toward us. The Great Conjunction carries the promise of hope.

### Crossing the Threshold

We have clearly begun the process of collectively crossing the threshold between worlds. In so doing, we will inevitably be faced with the darkness within our own souls. This can happen either gradually or suddenly. And it marks our encounter with what is called our "double." At the threshold stands Michael (the Lesser Guardian of the Threshold), who reveals to us our personal contribution to the darkness of the world (i.e., our double). This Michaelic Guardian, in turn, has his own evil caricature, which is a Minotaur-like being. For, not only does each of us have our personal double; there also exists the *collective* double of humanity.

The Antichrist sheathes himself in the prevailing darkness of humanity's collective double, and he has been loosed. "Minotaur" is another imagination for the sometimes overladen concept of "Antichrist." Using yet another metaphor, we could say that this being is our very own Golden Calf. Like Aaron's people at the time when Moses was receiving the Ten Commandments, we, too, have all contributed our gold—our wisdom—to materialism's many idols. Now this Calf has grown into a demonic Minotaur, by means of which he has autonomously arisen. He bears a frightful authority *that can paralyze free will*. We have long been wandering in his labyrinth, disempowered by having fallen prey to his ubiquitous allurements. Although we are afraid of the labyrinth's mindless insanity, we are even more afraid of facing the true Guardian—a being who asks us to redeem our error. The Minotaur, on the other hand, asks for nothing; he simply feeds upon us.[37]

If we choose to be lost eternally in the shadow world that riddles the maze, we will eventually fall into its yawning abyss. So many of us have already fallen! What else explains the plethora of psychotic epidemics and senseless violence? The veins running through the labyrinth bear the bloodless chill of the collective double's circulation. Round and round we go, seemingly seeking escape—when, in truth, we would rather wander here than suffer our darkness into light. We are, however, allowed only so many seasons of time before the Sun Demon lays hold of us, grinding our "I" to bits with the pointed steel of his sharp teeth.

The labyrinth is haunted. From the distant hours of time, ghostlike figures reach out to us, longing to live again through the life still remaining in us. Although they are naught but chimeras of past ages, they are also like unto the "walking dead," propelled by their masters—who have stolen, and inverted, life forces. In the wake of this loss, our consciousness is dragged under. These specters are, in actuality, *zombies of darkness*. Each of us owns some of them. And in an insidious attempt to render the Minotaur's presence palatable, contemporary literature and Hollywood films are making these beings familiar to us. Such familiarity entrains human souls, often from very

---

37 Watch for the author's forthcoming book, *The Hermit, the Minotaur, and the Beast: Generational Influences over the Next Three Decades.*

young ages, to develop a fondness for Ahriman's bedeviled vampires.

*We are in a process of continually crossing the threshold between worlds.* This is an evolutionary necessity that begs the question: Where is Ariadne's thread?[38] Is there not more to this threshold experience besides the rasping, grasping specters? Indeed, there is. For, that which was Ariadne's thread in the age of Taurus has become something else since the time of Christ. In a sense, we could even say that Ariadne's thread was a *prefiguring* of Christ's descent into Hell.

When Christ descended into Hell, he left behind a Grail thread as he wove his way into the very depths of the inner Earth. This is the thread of Ariadne in our time. This Grail thread shines with an eternal light, indelibly permeating the entirety of the subearthly realms with the memory of his presence. Christ's presence literally permeated *all* material substance, and it eternally holds the resurrecting force that heals every single cell in the being of the collective double of humanity. As the greatest of all labyrinthine Minotaurs, the Antichrist lures souls away from this eternal imprint. Posing as a sheep, this wolf savagely devours— while endlessly promising riches and reward. Thus can he work unseen within the cloak of our collective double, in which we find a reflection of what also lives in us. Facing this reality can cripple what would otherwise be our intuition.

As Jupiter and Saturn again come into conversation, we are to pick up this Grail thread and find our way to the labyrinth's center, wherein awaits the true Guardian. Can we face him? Despite standing before all our own darkness, we are to maintain *spiritual presence of mind.* Then we will notice that there is a tiny pinprick of light at the deepest center of this darkness. Through this, on the other side, we see the Greater Guardian—Christ—waiting to receive us into the arms of promise.

### Water into Wine

At the first of the seven archetypal healings by Jesus Christ, the turning of water into wine at the wedding in Cana, the Sun stood at 8° Capricorn.[39] The 2020 Great Conjunction finds Jupiter and Saturn at 5° Capricorn, a mere 3° from where the Sun was at that time. Moreover, at 9° Capricorn, the above-mentioned second Saturn return of the Middle Eastern child falls just past the Sun's memory of this miracle. To enliven the human "I," Christ brought down the wine of divine Love in Cana. The Antichrist, in contrast, sends upward the intoxicating wine of evil possession, through which the "I" is captured and then—eventually—destroyed.

The miracle of turning water into wine can help us meet what may indeed be an urgent, if not dire, situation. In Cana, the old wine had become barren; Christ therefore offers a *new* wine. By analogy, we can see that the historic lineage of our collective history, as well as the egoistic blood that now runs in our veins, must make a drastic turn. We are to raise ourselves above the materialistic labyrinth and become filled with spirit-wine—i.e., with the wine of the Grail that flows from above into the below. As a never-ending source of life from Shambhala, which rests in the heart of Our Mother, the Grail wine also flows magically from worlds below. Yet, if we cannot find our vertical alignment with Christ's spiritual River of Life, we may indeed find ourselves in a situation from which it is too late to turn back. History, we know, is filled with national catastrophes that erupted due to people not believing the early warning signs of doom—until it was too late.

In light of the Virgin principle of Force[40] being the principle of cooperation with the Holy Spirit (Jupiter), we can imagine that the wine at the wedding of Cana was not created anew. *Rather it*

---

38 "Ariadne's thread" is an analogy for the Sophianic wisdom that leads human souls out of the labyrinth.

39 At the birth of the "Middle Eastern child," Mars was exactly conjunct the position of the Sun in Cana, thus representing his *anti*-Michael spirit. Moreover, Saturn stood only 1° away —at 9° Capricorn. *Indeed, a poisonous wine may yet pour from him.*

40 See the Letter Meditation on the 11th Arcanum in Anon., *Meditations of the Tarot.*

*was the resurrection of the water of life into the fire of spirit.* Who guards the water of life? It is Our Mother, who worked through the Holy Virgin Mary when Mary stood at Christ's side as he turned the water into wine. The Holy Spirit (Jupiter) and the Virgin Mary (Saturn) created the vessel into which the new wine streamed into time. This is a profound metaphor for the inherent potential of the 2020 Great Conjunction.

Following upon the miracle of turning water into wine at the wedding at Cana, a new revelation stream opened. St. Paul would be blind for three days after encountering its light outside the gates of Damascus. This is exactly the place to which this year's conjunction calls us; for it is here, before this gateway to the gods (Capricorn), that we will find the unceasing Grail River of Truth.

## Modern Technology vs. Resonance Technology

Freedom bears the privilege of dissent, which is the ability to resist any overreach that a government or individuality might tyrannically impose upon a people. The absence of this freedom is daunting to contemplate:

> In the English-speaking world, it will thus become possible [through new technology] to render nine-tenths of human labor superfluous. But mechanical occultism will not only provide the possibility of dispensing with nine-tenths of the work presently done by human hands; *it will also make it possible to paralyze every uprising of the dissatisfied masses of humanity.*[41]

Again, our attention is drawn to the fact that the launch of 5G technologies are coincident with the second Saturn return of a being we are contemplating. It is, therefore, extraordinarily chilling that the possibility of paralyzing "every uprising" was part of Steiner's prophecy.

The new wine of Cana lies dormant in our blood, nourished by truth, goodness, and beauty. Sustained by virtue, it rises from the heart as it sublimes into a spiritual force that listens to God. This is called *the etherization of the blood.*[42]

How do we begin to protect our children, ourselves, and Natura from the damaging climate these techno-fields continue to create? We must build our inner resonance technology; that is, we must turn our mind's eye to the fiery edge where light abundantly flows into all who seek its mercy. We are to become practitioners who cultivate *living* etheric energy.

Hermeticists are unceasingly faithful to the Hermetic axiom: *As above, so also below.* Thus does the instreaming light find a reciprocal action in worlds below. For the Mother's loving warmth streams ever upward through our feet, toward our heart, awakening a direct knowing that shakes our memory from its sleep. We can experience this ascending Force by actually walking on the Earth in consciousness of the upstreaming warmth flowing from her presence. Our Mother offers gifts profusely, literally placing them at our feet. Lo, how we ignore these! On the first day of the *Chymical Wedding of Christian Rosenkreutz,* an old man spoke to him the following words:

> If the poor human race
> Were not so arrogant,
> It would have been given much good
> From my mother's heritage.
> But because the human race will not take heed,
> It lies in such straits
> And must be held in prison.

Modern technologies constitute a direct assault against the Earth's newly awakened activity. They also attack newly streaming dispensations that are flowing from angelic realms. The beings behind these technologies are grievously dark, and are foreign to the Earth proper. In the northern land of the Eagle, the death cult of materialism has so embedded itself that, for many, even the mention of developing new soul organs is contemptuously dismissed, and the notion of the awakening of Shambhala would be

---

41 Steiner, *The Challenge of the Times,* lect. 3 (italics added—CML).

42 See Steiner, "The Etherization of the Blood" in *Esoteric Christianity and the Mission of Christian Rosenkreutz.*

considered equally absurd. Students of Christian Rosenkreutz know otherwise.

Rosenkreutz directed his pupils to the activity of the inner Earth mysteries. As the reincarnated Lazarus, his grasp of etheric technologies was indisputable; and regardless of whether he is incarnated or not, his etheric body is active. Moreover, we remember that consequent to his being raised from the dead by Christ, he bears the seed of Christ's etheric body (his *Buddhi* sheath—i.e., his purified etheric body). Furthermore, he is very closely aligned with John the Baptist: the first Adam, the baptizer of Christ.

Many have experienced that the resurrection of the Rosicrucian mysteries can be found in Valentin Tomberg's anonymous magnum opus, *Meditations on the Tarot*. The third Arcanum, The Empress, reveals the secrets of sacred magic—i.e., moral etheric technologies.

## Evil's Head Start

Much has already been prepared through *materialistic* technology. As we plummet into the seductive world of 5G wireless systems, however, the stakes are severely raised. It is likely that the intensity of this new level of destructive assault will critically inhibit the further development of humanity's spiritual antennae. A time will come when the question posed may be: Can we practice resonance and moral technological magic under the deadening conditions 5G will set upon us? *Moral* technology, on the other hand, streams from Christ, who is now within the Earth's etheric aura. We must continue to believe that his protection, as Lord of the Elements, does not wane.

Rudolf Steiner made it perfectly clear that the incarnation of Ahriman would be unavoidable, for it is a necessity of evolution. What he left open-ended is the *greater* danger, which is that this being's incarnation could pass by unnoticed. *Is this already happening?* Such obliviousness would signify that there are not even "ten righteous humans" in the entire world. By analogy, ten refers to the fact that there were not enough who saw—who *witnessed*—what was happening. There was thus no opposition, no awakening, and no change.

*The possibility exists, therefore, that Ahriman's incarnation could indeed go unnoticed.* This fact reveals what may be the very subtle (although devastating) nature of the event, as well as its incredibly sinister potential.

## Spiders and the World Wide Web

Rudolf Steiner could gaze into the future and bear witness to the technological web that he foresaw would rise against the new Christ mystery:

> And from the Earth there will spring forth a terrible brood of beings, a brood of automata of an order of existence lying between the mineral and the plant kingdoms, and possessed of an overwhelming power of intellect.
>
> This swarm will seize upon the Earth. It will spread over the Earth like a network of ghastly, spider-like creatures—of an order lower than that of plant existence, but possessed of overpowering wisdom. These spidery creatures will all be interlocked with one another. *And in their outward movements they will imitate the thoughts that people have spun from the shadowy intellect that has not allowed itself to be quickened by the new form of imaginative knowledge—by spiritual science.* All the thoughts that lack substance and reality will then be endowed with being.
>
> The Earth will be surrounded—as it is now with air and as it sometimes is with swarms of locusts—with a brood of terrible spider-like creatures that are half-mineral and half-plant. They will be interweaving with masterly intelligence, it is true, but *with intensely evil intent.* And insofar as people have not allowed their shadowy intellectual concepts to be quickened to life, their existence will be united not with the beings who have been trying to descend since the last third of the nineteenth century, but with this ghastly brood of half mineral, half plantlike creatures. They will have to live together with these spider-like creatures and continue their cosmic existence within the order of evolution into which this brood will then enter.[43]

---

43 Steiner, "A Picture of Earth-Evolution in the Future" (May 13, 1921), *The Golden Blade*, 1960 (italics added—CML). Also in Steiner, *Materialism and the Task of Anthroposophy*, pp. 263ff.

These are frightful imaginations. Doesn't the World Wide Web and social media exemplify this? Look at how these have progressed, even just recently—as our lives are constantly tracked, monitored, and measured! The ubiquity and intrusive nature of current technologies, as well as developments from Facebook to "wire the world," will be drastically accelerated with 5G technologies.[44] This imminent reality should "shake us to the very depths of our souls, like the explosion of a bomb." *In the near future, the attention of every child from kindergarten age onward will become ever more absorbed by the spider's web.*

What is headed toward us will eventually reach a "tipping point," after which we will no longer have choice. For, due to the inability of many of us to be "apocalyptists" of our time (i.e., failing to name evil as it is occurring), every advancing encroachment draws us closer to spiritual asphyxiation. Such technologies seek to achieve *a total eclipse of spirit.* This is the signature of the "air trial," which brings the War of All against All. Steiner mentioned that this could indeed arrive 5,000 years before its intended time.

The vantage of hindsight will be of no use. We are so very near this dangerous edge! And although it is inevitable that this kind of materialistic–ahrimanic technology will be with us into the far-distant future, the necessity for us to develop resonance and moral technologies has taken on renewed urgency.[45]

We do well to imagine the great transformation that could occur if humanity awakens to the spiritual ideals this year's Great Conjunction promises.

### Sophia's Force

Sophia's "Force" is an analogy for the moral ether that streams transfiguring energies into human souls:

> There is not a shadow of doubt for anyone who takes the spiritual life of humankind seriously, even if they are short of authentic spiritual experience, that the Blessed Virgin [Saturn] is not an ideal only, nor a mental image only, nor an archetype of the unconscious (of depth-psychology), nor, lastly, an occultistic *egregore* (a collective astral creation of believers), but rather a concrete and living individuality—like you or I—who loves, suffers, and rejoices.[46]

The Holy Virgin represents a Saturnine "Force"; and when we accept her blessed mantle, we may gradually find ourselves engaging in an alchemical wedding, like that of Christian Rosenkreutz. Such a wedding is Hermetic; it is the marriage between the lower and higher "I." It is like unto a coronation of our soul as we receive the *manas* light—*initiation*:

> And it is authentic victory that one must hope for and wait for in the conflict that tradition represents as the struggle between the Archistrategist Michael and the dragon. The day when it is achieved will be the day of a new festival—the festival of the coronation of the Virgin *on Earth.* For then the principle of opposition will be replaced on Earth by that of collaboration. This will be the triumph of life over electricity. And cerebral intellectuality will then bow before Wisdom (Sophia) and will unite with her.[47]

The principle of electricity is the opposite of the principle of collaboration, for the latter serves to increase inner resonance and the presence of the moral ether. It is an actual Force "to overcome every subtle thing." Modern technology operates on the principle of electricity and magnetism—i.e., through dead light and dead sound. The moral ether, on the other hand, develops as we increase our inner resonance technology through meditation, eurythmy, and spiritual–religious efforts of all kinds.[48] Indeed, resonance with higher worlds creates an effective power for overcoming death technology: "The 'subtle things' to overcome are

---

44 See the article by Lev Grossman, "Inside Facebook's Plan to Wire the World" (http://time.com/facebook-world-plan).

45 Emberson, *From Gondishapur to Silicon Valley.*

46 Anon., *Meditations on the Tarot,* p. 280.

47 Ibid., pp. 282–283.

48 "Religion" here does not refer to denomination. Rather does it signify the soul's understanding of our primal relationship to spirit—as well as to the many petals of the World's Rose that celebrate this primacy in many different forms.

the intellectual forces of temptation based on *doubt,* the psychic forces of temptation based on *sterile enjoyment,* and the electrical forces of temptation based on *power.*"[49] Doubt, sterile enjoyment, and power constitute the "technology" of temptation. Inverse to these elements are *faith, devotion,* and *powerlessness.* Powerlessness, in this sense, is the surrender to that which is higher—which measures the supreme accomplishment of true Power.

As we develop inner radiance—and as the moral ether streams into us—we find the benediction of spirit. This ether originates from Virgin Nature as an elixir from the Grail. Long has this been imprisoned in both the heights and the depths.

### The Moral Ether

Resonance technology prepares us to receive the moral ether that can actually move, through us, into the world. Whereas resonance technology protects us from destructive modern technologies entering our field, the moral ether can transfigure the world through its *emollient action*—which moves effortlessly through physical, psychic, and mental barriers.

As our resonance field increases, our hearts begin to open to our perfect self, which is like unto a star dwelling above our heads. And as we grow into consciousness of this self, we diminish the effects issuing from all negative barriers. Moreover, when communities work together in creating such fields, they are engaged in what can be called the "fish communion."[50] *This communion weaves the binding power of love among community members, shielding them from the* egregores *that would otherwise cause harm.*[51]

The minions of the Antichrist use arbitrary and dark magic to lure humankind into a false kingdom. As a result, we are now living in the winter of the Piscean age—and in the brief second (from an evolutionary perspective) that human beings have occupied Earth, we have nearly destroyed her. Moral technology, on the other hand, lures no one. Rather, those who wield the sacred magic of this Force move freely between higher and lower worlds, uniting their consciousness with the phenomena of the archetypal world. This enables them to bring urgently needed healing to Earth existence.

The Virgin Sophia, architect of all creation, tells us that our current perilous situation does not need to continue endlessly. For, communion with her is a harbinger of the Aquarian age soon to come—as is also true of the *fish communion* that ignites sisterhood and brotherhood. From the ashes of the old, the new will arise.

> [Virgin-Sophia represents and is] the principle of springtime, i.e., that of creative spiritual élan and spiritual flourishing. The prodigious flourishing of philosophy and the arts in ancient Athens took place under the sign of the Virgin. Similarly, the flourishing of the Renaissance at Florence was under the vernal sign of the Virgin. Also, Weimar at the beginning of the nineteenth century was a place where the breath of the Virgin perceptibly moved hearts and minds.... The sickness of the West today is that it is more and more lacking creative élan.[52]

Ever more physicists are turning to the *qualitative* world of essence. We must pray that science will again place its theorems upon the altar of Infinity, so that we may free ourselves from the *quantitative* yoke of ahrimanic abstraction. Then will the human race remember that not only are we truly "born from the Divine"; we will also eventually slay the black rider of the Apocalypse. This is the rider who marches through the world while holding the scales that measure everything— even the worth of a human soul!

In our current Age of Michael, many are called to pick up the sword of truth, which is not unlike the flaming sword of the Cherubim who guard the Tree of Life in Paradise. Without this commitment to Michael, evil's power binds us. It creates obstacles to our free movement: physically, psychically,

---

49 Anon., *Meditations on the Tarot,* p. 283.

50 Christ offered his disciples the fish communion after his resurrection.

51 *Egregore* is a term denoting a certain class of human-generated demons that attack communities of people who are devoted to spiritual endeavors. For more on this topic, see Daniel Andreev, *The Rose of the World.*

52 Anon., *Meditations on the Tarot,* p. 291.

and spiritually. We can, of course, still move horizontally in the sense-world; but vertical movement, *hermetic* movement, is arrested. Whereas true Power is selfless, and is thus willing to crucify itself for the good of the whole, mere worldly power is selfish—in that it will crucify others for the sake of its nefarious agendas.

The approaching age of Aquarius (ruled by Saturn) bestows the overlighting virtue of a tempering silence through which, on the wings of creative élan, we are urged to "leap" into the void of the unknown. By cultivating this virtue, even now, we will begin to experience the hand of peace that reaches into our time from the angelic urns of the Angel–human (Aquarius). Blessings of incomparable measure await us.

### The Invisible Mark of the Beast

The true power of community, into which Sophia's Force weaves all together, is countered by splintering forces of divisiveness. Such tactics are the invisible mark of the beast. The Michaelic battle now in process must not be waged *between* people. It is to be waged first in our own soul; and only then is it to be waged against the objective evil in the world. *Willingness to engage*, within and without, marks the fertile ground upon which stand the true disciples of Christ—who unyieldingly unmask the beings of darkness without disturbing the constructive field of vital forces:

> Criticism and polemicism are mortal enemies of the spiritual life. [Indeed, they are a mark of the Beast,] for they signify the substitution of destructive electrical energy for constructive vital force. A complete change of the inspiring and motivating source takes place when a person or spiritual movement becomes engaged in the way of rivalry—with the criticism and polemicism that it comprises. Once carried away by electricity, "bearing witness against thy neighbor" will always be essentially and intrinsically false.[53]

Although such mortal enemies of the spiritual life surround us, we must not be counted among them.

---

53 Ibid., p. 300.

### The Star: The 17th Arcanum

Humility is the prerequisite for discipleship. Knowledge of Heaven's vertical causality—spoken through the movements of the stars—sheds wisdom upon all souls who look upward. This primacy of being is, in essence, the very meaning of Star Wisdom; and it is this that ensures our virtue as readers of the starry script. The entirety of the heavens is, in truth, the mantle of Sophia's wisdom. In learning how to speak to the stars, we are reminded that there is something far greater than our "little selves," and this is what we are to serve. Furthermore, as we kneel in our own Gethsemanes, and even prostrate ourselves before the mercy of Christ, star beings help us to weed the gardens of our souls.

Capricorn, representative of the Star Arcanum, commissions us to bless the Earth with the grandeur of new imaginations. We are wise to not underestimate the courage necessary if we are to represent the hitherto unknown. If we retreat from such a task, we may find cowardice engulfing us in doubt and despair. *It is better to act prudently than it is to await endlessly for confirmation, for action itself reveals to us the next step forward.*

We began this year with the conjunction of Pluto and Saturn in Sagittarius. As we turn toward the year's end, and to the conjunction of Jupiter and Saturn, we bring with us the Archer's razor-thin focus on Truth. Saturn has now entered Capricorn—and with the gifts bestowed from the beings of Sagittarius, we turn to Capricorn's holy Waters of life. Are our quivers filled with Truth's arrows, in readiness to climb the high mountain into realms where the thinking of the gods holds sway? We will be tested!

Capricorn represents continuity of growth—i.e., the sap of life that is ever flowing. And from where do these nourishing waters originate? From the high mountain springs. There are two sources of water: the holy Waters above, and the muddy waters of the serpent below.

> Just as there is Fire and fire, i.e., the celestial Fire of divine love and the fire of electricity due to friction, so there is also Water and water, i.e., the celestial Water of the sap of growth,

progress, and evolution and the lower water of instinctivity—the "collective unconscious," engulfing collectivity—which is the water of floods and drowning.[54]

As the influences of this Great Conjunction dawn, we seek the breath of the Holy Spirit (Jupiter) and the protecting mantle of the Holy Virgin (Saturn). All depends on the kind of growth we desire, for the process of continuity demands that we choose between the two waters. Both of these waters flow in our veins: one stream we must draw upward and cleanse; the other is already godly. Here the principle of dualism lives inside us.

When we climb, however, to the summit of the mountain (Capricorn), we see far—we rise above what dualism would otherwise obscure. In a sense, we could say that our star draws nearer to us, gaining radiance as it shines perpetually above our head. From this vantage, we gain the ability to "nail opposites together." The artistry of this capacity necessitates the union of light and will— i.e., not only must we see far; we must also act! *We must suffer duality until a third light breaks through, illumining the rainbow of reconciliation that streams from the holy Waters of spirit.* Was this not Steiner's hope in his admonition for collaboration between Aristotelians and Platonists?

And is not the rainbow the sign given to Noah? Indeed, it was! We are to build a new Ark and billow our sails upon the winds of pneumatism.[55] All those called to board this spirit-vessel have made a covenant with their heart, through which they may enter into the greatest mysteries of our time. There are 22 portholes in this Ark, each one an icon leading into the sacred magic of Christian Hermeticism. We find these 22 icons as the spiritual exercises offered in the book *Meditations on the Tarot.* Through cultivating them, we may commune with the moral ether as we enter the School of the Archangel Jesus (i.e., the "Christ School").

In preparation for the opening of this School, Choreocosmos has been developing for approximately 22 years. Looking in from without, one sees not what this form of eurythmy bestows. For if one is to be graced with passage into the 22 secrets it holds, one must *enter into it*—and this happens only gradually. Through this new community dance form, the sacred magic of Christian Hermetic teachings can open us to the holy Waters of the Grail.

### Holy Waters

Holy Waters unite what formerly appeared dualistically, revealing possibilities hitherto unimaginable. If we cannot sustain the intensity of suffering duality, however, we may find the unholy mud of the serpent rising, demanding that we take one side or the other. Thus will we remain on the terrestrial tarmac—when instead we could have taken flight! Are we willing to rise above the divisiveness and noise caused by one duality fighting against another? Senselessness has become the norm, for the mud seems so much more satisfying and requires so little effort.

True suffering—when unavoidable—is to be embraced, for it serves to open the heart and strengthen the will. As the Sinless One, Jesus Christ had no personal cause to suffer. It is unimaginable, however, to grasp the significance of how he freely bore the suffering of all humanity, throughout all time. To gain such understanding, we must advance in the process of evolution; then will we come to understand how suffering, in its higher aspect, is often actually *the inner experience of healing our brokenness.*

If we know that there is a choice, we may feel inspired to await the emergence of the full rainbow as it begins to arc across the wide expanse of the heavens. This requires that we also muster a sense of hope. The light of hope, in turn, gives us the power to dare. As a transfiguring light-force, it thus moves and directs spiritual evolution in the world:

> Hope is for spiritual evolution what the instinct of reproduction is for biological evolution. It is the force and the light of the *final cause* of the world or, if you wish, the force and the

---

54 Ibid., p. 469.

55 Pneumatism, the worldview of Aquarius (which is ruled by Saturn), is the sole belief that beings with ideas need to embody an active spirit that is able to do things.

light of the ideal of the world—the magical radiation of the "Omega point," according to Teilhard de Chardin. This "Omega point" toward which spiritual evolution is tending—or that of the "noosphere," which surges triumphantly above the "barysphere" and "biosphere"—is the central point of the hope of the "personalizing world." It is the point of complete unity of the outer and inner, of matter and spirit, i.e., the God–Man, *the resurrected Jesus Christ,* just as the "Alpha point," the prime mover or the effective cause, is the Word which sets in motion electrons, atoms, molecules—i.e., movement *directed* toward their association into planets, organisms, families, races, and kingdoms.[56]

*We are all striving to arrive where our true self already awaits us.* As is the hope of all mothers, we must believe that the future will be more glorious than the present. It is also the hope of Our Mother, who dwells in the heart of the Earth, praying that her children will turn to the School of Christ—which leads us into the revelatory School of Sophia, who is the Divine Daughter in the heights.[57] For when the Mother responds to our efforts in Christian Hermetic magic, we enter into a third level of depth: the Shambhala path begins to open.[58] This path can be seen as an aspect of the School of Sophia, *the Shambhala School,* which also has 22 icons that find their inspirations in the 22 chapters of the book of Revelation.

From a certain vantage, the choice is simple: Do we or do we not want to evolve? If we answer affirmatively, we choose the holy Waters over the mud of the serpent. Having made this choice, we will find ourselves becoming enveloped in an atmosphere of grace.

### The Eclipse Force

The stunted, materialistic attitude of soul stands inherently against the temerity required to think with the gods. In light of the eternal aims of gods, the alternative to obedience is to unite with matter as it continues to decay. In so doing, however, the soul's feeling becomes paralyzed. This is the grievous mistake of all who descend into the physical realm to such an extent that they unite with the instinctive forces of the physical body—i.e., *they sensualize the spirit.* In Revelation, such persons are called "Nicolaitans."

The grounds of eternity will not be found if we succumb to the eclipse force, which opposes Capricorn from the lower echelons of the constellation of Cancer. This is a force the adversaries will use against us as a countermeasure to progress. Where this occurs, we are deadened, hardened, and yet know this not. We are then caught in regressive movement, like the crab (Cancer), fleeing from one abstraction to another; and we suffer no guilt as we idly stand by while creation is mechanized and the Mother is brutalized. We then treat creation's most magnificent work of art as if it were one vast system operating under purely physical laws.

> What is most characteristic of this state [regression into facts drawn only from the sense world] is that *intelligence no longer moves forward but backward.* It looks to the least developed and the most primitive for the cause and explanation of what is most developed and most advanced in the process of evolution. Thus, it looks for the effective cause of the world not in the heights of creative consciousness but rather in the depths of the unconscious—instead of going forward and elevating itself toward God, it retreats into matter.[59]

Materialism is literally the *eclipse force,* under which we collectively live. It reduces us to an intellectuality that mechanizes and abstracts what would otherwise be perceived as the ineffable grandeur of Nature as well as the spiritual potential within every human being. At the beginning of the letter to the church of Sardis (Rev. 3:1–6), we hear of the One who has the seven spirits and the seven stars. This is the message related to our current cultural epoch. We are to follow him.

---

56 Ibid., p. 472.

57 See Powell, *The Most Holy Trinosophia and the New Revelations of the Divine Feminine.*

58 Robert Powell, in conjunction with several friends, is currently developing this path at his new home in Ecuador.

59 Ibid., p. 523.

When we remember the seven spirits, we awaken to our inner spiritual potential; and when we remember the seven stars, we awaken to the sacred biography of the Earth. *Evolution will slough off those who are deaf to creation's sublime anthem.* Such people are terrified of surrendering their lower ego-being in order to tread the path of the morning star, the path leading to the New Jerusalem—for without their egoism, they would be naked.

At this time in history, those who continue to choose the principle of the eclipse will find themselves bound to live the destiny of Narcissus, forever gazing at their own reflection (e.g., our "selfie" culture) while the process of evolution proceeds without them. In death they will be blind and deaf, for they must then live in a prison of their own making, suffering in loneliness—despite the fact that they are surrounded by a multitude of the faithful. *If we disallow our conversion, we will dig a hole in which we then must live.* "[This is] because the Moon is the principle of *reflection*: just as it reflects the light of the Sun, so does human intelligence reflect the creative light of conscience—and the latter is eclipsed when 'materialistic intellectuality' prevails."[60]

### The Tyranny of Egoism

Hermeticists see profundity in the most ordinary of known things. This is one of the secrets that reveals how they overcome intellectual rigidity; for, as they live from wonder to wonder, the surface state of intelligence gives way to the soaring wings of moral conscience.

In times past we felt the movements of the stars within us. As we fell further into material realms, however, we lost this intimacy.

Let us imagine the current Jupiter–Saturn conjunction as a resonant field created by two planetary spheres coming into a unique relationship. Referred to as "coherence," this signifies the unification of planetary waves, whereby a consistent field is formed that sustains and strengthens the duration of their effects. *Through this unified field, intangible patterns interpenetrate terrestrial worlds while communicating the noble aims of the gods.* Such communication is heard in the heart of the Hermeticist. The miracle of the communion of planetary influences does not escape them.

In the case of coherence between Jupiter and Saturn, we experience this influence in our third-eye (Jupiter) and crown (Saturn) chakras. Wisdom thereby unites with strength. As participants in cosmic realities, our third-eye is quickened, calling forth a reciprocal opening in our crown chakra—a spiritual organ that is opened only through heavenly deeds enacted *upon* us, rather than by direct efforts of our own human will.

Now, let us imagine the *closed* third eye. In this case, instead of being imbued with the instreaming imaginations of wisdom, we are filled with the tyranny of egoism. And in a soul arrested in egoism, what is missing is obedience to anything spiritual. Not only will we *not* find the benediction of Grace; we most likely will also experience its opposite: *an ascending "anti-benediction" of cunning illusions, bestowing an arrogant worldly power that actually imprisons the soul.* The confining bars of this jail are forged from doubt, derision, and fear. Despite the fact that this imprisonment is naught but a temporary interlude in the great breath of Time, its effects are long lasting. They continue even after our death. Thus does this self-glorified state deliver souls into what is sometimes called "an eternal Hell"—i.e., a soul that is imprisoned in itself.

### Our Current Challenge

Many are tired of hearing of evil and about an Antichrist or Sun Demon. The term *Antichrist*, in particular, has become cliché. Empty phrases are a signature of our current "Word-poverty." We have previously re-imagined the Antichrist as a Minotaur, which perhaps re-enlivens our conceptual sense of him. We can also re-imagine the Sun Demon, and thereby re-enliven *his* attributes.

We could simply call the Sun Demon "the Spider," for he certainly has a web. The Minotaur's approach is to seek world dominion through full-spectrum dominance—i.e., through the possession and manipulation of financial institutions, the military,

---

60 Ibid., p. 494.

and governments. By means of economic–military tyranny, he may then take over the world. The Spider's influence is much more subtle, for *his* aim is to take over the human "I" and destroy it. Thereby he, himself, becomes a god. The Spider can also be likened to a kind of *cosmic* spider, whose web weaves ever more tightly as we go about our daily business. This arachnoid-like being is described in Rudolf Steiner's lectures to the priests: "The satanic forces are lying in wait, with the intention of changing the whole planetary system. If they were to succeed, the planetary system in whose orbits human beings are supposed to live would be taken away from those divine-spiritual powers, and sent off into quite other cosmic-evolutionary directions."[61]

At first, he captures human beings—like the spider captures flies. Ultimately, though, *he is determined to capture and disrupt the orbits of the planets.* As a consequence, Earth would inevitably separate from cosmic rhythms. The effects of this would be truly unimaginable.

When we look around, we see that darkness has insinuated itself everywhere. Whose work is this? A revolution in slow motion seems to be building. Will we learn from the lessons of history? Even if the incarnation may not yet be upon us, the ground is certainly being prepared. We can meet this challenge for ourselves, or for our children's future, but it *must* be met. We are gravely behind in comprehending the totality of evil's encroachment.

The possibility that the Antichrist may appear has been considered. Furthermore, he may now be fifty-eight years old, and—as 5G rises—may be reaching his second Saturn return. Because the current conjunction between Jupiter and Saturn is occurring so very near the amazing planetary alignment of his possible horoscope, it may indeed quicken what already lives within him. Moreover, as the Capricorn Moon of the Transfiguration stood where this Jupiter–Saturn conjunction occurs, we can imagine an *inversion* of the positive karma of this event.

The Great Conjunction resounds with the promise that we can take back what we have given over to Ahriman since the last Great Conjunction. We need not lose hope. Instead, we can birth *new* hope by living with the knowledge that *Christ lives in us.* As we then empower our "I" to face darkness, to name evil—and especially to open the gateway of the gods so that the elixir of life may pour upon us—we take back any authority we've sacrificed to the beast.

If the "eighth king" of Revelation emerges, we can unmask him.[62] *We can stop pretending that the time of a great crisis still lives somewhere in the future.* Living in apocalyptic times is *not* the problem; rather is it evolution's promise. The problem would arise, however, if we fail to notice that this is where we are.

Many have prophesied the emergence of exactly that which is now destroying our Earth as well as human souls…and spirits. With Christ, every labyrinth has both an entrance and an exit. There is no turning back; and we would not even *want* to—for our future lies in front of us, as does the Guardian. We have the courage to face our redemption. We must simply dare to find it!

### The Crossroads

Humanity stands at the crossroads between what was and what can be. Let us be vigilant as we enter the year 2020—for we stand at a momentously transformational turning point. Now, or at least eventually, we must overcome our fear of "stinging" into evil.[63] And without Michaelic initiative, we will remain under the influences of the Spider and the Minotaur.

As 2020 is cradled by two significant conjunctions involving Saturn, Jupiter, and Pluto, the stars are indeed speaking to us. Jupiter (the Holy Spirit) rules Pisces; Saturn (the Virgin Mary) rules Aquarius. Thus may the Great Conjunction reveal a bridge between our current age and the age to come—which is exemplified by the glyph of Pisces. We stand on this bridge. Light must be brought in;

---

61 Steiner, *The Book of Revelation and the Work of the Priest*, p. 159.

62 See "A Remarkable Alignment" in this essay.

63 See the discussion on this in the section titled "Fear's Role in the Culmination."

for if it is not, the darkness will find no opposition. Steiner gave us the foundation of the Michael School.[64] There are two other schools: the Christ School (the School of the Archangel Jesus) and the Sophia School (the Shambhala School).

As Saturn is involved in both of this year's major star events, *spirit recollection is critical.*

If we indeed live in a Grail era, we must find our way to Damascus and kneel before its gates. We must roll away the stone entombing the Christ— so that our spiritual eyes may open to his greatest enemies.

With the Sun conjunct Pluto in Sagittarius, Christ bestowed power on his disciples to go forth and cast out unclean spirits (Matt. 10:1–4). As the year begins we, too, shall be called upon to cast out unclean spirits. And as the year ends, we are called to *remember* that we are each a star, fallen from the First Star, and that we long to find our way home.

---

64 It was previously stated that the Christ School is related to the 22 Arcanum of *Meditations on the Tarot*, and that the Sophia School is related to the 22 chapters in the book of Revelation. From a certain perspective we might ask: Where are the missing three lessons in the Michael School?

<hr>

## EVENING MEDITATION

In the evening meditate on the Earth as a great radiant green star shining out into the cosmos, and allow the heart to speak:

*May this prayer from my warm heart unite*

*With the Earth's Light which reveres the Christ-Sun,*

*That I may find Spirit in the Light of the Spirit,*

*Breath of the Soul in the World's Breath,*

*Human Strength in the Life of the Earth.*

Given by Rudolf Steiner, March 9, 1924, to Maud B. Monges of Spring Valley, New York (translated by R Powell)

# WORKING WITH THE
## *STAR WISDOM CALENDAR*

### *Robert Powell, PhD*

In taking note of the astronomical events listed in the Star Calendar, it is important to distinguish between long- and short-term astronomical events. Long-term astronomical events—for example, Pluto transiting a particular degree of the zodiac—will have a longer period of meditation than would the five days advocated for short-term astronomical events such as the New and Full Moon. The following describes, in relation to meditating on the Full Moon, a meditative process extending over a five-day period.

### *Sanctification of the Full Moon*

As a preliminary remark, let us remind ourselves that the great sacrifice of Christ on the Cross—the Mystery of Golgotha—took place at Full Moon. As Christ's sacrifice took place when the Moon was full in the middle of the sidereal sign of Libra, the Libra Full Moon assumes special significance in the sequence of twelve (or thirteen) Full Moons taking place during the cycle of the year. In following this sequence, the Mystery of Golgotha serves as an archetype for *every* Full Moon, since each Full Moon imparts a particular spiritual blessing. Hence the practice described here of *Sanctification of the Full Moon* applies to every Full Moon. Similarly, there is also the practice of *Sanctification of the New Moon*, as described in *Hermetic Astrology, Volume 2: Astrological Biography*, chapter 10.

During the two days prior to the Full Moon, we can consider the focus of one's meditation to extend over these two days as *preparatory days* immediately preceding the day of the Full Moon. These two days can be dedicated to spiritual reflection and detachment from everyday concerns, as one prepares to become a vessel for the in-streaming light and love one will receive at the Full Moon, something that one can then impart further—for example, to help people in need, or to support Mother Earth in times of catastrophe. During these two days, it is helpful to hold an attitude of dedication and service and try to assume an attitude of receptivity that opens to what one's soul will receive and subsequently impart—an attitude conducive to making one a true *servant of the spirit*.

The day of the Full Moon is itself a day of *holding the sacred space*. In doing so, one endeavors to cultivate inner peace and silence, during which one attempts to contact and consciously hold the in-streaming blessing of the Full Moon for the rest of humanity. One can heighten this silent meditation by visualizing the zodiacal constellation–sidereal sign in which the Moon becomes full, since the Moon serves to reflect the starry background against which it appears.

If the Moon is full in Virgo, for example, it reminds us of the night of the birth of the Jesus child visited by the three magi, as described in the Gospel of St. Matthew. That birth occurred at the Full Moon in the middle of the sidereal sign of Virgo, and the three magi, who gazed up that evening to behold the Full Moon against the background of the stars of the Virgin, witnessed the soul of Jesus emerge from the disk of the Full Moon and descend toward Earth. They participated from afar, via the starry heavens, in the Grail Mystery of the holy birth.

In meditating upon the Full Moon and opening oneself to receive the in-streaming blessing from the starry heavens, we can exercise restraint by avoiding the formulation of what will happen or what one might receive from the Full Moon. Moreover, we can also refrain from seeking tangible results or effects connected with our attunement to the Full Moon. Even if we observe only the date but not the exact moment when the Moon is full, it is helpful to find quiet time to reflect alone or to use the opportunity for deep meditation on the day of the Full Moon.

We can think of the two days following the Full Moon as a *time of imparting* what we have received from the in-streaming of the full disk of the Moon against the background of the stars. It is now possible to turn our attention toward humanity and the world and endeavor to pass on any spiritual blessing we have received from the starry heavens. Thereby we can assist in the work of the spiritual world by transforming what we have received into goodwill and allowing it to flow wherever the greatest need exists.

It is a matter of *holding a sacred space* throughout the day of the Full Moon. This is an important time to still the mind and maintain inner peace. It is a time of spiritual retreat and contact with the spiritual world, of holding in one's consciousness the archetype of the Mystery of Golgotha as a great outpouring of Divine Love that bridges Heaven and Earth. Prior to the day of the Full Moon, the two preceding days prepare the sacred space as a vessel to receive the heavenly blessing. The two days following the day of the Full Moon are a time to assimilate and distribute the spiritual transmission received into the sacred space we have prepared.

One can apply the process described here as a meditative practice in relation to the Full Moon to any of the astronomical events listed in *Star Wisdom*, especially as most of these *remember* significant Christ Events. Take note, however, whether an event is long-term or short-term and adjust the period of meditative practice accordingly.

*To starry realms,*
*To the dwelling places of Gods,*
*Turns the Spirit gaze of my soul.*

*From starry realms,*
*From the dwelling places of Gods,*
*Streams Spirit power into my soul.*

*For starry realms,*
*For the dwelling places of Gods,*
*Lives my Spirit heart through my soul.*

—RUDOLF STEINER

# SYMBOLS USED IN CHARTS

| PLANETS | | ZODIACAL SIGNS | | ASPECTS | |
|---|---|---|---|---|---|
| ⊕ | Earth | ♈ | Aries (Ram) | ☌ | Conjunction 0° |
| ☉ | Sun | ♉ | Taurus (Bull) | ✳ | Sextile 60° |
| ☽ | Moon | ♊ | Gemini (Twins) | ☐ | Square 90° |
| ☿ | Mercury | ♋ | Cancer (Crab) | △ | Trine 120° |
| ♀ | Venus | ♌ | Leo (Lion) | ☍ | Opposition 180° |
| ♂ | Mars | ♍ | Virgo (Virgin) | | |
| ♃ | Jupiter | ♎ | Libra (Scales) | | |
| ♄ | Saturn | ♏ | Scorpio (Scorpion) | | |
| ♅ | Uranus | ♐ | Sagittarius (Archer) | | |
| ♆ | Neptune | ♑ | Capricorn (Goat) | | |
| ♇ | Pluto | ♒ | Aquarius (Water Carrier) | | |
| | | ♓ | Pisces (Fishes) | | |

| OTHER | | | |
|---|---|---|---|
| ☊ | Ascending (North) Node | | Sun Eclipse |
| ☋ | Descending (South) Node | | Moon Eclipse |
| P | Perihelion–Perigee | | Inferior Conjunction |
| A | Aphelion–Apogee | | Superior Conjunction |
| | Maximum Latitude | ⚷ | Chiron |
| | Minimum Latitude | | |

# TIME

The information relating to daily geocentric and heliocentric planetary positions in the sidereal zodiac is tabulated in the form of an ephemeris for each month, in which the planetary positions are given at 0 hours Universal Time (UT) each day.

Beneath the geocentric and heliocentric ephemeris for each month, the information relating to planetary aspects is given in the form of an aspectarian, which lists the most important aspects—geocentric and heliocentric–hermetic—between the planets for the month in question. The day and the time of occurrence of the aspect on that day are indicated, all times being given in Universal Time (UT), which is identical to Greenwich Mean Time (GMT). For example, zero hours Universal Time is midnight GMT. This time system applies in Britain; however, when summer time is in effect, one hour must be added to all times.

**In other time zones, the time has to be adjusted according to whether it is ahead of or behind Britain. For example, in Germany, where the time is one hour ahead of British time, an hour must be added; when summer time is in effect in Germany, two hours have to be added to all times.

Using the calendar in the United States, do the following subtraction from all time indications according to time zone:

- Pacific Time subtract 8 hours
  (7 hours for daylight saving time);
- Mountain Time subtract 7 hours
  (6 hours for daylight saving time);
- Central Time subtract 6 hours
  (5 hours for daylight saving time);
- Eastern Time subtract 5 hours
  (4 hours for daylight saving time).

This subtraction will often change the date of an astronomical occurrence, shifting it back one day. Consequently, since most of the readers of this calendar live on the American Continent, astronomical occurrences during the early hours of day *x* are sometimes listed in the Commentaries as occurring on days *x–1/x*. For example, an eclipse occurring at 03:00 UT on the 12th is listed as occurring on the 11–12th since in America it takes place on the 11th.[1]

## SIMPLIFYING THE PROCEDURE

The preceding procedure can be greatly simplified. Here is an example for someone wishing to know the zodiacal locations of the planets on Christmas Day, December 25, 2018. Looking at the December ephemeris, it can be seen that Christmas Day falls on a Tuesday. In the upper tabulation, the geocentric planetary positions are given, with that of the Sun indicated in the first column, that of the Moon in the second column, and so on. The position of the Sun is listed as 8°07' Sagittarius.

For someone living in London, 8°07' Sagittarius is the Sun's position at midnight, December 24–25, 2017—noting that in London and all of the United Kingdom, the Time Zone applying there is that of Universal Time–Greenwich Mean Time (UT–GMT).

For someone living in Sydney, Australia, which on Christmas Day is eleven hours ahead of UT–GMT, 8°07' Sagittarius is the Sun's position at 11 a.m. on December 25.

For someone living in California, which is eight hours behind UT–GMT on Christmas Day, 8°07' Sagittarius is the Sun's position at 4 p.m. on **December 24.**

For the person living in California, therefore, it is necessary to look at the entries for **December 26** to know the positions of the planets on December 25. The result is:

For someone living in California, which is eight hours behind UT–GMT on Christmas Day, the Sun's position at 4 p.m. on December 25 is 9°08' Sagittarius and, by the same token, the Moon's position on Christmas Day at 4 p.m. on December

---

1 See *General Introduction to the Christian Star Calendar: A Key to Understanding* for an in-depth clarification of the features of the calendar in *Star Wisdom*, including indications about how to work with it.

25 is 24°08' Pisces—these are the positions alongside December 26 at midnight UT–GMT—and eight hours earlier equates with 4 p.m. on December 25 in California.

From these examples it emerges that the **planetary positions as given in the ephemeris** can be utilized, but that according to the Time Zone one is in, **the time of day is different** and also for locations West of the United Kingdom **the date changes** (look at the date following the actual date).

Here is a tabulation in relation to the foregoing example of December 25 (Christmas Day).

## UNITED KINGDOM, EUROPE, AND ALL LOCATIONS WITH TIME ZONES EAST OF GREENWICH

Look at what is given alongside December 25— these entries indicate the planetary positions at these times:

- 12:00 a.m. (midnight December 24–25) in London (UT–GMT)
- 01:00 a.m. in Berlin (CENTRAL EUROPEAN TIME, which is one hour ahead of UT–GMT)
- 11:00 a.m. in Sydney (AUSTRALIAN EASTERN DAYLIGHT TIME, which is eleven hours ahead of UT–GMT)

## CANADA, USA, CENTRAL AMERICA, SOUTH AMERICA, AND ALL LOCATIONS WITH TIME ZONES WEST OF GREENWICH

Look at what is given alongside December 26— these entries indicate the planetary positions at these times:

- 7:00 p.m. in New York (EASTERN STANDARD TIME, which is five hours behind UT–GMT)
- 6:00 p.m. in Chicago (CENTRAL STANDARD TIME, which is six hours behind UT–GMT)
- 5:00 p.m. in Denver (MOUNTAIN STANDARD TIME, which is seven hours behind UT–GMT)

- 4:00 p.m. in San Francisco (PACIFIC STANDARD TIME, which is eight hours behind UT–GMT)
- **IF SUMMER TIME IS IN USE,** add **ONE HOUR**—FOR EXAMPLE:
- 8:00 p.m. in New York (EASTERN DAYLIGHT TIME, which is four hours behind UT–GMT)
- 7:00 p.m. in Chicago (CENTRAL DAYLIGHT TIME, which is five hours behind UT–GMT)
- 6:00 p.m. in Denver (MOUNTAIN DAYLIGHT TIME, which is six hours behind UT–GMT)
- 5:00 p.m. in San Francisco (PACIFIC DAYLIGHT TIME, which is seven hours behind UT–GMT)

Note that in the preceding tabulation, the time given in Sydney on Christmas Day, December 25, is in terms of Daylight Time. Six months earlier, on June 25, for someone in Sydney they would look alongside the entry in the ephemeris for June 25 and would know that this applies (for them) to

- 10:00 a.m. in Sydney (AUSTRALIAN EASTERN TIME, which is ten hours ahead of UT–GMT).

In these examples, it is not just the position of the Sun that is referred to. The same applies to the zodiacal locations given in the ephemeris for *all* the planets, whether geocentric (upper tabulation) or heliocentric (lower tabulation). *All that is necessary to apply this method of reading the ephemeris is to know the Time Zone in which one is and to apply the number of hours difference from UT–GMT.*

The advantage of using the method described here is that it greatly simplifies reference to the ephemeris when studying the **zodiacal positions of the planets**. However, for applying the time indications listed under "Ingresses" or "Aspects" it is still necessary to add or subtract the time difference from UT–GMT as described in the above paragraph denoted.

# COMMENTARIES AND EPHEMERIDES
## JANUARY – DECEMBER 2020

*Commentaries and Ephemerides by Joel Matthew Park,
including Monthly Stargazing Previews and
Astronomical Sky Watch by Julie Humphreys*

### COMMENTARIES

For this volume's commentaries on the significant alignments of 2020, I have adopted a somewhat different approach to previous editions. In past years, the focus has been on the exact alignment of two planets—whether it is conjunction, opposition, or square (the three alignments currently focused upon within this series). However, as research and experience can show, it is not only during the day or moment of exact alignment that the planets are expressive of synchronistic, archetypal, and spiritual phenomena; the demarcation of a broader period of activity extends usually well before and after the *moment* of exact alignment. For inner planets, this time period of opening up a window for particular archetypal beings to become active is relatively short. However, for the outermost and slowest moving planets, the windows that are opened by their interaction remain so over long periods of time, often coming to define certain historical periods (see, for example, *Cosmos and Psyche* by Richard Tarnas for an in-depth exploration of this phenomenon; see bibliography).

Taking this into account, I have indicated for each alignment the time period during which the two planets in question are within 5° of each other. In this way, we can begin to become aware of not just particular alignments occurring at scattered moments throughout the year, but also become aware of the living process leading up to, culminating in, and moving away from the exact moment of alignment. I have found this to lead to a more musical, interwoven experience of the movements of the planets; I hope it is equally enriching for the reader.

### STARGAZING

The following information is based on Eastern Standard Time and Eastern Daylight Time for the convenience of our North American readers. Please make the necessary adjustments for different time zones.

Observing the apparent path of the planets (called the ecliptic) before the background of the fixed stars of the zodiac requires denizens of the northern hemisphere to look southward. On the days of our spring and autumn equinoxes, this path will begin directly in the east, arch over the southern horizon, and end directly due west. On the other 363 or 364 days of the year, you'll observe that the planets rise slightly north or south of east, culminate east or west of south, and set south or north of west—however, their east–south–west trajectory remains roughly the same. It is a wonderful exercise throughout the year to simply notice where the planets rise, culminate, and set in reference to your fixed surroundings: trees, steeples, mountains, and so on.

## JANUARY 2020

### STARGAZING PREVIEW

The New Year begins with Mercury, Jupiter, Sun, Pluto and Saturn in Sagittarius; by month's end the Sun will be in Capricorn, and Mercury will have moved on to Aquarius. On New Year's Day you'll see Mars, in the first decan of Scorpio, rise around 0400, roughly three hours ahead of the Sun. As the Sun falls below the western horizon at 1630, you'll

SIDEREAL GEOCENTRIC LONGITUDES :     JANUARY  2020  Gregorian at 0 hours UT

| DAY | ☉ | ☽ | ☊ | ☿ | ♀ | ♂ | ♃ | ♄ | δ̂ | Ψ | ♇ |
|---|---|---|---|---|---|---|---|---|---|---|---|
| 1 WE | 14 ♐ 59 | 21 ♒ 8 | 13 ♊ 22R | 9 ♐ 22 | 19 ♑ 23 | 3 ♏ 22 | 11 ♐ 39 | 26 ♐ 23 | 7 ♈ 40R | 21 ♒ 15 | 27 ♐ 22 |
| 2 TH | 16 1 | 3 ♓ 1 | 13 22 | 10 57 | 20 37 | 4 2 | 11 53 | 26 30 | 7 40 | 21 16 | 27 24 |
| 3 FR | 17 2 | 14 53 | 13 22D | 12 32 | 21 50 | 4 43 | 12 7 | 26 37 | 7 39 | 21 17 | 27 26 |
| 4 SA | 18 3 | 26 49 | 13 22 | 14 7 | 23 4 | 5 23 | 12 21 | 26 44 | 7 39 | 21 19 | 27 28 |
| 5 SU | 19 4 | 8 ♈ 55 | 13 23 | 15 42 | 24 17 | 6 3 | 12 34 | 26 51 | 7 39 | 21 20 | 27 30 |
| 6 MO | 20 5 | 21 14 | 13 23 | 17 18 | 25 31 | 6 44 | 12 48 | 26 58 | 7 38 | 21 21 | 27 32 |
| 7 TU | 21 6 | 3 ♉ 50 | 13 24 | 18 55 | 26 44 | 7 24 | 13 2 | 27 5 | 7 38 | 21 23 | 27 34 |
| 8 WE | 22 8 | 16 46 | 13 25 | 20 32 | 27 57 | 8 5 | 13 16 | 27 12 | 7 38 | 21 24 | 27 36 |
| 9 TH | 23 9 | 0 ♊ 4 | 13 26 | 22 9 | 29 10 | 8 45 | 13 29 | 27 19 | 7 38 | 21 25 | 27 38 |
| 10 FR | 24 10 | 13 44 | 13 26 | 23 46 | 0 ♒ 23 | 9 26 | 13 43 | 27 26 | 7 38 | 21 27 | 27 40 |
| 11 SA | 25 11 | 27 44 | 13 26R | 25 24 | 1 36 | 10 6 | 13 57 | 27 33 | 7 38 | 21 28 | 27 42 |
| 12 SU | 26 12 | 12 ♋ 0 | 13 25 | 27 3 | 2 49 | 10 47 | 14 11 | 27 40 | 7 38D | 21 30 | 27 44 |
| 13 MO | 27 13 | 26 27 | 13 23 | 28 42 | 4 2 | 11 28 | 14 24 | 27 47 | 7 38 | 21 31 | 27 46 |
| 14 TU | 28 14 | 10 ♌ 59 | 13 21 | 0 ♑ 21 | 5 15 | 12 8 | 14 38 | 27 55 | 7 38 | 21 33 | 27 48 |
| 15 WE | 29 15 | 25 31 | 13 19 | 2 1 | 6 28 | 12 49 | 14 52 | 28 2 | 7 38 | 21 34 | 27 50 |
| 16 TH | 0 ♑ 16 | 9 ♍ 57 | 13 18 | 3 41 | 7 41 | 13 29 | 15 5 | 28 9 | 7 38 | 21 36 | 27 52 |
| 17 FR | 1 18 | 24 13 | 13 17 | 5 22 | 8 53 | 14 10 | 15 19 | 28 16 | 7 39 | 21 37 | 27 54 |
| 18 SA | 2 19 | 8 ♎ 17 | 13 16D | 7 3 | 10 6 | 14 51 | 15 32 | 28 23 | 7 39 | 21 39 | 27 56 |
| 19 SU | 3 20 | 22 7 | 13 17 | 8 45 | 11 18 | 15 31 | 15 46 | 28 30 | 7 39 | 21 41 | 27 58 |
| 20 MO | 4 21 | 5 ♏ 44 | 13 18 | 10 27 | 12 31 | 16 12 | 15 59 | 28 37 | 7 40 | 21 42 | 28 0 |
| 21 TU | 5 22 | 19 7 | 13 20 | 12 9 | 13 43 | 16 53 | 16 13 | 28 44 | 7 40 | 21 44 | 28 2 |
| 22 WE | 6 23 | 2 ♐ 16 | 13 21 | 13 52 | 14 56 | 17 34 | 16 26 | 28 51 | 7 41 | 21 46 | 28 4 |
| 23 TH | 7 24 | 15 14 | 13 21R | 15 35 | 16 8 | 18 15 | 16 40 | 28 58 | 7 41 | 21 47 | 28 6 |
| 24 FR | 8 25 | 27 59 | 13 21 | 17 18 | 17 20 | 18 55 | 16 53 | 29 5 | 7 42 | 21 49 | 28 8 |
| 25 SA | 9 26 | 10 ♑ 33 | 13 18 | 19 2 | 18 32 | 19 36 | 17 7 | 29 13 | 7 43 | 21 51 | 28 10 |
| 26 SU | 10 27 | 22 55 | 13 14 | 20 45 | 19 44 | 20 17 | 17 20 | 29 20 | 7 44 | 21 53 | 28 12 |
| 27 MO | 11 28 | 5 ♒ 8 | 13 10 | 22 29 | 20 56 | 20 58 | 17 33 | 29 27 | 7 44 | 21 54 | 28 14 |
| 28 TU | 12 29 | 17 11 | 13 4 | 24 12 | 22 8 | 21 39 | 17 46 | 29 34 | 7 45 | 21 56 | 28 16 |
| 29 WE | 13 30 | 29 8 | 12 59 | 25 55 | 23 19 | 22 20 | 18 0 | 29 41 | 7 46 | 21 58 | 28 18 |
| 30 TH | 14 31 | 11 ♓ 0 | 12 54 | 27 37 | 24 31 | 23 1 | 18 13 | 29 48 | 7 47 | 22 0 | 28 20 |
| 31 FR | 15 32 | 22 51 | 12 50 | 29 18 | 25 42 | 23 42 | 18 26 | 29 54 | 7 48 | 22 2 | 28 22 |

## INGRESSES :

| | | | |
|---|---|---|---|
| 1 | ☽ → ♓ 17:54 | 19 | ☽ → ♏ 13:50 |
| 4 | ☽ → ♈ 6:20 | 21 | ☽ → ♐ 19:49 |
| 6 | ☽ → ♉ 16:46 | 24 | ☽ → ♑ 3:49 |
| 8 | ☽ → ♊ 23:52 | 26 | ☽ → ♒ 13:52 |
| 9 | ♀ → ♒ 16:20 | 29 | ☽ → ♓ 1:45 |
| 11 | ☽ → ♋ 3:51 | 31 | ☿ → ♒ 10: 4 |
| 13 | ☽ → ♌ 5:52 | | ☽ → ♈ 14:25 |
| | ☿ → ♑ 18:55 | | ♄ → ♑ 19: 6 |
| 15 | ☽ → ♍ 7:25 | | |
| | ☉ → ♑ 17:31 | | |
| 17 | ☽ → ♎ 9:48 | | |

## ASPECTS & ECLIPSES :

| | | | | | |
|---|---|---|---|---|---|
| 1 ☽ ☌ Ψ 0:15 | 10 ☉ ☌s ☿ 15:18 | | 14 ☽ ☍ Ψ 17:27 | 24 ☽ ☌ ♇ 0:16 | |
| 2 ☽ ☌ A 1:31 | ☽ ● PN 19: 9 | | 16 ☽ ◻N ☊ 5:34 | ☽ ☌ ♄ 2: 7 | |
| ☿ ☌ ♃ 16:40 | ☉ ☍ ☽ 19:20 | | 17 ☉ □ ☽ 12:57 | ☉ ☌ ☽ 21:40 | |
| ☽ ◻S ☊ 20:56 | ☽ ☍ ☿ 19:32 | | ☽ ☍ δ̂ 22:54 | 25 ☽ ☌ ☿ 19: 5 | |
| 3 ☉ □ ☽ 4:44 | ☽ ☍ ♄ 23:42 | | 18 ☿ □ δ̂ 8:29 | 27 ♀ □ ♂ 1:36 | |
| ☿ ☍ ☊ 12:45 | ☽ ☍ ♇ 23:56 | | 20 ☽ ☌ ♂ 19:45 | ♀ ☌ Ψ 20: 6 | |
| 4 ☽ ☌ δ̂ 21:30 | 12 ☿ ☌ ♄ 9:50 | | ♂ □ Ψ 10:46 | 28 ☽ ☌ Ψ 9:33 | |
| 7 ☽ ☍ ♂ 7: 4 | ☿ ☌ ♇ 10: 9 | | ☽ ☌ ♀ 11: 0 | | |
| 8 ♃ ☍ ☊ 16:54 | ♄ ☌ ♇ 16: 2 | | 22 ☽ ☌ ☋ 20:30 | 29 ☽ ☌ A 21:21 | |
| 9 ☽ ☌ ☊ 23:28 | 13 ☉ ☌ ♇ 13:14 | | 23 ☽ ☌ ♃ 2:43 | 30 ☽ ◻S ☊ 3:50 | |
| ☽ ☍ ♃ 23:58 | ☽ ☍ ♀ 13:40 | | ☉ □ δ̂ 6:51 | | |

SIDEREAL  HELIOCENTRIC  LONGITUDES :     JANUARY  2020  Gregorian at 0 hours UT

| DAY | Sid. Time | ☿ | ♀ | ⊕ | ♂ | ♃ | ♄ | δ̂ | Ψ | ♇ | Vernal Point |
|---|---|---|---|---|---|---|---|---|---|---|---|
| 1 WE | 6:40:29 | 27 ♏ 25 | 9 ♓ 24 | 15 ♊ 0 | 9 ♎ 7 | 11 ♐ 2 | 27 ♐ 30 | 10 ♈ 18 | 22 ♒ 59 | 27 ♐ 44 | 4 ♓ 58'51" |
| 2 TH | 6:44:26 | 0 ♐ 10 | 11 0 | 16 1 | 9 36 | 11 7 | 27 31 | 10 19 | 22 59 | 27 44 | 4 ♓ 58'51" |
| 3 FR | 6:48:22 | 2 56 | 12 35 | 17 2 | 10 4 | 11 12 | 27 33 | 10 19 | 23 0 | 27 44 | 4 ♓ 58'51" |
| 4 SA | 6:52:19 | 5 43 | 14 11 | 18 4 | 10 33 | 11 17 | 27 35 | 10 20 | 23 0 | 27 45 | 4 ♓ 58'51" |
| 5 SU | 6:56:15 | 8 31 | 15 47 | 19 5 | 11 2 | 11 22 | 27 37 | 10 21 | 23 0 | 27 45 | 4 ♓ 58'51" |
| 6 MO | 7: 0:12 | 11 21 | 17 22 | 20 6 | 11 31 | 11 27 | 27 39 | 10 21 | 23 1 | 27 45 | 4 ♓ 58'51" |
| 7 TU | 7: 4: 9 | 14 12 | 18 58 | 21 7 | 12 0 | 11 32 | 27 41 | 10 22 | 23 1 | 27 46 | 4 ♓ 58'51" |
| 8 WE | 7: 8: 5 | 17 4 | 20 33 | 22 8 | 12 29 | 11 37 | 27 42 | 10 23 | 23 1 | 27 46 | 4 ♓ 58'50" |
| 9 TH | 7:12: 2 | 19 59 | 22 9 | 23 9 | 12 58 | 11 42 | 27 44 | 10 23 | 23 2 | 27 46 | 4 ♓ 58'50" |
| 10 FR | 7:15:58 | 22 55 | 23 45 | 24 10 | 13 27 | 11 46 | 27 46 | 10 24 | 23 2 | 27 46 | 4 ♓ 58'50" |
| 11 SA | 7:19:55 | 25 55 | 25 21 | 25 12 | 13 56 | 11 51 | 27 48 | 10 25 | 23 3 | 27 47 | 4 ♓ 58'50" |
| 12 SU | 7:23:51 | 28 56 | 26 56 | 26 13 | 14 26 | 11 56 | 27 50 | 10 26 | 23 3 | 27 47 | 4 ♓ 58'50" |
| 13 MO | 7:27:48 | 2 ♑ 1 | 28 32 | 27 14 | 14 55 | 12 1 | 27 51 | 10 26 | 23 3 | 27 47 | 4 ♓ 58'50" |
| 14 TU | 7:31:44 | 5 9 | 0 ♈ 8 | 28 15 | 15 24 | 12 6 | 27 53 | 10 27 | 23 4 | 27 48 | 4 ♓ 58'50" |
| 15 WE | 7:35:41 | 8 21 | 1 44 | 29 16 | 15 53 | 12 11 | 27 55 | 10 27 | 23 4 | 27 48 | 4 ♓ 58'49" |
| 16 TH | 7:39:38 | 11 36 | 3 19 | 0 ♋ 17 | 16 23 | 12 16 | 27 57 | 10 28 | 23 4 | 27 48 | 4 ♓ 58'49" |
| 17 FR | 7:43:34 | 14 56 | 4 55 | 1 18 | 16 52 | 12 21 | 27 59 | 10 29 | 23 5 | 27 49 | 4 ♓ 58'49" |
| 18 SA | 7:47:31 | 18 20 | 6 31 | 2 19 | 17 22 | 12 26 | 28 1 | 10 29 | 23 5 | 27 49 | 4 ♓ 58'49" |
| 19 SU | 7:51:27 | 21 48 | 8 7 | 3 20 | 17 51 | 12 31 | 28 2 | 10 30 | 23 5 | 27 49 | 4 ♓ 58'49" |
| 20 MO | 7:55:24 | 25 22 | 9 43 | 4 22 | 18 21 | 12 36 | 28 4 | 10 31 | 23 6 | 27 49 | 4 ♓ 58'49" |
| 21 TU | 7:59:20 | 29 1 | 11 19 | 5 23 | 18 50 | 12 41 | 28 6 | 10 31 | 23 6 | 27 50 | 4 ♓ 58'49" |
| 22 WE | 8: 3:17 | 2 ♒ 46 | 12 55 | 6 24 | 19 20 | 12 46 | 28 8 | 10 32 | 23 7 | 27 50 | 4 ♓ 58'48" |
| 23 TH | 8: 7:13 | 6 37 | 14 31 | 7 25 | 19 49 | 12 51 | 28 10 | 10 33 | 23 7 | 27 50 | 4 ♓ 58'48" |
| 24 FR | 8:11:10 | 10 35 | 16 7 | 8 26 | 20 19 | 12 56 | 28 11 | 10 33 | 23 7 | 27 51 | 4 ♓ 58'48" |
| 25 SA | 8:15: 7 | 14 39 | 17 43 | 9 27 | 20 49 | 13 1 | 28 13 | 10 34 | 23 8 | 27 51 | 4 ♓ 58'48" |
| 26 SU | 8:19: 3 | 18 51 | 19 19 | 10 28 | 21 19 | 13 6 | 28 15 | 10 34 | 23 8 | 27 51 | 4 ♓ 58'48" |
| 27 MO | 8:23: 0 | 23 11 | 20 56 | 11 29 | 21 49 | 13 11 | 28 17 | 10 35 | 23 8 | 27 52 | 4 ♓ 58'48" |
| 28 TU | 8:26:56 | 27 38 | 22 32 | 12 30 | 22 18 | 13 15 | 28 19 | 10 36 | 23 9 | 27 52 | 4 ♓ 58'48" |
| 29 WE | 8:30:53 | 2 ♓ 14 | 24 8 | 13 31 | 22 48 | 13 20 | 28 20 | 10 36 | 23 9 | 27 52 | 4 ♓ 58'48" |
| 30 TH | 8:34:49 | 6 59 | 25 44 | 14 32 | 23 18 | 13 25 | 28 22 | 10 37 | 23 9 | 27 52 | 4 ♓ 58'47" |
| 31 FR | 8:38:46 | 11 52 | 27 20 | 15 33 | 23 48 | 13 30 | 28 24 | 10 38 | 23 10 | 27 53 | 4 ♓ 58'47" |

## INGRESSES :

| | |
|---|---|
| 1 | ☿ → ♐ 22:29 |
| 12 | ☿ → ♑ 8:17 |
| 13 | ♀ → ♈ 22: 2 |
| 15 | ⊕ → ♋ 17:16 |
| 21 | ☿ → ♒ 6:21 |
| 28 | ☿ → ♓ 12:25 |

## ASPECTS (HELIOCENTRIC +MOON(TYCHONIC)) :

| | | | | | |
|---|---|---|---|---|---|
| 1 ☽ ☌ Ψ 3:44 | 6 ☿ ☌ ♃ 0:51 | ☿ ☌ Ψ 14:52 | 17 ☽ □ ♂ 6: 5 | 23 ☽ ☌ Ψ 23:44 | 31 ☿ □ ♃ 8: 1 |
| ☽ □ ☿ 16:31 | 8 ☽ □ Ψ 11:22 | ☽ □ ♄ 6:23 | ☽ □ ♃ 10: 9 | 24 ☽ ☌ ♄ 0:23 | ☽ □ ♇ 10: 9 |
| 2 ♀ □ ♃ 1:52 | 9 ☽ ☍ ♃ 20:34 | ☽ ☌ δ̂ 21:22 | 18 ☽ ☌ δ̂ 3:47 | 25 ☽ □ δ̂ 0: 2 | ☽ □ ♄ 11:14 |
| ☽ □ ♃ 16:30 | 10 ♄ ☌ ♂ 6:57 | ☿ ☌ ♂ 16: 5 | ☽ ☌ ♂ 16:16 | ☽ □ ♀ 15:56 | |
| ☽ ☌ ♀ 18:39 | ♀ □ ♃ 14:16 | ☽ ☍ ♀ 20:34 | ☽ □ ☿ 23:14 | ☽ ☌ δ̂ 20:43 | |
| 3 ♂ ☍ ♃ 12:38 | ☽ ☌ ♀ 15:18 | | 19 ☽ ◻ ☊ 11:50 | 26 ⊕ ☌ δ̂ 2:36 | |
| 4 ☽ ☌ ♄ 1:31 | 11 ☽ ☍ ♃ 0: 5 | 13 ⊕ ☍ ♇ 13:14 | 20 ♀ ☌ δ̂ 11:56 | ☿ ☌ Ψ 23:47 | |
| ☽ □ Ψ 1:50 | ☽ ☍ ♂ 0: 7 | ⊕ ☍ ♄ 15:14 | 21 ☽ □ Ψ 7:14 | 27 ♀ ☌ ♂ 19:12 | |
| ⊕ ☌ P 4:46 | 12 ☽ ☌ ♂ 4:11 | 14 ☽ ☍ Ψ 19:56 | 22 ☽ ☌ ♃ 19:31 | 28 ☽ ☌ Ψ 11:57 | |
| 5 ☽ ☌ δ̂ 2:48 | | 15 ☿ □ δ̂ 15:38 | | 29 ☽ ☌ ♀ 10:23 | |
| ☽ ☍ ♂ 4:20 | | 16 ☽ □ ♃ 3:53 | | 30 ☽ □ ♃ 4:57 | |

find Venus low in the southwestern sky. Now an evening star, she'll only be visible after sunset; at this time, the nearly First Quarter Moon will be high in the south.

Just before midnight on the 2nd, the Moon will reach its First Quarter at 17° Pisces, meaning that its right half will be illuminated by the Sun. It will rise around 1130 and be overhead, due south, as the Sun sets, finally dropping below the western horizon around 2300.

The Full Moon on the 10th will be below the star *Castor* (25° Gemini), found at the upper eastern corner of the constellation. And what a special one this will be—as India and surrounding lands will experience a Penumbral Lunar Eclipse that will last over four hours.

The 17th will bring the Last Quarter Moon; having just entered Libra, you'll see the left half of the Moon illumined as it rises in the east around 0100, three hours ahead of Mars. By the 20th, the Moon will catch up to Mars, and on the following morning you'll see Mars, in the middle decan of Scorpio, rise just ahead of the Moon. As they move higher above the horizon, you'll have a few hours before dawn to gaze at *Antares,* the heart of the Scorpion, below Mars. Both have a reddish hue, but *Antares* twinkles, seeming to wax and wane in brightness.

January's New Moon at 9° Capricorn will take place on the 24th. Between the setting of Venus at 2000 and the rising of Mars at 0400 on the 25th, the night sky will be free of both moonlight and other visible planets—in the absence of cloud cover, the stars should be beautiful! Between these hours you'll be able to see the Bull and Orion move from culmination to setting as Leo rises to its apex from the eastern horizon.

On the 26th, Venus and Mars will form a perfect square aspect, and between Venus setting and Mars rising, you'll again find the night sky free of classical (visible) planets. On the 27th you'll find the Moon, almost conjunct Venus, setting at 2000, quickly followed by Neptune (invisible to the naked eye) and Venus, at 22° Aquarius. On the actual day of the Moon–Venus conjunction, the 28th, Venus will set about twenty minutes ahead of the Moon.

Orion will be high in the southeast at sunset; the Hunter sets in the west at approximately 0400, three hours before dawn.

## JANUARY COMMENTARIES

**Note:** Rudolf Steiner gave a series of verse meditations for deepening into the realities of the seven planets moving among the twelve constellations. We find this in the booklet titled *Twelve Cosmic Moods.* As planets ingress into different constellations, different moods are reflected in the human soul. In accord with such ingresses, the appropriate line of the relevant Cosmic Mood has been highlighted in bold.

*Greetings to you, dear reader!* As I write these words, we are heading into the summer of 2019. The earliest that you could possibly be reading this is November 2019. What is the mood of the world at this time? What is the mood in our communities? In our own biographies, our own souls? Are we feeling a great heaviness? A feeling of impending doom, perhaps? Do we get the sense that fate is driving us into a corner, to a place in which we will be forced to make a severe choice? Are we becoming aware of the Darkness to a heightened degree— whether it is objective Evil in the world, or our own powerful Shadow? Perhaps we feel on the one hand overwhelmed by this, and on the other driven to new levels of actuating our Higher Self—to develop the courage to face what seems insurmountable, and actually rise to it! Where are we in the cosmic cycle, and what signs can the movements of the planets give us as to what wishes to manifest at this time in our lives?

One of the most powerful meetings that can take place in the heavens is that between Pluto and Saturn. Over the course of the twentieth century, they were conjunct in 1914–15, 1947, and 1982–83. Richard Tarnas, in his massive *Cosmos and Psyche,* characterizes their archetypal manifestation as such:

> …the positive potential of the archetypal complex associated with Saturn–Pluto alignments seemed to be inextricably intertwined with

confronting its negative manifestations: moral discernment and wisdom born from difficult experience and suffering; fortitude and courageous acts of will in the face of darkness, evil, danger, and death; a capacity for sustained effort and determination; disciplined control of intense energies both inner and outer. Generally speaking, the Saturn–Pluto complex appeared to press the psyche, individual or collective, toward the forging of a deeper and stronger structure of moral consciousness.[1]

It is this powerful interaction that has dominated the overall psychic and spiritual atmosphere for some time, and will continue to do so into the year 2020. From a heliocentric perspective, Saturn and Pluto are within 5° of each other from June 26, 2019 through July 27, 2020. Geocentrically, they were within 5° of each other from February 24 through July 14, 2019, and again between November 8, 2019 and March 17, 2020. **Saturn and Pluto are conjunct at 27°40' Sagittarius on January 12, 2020.**

On the psycho–biological level, Saturn represents Death and Pluto the Devil. It is very likely that many of us, in our personal and social lives, are experiencing the heaviness and intensity of this combination of archetypal forces. On a higher level, however, we can see this as a meeting of Gnosis (Saturn) with Evil (Pluto)—our consciousness of Evil, our recognition of its activity (if we are bold enough to give it the knowing glance) disenchants us, and undoes the potentially destabilizing and destructive force that Evil can have on us and in the world.

Yet we can behold and absorb the higher aspects, the psychospiritual aspects of these two archetypal beings as well. For Saturn, in her highest aspect, reveals to us the Virgin Mary, who prays for us sinners, now and at the hour of our death. Pluto, in his highest aspect, is the Empyrean, the Holy Fire, the Father–foundation of the World. We have before us a meeting of the Virgin Mother, who reminds us to honor Earth below, and the Holy Father, who draws our gaze to the highest heights above. The mantra for this time period is, "Honor your Father and your Mother." Are we honoring the timeless reality of the spiritual world as well as the needs of Mother Nature? Are we cultivating both spontaneous intuition as well as dedication to the Perennial Tradition? What is out of balance in our lives? How is the meeting of Mother and Father drawing our attention to this lack of balance? What are we repressing, and potentially projecting onto others?

This time period, as difficult as it can be, opens up to us a vast opportunity—to return to the source, to *both* the Father Above and the Mother Below—not *only* one or the other, nor as opposing principles, but alchemically wed to each other. Perhaps the extremely negative manifestation of this archetypal meeting hinges on our lack of will to step away from our folly, and return to the twofold source of wholeness and meaning.

The Twelve Holy Nights are a potent time in the cycle of the year; they both summarize the preceding year and plant the seeds for the coming one. These twelve nights provide a kind of open door to the spiritual world, a thinning of the veil; one is given the opportunity to engage more intimately with the spiritual world and receive wisdom and guidance for the unfolding of life's path. During the transition from 2019 to 2020, special alignments are occurring which make this time period even more potent than usual.

The Sun and Jupiter are close to conjunction from December 21 through January 2. They reach exact alignment on **December 27: Sun conjunct Jupiter 10° Sagittarius.** Concurrently with this alignment, we see the **Sun 13° Sagittarius opposite Node 13° Gemini on December 30;** they spend the days of December 25 through January 4, essentially the entirety of the Holy Nights, in close opposition. Finally, we see **Jupiter 13° Sagittarius opposite Node 13° Gemini on January 8.** They spend a longer time in close opposition: from December 18 through January 29, over a month.

What occurs annually during the Holy Nights as the thinning of the veil between the human and spiritual worlds is the hallmark of the rhythm of the Moon's Node (18.61 years). At the Nodal return,

---

1 Tarnas, *Cosmos and Psyche*, p. 285.

one receives a reminder, a living picture of one's mission for the current lifetime. And here we see over the course of the entirety of the Holy Nights, the Sun conjunct Jupiter, opposite the Node. We feel the special interaction of Jupiter and the Sun—creative thinking and radiant willing, head and heart joining together. The Node gives us a clear vision (Jupiter) of the mission of our Higher Self (Sun). Let us be filled with potent imaginations with which to begin the new year!

Jupiter can be thought of as an outer expression of the Holy Spirit, while the Sun expresses to us the Risen Christ. During the original Pentecost, Mary–Sophia sat amid the 12 disciples, and through her sacred heart transmitted to each of the disciples an individualized, personal experience of the Risen Christ—the gift of the Holy Spirit. We can imagine the Node as Mary–Sophia, and the Sun and Jupiter as the Paraclete, the Comforter given to each of us during these Holy Nights.

The aspect of Jupiter in Sagittarius opposite Node in Gemini is particularly potent: this same aspect, in the same sign, occurred during Parzival's second visit to the Grail Castle on May 26, 810.[2] We see here an archetypal expression of the clarity of insight and will created through the conversation between Jupiter and Node. During the opposition of these two planetary phenomena during the life of Parzival, he reunited with his estranged brother, asked the healing question of his uncle, King Anfortas, and himself became the new Grail King. Additionally, his brother Feirfiz came to know the Grail and the Grail Bearer, Repanse de Schoye; the two of them later became the parents of the reincarnated Lazarus, Prester John, in India. A great reordering of destiny is made possible at this time!

Between December 30 and January 6, we see Mercury and Jupiter close to conjunction, with an exact conjunction on **January 2: Mercury conjunct Jupiter, 11° Sagittarius.** During essentially the same period, Mercury and Node are in close opposition: they come to exact opposition on **January 3:**

**Mercury 13° Sagittarius opposite Node 13° Gemini.** Both of these aspects involving Mercury continue the recollection of the healing of Anfortas in the ninth century, although on that day Mercury was *opposite* its position currently: it was in Gemini, conjunct the Node and opposite Jupiter. The travels of Mercury culminate by joining the Sun; they are in close conjunction from January 2–18. **The Superior Conjunction of Sun and Mercury is 25° Sagittarius on January 10.**

Here we can feel the continuation of the story begun by Sun, Jupiter, and Node during the Holy Nights. The Sun and Mercury, each in their turn, come into alignment with Jupiter and Node. The Sun represents our Higher or Transcendental Self; Mercury the Lower or Empirical Self. New inspirations flow first into our Higher Self, as the Sun aspects Jupiter and Node in late December; this is followed by the same inspirations flowing into our Lower Self, as Mercury aspects the same two planets during the first few days of the year.

This is the story woven into us during the Holy Nights, culminating in the celebration of **Epiphany on January 6.** This Christian festival celebrates three events: the visit of the Three Magi to the newborn Master Jesus; the Baptism of Christ, inaugurating his ministry as God–Man; and the Parousia, the presence of Christ in the modern time. In fact, the season of Advent through Epiphany was, until the Middle Ages, a festival of the *future*, looking toward Christ's imminent return, rather than a festival of the *past*, honoring his first coming. When we celebrate this day with the birth, ministry, and return simultaneously in mind, we resolve the three streams of time: past, present, and future. This is contained in the Rosicrucian Mantra: *Ex deo nascimur; In Christo murmur; Per spiritum sanctum revivisimus.* We can begin the new year with this resolution at the core of our thoughts, feelings, and decisions.

Exiting the Holy Nights and Epiphany, the story woven by Sun, Mercury, Jupiter, and Node culminates between January 8, when Jupiter is exactly opposite the Node, and January 10, during the Superior Conjunction of Sun and Mercury. Especially during the latter, we feel the possibility of a

---

2 Park, "First Steps toward a Grail Timeline," *Cosmology Reborn: Star Wisdom,* vol 1.

"seeing together" of the Higher Eye and the Lower eye, of bringing the likeness of the lower self into cooperation with the image of the higher self.

A Superior Conjunction of the Sun and Mercury sees Mercury on the far side of the Sun from the geocentric perspective. It receives intuitive ferment from the Cosmos; what is taken up on an intuitive level will then come to fully conscious engagement during the Inferior Conjunction on February 25. Remember, what is given to us on an intuitive level is usually provided via symbolic synchronicities, seemingly insignificant coincidences happening in our day-to-day that pass us by if we aren't paying attention. We are to cultivate and unite the capacity to have the simple, wide-eyed wonder and receptivity of the child, with an ever keener quality of perception.

A Superior Conjunction occurred in Sagittarius, close to this degree, on December 8–9 AD 30. During this time, Christ healed two blind men and one man kept under possession by pagan sorcerers, who used him as a puppet to prove their power and knowledge. Christ set him free. Subsequently, the Pharisees used these healings to argue that Christ's power over demons came from his ability to bargain with them, to make a "deal with the Devil." Christ later excoriated them by saying, "Every kingdom divided against itself shall not stand. And if Satan cast out Satan, he is divided against himself. How then shall his kingdom stand? And if I by Beelzebub cast out devils, by whom do your children cast them out?"[3] Stand strong in deeds born of conscience!

**January 9:** Venus enters Aquarius:

> May what is bounded yield to the boundless.
> What feels the lack of bounds, may it create
> Bounds for itself in its depths;
> May it raise itself in the current,
> As wave, flowing forth, sustaining itself,
> In becoming, shaping itself to existence.
> Set yourself bounds, oh boundless!

In the aftermath of the Holy Nights and the intensity of new insights and inspirations that we may have experienced, a shadow side comes with it. Perhaps we are experiencing inflationary tendencies, giving into delusion, "playing around" rather than seeing true synchronicity. Venus's ingress to Aquarius heightens our feeling of lacking bounds, reminding us to stay grounded.

**January 10: Full Moon, 25° Gemini (Lunar Eclipse)**
Simultaneous with the Superior Conjunction on January 10 is the Full Moon in Gemini—within 6° of Sirius, the brightest star in the heavens. This Full Moon is not only reflecting the light of the Sun, but of Mercury also. With Sirius close by, this enhances our ability to bring into devotional reflection everything that has built up amongst Jupiter, Node, Mercury and Sun over the course of the past few weeks.

The cycle of the Moon was of great importance in ancient astrology. The Moon acts as a kind of transmitter or filter for the cosmic forces radiating from the different planetary spheres. In our time, we can understand this as a cycle of transmission, beginning with 1) the Risen Christ from the realm of the Sun; 2) the Holy Trinity from the realm of the Moon; 3) Archangel Michael from the realm of Mars; 4) the Healers of Humanity from the realm of Mercury; 5) the Holy Spirit from the realm of Jupiter; 6) Christ Crucified from the realm of Venus; and 7) the Virgin Mary from the realm of Saturn. These seven stages of transmission repeat four times during one Lunar month, beginning with the day after the New Moon, and ending the day before. The Full Moon transmits to us the influence of the Virgin Mary from the realm of Saturn. We can imagine that this Full Moon is pointing our attention to the conjunction of Saturn and Pluto, and all of the inner upheaval it asks of us.[4]

A Full Moon close to this degree occurred on December 10 AD 29:

> When the sabbath began, he taught in the synagogue taking for his subject a parable upon the waving branches of a tree scattering around their blossoms and bearing no fruit. By this parable

---

3  Brentano, *The Visions of Anne Catherine Emmerich*, vol. 2, p. 173.

4  Powell, "Classics in Astrosophy: The Lunar Calendar, Part. 1," *Journal for Star Wisdom*, 2018.

Jesus intended to rebuke the inhabitants, who for the most part had not become better after having received John's baptism. They allowed the blossoms of penance to be scattered by every wind without bearing fruit. Such were they here. Jesus chose this similitude because these people found their support chiefly in the cultivation of fruit. They had to carry it far away for sale, as no highroad passed near their isolated city. They were also largely engaged in coarse embroidery and the manufacture of covers.[5]

This is in line with the challenge presented to us by Saturn and Pluto at this time—will we hold steadfast and allow our blossoms to bear fruit, or scatter them to the wind? A lunar eclipse makes this especially challenging—the light of the Sun is no longer reflected, i.e., the guidance of the Higher Self is temporarily blocked, and terrestrial (materialistic) intellectuality may hold sway.

In the *Wandering Fool*, the anonymous author describes the light of the Moon (i.e., the light she produces, not the light she reflects) as the light of memory. Ritual, religion, and tradition are spiritual memory, the light that shines when all other lights have gone out.[6] In our time, as the path to the Mother in the heart of the Earth is opening back up for humanity, we can begin to experience a Lunar Eclipse as a potent time to remember the Mother.

**January 11:** Uranus stations direct, 7°38' Aries: Uranus was at this degree on April 24, 1935, just days after the fateful General Annual Meeting of the Anthroposophical Society, during which Ita Wegman and Elisabeth Vreede (not to mention 2,000 other members) were excluded from the Anthroposophical Society. This unfortunate turn of events would have extremely detrimental consequences for the world. As Elisabeth Vreede remarked after the expulsion: "The dam that held back National Socialism is now broken."

In January 1936, Uranus was in almost exactly the same position: stationing direct at 7° Aries. Shortly after this time, John Maynard Keynes published his last and enormously influential book

*The General Theory of Employment, Interest and Money*, which would bring about the so-called Keynesian Revolution in economic theory. It laid the foundation for the neoliberal macroeconomic model that has dominated the world ever since World War II.

Uranus at this degree warns us of the dangers of closed systems, of the destructive folly to which we succumb when we refuse to emerge from narrow paradigms that merely reflect our own ulterior motives. Instead, let us be Gardeners and Fools of Love.

After having come together for the Superior Conjunction on January 10, the Sun and Mercury continue on their journey together, having aligned the intentions of the Higher Self with the Lower Self. Soon afterward, however, the true test comes about. Between January 9 and 15, Mercury is close to conjunction with Saturn and Pluto; on **January 12, Mercury is conjunct both Saturn and Pluto, 27° Sagittarius.** One day later, **January 13, Sun is conjunct Saturn and Pluto** as well; it is within their general orb from January 8 to 19.

We have been filled with the nourishing inspirations of the Holy Nights, of the Node in Gemini, of Jupiter in Sagittarius. Now we stand before Saturn and Pluto; we can think of these two as Guardians of the Threshold. Can our lofty spiritual inspirations withstand the blunt force of reality? We must come to terms with the fact that spiritual development hinges on sacrifice; this occurs either through a sacrifice of others or of ourselves. We can, and sometimes must, sacrifice others through the asocial withdrawal from the world that inner work requires. The alternative is to choose to sacrifice ourselves—to place what is unresolved on the altar of conscience. If we can face and integrate that which requires transformation, and confront the shadow with boldness, it is transmuted into new capacities, which we then put to the *service of* the outer world.

On a higher level, we can think of the Sun as representative of the Risen Christ; Mercury as representative of the initiate, the shepherd of humanity;

---

5 Brentano, *The Visions of Anne Catherine Emmerich*, vol. 1, p. 375.

6 Anon. *The Wandering Fool*, p. 92.

Saturn as the Virgin Mary; and Pluto as the Father. Here we have the Holy Family of Virgin Mother, Risen Son, and Divine Father, with the enlightened and transfigured human being standing with them—the Prodigal Son of the Cosmos returned to his origin. Can we experience the trial of this time as a sort of homecoming? As with the Prodigal, this hinges on our own humility and ability to face reality head-on.

The healing question at the time of Parzival was "What ails thee?" In our time, 1,200 years later, this has changed. We cannot help the other without invitation, whether implicit or explicit—and the flipside to this is that the other cannot help *us* without invitation. The healing question of our time is therefore, "Can you help me? What ails *me?*" To live in vulnerability, to need the active assistance of other people is the hard lesson of our time. In the expression of our needs to the other, we place ourselves in an uncomfortable state—we have placed our fate in the hands of someone else. The reality is, this is *always* the case—every aspect of our existence somehow depends on the activity of other beings. In order to approach a state of freedom, we must come to an active recognition of and participation with this reality. The Prodigal Son is the perfect expression of this path to freedom.

**January 13: Mercury enters Capricorn; January 15: Sun enters Capricorn:**

> May what is coming, rest on what has been.
> May what has been, surmise what is to come,
> For a vigorous present existence.
> Through inward life-withstanding
> May world-beings' guard grow strong,
> May life's working might blossom forth,
> May what has been endure what is to come!

The combination of these two lines—"May what is coming, rest on what has been, / for a vigorous present existence"—doesn't the mood of these words bring us right to the heart of "Honor your Father and your Mother, and you shall live a long life"? Our creativity can only thrive (live a "vigorous present existence") if it swims in the current of Living Tradition.

Between January 15 and 21, Mercury is square to Uranus. The alignment is exact on **January 18, with Mercury 7°39' Capricorn square Uranus 7°39' Aries.** Following on the heels of this alignment, the Sun is square Uranus between January 18 and 28. Their alignment is exact on **January 23: Sun 7°41' Capricorn square Uranus 7°41' Aries.** As we head into the final week of January, the alignment between Jupiter and the Node begins to loosen; by January 29, they will have drifted apart. At the same time, we can feel both Mercury and the Sun coming into a dynamic tension with Uranus. The beneficent inspirations of Jupiter and the Node begin to wane; meanwhile, we are confronted with the temptation presented to us by Uranus. Uranus can provide what on the surface are enticing and scintillating flashes of brilliance. These are extremely attractive to the Lower Self inasmuch as it remains trapped in its own subjectivity. It takes courage and openness to allow these surface flashes to take on their full reality: lightning flashes of Truth meant to shatter our delusions. A feeling of inner and outer restlessness, a rebellious attitude, can overtake us during such aspects; however, if we can summon the fortitude to set aside quiet moments to *breathe* on a soul and spiritual level, the same aspect can fire the will and the imagination in a fruitful way.

A similar aspect, but with Sun and Mercury in Taurus and Uranus in Leo, occurred between May 5 and 11 AD 33, the days immediately preceding the Ascension:

> Jesus communicated with the apostles quite naturally in these last days. He ate and prayed with them, walked with them in many directions, and repeated all that he had before told them. He appeared also to Simon of Cyrene as he was working in a garden between Bethphage and Jerusalem. Jesus, resplendent with light, approached him as if floating in the air. Simon fell on his knees and kissed the ground at Jesus's feet, who signed to him with his hand to keep silence, and then vanished. Some others that were working nearby likewise saw Jesus, and they too fell on their knees like Simon. When Jesus was walking with the apostles around

Jerusalem, some of the Jews perceived the apparition, and were terrified. They ran to hide themselves, or to shut themselves up in their houses. Even the apostles and disciples accompanied him with a certain degree of timidity, for there was in him something too spiritual for them. Jesus appeared also in other places, Bethlehem and Nazareth for instance, to those especially with whom he and his blessed Mother had formerly had contact. He scattered blessings everywhere, and they that saw him believed and joined the apostles and disciples.[7]

**January 24: New Moon 8° Capricorn.** The New Moon was in Capricorn, close to this degree, on December 24 AD 29. Anne Catherine Emmerich witnessed the summons of the disciple Phillip on this day, "…who was backward and humble…[he] hung behind, not certain as to whether he should or should not follow. Jesus, who was going on before, turned his head and, addressing Phillip, said: 'Follow me!' at which words Phillip went on joyously with the others. There were about twelve in the little band." She also witnessed Christ's teaching on the subject of "Vocation and Correspondence":

He alluded to their own vocation, telling them to hold themselves in readiness. They would, he continued, have to forsake all when he called them. He would provide for them, they should suffer no want. They might still continue their customary occupations, because as the Passover was now approaching he would have to discharge other affairs. But when he should call them, they should follow him immediately. The disciples questioned him unrestrainedly as to how they should manage with regard to their families. Peter, for instance, said that just at present he could not leave his old stepfather, who was also Phillip's uncle. But Jesus relieved his anxiety by his answer, that he would not begin before the Passover feast; that only insofar as the heart was concerned, should they detach themselves from their occupations; that exteriorly they should continue them until he called them. In the meantime, however, they should

take the necessary steps toward freeing themselves from their different avocations.[8]

The message of this New Moon is to be like Phillip: in all humility to hold back until we are called, and yet have the detachment and subsequent readiness to, at a moment's notice, take up the call of the Master. This New Moon is conjunct the Sun square Uranus referred to above; all three planets—Moon, Sun, and Mercury—are therefore in dynamic tension with Uranus, the transmitter of Cosmic Imaginations at this time.

Whereas the other phases of the Moon are related to one of the seven planetary rulers (see commentary on the Full Moon), the New Moon is unique. It represents a pause, an opening in the circle that creates a spiral. New influences can stream in during this time from the celestial heights of Sophia and the Divine Father. We can particularly take in the influence of the outer planets (Uranus, Neptune, and Pluto) during the New Moon as expressions of the realm of the Midnight Hour, of new beginnings—"Ex Deo Nascimur." We have already taken note of Saturn and Pluto's conjunction earlier in our meditations, as well as Mercury, Sun and Moon coming into dynamic tension with Uranus. We can also focus our attention on Neptune…

Between January 17 and February 4, Mars and Venus are within 5° of square alignment. This square is exact on **January 27: Mars 20° Scorpio square Venus 20° Aquarius.** Almost simultaneously, Venus comes into conjunction with Neptune between January 23 and February 1. **Venus and Neptune are exactly conjunct somewhat later on January 27, also 20° Aquarius.** Slower moving Mars, after first coming into square alignment with Venus, then squares Neptune between January 20 and February 5; this alignment is exact on **January 28: Mars 21° Scorpio square Neptune 21° Aquarius.**

With Mars in Libra, and Venus and Neptune in Capricorn, this same alignment (Mars square Venus conjunct Neptune) occurred on December 1 AD 29. This was the day after Christ successfully passed through the three temptations in the wilderness, as

<hr>

7   Brentano, *The Visions of Anne Catherine Emmerich,* vol. 3, p. 409.

8   Ibid., vol. 1, p. 382.

well as the fourth temptation. The fourth temptation is the megalomania that accompanies spiritual victories small and great; the greater the victory, the greater the temptation to self-glorification. Venus is related to victory over temptation; Mars to victory over megalomania; Neptune is Nyx, Night—the Divine Mother of the World who watches over us during this trial. Inversely, these three planets are related to *yielding to* temptation (Venus); *yielding to* megalomania (Mars); and the intoxication of the subconscious (Neptune). Take care!

While at the time of Christ, the archetypal drama was playing out in the form of confrontation with the Guardian of the Threshold (Libra) in the wilderness (Capricorn) for the sake of proving both human and cosmic Justice, this same drama unfolds with different scenery in our time. The concern now is the transformation (Aquarius) of the Scorpion into the Dove (Scorpio) for the sake of wholeness, reintegration, redemption. Seek to transform reductive intellectualizing into inspiration—"think together" with your Angel. Seek to transform the narrowness of fear and defensiveness into the flow of living waters. Seek to transform the outer world into a work of art rather than a mere technocracy.

**January 31:** Mercury enters Aquarius; Saturn enters Capricorn: **"Create bounds for itself in its depths..."** (See January 9 for full verse.)

**"May life's working might blossom forth."** (See January 13–15 for full verse.) We end the month with a double-edged injunction—we are reminded that for life's working might to blossom forth, boundaries must be self-created. The contracting movement of setting boundaries yields the countermovement of expansion.


# FEBRUARY 2020

## STARGAZING PREVIEW

February starts with a First Quarter Moon at 17° Aries, which will rise and set at about 1100 and 0100, respectively. After its setting, the sky will remain devoid of classical planets until Mars, at 25°

Scorpio, rises at 0400. Jupiter and Saturn, also, will crest the eastern horizon before the 0700 sunrise.

The Full Moon at 25° Cancer on the 9th will appear larger and brighter than is usual due to its relative proximity to the Earth. It will have the night sky to itself between 2100, when Venus sets, and the rising of Mars at 0400. Enjoy watching the Moon lead the Lion across the sky from east to west!

The Last Quarter Moon (1° Scorpio) will occur on the 15th; watch it rise at about 0100; Mars, Jupiter, and Saturn will follow at 0500 and 0530, respectively. Ninety minutes later, the Sun will top the eastern horizon, marking the same zodiacal degree as it did at the Healing of the Paralyzed Man, on January 19, 31 CE. When the Moon rises at 0100 on the following morning, Orion will be low in the west and Leo will be ruling from high above the southern horizon.

The Moon catches up with Mars on the 18th (6° Sagittarius), Jupiter on the 19th (22° Sagittarius), Saturn on the 20th (2° Capricorn), before reaching the Sun (February's New Moon, 9° Aquarius) on the 23rd.

The 27th finds a special conjunction between the Moon and Venus at 27° Pisces, the classical exaltation point of Venus, making her influence particularly strong. As the Moon will be just past the conjunction at the time of their setting, Venus will disappear below the western horizon first.

Orion rises at 1100 and sets at 0200, at which time all the planets of our solar system will be hiding below the horizon.

## FEBRUARY COMMENTARIES

**February 2: Christian Celebration of Candlemas:** Today we honor the halfway point between the Winter Solstice and the Spring Equinox. In ancient times, this was celebrated as the festival of Imbolc, one of the four main Celtic festivals in honor of the goddess Brigid. Brigid was the Mother Goddess of the dawn, of healing, fertility, poetry, and smith craft. In the temples of Brigid, the priestesses guarded the Eternal Flame. St. Brigid of Ireland became the Christian personification of this other-worldly deity, carrying a deep relationship to the same realms borne by the pagan goddess: healing, metalwork, and poetry (specifically, illuminated manuscripts). St. Brigid and her nuns maintained the perpetual flame at their sanctuary in Kildare. The cross of St. Brigid resembles a vortex—that which was given to us during the Holy Nights, that which is new to the world, begins to mingle more concretely with that which has already been there from the past. The midpoint between Christmas and Easter finds us in the vortex of metamorphosis. This vortex-like cross might also remind us of the root chakra, the portal to the realm of the Mother below. While this is the realm of Life, it is also the realm of our accumulated negative karma—our shadow, which must be confronted before entry to the Mother's realm.

Candlemas, in the Christian tradition, celebrates that which is recounted in Luke 2:22–39. Forty days after the birth of Christ, he was taken to the Temple in order to be presented, and for Mary to perform the ritual sacrifice of purification. Mary, like Brigid, guards the Eternal Flame which is Christ. He is born into the world in the darkness of the dead of Winter, and is only brought out to meet the outer world at the midway point to Spring. Perhaps we have been protectively cultivating something new since the Holy Nights. Now is the time to take the first steps to making it an outer, objective reality.

The Feast of the Purification of the Virgin Mary—Candlemas—is, along with other Marian celebrations (such as the Feast of the Immaculate Conception on December 8, the Feast of the Assumption on August 15, and the Feast of the Annunciation on March 25) becoming of greater significance during this time of Christ's Parousia. The Virgin Mary appeared to the Conceptionist sister Mother Mariana de Jesus Torres in Quito, Ecuador many times between February 2, 1594 and February 2, 1634. She delivered to Mother Mariana dire prophecies relating to the times we live in now, many of which in specific detail have come to pass. She requested a statue, dedicated to "Our Lady of Good Success," be built for the sake of the adoration of the Virgin Mary:

"Now I ask and command you to have a statue to be made for the consolation and preservation of my convent and for those faithful souls of that epoch during which there will be a great devotion to me, for I am the Queen of Heaven under many invocations… With the making of this statue I will favor not only my convent, but also the people of Quito— and all the people throughout the centuries."

Our Lady of Good Success also told Mother Mariana that this statue was to be made, for these reasons:

"First so that men in the future might realize how powerful I am in placating Divine Justice and obtaining mercy and pardon for every sinner who comes to me with a contrite heart. For I am the Mother of Mercy and in me there is only goodness and love."

"And second …when tribulations of spirit and sufferings of the body oppress them and they seem to be drowning in this bottomless sea let them gaze at my holy image and I will always be there ready to listen to their cries and soothe their pain. Tell them that they should always run to their Mother with confidence and love… "

Our Lady of Good Success had requested that a certain sculptor, Francisco del Castillo, who was known not only for his artistic ability but also for his virtue and devotion to the Blessed Mother, create the statue. This sculptor worked long and hard on this statue. When he was about to put the finishing coat of paint on the statue he decided he would go to find the best paints he could acquire that would be the most fitting for the faces of Mother of God and the Infant Jesus.

While he was gone something miraculous happened. From the very first apparition, Our Lady had promised that she, herself, would see to the completion of this statue. While the sculptor was away, Mother Mariana and the other sisters went to the choir loft to implore Our Lady of Good Success to keep her promise.

Later that night, Mother Mariana found the upper choir loft illuminated with heavenly brilliance. The Archangels Michael, Raphael and Gabriel appeared and bowed reverently before the Blessed Trinity as if acceding to a command. Then they stood before the Queen of Heaven and saluted her. The Archangels, along with St.

## SIDEREAL GEOCENTRIC LONGITUDES :   FEBRUARY 2020 Gregorian at 0 hours UT

| DAY | ☉ | ☽ | ☊ | ☿ | ♀ | ♂ | ♃ | ♄ | ♅ | ♆ | ♇ |
|---|---|---|---|---|---|---|---|---|---|---|---|
| 1 SA | 16 ♑ 33 | 4 ♈ 45 | 12 ♊ 48R | 0 ♒ 58 | 26 ♒ 54 | 24 ♏ 22 | 18 ♐ 39 | 0 ♑ 1 | 7 ♈ 49 | 22 ♒ 4 | 28 ♐ 24 |
| 2 SU | 17 34 | 16 47 | 12 47 | 2 36 | 28 5 | 25 3 | 18 52 | 0 8 | 7 50 | 22 6 | 28 25 |
| 3 MO | 18 35 | 29 2 | 12 48D | 4 13 | 29 16 | 25 44 | 19 5 | 0 15 | 7 51 | 22 8 | 28 27 |
| 4 TU | 19 36 | 11 ♉ 34 | 12 49 | 5 47 | 0 ♓ 27 | 26 25 | 19 18 | 0 22 | 7 53 | 22 10 | 28 29 |
| 5 WE | 20 37 | 24 27 | 12 51 | 7 18 | 1 38 | 27 6 | 19 31 | 0 29 | 7 54 | 22 12 | 28 31 |
| 6 TH | 21 38 | 7 ♊ 46 | 12 52 | 8 46 | 2 49 | 27 47 | 19 44 | 0 36 | 7 55 | 22 14 | 28 33 |
| 7 FR | 22 38 | 21 32 | 12 51R | 10 10 | 4 0 | 28 29 | 19 56 | 0 42 | 7 56 | 22 16 | 28 35 |
| 8 SA | 23 39 | 5 ♋ 45 | 12 49 | 11 29 | 5 10 | 29 10 | 20 9 | 0 49 | 7 58 | 22 18 | 28 37 |
| 9 SU | 24 40 | 20 20 | 12 45 | 12 43 | 6 21 | 29 51 | 20 22 | 0 56 | 7 59 | 22 20 | 28 39 |
| 10 MO | 25 41 | 5 ♌ 13 | 12 40 | 13 51 | 7 31 | 0 ♐ 32 | 20 34 | 1 3 | 8 1 | 22 22 | 28 40 |
| 11 TU | 26 41 | 20 14 | 12 33 | 14 51 | 8 41 | 1 13 | 20 47 | 1 9 | 8 2 | 22 24 | 28 42 |
| 12 WE | 27 42 | 5 ♍ 14 | 12 26 | 15 44 | 9 51 | 1 54 | 20 59 | 1 16 | 8 4 | 22 26 | 28 44 |
| 13 TH | 28 43 | 20 4 | 12 19 | 16 29 | 11 1 | 2 35 | 21 12 | 1 23 | 8 6 | 22 28 | 28 46 |
| 14 FR | 29 43 | 4 ♎ 37 | 12 15 | 17 5 | 12 11 | 3 16 | 21 24 | 1 29 | 8 7 | 22 30 | 28 48 |
| 15 SA | 0 ♒ 44 | 18 49 | 12 12 | 17 31 | 13 21 | 3 58 | 21 36 | 1 36 | 8 9 | 22 33 | 28 49 |
| 16 SU | 1 45 | 2 ♏ 39 | 12 11 | 17 47 | 14 30 | 4 39 | 21 48 | 1 42 | 8 11 | 22 35 | 28 51 |
| 17 MO | 2 45 | 16 8 | 12 12D | 17 52 | 15 39 | 5 20 | 22 1 | 1 49 | 8 13 | 22 37 | 28 53 |
| 18 TU | 3 46 | 29 16 | 12 13 | 17 47R | 16 49 | 6 1 | 22 13 | 1 55 | 8 14 | 22 39 | 28 55 |
| 19 WE | 4 46 | 12 ♐ 8 | 12 14R | 17 32 | 17 58 | 6 43 | 22 25 | 2 1 | 8 16 | 22 41 | 28 56 |
| 20 TH | 5 47 | 24 46 | 12 13 | 17 7 | 19 6 | 7 24 | 22 37 | 2 8 | 8 18 | 22 43 | 28 58 |
| 21 FR | 6 47 | 7 ♑ 12 | 12 10 | 16 33 | 20 15 | 8 5 | 22 48 | 2 14 | 8 20 | 22 46 | 29 0 |
| 22 SA | 7 48 | 19 30 | 12 4 | 15 50 | 21 24 | 8 47 | 23 0 | 2 20 | 8 22 | 22 48 | 29 1 |
| 23 SU | 8 48 | 1 ♒ 39 | 11 56 | 14 59 | 22 32 | 9 28 | 23 12 | 2 27 | 8 24 | 22 50 | 29 3 |
| 24 MO | 9 49 | 13 42 | 11 45 | 14 3 | 23 40 | 10 9 | 23 24 | 2 33 | 8 27 | 22 52 | 29 5 |
| 25 TU | 10 49 | 25 40 | 11 33 | 13 2 | 24 48 | 10 51 | 23 35 | 2 39 | 8 29 | 22 54 | 29 6 |
| 26 WE | 11 50 | 7 ♓ 34 | 11 21 | 11 59 | 25 56 | 11 32 | 23 47 | 2 45 | 8 31 | 22 57 | 29 8 |
| 27 TH | 12 50 | 19 25 | 11 10 | 10 54 | 27 3 | 12 14 | 23 58 | 2 51 | 8 33 | 22 59 | 29 9 |
| 28 FR | 13 50 | 1 ♈ 17 | 11 1 | 9 49 | 28 11 | 12 55 | 24 9 | 2 57 | 8 35 | 23 1 | 29 11 |
| 29 SA | 14 50 | 13 11 | 10 53 | 8 46 | 29 18 | 13 36 | 24 20 | 3 3 | 8 38 | 23 3 | 29 13 |

### INGRESSES :

| | | | |
|---|---|---|---|
| 3 | ☽ → ♉ | 1:52 | |
| | ♀ → ♓ | 14:44 | |
| 5 | ☽ → ♊ | 10: 5 | |
| 7 | ☽ → ♋ | 14:23 | |
| 9 | ♂ → ♐ | 5:25 | |
| | ☽ → ♌ | 15:37 | |
| 11 | ☽ → ♍ | 15:37 | |
| 13 | ☽ → ♎ | 16:19 | |
| 14 | ☉ → ♒ | 6:36 | |
| 15 | ☽ → ♏ | 19:20 | |
| 18 | ☽ → ♐ | 1:21 | |
| 20 | ☽ → ♑ | 10: 3 | |
| 22 | ☽ → ♒ | 20:43 | |
| 25 | ☽ → ♓ | 8:43 | |
| 27 | ☽ → ♈ | 21:24 | |
| 29 | ♀ → ♈ | 15: 6 | |

### ASPECTS & ECLIPSES :

| | | |
|---|---|---|
| 1 ☽ ☌ ♅ 6: 8 | 12 ☽ ☍ ♀ 8: 5 | ♀ □ ♃ 16:58 |
| 2 ☉ □ ☽ 1:40 | ☽ ⊼ ☊ 11:31 | 24 ☽ ☌ ☿ 0:38 |
| 5 ☽ ☍ ♂ 5: 6 | 14 ♀ □ ☊ 1:11 | ☽ ☌ ♆ 18:25 |
| 6 ☽ ☌ ☊ 8:58 | ☽ ☍ ♅ 5:52 | 25 ♂ ☍ ☊ 19: 5 |
| ☽ ☍ ♃ 21:12 | 15 ☉ □ ☽ 22:16 | 26 ☉ ☌ ♅ 1:43 |
| 7 ☽ ☍ ♆ 12: 1 | 18 ☽ ☌ ♂ 13:15 | ☿ ⊼ ☊ 7:32 |
| ☽ ☍ ♄ 15:42 | 19 ☽ ☌ ☋ 0:10 | ☽ ☌ A 11:40 |
| 9 ☉ ☍ ☽ 7:32 | ☽ ☌ ♃ 19:48 | 27 ☽ ☌ ♀ 17: 4 |
| 10 ☽ ☍ ☿ 14:49 | 20 ☽ ☌ ♆ 8: 5 | 28 ☽ ☌ ♅ 14:48 |
| ☽ ☌ P 20:31 | ☽ ☌ ♄ 14:17 | ♀ □ ♆ 22: 2 |
| 11 ☽ ☍ ♆ 3:28 | 23 ☉ ☌ ☽ 15:30 | |

## SIDEREAL HELIOCENTRIC LONGITUDES :   FEBRUARY 2020 Gregorian at 0 hours UT

| DAY | Sid. Time | ☿ | ♀ | ⊕ | ♂ | ♃ | ♄ | ♅ | ♆ | ♇ | Vernal Point |
|---|---|---|---|---|---|---|---|---|---|---|---|
| 1 SA | 8:42:42 | 16 ♓ 54 | 28 ♈ 57 | 16 ♋ 34 | 24 ♎ 19 | 13 ♐ 35 | 28 ♐ 26 | 10 ♈ 38 | 23 ♒ 10 | 27 ♐ 53 | 4 ♓ 58'47" |
| 2 SU | 8:46:39 | 22 6 | 0 ♉ 33 | 17 35 | 24 49 | 13 40 | 28 28 | 10 39 | 23 11 | 27 53 | 4 ♓ 58'47" |
| 3 MO | 8:50:36 | 27 26 | 2 9 | 18 36 | 25 19 | 13 45 | 28 30 | 10 40 | 23 11 | 27 54 | 4 ♓ 58'47" |
| 4 TU | 8:54:32 | 2 ♈ 56 | 3 46 | 19 36 | 25 49 | 13 50 | 28 31 | 10 40 | 23 11 | 27 54 | 4 ♓ 58'47" |
| 5 WE | 8:58:29 | 8 34 | 5 22 | 20 37 | 26 19 | 13 55 | 28 33 | 10 41 | 23 12 | 27 54 | 4 ♓ 58'47" |
| 6 TH | 9: 2:25 | 14 21 | 6 58 | 21 38 | 26 50 | 14 0 | 28 35 | 10 42 | 23 12 | 27 55 | 4 ♓ 58'46" |
| 7 FR | 9: 6:22 | 20 16 | 8 35 | 22 39 | 27 20 | 14 5 | 28 37 | 10 42 | 23 12 | 27 55 | 4 ♓ 58'46" |
| 8 SA | 9:10:18 | 26 17 | 10 11 | 23 40 | 27 51 | 14 10 | 28 39 | 10 43 | 23 13 | 27 55 | 4 ♓ 58'46" |
| 9 SU | 9:14:15 | 2 ♉ 25 | 11 48 | 24 40 | 28 21 | 14 15 | 28 40 | 10 44 | 23 13 | 27 55 | 4 ♓ 58'46" |
| 10 MO | 9:18:11 | 8 37 | 13 24 | 25 41 | 28 52 | 14 20 | 28 42 | 10 44 | 23 13 | 27 56 | 4 ♓ 58'46" |
| 11 TU | 9:22: 8 | 14 53 | 15 1 | 26 42 | 29 22 | 14 25 | 28 44 | 10 45 | 23 14 | 27 56 | 4 ♓ 58'46" |
| 12 WE | 9:26: 5 | 21 12 | 16 38 | 27 43 | 29 53 | 14 30 | 28 46 | 10 46 | 23 14 | 27 56 | 4 ♓ 58'46" |
| 13 TH | 9:30: 1 | 27 31 | 18 14 | 28 43 | 0 ♏ 24 | 14 35 | 28 48 | 10 46 | 23 15 | 27 57 | 4 ♓ 58'45" |
| 14 FR | 9:33:58 | 3 ♊ 50 | 19 51 | 29 44 | 0 54 | 14 40 | 28 50 | 10 47 | 23 15 | 27 57 | 4 ♓ 58'45" |
| 15 SA | 9:37:54 | 10 7 | 21 28 | 0 ♌ 45 | 1 25 | 14 45 | 28 51 | 10 48 | 23 15 | 27 57 | 4 ♓ 58'45" |
| 16 SU | 9:41:51 | 16 20 | 23 4 | 1 45 | 1 56 | 14 50 | 28 53 | 10 48 | 23 16 | 27 58 | 4 ♓ 58'45" |
| 17 MO | 9:45:47 | 22 28 | 24 41 | 2 46 | 2 27 | 14 55 | 28 55 | 10 49 | 23 16 | 27 58 | 4 ♓ 58'45" |
| 18 TU | 9:49:44 | 28 29 | 26 18 | 3 46 | 2 58 | 15 0 | 28 57 | 10 50 | 23 16 | 27 58 | 4 ♓ 58'45" |
| 19 WE | 9:53:40 | 4 ♋ 24 | 27 55 | 4 47 | 3 29 | 15 5 | 28 59 | 10 50 | 23 17 | 27 58 | 4 ♓ 58'45" |
| 20 TH | 9:57:37 | 10 10 | 29 32 | 5 47 | 4 0 | 15 10 | 29 0 | 10 51 | 23 17 | 27 59 | 4 ♓ 58'44" |
| 21 FR | 10: 1:34 | 15 48 | 1 ♊ 8 | 6 48 | 4 31 | 15 14 | 29 2 | 10 52 | 23 17 | 27 59 | 4 ♓ 58'44" |
| 22 SA | 10: 5:30 | 21 16 | 2 45 | 7 48 | 5 2 | 15 19 | 29 4 | 10 52 | 23 18 | 27 59 | 4 ♓ 58'44" |
| 23 SU | 10: 9:27 | 26 35 | 4 22 | 8 49 | 5 33 | 15 24 | 29 6 | 10 53 | 23 18 | 28 0 | 4 ♓ 58'44" |
| 24 MO | 10:13:23 | 1 ♌ 44 | 5 59 | 9 49 | 6 5 | 15 29 | 29 8 | 10 54 | 23 19 | 28 0 | 4 ♓ 58'44" |
| 25 TU | 10:17:20 | 6 44 | 7 36 | 10 50 | 6 36 | 15 34 | 29 10 | 10 54 | 23 19 | 28 0 | 4 ♓ 58'44" |
| 26 WE | 10:21:16 | 11 34 | 9 13 | 11 50 | 7 7 | 15 39 | 29 11 | 10 55 | 23 19 | 28 1 | 4 ♓ 58'44" |
| 27 TH | 10:25:13 | 16 15 | 10 50 | 12 50 | 7 39 | 15 44 | 29 13 | 10 56 | 23 20 | 28 1 | 4 ♓ 58'44" |
| 28 FR | 10:29: 9 | 20 46 | 12 27 | 13 51 | 8 10 | 15 49 | 29 15 | 10 56 | 23 20 | 28 1 | 4 ♓ 58'43" |
| 29 SA | 10:33: 6 | 25 9 | 14 4 | 14 51 | 8 42 | 15 54 | 29 17 | 10 57 | 23 20 | 28 1 | 4 ♓ 58'43" |

### INGRESSES :

| | | | |
|---|---|---|---|
| 1 | ♀ → ♉ | 15:47 | |
| 3 | ☿ → ♈ | 11:15 | |
| 8 | ☿ → ♉ | 14:35 | |
| 12 | ♂ → ♏ | 5:36 | |
| 13 | ☿ → ♊ | 9:24 | |
| 14 | ⊕ → ♌ | 6:21 | |
| 18 | ☿ → ♋ | 6: 5 | |
| 20 | ♀ → ♊ | 7: 2 | |
| 23 | ☿ → ♌ | 15:48 | |

### ASPECTS (HELIOCENTRIC +MOON(TYCHONIC)) :

| | | | | |
|---|---|---|---|---|
| 1 ☽ ☌ ♅ 11:47 | ☽ ☍ ♄ 12: 4 | ☽ □ ♃ 15: 2 | ☽ ☍ ♀ 17:45 | 24 ☽ ☌ ♆ 19:15 |
| ♂ ☌ ☋ 18:20 | ☿ ☌ ☊ 13: 9 | 13 ☽ □ ♆ 12:56 | ☿ ☍ ♇ 21:54 | ☿ □ ♂ 23:15 |
| 2 ☽ ☍ ♂ 16:27 | 8 ☿ ☍ ♂ 6:41 | ☽ □ ♄ 14:22 | 18 ☿ ☍ ♄ 1:51 | 25 ♃ ☌ ☋ 22: 9 |
| 3 ☿ □ ♆ 2: 0 | ☽ □ ♅ 8:15 | ♄ ☌ ☋ 20:30 | 19 ☽ ☌ ♃ 5:35 | 26 ☿ ☌ ⊕ 1:43 |
| ☿ □ ♄ 4:40 | 9 ☽ □ ♂ 13:26 | 14 ☽ ☍ ♅ 10:21 | 20 ☿ □ ♅ 2:51 | ☽ □ ♀ 3:52 |
| ☽ ☌ ♀ 6:55 | 10 ☽ □ ☿ 9:21 | 15 ♀ ☌ ☊ 5:39 | ☽ ☌ ♆ 6:10 | ☽ □ ♃ 16:28 |
| 4 ☽ □ ♆ 21:40 | ☽ □ ♀ 14:41 | ☿ ☍ ♃ 18: 6 | ☽ ☌ ♄ 8:10 | 27 ☽ □ ♆ 17:24 |
| 5 ☿ ☌ ♅ 8:50 | 11 ☿ ☌ ♀ 0:39 | ☽ ☌ ♂ 22:40 | 21 ☽ □ ♅ 7: 6 | ☽ □ ♄ 19:53 |
| 6 ☽ ☍ ♃ 11: 1 | ☽ ☍ ♆ 4:47 | 16 ♀ □ ♆ 2:47 | 22 ☽ ☍ ☿ 6:15 | 28 ☿ ☍ ♆ 13:57 |
| 7 ☽ ☍ ♆ 10:52 | 12 ☿ ☌ P 5:53 | ⊕ □ ♂ 8:39 | ☿ ⊼ ☊ 10:11 | ☽ ☌ ♅ 19:30 |
| ☿ □ ⊕ 11:30 | ☿ □ ♆ 7:44 | 17 ☽ □ ♆ 12:58 | 23 ☽ □ ♂ 8: 5 | |

Francis, drew near to the statue to miraculously finish it. Instantaneously completed, the statue was enveloped in light brighter than the Sun and became animated as Our Queen and Mother entered into it singing the "Magnificat." This most lovely of all visions took place at 3 o'clock on the morning of January 16, 1611.

Our Lady specifically requested that her name be "Mary of Good Success of the Purification and Candlemas" and that this date, February 2, should be especially remembered since this date had always brought "great gifts and mercies" from Our Lady.

On Feb 2, 1611, the day of the formal institution of the official devotion, the good bishop bestowed upon Our Lady of Good Success the keys of the cloister and the crosier into the hands of the miraculous statue with great reverence and honor, [and] invoked her saying:

"My Lady, I deliver to Thee the Church... My Lady and my Mother, I deliver to Thee my soul. Open to me the doors of Heaven, for the life remaining to me is quite brief... Queen of Heaven and Earth, Thou who dost remain in Thy sanctuary governing Thy beloved flock, do not forget Thy poor children who are pilgrims on this Earth, exposed to falls at every step. Let Thy arm sustain us and let the sweet love of Thy maternal Heart console us in our deep tribulations."[9]

There are many other marvelous details to this story. For example, she prophesied that the dogma of papal infallibility would be instituted by the same Pope who would proclaim the dogma of the Immaculate Conception. This occurred in the nineteenth century, under Pope Pius IX. Interestingly, there are only two dogmas proclaimed by the Pope that are universally considered proclamations "*ex cathedra*" (i.e., infallible): the dogma of the Immaculate Conception of the Virgin Mary given through Pope Pius IX in 1854, and the dogma of the Assumption of the Virgin Mary given through Pope Pius XII in 1950.[10] It would seem that the (thus far rare) ability

of the Pope to speak as representative of the spiritual world is directly related to the establishment of the devotion to the Divine Feminine!

**February 3: Venus enters Pisces.**

> In losing, may loss be found,
> In winning may gain be lost,
> in comprehending seek to grasp
> And maintain in maintaining.
> Through coming to existence upraised,
> Through existing to become interlaced,
> May loss be gain in itself!

The first part of the year led us to be focused primarily on our aims and intentions, our imaginations, and our activities in the world. Toward the end of January, the forces of Venus came to the fore—and particularly in relationship to Mars and Neptune, Venus brings about an increased awareness of our inner life of feeling, of devotion, of interest in the other, and of self-sacrifice. Inversely, it can bring about an increased self-focus, illusion, vanity, jealousy and competitiveness. As Venus enters Pisces, we can remind ourselves that "winning"— i.e., true success—is not a matter of gain, whether in regard to money and possessions, or knowledge, or acclaim. True success is only possible when we cultivate our ability to be an open doorway for living water to flow through us. This opening can only be created through devotedly allowing life to *carve out* a space within us—gain does no good here.

**February 9: Mars enters Sagittarius.**

> Growth attains power of existence,
> In existence growth's power dies.
> Attainment concludes joyful striving
> In life's active force of will.
> World activity matures in dying,
> Forms vanish in reforming.
> May existence feel existence!

In addition to the influences of Venus taking on a greater role since the end of January, Mars also becomes a greater force in our lives. Mars is related to courage, morality, speech, and justice. Mars is no longer the God of War, but Michael, the Cosmic

---

9 Heckenkamp, Kathleen M. "Our Lady of Good Success," https://www.ourladyofgoodsuccess.com /pages/history.

10 Pope John Paul II. "The Holy Spirit Assists the Roman Pontiff" (1993).

Intelligence who slays the dragon of ease, complacency, confusion, and obstruction. At this time, Michael lends us the "active forces of will" to carry the Eternal Flame into the world.

**Full Moon 24°59' Cancer:** The Full Moon was close to this degree in Cancer January 7–8 AD 30:

> Jesus gave an instruction on gratitude. After the sabbath, Jesus returned to his mother, with whom he conversed alone far into the night. He spoke of his future movements: he would first go to the Jordan, then celebrate Passover at Jerusalem, afterward call his apostles, and make his public appearance. He predicted the persecution he should endure at Nazareth, alluded to his career after that, and explained in what way she and the other women should bear a part in it.[11]

This Full Moon encourages us to exercise foresight, but not in any vague or sweeping sense—to exercise attention to detail, detachment in the face of what will inevitably go wrong, yet courage to proceed. Crucial to all of this is active dialogue and collaboration with those with whom we live and work. The qualities of Venus in Pisces and Mars in Sagittarius bolster the openness and courage required.

Between February 10 and 18, Venus is square to the Node. The square is exact on **February 14: Venus 12° Pisces square Node 12° Gemini.** Venus and Node were square in the same signs of the Zodiac at the death of Mary the Silent on April 8 AD 30. Who was Mary the Silent? At the time of Christ, there were four siblings closely connected with him: Lazarus, the eldest; Martha the next eldest; Mary, whom they called "the Silent"; and finally Mary, the youngest, whom they called "Magdalene." Anne Catherine Emmerich describes this third child and sibling of Lazarus:

> Like the aged Essene Eliud of Nazareth—the type of the mystic living in contemplative solitude—we find among the holy women Lazarus's middle sister, *Silent Mary.* She has her own quarters with an enclosed garden on the grounds of the Bethany estate of Martha. Her family considers her mentally handicapped, but Jesus judges differently, telling Eliud, "She is not for this world, therefore is she now altogether secluded from it. But she has never committed a sin. If I should speak to her, she should perfectly comprehend the greatest mysteries."
>
> Jesus has with her two long private and very profound conversations, in which she speaks ecstatically of the mysteries of the Trinity and of the Incarnation. Jesus interrupts her now and then with a prayer of gratitude to the heavenly Father, then blesses her and predicts her impending liberation from earthly life; this occurs in April of AD 30, in the presence of the blessed Virgin and the other holy women.[12]

She goes on to describe the day of her death:

> Jesus kept the sabbath at Lazarus's, in Bethany, whither he had retired after the tumult occasioned by the cures wrought in the temple. After the sabbath, the Pharisees went to the house of Mary Mark in Jerusalem, thinking to find Jesus there and to take him into custody. They were, however, disappointed. They did not find him, but only his mother and the other holy women whom, as the followers of Jesus, they commended with harsh words to leave the city. The mother of Jesus and the other women became greatly troubled at hearing this, and in tears hurried to Martha in Bethany. Mary, weeping, entered the room wherein Martha was with her sick sister, Mary the Silent. The latter was again quite rapt in ecstasy. All that she had hitherto seen in spirit, she now beheld about to be fulfilled. She could no longer endure the pain it caused her, and she died in the presence of Mary, Mary Cleophas, Martha, and the other women.
>
> Nicodemus, in spite of the open persecution directed against Jesus, visited him during these days by invitation of Lazarus. I saw Jesus during the night reclining beside him on the ground and instructing him (John 3:1–21).[13]

Estelle Isaacson recounts the death of Silent Mary from another perspective:

---

11 Brentano, *The Visions of Anne Catherine Emmerich,* vol. 1, p. 393.

12 Ibid., p. 90.

13 Ibid., p. 424.

On the day Silent Mary died...[she] witnessed all that transpired from outside her body. Her thoughts went something like this:

*They did not know me; they did not know why I was here. I was nothing more than an afterthought, for rarely did anyone visit me or consider me...but I have no resentment. I know I was here as a channel for love, and to prepare Jesus for his path.*

I saw that by incarnating with Jesus, and by having so deep a connection with him, Silent Mary was able to follow him intimately as his apostle in the spirit—as one who witnessed everything Jesus did.

When Silent Mary crossed over the threshold, the Blessed Mother was with her, one hand on her head, the other over her heart. She blessed her and prayed for her continuously as Silent Mary stepped out from the physical and into the spiritual realm.

And then everything became so crystal clear to Silent Mary's soul. She rejoiced over the life she had lived. She was taken into the bosom of an angel. Wherever she traveled thereafter, and whatever she saw, she experienced from within the bosom of the angel.

Her soul contains the record of all that Jesus Christ did, for she saw it all...Jesus Christ and Silent Mary remained in communion with each other. She brought souls to him, both the departed and the living. She was so happy to be with him, working with him from the other side.[14]

Clearly, this aspect is accompanied by pain and sorrow. The sphere of Venus is expressed most archetypally in Christ's crucifixion—the highest outpouring of Love for the other, amid the greatest level of pain and sacrifice. It is this aspect of Venus which is exemplified here, both in the suffering of the holy women, as well as the painful death of Mary the Silent. On the other hand, the calming dynamic that can be created between Venus and Node is revealed to us in the illuminating nighttime conversation that took place subsequently between Nicodemus and Christ. Venus's dynamic tension with Node facilitated a baptism by water (Venus) and spirit (Node).

---

14 Isaacson, *Through the Eyes of Mary Magdalene,* vol. 1, pp. 245–246.

**February 14:** Sun enters Aquarius: **"May what is bounded yield to the boundless."** (See January 9 for full verse).

In the context of the above memories, the verse for Sun in Aquarius reveals itself in a new light. Nicodemus was bounded by the traditions, rites and expectations of the Hebrew leadership. His nighttime conversation with Christ forced him not just to reevaluate his core beliefs and attitudes, but threw him into a totally different way of experiencing the world—the way of Initiation, of being "born again." What was bounded in him (empty tradition) yielded to the boundless (Christ).

Similarly, Mary the Silent spent her entire life in the external bounds of developmental disability. She was seen as not just uneducated, but unteachable, by her family and culture. Yet within her lived the deepest mysteries of Christ. During her entire incarnation, an inner life was being cultivated that ultimately could not be contained by an earthly body. Her death, while externally tragic to those around her, was a triumph of the spirit—yielding to the boundless, she could finally experience her Self in its proper element.

At the end of January, we created bounds for ourselves in our depths. Like the gardener starting his seedlings, we had to take what came out of the Holy Nights and put it in a protective space for its healthy development. But like the seedling that is outgrowing its pot and requires transplanting, so too with our new initiatives for the year. Whatever has become too fixed or rigid in our inner or outer life—now is the time for it to fall away so that growth can proceed.

Between February 15 and 19, Mercury comes within 5° of Neptune in Aquarius. This approach is short-lived, as **Mercury stations retrograde on February 17–18, 17°52' Aquarius.** Mercury was at this degree on January 24–25 AD 33:

Jesus journeyed on with the three apostles and reached a strong castle (Alexandrium) surrounded by moats, or ponds with discharging channels attached. It seemed that there were baths here, and I saw all kinds of vaults and massive walls. When Jesus manifested his intention to enter the castle, the apostles made objections to his doing so. He might, they said, rouse indignation and give occasion for scandal. Jesus rejoined that if they did not want to accompany him, they should suffer him to enter alone, and so he went in. It contained all sorts of people, some of whom appeared to be prisoners, others sick and infirm. Guards were standing at the gates, for the inmates dared not go out alone. Several always went together and attended by a guard. They were obliged to work in the country around the castle, clearing the fields and digging trenches. When Jesus with the apostles attempted to pass through the gate, the guards stopped them, but at a word from him, they respectfully allowed him to enter. The inmates assembled around him in the courtyard, where he spoke with them and separated several from the rest. From the city, which was not far off, Jesus summoned two men who appeared to be officers of the law, for they had little metallic badges hanging on straps from their shoulders. Jesus spoke with them, and it looked as if he were giving bail for those that he had separated from the rest of the inmates. Later on, I saw him leaving the castle with five and twenty of those people, and with them and the apostles traveling up the Jordan the whole night. This hurried march brought him to a little city in which he restored to their wives and children several of the prisoners lately freed.[15]

Retrograde Mercury is a good time to go back and retrace our steps, to reassess our thoughts, feelings, and actions that may have been foolhardy or inconsiderate. Sometimes this takes boldness, and to others might seem like a fruitless or even dangerous activity. What or who has been imprisoned that shouldn't have been? How can we set them free?

At the same time that Mercury turns retrograde, Venus leaves behind the square relationship with the Node that lasted from February 10 to 18, and begins to come into square relationship with Jupiter, a tension that lasts from February 18 to 29. The square is exact on **February 23, Venus 23° Pisces square Jupiter 23° Sagittarius.** Mercury's retrograde turn, therefore, has to do with our devotional life (Venus) turning from the clarity of Spirit Beholding (Node) to the more grounded, but still creative, thinking activity of Jupiter. Venus square Node is inward; Venus square Jupiter turns with magnanimity toward the wider community, and begins forming a plan of action born from soul warmth and geniality.

Venus and Jupiter were square within 5° of their positions today on May 9–10, 810. May 9, 810 was Ascension Thursday. Important events took place in the days surrounding this Ascension Day. It was just a few days prior to this that Gawan had set free those kept under enchantment by Klingsor in his Chastel Marveille. After this adventure (on May 7), in spite of suffering great wounds, Gawan wished to win the love of the spiteful lady Orgeleuse. She was under the oppressive hand of King Gramoflanz, who Gawan challenged to a duel. Not only did Gawan wish to strike down Gramoflanz to win the love of Orgeleuse, Gramoflanz wished to take vengeance on Gawan. He wrongly believed that Gawan's father, King Lot, had murdered his father, Irot. And so they planned to meet for battle sixteen days later, on May 23.

Gawan sent a squire to the campgrounds of King Arthur and Queen Ginover in order to ask them for their aid in meeting Gramoflanz and his hosts in battle. The lad sets out the next morning, arriving on Ascension Thursday (May 9), and delivers the letter from Gawan to Ginover: "It was early of a morning when he took his errand in hand. The Queen was in chapel reading her psalter on bended knee. The squire knelt before her and offered her a joyful gift. She took the letter from his hand and saw writing on it which she recognized before the youth she saw kneeling there could name his lord."[16] Chapters 12 to 13 of Eschenbach's telling of the tale recount the events of this time period more fully.[17]

We can see quite clearly here what Venus in Pisces square Jupiter in Sagittarius can bring about—bold plans for the sake of love and redemption!

---

15 Brentano, *The Visions of Anne Catherine Emmerich,* vol. 2, pp. 525–26.

16 Eschenbach, Wolfram von. *Parzival,* p. 323.

17 Joel Park, "First Steps Toward a Grail Timeline," *Cosmology Reborn: Star Wisdom,* vol 1.

**February 23: New Moon 9° Aquarius.** As Venus reaches the exact square with Jupiter, a New Moon occurs in Aquarius. Once again we can orient our inner life to the cosmic realms of the Father and Daughter (Divine Sophia) in the Heights. The Moon makes an opening in the spiral for the influences of the transpersonal planets to shine through (Uranus, Neptune, Pluto). Mercury was recently making his approach to Neptune, but drew back. Something in the subconscious depths is not ready to be brought to consciousness. Looking ahead, we can see both Jupiter and Venus coming into relationship with Pluto after their square (see below). It is time for joyful self-sacrifice to be amplified to a much higher degree.

A New Moon in Aquarius (with Mercury and Neptune close by) occurred on January 19 AD 33. Christ had been on a four month long journey south to Egypt, and was just returning to Israel at this time—specifically to Ephraim, the region of Jacob's Well. Anne Catherine Emmerich writes:

> On the journey...Jesus did not confine himself to the straight route. He went to different localities, different towns and houses, consoling the inhabitants, healing the sick, and exhorting all to follow him. The apostles and disciples likewise did not take the direct road to the places to which they were sent, but turned off into the farms and houses lying along their way in order to announce Jesus's coming. It was as if all who sighed after salvation were to be again stirred up, as if the sheep that had strayed in the forest had come back, to be gathered again by the shepherd servants into one herd.[18]

A similar mood prevails here as to that of the memory of Gawan above—a gathering in and gathering together, of reuniting in order to set the stage for what needs to come next. Take note that this New Moon occurs within 1° of the meridian of the megastar Deneb, one of the most powerful megastars in the galaxy, at 10° Aquarius. The Sun was aligned with this megastar at the miracle of the Feeding of the Five Thousand, an event that, perhaps more strongly than any other, captures

the majesty and magnanimity of gathering up and gathering in—true communion of love.

Right now, with the Sun, Mercury, Moon and Neptune all in Aquarius, a "Hermetic Conversation" is taking place to which we can also have access, and to which we can contribute. Its goal is the spontaneous emergence from the spiritual depths of the human being what can take form as sacred art, sacred science, and sacred ritual in the world.

As the month of February comes to a close, Venus and Jupiter maintain their square alignment, and other planetary relationships come to the aid of their impulse to reach out in love to the wider community. From February 19 to March 3, Mars comes into opposition with the Node. This is exact on **February 25, Mars 11° Sagittarius opposite Node 11° Gemini.** Note that we now have Mars, Saturn, Pluto *and* Jupiter all within 30° of each other—quite the stellium! (On the 19th and 20th, the Moon was with them as well). Michael (Mars) comes to the defense of Mary (Saturn) on behalf of the Father (Pluto) so she can become the mediatrix for the Holy Spirit (Jupiter). A true cosmic drama!

Mars in Sagittarius opposed Node in Gemini on February 17 AD 30:

> ...Jesus taught in the school of Chisloth. Andrew instructed the children in an adjacent hall, and recounted to the strangers crowding in all that he had seen and heard of Jesus. Jesus took for his subject vanity and presumption. He performed no cures that day because, as he said, they thought themselves better than others, and attributed to their own merit his coming to teach in their city; whereas he would have them know that he had been led thereto by his knowledge of their misery and his desire to humble and convert them.
>
> The preaching ended, Jesus went out into the court in front of the synagogue, in which there were little cells belonging to it. They were like sentry boxes in a courtyard. Here, he cured of convulsions and other ills numerous children brought to him by their mothers. He cured them because they were innocent. He cured several women also who humbled themselves before him,

---

18 Brentano, *The Visions of Anne Catherine Emmerich,* vol. 2, p. 523.

saying: "Lord, hearken to my fault, my transgression!" They cast themselves down in the hall before him and bewailed their sins. Among them were some afflicted with an issue of blood, and others tormented by evil inclinations from which they implored to be freed.[19]

Let us take heed of the warning of this day in the life of Christ, and of Mars opposite Node: beware of vanity and presumption. Become like a little child, practice humility and accurate self-knowledge, especially of shortcomings and imbalances. Ask of others the healing question: "Can you help me?"

During the same time period that Mars is opposite Node and Venus square Jupiter, the Sun and Mercury come into Inferior Conjunction. They are close to conjunction between February 23 and 28; **the Inferior Conjunction of Sun and Mercury is exact on February 26, Ash Wednesday, 11°50' Aquarius.** During a Superior Conjunction, the Sun is in between the Earth and Mercury; Mercury spends time on the far side of the Sun, communicating with the wider starry spheres. During an Inferior Conjunction, Mercury is between the Sun and Earth; he sends down as new ideas, impulses and intuitions that which he has gathered up during his time on the far side of the Sun.

Interestingly, there were no Inferior Conjunctions in Aquarius during Christ's ministry. A Superior Conjunction occurred in Aquarius on February 15 AD 31. Three days prior saw Christ's healing of the Syrophoenician woman:

[Christ] was followed by an old pagan woman from Ornithopolis, who was crippled on one side…she begged him to come and heal her daughter, who was possessed. Jesus replied that it was not yet time…Later that afternoon, [she] approached Jesus and again begged him to drive the unclean spirit out of her daughter. There then followed the exorcism of her daughter, as described in Matthew 15:21–28. Jesus asked her whether she herself wished to be healed, but the Syrophoenician woman replied that she was not worthy, and that she asked only for her daughter's cure. Then Jesus laid one hand upon her head, the other upon her side, and said: "Straighten up! May it be done to you as you also will it to be done! The devil has gone out of your daughter." The woman stood upright and cried out: "O Lord, I see my daughter lying in bed well and at peace!"[20]

This healing occurred on February 12. On February 15, Christ and his disciples made the hours-long journey northwest to Ornithopolis to be hosted by the Syrophoenician woman and her daughter in gratitude for Christ's healing of their afflictions. This woman was a widow of a wealthy merchant in a pagan city; the two women threw a magnificent banquet in Christ's honor, inviting the local elderly Jews to their pagan feast as a sign of peace. Christ and his followers were showered with expensive gifts by the two women, gifts which they sold, giving the money to the poor. The daughter, who had been healed of possession which brought about convulsions and violent spells, honored Christ in particular: "During the meal, the lady with her daughter and relatives entered to give thanks for the cures wrought among them, their servants following with presents in ornamented caskets, which they bore between them on tapestry. The daughter, veiled, stepped behind Jesus, broke a little vial of precious ointment over his head, and then modestly returned to her mother."[21]

During the Superior Conjunction, we recalled the Pharisees excoriating Christ for casting out demons; today we remember one who was set free of her demons showing the highest honor to Christ. Today is Ash Wednesday, marking the beginning of the trials of Lent leading up to the joy of Easter. We can only honor that which is higher than ourselves if we exercise humility. The meditation for Ash Wednesday is, "Remember you are dust, and to dust you shall return." Ruminate on the multivalent meanings of this phrase today, so that you are prepared to honor that which is highest rather than tearing it down.

As Mars comes into opposition with the Node, and the Inferior Conjunction takes place with the

---

19 Ibid., vol. 1, p. 406.

20 Ibid., p. 309.
21 Ibid., p. 311.

Moon close by, the square alignment of Venus with Jupiter begins to dissolve. The rapidly paced Venus comes into square alignment with Pluto between February 24 and March 4; this square alignment is exact on **February 28, Venus 29° Pisces square Pluto 29° Sagittarius.** Once again, our inner gaze is drawn to the events of January 19 AD 33 (see entry for the New Moon in Aquarius above). The sacrificial gesture of Venus is working dynamically with the Fire of Love: Pluto, the Empyrean.

The slower moving Jupiter begins to come into conjunction with Pluto beginning on February 28. They are within 5° of each other until August 27, with exact alignments occurring on both April 5 and June 30. Due to retrograde movement, they move apart from each other after August 27. However, they are once again in alignment between September 22 and December 13, with a final exact conjunction on November 12. Heliocentrically, they are within 5° of each other from May 29 to October 2, with the exact alignment occurring July 31.

The year begins with the historically harrowing conjunction of Saturn and Pluto. As Saturn moves *out* of conjunction with Pluto, Jupiter moves *into* conjunction with Pluto. The combination of these two forces is completely different than that of Saturn and Pluto. Pluto has the effect of amplification and magnification when it aligns with another planet. When it comes to Saturn, the qualities of heaviness, rigidity, death, conscience, and fortitude are amplified to an uncomfortable degree. However, the pendulum swings almost in the complete opposite direction when it comes to Jupiter. Jupiter has to do with wisdom, creativity, generosity, magnanimity, and geniality. Jupiter is expansion in contrast to Saturnine contraction.

Conjunctions of Pluto and Jupiter happen every 12 to 13 years; the last time they were conjunct was between 2007 and 2008. We remember this time as one of blossoming hope in the possibilities of the united effort of groups of conscientious people. A positive energy permeated the country. Yet at the same time, the double of the Jupiter–Pluto conjunction cropped up—inflation, megalomania, mass consciousness that lacks discernment of barely perceptible subterranean currents influencing outer appearances. The danger is that addressed by the Anonymous author of *Meditations on the Tarot* in both the Letter Meditation on the 15th Arcanum, The Devil, and the 22nd Arcanum, The World: putting joy before truth, and allowing intoxication produced by addiction to positive feelings to hold sway rather than the three vows of obedience, poverty, and chastity.

The gesture of 2020 is a movement from the almost unbearable trials that come with Saturn–Pluto conjunctions, to the joy of overcoming the trials—and the danger of megalomania that comes with triumph—in the middle portion of the year, during the Jupiter–Pluto conjunction. Finally, the year ends with the magnificent Great Conjunction of Saturn and Jupiter, a meeting that always portends great cultural shifts. After swinging from one end of the pendulum to the other, humanity is given the opportunity by the cosmic movements to reach a place of Balance between the Severity of Saturn and the Mercy of Jupiter.

**February 29:** Venus enters Aries

> Arise, O shining light,
> Take hold of growth's being,
> lay hold of forces weaving.
> Ray out awakening life.
> In face of resistance, succeed—
> In stream of time, recede,
> O shining light, abide!

We began the month with Venus entering Pisces, with the reminder that true success involves the loss of gain. Now we end the month with Venus's ingress into the constellation Aries. Venus in Pisces may have given us the feeling of being between a rock and a hard place, of needing to make uncomfortable choices. As Venus moves into Aries, we may experience a feeling not only of relief, but of jubilation. Taking hold of growth's being takes us into the realm of eternal childhood, of innocence and joy.

# MARCH 2020

## STARGAZING PREVIEW

On the 2nd, the First Quarter Moon, slightly above and to the left of *Aldeberan*, the eye of the Bull, will be overhead as the Sun sets at 1800. On the following day, Venus will square Saturn, though they won't be visible at the same time: in the southwest at sunset, Venus will drift under the horizon at about 2130, while Saturn rises in the east at 0430, two hours before dawn.

Our March Full Moon on the 9th, at 25° Leo—its position at the birth of Rudolf Steiner—will have the night sky to itself between the setting of Venus (2230) and the rising of Mars (0430). And, as night follows day, so does the Last Quarter Moon appear about a week after the Full Moon. The Moon on the 16th, in the last degree of Scorpio, will rise into a planet-free sky at about 0230, beginning its Last Quarter phase a few hours later, from the first degree of the Archer.

The 18th will be a very special day as the Moon passes Mars, Jupiter, and Saturn! Getting up early will be worth your while, so bundle up, fill your mug, and head out the door: the Moon will rise at 0400, and within forty minutes, Mars, Jupiter, and Saturn will follow it in a tight cluster. All four will be at nearly the same declination and within eight zodiacal degrees of each other. And, by the time Saturn rises, the Moon will have passed Mars. Truly, it's unusual to have so much "show" packed into forty minutes!

On Friday the 20th, Mars and Jupiter will be conjunct at 28° Sagittarius; they rise at 0400, less than a half hour before Saturn. The New Moon on the 24th (9° Pisces) means that the night sky will be without planets between 2300 and 0400; Leo will be visible throughout this time.

Sunset on the 27th will reveal the Moon below and to the right of Venus (29° Aries). On the following evening, the Moon will have just moved into Taurus and will therefore be to Venus's left. The planet of love will reach the Bull early on the 29th. Finally, on the 31st, Mars will pass above Saturn at 6° Capricorn. Early in the morning, before the conjunction, you'll be able to see them rise—Mars slightly ahead of Saturn at about 0340.

You'll find Orion high in the southwest at sunset; the Hunter will set at 0100.

## MARCH COMMENTARIES

We ended the previous month with Venus and Jupiter moving out of square alignment. Mars came into opposition with the Node; Sun and Mercury reached Inferior Conjunction; and finally, first Venus and then Jupiter came into alignment with Pluto. Slower moving Jupiter will take a few months to come into exact conjunction with Pluto; on the other hand, Venus's square alignment with Pluto will only last through March 4 of this month. At the same time, due to the continuing proximity of Saturn and Pluto, Venus also comes into square alignment with Saturn between February 27 and March 8. The square is exact on **March 3, Venus 3° Aries square Saturn 3° Capricorn**. Venus's journey continues: first, in square to Jupiter, it remembered the time of Parzival, and the gathering together of the Arthurian Knights. Then, in square to Pluto, it remembered Christ's homecoming from his journeys in Egypt, once again a gesture of gathering many different souls together in a kind of reunion. Now, Venus is square Saturn. A highly devotional mood can be created in the dynamic tension between the Crucified Christ (Venus) and the Virgin Mary (Saturn). Venus was square Saturn as Christ *began* the journey to Egypt with three youths and about a dozen shepherds. This star memory took place on September 17 AD 32, about a week into their journey, and just a few days before they reached Mensor, the Gold King:

> This journey was a very lonely one, for on the whole length of the route they did not meet one dwelling house. The road was, however, distinctly marked out, and there was no chance of the traveler's losing his way in the desert. Trees lined the roadside bearing edible fruits the size of figs, and here and there were found berries. At certain points, marking one day's journey, resting places were formed. They consisted of a covered well surrounded by trees, whose tops were drawn together in a large hoop, their hanging

branches thus forming an arbor. These resting places were furnished with conveniences for making a fire and passing the night. During the great noonday heat, Jesus and the youths rested at one of these wells and refreshed themselves with some fruit. Each time they thus paused on their journey, Jesus and the youths washed one another's feet. The Lord never permitted any of the others to touch him. The youths, drawn by his goodness, at times treated Jesus with child-like confidence, but again, when they thought of his miracles, his divinity, they cast timid and frightened glances toward him and looked at one another.[22]

Our path has been made straight before us. Comfort and restoration is ready at hand. A mood of absolute security, yet holy awe, almost dread, permeates the spiritual atmosphere.

As the square alignment between Saturn and Venus begins to loosen, the Sun and Neptune begin to come into conjunction. This is exact on **March 8, Sun conjunct Neptune 23° Aquarius.** This is a powerful meeting; the Sun, who embodies the Transcendent Self and the Resurrected Christ, comes into direct contact with Neptune, the Goddess Night, the wellspring of Inspiration. We see these two planets working most powerfully, most archetypally on August 16 AD 44, at the Assumption of the Virgin Mary:

I saw a broad pathway of light descend from Heaven and rest upon the tomb. In it were circles of glory full of angels, in the midst of whom the resplendent soul of the blessed Virgin came floating down. Before her went her divine Son, the marks of his wounds flashing with light. In the innermost circle, that which surrounded the holy soul of Mary, the angels appeared like the faces of very young children; in the second circle, they were like those of children from six to eight years old; and in the outermost, like the faces of youths, I could clearly distinguish only the face, the rest of the figure consisting of perfectly transparent light. Encircling the head of the blessed Virgin like a crown was a choir of blessed spirits. I know not what those present saw of all this. But I saw that some gazed up in amazement and adoration, while others cast themselves prostrate in fright upon the Earth. These apparitions, becoming more and more distinct as they approached nearer, floated over the grotto, and another pathway of light issued from it and arose to the Heavenly Jerusalem. The blessed soul of Mary, floating before Jesus, penetrated through the rock and into the tomb, out of which she again arose radiant with light in her glorified body and, escorted by the entire multitude of celestial spirits, returned in triumph to the Heavenly Jerusalem.[23]

At this event, Neptune was very close to where it is in Aquarius today, while the Sun was opposite in Leo. We are being carried from the respite and renewal brought forth from the Venus and Saturn square into something more like a resurrection. Simultaneous with this aspect between Sun and Neptune comes the conjunction between Venus and Uranus, which builds from March 4 until it too becomes exact on **March 8, Venus conjunct Uranus 8°58' Aries,** with the conjunction staying close until March 13. These two planets were conjunct between July 25 and 26 AD 32—the seventh archetypal healing miracle of Christ, the Raising of Lazarus from the Dead:

At that instant Jesus raised his eyes to Heaven, prayed aloud, and called out in a strong voice: "Lazarus, come forth!" At this cry, the corpse arose to a sitting position....Lazarus, as if waking from lethargy, rose from the coffin and stepped out of the grave, tottering and looking like a phantom...Like one walking in sleep, he approached the door, passed the Lord and went out to where his sisters and the other women had stepped back in fright as before a ghost. Without daring to touch him, they fell prostrate on the ground. At the same instant, Jesus stepped after him out of the vault and seized him by both hands, his whole manner full of loving earnestness....

Lazarus moved along more like one floating than walking, and he still had all the appearance of a corpse. Jesus walked by his side...At this moment, Lazarus threw himself prostrate on the Earth before Jesus, like one about to be

---

22 Ibid., pp. 499–500.

23 Ibid., vol. 3, p. 427.

SIDEREAL GEOCENTRIC LONGITUDES :     MARCH 2020 Gregorian at 0 hours UT

| DAY | ☉ | ☽ | ☊ | ☿ | ♀ | ♂ | ♃ | ♄ | ⛢ | ♆ | ♇ |
|---|---|---|---|---|---|---|---|---|---|---|---|
| 1 SU | 15♒51 | 25♈11 | 10♊49R | 7♒47R | 0♈25 | 14♐18 | 24♐31 | 3♑9 | 8♈40 | 23♒6 | 29♐14 |
| 2 MO | 16 51 | 7♉22 | 10 47 | 6 51 | 1 31 | 14 59 | 24 42 | 3 14 | 8 42 | 23 8 | 29 16 |
| 3 TU | 17 51 | 19 49 | 10 47D | 6 1 | 2 38 | 15 41 | 24 53 | 3 20 | 8 45 | 23 10 | 29 17 |
| 4 WE | 18 51 | 2♊35 | 10 47 | 5 17 | 3 44 | 16 22 | 25 4 | 3 26 | 8 47 | 23 13 | 29 18 |
| 5 TH | 19 51 | 15 47 | 10 47R | 4 39 | 4 50 | 17 4 | 25 15 | 3 32 | 8 50 | 23 15 | 29 20 |
| 6 FR | 20 51 | 29 28 | 10 45 | 4 8 | 5 56 | 17 45 | 25 26 | 3 37 | 8 52 | 23 17 | 29 21 |
| 7 SA | 21 51 | 13♋38 | 10 42 | 3 44 | 7 1 | 18 27 | 25 36 | 3 43 | 8 55 | 23 19 | 29 23 |
| 8 SU | 22 51 | 28 16 | 10 35 | 3 26 | 8 7 | 19 8 | 25 47 | 3 48 | 8 58 | 23 22 | 29 24 |
| 9 MO | 23 51 | 13♌18 | 10 26 | 3 16 | 9 12 | 19 50 | 25 57 | 3 54 | 9 0 | 23 24 | 29 25 |
| 10 TU | 24 51 | 28 34 | 10 15 | 3 11 | 10 16 | 20 31 | 26 7 | 3 59 | 9 3 | 23 26 | 29 27 |
| 11 WE | 25 51 | 13♍53 | 10 4 | 3 14D | 11 21 | 21 13 | 26 17 | 4 4 | 9 6 | 23 28 | 29 28 |
| 12 TH | 26 51 | 29 4 | 9 54 | 3 22 | 12 25 | 21 54 | 26 27 | 4 9 | 9 8 | 23 31 | 29 29 |
| 13 FR | 27 51 | 13♎57 | 9 46 | 3 36 | 13 28 | 22 36 | 26 37 | 4 15 | 9 11 | 23 33 | 29 30 |
| 14 SA | 28 51 | 28 25 | 9 41 | 3 55 | 14 32 | 23 18 | 26 47 | 4 20 | 9 14 | 23 35 | 29 32 |
| 15 SU | 29 51 | 12♏25 | 9 38 | 4 19 | 15 35 | 23 59 | 26 57 | 4 25 | 9 17 | 23 38 | 29 33 |
| 16 MO | 0♓50 | 25 58 | 9 37 | 4 48 | 16 38 | 24 41 | 27 6 | 4 30 | 9 19 | 23 40 | 29 34 |
| 17 TU | 1 50 | 9♐5 | 9 37 | 5 22 | 17 40 | 25 23 | 27 16 | 4 35 | 9 22 | 23 42 | 29 35 |
| 18 WE | 2 50 | 21 51 | 9 37 | 6 0 | 18 42 | 26 4 | 27 25 | 4 39 | 9 25 | 23 44 | 29 36 |
| 19 TH | 3 50 | 4♑20 | 9 35 | 6 42 | 19 44 | 26 46 | 27 34 | 4 44 | 9 28 | 23 47 | 29 37 |
| 20 FR | 4 49 | 16 36 | 9 31 | 7 27 | 20 46 | 27 28 | 27 43 | 4 49 | 9 31 | 23 49 | 29 38 |
| 21 SA | 5 49 | 28 42 | 9 23 | 8 16 | 21 47 | 28 9 | 27 52 | 4 53 | 9 34 | 23 51 | 29 39 |
| 22 SU | 6 48 | 10♒42 | 9 13 | 9 9 | 22 47 | 28 51 | 28 1 | 4 58 | 9 37 | 23 53 | 29 40 |
| 23 MO | 7 48 | 22 37 | 9 0 | 10 4 | 23 48 | 29 33 | 28 10 | 5 2 | 9 40 | 23 55 | 29 41 |
| 24 TU | 8 47 | 4♓30 | 8 46 | 11 2 | 24 47 | 0♑14 | 28 18 | 5 7 | 9 43 | 23 58 | 29 42 |
| 25 WE | 9 47 | 16 22 | 8 31 | 12 3 | 25 47 | 0 56 | 28 27 | 5 11 | 9 46 | 24 0 | 29 43 |
| 26 TH | 10 46 | 28 15 | 8 17 | 13 7 | 26 46 | 1 38 | 28 35 | 5 15 | 9 49 | 24 2 | 29 44 |
| 27 FR | 11 46 | 10♈9 | 8 5 | 14 13 | 27 44 | 2 19 | 28 43 | 5 20 | 9 52 | 24 4 | 29 45 |
| 28 SA | 12 45 | 22 6 | 7 55 | 15 21 | 28 42 | 3 1 | 28 52 | 5 24 | 9 56 | 24 7 | 29 46 |
| 29 SU | 13 45 | 4♉10 | 7 49 | 16 32 | 29 40 | 3 43 | 28 59 | 5 28 | 9 59 | 24 9 | 29 47 |
| 30 MO | 14 44 | 16 23 | 7 45 | 17 44 | 0♉37 | 4 24 | 29 7 | 5 32 | 10 2 | 24 11 | 29 47 |
| 31 TU | 15 43 | 28 49 | 7 44 | 18 59 | 1 34 | 5 6 | 29 15 | 5 35 | 10 5 | 24 13 | 29 48 |

### INGRESSES :

| | | | |
|---|---|---|---|
| 1 | ☽→♉ | 9:32 | |
| 3 | ☽→♊ | 19:11 | |
| 6 | ☽→♋ | 0:55 | |
| 8 | ☽→♌ | 2:47 | |
| 10 | ☽→♍ | 2:14 | |
| 12 | ☽→♎ | 1:28 | |
| 14 | ☽→♏ | 2:39 | |
| 15 | ☉→♓ | 3:45 | |
| 16 | ☽→♐ | 7:18 | |
| 18 | ☽→♑ | 15:36 | |
| 21 | ☽→♒ | 2:35 | |
| 23 | ☽→♓ | 14:53 | |
| | ♂→♑ | 15:47 | |
| 26 | ☽→♈ | 3:32 | |
| 28 | ☽→♉ | 15:45 | |
| 29 | ♀→♉ | 8:23 | |
| 31 | ☽→♊ | 2:16 | |

### ASPECTS & ECLIPSES :

| | | |
|---|---|---|
| 2 | ☉□☽ | 19:56 |
| 3 | ♀□♄ | 16:43 |
| 4 | ☽☌☊ | 14:59 |
| 5 | ☽☍♂ | 2:23 |
| | ☽☍♃ | 16:54 |
| | ☽☍♆ | 23:48 |
| 6 | ☽☍♄ | 7:10 |
| 8 | ☽☍♀ | 8:11 |
| | ☉☌♆ | 12:31 |
| | ♀☌⛢ | 19:35 |
| 9 | ☽☍♆ | 15:56 |
| | ☉☍☽ | 17:46 |
| 10 | ☽☌P | 6:45 |
| | ☽⛢☊ | 18: 5 |
| 12 | ☽☍⛢ | 16:12 |
| | ☽☍♀ | 23: 9 |
| 16 | ☉□☽ | 9:33 |
| 17 | ☽☌♅ | 0:58 |
| 18 | ☽☌♂ | 8:31 |
| | ☽☌♃ | 10:46 |
| | ♀☌♇ | 14:52 |
| 19 | ☽☌♄ | 0:47 |
| 20 | ♂☌♃ | 11:34 |
| 21 | ☽☌☿ | 20:37 |
| 23 | ☽☌♆ | 2:38 |
| | ☉☌♀ | 5:11 |
| | ☉□♇ | 23:27 |
| 24 | ☽⛢☊ | 8:25 |
| | ☉☌☽ | 9:27 |
| | ☽☌A | 15:14 |
| 26 | ☽☌⛢ | 23:27 |
| 28 | ☽☌♀ | 14:19 |
| 31 | ☽☌☊ | 16:52 |
| | ♂☌♄ | 18:30 |

SIDEREAL HELIOCENTRIC LONGITUDES :     MARCH 2020 Gregorian at 0 hours UT

| DAY | Sid. Time | ☿ | ♀ | ⊕ | ♂ | ♃ | ♄ | ⛢ | ♆ | ♇ | Vernal Point |
|---|---|---|---|---|---|---|---|---|---|---|---|
| 1 SU | 10:37: 3 | 29♌24 | 15♊42 | 15♌51 | 9♏13 | 15♐59 | 29♐19 | 10♈58 | 23♒21 | 28♐2 | 4♓58'43" |
| 2 MO | 10:40:59 | 3♍31 | 17 19 | 16 52 | 9 45 | 16 4 | 29 20 | 10 58 | 23 21 | 28 2 | 4♓58'43" |
| 3 TU | 10:44:56 | 7 30 | 18 56 | 17 52 | 10 17 | 16 9 | 29 22 | 10 59 | 23 21 | 28 2 | 4♓58'43" |
| 4 WE | 10:48:52 | 11 22 | 20 33 | 18 52 | 10 48 | 16 14 | 29 24 | 11 0 | 23 22 | 28 3 | 4♓58'43" |
| 5 TH | 10:52:49 | 15 8 | 22 10 | 19 52 | 11 20 | 16 19 | 29 26 | 11 0 | 23 22 | 28 3 | 4♓58'43" |
| 6 FR | 10:56:45 | 18 47 | 23 48 | 20 52 | 11 52 | 16 24 | 29 28 | 11 1 | 23 22 | 28 3 | 4♓58'42" |
| 7 SA | 11: 0:42 | 22 21 | 25 25 | 21 52 | 12 24 | 16 29 | 29 29 | 11 2 | 23 23 | 28 3 | 4♓58'42" |
| 8 SU | 11: 4:38 | 25 49 | 27 2 | 22 52 | 12 56 | 16 34 | 29 31 | 11 2 | 23 23 | 28 4 | 4♓58'42" |
| 9 MO | 11: 8:35 | 29 13 | 28 39 | 23 52 | 13 28 | 16 39 | 29 33 | 11 3 | 23 24 | 28 4 | 4♓58'42" |
| 10 TU | 11:12:32 | 2♎32 | 0♋17 | 24 52 | 14 0 | 16 44 | 29 35 | 11 3 | 23 24 | 28 4 | 4♓58'42" |
| 11 WE | 11:16:28 | 5 40 | 1 54 | 25 52 | 14 32 | 16 49 | 29 37 | 11 4 | 23 24 | 28 5 | 4♓58'42" |
| 12 TH | 11:20:25 | 8 57 | 3 32 | 26 52 | 15 4 | 16 54 | 29 39 | 11 5 | 23 25 | 28 5 | 4♓58'42" |
| 13 FR | 11:24:21 | 12 4 | 5 9 | 27 52 | 15 37 | 16 59 | 29 40 | 11 5 | 23 25 | 28 5 | 4♓58'41" |
| 14 SA | 11:28:18 | 15 8 | 6 46 | 28 51 | 16 9 | 17 4 | 29 42 | 11 6 | 23 25 | 28 6 | 4♓58'41" |
| 15 SU | 11:32:14 | 18 9 | 8 24 | 29 51 | 16 41 | 17 9 | 29 44 | 11 7 | 23 26 | 28 6 | 4♓58'41" |
| 16 MO | 11:36:11 | 21 7 | 10 1 | 0♍51 | 17 14 | 17 14 | 29 46 | 11 7 | 23 26 | 28 6 | 4♓58'41" |
| 17 TU | 11:40: 7 | 24 3 | 11 39 | 1 51 | 17 46 | 17 19 | 29 48 | 11 8 | 23 26 | 28 6 | 4♓58'41" |
| 18 WE | 11:44: 4 | 26 56 | 13 16 | 2 50 | 18 19 | 17 24 | 29 49 | 11 9 | 23 27 | 28 7 | 4♓58'41" |
| 19 TH | 11:48: 1 | 29 48 | 14 54 | 3 50 | 18 51 | 17 29 | 29 51 | 11 9 | 23 27 | 28 7 | 4♓58'41" |
| 20 FR | 11:51:57 | 2♏38 | 16 31 | 4 50 | 19 24 | 17 34 | 29 53 | 11 10 | 23 28 | 28 7 | 4♓58'41" |
| 21 SA | 11:55:54 | 5 27 | 18 9 | 5 49 | 19 57 | 17 39 | 29 55 | 11 11 | 23 28 | 28 8 | 4♓58'40" |
| 22 SU | 11:59:50 | 8 14 | 19 46 | 6 49 | 20 30 | 17 44 | 29 57 | 11 11 | 23 28 | 28 8 | 4♓58'40" |
| 23 MO | 12: 3:47 | 11 1 | 21 24 | 7 49 | 21 2 | 17 49 | 29 59 | 11 12 | 23 29 | 28 8 | 4♓58'40" |
| 24 TU | 12: 7:43 | 13 46 | 23 1 | 8 48 | 21 35 | 17 54 | 0♑0 | 11 13 | 23 29 | 28 9 | 4♓58'40" |
| 25 WE | 12:11:40 | 16 32 | 24 39 | 9 48 | 22 8 | 17 59 | 0 2 | 11 13 | 23 30 | 28 9 | 4♓58'40" |
| 26 TH | 12:15:36 | 19 16 | 26 16 | 10 47 | 22 41 | 18 4 | 0 4 | 11 14 | 23 30 | 28 9 | 4♓58'40" |
| 27 FR | 12:19:33 | 22 1 | 27 54 | 11 46 | 23 14 | 18 9 | 0 6 | 11 15 | 23 30 | 28 9 | 4♓58'40" |
| 28 SA | 12:23:30 | 24 46 | 29 31 | 12 46 | 23 47 | 18 14 | 0 8 | 11 15 | 23 30 | 28 10 | 4♓58'39" |
| 29 SU | 12:27:26 | 27 31 | 1♌9 | 13 45 | 24 21 | 18 19 | 0 9 | 11 16 | 23 31 | 28 10 | 4♓58'39" |
| 30 MO | 12:31:23 | 0♐16 | 2 46 | 14 45 | 24 54 | 18 24 | 0 11 | 11 17 | 23 31 | 28 10 | 4♓58'39" |
| 31 TU | 12:35:19 | 3 2 | 4 24 | 15 44 | 25 27 | 18 29 | 0 13 | 11 17 | 23 32 | 28 11 | 4♓58'39" |

### INGRESSES :

| | | |
|---|---|---|
| 1 | ☿ → ♍ | 3:28 |
| 9 | ☿ → ♎ | 5:38 |
| | ♀ → ♋ | 19:51 |
| 15 | ⊕ → ♍ | 3:29 |
| 19 | ☿ → ♏ | 1:40 |
| 23 | ♄ → ♑ | 18:51 |
| 28 | ♀ → ♌ | 7: 3 |
| 29 | ☿ → ♐ | 21:41 |

### ASPECTS (HELIOCENTRIC +MOON(TYCHONIC)) :

| | | |
|---|---|---|
| 1 | ♀☌♃ | 4:35 |
| 2 | ☽☌♂ | 4:50 |
| 3 | ☽□♆ | 6:44 |
| 4 | ☽□☿ | 22:22 |
| 5 | ☽☌♃ | 0:57 |
| | ☿□♃ | 7:54 |
| | ☽☌♀ | 12:50 |
| | ☽☍♇ | 21:33 |
| | ☽☍♄ | 23:59 |
| 6 | ☽□⛢ | 19:38 |
| 8 | ⊕☍♆ | 12:31 |
| 1 | ☿☌♀ | 15:14 |
| | ☿□♆ | 15:48 |
| | ☿□♀ | 16:20 |
| 9 | ☽□♂ | 0:16 |
| | ☿□♄ | 2:26 |
| | ♀☍♄ | 13:28 |
| | ♂☌♅ | 15:53 |
| 11 | ☽☌♃ | 4:37 |
| | ☽□♆ | 22:25 |
| 12 | ☽□♄ | 0:54 |
| | ☿☌♀ | 16:24 |
| | ☽☍⛢ | 19:19 |
| | ☽☌☿ | 20: 6 |
| 15 | ☽☌♂ | 7:47 |
| | ☽□♆ | 19:27 |
| 16 | ♇□⛢ | 16:24 |
| 17 | ☽☌♃ | 15:29 |
| 18 | ☽☌♆ | 11:58 |
| 19 | ☽□⛢ | 13:19 |
| | ☽☍♀ | 23:49 |
| 20 | ♀☌P | 4:31 |
| 21 | ☽□♄ | 17:34 |
| 22 | ☽□♂ | 20:39 |
| 23 | ☽☌♀ | 1:43 |
| 25 | ☽☌♃ | 3:16 |
| 26 | ☽□♀ | 3:41 |
| 27 | ☽☌⛢ | 2:13 |
| | ☿☌A | 6:24 |
| | ☉□♀ | 11:35 |
| | ☿□♀ | 13: 1 |
| | ☿☌♂ | 13:23 |
| 28 | ☽□♀ | 17: 6 |
| 30 | ☽□♆ | 13:51 |
| | ☽☍♂ | 17:15 |
| 31 | ☽☍♀ | 10:17 |

received into a religious order.... Jesus laid his right hand on his head and breathed upon him seven times. The Lord's breath was luminous. I saw a dark vapor withdrawing as it were from Lazarus, and the devil under the form of a black winged figure, impotent and wrathful, clearing the circle backward and mounting on high. By this ceremony, Jesus consecrated Lazarus to his service, purified him from all connections with the world and sin, and strengthened him with the gifts of the Holy Spirit.[24]

We enter fully into the power and mystery of resurrection with this aspect. Uranus has a Promethean energy, like a bolt of celestial lightning, or a comet. Combined with the devotional self-sacrifice and feminine emollient action of Venus, it is like an alchemical marriage of water and fire. The potential is laid for powerful deeds of love during this week leading up to March 13.

**March 9: Full Moon, 24° Leo.** This Full Moon occurs with Neptune and the Sun still within 1° of each other. The Full Moon occurred close to these degrees, with Neptune just ingressing into Aquarius, on February 2–3 AD 33. On the 2nd, Christ cured a possessed youth who had been abused by his parents:

When Jesus again commanded the possessed to come to him, he did so and cast himself full length at his feet. Jesus passed over him twice, first one foot and then the other, as if treading him underfoot, and I saw rising from the open mouth of the possessed a black spiral vapor which disappeared in the air. In this rising exhalation I remarked three knots, the last of which was the darkest and strongest. These three knots were connected together by one strong thread and many finer ones. I can compare the whole thing to nothing better than to three censers one above the other, whose clouds of smoke, issuing from different openings, at last united with one another.[25]

And on the 3rd: "One man affected with edema he stroked over the head and body with his hand, and the swelling immediately went down. The water poured from his whole person in a stream of perspiration."[26] Today, we may find that emotions we have been bottling up will be able to find a healthy release; problems we haven't been able to solve can be taken into the night, and new solutions may arise as we wake. Have the boldness to take advantage of this opportunity for the suture to be applied so that healing can begin.

**March 12: Mercury stations direct 3°26' Aquarius.** Mercury was at this degree on January 16–17 AD 33, just as Christ was returning from his months-long expedition to Egypt to visit the two surviving Magi with three youths Eliud, Silas, and Eremenzear:

As Jesus was journeying with the new disciples from the shepherd village..., I frequently saw him standing still and giving them animated instructions. He ordered Eliud, Silas, and Eremenzear to disclose to no one where they had gone with him nor what had befallen them on that journey, and he told them some of the reasons for silence on those subjects. I saw Eremenzear holding the sleeve of Jesus's robe and begging to be allowed to write down something about it. Jesus replied that he might do so after his death, but ordered him at the same time to leave the writing with John. I cannot help thinking that a part of that writing is still in existence somewhere.[27]

Later, when the four of them had rejoined the twelve apostles, Emmerich sees that "Jesus was displeased at the apostles' desire to find out from the three youths where he had been and what he had done. They were much vexed at the youths' silence on being questioned."[28]

Aquarius carries the virtue of meditative power that is born of discretion. Especially when it comes to Mercury, who in his lower aspect is a trickster, a liar, and a swindler with a loose tongue, we are reminded at this time to watch our speech. Right speech is true, necessary, kind, and clear, and delivered to the right person at the right time. Take care!

---

24 Ibid., vol. 2, p. 479.
25 Ibid., p. 529.
26 Ibid., p. 529.
27 Ibid., p. 522.
28 Ibid., p. 523.

**March 15: Sun enters Pisces. "In losing, may loss be found."** (See February 3 for the full verse)

The first line of the verse of Pisces, focusing on the Sun, invites us to an experience related to the second line, related to Venus: "In winning, may gain be lost." These two lines are like two sides of the same coin. Here we are challenged to recognize that losing is not a failure. It is not just a way, but *the* way to discover loss. The experience of loss is crucial for human development, on every level. Without the concrete experience of loss, we make no room for that which is new to take form within us. Nature abhors a vacuum, but Spirit abhors a fullness. The miracle, the presence of the Spirit, can only occur via loss.

As we move into the second quarter of the year on March 19–20 with the Spring Equinox, let's take stock of where we have been and where we are going. We began the year by pointing out the proximity of Saturn and Pluto, and the intensity that can be called forth by the combined forces of their spheres. At first, Jupiter and the Descending Node were close by, but as the year has worn on, Jupiter has drawn closer to Pluto and Saturn, and the Descending Node (which regresses through the signs) has moved farther away from aspecting these other three slow moving phenomena.

The Descending Node, Jupiter, Saturn, and Pluto are all more or less straddling the signs of Sagittarius and Capricorn during this time period. Therefore, this becomes a potent region of the starry heavens: as other faster moving planets pass through this boundary between the two signs, they aspect all four of these slower moving phenomena, each activating different modes of expression particular to their own archetypal being. At the beginning of the year, we experienced the Sun and Mercury passing through this Sagittarius–Capricorn boundary. The archetypal forces of the Node, Jupiter, Saturn, and Pluto were living more so in the regions of the "I" (Sun) and Thinking (Mercury). This period of digesting the previous year, and envisioning and planning the coming year, dominated the end of 2019 up through late January.

In the latter half of January, Mars (Willing) and Venus (Feeling) came into square alignment. Faster moving Venus then proceeded to aspect all of the slower moving planets, including Neptune in Aquarius and Uranus in Aries. This time period sets the stage for us to develop the feminine side enhanced by Venus: on an internal level, submerging our inner life to depths of feeling rather than keeping it merely intellectual–conceptual; and on an external level, reaching out in dialogue to the wider community, expressing our needs and striving to hear and meet the needs of others. This culminated in the Venus–Uranus conjunction on March 8.

We now approach the third level of experience around the Sagittarius–Capricorn boundary. Mars, the bearer of masculine energy, follows more slowly after the Sun, Mercury, and Venus. We experience Mars on an outer level in practical and creative deeds, and on an inner level in the experience of contrition. The two meet in the realm of moral courage. While there is certainly an active side to Venus, she is primarily enhancing the realm of emotional depth; and while there is an inner aspect to Mars, he is primarily enhancing the realm of action, of *doing*. It is this Mars energy that prevails from approximately the middle of March through the beginning of April. We exit winter and enter spring with might.

Between March 11 and 29, Mars is close to conjunction with Jupiter. On **March 20, Mars is exactly conjunct Jupiter, 27°43' Sagittarius.** An awesome spiritual energy can be harnessed in the meeting of these two, especially in the realm of the Archer. Think of a mighty and generous King meeting once again with his most trusted Knight after two years apart. Note that these energies are "awesome" and not necessarily good or bad—e.g., think on the other hand of a tyrant meeting once again with his most trusted attack dog! Beware megalomania and aggression during this time; strive to uphold your royal inheritance as a son or daughter of the Gods, and cleave to the Knight's standard of courage, fidelity, and righteousness.

Some star memories that can aid us in steering these energies in the right directions: first of all, the events of January 17 AD 31. On this day, the disciples steeled themselves to retrieve the remains of John the Baptist (all but his head, which was not retrieved until months later) from Herod's castle. It took great courage for them to enter the "belly of the beast," and should have been quite an arduous task; yet their way was made clear through the aid of the discarnate spirit of Elizabeth, the mother of John. All went miraculously smoothly. They then proceeded with many others (including the Essenes) to hold a funeral service and burial for John the Baptist. Truly a magnanimous deed of courage!

Mars and Jupiter were conjunct almost exactly opposite today's degree, in Gemini, on April 19–20 AD 33. This was the heart of the 40 days that Christ spent with his followers after his Resurrection. This time period represents clearly the power and majesty accompanying the Mars–Jupiter conjunction.

Finally, Mars and Jupiter were conjunct on Whitsun day, May 25, 804. This was around the time that Parzival more or less single-handedly defended the besieged city of Belrepeire (modern day Montpellier), winning the hand of the lady Condwiramurs. After the victory, on Whitsun, Arthur came with his retinue for a celebration of both the victory and the marriage of Parizival and Condwiramurs. Once again, a prime example of deeds of courage born of love! (See Chapter 4 of Eschenbach's *Parzival* for a full account).

After and during the conjunction with Jupiter, from March 15 to 30, Mars is close to conjunction with Pluto. This is exact on **March 23, Mars conjunct Pluto 29°41' Sagittarius.** Simultaneously, the Sun is square the Node between March 19 and 28. This is also exact on **March 23, Sun 8°46' Pisces square Node 8°46' Gemini.** Remarkably, both of these aspects, in the same signs of the Zodiac, were present along with a New Moon in Pisces between February 21 and 24 AD 30. The **New Moon, 9°11' Pisces occurs on March 24.**

Specifically, the New Moon occurred on February 21. On this day, Christ was teaching in a fruitful valley south of Jezreel, an "uncommonly productive and charming fruit region."[29] An abundant spring formed in this valley, over which a chapel had been built; from this main spring, many others branched off, until finally flowing into the Jordan River. The poor people who, living in tents, were the custodians of the orchards in this valley, were overjoyed and touched that Christ would bother to visit with such humble people. Some guiding images from the opening in the spiral of the New Moon in Pisces might be: flowing springs of water; abundant fruitful valleys; humility and gratitude.

Christ and his disciples then traveled from the valley below Jezreel to the hillside town of Shunem. It is this day that is remembered by Mars conjunct Pluto:

> The multitude that here pressed around Jesus was simply astonishing, and it was ever on the increase. The people surrounded him everywhere, cast themselves down before him, crying and shouting that a new prophet had arisen, one sent by God! Many were sincere in their acclamations, but others followed through curiosity and shouted merely to swell the noise. The crowd was so dense that it was almost like an insurrection, and because here in Galilee the excitement was daily increasing, Jesus resolved soon to leave it….
>
> When Jesus, on the morning of the following day, started with his disciples for the teacher's chair, the whole place was alive with excitement. They had brought numbers of sick in liters, and had placed them all along the road leading up the hill. Jesus ascended through the clamoring multitude, healing as he went. The people had mounted to the roofs, the better to see and hear all that he would do and say. From the teacher's chair on the top of the hill the view was magnificent, stretching off toward Tabor. Jesus inveighed against the pride and presumption of the Shumenites who, instead of being converted, doing penance, and keeping the commandments of God, broke forth into vain shouts over the prophet that had come among them, sent from God, for they attributed his coming as an honor due their own merit, whereas he had come in order to convince them of their sins.[30]

---

29 Ibid., vol. 1, p. 407.

30 Ibid., pp. 407–408.

We see here the dark side of the Mars–Pluto energy: vanity, insurrection, and the overzealous masses. On the other hand, we see the positive side in the admonitions of Christ. The square alignment of Sun and Node remembers the following day, February 24, when Christ moved on to the more modern and Romanized city of Ulama. Here he healed the sick and possessed, and was met with somewhat more restrained turbulence. He continued in his severe rebuke of vanity and pride, teaching on the value of simplicity, respect for one's parents, and the benefits of penance and instruction.

Our lesson during these latter days of March: beware of vanity and pride; cultivate simplicity, humility, and gratitude.

**March 23: Mars enters Capricorn. "Through inward life-withstanding…"** (See Jan. 13–15 for the full verse)

Mars in Capricorn is all about composure. We can bring to our imagination the 7th Arcanum, The Chariot. Is the Charioteer in this image effortlessly guiding the horses pulling his chariot? Why isn't he holding the reins? Has he dropped them due to lack of full consciousness, or distraction? Or does he have such an intuitive relationship with the horses that he doesn't need them? We can bring this Arcanum into conversation with the 17th Arcanum, The Star. With the effortless innocence and wonder of the small child, the woman in The Star maintains the flow of water from the two vases into the greater stream. May the Charioteer be imbued with this same effortless composure!

**March 25: Christian Celebration of the Feast of the Annunciation.** Today marks the celebration of the second major Marian festival after Candlemas, the Feast of Purification. We remember the Archangel Gabriel appearing to the Virgin Mary, revealing to Mary that in nine months she would become the Virgin Mother of God. We can meditate upon Mary's words at this occasion: *"Ecce ancilla Domini; mihi fiat secundum verbum tuum"* (Behold I am the handmaid of the Lord; let it be to me according to your word, Luke 1:38). These words contain the fundamental Arcanum (i.e., the Key to the Mystery) of Sacred Magic.

**March 29:** Venus enters Taurus.

> Become bright, radiant being,
> Feel growth's power.
> Weave life's thread
> In creative world existence,
> In thoughtful relation,
> In shining life contemplation.
> O radiant being, appear!

We might combine these two mantra into one: "Through inward life-withstanding, feel growth's power." At first, keeping ourselves (that is, our impulsive–instinctual nature) in check feels like an affront to a feeling we usually associate with freedom. The feeling that has largely become associated with freedom in the modern age is generally nothing more than licentiousness, the ability to do whatever we feel like, as soon as possible. In truth, this is the opposite of freedom. If a plant were to grow wherever and however it pleased, rather than toward the Sun, it would never raise itself above the compost heap. Growth's power resides in the rhythmic alteration of expansion and contraction, toward a specific aim. This is what we begin to be able to experience through self-mastery: the ability to open ourselves up completely at times to the joy and pleasure offered by life, while at other times effortlessly reining ourselves in and cultivating a rich, devotional inner life. The experience of mastering the capacity to keep oneself in check stops feeling like a chore or a torment, and begins to feel like what it is: the practice of true freedom.

After Mars ingresses into Capricorn, it begins to draw near to Saturn. They are in close proximity from March 23 to April 7.

**Mars and Saturn are conjunct on March 31, 5°35' Capricorn.** Mars and Saturn were conjunct on April 30 AD 29. During this time in the life of Christ, his father Joseph had just died, less than a month prior. It was around this time that John the Baptist first emerged from the wilderness to proclaim the coming of Christ. Saturn, as the classical planet with the longest and slowest journey around the

Sun, could be thought of as the "highest" of the visible planets. Especially in the sign of Capricorn, the Goat (a sign in which she is at home) we can imagine her as being on a great height, her gaze extending all around her. It is hindsight, insight, and foresight that belong to her—these three together are Wisdom. On the other hand, Mars has everything to do with speaking and listening, with the bringing into manifestation of Truth via the Word. Both Saturn and Mars, however, have to do with morality and conscience. When they join together in Capricorn, they seem to announce the time of a new infusion of Truth and Wisdom from beyond the stream of time, *into* this stream of time. For example, over the course of the twentieth century Mars and Saturn were conjunct in Capricorn at the turn of 1903–04, when Rudolf Steiner first began to publish his spiritual scientific discoveries; between 1932 and 1934, when Valentin Tomberg began to publish his Anthroposophic meditations on the Bible; in 1962, when the Anonymous author was hard at work on the 22 Letter Meditations on the Major Arcana of the Tarot of Marseilles; and in 1992, the year that the inspiration to establish the Sophia Foundation first came into being. What might this year's meeting of Mars and Saturn in Capricorn be heralding? "Change your thinking, for the time is at hand!"

# APRIL 2020

## STARGAZING PREVIEW

The month begins and ends with a First Quarter Moon; on the 1st, the 17° Gemini Moon will set around 0200, two hours before Jupiter, Saturn and Mars rise in a seven-degree cluster that spans the last degree of Sagittarius and the first six of Capricorn. Pluto is right there, too, but is of course invisible to the naked eye. Sunset's at 1930, and Venus, still an evening star, sets four hours later.

Jupiter moves into Capricorn on the 6th. Late on Tuesday the 7th, the Full Virgo Moon will be high in the southeast at midnight. Jupiter will rise into the night sky three hours later.

The 14th brings the Last Quarter Moon (0° Capricorn), which will pass by Jupiter that same evening. At 0230 the following morning, Jupiter will rise first, followed by the waning Moon, then Saturn and Mars. Also on the 15th, the Moon will find Saturn, followed by the Moon–Mars conjunction early on the 16th. Before the Sun rises around 0630, look up, because this stellium, Jupiter–Saturn–Mars–Moon, will be high in the south. You might even get a peek at Mercury, which will be up and about in the east 45 minutes before the Sun.

April's New Moon will occur late on the 22nd, at 8° Aries, and, rest assured, Uranus will be right there with them, at 11°! Spica (29° Virgo), Mary's star, will be roughly overhead, high in the south, at midnight. And speaking of the night of the 22nd, this will be the peak of the Lyrid meteor showers! If you're checking them out at midnight, look to the northeast. These showers are particularly special because they originate from a comet discovered in 1861, the year of Rudolf Steiner's birth. On the 26th, the Moon will sail below Venus at 22° Taurus; later, Venus will set first, at 2300.

The month ends with its second First Quarter Moon, this time at 16° Cancer; Jupiter and Saturn rise just before the Moon sets. You'll be able to see Orion for only a few hours after sunset; Venus will be above the Hunter, aligned with *Rigel*, the star marking his left foot—as the Sun was at the Ascension.

## APRIL COMMENTARIES

Starting on the last day of March, two different aspects begin to take shape over the course of the first two weeks of April. Between March 31 and April 17, Mercury is conjunct Neptune; this aspect is exact on **April 4, Mercury conjunct Neptune 24°22' Aquarius**. At the same time, between March 31 and April 15, Mars comes into square alignment with Uranus; this alignment is exact on **April 7, Mars 10° Capricorn square Uranus 10° Aries**. While both of these powerful alignments are coming in and out of focus, the Jupiter–Pluto conjunction that has been building since late February culminates in an exact conjunction on **April 5, Palm Sunday, Jupiter conjunct Pluto 29°52' Sagittarius**.

Let's look first at the conjunction of Mercury and Neptune. These two planets were conjunct, albeit in Capricorn, on January 29 AD 31, after the fourth miracle of the Feeding of the Five Thousand, and during the fifth miracle of the Walking on Water. What a perfect image for the meeting of these two archetypal beings—Mercury, the wing-footed messenger (Walking) with Neptune, the unfathomable ocean (Water) of spiritual depth on the one hand, and the yet-to-be integrated forces of the unconscious on the other. Anne Catherine Emmerich describes this miracle:

> …Jesus walked on the sea in a direction from northeast to southwest. He was shining with light. Rays darted from him, and one could see his image reversed in the water under his feet…He appeared to be gliding along more rapidly than in ordinary walking, and wherever he approached, the sea became calm. But a fog rested upon the water, so that he could be seen only at a certain distance. Although they had once before seen him thus walking, still the unusual and specter-like sight filled them with terror, and they uttered a great cry.
>
> Jesus allowed Peter to come to him on the water in order to humble him, for he knew very well that he was going to sink. Peter was very fiery and strong in believing, and in his zeal he wanted to give a testimony of his faith to Jesus and the disciples. By his sinking, he was preserved from pride. The others had not sufficient confidence to wish to follow his example and, while wondering at Peter's faith, they could see that although it excelled their own it was not yet what it ought to be.[31]

As the time of Lent, a time of trial, winds to a close, let us continue to strive for boldness in our thoughts, words, and actions. At the same time, let us strive to have gratitude for our lack of complete success, as this is a sure protection against the dangers of inflation and self-glorification.

The day after this exact conjunction of Mercury and Neptune, April 5, is **Palm Sunday.** It is very fitting that there is a Jupiter–Pluto conjunction on this day: during the entirety of the time period from the actual Palm Sunday (which occurred on

---

31 Ibid., vol. 2, p. 301.

Thursday, March 19 AD 33, over two weeks prior to Easter) until Easter Sunday, Jupiter and Pluto were in opposition, with Pluto in Sagittarius like it is today, and Jupiter in Gemini. Palm Sunday, Good Friday, and Easter Sunday each show a different side of the multifaceted reality of the meeting of the beings of Jupiter and Pluto. Pluto tends to magnify the qualities of whatever planet it aspects. On Palm Sunday we see the kingly aspect of Jupiter magnified in Christ's entry to Jerusalem; we see the magnanimity of Jupiter magnified in the joyous rapture of the crowd. On the other hand, on Good Friday we see more of the lower, Hades aspect of Pluto coming to the fore: the unredeemed forces of the unconscious rumbling up through the masses (still related to Jupiter, in the aspect of expansiveness). This mob-consciousness resulted in a guilty murderer going free so that the innocent God–Man could be put to death. Finally, on Easter Sunday we see a kind of union of these two prior manifestations on a more sublime level: Christ returns to life as the true, heavenly King, rather than in the illusory role of temporal king which was bestowed on him on Palm Sunday by the masses. The very deed that facilitated this true return of the King was the overcoming and redemption of the Underworld (Pluto). We can carry the mood of the Jupiter–Pluto conjunction with us for the entirety of the Holy Week, as we relive the eight archetypal memories of each day:

| | |
|---|---|
| Sunday: | Palm Sunday |
| Monday: | Cleansing of the Temple |
| Tuesday: | Enmity of the Pharisees |
| Wednesday: | Magdalene's Last Anointing |
| Thursday: | Last Supper and Betrayal |
| Friday: | The Passion |
| Saturday: | Harrowing of Hell |
| Sunday: | Resurrection |

On the Tuesday of Holy Week, April 7, Mars and Uranus are exactly square. These two planets were very close to square alignment during the Wedding at Cana, and came into exact alignment a few days after the miracle of the Changing of Water into Wine: January 2 AD 30. We can almost see the blinding light of Uranus (the pure white "water" of

SIDEREAL  GEOCENTRIC  LONGITUDES :     APRIL  2020  Gregorian at 0 hours UT

| DAY | ☉ | ☽ | ☊ | ☿ | ♀ | ♂ | ♃ | ♄ | ♅ | ♆ | ♇ |
|---|---|---|---|---|---|---|---|---|---|---|---|
| 1 WE | 16 ♓ 42 | 11 ♊ 32 | 7 ♊ 44R | 20 ♒ 16 | 2 ♉ 30 | 5 ♑ 48 | 29 ♐ 22 | 5 ♑ 39 | 10 ♈ 8 | 24 ♒ 15 | 29 ♐ 49 |
| 2 TH | 17 42 | 24 38 | 7 44 | 21 34 | 3 25 | 6 30 | 29 30 | 5 43 | 10 12 | 24 17 | 29 50 |
| 3 FR | 18 41 | 8 ♋ 10 | 7 43 | 22 55 | 4 20 | 7 11 | 29 37 | 5 46 | 10 15 | 24 19 | 29 50 |
| 4 SA | 19 40 | 22 10 | 7 39 | 24 17 | 5 14 | 7 53 | 29 44 | 5 50 | 10 18 | 24 22 | 29 51 |
| 5 SU | 20 39 | 6 ♌ 38 | 7 33 | 25 41 | 6 8 | 8 35 | 29 51 | 5 53 | 10 21 | 24 24 | 29 52 |
| 6 MO | 21 38 | 21 32 | 7 25 | 27 7 | 7 1 | 9 16 | 29 58 | 5 57 | 10 25 | 24 26 | 29 52 |
| 7 TU | 22 37 | 6 ♍ 44 | 7 15 | 28 34 | 7 53 | 9 58 | 0 ♑ 5 | 6 0 | 10 28 | 24 28 | 29 53 |
| 8 WE | 23 36 | 22 4 | 7 4 | 0 ♓ 3 | 8 44 | 10 40 | 0 11 | 6 3 | 10 31 | 24 30 | 29 53 |
| 9 TH | 24 35 | 7 ♎ 21 | 6 54 | 1 34 | 9 35 | 11 21 | 0 17 | 6 6 | 10 35 | 24 32 | 29 54 |
| 10 FR | 25 34 | 22 23 | 6 46 | 3 6 | 10 25 | 12 3 | 0 24 | 6 9 | 10 38 | 24 34 | 29 54 |
| 11 SA | 26 33 | 7 ♏ 3 | 6 40 | 4 40 | 11 15 | 12 45 | 0 30 | 6 12 | 10 41 | 24 36 | 29 55 |
| 12 SU | 27 32 | 21 14 | 6 37 | 6 15 | 12 3 | 13 27 | 0 36 | 6 15 | 10 45 | 24 38 | 29 55 |
| 13 MO | 28 30 | 4 ♐ 56 | 6 36 | 7 52 | 12 51 | 14 8 | 0 41 | 6 18 | 10 48 | 24 40 | 29 56 |
| 14 TU | 29 29 | 18 10 | 6 36D | 9 31 | 13 38 | 14 50 | 0 47 | 6 20 | 10 52 | 24 42 | 29 56 |
| 15 WE | 0 ♈ 28 | 0 ♑ 59 | 6 37R | 11 11 | 14 24 | 15 32 | 0 52 | 6 23 | 10 55 | 24 44 | 29 56 |
| 16 TH | 1 27 | 13 28 | 6 36 | 12 53 | 15 9 | 16 13 | 0 58 | 6 25 | 10 58 | 24 46 | 29 57 |
| 17 FR | 2 25 | 25 42 | 6 33 | 14 36 | 15 53 | 16 55 | 1 3 | 6 28 | 11 2 | 24 48 | 29 57 |
| 18 SA | 3 24 | 7 ♒ 44 | 6 28 | 16 21 | 16 36 | 17 37 | 1 8 | 6 30 | 11 5 | 24 49 | 29 57 |
| 19 SU | 4 23 | 19 40 | 6 21 | 18 8 | 17 18 | 18 18 | 1 12 | 6 32 | 11 9 | 24 51 | 29 57 |
| 20 MO | 5 21 | 1 ♓ 32 | 6 11 | 19 56 | 17 59 | 19 0 | 1 17 | 6 34 | 11 12 | 24 53 | 29 57 |
| 21 TU | 6 20 | 13 23 | 6 0 | 21 46 | 18 39 | 19 42 | 1 21 | 6 36 | 11 16 | 24 55 | 29 58 |
| 22 WE | 7 18 | 25 15 | 5 48 | 23 37 | 19 17 | 20 23 | 1 25 | 6 38 | 11 19 | 24 57 | 29 58 |
| 23 TH | 8 17 | 7 ♈ 11 | 5 37 | 25 30 | 19 55 | 21 5 | 1 30 | 6 40 | 11 22 | 24 59 | 29 58 |
| 24 FR | 9 15 | 19 10 | 5 28 | 27 25 | 20 31 | 21 46 | 1 33 | 6 42 | 11 26 | 25 0 | 29 58 |
| 25 SA | 10 14 | 1 ♉ 16 | 5 20 | 29 21 | 21 6 | 22 28 | 1 37 | 6 43 | 11 29 | 25 2 | 29 58 |
| 26 SU | 11 12 | 13 29 | 5 15 | 1 ♈ 19 | 21 40 | 23 9 | 1 41 | 6 45 | 11 33 | 25 4 | 29 58R |
| 27 MO | 12 11 | 25 52 | 5 13 | 3 18 | 22 12 | 23 51 | 1 44 | 6 46 | 11 36 | 25 6 | 29 58 |
| 28 TU | 13 9 | 8 ♊ 26 | 5 13D | 5 20 | 22 43 | 24 32 | 1 47 | 6 48 | 11 40 | 25 7 | 29 58 |
| 29 WE | 14 7 | 21 15 | 5 14 | 7 22 | 23 12 | 25 14 | 1 50 | 6 49 | 11 43 | 25 9 | 29 58 |
| 30 TH | 15 6 | 4 ♋ 22 | 5 15 | 9 26 | 23 40 | 25 55 | 1 53 | 6 50 | 11 47 | 25 10 | 29 58 |

### INGRESSES :

2 ☽ → ♋ 9:36  
4 ☽ → ♌ 13:5  
6 ♃ → ♑ 7:20  
  ☽ → ♍ 13:25  
7 ☿ → ♓ 23:11  
8 ☽ → ♎ 12:26  
10 ☽ → ♏ 12:22  
12 ☽ → ♐ 15:15  
14 ☉ → ♈ 12:36  
  ☽ → ♑ 22:7  
17 ☽ → ♒ 8:32  
19 ☽ → ♓ 20:54  
22 ☽ → ♈ 9:34  
24 ☽ → ♉ 21:29  
25 ☿ → ♈ 7:57  
27 ☽ → ♊ 7:57  
29 ☽ → ♋ 16:3

### ASPECTS & ECLIPSES :

1 ☉ □ ☽ 10:20  
2 ☽ ☍ ♃ 8:47  
  ☽ ☍ ♆ 9:18  
  ☽ ☍ ♄ 19:48  
  ☽ ☍ ♂ 22:12  
4 ☿ ☌ ♆ 1:20  
5 ♃ ☌ ♆ 1:52  
6 ☽ ☍ ♆ 4:37  
  ☽ ☍ ☿ 9:47  
7 ☽ ⊡N ☊ 0:48  
  ☽ ☌ P 18:13  

  ♂ □ ♅ 18:46  
8 ☉ ☍ ☽ 2:34  
9 ☽ ☍ ♅ 5:8  
11 ☽ ☍ ♀ 7:26  
12 ☿ □ ☊ 5:23  
13 ☽ ☌ ☋ 2:58  
14 ☉ □ ♇ 11:0  
  ☽ ☌ ♇ 22:0  
  ☉ □ ☽ 22:55  
  ☽ ☌ ♃ 23:46  
15 ☽ ☌ ♄ 10:19  

  ☉ □ ♃ 10:58  
16 ☽ ☌ ♂ 5:40  
19 ☽ ☌ ♆ 10:31  
20 ☽ ⊡S ☊ 9:17  
  ☽ ☌ A 18:49  
21 ☉ □ ♄ 6:59  
  ☽ ☌ ☿ 20:4  
23 ☉ ☌ ☽ 2:24  
  ☽ ☌ ♅ 8:27  
25 ☿ □ ♇ 7:32  
26 ☿ □ ♃ 4:30  

  ☉ ☌ ♅ 8:58  
  ☽ ☌ ♀ 16:37  
27 ☽ ☌ ☊ 17:53  
28 ☿ □ ♄ 17:26  
29 ☽ ☍ ♆ 15:59  
  ☽ ☍ ♃ 19:28  
30 ☽ ☍ ♄ 4:26  
  ☉ □ ☽ 20:37

SIDEREAL  HELIOCENTRIC  LONGITUDES :     APRIL  2020  Gregorian at 0 hours UT

| DAY | Sid. Time | ☿ | ♀ | ⊕ | ♂ | ♃ | ♄ | ♅ | ♆ | ♇ | Vernal Point |
|---|---|---|---|---|---|---|---|---|---|---|---|
| 1 WE | 12:39:16 | 5 ♐ 49 | 6 ♌ 1 | 16 ♍ 43 | 26 ♏ 0 | 18 ♐ 34 | 0 ♑ 15 | 11 ♈ 18 | 23 ♒ 32 | 28 ♐ 11 | 4 ♓ 58'39" |
| 2 TH | 12:43:12 | 8 37 | 7 39 | 17 42 | 26 34 | 18 39 | 0 17 | 11 19 | 23 32 | 28 11 | 4 ♓ 58'39" |
| 3 FR | 12:47: 9 | 11 26 | 9 16 | 18 41 | 27 7 | 18 44 | 0 19 | 11 19 | 23 33 | 28 12 | 4 ♓ 58'39" |
| 4 SA | 12:51: 5 | 14 17 | 10 54 | 19 41 | 27 41 | 18 49 | 0 20 | 11 20 | 23 33 | 28 12 | 4 ♓ 58'38" |
| 5 SU | 12:55: 2 | 17 10 | 12 31 | 20 40 | 28 14 | 18 54 | 0 22 | 11 21 | 23 33 | 28 12 | 4 ♓ 58'38" |
| 6 MO | 12:58:59 | 20 5 | 14 9 | 21 39 | 28 48 | 18 59 | 0 24 | 11 21 | 23 34 | 28 12 | 4 ♓ 58'38" |
| 7 TU | 13: 2:55 | 23 1 | 15 46 | 22 38 | 29 22 | 19 4 | 0 26 | 11 22 | 23 34 | 28 13 | 4 ♓ 58'38" |
| 8 WE | 13: 6:52 | 26 1 | 17 24 | 23 37 | 29 55 | 19 9 | 0 28 | 11 23 | 23 34 | 28 13 | 4 ♓ 58'38" |
| 9 TH | 13:10:48 | 29 2 | 19 1 | 24 36 | 0 ♐ 29 | 19 14 | 0 29 | 11 23 | 23 35 | 28 13 | 4 ♓ 58'38" |
| 10 FR | 13:14:45 | 2 ♑ 7 | 20 39 | 25 34 | 1 3 | 19 19 | 0 31 | 11 23 | 23 35 | 28 14 | 4 ♓ 58'38" |
| 11 SA | 13:18:41 | 5 16 | 22 16 | 26 33 | 1 37 | 19 24 | 0 33 | 11 25 | 23 36 | 28 14 | 4 ♓ 58'37" |
| 12 SU | 13:22:38 | 8 27 | 23 53 | 27 32 | 2 11 | 19 29 | 0 35 | 11 25 | 23 36 | 28 14 | 4 ♓ 58'37" |
| 13 MO | 13:26:34 | 11 43 | 25 31 | 28 31 | 2 45 | 19 34 | 0 37 | 11 26 | 23 36 | 28 15 | 4 ♓ 58'37" |
| 14 TU | 13:30:31 | 15 2 | 27 8 | 29 30 | 3 19 | 19 39 | 0 39 | 11 27 | 23 37 | 28 15 | 4 ♓ 58'37" |
| 15 WE | 13:34:28 | 18 26 | 28 45 | 0 ♎ 29 | 3 53 | 19 44 | 0 40 | 11 27 | 23 37 | 28 15 | 4 ♓ 58'37" |
| 16 TH | 13:38:24 | 21 55 | 0 ♍ 22 | 1 27 | 4 27 | 19 49 | 0 42 | 11 28 | 23 37 | 28 15 | 4 ♓ 58'37" |
| 17 FR | 13:42:21 | 25 29 | 2 0 | 2 26 | 5 2 | 19 54 | 0 44 | 11 29 | 23 38 | 28 16 | 4 ♓ 58'37" |
| 18 SA | 13:46:17 | 29 8 | 3 37 | 3 25 | 5 36 | 19 59 | 0 46 | 11 29 | 23 38 | 28 16 | 4 ♓ 58'37" |
| 19 SU | 13:50:14 | 2 ♒ 53 | 5 14 | 4 23 | 6 10 | 20 4 | 0 48 | 11 30 | 23 38 | 28 16 | 4 ♓ 58'36" |
| 20 MO | 13:54:10 | 6 44 | 6 51 | 5 22 | 6 45 | 20 9 | 0 49 | 11 31 | 23 39 | 28 17 | 4 ♓ 58'36" |
| 21 TU | 13:58: 7 | 10 42 | 8 28 | 6 20 | 7 19 | 20 14 | 0 51 | 11 31 | 23 39 | 28 17 | 4 ♓ 58'36" |
| 22 WE | 14: 2: 3 | 14 47 | 10 5 | 7 19 | 7 54 | 20 19 | 0 53 | 11 32 | 23 40 | 28 17 | 4 ♓ 58'36" |
| 23 TH | 14: 6: 0 | 18 59 | 11 42 | 8 18 | 8 29 | 20 24 | 0 55 | 11 33 | 23 40 | 28 18 | 4 ♓ 58'36" |
| 24 FR | 14: 9:57 | 23 19 | 13 19 | 9 17 | 9 3 | 20 29 | 0 57 | 11 33 | 23 40 | 28 18 | 4 ♓ 58'36" |
| 25 SA | 14:13:53 | 27 47 | 14 56 | 10 14 | 9 38 | 20 34 | 0 59 | 11 34 | 23 41 | 28 19 | 4 ♓ 58'35" |
| 26 SU | 14:17:50 | 2 ♓ 23 | 16 33 | 11 13 | 10 13 | 20 39 | 1 0 | 11 34 | 23 41 | 28 19 | 4 ♓ 58'35" |
| 27 MO | 14:21:46 | 7 7 | 18 10 | 12 11 | 10 47 | 20 44 | 1 2 | 11 35 | 23 41 | 28 19 | 4 ♓ 58'35" |
| 28 TU | 14:25:43 | 12 1 | 19 47 | 13 10 | 11 22 | 20 49 | 1 4 | 11 36 | 23 42 | 28 19 | 4 ♓ 58'35" |
| 29 WE | 14:29:39 | 17 4 | 21 24 | 14 8 | 11 57 | 20 54 | 1 6 | 11 36 | 23 42 | 28 19 | 4 ♓ 58'35" |
| 30 TH | 14:33:36 | 22 15 | 23 1 | 15 6 | 12 32 | 20 59 | 1 8 | 11 37 | 23 42 | 28 20 | 4 ♓ 58'35" |

### INGRESSES :

8 ♂ → ♐ 3:13  
9 ☿ → ♑ 7:30  
14 ⊕ → ♎ 12:21  
15 ♀ → ♍ 18:27  
18 ☿ → ♒ 5:35  
25 ☿ → ♓ 11:40

### ASPECTS (HELIOCENTRIC +MOON(TYCHONIC)) :

1 ☽ ☍ ♃ 13:2  
2 ☽ ☍ ♇ 6:22  
  ☽ ☍ ♄ 10:8  
3 ⊕ □ ♃ 1:2  
  ☽ □ ♅ 5:29  
5 ☽ ☌ ♀ 10:44  
  ☿ ☌ ♃ 14:43  
6 ☽ ☍ ♆ 3:14  
  ☽ □ ♂ 11:58  
  ☿ □ ⊕ 19:12  
7 ☽ □ ♃ 19:24  

8 ☽ □ ☿ 7:41  
  ☽ □ ♆ 9:38  
  ☽ □ ♄ 13:11  
  ☿ ☌ ♆ 17:32  
9 ☽ ☍ ♅ 6:24  
  ☿ ☌ ♄ 11:27  
10 ♀ ⊡N ☊ 17:42  
11 ♀ ☍ ♇ 19:42  
12 ☽ □ ♆ 4:4  
  ☽ □ ♀ 5:11  
  ⊕ □ ♇ 17:15  

  ☽ ☌ ♂ 19:56  
  ☿ □ ♅ 21:57  
14 ☽ ☌ ♃ 2:44  
  ☽ ☌ ♇ 18:48  
  ☽ ☌ ♄ 23:23  
15 ⊕ □ ♄ 5:0  
  ☽ □ ♅ 20:5  
16 ☿ ⊡S ☊ 11:4  
  ☽ ☌ ☿ 23:23  
19 ☽ ☌ ♆ 8:2  
  ♀ □ ♂ 21:34  

20 ☽ □ ♂ 11:6  
  ☽ ☍ ♀ 12:29  
21 ☽ □ ♃ 13:57  
22 ☽ □ ♇ 6:7  
  ☽ □ ♄ 11:22  
23 ☽ ☌ ♅ 8:45  
24 ☿ ☌ ♆ 1:56  
26 ⊕ ☍ ♅ 8:58  
  ☽ □ ♆ 19:48  
27 ☿ □ ♂ 20:27  
28 ☽ ☍ ♂ 5:48  

  ☽ □ ☿ 11:6  
  ♀ □ ♃ 16:10  
  ☽ ☍ ♃ 23:20  
29 ☽ □ ♀ 0:18  
  ☽ ☍ ♆ 13:0  
  ☿ □ ♃ 18:4  
  ☽ ☍ ♄ 18:6  
30 ☿ ☍ ♀ 4:55  
  ☽ □ ♅ 12:59

logic) dynamically blending with the red of Mars (the "wine" of heart thinking, of logic infused with morality and love). The first two days of January in AD 30 were fasting days:

> I saw the cooking done in advance. All the fires were covered, and the windows not absolutely necessary were closed. In the homes of the rich, there were little receptacles on the hearth in which, covered with hot ashes, the food kept warm. Jesus kept these fasts in Capernaum where, too, he taught in the synagogue. Twice a day, the sick were brought to him, and he cured them. The disciples from Bethsaida went home, but some of them afterward returned. Jesus traversed the country around teaching, but in the hours of rest he stayed with Mary.[32]

Both the aspects of Mercury–Neptune and Jupiter–Pluto conjunction may have brought some healthy stimulation into our lives. However, now as we settle into the Holy Week, perhaps we too should make the space for "fasting days"—if not a literal fast from food, a fast from anything extraneous. Keep life as simple and quiet as possible to make room for properly honoring this week. Have a silent supper, or a foot washing. Cultivate a somber mood.

**April 6: Jupiter enters Capricorn. "May world-beings' guard grow strong."** (See January 13–15 for the full verse)

**April 7: Mercury enters Pisces. "In comprehending seek to grasp."** (See February 3 for the full verse)

Over the course of the year thus far, we have moved through three different motifs. From the end of December into January, the focus was on the stimulation of the Ego (Sun) and our life of thought (Mercury)—or one might say on the Transcendental Self and its companion, the Empirical Self. From January into February, the focus deepened to the life of feeling (Venus); in March, we entered the realm of the will, of bringing the inspirations from the Holy Nights into some level of action and realization. This has culminated as we enter into the Holy Week. The focus moves once again to the level of the Ego and

thinking—of Sun and Mercury. It is time to once again pause, take stock, and reorient.

We are reminded of this in both of the lines above. The "world-beings" in Jupiter's mantra are guarding the past, established tradition, the foundation upon which we build. It's time to stop in the midst of our activity and make sure that what we've done so far sets a solid foundation, that it will actually last, before we go any further. We do this through Mercury's injunction to not only comprehend, but *grasp*. The goal is for our thinking to not merely flit about or get lost down blind alleys, but to be infused with the vitality of the will to the point that we experience a *grasping* of thoughts.

The mood of quiet encouraged above facilitates our ability to pause and take stock.

**April 8: Full Moon, 23°42' Virgo.** The Full Moon in Virgo recalls the celebration of the Purim festival, honoring Esther (both March 7 AD 30 and February 26 AD 31):

> At the commencement of the Festival of Purim, a musical instrument, which stood on three feet, was again played on the roof of the synagogue. It was hollow with pipes running through it, the ends extending both above and below. By pushing the pipes in and out, the music was produced. Children, too, were playing harps and flutes. Today, in commemoration of Esther, the women and young maidens enjoyed certain rights and privileges in the synagogue. They were not separated from the men, they could even approach where the priests were. There was a procession in the synagogue of children dressed fancifully, some in white, others in red. Then a maiden entered wearing around her neck an ornament somewhat frightful looking. It was a blood-red circle around her throat, as if she had been beheaded, and from it, hung on her white garments, numerous knots of blood-red threads, like so many streaks of blood from the wounded neck. She wore a magnificent mantle borne by train bearers and appeared to be enacting the principal part in some drama. Children and maidens followed her. She wore a high, pointed ornament on the forepart of her head and a long veil. In her hand she carried something, whether a sword or a scepter, I do

---

32 Ibid., vol. 1, p. 390.

not know. She was tall, and a maiden of great beauty....

There was with her a maiden, who carried a beautiful basket containing presents for the chief priest. She presented to him many precious little shields, such as the priests wore sometimes on the forehead or the breast. In one corner of the synagogue, concealed by a curtain, lay upon a bed of state the effigy of a man, whose head the maiden struck off and took to the chief priest. Then, making use of the privilege granted to females on that day, she rebuked the priests for the principal faults they had committed during the year. That done, she withdrew.[33]

What an Arcanum this celebration is, so rich with archetypal rites and imagery! Note that today is the Wednesday of Holy Week, during which we honor Magdalene's last anointing of Christ, a deed which caused uproar with some of the disciples, particularly Judas. On this day as well (April 1 AD 33) the Moon was in Virgo, albeit not full. Clearly both the Full Moon in Virgo, as well as the Wednesday of Holy Week, are days to honor and ponder the mighty Mystery of the Feminine! Are we making room for the Feminine to speak her peace, perhaps even to offer us an overdue rebuke?

Between April 9 and 15, Mercury comes into square alignment with the Node; once again the "window into the spiritual world" created by the Moon's Ascending Node creates a dynamic tension with our day-to-day thoughts and observations (Mercury). This alignment is exact on **April 12, Easter Sunday: Mercury 6° Pisces square Node 6° Gemini.** The mood of this day is a joyous one, perhaps the most joyous and victorious mood of the whole year. The alignment of Jupiter and Pluto aids us in tapping into the wellspring of this triumph. However, the square of Mercury in Pisces to Node in Gemini enhances a mood that has been encouraged throughout the whole week: pausing, taking stock, reorienting.

Mercury and Node were in the same signs, approaching exact square alignment, on March 29, 810. On this day, Parzival had let go the reins of his horse and was wandering aimlessly through the woods. He had given up on his quest, on his life, on God. He keenly felt the shame of youthful failure (he was barely 21 years of age) that had come upon him after being harshly reprimanded by the intimidating Cundrie over four years prior. Fate and the good spirits drew him to the shelter of a middle-aged man who lived life as a hermit, a former soldier named Trevrizent, serving penance as a solitary monk due to his own failure to uphold his knightly vows.

Parzival finds solace with this man and his humble dwelling on several levels. First of all, he is told that it is Good Friday—for the first time in several years, his consciousness is brought back to awareness of the liturgical year, the living memory of Christ. He then discovers, as conversation goes on, that this man Trevrizent is his uncle, the brother of his deceased mother Herzeloyde. Above all, he comes to understand the strange experience he had had four and a half years prior (on September 25, 805) at the Grail Castle: that the wounded man he witnessed was also his uncle, King Anfortas; and that Parzival, and only Parzival, could heal him through the magic of questioning.

After spending a few days with Trevrizent, Parzival rides forth with focus, energy, and purpose like he has never had before—both hands are now firmly holding the reins! On this Resurrection Sunday, may whatever quiet space we have been able to cultivate pay off as fruitfully as Parzival's. May we know with a certainty we have never yet experienced who we are and the nature of the tasks ahead of us, feeling more than adequately equipped to ride forth and meet the world (see Eschenbach's *Parzival*, chap. 9, for further context).

Almost simultaneously with the Mercury–Node aspect occurring over Easter, the Sun comes into square alignment, in turn, with Pluto and Jupiter. Between April 9 and 19 Sun is square Pluto; this alignment is exact on **April 14, Sun 29°56' Pisces square Pluto 29° 56' Sagittarius.** Immediately after this, the **Sun enters Aries.** Between April 9 and

---

33 Ibid., p. 413.

12, the Sun is square Jupiter, and this alignment is exact on **April 15: Sun 0°52' Aries square Jupiter 0°52' Capricorn.** Shortly after this, between April 15 and 26, the Sun squares Saturn; this is exact on **April 21, Sun 6° Aries square Saturn 6° Capricorn.**

The Sun in dynamic tension with Pluto offers the possibility of extremely clear and practical foresight. These two planets were very close to where they are today on March 7 AD 33, during which Christ gave specific details of what would become of himself and his disciples in the next month, the next six months, and even the next years. Each of them was given ample opportunity to question Christ and clarify all the indications he gave as to the immediate future. Our capacities for foresight are heightened at this time.

After this square with Pluto, the Sun enters Aries: **"Arise, Oh Shining Light!"** As our Easter meditation emphasized, the time has come to emerge from the womb of quiet reflection that we have cultivated during Holy Week—it is time for our Shining Light to arise. Like Parzival setting out from Trevrizent's hermitage, or the disciples receiving their specific guidance from Christ before his Passion, we are given the opportunity from the star memories of these days to receive the same degree of sharp clarity.

Just as the Sun ingresses into Aries, it comes into exact square alignment with Jupiter, another triumphant alignment. The Sun was in Capricorn and Jupiter in Aries in late December AD 30. It was during this time that the recalcitrant Mary Magdalene once again came to hear Christ speak:

[Christ]…said that the Queen of Sheba had come from the South to hear the wisdom of Solomon, but here was one greater than Solomon. And lo, the wonder! Children that had never yet spoken, babes in their mothers' arms, cried out from time to time during the instruction: "Jesus of Nazareth! Holiest of prophets! Son of David! Son of God!" Which words caused many of the hearers, among them Magdalene, to tremble with fear. Making allusion to Magdalene, Jesus said that when the devil has been driven out and the house has been swept, he returns with six other demons, and rages worse than before. These words terrified Magdalene.…

Magdalene also, from her splendid seat upon which she had attracted all eyes, fell in violent convulsions…just then some persons near her cried out: "Stop, Master! Stop! This woman is dying." Jesus interrupted his discourse to reply: "Place her on her chair! The death she is now dying is a good death, and one that will vivify her!"

After falling into convulsions two more times, she was led to the inn of the holy women in order to recover. While not entirely cured, she was profoundly impressed, and set aside her frivolous attire, donning a veil. Later Christ came to speak to her again, and she experienced convulsions for a fourth time.

She was now like one distracted. She cried and wept. She ran through the public streets saying to all she met that she was a wicked creature, a sinner, the refuse of humanity. The holy women had the greatest trouble to quiet her. She tore her garments, disarranged her hair, and hid her face in the folds of her veil. When Jesus returned to his inn with the disciples and some of the Pharisees, and while they were taking some refreshments standing, Magdalene escaped from the holy women, ran with streaming hair and uttering loud lamentations, made her way through the crowd, cast herself at Jesus's feet, weeping and moaning, and asked if she might still hope for salvation. The Pharisees and disciples, scandalized at the sight, said to Jesus that he should no longer suffer this reprobate woman to create disturbance everywhere, that he should send her away once for all. But Jesus replied: "Permit her to weep and lament! Ye know not what is passing in her"—and he turned to her with words of consolation. He told her to repent from her heart, to believe and to hope, for that she should soon find peace. Then he bade her depart with confidence.[34]

This was on December 26 AD 30. On the next day, December 27, she fainted three more times in the presence of Christ. After recovering, pale and weak, from the last fainting, she finally achieved full and permanent redemption.

---

34 This and previous quote, Brentano. *The Visions of Anne Catherine Emmerich* vol. 2, pp. 189–190.

As the Sun and Saturn come into square align-ment, they recall the events in the first days after the Resurrection. At this time, Sun was in Aries square Saturn in Cancer, opposite to its position today. During this time we see a very different Mary Magdalene—yet somehow similar to the one described above:

> Magdalene, in her sorrow and love, was above all fear. She was perfectly heroic and without a thought of danger. She took no rest, but often left the house, hurried through the street with streaming hair, and wherever she found listen-ers, whether in their homes or in public places, she accused them as the murderers of the Lord, vehemently recounting all they had done to the Savior, and announcing to them his resurrection. If she found no one to listen to her, she wandered through the gardens and told it to the flowers, the trees, and the fountains. Oftentimes a crowd gathered around her, some offering her compas-sion, others insulting her on account of her past life. She was little esteemed by the crowd, for she had once given great scandal. I saw that her present violent conduct scandalized some of the Jews, and about five of them wanted to seize her, but she passed straight through them and went on as before. She had lost sight of the whole world, she sighed only after Jesus.[35]

**April 23: New Moon 8° Aries.** The New Moon in Aries carries the impulse of "opening the spi-ral" and bringing in new impulses to a particularly potent degree. The New Moon was in Aries on April 17 AD 33. On this day, the disciples were cel-ebrating the Mass:

> They spoke in words full of mystery of their rela-tions to the mother of the Lord and what she should be to them.... I saw the blessed Virgin hovering over the assembly in a shining, out-spread mantle whose folds embraced them all, and on her head descended a crown from the most holy Trinity through the open heavens above her.... I had the conviction that Mary was the legitimate head of them all, the temple that enclosed them all.
>
> When midnight had sounded, the blessed Virgin, kneeling, received the blessed sacrament

from Peter.... Mary was penetrated with light and splendor.... Here standing she recited the Magnificat, the Canticle of the three youths in the fiery furnace (Daniel 3:23–37), and the 130th Psalm. The day was beginning to dawn when I saw Jesus entering through the closed doors. He spoke long to her, telling her that she was to help the apostles, and explaining what she was to be to them. He gave her power over the whole church, endued her with his strength, his protecting influence, and it was as if his light flowed in upon her, as if he penetrated her through and through.[36]

The might of the Feminine that streamed in dur-ing the Virgo Full Moon continues to heighten in its potency. A good meditation for the day might be exactly what was spoken by Mary: the Magnificat (Luke 1:46–55), Daniel 3:23–37, and Psalm 130.

During the first weeks of Eastertide, the Sun (the Higher Self) made contact with Pluto (the Fire of Love vs the volcanic instinctual life), Jupiter (the Holy Spirit, imaginative thinking), and Saturn (Vir-gin Mary, Wisdom, Death) in turn. Over the latter part of April, Mercury (the Lower Self) will make the same journey—what exists on a purely intuitive level of the Ego bubbles into the daylight consciousness of our thought life. Between April 23 and 27, Mer-cury is square Pluto. This aspect is exact on **April 25, Mercury 29°58' Pisces square Pluto 29°58' Sagit-tarius.** Immediately after this exact square, Mercury ingresses into Aries and Pluto stations retrograde.

Simultaneously, between April 23 and 28, Mer-cury is square Jupiter. The alignment is exact on **April 26, Mercury 1°41' Aries square Jupiter 1°41' Capricorn.** Subsequently, between April 26 and May 1, Mercury is square Saturn. This alignment is exact on **April 28, Mercury 6°48' Aries square Saturn 6°48' Capricorn.** Meanwhile, the Sun con-tinues on his journey: between April 20 and May 1, the Sun is conjunct Uranus. This alignment is exact on **April 26, Sun and Uranus 11°33' Aries.**

Mercury square Pluto brings us once again to Mary Magdalene. These two planets were square

---

35 Ibid., vol. 3, p. 397.

36 Ibid., pp. 406–407.

in the same signs of the Zodiac on April 1 AD 33, during Magdalene's last anointing of Christ. We can see here a dual aspect: Mercury as priest or priestess, and Pluto as the Empyrean, the Fire of Love together lay the foundation for Magdalene playing the role of anointing priestess on behalf of Christ, fired by Love. On the other hand, Mercury is the archetype of thieves, merchants, and liars, while Pluto's darker side deals with the unresolved and violent energy of the instinctual life. Here we have the foundation laid for the rage that Judas (the treasurer) felt at the money wasted by Magdalene on the costly spikenard oil used to anoint Christ's head and feet—a rage which was the catalyst for his accepting the offer of 30 silver pieces to betray Christ.

**April 25: Mercury enters Aries**; Pluto stations retrograde, 29°58' Sagittarius. **"Lay hold of forces weaving."**

Like Parzival setting out from Trevrizent's hermitage, we are reminded to take hold of the reins— the "forces weaving" at work outside of our normal level of awareness—instead of riding dejectedly with the reins slack. However, we needn't think that this requires any grandstanding or obvious outer activity. Pluto's movement retrograde reminds us of this. On March 26 AD 33, Pluto turned retrograde in Sagittarius. This was the day that witnessed the "Widow's Mite" (as told in Mark 12:41–44). Her meager contribution to the temple treasury meant more than any of the grand offerings of the rich and powerful—it was not the quantity, but the *quality* of her gift that made the difference. Today is a good day to pay attention to the seemingly insignificant, which secretly holds the potential for the miraculous.

※

Mercury carries on its journey, coming into square alignment with Jupiter on April 26. Simultaneously, the Sun comes into conjunction with Uranus. The Sun and Uranus were conjunct on August 3 AD 30, during the second of Christ's healing miracles: the Healing of the Nobleman's Son. According to Valentin Tomberg,[37] while the first healing miracle of

Changing Water into Wine had to do with seeding the necessary spiritual potential for the future, the second healing miracle had to do with the redemption of the past. In the healing of physical–biological heritage between father and son during this miracle, a wider healing was initiated involving healing the *psychospiritual* heritage, the flow of Tradition. Again our hearts are awoken to the mandate "Honor Thy Father and Mother." While Rudolf Steiner accomplished the modern iteration of the first healing miracle by seeding the future through Anthroposophy, Valentin Tomberg accomplished the modern iteration of the second miracle by entering the Catholic Church and infusing it with Hermeticism—ultimately resulting in *Meditations on the Tarot*.[38]

Mercury square Jupiter carries with it a similar gesture of honoring and remembering—this aspect occurred on January 16 AD 31, when some of the disciples were venturing to rescue the remains of the recently murdered John the Baptist. They too had the task of preserving the past (the ministry of John) while linking it onto the present and the future. John became the guiding light from across the threshold for the twelve disciples after his death, and in our own time plays a very similar role. Mercury is square Jupiter on the 26th; a few days later he is square to Saturn, on April 28. Mercury was in Aries, square to Saturn in Cancer rather than Capricorn, on April 20 AD 33. This was just over two weeks after the Resurrection, a time when the new Tradition came to be established on Earth. We might see Mercury as Peter, the first High Priest, and Saturn as the Virgin Mary, the masculine and feminine pillars of the Church. They sought to embody the archetypal rite of spiritual respiration—Holy Communion—during this time. Focus on the crown center as Divine Feminine, the Pillar of Severity; focus on the solar plexus center as Divine Masculine, the Pillar of Mercy; cultivate spiritual respiration through these two centers.

---

37 Tomberg, *Christ and Sophia*, pp. 247–249.

38 See the article series "The Seven Miracles:" https://treehouse.live/2017/06/10/the-seven-miracles-part-1/; https://treehouse.live/2017/06/14/the-seven-miracles-part-2/; https://treehouse.live/2017/06/17/the-seven-miracles-part-3/.

# MAY 2020

## STARGAZING PREVIEW

The month of May begins at midnight with a merry waxing Cancer Moon alone in the sky; Jupiter and Saturn, in the first decan of Capricorn, will have risen by 0200. On the 4th, Mercury moves behind the Sun, marking the start of its phase as an evening star. Mars enters Aquarius on the following day.

The night of the 6th brings us the peak of the Eta Aquarid meteor showers, courtesy of the dust of Halley's Comet. The Moon, near Full, will brighten the sky enough to interfere with visibility, but for your best shot at viewing, look to the northeast around midnight.

Our May Full Moon takes place on the 7th, at 22° Libra—it will be in the southeast when Venus sets at 2230. On the 12th, the Moon will again be in the first decan of Capricorn, passing below Jupiter, then Saturn, just before Saturn begins its yearly retrograde movement; you'll find them high in the south before sunrise.

The Last Quarter Moon will happen on the 14th in the last degree of Capricorn. On this same day, Venus moves retrograde at 27° Taurus, the point of the zodiac aligned with *Bellatrix* (the left shoulder of Orion) and *Mintaka* (the star marking the left side of his belt)—though she'll be high above them. (When we speak of the stars of Orion, those on his left are on our right, and vice versa). Jupiter begins its seasonal retrograde movement on this day, at 2° Capricorn. The first moments of the 15th will reveal a Moon–Mars conjunction at 6° Aquarius; they'll rise just after 0200, Mars above the Moon.

May's New Moon (7° Taurus) falls on the 22nd, and this means that without moonlight, Jupiter and Saturn, which rise by 0100, and Mars, above the horizon an hour later, will be very bright indeed. Look for the Lion high in the south at sunset.

Late on the 23rd, the Moon will catch up to Venus, but they might be too difficult to see, as they set little more than an hour after our Sun. The 29th will bring us the First Quarter Moon in Leo; you'll find them overhead, due south, as the Sun sets. Sunlight hides Orion from view this month.

## MAY COMMENTARIES

Toward the end of April, on the 28th, Jupiter and Saturn come within 5° of each other. They remain close through June 7, but due to retrograde movement of both planets beginning later in May, they drift apart from each other. Geocentrically, their exact conjunction will not take place until December; heliocentrically, in November. This is an epochal meeting in the heavens, one that has been known to be of great importance since the earliest days of astrology. Perhaps, for the next few months, we receive a foretaste of what will not come to full fruition until the year's end.

Over the course of April, our soul was directed once again to the realm of the Self (Sun) and thinking (Mercury). As we move into May, these two realms of soul are more and more brought into relation with the realm of feeling (Venus). This is especially shown in the dominating aspect of the month, Venus square Neptune. These two planets already began to come into square relationship at the end of April, on the 23rd. This alignment is exact on **May 4, Venus 25° Taurus square Neptune 25° Aquarius.** However, the two remain in close alignment after this; at first, Venus begins to drift away, but then turns retrograde on the 13th. The two are exactly square once again on May 20, and finally drift out of alignment by May 31.

Venus is the realm of beauty, art, health and balance, and love—particularly the brotherly and sisterly love of community. It is the realm of the union of above and below, of effort and grace. It is best expressed in the imagination of Christ Crucified, with Mary and John at the foot of the cross. Neptune is Nyx, Night, the Mother Goddess, the "Virgin of Dark Perfection." She is the prime mover, the origin, the depths, the ocean, the sub- and super-conscious. She is the wellspring of inspiration. On the other hand, Venus is jealousy, backbiting, and vanity; Neptune is the temptation to "cast oneself down from the heights," into the murky realms of the instinctual, of pleasure for pleasure's sake.

Venus and Neptune were square (in Aries and Capricorn respectively) on March 15 AD 31:

Today Jesus delivered the so-called Sermon on the Mount [Matt. 5:1–7; 29], signifying the conclusion of his presentation of the beatitudes, which had begun on the Mount of Beatitudes on Kislev 13 [Nov. 28 AD 30]. Then, toward evening, there took place the feeding of the four thousand [Matt. 15:32–39]. Jesus took leave of the people who shed tears of thanks. He made his way back to the lake with the disciples. Before they could board their ship, they were met by a group of Pharisees who demanded Jesus to show them a sign from Heaven. He replied as recorded in Matthew 16:1–4, saying that, after a certain number of weeks [actually 107], they would be given the sign of Jonah [Matt. 12:40]. Jesus and the disciples then boarded Peter's ship and rowed out onto the lake, where they spent the night.[39]

Represented so clearly to us on this day is the positive aspect of Venus square Neptune in both the teaching of the Beatitudes, as well as the miracle of the feeding of the four thousand. Whereas the feeding of the five thousand, which had taken place about two months prior, took five loaves and two fishes, and left twelve baskets of leftovers, this miracle took seven loaves and seven fishes, with seven baskets of leftovers. Whereas the feeding of the five thousand has something more to do with the healing of both the Self of Humanity as well as the *structure* and *senses* of the physical body, this subsequent feeding had more to do with healing the course of time and of the actual *health* and *wellbeing* of the human body—a healing more on an elemental rather than physical–material level. One might also say this healing had more to do with the human as a being of Soul—the Soul being an expression of the seven-fold nature of the planets—rather than as a being of Spirit—the Spirit being an expression of the twelve worldviews of the cosmos. It is this Divine Feminine aspect of the human being that is comforted by Venus and Neptune, an aspect that is brought to wholeness through the Nine Beatitudes.

---

39 Brentano, *The Visions of Anne Catherine Emmerich*, vol. 2, p. 323.

The Pharisees, on the other hand, represent to us the dark side of jealousy, and the temptation to "prove oneself" through foolhardy actions. Take care!

While this aspect is still taking form, we begin the month with Mercury conjunct Uranus. They begin to approach close to each other on April 28; on **May 1, Mercury is exactly conjunct Uranus, 11°50' Aries.** After this, they drift apart again, moving beyond 5° apart by May 3. When the Sun, the Higher Self, was conjunct Uranus a week ago, we remembered the second Healing Miracle, the Healing of the Nobleman's Son. Today recalls the events of August 21–22 AD 32:

On the mountains near this place, Sichar-Kedar, there were whole rows of beehives. The declivity of the mountain was terraced, and on the terraces resting against the mountain stood numerous square, flat-roofed beehives about seven feet in height, the upper part ornamented with knobs. They were placed in several rows, one above the other. They were not rounded in the back, but pointed like a roof, and they could be opened from top to bottom on the shelf side. The whole apiary was encoded by a fine trellis of woven reeds. Between these stacks of hives there were steps leading up to the terraces, and to the railings on either side bushes bearing white blossoms and berries were trained. One could mount from terrace to terrace, upon each of which were similar arrangements for bees.

Jesus related the parable of the king's son who came to discharge all the debts of his subjects...He told them also that his father had given him a vineyard which had to be cultivated and pruned, and that he was looking for laborers to replace the useless, lazy servants whom he was going to chase away, and who were fitting images of the branches they had neglected to prune. Then he explained to them the cutting away of the vine stock, spoke of the quantity of useless wood and foliage, and of the small number of grapes. [He] told the people that they too ought to cultivate [the vine]. They replied quite innocently that the country was not adapted to vine culture. But Jesus responded that they ought to plant it on that side of the mountain occupied by the apiary, for that was an excellent

SIDEREAL GEOCENTRIC LONGITUDES :   MAY 2020 Gregorian at 0 hours UT

| DAY | ☉ | ☽ | ☊ | ☿ | ♀ | ♂ | ♃ | ♄ | ⛢ | ♆ | ♇ |
|---|---|---|---|---|---|---|---|---|---|---|---|
| 1 FR | 16 ♈ 4 | 17 ♋ 51 | 5 ♊ 15R | 11 ♈ 31 | 24 ♉ 6 | 26 ♑ 37 | 1 ♑ 56 | 6 ♑ 51 | 11 ♈ 50 | 25 ♒ 12 | 29 ♐ 58R |
| 2 SA | 17 2 | 1 ♌ 42 | 5 14 | 13 38 | 24 30 | 27 18 | 1 58 | 6 52 | 11 53 | 25 14 | 29 57 |
| 3 SU | 18 0 | 15 57 | 5 11 | 15 46 | 24 53 | 27 59 | 2 0 | 6 53 | 11 57 | 25 15 | 29 57 |
| 4 MO | 18 58 | 0 ♍ 34 | 5 7 | 17 54 | 25 13 | 28 41 | 2 2 | 6 53 | 12 0 | 25 17 | 29 57 |
| 5 TU | 19 57 | 15 28 | 5 0 | 20 3 | 25 32 | 29 22 | 2 4 | 6 54 | 12 4 | 25 18 | 29 57 |
| 6 WE | 20 55 | 0 ♎ 32 | 4 54 | 22 13 | 25 49 | 0 ♒ 3 | 2 6 | 6 55 | 12 7 | 25 20 | 29 56 |
| 7 TH | 21 53 | 15 36 | 4 48 | 24 23 | 26 4 | 0 44 | 2 8 | 6 55 | 12 11 | 25 21 | 29 56 |
| 8 FR | 22 51 | 0 ♏ 32 | 4 43 | 26 34 | 26 17 | 1 26 | 2 9 | 6 55 | 12 14 | 25 23 | 29 56 |
| 9 SA | 23 49 | 15 9 | 4 40 | 28 44 | 26 28 | 2 7 | 2 10 | 6 56 | 12 17 | 25 24 | 29 55 |
| 10 SU | 24 47 | 29 23 | 4 38 | 0 ♉ 53 | 26 36 | 2 48 | 2 11 | 6 56 | 12 21 | 25 25 | 29 55 |
| 11 MO | 25 45 | 13 ♐ 11 | 4 38D | 3 2 | 26 43 | 3 29 | 2 12 | 6 56 | 12 24 | 25 27 | 29 55 |
| 12 TU | 26 43 | 26 31 | 4 40 | 5 9 | 26 47 | 4 10 | 2 12 | 6 56R | 12 28 | 25 28 | 29 54 |
| 13 WE | 27 41 | 9 ♑ 26 | 4 41 | 7 16 | 26 49 | 4 51 | 2 13 | 6 56 | 12 31 | 25 29 | 29 54 |
| 14 TH | 28 38 | 22 0 | 4 42 | 9 20 | 26 48R | 5 32 | 2 13 | 6 56 | 12 34 | 25 31 | 29 53 |
| 15 FR | 29 36 | 4 ♒ 16 | 4 42R | 11 23 | 26 45 | 6 13 | 2 13R | 6 55 | 12 38 | 25 32 | 29 53 |
| 16 SA | 0 ♉ 34 | 16 20 | 4 41 | 13 23 | 26 40 | 6 54 | 2 13 | 6 55 | 12 41 | 25 33 | 29 52 |
| 17 SU | 1 32 | 28 16 | 4 38 | 15 22 | 26 32 | 7 35 | 2 12 | 6 54 | 12 44 | 25 34 | 29 51 |
| 18 MO | 2 30 | 10 ♓ 7 | 4 34 | 17 18 | 26 22 | 8 16 | 2 12 | 6 54 | 12 48 | 25 35 | 29 51 |
| 19 TU | 3 28 | 21 59 | 4 29 | 19 11 | 26 10 | 8 57 | 2 11 | 6 53 | 12 51 | 25 37 | 29 50 |
| 20 WE | 4 25 | 3 ♈ 54 | 4 23 | 21 1 | 25 55 | 9 37 | 2 10 | 6 52 | 12 54 | 25 38 | 29 50 |
| 21 TH | 5 23 | 15 55 | 4 18 | 22 49 | 25 38 | 10 18 | 2 9 | 6 51 | 12 57 | 25 39 | 29 49 |
| 22 FR | 6 21 | 28 3 | 4 14 | 24 33 | 25 18 | 10 58 | 2 8 | 6 50 | 13 1 | 25 40 | 29 48 |
| 23 SA | 7 18 | 10 ♉ 20 | 4 11 | 26 15 | 24 56 | 11 39 | 2 6 | 6 49 | 13 4 | 25 41 | 29 47 |
| 24 SU | 8 16 | 22 47 | 4 9 | 27 53 | 24 32 | 12 19 | 2 5 | 6 48 | 13 7 | 25 42 | 29 47 |
| 25 MO | 9 14 | 5 ♊ 26 | 4 8D | 29 29 | 24 6 | 13 0 | 2 3 | 6 47 | 13 10 | 25 43 | 29 46 |
| 26 TU | 10 11 | 18 18 | 4 9 | 1 ♊ 1 | 23 38 | 13 40 | 2 1 | 6 45 | 13 13 | 25 44 | 29 45 |
| 27 WE | 11 9 | 1 ♋ 22 | 4 10 | 2 30 | 23 8 | 14 20 | 1 58 | 6 44 | 13 17 | 25 45 | 29 44 |
| 28 TH | 12 7 | 14 42 | 4 12 | 3 56 | 22 36 | 15 1 | 1 56 | 6 42 | 13 20 | 25 45 | 29 43 |
| 29 FR | 13 4 | 28 17 | 4 14 | 5 18 | 22 3 | 15 41 | 1 53 | 6 41 | 13 23 | 25 46 | 29 43 |
| 30 SA | 14 2 | 12 ♌ 8 | 4 14 | 6 38 | 21 29 | 16 21 | 1 51 | 6 39 | 13 26 | 25 47 | 29 42 |
| 31 SU | 14 59 | 26 15 | 4 13R | 7 53 | 20 53 | 17 1 | 1 48 | 6 37 | 13 29 | 25 48 | 29 41 |

INGRESSES :

| | | |
|---|---|---|
| 1 ☽→♌ 21: 5 | 19 ☽→♈ 16: 9 | |
| 3 ☽→♍ 23: 4 | 22 ☽→♉ 3:50 | |
| 5 ♂→♒ 22: 7 | 24 ☽→♊ 13:43 | |
| ☽→♎ 23: 9 | 25 ☿→♊ 8: 1 | |
| 7 ☽→♏ 23: 8 | 26 ☽→♋ 21:30 | |
| 9 ☿→♉ 14: 7 | 29 ☽→♌ 3: 0 | |
| 10 ☽→♐ 1: 2 | 31 ☽→♍ 6:17 | |
| 12 ☽→♑ 6:23 | | |
| 14 ☽→♒ 15:35 | | |
| 15 ☉→♉ 9:50 | | |
| 17 ☽→♓ 3:30 | | |

ASPECTS & ECLIPSES :

| | | | |
|---|---|---|---|
| 1 ☿☌⛢ 3:39 | 10 ☽☌☋ 9: 2 | ♀□♆ 22:31 | 30 ☉□☽ 3:28 |
| ☽☍♂ 16: 3 | 11 ☿□♂ 7:32 | 22 ☿☌♀ 8:39 | ☽☍♂ 7:33 |
| 3 ☽☍♆ 15:21 | 12 ☽☌♇ 6:12 | ☿□♆ 15:47 | ☽☍♆ 23:13 |
| 4 ♀□♆ 4:23 | ☽☌♃ 10:28 | ☉☌☽ 17:37 | 31 ☽⊟☊ 13:20 |
| ☽⊟☊ 7:18 | ☽☌♄ 19:16 | 24 ☽☌♀ 3:13 | |
| ☉⊟☿ 21:40 | 14 ☉□☽ 14: 1 | ☽☌☿ 11: 8 | |
| 6 ☽☌P 2:57 | 15 ☽☌♂ 4: 4 | ☽☌☊ 21:33 | |
| ☽☍⛢ 18:30 | 16 ☽☌♆ 18:33 | 26 ☽☍♇ 21: 1 | |
| 7 ☉☍☽ 10:44 | 17 ☽⊟☊ 12:48 | 27 ☽☍♃ 1: 5 | |
| ☽☍☿ 16:29 | 18 ☽☌A 7:44 | ☽☍♄ 9:41 | |
| 9 ☽☍♀ 19:12 | 20 ☽☌⛢ 18: 5 | 28 ☿☌☊ 4:40 | |

SIDEREAL HELIOCENTRIC LONGITUDES :   MAY 2020 Gregorian at 0 hours UT

| DAY | Sid. Time | ☿ | ♀ | ⊕ | ♂ | ♃ | ♄ | ⛢ | ♆ | ♇ | Vernal Point |
|---|---|---|---|---|---|---|---|---|---|---|---|
| 1 FR | 14:37:32 | 27 ♓ 36 | 24 ♍ 37 | 16 ♎ 5 | 13 ♐ 7 | 21 ♐ 4 | 1 ♑ 9 | 11 ♈ 38 | 23 ♒ 43 | 28 ♐ 20 | 4 ♓ 58'35" |
| 2 SA | 14:41:29 | 3 ♈ 6 | 26 14 | 17 3 | 13 42 | 21 9 | 1 11 | 11 38 | 23 43 | 28 20 | 4 ♓ 58'35" |
| 3 SU | 14:45:26 | 8 45 | 27 51 | 18 1 | 14 18 | 21 14 | 1 13 | 11 39 | 23 44 | 28 21 | 4 ♓ 58'34" |
| 4 MO | 14:49:22 | 14 32 | 29 27 | 18 59 | 14 53 | 21 19 | 1 15 | 11 40 | 23 44 | 28 21 | 4 ♓ 58'34" |
| 5 TU | 14:53:19 | 20 26 | 1 ♎ 4 | 19 57 | 15 28 | 21 24 | 1 17 | 11 40 | 23 44 | 28 21 | 4 ♓ 58'34" |
| 6 WE | 14:57:15 | 26 28 | 2 40 | 20 55 | 16 3 | 21 29 | 1 19 | 11 41 | 23 45 | 28 21 | 4 ♓ 58'34" |
| 7 TH | 15: 1:12 | 2 ♉ 35 | 4 17 | 21 53 | 16 39 | 21 34 | 1 20 | 11 42 | 23 45 | 28 22 | 4 ♓ 58'34" |
| 8 FR | 15: 5: 8 | 8 48 | 5 53 | 22 51 | 17 14 | 21 39 | 1 22 | 11 42 | 23 45 | 28 22 | 4 ♓ 58'34" |
| 9 SA | 15: 9: 5 | 15 4 | 7 30 | 23 49 | 17 50 | 21 44 | 1 24 | 11 43 | 23 46 | 28 22 | 4 ♓ 58'34" |
| 10 SU | 15:13: 1 | 21 23 | 9 6 | 24 47 | 18 25 | 21 49 | 1 26 | 11 44 | 23 46 | 28 23 | 4 ♓ 58'33" |
| 11 MO | 15:16:58 | 27 42 | 10 42 | 25 45 | 19 1 | 21 54 | 1 28 | 11 44 | 23 46 | 28 23 | 4 ♓ 58'33" |
| 12 TU | 15:20:55 | 4 ♊ 1 | 12 18 | 26 43 | 19 36 | 21 59 | 1 29 | 11 45 | 23 47 | 28 23 | 4 ♓ 58'33" |
| 13 WE | 15:24:51 | 10 17 | 13 55 | 27 41 | 20 12 | 22 4 | 1 31 | 11 46 | 23 47 | 28 23 | 4 ♓ 58'33" |
| 14 TH | 15:28:48 | 16 30 | 15 31 | 28 39 | 20 48 | 22 9 | 1 33 | 11 46 | 23 48 | 28 24 | 4 ♓ 58'33" |
| 15 FR | 15:32:44 | 22 38 | 17 7 | 29 37 | 21 24 | 22 14 | 1 35 | 11 47 | 23 48 | 28 24 | 4 ♓ 58'33" |
| 16 SA | 15:36:41 | 28 40 | 18 43 | 0 ♏ 35 | 21 59 | 22 19 | 1 37 | 11 48 | 23 48 | 28 24 | 4 ♓ 58'33" |
| 17 SU | 15:40:37 | 4 ♋ 34 | 20 19 | 1 33 | 22 35 | 22 24 | 1 39 | 11 48 | 23 49 | 28 25 | 4 ♓ 58'33" |
| 18 MO | 15:44:34 | 10 20 | 21 55 | 2 30 | 23 11 | 22 29 | 1 40 | 11 49 | 23 49 | 28 25 | 4 ♓ 58'32" |
| 19 TU | 15:48:30 | 15 57 | 23 31 | 3 28 | 23 47 | 22 34 | 1 42 | 11 50 | 23 49 | 28 25 | 4 ♓ 58'32" |
| 20 WE | 15:52:27 | 21 26 | 25 7 | 4 26 | 24 23 | 22 39 | 1 44 | 11 51 | 23 50 | 28 26 | 4 ♓ 58'32" |
| 21 TH | 15:56:24 | 26 44 | 26 42 | 5 24 | 24 59 | 22 44 | 1 46 | 11 51 | 23 50 | 28 26 | 4 ♓ 58'32" |
| 22 FR | 16: 0:20 | 1 ♌ 53 | 28 18 | 6 21 | 25 35 | 22 49 | 1 48 | 11 52 | 23 50 | 28 26 | 4 ♓ 58'32" |
| 23 SA | 16: 4:17 | 6 52 | 29 54 | 7 19 | 26 12 | 22 54 | 1 50 | 11 52 | 23 51 | 28 26 | 4 ♓ 58'32" |
| 24 SU | 16: 8:13 | 11 42 | 1 ♏ 30 | 8 17 | 26 48 | 22 59 | 1 51 | 11 53 | 23 51 | 28 27 | 4 ♓ 58'32" |
| 25 MO | 16:12:10 | 16 23 | 3 5 | 9 14 | 27 24 | 23 4 | 1 53 | 11 54 | 23 52 | 28 27 | 4 ♓ 58'31" |
| 26 TU | 16:16: 6 | 20 54 | 4 41 | 10 12 | 28 0 | 23 10 | 1 55 | 11 55 | 23 52 | 28 27 | 4 ♓ 58'31" |
| 27 WE | 16:20: 3 | 25 17 | 6 16 | 11 10 | 28 37 | 23 15 | 1 57 | 11 55 | 23 52 | 28 28 | 4 ♓ 58'31" |
| 28 TH | 16:23:59 | 29 31 | 7 52 | 12 7 | 29 13 | 23 20 | 1 59 | 11 56 | 23 53 | 28 28 | 4 ♓ 58'31" |
| 29 FR | 16:27:56 | 3 ♍ 38 | 9 28 | 13 5 | 29 50 | 23 25 | 2 0 | 11 56 | 23 53 | 28 28 | 4 ♓ 58'31" |
| 30 SA | 16:31:53 | 7 37 | 11 3 | 14 2 | 0 ♑ 26 | 23 30 | 2 2 | 11 57 | 23 53 | 28 29 | 4 ♓ 58'31" |
| 31 SU | 16:35:49 | 11 29 | 12 38 | 15 0 | 1 3 | 23 35 | 2 4 | 11 58 | 23 54 | 28 29 | 4 ♓ 58'31" |

INGRESSES :

| | |
|---|---|
| 1 ☿→♈ 10:32 | |
| 4 ♀→♎ 8: 8 | |
| 6 ☿→♉ 13:53 | |
| 11 ☿→♊ 8:43 | |
| 15 ⊕→♏ 9:34 | |
| 16 ☿→♋ 5:24 | |
| 21 ☿→♌ 15: 7 | |
| 23 ♀→♏ 1:31 | |
| 28 ☿→♍ 2:46 | |
| 29 ♂→♑ 6:45 | |

ASPECTS (HELIOCENTRIC +MOON(TYCHONIC)) :

| | | | | |
|---|---|---|---|---|
| 1 ☿□♇ 3:12 | 6 ☽□♄ 1:14 | ☽☌♄ 9:10 | ☽□♂ 3:49 | ☿☍♆ 16:11 |
| ☿□♄ 15:40 | ☽☌♀ 3:48 | 13 ☽□⛢ 4:23 | ☽□♇ 12:59 | ♂☌♇ 17:54 |
| 3 ♀□♇ 7:26 | ☽☍⛢ 17:45 | ☽□♀ 9:42 | ☽□♄ 19:38 | ☽☍♆ 18:41 |
| ☿☌⛢ 12: 9 | 8 ☽☍☿ 23:45 | 14 ☿☍♂ 18:35 | 20 ☿⊟☊ 9:30 | ☽☍♂ 18:43 |
| ☽☍♆ 12:50 | 9 ☽□♆ 14:25 | ☿☍♃ 22:25 | ☽☌⛢ 15:54 | 27 ☽☍♄ 1: 2 |
| 4 ☿☍⊕ 21:40 | 10 ☿☌P 5:11 | 15 ☿☍♇ 22:59 | ☿□♀ 23:48 | ☽□⛢ 19: 2 |
| ☽□♂ 23:59 | ☿□♆ 9: 4 | 16 ☿☍♄ 12: 0 | 22 ☽☍♀ 0:35 | 29 ☽□♀ 21:53 |
| 5 ♀□♄ 3:17 | 11 ☽☌♂ 10:52 | ☽☌♆ 15: 1 | ☽□☿ 12:45 | 30 ☽☍♆ 20: 0 |
| ☽□♃ 9:31 | ♀☍⛢ 15:38 | ♂☌♃ 15:26 | 23 ☿□⊕ 2:43 | |
| ☿☌☊ 12:26 | ☽☌♃ 15:42 | 18 ☿□⛢ 6:16 | 24 ☽□♆ 2: 2 | |
| ☽□♇ 20:32 | 12 ☽☌♇ 3:25 | 19 ☽□♃ 1:11 | 26 ☽☍♃ 9: 2 | |

exposure for it, and then he related a parable treating of bees.[40]

In truth, the second miracle and Christ's teachings on this day address the same soul–spiritual reality. What is being called into question is the relationship between the autonomous self or individuality (the nobleman, the fruit of the vine) and the psyche, the subconscious life of soul (the beehive, the Son of the Nobleman). Our sense of individuality must live in harmony with our entire soul life—in Jung's terms, it must achieve ever more comprehensive degrees of individuation—if it is to be "fruitful." Mercury conjunct Uranus gives us a further opportunity to achieve our reintegration.

The Sun (as Higher Self) has held cosmic conversation with Pluto, Jupiter, Saturn and Uranus in turn. Mercury (as Empirical Self) followed in his wake, bringing what occurred on a more intuitive level into the full light of consciousness (that is, into the form of thought). Between April 30 and May 9, they finally begin to reconvene, to communicate directly with each other. An Inferior Conjunction of the Sun and Mercury took place on February 25; on that day, Mercury stood between the Sun and Earth, acting as a sort of sieve or translator of the Sun's inspiring might.

**May 4, it is a Superior Conjunction of Sun and Mercury, 19° Aries.** Mercury is on the far side of the Sun from the point of view of the Earth. We might imagine that today Mercury is performing the same translating or filtering activity, but this time it is on behalf of the Sun himself. Mercury draws in spiritual motivations from the entire cosmos beyond the Solar System, and filters it down to the Sun Sphere. During the next Inferior Conjunction, on June 3, these same inspirations will once again be filtered down to the Earth Sphere.

Note that today is also the exact square of Venus and Neptune, an alignment that dominates the whole month of May (see above). This is already a potent alignment, but is only increased in its potency by the conjunction of Mercury and Sun in Aries. These two planets were conjunct (albeit in Inferior rather than Superior Conjunction) on April

3 AD 31: the Transfiguration of Christ on Mount Tabor.

Anne Catherine Emmerich's description of this event is lengthy yet powerful, and ought to be read in full. She speaks in detail of Christ's instructing Peter, James, and John in the Lord's Prayer. From her description, one wonders if the content of Valentin Tomberg's *Lord's Prayer Course* offers us a glimpse into what was given on this day by Christ. She goes on to describe his actual transformation while he instructs:

> Jesus began again his instructions, and along with the angelic apparitions flowed alternate streams of delicious perfumes, of celestial delights and contentment over the apostles. Jesus meantime continued to shine with ever-increasing splendor, until he became as if transparent...
>
> I saw a shining pathway reaching from Heaven to Earth, and on it angelic spirits of different choirs, all in constant movement. Some were small, but of perfect form; others were merely faces peeping forth from the glancing light; some were in priestly garb, while others looked like warriors. Each had some special characteristic different from that of the others, and from each radiated some special refreshment, strength, delight, and light. They were in constant action, constant movement...[41]

While both the biblical account and depiction of this event show only Moses and Elijah, one on either side of Christ, Emmerich recounts the appearance of a third figure: Malachi. While Moses and Elijah are more human, passionate, and personable with Christ, Malachi is "more ethereal, more spiritual...like an angel, the personification of strength and repose." Rather than conversing with Christ, he remains silent.

This day, and the wider time period surrounding it, provides great opportunity for renewal and reintegration. It holds the possibility of being the culmination of an inner awakening that began one month prior, on Palm Sunday.

**May 5: Mars enters Aquarius. "May it raise itself in the current."** Yesterday's meditations on Transfiguration are only bolstered by Mars entering

---

40 Ibid., pp. 488–489.

41 Ibid., pp. 338–339.

Aquarius. This ingress offers us the image of the formless coalescing into the formed and raising itself up out of the water, out of the depths. Rather than feeling swept away by the chaotic tide of life, we can swim with this tide, and ride the wave.

**May 7: Full Moon, 22°19' Libra.** The Full Moon in Libra remembers Christ's Crucifixion (April 3 AD 33). But it also remembers a Passover held in Lazarus's house two years prior, on March 27 AD 31:

> During the supper Jesus taught and explained. He delivered an exceedingly beautiful instruction on the vine, on its cultivation, on the extermination of the bad, the planting of better shoots, and the pruning of the same after every new growth. He then turned to the apostles and disciples and told them that they were the shoots of which he spoke, that the Son of Man was the true vine, and that they must remain in him; that when he would be subjected to the wine press they must continue to make known the knowledge of the true vine, namely, himself, and plant all the vineyards with the same.[42]

Once again, we are brought into awareness of the image of the vine. Not only does our individuality (the fruit) need to be in touch with the wider realm of soul (colony of bees), it also needs to have a healthy connection to the "true vine," to the "Self of Selves" that is Christ. Our individuality tends to be an exercise in pure subjectivity—like Cain, we assume that whatever arbitrary creations proceed from us are worthwhile, simply because we have made them. Yet our ultimate goal is to create authentically—i.e., to create in concordance with the aims and methods of the "Self of Selves," the True Vine. Only then can we bear "good fruit."

**May 9: Mercury enters Taurus. "Weave life's thread."** (See March 29 for the full verse.)

Mercury in Taurus asks us to not just participate passively in the weaving of our biography, but actively take up life's thread and weave it ourselves. This is not as simple a task as it sounds. In reality, our destiny unfolds through an ongoing process of exchange between the "depth world"—i.e., the depths of our unconscious life, and the heights of

the spiritual world—and the "surface world," the plane of our day-to-day lives. In order to begin to actively take up life's thread, it is more than a matter of setting goals and working toward them. We must begin to cultivate the ability to converse with the depth world (the archetypal plane) consciously, establishing regular contact between the two worlds.

Between May 7 and 14, Mercury and Mars come into square alignment. This alignment is exact on **May 11: Mercury 3°29' Taurus square Mars 3°29' Aquarius.** A powerful dynamic tension is created between these two, effecting both speech and action. We can imagine that a certain combination of influence from these two spheres is special to the role of a great teacher or prophet: Mercury is Hermes, the Teacher, Priest, and Doctor, while Mars is the power of the Word. These two were square on October 29 AD 30, albeit with Mercury across from Taurus, in Scorpio, during which Christ taught on one of the great Hebrew prophets:

> He alluded to Elisha, who had formerly taught in this same place. The Syrians sent to take him prisoner were struck with blindness. Then Elisha conducted them to Samaria into the hands of their enemies, but far from allowing them to be put to death, he entertained them hospitably, restored their sight, and sent them back to their king. Jesus applied this to the Son of Man and the persecution he endured from the Pharisees. He spoke also for a long time of prayer and good works, related the parable of the Pharisees and the Publican, and told his hearers that they ought to adorn and perfume themselves on their fast days instead of parading their piety before the people. The inhabitants of this place, who were very much oppressed by the Pharisees and Sadducees, were greatly encouraged by Jesus's teaching. But the Pharisees and Sadducees, on the contrary, were enraged upon seeing the joyous multitude and hearing the words of Jesus.[43]

Here the Pharisees and Sadducees represent the darker side of Mercury square Mars. Keep aware

---

42 Ibid., p. 333.

43 Ibid., p. 93.

of your anger during these days. Aspire to respond to angry speech and action arising within yourself, and brought toward you from without by others, in the way of Elisha—with a fortitude and wisdom that does not lead to punishment or discipline, but, being imbued with love, leads to transformation. Bring calm to the storm.

**May 15: Jupiter stations retrograde, 2°13' Capricorn.** Jupiter spends a good part of this year wavering on the cusp of Sagittarius and Capricorn. The last time Jupiter walked this tightrope was in the early months of 1961. Jupiter stationed retrograde in Capricorn on May 28. John F. Kennedy had just been elected, and was actively attempting rapprochement with the USSR, much to the disdain of the intelligence agencies thirsty for the destruction of the Slavic world. The Civil Rights movement was in full swing. On the exact day of Jupiter's stationing retrograde, the British human rights activist Peter Benenson published the article "The Forgotten Prisoners," later seen as the founding of the organization Amnesty International. This is a good sign under which to extend radical gestures of peace.

Conversely, on May 25 President Kennedy announced his plan to put a man on the Moon before the end of the decade under the Apollo program. On May 15, J. Heinrich Matthaei performed the Poly-U-Experiment and became the first person to recognize and understand the genetic code—the birthdate of modern genetics. This is also a sign under which great discovery—at the dire cost of further detachment from and abstraction of Living Reality—can unfold.

**Sun enters Taurus: "Become bright, radiant being."** (See March 29 for full verse.)

The Sun entering Taurus encourages us once again to enter into the experience called up within us by dwelling on the event of the Transfiguration of Christ on Mount Tabor. Within us dwells a bright, radiant being—the Transcendent Self, which remains unsullied throughout all of our lifetimes. She is the bearer of all of our positive karma. As we move through Eastertide, looking earnestly toward Whitsun, we can exercise our ability to let this radiant being become brighter and brighter.

**Ascension Thursday is May 21 this year.** This can be a time of trial; the disciples experienced this as a loss, as a great letdown after the intense spiritual presence they had felt with them for the 40 days after Christ's resurrection. They felt confused and abandoned. This year, we can keep with us once again the star memory of the events of March 15 AD 31—the Feeding of the Four Thousand (see commentary at the beginning of May). Venus and Neptune, which were square on that day, are square on **May 20, Venus 25°38' Taurus square Neptune 25°38' Aquarius.** Simultaneously, between May 19 and 25, Mercury gradually comes to join Venus at her side. The two of them are exactly conjunct on **May 22: Mercury and Venus 25°40' Taurus.** This means that on the same day, **May 22, Mercury 25°40' Taurus is square Neptune 25°40' Aquarius.** This is a special meeting in the heavens—a conversation can occur amongst these three that is simultaneously soothing and stimulating.

Mercury and Venus were conjunct on April 6 AD 33. This was the day after the resurrection; many were still in the throes of processing the horrific events of Good Friday, only to be thrown into further confusion by the rumors of the resurrection. Two disciples, Luke and Cleophas, were on the road to Emmaus, speaking quietly together of these taboo subjects and consoling each other in their confusion and sadness. Later a stranger came to join them in their walk, and they invited him to supper. They did not realize it, but this stranger was the Risen Christ:

Jesus reclined at the table with the two disciples and ate with them of the cake and honey. Then taking the small cake, the ribbed one, he broke off a piece that he afterward divided into three with the short, white bone knife. These he laid on the little plate, and blessed. Then he stood up, elevated the plate on high with both hands, raised his eyes, and prayed. The two disciples stood opposite him, both intensely moved, and as it were transported out of themselves. When Jesus broke the little pieces, they opened their mouth and stretched forward toward him. He reached his hand across the table and laid the particle in their mouth. I saw that as he raised his hand with the third morsel to his own mouth, he disappeared. I cannot say that he really received it. The morsels shone with light after he had blessed them. I saw the two disciples standing a little while as if stupefied, and then casting themselves with tears of emotion into each other's arms.[44]

Mercury was square to Neptune on May 11 AD 31:

Today, Jesus and the disciples took a walk with seven (formerly pagan) philosophers who had received baptism. The latter asked him about the Persian king Djemschid, who had received a golden blade from God with which he had divided many lands and shed blessings everywhere. Jesus replied that Djemschid had been a leader who was wise and intelligent in things of the sense world. He spoke of Djemschid as a false type of Melchizedek, who was truly a priest and a king to whom they should turn their attention. The sacrifice of bread and wine which Melchizedek had offered would be fulfilled and perfected and would endure until the end of the world.[45]

Another memory of rich conversation, and one too that ultimately revolves around the sacramental taking of bread communally. Clearly, the antidote to whatever trial may confront us over the course of the ten days between Ascension and Whitsun is counteracted by the willingness to have rich, in-depth conversation. Conversation is the archetypal social phenomenon according to Rudolf Steiner. When entered into properly, it is analogous, in the realm of soul, to what the communal taking of the sacrament is for the body.

**May 22: New Moon 7°3' Taurus.** The New Moon was in Taurus on May 17 AD 33. This was three days after the Ascension of Christ, and a week prior to Whitsun. Once again we are brought into the sorrowful space left by Christ's absence:

The apostles and disciples now felt themselves alone. They were at first restless and like people forsaken. But by the soothing presence of the blessed Virgin they were comforted, and putting entire confidence in Jesus's words that she would be to them a mediatrix, a mother, and an advocate, they regained peace of soul.[46]

Mary continues to be the mediatrix, not only between us human beings and the spiritual world, but also between us and nature, and perhaps most crucially of all in our time, between and amongst each other. In living conversation, it is the Holy Silence that is Mary that allows for true exchange and reciprocity to exist between conflicting points of view. It is into the vessel created by us in conversation, with the Mediatrix in the center, that the descending Dove, the Holy Spirit, can alight.

**May 25:** Mercury enters Gemini;

> Reveal thyself, Sun life,
> Set repose in movement,
> Embrace joyful striving
> Toward life's mighty weaving,
> Toward blissful world knowing,
> Toward fruitful ripe-growing.
> O Sun life, endure!

Mercury triumphantly strides into Gemini, a sign in which it finds its home (the other domicile of Mercury is Virgo). Gemini, the Twins, reveals to us the mysteries of love, friendship, and cooperation. One aspect of Mercury reminds us of the talkative, sanguine, and congenial young child. It is this childlike spirit of friendship that is fostered here. The word "striving" makes us think of strenuous effort; yet paired with the qualifier "joyful," suddenly the burden is made light. With the instruction to "embrace," a warm and devotional gesture underpins this striving. Mercury in Gemini is warm, bright, and hard-working. "Make every burden easy and every yoke light."

As the month of May comes to a close, after Mercury's ingress into Gemini, he winds closer and closer to the Moon's Ascending Node. They are within 5° of each other between May 25 and June

---

44 Brentano, *The Visions of Anne Catherine Emmerich,* vol. 3, p. 394.

45 Ibid., vol. 2, p. 374.

46 Ibid., vol. 3, p. 412.

1. They meet each other on **May 28, Mercury conjunct Node 4°12' Gemini.** This conjunction is still relatively close all the way through to **Whit Sunday (Pentecost), May 31, 2020.**

Mercury ingressed into Gemini on May 6, 810. It was around this time that Gawan was confronting the bewildering and hazardous trials of the "Castle of Marvels." This was a fortress belonging to the black magician Klingsor, where he held in silent captivity many women from the surrounding countryside. Mercury continued to draw closer to the Node over the course of the month of May, during which Gawan won the hand of his love Orgeleuse, and Parzival was reunited with the retinue of the Knights of the Round Table as well as his estranged half-brother Feirefiz. Mercury and Node were within 3° of each other on May 26, 810, when both Parzival and Feirefiz rode together to the Grail Castle. It was on this day that Parzival fulfilled his destiny, asking King Anfortas the healing question, "What ails thee?" Feirefiz, too, found his destiny, for here he met his future bride Repanse de Schoye (the reincarnated Magdalene). The two of them would wed soon after, and eventually settle in India, where their son Prester John (the reincarnated Lazarus) would become a teacher of esoteric Christianity.

The events of the last chapters of *Parzival* are exemplary of the injunction to "embrace joyful striving." This could be a motto for Parzival's whole biography. As we gather together on May 31 to celebrate Whitsun, let us remember that this is the festival that transitions us out of the Raphaelic time of year, a time of healing, into the Urielic time of year. Uriel is the archangel who guards the mysteries of the social life and of morality. Whereas Easter was about healing that which is ill within humanity, nature, and subnature, Pentecost is about the archetypal social phenomenon—meeting soul to soul via conversation. In Parzival's time, this conversation could be sparked through the healing question: "What ails thee?"—that is, "How can I help you?" In our time it is different. We are less and less able to offer the helping hand to another unless they open the door for us first. Therefore it is up to each of us: we must find the way to become vulnerable enough to open the door for the helpful opinion of the other. The Grail Question of our time needs to be, "What ails *me*? Can you help me, please?" If we can give this question as an offering to other people, we might be surprised at the possibilities that are opened up through it. May we cultivate the practice of entering this vulnerable space on this Whitsun, joyfully striving to create a living *E Pluribus Unum*: out of many, One—harmony in difference.

Today also marks the Christian celebration of the third major Marian festival of the year, the Visitation. We remember Mary's visit to her cousin Elizabeth, who was six months pregnant with John the Baptist, the cousin of Jesus. The two soul twins drew near to each other as their mothers drew close, and John leapt in the womb with joy. We can meditate today on the words of the Magnificat:

> My soul magnifies the Lord,
> And my spirit rejoices in God my Savior,
> For he has regarded the low estate of
>     his handmaiden.
> For behold, henceforth all generations
>     will call me blessed...
> He has scattered the those who have
>     proud thoughts in their hearts,
> He has put down the mighty from
>     their thrones,
> And he has exalted those of low degree.
> He has filled the hungry with good things,
> And the rich he has sent away empty-handed.
>                 (Luke 1: 46–48, 51–53).

What a wonderful coincidence that the fixed festival of Visitation, which always falls on May 31, would fall on the moving feast of Whit Sunday (Pentecost)—in which Mary was the central Mediatrix of the Holy Spirit. Today we honor and remember Our Lady.

# JUNE 2020

## STARGAZING PREVIEW

On the 1st of the month we'll find Jupiter and Saturn only 5° apart, six months away from their conjunction on the winter solstice. Venus and the Sun meet in an inferior conjunction on the 3rd (18° Taurus). The Scorpio Full Moon on the 5th will create a Penumbral Lunar Eclipse that will be centered over western China and will last for over three hours.

Three days later, on the 8th, the Moon will pass in front of and slightly below both Jupiter and Saturn. The Moon will have already moved beyond Jupiter at the time of Jupiter's rising at 2300, and ten minutes later you'll be able to see the Moon and Saturn crest the horizon in perfect conjunction. At sunrise (0530) on the following day, these three will be low in the west and Mars, in the last decan of Aquarius, will be high in the south.

The 12th marks the day that the Moon catches up to Mars. The Moon rises just before Mars (around 0100) on this day—most of its right half will be darkened; if you're up at the same time on the 13th, you'll be able to see Mars rise moments ahead of the Moon, which will reach its Last Quarter in Aquarius several hours later. Mars moves into Pisces late on the 19th.

Our June New Moon (5° Gemini) on the 21st will result in an Annular Solar Eclipse lasting as much as 38 seconds; Nepal will be the area most affected. Can you imagine being on Everest during a solar eclipse? Though the climbing season will be over by then, may we pray for all of the climbers in our lives, as well as the snow leopards and Himalayan tahrs of the region!

Venus stations direct on the 25th (10° Taurus), which means that when we next see her, she'll be a morning star. The 28th brings us a First Quarter Moon at 12° Virgo. When it sets around 0100, you'll be able to watch Mars, from across the zodiacal circle, rise in the east.

## JUNE COMMENTARIES

The month of April was a time during which new levels of realization became accessible to the Self, particularly in its reflective activity of thinking, as the Sun (Self) and Mercury (Thinking) were involved in the major aspects of the month. Then in May, Venus joined the other two; a weaving together of thinking and feeling—what one might call "heart thinking"—was given support during this month, encouraging empathic, soulful conversation in the light of Whitsun and the Visitation on May 31.

As we move into the month of June, Mars becomes more dominant in the major aspects of the month, giving emphasis to the realm of the will, to action. The longest lasting aspect is the square of Sun and Mars. The two are already coming into alignment as of May 20; this alignment lasts until June 22. It is exact on **June 6, Sun 20°58' Taurus square Mars 20°58' Aquarius.** Sun and Mars were square on March 12 AD 30, the death day of Eliud the Essene:

> Jesus visited a venerable old man named Eliud on Tuesday, September 6 AD 29, just outside of Nazareth. He was a widower, the son of a brother of Zechariah, and looked after by his daughter and a nephew of Zechariah. Jesus is with him for twelve days, conversing in his home and undertaking together a private journey through Southern Galilee, during which they visit a leper settlement, a healing pool, and several towns. They never leave each other's side, and on the last night, in the field of Jezebel, Jesus appears to Eliud in transfigured form. Why this singular distinction and preference for one person? Anne Catherine Emmerich received an answer to this question which can shed its clarifying light also upon all other such private conversations that Jesus held: all the private individuals whom the evangelists mention by name, and with whom the Master spent extended periods of time, are "types" of humanity, representing very specific groups in human history, as also certain states that recur ever and again in human souls as well as specific gifts and vocations (even misdirected ones, as in the case of Judas Iscariot). Eliud is the type of a mystic

living in a state of mature private illumination, as a result of which he is granted a particularly intimate contact with Jesus. Accordingly, Jesus's conversations with Eliud deal with things he did not share with the public at large, or even in a small circle. When they part company, Jesus gives Eliud a special blessing and accepts him into the community of his new kingdom. And shortly before his death, the weakened Eliud receives the divine consolation of speaking one last time with Jesus, who passes the entire night in his Capernaum lodging.[47]

The day after Eliud's death, Christ performs the miracle of effortlessly and discreetly multiplying a loaf of bread by handing out pieces of it to those he passed while walking. Eliud represents a certain state of soul, that of mature private illumination. Here, as Sun squares Mars, we remember his *passing*, and the unseen miracle that occurs the next day. Perhaps it is time for us to emerge from a more contemplative state of soul, to "put to death" our private illumination, so that it can resurrect in the form of *deeds*—deeds that very likely will go unnoticed by the outer world, but will be to great effect.

While the above aspect lasts for about a month (May 20–June 22), it is of particular potency at the start of June. As June begins, the Sun comes into conjunction with Venus; and since the Sun is also square Mars during this time, this means that Venus too comes into square alignment with Mars. This is a beautiful arrangement displaying the dying Christ (Venus) resurrecting (Sun) through overcoming the depths (Mars).

Between May 29 and June 6, Venus and Mars are in square alignment, while the Sun and Venus are close to conjunction from May 31 through June 6. **On June 3, Venus 19° Taurus squares Mars 19° Aquarius; and Sun and Venus are conjunct 18° Taurus.** Keep in mind that Venus is currently retrograde, so it squares Mars prior to its conjunction with the Sun. The Venus–Mars alignment recalls the raising of Martialis, the Youth of Nain, on November 13 AD 30:

Jesus called for water and a little branch. Someone brought to a disciple, who handed them to Jesus, a little vessel of water and a twig of hyssop. Jesus took the water and said to the bearers: "Open the coffin and loosen the bands!" While this command was being executed, Jesus raised his eyes to Heaven and said: "I confess to thee, O Father, Lord of Heaven and Earth, because thou hast hidden these things from the wise and the prudent, and hast revealed them to little ones. Yea, Father, for so it hath seemed good in thy sight. All things are delivered to me by my Father, and not one knoweth the Son but the Father; neither doth anyone know the Father but the Son, and he to whom it shall please the Son to reveal to him. Come to me, all you that labor and are burdened, and I will refresh you. Take up my yoke upon you, and learn of me, because I am meek and humble of heart, and you shall find rest to your souls, for my yoke is sweet, and my burden light!" When the bearers removed the cover, I saw the body wrapped like a babe in swaddling clothes and lying in the coffin. Supporting it in their arms, they loosened the bands, drew them off, uncovered the face, unbound the hands, and left about it only one linen covering. Then Jesus blessed the water, dipped the little branch into it, and sprinkled the crowd. Thereupon I saw numbers of small, dark figures like insects, beetles, toads, snakes, and little black birds issuing from many of the bystanders. The crowd became purer and brighter. Jesus then sprinkled the dead youth with the little branch, and with his hand made the sign of the cross over him, upon which I beheld a murky, black, cloud-like figure issuing from the body. Jesus said to the youth, "Arise!" He arose to a sitting posture, and gazed around him in questioning astonishment.[48]

While Venus square Mars is a powerful force for deeds of restoration and purification in the world (as witnessed to by the above recollection), Sun conjunct Venus is radiantly devotional—however, jealousy and avarice, the dark side of Venus, can also manifest. These two were conjunct on March 20 AD 33:

---

47 Brentano, *The Visions of Anne Catherine Emmerich*, vol. 1, p. 60.

48 Ibid., vol. 2, p. 142.

## SIDEREAL GEOCENTRIC LONGITUDES :   JUNE 2020 Gregorian at 0 hours UT

| DAY | ☉ | ☽ | ☊ | ☿ | ♀ | ♂ | ♃ | ♄ | ♅ | ♆ | ♇ |
|---|---|---|---|---|---|---|---|---|---|---|---|
| 1 MO | 15 ♉ 57 | 10 ♍ 37 | 4 ♊ 12R | 9 ♊ 6 | 20 ♉ 17R | 17 ♒ 40 | 1 ♑ 44R | 6 ♑ 35R | 13 ♈ 32 | 25 ♒ 48 | 29 ♐ 40R |
| 2 TU | 16 54 | 25 10 | 4 10 | 10 15 | 19 40 | 18 20 | 1 41 | 6 33 | 13 35 | 25 49 | 29 39 |
| 3 WE | 17 52 | 9 ♎ 49 | 4 8 | 11 20 | 19 2 | 19 0 | 1 38 | 6 31 | 13 38 | 25 50 | 29 38 |
| 4 TH | 18 49 | 24 29 | 4 7 | 12 22 | 18 24 | 19 39 | 1 34 | 6 29 | 13 41 | 25 50 | 29 37 |
| 5 FR | 19 47 | 9 ♏ 3 | 4 5 | 13 20 | 17 47 | 20 19 | 1 30 | 6 27 | 13 44 | 25 51 | 29 36 |
| 6 SA | 20 44 | 23 24 | 4 4 | 14 14 | 17 9 | 20 58 | 1 26 | 6 24 | 13 47 | 25 52 | 29 35 |
| 7 SU | 21 41 | 7 ♐ 27 | 4 4D | 15 5 | 16 32 | 21 38 | 1 22 | 6 22 | 13 50 | 25 52 | 29 34 |
| 8 MO | 22 39 | 21 10 | 4 5 | 15 51 | 15 56 | 22 17 | 1 18 | 6 19 | 13 53 | 25 53 | 29 33 |
| 9 TU | 23 36 | 4 ♑ 29 | 4 6 | 16 34 | 15 21 | 22 56 | 1 13 | 6 17 | 13 56 | 25 53 | 29 32 |
| 10 WE | 24 34 | 17 27 | 4 7 | 17 13 | 14 47 | 23 35 | 1 8 | 6 14 | 13 58 | 25 54 | 29 31 |
| 11 TH | 25 31 | 0 ♒ 4 | 4 7 | 17 47 | 14 15 | 24 14 | 1 4 | 6 11 | 14 1 | 25 54 | 29 29 |
| 12 FR | 26 28 | 12 23 | 4 8 | 18 17 | 13 44 | 24 53 | 0 59 | 6 9 | 14 4 | 25 54 | 29 28 |
| 13 SA | 27 26 | 24 29 | 4 8R | 18 43 | 13 15 | 25 32 | 0 54 | 6 6 | 14 7 | 25 55 | 29 27 |
| 14 SU | 28 23 | 6 ♓ 27 | 4 8 | 19 4 | 12 48 | 26 10 | 0 48 | 6 3 | 14 9 | 25 55 | 29 26 |
| 15 MO | 29 20 | 18 20 | 4 7 | 19 21 | 12 23 | 26 49 | 0 43 | 6 0 | 14 12 | 25 55 | 29 25 |
| 16 TU | 0 ♊ 17 | 0 ♈ 13 | 4 7 | 19 33 | 12 0 | 27 27 | 0 37 | 5 56 | 14 15 | 25 56 | 29 23 |
| 17 WE | 1 15 | 12 10 | 4 6 | 19 41 | 11 40 | 28 5 | 0 32 | 5 53 | 14 17 | 25 56 | 29 22 |
| 18 TH | 2 12 | 24 16 | 4 6 | 19 44 | 11 21 | 28 43 | 0 26 | 5 50 | 14 20 | 25 56 | 29 21 |
| 19 FR | 3 9 | 6 ♉ 32 | 4 6 | 19 43R | 11 5 | 29 21 | 0 20 | 5 47 | 14 22 | 25 56 | 29 20 |
| 20 SA | 4 7 | 19 1 | 4 6D | 19 37 | 10 51 | 29 59 | 0 14 | 5 43 | 14 25 | 25 56 | 29 18 |
| 21 SU | 5 4 | 1 ♊ 45 | 4 6 | 19 27 | 10 40 | 0 ♓ 37 | 0 7 | 5 40 | 14 27 | 25 56 | 29 17 |
| 22 MO | 6 1 | 14 44 | 4 6R | 19 13 | 10 31 | 1 14 | 0 1 | 5 36 | 14 30 | 25 56 | 29 16 |
| 23 TU | 6 58 | 27 58 | 4 6 | 18 54 | 10 25 | 1 52 | 29 ♐ 55 | 5 33 | 14 32 | 25 56 | 29 15 |
| 24 WE | 7 56 | 9 ♋ 26 | 4 6 | 18 32 | 10 21 | 2 29 | 29 48 | 5 29 | 14 35 | 25 56R | 29 13 |
| 25 TH | 8 53 | 25 8 | 4 5 | 18 7 | 10 19 | 3 6 | 29 41 | 5 26 | 14 37 | 25 56 | 29 12 |
| 26 FR | 9 50 | 9 ♌ 0 | 4 5 | 17 38 | 10 19D | 3 43 | 29 35 | 5 22 | 14 39 | 25 56 | 29 11 |
| 27 SA | 10 47 | 23 2 | 4 4 | 17 7 | 10 22 | 4 19 | 29 28 | 5 18 | 14 42 | 25 56 | 29 9 |
| 28 SU | 11 45 | 7 ♍ 11 | 4 4 | 16 34 | 10 27 | 4 56 | 29 21 | 5 14 | 14 44 | 25 56 | 29 8 |
| 29 MO | 12 42 | 21 25 | 4 4D | 15 59 | 10 34 | 5 32 | 29 14 | 5 10 | 14 46 | 25 56 | 29 7 |
| 30 TU | 13 39 | 5 ♎ 42 | 4 4 | 15 24 | 10 44 | 6 8 | 29 7 | 5 6 | 14 48 | 25 56 | 29 5 |

### INGRESSES :

| | | |
|---|---|---|
| 2 ☽ → ♎ 7:55 | 22 ♃ → ♐ 4:16 | |
| 4 ☽ → ♏ 9: 3 | 23 ☽ → ♋ 3:39 | |
| 6 ☽ → ♐ 11:11 | 25 ☽ → ♌ 8:27 | |
| 8 ☽ → ♑ 15:50 | 27 ☽ → ♍ 11:49 | |
| 10 ☽ → ♒ 23:53 | 29 ☽ → ♎ 14:25 | |
| 13 ☽ → ♓ 11: 1 | | |
| 15 ☉ → ♊ 16:40 | | |
| ☽ → ♈ 23:33 | | |
| 18 ☽ → ♉ 11:16 | | |
| 20 ♂ → ♓ 0:31 | | |
| ☽ → ♊ 20:44 | | |

### ASPECTS & ECLIPSES :

| | | | |
|---|---|---|---|
| 3 ♀ □ ♂ 0:39 | ☽ ☌ ♃ 18: 4 | ☉ ☌ ☊ 23:43 | ☽ ☍ ♂ 20: 0 |
| ☽ ☌ P 3:33 | 9 ☽ ☌ ♄ 3:15 | 21 ☽ ☌ ☊ 4:23 | 28 ☉ □ ☽ 8:14 |
| ☽ ☍ ♅ 6:15 | 11 ☉ □ ♆ 9:46 | ☉ ● A 6:38 | 30 ☽ ☌ P 1:48 |
| ☉ ☌ ♀ 17:42 | 13 ☽ ☌ ♂ 2:11 | ☉ ☌ ☽ 6:40 | ♃ ☌ ♇ 6:42 |
| 5 ☽ ☍ ♀ 13:56 | ☽ ☌ ♆ 2:50 | 22 ☽ ☌ ☿ 8: 0 | ☽ ☍ ♅ 15:19 |
| ☉ ☍ ☽ 19:11 | ☉ □ ☽ 6:22 | 23 ☽ ☍ ♇ 2:17 | |
| ☽ ☌ PN 19:21 | ♂ ☌ ♆ 14:26 | ☽ ☍ ♃ 3:27 | |
| 6 ☽ ☌ ☋ 18:10 | ☽ ∥ ☊ 19:19 | ☽ ☍ ♄ 13:29 | |
| ☉ □ ♂ 19: 9 | 15 ☽ ☌ A 0:42 | 26 ♂ □ ☊ 14:11 | |
| 7 ☽ ☍ ☿ 14: 4 | 17 ☽ ☌ ♅ 4:14 | 27 ☽ ☍ ♆ 4:56 | |
| 8 ☽ ☌ ♇ 14:59 | 19 ☽ ☌ ♀ 8:38 | ☽ ∥ ☊ 18:43 | |

## SIDEREAL HELIOCENTRIC LONGITUDES :   JUNE 2020 Gregorian at 0 hours UT

| DAY | Sid. Time | ☿ | ♀ | ⊕ | ♂ | ♃ | ♄ | ♅ | ♆ | ♇ | Vernal Point |
|---|---|---|---|---|---|---|---|---|---|---|---|
| 1 MO | 16:39:46 | 15 ♍ 14 | 14 ♏ 14 | 15 ♏ 57 | 1 ♑ 39 | 23 ♐ 40 | 2 ♑ 6 | 11 ♈ 58 | 23 ♒ 54 | 28 ♐ 29 | 4 ♓ 58'30" |
| 2 TU | 16:43:42 | 18 54 | 15 49 | 16 55 | 2 16 | 23 45 | 2 8 | 11 59 | 23 54 | 28 29 | 4 ♓ 58'30" |
| 3 WE | 16:47:39 | 22 27 | 17 24 | 17 52 | 2 53 | 23 50 | 2 10 | 12 0 | 23 55 | 28 30 | 4 ♓ 58'30" |
| 4 TH | 16:51:35 | 25 56 | 19 0 | 18 50 | 3 29 | 23 55 | 2 11 | 12 0 | 23 55 | 28 30 | 4 ♓ 58'30" |
| 5 FR | 16:55:32 | 29 19 | 20 35 | 19 47 | 4 6 | 24 0 | 2 13 | 12 1 | 23 56 | 28 30 | 4 ♓ 58'30" |
| 6 SA | 16:59:28 | 2 ♎ 38 | 22 10 | 20 45 | 4 43 | 24 5 | 2 15 | 12 2 | 23 56 | 28 31 | 4 ♓ 58'30" |
| 7 SU | 17: 3:25 | 5 52 | 23 45 | 21 42 | 5 20 | 24 10 | 2 17 | 12 2 | 23 56 | 28 31 | 4 ♓ 58'30" |
| 8 MO | 17: 7:22 | 9 3 | 25 21 | 22 39 | 5 57 | 24 15 | 2 19 | 12 3 | 23 57 | 28 31 | 4 ♓ 58'29" |
| 9 TU | 17:11:18 | 12 10 | 26 56 | 23 37 | 6 34 | 24 20 | 2 20 | 12 4 | 23 57 | 28 32 | 4 ♓ 58'29" |
| 10 WE | 17:15:15 | 15 14 | 28 31 | 24 34 | 7 11 | 24 25 | 2 22 | 12 4 | 23 57 | 28 32 | 4 ♓ 58'29" |
| 11 TH | 17:19:11 | 18 14 | 0 ♐ 6 | 25 32 | 7 48 | 24 30 | 2 24 | 12 5 | 23 58 | 28 32 | 4 ♓ 58'29" |
| 12 FR | 17:23: 8 | 21 13 | 1 41 | 26 29 | 8 25 | 24 35 | 2 26 | 12 5 | 23 58 | 28 32 | 4 ♓ 58'29" |
| 13 SA | 17:27: 4 | 24 8 | 3 16 | 27 26 | 9 2 | 24 40 | 2 28 | 12 6 | 23 58 | 28 33 | 4 ♓ 58'29" |
| 14 SU | 17:31: 1 | 27 2 | 4 51 | 28 23 | 9 39 | 24 45 | 2 30 | 12 7 | 23 59 | 28 33 | 4 ♓ 58'29" |
| 15 MO | 17:34:57 | 29 54 | 6 26 | 29 21 | 10 16 | 24 50 | 2 31 | 12 7 | 23 59 | 28 33 | 4 ♓ 58'29" |
| 16 TU | 17:38:54 | 2 ♏ 44 | 8 1 | 0 ♐ 18 | 10 53 | 24 55 | 2 33 | 12 8 | 23 59 | 28 34 | 4 ♓ 58'28" |
| 17 WE | 17:42:51 | 5 32 | 9 36 | 1 15 | 11 30 | 25 0 | 2 35 | 12 9 | 24 0 | 28 34 | 4 ♓ 58'28" |
| 18 TH | 17:46:47 | 8 20 | 11 11 | 2 13 | 12 8 | 25 6 | 2 37 | 12 9 | 24 0 | 28 34 | 4 ♓ 58'28" |
| 19 FR | 17:50:44 | 11 6 | 12 46 | 3 10 | 12 45 | 25 11 | 2 39 | 12 10 | 24 1 | 28 35 | 4 ♓ 58'28" |
| 20 SA | 17:54:40 | 13 52 | 14 21 | 4 7 | 13 22 | 25 16 | 2 40 | 12 11 | 24 1 | 28 35 | 4 ♓ 58'28" |
| 21 SU | 17:58:37 | 16 37 | 15 56 | 5 5 | 14 0 | 25 21 | 2 42 | 12 11 | 24 1 | 28 35 | 4 ♓ 58'28" |
| 22 MO | 18: 2:33 | 19 22 | 17 31 | 6 2 | 14 37 | 25 26 | 2 44 | 12 12 | 24 2 | 28 35 | 4 ♓ 58'28" |
| 23 TU | 18: 6:30 | 22 6 | 19 6 | 6 59 | 15 15 | 25 31 | 2 46 | 12 13 | 24 2 | 28 36 | 4 ♓ 58'27" |
| 24 WE | 18:10:26 | 24 51 | 20 41 | 7 56 | 15 52 | 25 36 | 2 48 | 12 13 | 24 2 | 28 36 | 4 ♓ 58'27" |
| 25 TH | 18:14:23 | 27 36 | 22 15 | 8 54 | 16 30 | 25 41 | 2 50 | 12 14 | 24 3 | 28 36 | 4 ♓ 58'27" |
| 26 FR | 18:18:20 | 0 ♐ 22 | 23 50 | 9 51 | 17 7 | 25 46 | 2 51 | 12 15 | 24 3 | 28 37 | 4 ♓ 58'27" |
| 27 SA | 18:22:16 | 3 8 | 25 25 | 10 48 | 17 45 | 25 51 | 2 53 | 12 15 | 24 3 | 28 37 | 4 ♓ 58'27" |
| 28 SU | 18:26:13 | 5 55 | 27 0 | 11 45 | 18 22 | 25 56 | 2 55 | 12 16 | 24 4 | 28 37 | 4 ♓ 58'27" |
| 29 MO | 18:30: 9 | 8 43 | 28 35 | 12 42 | 19 0 | 26 1 | 2 57 | 12 17 | 24 4 | 28 37 | 4 ♓ 58'27" |
| 30 TU | 18:34: 6 | 11 32 | 0 ♑ 10 | 13 40 | 19 37 | 26 6 | 2 59 | 12 17 | 24 5 | 28 38 | 4 ♓ 58'26" |

### INGRESSES :

| |
|---|
| 5 ☿ → ♎ 4:54 |
| 10 ♀ → ♐ 22:28 |
| 15 ☿ → ♏ 0:53 |
| ⊕ → ♐ 16:25 |
| 25 ☿ → ♐ 20:52 |
| 29 ♀ → ♑ 21:32 |

### ASPECTS (HELIOCENTRIC +MOON(TYCHONIC)) :

| | | | | |
|---|---|---|---|---|
| 1 ☽ ☌ ☿ 10:15 | ☿ □ ♄ 21:12 | ☽ ☍ ♅ 13:57 | 19 ☽ ☍ ☿ 11:21 | ♀ ☌ ♃ 6:55 |
| ♂ ☌ ♄ 18:17 | ☽ ☌ ♀ 21:40 | ☽ □ ☿ 18:32 | 20 ☽ □ ♆ 9:29 | ☽ □ ♀ 21:18 |
| ☽ □ ♃ 21:39 | 6 ☽ □ ♆ 0:54 | 12 ☿ ☌ ♅ 19: 8 | 22 ☽ ☍ ♀ 5:46 | 29 ♀ ☌ ♇ 0:40 |
| 2 ☽ □ ♇ 5:27 | ☿ ☌ ♂ 19: 1 | ☽ ☌ ♆ 22:57 | ☽ ☍ ♃ 19:33 | ☽ □ ♃ 7:46 |
| ☽ ☌ ♄ 11:26 | 7 ☽ ☌ ♆ 2:43 | 13 ☽ ☍ ♀ 20:17 | 23 ☽ ☍ ♇ 1: 8 | ☽ ☍ ♆ 12: 6 |
| ☽ ☌ ♂ 12: 9 | 8 ☽ ☌ ♂ 5:32 | 15 ☽ □ ♆ 13:14 | ☿ ☌ A 5:37 | ☽ □ ♀ 13:31 |
| 3 ☽ ☍ ♅ 3:33 | ☽ ☌ ♆ 13:10 | ☽ □ ♆ 20:39 | ☽ ☍ ♄ 8:37 | ☽ ☍ ♀ 19:24 |
| ☿ □ ♃ 9:40 | ☽ ☌ ♄ 20: 4 | 16 ☽ □ ♄ 4:43 | ☿ □ ♆ 16:53 | 30 ☽ ☍ ♅ 11: 4 |
| ♀ ☌ ⊕ 17:42 | ☿ ☍ ♅ 23:10 | ☽ □ ♂ 22:35 | 24 ☽ □ ♅ 1:23 | |
| 4 ☿ □ ♀ 18:12 | 9 ☽ ☌ ♂ 3:58 | ☽ ☌ ♅ 23:56 | ☽ ☍ ♂ 8:10 | |
| 5 ♀ ☌ ♇ 18:58 | ⊕ □ ♆ 8:29 | 18 ♂ □ ♅ 1: 7 | 27 ☽ ☍ ♆ 1:44 | |

Toward the end of [the meal], Magdalene, urged by love, gratitude, contrition, and anxiety, again made her appearance. She went behind the Lord's couch, broke a little flask of precious balm over his head and poured some of it upon his feet, which she again wiped with her hair. That done, she left the dining hall. Several of those present were scandalized, especially Judas…full of chagrin, [he] hurried back to Jerusalem that night. I saw him, torn by envy and avarice, running in the darkness over the Mount of Olives, and it seemed as if a sinister glare surrounded him, as if the devil were lighting his steps. He hurried to the house of Caiaphas, and spoke a few words at the door. He could not stay long in any one place…. This was the first definite step in his treacherous course.[49]

**June 5: Full Moon, 20°33' Scorpio (Lunar Eclipse).** The Full Moon was in Scorpio on the night of April 25–26 AD 31, as Christ and the disciples boarded boats to sail from Ornothopolis to Cyprus:

It was by starlight that Jesus, accompanied by all the travelers, went down to the harbor and embarked. The night was clear, and the stars looked larger than they do to us…Jesus stood near the mast of the ships that were fastened to the large one and, as they pushed off, he blessed both land and sea. Shoals of fishes swarmed after the flotilla, among them some very large ones with remarkable-looking mouths. They sported around and stretched their heads out of the water, as if hearkening to the instructions given by Jesus during the voyage.

The passage was so unusually rapid, the sea so smooth, and the weather so beautiful that the sailors, both Jews and pagans, cried out: "Oh, what an auspicious voyage! That is owing to thee, O prophet!" Jesus was standing near the mast. He commanded them silence and to give glory to the almighty God alone.[50]

We might continue to find that, like Christ effortlessly multiplying the bread (see memory of March 13 AD 31 above), our efforts seem to be coming together seamlessly. The risk is vanity, self-glorification, inflation. Remember how many other

individuals, known to us and unknown, are crucial to the unfolding of any of our intentions. We never act alone—and often things work out magnificently *despite* our efforts, not due to them!

The event of a lunar eclipse heightens the tension of this choice between the risk of inflation on the one hand (due to the eclipse of the Higher Self), and the active recognition and remembering of those upon whom we rely. This active recognition and remembering is the activity at the heart of the Moon's own light—the light of the Earth Mother—that is unveiled during a lunar eclipse.

In prior months (both January and April), the Sun's movements have been coordinated with Mercury's, usually with the Sun traversing a path prior to Mercury following along. We can envision this as our Higher Self—which manifests itself typically both in our spontaneous intuitive capacities as well as in the seemingly chance occurrences of our biography—forging ahead, making a path for our Lower Self—which manifests itself in our waking consciousness, our life of thought—to make sense of our experiences and intuitions only after the fact.

June is different. Here we have *Mars aspects* following in the wake of the Sun's. This means our sense of self-realization and understanding is not going to occur through conscious thought, but only through word and deed. We feel our Self *living* in our will, rather than in our internal monologue.

From June 6 to 16, the Sun comes into square alignment with Neptune. This alignment is exact on **June 11, Sun 25°54' Taurus square Neptune 25°54' Aquarius.** Meanwhile, between June 5 and 21, Mars is conjunct Neptune; this alignment is exact on **June 13, Mars conjunct Neptune 25°55'.** Neptune's higher aspect has to do with the depths of inspiration from the Goddess Night, a level of inspiration of the highest degree. However, the shadow side of Neptune is as dangerous as its higher aspect is transformative. It has to do with the insidious underbelly, subterfuge, possession, and manipulation. Sun square Neptune might enable the unveiling of this underbelly through shining the powerful

---

49 Ibid., vol. 3, p. 10.
50 Ibid., vol. 2, p. 354.

light of the Sun into the darkness. We see this on April 19 AD 31:

> Today, Jesus continued his "Sermon on the Mount." The Pharisees began to proclaim Jesus as a "disturber of the peace," saying that they had the sabbath, the festival days, and their own teaching, and that they did not need the innovations of this upstart. They threatened to complain to Herod—who would certainly put a stop to Jesus's activities. Jesus answered that he would continue to teach and heal, in spite of Herod, until his mission was complete. Eventually, the pressure of the crowd forced the Pharisees to leave so that Jesus could continue his teaching undisturbed. After the sermon had ended and the crowd had dispersed, Jesus taught the disciples concerning the character of the Pharisees and how they should conduct themselves in relation to them. That evening, as Jesus and the disciples ate together, Lazarus told of the journey the women had made to Machaerus from Hebron and Jerusalem. Indeed, one of them, Johanna Chusa, had just succeeded in recovering the head of John the Baptist from Herod's castle.[51]

Christ shines this light both in his response to the Pharisees as well as in his recommendations as to how to properly meet them. The holy women shine this light into the darkness in their recovery of the head of John the Baptist from Herod's garbage heap. Meanwhile, the conjunction of Mars and Neptune is recalled on August 15 AD 30:

> Today they went northward to the town of Gerasa, where they arrived that evening. Here he received a message sent by the holy Virgin on behalf of a widow of Nain who was possessed. This widow was an acquaintance of Maroni, the widow of Nain [and mother of Martialias] whom Jesus had visited there on Ab 14 [August 2 AD 30]. Receiving the message, Jesus healed the possessed woman from a distance.[52]

Here we see not only a light shining in the darkness, but the actual power of the Word (Mars) overcoming this darkness, in Christ healing the possessed woman from a distance. We may be confronted by the darkness during this time of the month—allow the Light and the Word to transform it!

**June 15: Sun enters Gemini. "Reveal thyself, Sun life."** (See May 25 for the full verse).

The life of the Sun is called upon to reveal itself. This implies that at other times of the year, the life of the Sun is veiled or hidden. One might associate this with a veiled or hidden identity; we might *feel* the life of the Sun throughout the year without *knowing* who or what this life is. Sun in Gemini, therefore, only enhances our ability to "shine a light into the darkness." A meditative exercise for the day might be to move imaginatively into who exactly—what being or beings—lives within the life of the Sun.

**June 18: Mercury stations retrograde, 19°44' Gemini.** Mercury was at this degree on the evening of June 6–7 AD 31:

> [Christ] rebuked the Pharisees for subjugating the people with the heavy duties that they themselves did not perform.
>
> [The next day] in the afternoon, Jesus and the disciples went to Nain. Here on Heshvan 28 [November 13 AD 30—see commentary for June 3], he had raised the youth Martialis from the dead. Martialis's mother—the rich widow Maroni—had put one of her properties at Jesus's disposal to be used by him and his disciples as an inn. Jesus and the disciples visited this house. Martha, Mary Magdalene, Veronica, Johanna Chusa, and Mara the Suphanite were waiting there.[53]

Mercury brings us once again to the rebuke of the Pharisees, as well as to the aftermath of the raising of Martialis. Perhaps today we can gratefully reap the benefits of the purification and transformation in which we engaged at the start of the month.

---

51 Ibid., pp. 348–349.
52 Ibid., p. 16.

53 Ibid., p. 395.

Mars and the Sun continue their journey, maintaining a 90° angle between them as they aspect other stellar phenomena. Between June 14 and 25, the Sun comes into conjunction with the Node. This alignment is exact on **June 19, Sun conjunct Node 4°6' Gemini.** These two were conjunct on March 27 AD 33:

> Jesus exhorted the apostles not to give way to their natural fears upon what he had said to them, namely, that they would all be dispersed; they should not forget their neighbor and should not allow one sentiment to veil, to stifle another; and here he made use of the similitude of a mantle. In general terms he reproached some of them for murmuring at Magdalene's anointing. Jesus probably said this in reference to Judas's first definitive step toward his betrayal, which had been taken just after that action of hers—also, as a gentle warning to him for the future, since it would be after Magdalene's last anointing that he would carry out his treacherous design. That some others were scandalized at Magdalene's prodigal expression of love arose from their erroneous severity and parsimony. They regarded this anointing as a luxury so often abused at worldly feasts, while overlooking the fact that such an action performed on the Holy of Holies was worthy of the highest praise.[54]

We return here to one of the main themes of this month: the radical devotional gesture of Mary Magdalene, and its unfortunate lack of approval—or worse—by those witnessing. We should pay heed to the exhortation to be gentle as doves: acting out of conscience without fear or hesitation, yet being as wise as serpents: seeing quite clearly the potentially disturbing effect our conscientious behavior might have on those who are less than conscientious.

**June 20: Summer Solstice; Mars enters Pisces. "And maintain in maintaining."** (See February 3 for the full verse).

Before Mars can continue to indirectly follow the course set out by the Sun, it must ingress into Pisces. There is nothing in the way of grandeur here; the phrase "maintain in maintaining" conjures up images of slow, steady, and rhythmic labor. Keeping a space tidy; creating a moment of silence or

blessing before and after a meal; dutifully practicing an exercise, whether physical or spiritual. These seemingly simple and insignificant tasks requiring timely repetition are often the hardest and most crucial to stick to. Mars in Pisces aids in the effort.

**June 21: New Moon 5°20' Gemini (Solar Eclipse).** Today's New Moon carries on directly with the star memory from just a few days ago. Mercury recalled the events of June 6–7 AD 31; on June 8, there was also a New Moon in Gemini:

> Jesus visited several people in Nain and then went to Maroni's garden. Here he gave the holy women advice about their inner life and their work serving the community of Christians. When on the sabbath Jesus returned to the synagogue, he did not go to the teacher's chair but stood with his disciples in the place in which traveling teachers were accustomed to stand. But after bidding him welcome and the prayers being said, the rabbis constrained him to take his place before the open rolls of scripture and to read therefrom....[The Pharisees] recommended him to be quiet and not to disturb the sabbath with his cures. It would be just as well for him, they said, to go back whence he came and to forbear creating any excitement. Jesus replied that he would fulfill the duties of his mission, journeying and teaching until his hour had arrived. The Pharisees...were full of spite against him, because his doctrine and charity drew after him all the poor, the miserable and the simple-hearted, whom their own severity alienated.[55]

This star memory brings us back to our other themes this month: the raising of the Youth of Nain and its consequences, and facing the enmity of the Pharisees. Cultivate the ability to strike the balance between an unassuming humility and an unwavering steadfastness in the face of undue criticism. This challenge is particularly strong during a solar eclipse; at this time, both the light of the Sun *and* of the Moon is occluded. We feel detached from both Father and Mother; our lower impulses can come to the fore in a particularly strong way. The antidote is to consciously cultivate good will and right action during a solar eclipse—to shine a light

---

54 Ibid., vol. 3, p. 15.

55 Ibid., vol. 2, p. 396.

in response to and in honor of the darkened Father Sun and Mother Moon.

**June 22: Retrograde Jupiter enters Sagittarius. "World activity matures in dying."** (See February 9 for full verse).

This is a sobering reminder that all activity, both inner and outer, finds its maturity and fulfillment in death. If we can begin to view all of our activity as a preparation for death, it might drastically change what types of activity we engage in. In a way, this phrase encapsulates many of the themes from this month: the death of Eliud, which was a complete maturation of his inner activity of mysticism; the raising of the Youth of Nain, the fruit of an untimely death; and the ministrations of Magdalene, unwittingly preparing Christ for his own death on the Cross.

**June 23: Neptune stations retrograde, 25°56' Aquarius.** Neptune stationed retrograde on May 3 AD 30. Anne Catherine Emmerich recounts the beautiful story of an envoy, sent by Christ to the King of Abgar to request a healing for the king:

> He had an eruption that had settled in his feet and rendered him lame.... The young man commissioned to bear the king's letter to Jesus was an artist, and he had received commands to bring back Jesus's portrait if he would not come himself. I saw him vainly trying to reach Jesus.... Then Jesus bade one of the disciples to make room for the man that was going around people unable to push his way to the front, and he pointed out a platform nearby to which he should be conducted....
>
> The envoy, overjoyed at being able at last to see Jesus, at once produced his drawing materials, rested his tablet on his knee, regarded Jesus with great admiration and attention, and set to work. The tablet before him was white as if made of wax. He began by sketching with a pencil the outlines of Jesus's head and beard. Then it looked as if he spread over his work a layer of wax in which to receive the impression of the sketch....
>
> Jesus continued his discourse a while longer, and then sent the disciples to say to the envoy that he might now approach and deliver his message.... The picture at which he had been working was hanging by a strap on his left arm. It was like a shield in the form of a heart.... The part of the letter containing the writing was stiff; the envelope pliable, as if of some kind of stuff, either leather or silk. I saw, too, that it was bound by a string.
>
> When Jesus had read the letter, he turned the other side of the stiff part and, drawing from his robe a coarse pencil out of which he pushed something, he wrote several words in tolerably large characters, and then folded it again. After that he called for some water, bathed his face, pressed the soft stuff in which the letter had been folded to his sacred countenance, and returned it to the envoy. The latter applied it to the picture he had vainly tried to perfect, when behold! The likeness instantly became a facsimile of the original.[56]

Retrograde Neptune opens the door for the unexpected and the seemingly impossible to occur! Artistic inspiration is heightened, particularly in the realm of sacred art.

**June 24: The Christian Celebration of St. John's Day.**

**June 25: Venus stations direct, 10°19' Taurus.** Today is the Feast of St. John. The Urielic season inaugurated by Whitsun finds its next octave of expression on this day. The truly social gesture is in the words of John the Baptist: "I must decrease, that he may increase." John spoke this in reference to Christ; when we see Christ in the other person, this phrase applies universally. The image that Steiner gave on October 12, 1923, for the celebration of the Urielic season was the reddish-gold realm of the Father in the heights, and the bluish-silver realm of the Mother in the depths. The Mother is surrounded by human error; in between, admonishing Uriel in the form of a dove alchemically transmutes human error into human virtue, creating the golden realm above. In the transformation of vice into virtue, we can achieve the reconnection of the Above and the Below.[57]

---

56 Ibid., vol. 1, pp. 458–459.
57 Steiner, *The Four Seasons and the Archangels*, lect. 4.

This is remembered in the life of Mary Magdalene, the archetypal penitent. Venus at this degree recalls Magdalene on March 24 AD 31:

> Jesus taught this morning and afternoon (at the close of the sabbath) in the castle. In between, he walked in the garden. Mary Magdalene followed him everywhere, full of love and contrition. She sat at his feet to take in his words. Since her final conversion, she had changed greatly in her countenance and bearing.[58]

Between June 18 and July 5, Mars is square the Node; this alignment is exact on **June 26, Mars 4°5' Pisces square Node 4°5' Gemini**. These two were square on November 8 AD 30, another significant date in the life of Mary Magdalene:

> Around ten o'clock Jesus arrived at the mountain, where there was a teacher's chair. He delivered a powerful discourse, culminating with the words: "Come! Come to me, all who are weary and laden with guilt! Come to me, O sinners! Do penance, believe, and share the kingdom with me!" At these words, Mary Magdalene was deeply moved inwardly, and Jesus, perceiving her agitation, addressed his hearers with some words of consolation—words actually meant for Mary Magdalene—and she was converted. That evening, a Pharisee named Simon Zabulon invited Jesus to a banquet. During the meal, Mary Magdalene entered the room carrying a flask of ointment, with which she anointed Jesus's head (Luke 7:36–50).[59]

**June 30: Jupiter conjunct Pluto 29°5' Sagittarius.** Jupiter and Pluto are conjunct for the second of three times this year. The first time was on April 5, and the third and last time will be on November 12. This is due to their retrograde movement from the geocentric perspective. Heliocentrically, there is no retrograde movement; from this point of view, the two have been within 5° of each other since May 29, and will be until October 2. Their heliocentric conjunction occurs on July 31.

Are we beginning to feel a sense of triumph and glory that is overcoming the feelings of rigidity, death, and heaviness that have held sway for the last year during the height of the Saturn–Pluto conjunction? Perhaps there are times when this feeling of jubilation gets out of hand and leans in the direction of mob-consciousness or megalomania? Cultivate humility, and performing right action on the sly, without any expectation of recognition or gratitude. On the other hand, we can strive to have a keen awareness for the right action of others, offering recognition and gratitude to the other person rather than ourselves.

# JULY 2020

## STARGAZING PREVIEW

For those of us in the northern hemisphere, summer is on, and the 5th brings a Penumbral Lunar Eclipse to the Americas! Though Argentina will be able to see the shadow that the Earth will cast over the Moon for the longest period of time (almost three hours), all of the Andes, Central America, Mexico, and the eastern seaboard of the United States will experience this special Full Moon at 19° Sagittarius—its exact position at the conception of the Blessed Virgin. Furthermore, the Sun, at 19° Gemini, will be aligned with the star *Sirius*, found below and to the left of Orion; Steiner referred to it as the star of Zarathustra, the great initiate who later incarnated as the Solomon Jesus—the child to whom the Blessed Virgin gave birth in 6 BC. Later on the 5th, the Moon will conjunct Jupiter: watch them rise at 2100, followed by Saturn twenty minutes later. On the 6th, the Moon will find Saturn, and in the evening, watch Saturn rise twenty minutes before the waning Moon.

The Moon and Mars, at 13° Pisces, will be together in conjunction on the 11th. Not only was the Moon at this degree as Jesus stilled the Sea of Galilee and called to Peter and Andrew, "Come and follow me, I will make you fishers of men"—but Mars was at 13° Pisces at the Commissioning of the Disciples. As the day ends, watch Mars rise eight minutes ahead of the Moon, and don't forget to look high in the southern sky, where you'll see Jupiter

---

58 Brentano, *The Visions of Anne Catherine Emmerich*, vol. 2, p. 329.
59 Ibid., p. 107.

and Saturn straddling the Sagittarius–Capricorn cusp. After moonset on the 12th, the Moon will reach its Last Quarter (26° Pisces).

On the 14th, Jupiter will be "Full"—opposite the Sun, and therefore at its brightest. Watch it be the first to rise after sunset. The Moon finds Venus in the central decan of the Bull on the 17th; now that Venus is a morning star, observe as they rise together at about 0230 (I did say morning!). At this time, Mars will be high in the southeast, while you'll find Jupiter and Saturn due southwest.

July's New Moon (3° Cancer) occurs on the 20th, when Saturn will be directly across the zodiacal circle. Around noon on the 27th, the First Quarter Moon will shine from Libra; you'll be able to see it high in the south at dusk.

## July Commentaries

During the month of May, Sun and Mercury (Higher and Lower Self) were moving in tandem with each other, descending into and uniting with the realm of loving devotion (Venus). Over the course of June, the Higher Self (Sun) began to find its self-realization in the realm of action (Mars) rather than thought (Mercury), as the wing-footed messenger of the gods sped far ahead of the Sun's path. On the 18th, he turned retrograde and began his return to the Sun. Between June 27 and July 4, Mercury and the Sun are once again within 5° of each other. The inferior conjunction of Sun and Mercury is exact on the night of **June 30–July 1: Sun and Mercury 14° Gemini.** The inspirations from the wider cosmos that Mercury has been gathering up as he winds his way around the Sun he now transmits to both Sun and Earth, acting as both intermediary between and messenger to the two of them.

A superior conjunction of Sun and Mercury occurred in Gemini on June 1 AD 31, recalling the visit of Christ and his disciples to the suburbs of the Levitical city Misael:

> To the north of the suburb and on a declivity halfway up the height lay the beautiful pleasure garden of Misael, commanding a magnificent view of the gulf. Higher up on the hill one could see the pond, or swamp, of Cendevia and Libnath, the "City of Waters," which was an hour

and a half distant. It was nearer the sea, which here makes a bend into the land, than Misael, which was a couple of hours from the sea. Debbaseth was five hours to the east of the Kishon, and Nazareth about seven. Jesus walked in the garden with his disciples and related the parable of a fisherman that went out to sea to fish, and took five hundred and seventy fishes. He told them that an experienced fisherman would put into pure water the good fish found in bad, that like Elijah he would purify the springs and wells, that he would remove good fish from bad water, where the fish of prey would devour them, and that he would make for them new spawning ponds in better water. Jesus introduced into the parable also the accident that had happened on the sandbank to those that, out of self-will, had not followed the master of the vessels. The Cypriotes who had followed Jesus could not restrain their tears when they heard him speak of the laborious task of transporting fish from bad to good water. Jesus mentioned clearly and precisely the number "five hundred and seventy good fish" that had been saved, and said that that was indeed enough to pay for the labor.[60]

Careless (and therefore destructive) acts are so easy; indeed, this is intrinsic to their semi- or unconscious origin, that they require no inner or outer effort. Conversely, the reclamation required to undo a mess created by carelessness and inattention calls up the greatest amount of inner and outer will. The number 570 is both a riddle and an answer to a riddle. What is the qualitative essence of the numbers involved here, such as five, seven, ten and twelve? How are they cooperating in the number 570? The sign of Gemini, like a school of fish, is a sign of cooperation. Together we can cultivate the social will needed for reclamation.

**July 5: Full Moon 18°36' Sagittarius (Lunar Eclipse).** Once again, the Full Moon brings with it a lunar eclipse (the third of the year). As we have noted before, a lunar eclipse hides from us the light of the Sun (celestial illumination, formative thoughts from the future) and exposes us to the normally veiled light of the Moon (terrestrial illumination,

---

60 Ibid., p. 393.

# SIDEREAL GEOCENTRIC LONGITUDES : JULY 2020 Gregorian at 0 hours UT

| DAY | ☉ | ☽ | ☊ | ☿ | ♀ | ♂ | ♃ | ♄ | ♅ | ♆ | ♇ |
|---|---|---|---|---|---|---|---|---|---|---|---|
| 1 WE | 14♊36 | 19♎58 | 4♊5 | 14♊47R | 10♉55 | 6♓44 | 29♐0R | 5♑2R | 14♈50 | 25♒55R | 29♐4R |
| 2 TH | 15 33 | 4♏11 | 4 6 | 14 11 | 11 8 | 7 20 | 28 52 | 4 58 | 14 52 | 25 55 | 29 2 |
| 3 FR | 16 31 | 18 17 | 4 6 | 13 36 | 11 24 | 7 55 | 28 45 | 4 54 | 14 54 | 25 55 | 29 1 |
| 4 SA | 17 28 | 2♐13 | 4 7 | 13 3 | 11 41 | 8 31 | 28 38 | 4 50 | 14 56 | 25 55 | 29 0 |
| 5 SU | 18 25 | 15 56 | 4 7R | 12 31 | 12 0 | 9 6 | 28 30 | 4 46 | 14 58 | 25 54 | 28 58 |
| 6 MO | 19 22 | 29 23 | 4 6 | 12 2 | 12 21 | 9 41 | 28 23 | 4 42 | 15 0 | 25 54 | 28 57 |
| 7 TU | 20 19 | 12♑33 | 4 4 | 11 36 | 12 44 | 10 16 | 28 15 | 4 38 | 15 2 | 25 53 | 28 55 |
| 8 WE | 21 17 | 25 25 | 4 2 | 11 14 | 13 9 | 10 50 | 28 7 | 4 33 | 15 4 | 25 53 | 28 54 |
| 9 TH | 22 14 | 8♒0 | 3 59 | 10 56 | 13 35 | 11 24 | 28 0 | 4 29 | 15 6 | 25 52 | 28 52 |
| 10 FR | 23 11 | 20 19 | 3 57 | 10 42 | 14 2 | 11 58 | 27 52 | 4 25 | 15 7 | 25 52 | 28 51 |
| 11 SA | 24 8 | 2♓26 | 3 54 | 10 33 | 14 31 | 12 32 | 27 44 | 4 21 | 15 9 | 25 51 | 28 49 |
| 12 SU | 25 5 | 14 24 | 3 53 | 10 28 | 15 2 | 13 6 | 27 37 | 4 16 | 15 11 | 25 51 | 28 48 |
| 13 MO | 26 3 | 26 17 | 3 52 | 10 29D | 15 34 | 13 39 | 27 29 | 4 12 | 15 12 | 25 50 | 28 47 |
| 14 TU | 27 0 | 8♈10 | 3 53D | 10 35 | 16 7 | 14 12 | 27 21 | 4 8 | 15 14 | 25 49 | 28 45 |
| 15 WE | 27 57 | 20 9 | 3 54 | 10 47 | 16 42 | 14 45 | 27 14 | 4 3 | 15 16 | 25 49 | 28 44 |
| 16 TH | 28 54 | 2♉16 | 3 55 | 11 3 | 17 18 | 15 17 | 27 6 | 3 59 | 15 17 | 25 48 | 28 42 |
| 17 FR | 29 51 | 14 37 | 3 57 | 11 26 | 17 55 | 15 49 | 26 58 | 3 54 | 15 18 | 25 47 | 28 41 |
| 18 SA | 0♋49 | 27 15 | 3 58 | 11 54 | 18 33 | 16 21 | 26 50 | 3 50 | 15 20 | 25 47 | 28 39 |
| 19 SU | 1 46 | 10♊12 | 3 58R | 12 27 | 19 12 | 16 53 | 26 43 | 3 45 | 15 21 | 25 46 | 28 38 |
| 20 MO | 2 43 | 23 30 | 3 57 | 13 6 | 19 53 | 17 24 | 26 35 | 3 41 | 15 23 | 25 45 | 28 36 |
| 21 TU | 3 41 | 7♋7 | 3 54 | 13 50 | 20 34 | 17 55 | 26 27 | 3 37 | 15 24 | 25 44 | 28 35 |
| 22 WE | 4 38 | 21 2 | 3 51 | 14 40 | 21 17 | 18 26 | 26 20 | 3 32 | 15 25 | 25 43 | 28 34 |
| 23 TH | 5 35 | 5♌11 | 3 46 | 15 35 | 22 0 | 18 56 | 26 12 | 3 28 | 15 27 | 25 42 | 28 32 |
| 24 FR | 6 32 | 19 29 | 3 42 | 16 35 | 22 44 | 19 26 | 26 5 | 3 23 | 15 27 | 25 42 | 28 31 |
| 25 SA | 7 30 | 3♍51 | 3 38 | 17 40 | 23 30 | 19 55 | 25 57 | 3 19 | 15 28 | 25 41 | 28 29 |
| 26 SU | 8 27 | 18 12 | 3 35 | 18 51 | 24 15 | 20 24 | 25 50 | 3 14 | 15 29 | 25 40 | 28 28 |
| 27 MO | 9 24 | 2♎30 | 3 33 | 20 6 | 25 2 | 20 53 | 25 42 | 3 10 | 15 30 | 25 39 | 28 26 |
| 28 TU | 10 22 | 16 40 | 3 33D | 21 27 | 25 50 | 21 22 | 25 35 | 3 6 | 15 31 | 25 38 | 28 25 |
| 29 WE | 11 19 | 0♏41 | 3 34 | 22 52 | 26 38 | 21 50 | 25 28 | 3 1 | 15 32 | 25 37 | 28 24 |
| 30 TH | 12 16 | 14 33 | 3 36 | 24 11 | 27 27 | 22 17 | 25 21 | 2 57 | 15 33 | 25 35 | 28 22 |
| 31 FR | 13 14 | 28 14 | 3 37 | 25 55 | 28 17 | 22 44 | 25 14 | 2 53 | 15 34 | 25 34 | 28 21 |

## INGRESSES :

| | | | |
|---|---|---|---|
| 1 ☽→♏ 16:54 | 24 ☽→♍ 17:34 | | |
| 3 ☽→♐ 20:8 | 26 ☽→♎ 19:47 | | |
| 6 ☽→♑ 1:6 | 28 ☽→♏ 22:49 | | |
| 8 ☽→♒ 8:41 | 31 ☽→♐ 3:8 | | |
| 10 ☽→♓ 19:9 | | | |
| 13 ☽→♈ 7:30 | | | |
| 15 ☽→♉ 19:32 | | | |
| 17 ☉→♋ 3:34 | | | |
| 18 ☽→♊ 5:8 | | | |
| 20 ☽→♋ 11:31 | | | |
| 22 ☽→♌ 15:14 | | | |

## ASPECTS & ECLIPSES :

| | | | |
|---|---|---|---|
| 1 ☉☌♇ 2:51 | 11 ☽☌☊ 2:56 | 20 ☽☍♃ 5:26 | ☿□♂ 21:44 |
| 2 ☽☌♂ 12:0 | ☽☌♂ 21:15 | ☽☍♅ 9:3 | ☽☍♂ 22:3 |
| 4 ☽☌♅ 3:17 | ☉□☽ 22:4 | ☉☌☽ 17:31 | 30 ☿☍♂ 14:16 |
| ☽☍☿ 18:11 | 12 ☽☌A 19:14 | ☽☌♄ 17:53 | 31 ☿☌♀ 0:6 |
| 5 ☽⚹PN 4:27 | ☉□☽ 23:27 | ☉☍♄ 22:26 | ☽☌♅ 9:32 |
| ☉☍☽ 4:43 | 14 ☉☍♃ 7:57 | 24 ☽☍♆ 10:22 | |
| ☽☌♃ 22:11 | ☽☌♅ 14:12 | ☽☍☊ 23:38 | |
| ☽☌♆ 23:12 | 15 ☽☌♆ 23:12 | 25 ☽☌P 4:57 | |
| 6 ☽☌♄ 9:34 | 17 ☽☌♀ 6:39 | 26 ☽☍♀ 3:48 | |
| 8 ☿□♂ 10:40 | 18 ☽☌☊ 12:31 | 27 ☉□☽ 12:31 | |
| 10 ☽☌♆ 10:56 | 19 ☽☌☿ 4:17 | ♀□♆ 17:58 | |

# SIDEREAL HELIOCENTRIC LONGITUDES : JULY 2020 Gregorian at 0 hours UT

| DAY | Sid. Time | ☿ | ♀ | ⊕ | ♂ | ♃ | ♄ | ♅ | ♆ | ♇ | Vernal Point |
|---|---|---|---|---|---|---|---|---|---|---|---|
| 1 WE | 18:38:2 | 14♐23 | 1♑45 | 14♐37 | 20♑15 | 26♐11 | 3♑1 | 12♈18 | 24♒5 | 28♐38 | 4♓58'26" |
| 2 TH | 18:41:59 | 17 16 | 3 19 | 15 34 | 20 53 | 26 16 | 3 2 | 12 19 | 24 5 | 28 38 | 4♓58'26" |
| 3 FR | 18:45:55 | 20 11 | 4 54 | 16 31 | 21 30 | 26 21 | 3 4 | 12 19 | 24 6 | 28 39 | 4♓58'26" |
| 4 SA | 18:49:52 | 23 7 | 6 29 | 17 28 | 22 8 | 26 26 | 3 6 | 12 20 | 24 6 | 28 39 | 4♓58'26" |
| 5 SU | 18:53:49 | 26 7 | 8 4 | 18 26 | 22 46 | 26 32 | 3 8 | 12 21 | 24 6 | 28 39 | 4♓58'26" |
| 6 MO | 18:57:45 | 29 9 | 9 39 | 19 23 | 23 24 | 26 37 | 3 10 | 12 21 | 24 7 | 28 40 | 4♓58'26" |
| 7 TU | 19:1:42 | 2♑14 | 11 14 | 20 20 | 24 2 | 26 42 | 3 11 | 12 22 | 24 7 | 28 40 | 4♓58'26" |
| 8 WE | 19:5:38 | 5 22 | 12 49 | 21 17 | 24 39 | 26 47 | 3 13 | 12 23 | 24 7 | 28 40 | 4♓58'25" |
| 9 TH | 19:9:35 | 8 34 | 14 23 | 22 14 | 25 17 | 26 52 | 3 15 | 12 23 | 24 8 | 28 40 | 4♓58'25" |
| 10 FR | 19:13:31 | 11 49 | 15 58 | 23 12 | 25 55 | 26 57 | 3 17 | 12 24 | 24 8 | 28 41 | 4♓58'25" |
| 11 SA | 19:17:28 | 15 9 | 17 33 | 24 9 | 26 33 | 27 2 | 3 19 | 12 25 | 24 9 | 28 41 | 4♓58'25" |
| 12 SU | 19:21:24 | 18 33 | 19 8 | 25 6 | 27 11 | 27 7 | 3 21 | 12 25 | 24 9 | 28 41 | 4♓58'25" |
| 13 MO | 19:25:21 | 22 2 | 20 43 | 26 3 | 27 49 | 27 12 | 3 22 | 12 26 | 24 9 | 28 42 | 4♓58'25" |
| 14 TU | 19:29:18 | 25 36 | 22 18 | 27 0 | 28 27 | 27 17 | 3 24 | 12 27 | 24 10 | 28 42 | 4♓58'25" |
| 15 WE | 19:33:14 | 29 16 | 23 53 | 27 58 | 29 5 | 27 22 | 3 26 | 12 27 | 24 10 | 28 42 | 4♓58'24" |
| 16 TH | 19:37:11 | 3♒1 | 25 28 | 28 55 | 29 43 | 27 27 | 3 28 | 12 28 | 24 10 | 28 43 | 4♓58'24" |
| 17 FR | 19:41:7 | 6 52 | 27 3 | 29 52 | 0♒21 | 27 32 | 3 30 | 12 29 | 24 11 | 28 43 | 4♓58'24" |
| 18 SA | 19:45:4 | 10 51 | 28 38 | 0♑49 | 0 59 | 27 37 | 3 32 | 12 29 | 24 11 | 28 43 | 4♓58'24" |
| 19 SU | 19:49:0 | 14 56 | 0♒13 | 1 47 | 1 37 | 27 42 | 3 33 | 12 30 | 24 11 | 28 43 | 4♓58'24" |
| 20 MO | 19:52:57 | 19 8 | 1 48 | 2 44 | 2 15 | 27 48 | 3 35 | 12 31 | 24 12 | 28 44 | 4♓58'24" |
| 21 TU | 19:56:53 | 23 28 | 3 23 | 3 41 | 2 53 | 27 53 | 3 37 | 12 31 | 24 12 | 28 44 | 4♓58'24" |
| 22 WE | 20:0:50 | 27 56 | 4 58 | 4 38 | 3 31 | 27 58 | 3 39 | 12 32 | 24 13 | 28 44 | 4♓58'23" |
| 23 TH | 20:4:47 | 2♓32 | 6 33 | 5 36 | 4 9 | 28 3 | 3 41 | 12 33 | 24 13 | 28 45 | 4♓58'23" |
| 24 FR | 20:8:43 | 7 17 | 8 8 | 6 33 | 4 47 | 28 8 | 3 42 | 12 33 | 24 13 | 28 45 | 4♓58'23" |
| 25 SA | 20:12:40 | 12 11 | 9 43 | 7 30 | 5 25 | 28 13 | 3 44 | 12 34 | 24 14 | 28 45 | 4♓58'23" |
| 26 SU | 20:16:36 | 17 14 | 11 18 | 8 28 | 6 3 | 28 18 | 3 46 | 12 35 | 24 14 | 28 46 | 4♓58'23" |
| 27 MO | 20:20:33 | 22 26 | 12 53 | 9 25 | 6 41 | 28 23 | 3 48 | 12 35 | 24 14 | 28 46 | 4♓58'23" |
| 28 TU | 20:24:29 | 27 47 | 14 28 | 10 22 | 7 19 | 28 28 | 3 50 | 12 36 | 24 15 | 28 46 | 4♓58'23" |
| 29 WE | 20:28:26 | 3♈17 | 16 3 | 11 20 | 7 57 | 28 33 | 3 52 | 12 37 | 24 15 | 28 46 | 4♓58'22" |
| 30 TH | 20:32:22 | 8 56 | 17 39 | 12 17 | 8 35 | 28 38 | 3 53 | 12 37 | 24 15 | 28 47 | 4♓58'22" |
| 31 FR | 20:36:19 | 14 43 | 19 14 | 13 14 | 9 13 | 28 43 | 3 55 | 12 38 | 24 16 | 28 47 | 4♓58'22" |

## INGRESSES :

| | |
|---|---|
| 6 ☿→♑ 6:41 | |
| 15 ☿→♒ 4:46 | |
| 16 ♂→♒ 10:58 | |
| 17 ⊕→♑ 3:19 | |
| 18 ♀→♒ 20:47 | |
| 22 ☿→♓ 10:52 | |
| 28 ☿→♈ 9:45 | |

## ASPECTS (HELIOCENTRIC +MOON(TYCHONIC)) :

| | | | | | |
|---|---|---|---|---|---|
| 1 ☽□♂ 0:29 | ☽☌♀ 21:13 | ☽□♇ 4:52 | 20 ☽☍♃ 7:40 | 26 ☽□♃ 17:2 | ☿□⊕ 16:44 |
| ☿☌⊕ 2:51 | ☽□♅ 23:39 | ☿☍☊ 10:14 | ☽☍♇ 9:17 | ☽□♆ 17:42 | ☽□♆ 17:0 |
| ♀☌♄ 19:36 | 7 ☿☌♄ 7:28 | ☽□♄ 14:21 | ♀☌♂ 11:21 | 27 ☽□♄ 2:12 | 31 ♃☌♆ 18:8 |
| 3 ☽□♆ 9:57 | ♀□♅ 17:24 | 14 ⊕☌♃ 7:43 | ☽☍♄ 17:51 | ☽☍♅ 17:5 | |
| 4 ⊕☌A 19:54 | ☽☌♂ 22:29 | ☽☌♅ 8:35 | ⊕☌♄ 22:11 | 28 ☿□♃ 3:4 | |
| 5 ☿☌♃ 3:22 | 8 ♂☌☊ 1:17 | ☿☌♂ 22:34 | 21 ☿☌♆ 4:2 | ☿□♆ 4:21 | |
| ☽☌♃ 18:58 | 10 ☿□♅ 4:12 | 15 ☽□♀ 8:33 | ☽□♅ 9:22 | 29 ☿□♄ 2:29 | |
| ☿☌♇ 20:10 | ☽☌♆ 7:32 | ☽□♂ 18:41 | 22 ☽☍♂ 22:10 | ☽□♂ 13:9 | |
| ☽☌♇ 22:41 | ♀☌A 12:56 | ⊕☌♇ 18:49 | 23 ☽☍♀ 2:35 | 30 ☽□♀ 6:7 | |
| ☽☌☿ 23:26 | 12 ☿☌♀ 7:26 | 16 ☽□♅ 2:8 | 24 ☽☍♆ 7:55 | ⊕□♅ 8:30 | |
| 6 ☽☌♄ 6:50 | 13 ☽□♃ 1:51 | 17 ☽□♆ 18:13 | 25 ☽☍☿ 21:27 | ☿☌♅ 15:24 | |

dead thoughts of the material world). However, in our time, with the Presence of Christ occurring on the elemental plane of Mother Nature, we can begin to receive this light as the light of Mother Earth herself. We are best able to do this in a mood of recollection, usually accompanied by sorrow— the mood of the Prodigal Son bringing to full consciousness what he has for so long forgotten.

The Full Moon was in Sagittarius on May 25 AD 31. On this day, Christ and the disciples were journeying through Kyrenia and visiting with the family of Christ's disciple Mnason:

> One of Mnason's married sisters did not make her appearance, because her little daughter had died the day before. She sat closely veiled, lamenting near the corpse. The child could not (I cannot now recall on what account) be buried on that day; but on this, the next day, they were expecting the rabbis from Mallep to conduct the funeral, for it was there they had their graveyard. The child had attained a tolerably good size, although she had always been an invalid. She could neither speak nor walk with facility, but she understood all that was said to her. Mnason, who had visited her home from time to time, had spoken to Jesus about her. Jesus told him that she would soon die, and instructed him how to prepare her for death. Mnason prudently followed Jesus's directions at a time in which the mother was not present. He excited the child to faith in the Messiah, to hearty sorrow for her sins, and to the hope of salvation; he prayed with her, and anointed her with oil that Jesus had blessed. The child died a very good death. I saw her lying on a little bier near the veiled mother, just like a babe in swaddling clothes, her face covered. The casket in which she lay was shaped something like a trough. On her head was a wreath of flowers, and tiny bunches of aromatic herbs were laid closely around her. Her arms and hands also were wrapped in burial bands, but left free from the person. A little white staff rested in her arms. On the top of her was a bouquet made up of a large ear of corn, a vine leaf, a little olive branch, a rose, and foliage peculiar to the country. Several women visited the mother and mourned with her. By the child's side in the coffin they deposited playthings: two little flutes, a little crooked, spiral-shaped horn, a tiny bow spanned with a string, on top of which in a furrow lay a little wand like an arrow. In each arm, besides, the child held a short, gilded staff with a knob on top.
>
> When the rabbis came to conduct the corpse, the coffin was closed with a light lid, which, instead of being nailed, was fastened down with a cord. Four men carried it on poles. A lighted lamp in a horn–lantern was borne on a pole and was followed by a crowd of children and grown persons, who all pressed forward with no attention to order. Jesus and the disciples were standing outside the house watching the funeral. Jesus comforted the mother and relatives, and spoke of the resurrection.[61]

What touching imagery through which we can access the sorrowful Mother in the heart of the Earth, as well as the sorrowful Mother in the other people with whom we come into contact today. It is somehow incredibly heartening that not all deaths were immediately and miraculously undone by Christ; that the gesture of silently standing by and supporting one who is suffering is also represented to us by the God–Man. Strive to be this silent support for someone today.

For the month of June, the dominant aspect was Sun square Mars. This aspect brought our attention to the death of Eliud the Essene, who, according to Anne Catherine Emmerich, was chosen by Christ to represent both a "type" of human being and also a stage of spiritual progress: that of intense, private, and mystical illumination. During the month of July, a different but similar aspect holds sway: Mercury square Mars. While the Self (Sun) found its realization in action (Mars) during June, here we see the uniting of conscious thought (Mercury) and action (Mars). There is a great potential during this month to not only *do*, but *know what we are doing*; to not only *ponder* but to put ideas into action. Some of us tend to be doers, others primarily planners; July 2020 will be a good time for the two to get together and make things happen.

---

61 Ibid., p. 387.

Mercury and Mars are within 5° of square alignment from July 3 through August 1. This alignment is exact on **July 8: Mercury 10°50' Gemini, Mars 10°50' Pisces.** The two are conjunct once again on July 27, 10° farther along. This aspect occurred, with Mars in Sagittarius and Mercury in Pisces, on March 6 AD 30:

> The three rich youths of Nazareth who had once before vainly preferred their petition to him to be received as disciples came to him again, reiterating their request. They almost knelt to him, but he sent them away after pointing out certain conditions that had to be fulfilled before he would allow them to join his disciples. Jesus knew well that their views were wholly terrestrial, and that they could not understand him. They wanted to follow him because they saw in him a philosopher, a learned Rabbi. After a time spent in his school, they could, as they thought, shine with a more brilliant reputation and do honor to their city Nazareth. They were besides somewhat vexed at seeing him giving the preference to the poor sorts of Nazareth rather than to themselves.
>
> Until far into the night I saw Jesus with the old Essene, Eliud of Nazareth. The holy man looked as if he would soon die of old age. He was no longer able for much, indeed he was almost bedridden. Jesus leaned on his arm at the bedside and talked with him. Eliud was entirely absorbed in God.
>
> [The night before] I again saw Jesus praying with outstretched arms, and again appearing on the Sea of Galilee to bear help in a storm. This time the distress was much greater, and many more vessels were in danger. I saw Jesus laying his hand on the helm without the helmsman's seeing him.[62]

Once again we are asked to bring Eliud to our mind's eye, this time still alive and absorbed in contemplation of Christ. We see the challenge to those who have ulterior motives, and the stilling of the storm. During this month of bringing thought and action into dynamic interaction, we can challenge ourselves to cultivate an inner Eliud, uprooting whatever ulterior motives might be hiding within us. The more we can do this, the better able we too will be to "calm the storms" around us with our words and actions.

**July 12: Mercury stations direct, 10°28' Gemini.** Mercury was at this degree during the conjunction with the Sun on June 1 AD 31, referred to previously. It was also at this degree, square Mars, on May 23 AD 32, during which Christ and his disciples were journeying fast and far, staying with shepherds and healing as they went. Mercury was at this degree on May 15 AD 33, the day after the Ascension:

> Jesus at each instant shone more brightly and his motions became more rapid. The disciples hastened after him, but it was impossible to overtake him. When he reached the top of the mountain, he was resplendent as a beam of white sunlight. A shining circle, glancing in all the colors of the rainbow, fell from Heaven around him. The pressing crowd stood in a wide circle outside, as if blending with it. Jesus himself shone still more brightly than the glory about him. He laid the left hand on his breast and, raising the right, turned slowly around, blessing the whole world. The crowd stood motionless. I saw all receive the benediction. Jesus did not impart it with the flat, open hand, like the rabbis, but like the Christian bishops. With great joy I felt his blessing of the whole world.
>
> And now rays of light from above united with the glory emanating from Jesus, and I saw him disappearing, dissolving as it were in the light from Heaven, vanishing as he rose. I lost sight of his head first. It appeared as if one sun was lost in another, as if one flame entered another, as if a spark floated into a flame. It was as if one were gazing into the *full midday* splendors of the Sun, though this light was whiter and clearer. Full day compared with this would be dark. First, I lost sight of Jesus's head, then his whole person, and lastly his feet, radiant with light, disappeared in the celestial glory. I saw innumerable souls from all sides going into that light and vanishing on high with the Lord. I cannot say that I saw him becoming apparently smaller and smaller like something flying up in the air, for he disappeared as it were in a cloud of light.

---

62 Ibid., vol. 1, p. 413.

Out of that cloud, something like dew, like a shower of light, fell upon all below, and when they could no longer endure the splendor, they were seized with amazement and terror. The apostles and disciples, who were nearest to Jesus, were blinded by the dazzling glare. They were forced to lower their eyes, while many cast themselves prostrate on their faces. The blessed Virgin was standing close behind them and gazing calmly straight ahead.[63]

The Sun is now approaching opposition of planets with which it was conjunct in late December and early January. Between July 9 and 18, the Sun is opposed Jupiter; this alignment is exact on **July 14: Sun 27°21' Gemini opposite Jupiter 27°21' Sagittarius**. Meanwhile, between July 10 and 20, the Sun and Pluto come into opposition; this alignment is exact on **July 15: Sun 28°44' Gemini opposite Pluto 28°44' Sagittarius**. This is a sort of homecoming: the Sun is the outer expression of the Risen Christ, the Son. Jupiter is the outer expression of the Holy Spirit, and Pluto that of the Father. This is a good day to dwell within the Rosicrucian mantra: *Ex Deo Nascimur; In Christo Morimur; Per Spiritum Sanctum Reviviscimus*. A particularly triumphant and glorious mood accompanies these aspects.

The Sun and Jupiter were conjunct in Gemini on May 21 AD 32, once again recalling Christ's time traveling far and wide and staying with shepherds. Sun and Jupiter were opposed (albeit in Libra and Aries respectively) on September 30 AD 30, when Christ shared the parable of the Prodigal Son (Luke 15:11–32):

Next morning Jesus cured several sick persons, and taught in the synagogue. He also taught in a place to which those pagans that had received baptism and those still in expectation of the same were admitted. In his latter instruction he spoke so feelingly, so naturally, of the lost son, that one would have thought him the father who had found his son. He stretched out his arms, exclaiming: "See! See! He returns! Let us make ready a feast for him!" It was so natural that the people looked around, as if all that Jesus

was saying were a reality. When he mentioned the calf that the father had slaughtered for the newly found son, his words were full of mysterious significance. It was as if he said: "But what would not be that love which would lead the heavenly Father to give his own Son as a sacrifice, to save his lost children." The instruction was addressed principally to penitents, to the baptized, and to the pagans present, who were depicted as the lost son returning to his home. All were excited to joy and mutual charity. The fruit of Jesus's teaching was soon apparent at the celebration of the Feast of Tabernacles, in the good will and hospitality shown by the Jews to their pagan brethren. In the afternoon Jesus with his disciples and a crowd of the inhabitants took a walk outside the city and along by the Jordan, through the beautiful meadows and flowery fields in which the tents of the pagans stood. The parable they had just heard, that of the prodigal son, formed the subject of conversation, and all were cheerful and happy, full of love toward one another.[64]

Pluto and the Sun were opposed in the same signs as today on June 5 AD 32. Emmerich saw that "Jesus taught in the synagogue and on the streets of Jericho. Many tax collectors and sinners came to hear him, and the Pharisees plotted against him (Luke 15:1–2). The disciples were unhappy that Jesus associated with tax collectors and sinners. Because of this, Jesus told them the parables recorded in Luke 15:3–32."[65] These are the parables of the Lost Sheep—and once again, the Prodigal Son! This parable is a potent force upon which to meditate today.

**July 18: Sun enters Cancer.**

> Thou resting, glowing light,
> Create life warmth;
> Warm soul life
> To gain strength in test of trial,
> To become spirit-permeated,
> In peaceful light created.
> Thou glowing light, become strong!

---

63 Ibid., vol. 3, p. 411.

64 Ibid., vol. 2, p. 67.
65 Ibid., p. 472.

The light streaming from above, from the realm of the Father and the Daughter, Sophia, is an active, radiating light. On the other hand, the light streaming from below, from the realm of the Mother and Christ, is a "resting, glowing light," one that embraces, warms, and soothes rather than braces, inspires, and activates. The Sun in Cancer enhances our receptivity to this light, as well as our ability to bestow it on others. The mood of Eliud the Essene, or of those comforting the sister of Mnason, is called once again to the eye of the soul.

The Sun continues on his journey, coming into opposition with Saturn between July 16 and 25. This alignment is exact on **July 20, Sun 3°41' Cancer opposite Saturn 3°41' Capricorn.** Powers of memory are greatly enhanced with these two planets in these two signs, whether it is our day-to-day memory function, karmic memory, or Tradition—what one might call the living memory of the social body.

Saturn and Sun were opposed—although with Sun in Capricorn and Saturn in Cancer—on January 10 AD 33. During this time, Christ was at the end of his return journey from Egypt with seven young disciples. They passed through "Bethain, not far from Abraham's grave in the cave of Mecpelah, east of Mamre."[66] A few days later, traveling almost exclusively by night and in stealth, he would arrive at Jacob's well, the place appointed by him to meet with the apostles. He was greeted by Peter, Andrew, John, James, and Phillip.

Egypt, Abraham, Jacob…the entire history of the Hebrew people lived in the very body of Christ. His coming Passion was to extend, fulfill, and begin anew the living stream of Tradition. In order to properly prepare for this, he recapitulated in miniature the entire history of the Hebrew people in his journey to and back from Egypt during the end of AD 32 into the start of AD 33. If any of us has lost this living, golden thread, return to it: this is the message of the Prodigal Son. Before adding to the Tradition, honor what has come before—Wash the Feet of the Tradition—that is today's message.

**July 20: New Moon 3°25' Cancer.** The New Moon was in Cancer on July 19 AD 30, barely more than a day after John the Baptist's second arrest by Herod. Cancer can have the effect of bringing out the darker side of materialism, a crab hardened into its shell. With John's imprisonment and eventual death, we have power–lust (Herod) attempting to stifle Truth (John the Baptist) in the prison of materialistic, reductive thinking.

On the other hand, the New Moon was in Cancer on July 8 AD 31. On this day, Jesus travelled from Thantia to Datheman, a ruined citadel. The people of this region were firm believers in the sacred character of the Way of David:

> [It followed] the windings of the valley, [leading] down to the Jordan. This road was deep, a kind of hollow, in which water sometimes flowed. It ran through the solitudes of the mountains, and at several points along it were to be found places provided with troughs and stores of fodder for the camels, also rings for fastening them. When journeying through this country, Abraham saw a supernatural light on this road and had a vision, and when David, upon the advice of Jonathan, sought safety for his parents in the region of Mizpah, he lay concealed here with three hundred men, from which circumstance it received the name of David's Way. David here received from God a prophetic vision in which he saw the caravan of the three kings and heard, as if from the heavens open above him, melodious chanting proclaiming the praises of the promised Consoler of Israel. Malachi also, being obliged to flee after a battle, followed a mysterious light that led him to this region where, too, he lay hid for a time; and the three holy kings, giving rein to their camels upon leaving the confines of Sacha and entering this road, descended by it singing sweet hymns of thanksgiving.[67]

This star memory shows us the higher aspect of the New Moon in Cancer: that of protection, of shelter, and of the mysteries of the night.

Beginning on July 21, and lasting all the way through to November 28, Saturn and Pluto are

---

66 Ibid., p. 520.

67 Ibid., p. 465.

once again within 5° of each other, although they will not have another conjunction this year. Ten days after the start of this time period, Jupiter and Pluto achieve heliocentric conjunction. This means that all three of these planets are in extremely close alignment for the next few months. Saturn and Pluto were opposed from May AD 29 to 30, with Pluto in Sagittarius as it is today, centering on the Baptism in the Jordan, the Temptation in the Wilderness, and the first healing miracle of the Changing of Water into Wine. On the other hand, Jupiter and Pluto were opposed for approximately the last ten months of Christ's ministry, beginning with the last healing miracle of the Raising of Lazarus from the Dead, through the journeys to Egypt, and the entire Passion, Resurrection and Whitsuntide. We are living at a potent time when both of these moods, that prevailing at the start and at the end of the ministry of Christ, are very active.

Between July 21 and August 2, Venus and Neptune are once again square, for the third time since the beginning of May due to Venus's retrograde movement. This alignment is exact on **July 27, Venus 25°39' Taurus square Neptune 25°39' Aquarius.** Once again our inner gaze is drawn to the memory of the feeding of the four thousand and the rebuke of the Pharisees, as it was on May 4 and 27:

Here it was that Jesus concluded the eight beatitudes and delivered the so-called Sermon on the Mount. His words on this occasion were more than ordinarily forcible and impressive. Crowds of strangers and pagans were present, the whole multitude, exclusive of women and children, numbering about four thousand. Toward evening, Jesus paused in his teaching and said to John: "I have compassion on the multitudes, because they continue with me now three days, and have nothing to eat; but I will not send them away fasting lest they faint in the way." John replied: "We are far in the desert, and to bring bread this distance would be hard. Shall we gather for them the fruits and berries that are still on the trees around here?" Jesus answered by telling him to ask the other apostles how many loaves they had. The latter answered: "Seven loaves and seven little fishes." The fishes were, however, an arm in length. Upon receiving this answer, Jesus directed that the empty breadbaskets the people had brought with them, along with the loaves and fishes, should be laid upon the rocky ledge; after which he continued to teach a good half hour. He spoke very plainly of his being the Messiah, of the persecutions that awaited him, and of his approaching imprisonment. But on that day, he said, those mountains would quake and that rock (here he pointed to the stone ledge) whereupon he had announced the truth they had refused to receive, would split asunder. Then he cried woe to Capernaum, to Chorazin, and to many other places of that region. On the day of his arrest they should all become conscious of having rejected salvation. He spoke of the happiness of this region to which he had broken the bread of life, but added that the strangers passing through had carried away with them that happiness. The children of the house threw that bread under the table, while the stranger, the little whelps, as the Syrophoenician had called them, gathered up the crumbs, which were sufficient to vivify and enliven whole towns and districts. Jesus then took leave of the people. He implored them once more to do penance and amend their life, repeated his admonitions in the most forcible language, and informed them that this was the last time he would teach in those parts. The people wept. They were full of admiration at his words, although they did not comprehend them all.[68]

At the same time, Mercury and Mars are once again square: on **July 27, Mercury 20°53' Gemini squares Mars 20°53' Pisces.** We are reminded once again of Eliud, of the proud rich youths, and of the calming of the storm. Due to both of these dynamic aspects happening on the same day, the psychospiritual energy is volatile: handle with care! Beware feelings of resentment and jealousy; guard against potentially insensitive or violent speech. Withdraw and still your inner storms so that you are able to serve with a warm heart, and to speak the Truth without losing control.

As the month draws to a close, between July 27 and August 2, Mercury follows the Sun's path

---

68 Ibid., p. 323.

coming into opposition to Jupiter. The alignment is exact on **July 30, Mercury 25°21' Gemini opposite Jupiter 25°21' Sagittarius.** Many of this month's themes—of the return of the Prodigal, of the dynamic meeting of Martian action and Mercurial thinking, of following the "David's Way" laid out by Spirit and Tradition—are encapsulated in today's star memory. Mercury and Jupiter were opposite each other, in the same signs, when Parzival and Feirefiz returned to the Grail Castle on May 26, 810. Each found his destiny: Parzival healed Anfortas and himself became Grail King; Feirefiz wed the Grail Bearer Repanse de Schoye and subsequently fathered Prester John in India. A fitting end to a month of joy and dynamism.

# AUGUST 2020

## STARGAZING PREVIEW

The month begins with the Moon, Jupiter, and Saturn setting at 0400, two hours before dawn. And while you're looking up, don't miss Mars at culmination and Venus low in the east, high above but aligned with *Alnitak*, the easternmost star of Orion's belt. Later on the 1st, the Moon will pass close above Jupiter. On the 2nd, Venus will have moved into Gemini by the time it rises at 0230, and Jupiter, the Moon, and Saturn will set a few hours later. Before noon, the Moon will pass Saturn: that evening, these three will rise in Jupiter–Saturn–Moon order.

As the Sun is in Cancer, can the Capricorn Full Moon be far off? This will take place on the 3rd, and if you're able to rise early the next day (say, at 0330) and you look right to left, you'll have the privilege of seeing Jupiter, Saturn, the Moon (just past Full), Mars, and Venus arching across the starry vault.

The 4th will bring a square aspect between Mars and Jupiter; as mentioned, Jupiter will be setting around 0330 while Mars is at culmination. This month, Mars is greeted by the Moon on the 9th, at 27° Pisces; they'll rise together just before 2300, while Jupiter and Saturn are high above, due south. The waning Moon reaches its Last Quarter on the 11th (24° Aries)—meaning that it rises around midnight. The main attraction on the night of the 12th will be the peak of the Perseid meteor showers, which should be a fine show despite the Taurus moonlight. Look northeast in the first hours of the new day for optimal viewing. May our blood be fortified with Michaelic iron!

If, on the 15th, you've decided to "owl" into the wee hours, keep a lookout at 0220 for the rising of the Moon just ahead of Venus; on the following day, Venus will rise first. Late on the 18th the Moon will completely disappear as another lunar cycle begins at 1° Leo.

Mars moves into Aries on the following day. There is indeed something special about Mars, the ruler of Aries, in the first degree of the zodiac, making possible acts of leadership that benefit all of humanity. It is from this same degree that Mars will form a square aspect with Saturn on the 24th; if you're up at midnight, you'll see Mars in the southeast and Saturn, near Jupiter, in the southwest, marking the boundaries of one quarter of the 360° zodiacal circle.

August's First Quarter Moon in Scorpio will grace the night sky on the 25th, the same day that Venus and Jupiter will be facing each other in exact opposition—meaning that as Jupiter sets at about 0300, Venus will rise. As the month began with lunar conjunctions to Jupiter and Saturn, so shall it end! The Moon passes Jupiter on the 28th and Saturn on the 29th.

Orion will be visible in the east for an hour or two before sunrise.

## AUGUST COMMENTARIES

August continues precisely where July left off, with a strong emphasis on aspects involving Mercury and Mars. On July 30, Mercury began to follow the track laid out by the Sun—destiny has raced ahead of our conscious understanding, and now it runs to keep up. Mercury opposed Jupiter on that day; from July 29 through August 4, he also opposed Pluto. This alignment is exact on **August 1: Mercury 28°19' Gemini opposite Pluto 28°19' Sagittarius.** Many of the same themes that have arisen over the past month return to us with this aspect; the two planets were opposed in the same signs on June 2 AD 31, the day after the star memory from the Sun–Mercury conjunction at the beginning of the month of July when Christ taught regarding the good fish in the bad water. On June 2, his "teaching turned upon sacrifice for sin and upon Samson. He rehearsed the principal deeds of the latter, and spoke of him as of a saint whose life was prophetic. Samson, Jesus said, did not lose all his strength, for he had retained sufficient to do penance. His overturning of the pagan temple upon himself was owing to a special inspiration from God."[69]

The two were also opposed in these signs on June 16 AD 29, prior to Jesus of Nazareth's baptism in the Jordan River and the start of Christ's ministry. The day before, on June 15, Anne Catherine witnessed the following:

> After that I saw Jesus in Dothaim, a scattered little place northeast of Sepphoris, and in which there was a synagogue. The inhabitants were not bad, though very much neglected. Abraham had once owned fields there for his cattle intended for offerings. Joseph and his brethren used to guard their flocks in this same region, and it was here that the former was sold. Dothaim, at the time of our Lord, was but a sparsely settled place, but its soil was good and its meadows extended down to the Sea of Galilee. It contained a large building like a madhouse, in which many possessed lived. On Jesus's arrival, they became perfectly furious and dashed themselves almost to death. The keepers could not bind them. Jesus entered and spoke to them, and they became quite calm. He addressed to them a few more words, after which they quietly left the house and repaired to their several homes. The people were amazed at what they saw. They were unwilling for Jesus to depart, and one of them invited him to a marriage feast.[70]

Clearly an intense energy is unleashed with Mercury opposite Pluto—the combination of the volcanic fury of Pluto with the quicksilver of Mercury

makes for a bit of a whirlwind. An equally powerful inner force—the force of purity—is required to meet it properly.

Simultaneously with Mercury aspecting both Jupiter and Pluto, the Sun comes into square alignment with Uranus between July 28 and August 7. This alignment only intensifies the "whirlwind" nature of this time period. The Sun was square Uranus during the start of the forty days of temptation in the wilderness. The oppressive aspects of Uranus—the tendency to flashes of brilliance and spiritual illusion, leading to a kind of aridity of the soul—are heightened during this time period. Hold fast to your inner resources; those of you who have the good fortune to suffer this aridity in a group of trusted friends, treat each other as ministering Angels, confide in one another and take comfort and consolation from each other.

**August 2: Venus enters Gemini. "Set repose in movement."** (See May 25 for the full verse.)

**Mercury enters Cancer. "Warm soul life."** (See July 18 for the full verse.)

As Venus enters Gemini, she requests that the life of the Sun "set repose in movement," while Mercury entering Cancer asks for the resting, luminous glow to warm our life of soul. Perhaps there are areas of our inner life that have grown cold or dormant. The "resting, luminous glow" that is the life of the Sun is invited to enter in and set into movement that which we've allowed to repose. This is often felt as an uncomfortable or undesired occurrence, but if we can imagine the disturbance of our soul as akin to a seed sprouting to life in the soil, perhaps we can enter more lovingly into our own soul's development. It is this devotional surrender that can bring warmth to the soul.

**August 3: Full Moon 16°44' Capricorn.** There was a Full Moon in Capricorn on July 3 AD 30:

> In the court of the large mansion belonging to Simeon, there was a round, shallow basin from which the water overflowed into a surrounding trench. Here, too, the water was not good; it had a bad taste. Jesus blessed it, casting into it at the same time salt in lumps like stones. In

---

69 Ibid., p. 394.
70 Ibid., vol. 1, p. 297.

| SIDEREAL GEOCENTRIC LONGITUDES : AUGUST 2020 Gregorian at 0 hours UT | | | | | | | | | | | |
|---|---|---|---|---|---|---|---|---|---|---|---|
| DAY | ☉ | ☽ | ☊ | ☿ | ♀ | ♂ | ♃ | ♄ | ♅ | ♆ | ♇ |
| 1 SA | 14 ♋ 11 | 11 ♐ 44 | 3 ♊ 37R | 27 ♊ 33 | 29 ♉ 8 | 23 ♓ 11 | 25 ♐ 7R | 2 ♑ 48R | 15 ♈ 35 | 25 ♒ 33R | 28 ♐ 19R |
| 2 SU | 15 9 | 25 2 | 3 35 | 29 15 | 29 59 | 23 38 | 25 0 | 2 44 | 15 35 | 25 32 | 28 18 |
| 3 MO | 16 6 | 8 ♑ 8 | 3 31 | 1 ♋ 1 | 0 ♊ 50 | 24 4 | 24 53 | 2 40 | 15 36 | 25 31 | 28 17 |
| 4 TU | 17 3 | 21 2 | 3 25 | 2 50 | 1 43 | 24 29 | 24 47 | 2 35 | 15 37 | 25 30 | 28 15 |
| 5 WE | 18 1 | 3 ♒ 42 | 3 17 | 4 42 | 2 36 | 24 54 | 24 40 | 2 31 | 15 37 | 25 29 | 28 14 |
| 6 TH | 18 58 | 16 9 | 3 9 | 6 36 | 3 29 | 25 19 | 24 34 | 2 27 | 15 38 | 25 27 | 28 13 |
| 7 FR | 19 56 | 28 23 | 3 1 | 8 33 | 4 23 | 25 43 | 24 27 | 2 23 | 15 38 | 25 26 | 28 11 |
| 8 SA | 20 53 | 10 ♓ 27 | 2 54 | 10 32 | 5 18 | 26 7 | 24 21 | 2 19 | 15 38 | 25 25 | 28 10 |
| 9 SU | 21 51 | 22 24 | 2 48 | 12 32 | 6 13 | 26 30 | 24 15 | 2 15 | 15 39 | 25 23 | 28 9 |
| 10 MO | 22 48 | 4 ♈ 15 | 2 44 | 14 34 | 7 9 | 26 52 | 24 9 | 2 11 | 15 39 | 25 22 | 28 7 |
| 11 TU | 23 46 | 16 7 | 2 42 | 16 36 | 8 5 | 27 15 | 24 3 | 2 7 | 15 39 | 25 21 | 28 6 |
| 12 WE | 24 43 | 28 4 | 2 41D | 18 39 | 9 2 | 27 36 | 23 57 | 2 3 | 15 39 | 25 19 | 28 5 |
| 13 TH | 25 41 | 10 ♉ 10 | 2 42 | 20 42 | 9 59 | 27 57 | 23 52 | 1 59 | 15 40 | 25 18 | 28 4 |
| 14 FR | 26 39 | 22 31 | 2 43 | 22 45 | 10 57 | 28 18 | 23 46 | 1 55 | 15 40 | 25 17 | 28 2 |
| 15 SA | 27 36 | 5 ♊ 12 | 2 43R | 24 48 | 11 55 | 28 37 | 23 41 | 1 51 | 15 40 | 25 15 | 28 1 |
| 16 SU | 28 34 | 18 16 | 2 42 | 26 50 | 12 53 | 28 57 | 23 36 | 1 48 | 15 40R | 25 14 | 28 0 |
| 17 MO | 29 32 | 1 ♋ 45 | 2 39 | 28 52 | 13 52 | 29 15 | 23 31 | 1 44 | 15 40 | 25 12 | 27 59 |
| 18 TU | 0 ♌ 29 | 15 40 | 2 34 | 0 ♌ 53 | 14 51 | 29 33 | 23 26 | 1 40 | 15 40 | 25 11 | 27 57 |
| 19 WE | 1 27 | 29 57 | 2 26 | 2 52 | 15 51 | 29 51 | 23 22 | 1 37 | 15 39 | 25 10 | 27 56 |
| 20 TH | 2 25 | 14 ♌ 31 | 2 17 | 4 51 | 16 51 | 0 ♈ 7 | 23 17 | 1 33 | 15 39 | 25 8 | 27 55 |
| 21 FR | 3 23 | 29 16 | 2 8 | 6 49 | 17 51 | 0 23 | 23 13 | 1 30 | 15 39 | 25 7 | 27 54 |
| 22 SA | 4 20 | 14 ♍ 4 | 2 0 | 8 45 | 18 52 | 0 39 | 23 9 | 1 26 | 15 39 | 25 5 | 27 53 |
| 23 SU | 5 18 | 28 45 | 1 53 | 10 40 | 19 53 | 0 53 | 23 5 | 1 23 | 15 38 | 25 3 | 27 52 |
| 24 MO | 6 16 | 13 ♎ 15 | 1 49 | 12 34 | 20 54 | 1 7 | 23 1 | 1 20 | 15 38 | 25 2 | 27 51 |
| 25 TU | 7 14 | 27 30 | 1 47 | 14 26 | 21 56 | 1 21 | 22 57 | 1 17 | 15 38 | 25 0 | 27 50 |
| 26 WE | 8 12 | 11 ♏ 27 | 1 46D | 16 18 | 22 58 | 1 33 | 22 54 | 1 14 | 15 37 | 24 59 | 27 49 |
| 27 TH | 9 10 | 25 7 | 1 47 | 18 7 | 24 0 | 1 45 | 22 50 | 1 11 | 15 37 | 24 57 | 27 48 |
| 28 FR | 10 8 | 8 ♐ 31 | 1 47R | 19 56 | 25 3 | 1 56 | 22 47 | 1 8 | 15 36 | 24 56 | 27 47 |
| 29 SA | 11 6 | 21 42 | 1 46 | 21 43 | 26 6 | 2 6 | 22 44 | 1 5 | 15 35 | 24 54 | 27 46 |
| 30 SU | 12 4 | 4 ♑ 39 | 1 42 | 23 29 | 27 9 | 2 16 | 22 42 | 1 2 | 15 35 | 24 52 | 27 45 |
| 31 MO | 13 2 | 17 25 | 1 35 | 25 14 | 28 12 | 2 24 | 22 39 | 0 59 | 15 34 | 24 51 | 27 44 |

INGRESSES :

| | | | |
|---|---|---|---|
| 2 | ♀ → ♊ 0:38 | 19 | ☽ → ♌ 0: 5 |
| | ☽ → ♑ 9: 2 | | ♂ → ♈ 13:23 |
| | ☿ → ♋ 10:15 | 21 | ☽ → ♍ 1:10 |
| 4 | ☽ → ♒ 16:57 | 23 | ☽ → ♎ 2: 3 |
| 7 | ☽ → ♓ 3:11 | 25 | ☽ → ♏ 4:16 |
| 9 | ☽ → ♈ 15:22 | 27 | ☽ → ♐ 8:41 |
| 12 | ☽ → ♉ 3:51 | 29 | ☽ → ♑ 15:20 |
| 14 | ☽ → ♊ 14:14 | 31 | ☽ → ♒ 23:59 |
| 16 | ☽ → ♋ 20:55 | | |
| 17 | ☉ → ♌ 11:48 | | |
| | ☿ → ♌ 13:31 | | |

ASPECTS & ECLIPSES :

| | | | | | | | |
|---|---|---|---|---|---|---|---|
| 1 | ☿ ☍ ♇ 10:48 | 7 | ☽ ⊓S ☊ 9: 4 | | ☽ ☍ ♄ 23:58 | | ♀ ☍ ♃ 22:25 |
| | ☽ ☌ ♃ 23:56 | 9 | ☽ ☌ ♂ 8:34 | 17 | ☉ S☋ ☿ 15: 6 | 27 | ☽ ☌ ☋ 11:52 |
| 2 | ☽ ☌ ♇ 5:55 | | ☽ ☌ A 13:48 | 19 | ☉ ☌ ☽ 2:40 | 29 | ☽ ☌ ♃ 1:54 |
| | ☽ ☍ ☿ 8:51 | 10 | ☿ □ ♅ 12:50 | | ☽ ☌ ☿ 5:37 | | ☽ ☍ ♀ 8:49 |
| | ☉ □ ♅ 11:16 | | ☽ ☌ ♅ 23: 3 | 20 | ☽ ☍ ♆ 17:15 | | ☽ ☌ ♇ 11:10 |
| | ☽ ☌ ♄ 13:58 | 11 | ☉ □ ☽ 16:43 | 21 | ☽ N⊓ ☊ 4:35 | | ☽ ☌ ♄ 17:17 |
| 3 | ☉ ☍ ☽ 15:57 | 13 | ♂ □ ♇ 7: 0 | | ☽ ☌ P 10:50 | 30 | ♀ ☍ ♇ 13:25 |
| | ☿ ☍ ♄ 20:59 | 14 | ☽ ☌ ☊ 19:21 | 23 | ☽ ☍ ♂ 3:34 | | ☿ ☍ ♆ 18:48 |
| 4 | ♂ □ ♃ 13: 6 | 15 | ☽ ☌ ♀ 13:25 | 24 | ☽ ☍ ♅ 3:58 | | |
| 5 | ♀ ☌ ☊ 16:15 | 16 | ☽ ☍ ♃ 9:31 | | ♂ □ ♄ 18:20 | | |
| 6 | ☽ ☌ ♆ 18:11 | | ☽ ☍ ♇ 17:22 | 25 | ☉ □ ☽ 17:56 | | |

| SIDEREAL HELIOCENTRIC LONGITUDES : AUGUST 2020 Gregorian at 0 hours UT | | | | | | | | | | | |
|---|---|---|---|---|---|---|---|---|---|---|---|
| DAY | Sid. Time | ☿ | ♀ | ⊕ | ♂ | ♃ | ♄ | ♅ | ♆ | ♇ | Vernal Point |
| 1 SA | 20:40:16 | 20 ♈ 38 | 20 ♒ 49 | 14 ♑ 12 | 9 ♒ 52 | 28 ♐ 48 | 3 ♑ 57 | 12 ♈ 39 | 24 ♒ 16 | 28 ♐ 47 | 4 ♓ 58'22" |
| 2 SU | 20:44:12 | 26 39 | 22 24 | 15 9 | 10 30 | 28 54 | 3 59 | 12 39 | 24 17 | 28 48 | 4 ♓ 58'22" |
| 3 MO | 20:48: 9 | 2 ♉ 47 | 23 59 | 16 7 | 11 8 | 28 59 | 4 1 | 12 40 | 24 17 | 28 48 | 4 ♓ 58'22" |
| 4 TU | 20:52: 5 | 9 0 | 25 35 | 17 4 | 11 46 | 29 4 | 4 2 | 12 41 | 24 17 | 28 48 | 4 ♓ 58'22" |
| 5 WE | 20:56: 2 | 15 16 | 27 10 | 18 1 | 12 24 | 29 9 | 4 4 | 12 41 | 24 18 | 28 48 | 4 ♓ 58'22" |
| 6 TH | 20:59:58 | 21 35 | 28 45 | 18 59 | 13 2 | 29 14 | 4 6 | 12 42 | 24 18 | 28 49 | 4 ♓ 58'21" |
| 7 FR | 21: 3:55 | 27 54 | 0 ♓ 21 | 19 56 | 13 40 | 29 19 | 4 8 | 12 42 | 24 18 | 28 49 | 4 ♓ 58'21" |
| 8 SA | 21: 7:51 | 4 ♊ 12 | 1 56 | 20 54 | 14 18 | 29 24 | 4 10 | 12 43 | 24 19 | 28 49 | 4 ♓ 58'21" |
| 9 SU | 21:11:48 | 10 29 | 3 31 | 21 51 | 14 56 | 29 29 | 4 12 | 12 44 | 24 19 | 28 50 | 4 ♓ 58'21" |
| 10 MO | 21:15:45 | 16 41 | 5 7 | 22 49 | 15 34 | 29 34 | 4 13 | 12 44 | 24 19 | 28 50 | 4 ♓ 58'21" |
| 11 TU | 21:19:41 | 22 46 | 6 42 | 23 46 | 16 13 | 29 39 | 4 15 | 12 45 | 24 20 | 28 50 | 4 ♓ 58'21" |
| 12 WE | 21:23:38 | 28 50 | 8 18 | 24 44 | 16 51 | 29 44 | 4 17 | 12 46 | 24 20 | 28 51 | 4 ♓ 58'21" |
| 13 TH | 21:27:34 | 4 ♋ 44 | 9 53 | 25 42 | 17 29 | 29 50 | 4 19 | 12 46 | 24 21 | 28 51 | 4 ♓ 58'20" |
| 14 FR | 21:31:31 | 10 30 | 11 29 | 26 39 | 18 7 | 29 55 | 4 21 | 12 47 | 24 21 | 28 51 | 4 ♓ 58'20" |
| 15 SA | 21:35:27 | 16 7 | 13 4 | 27 37 | 18 45 | 0 ♑ 0 | 4 23 | 12 48 | 24 21 | 28 51 | 4 ♓ 58'20" |
| 16 SU | 21:39:24 | 21 35 | 14 40 | 28 35 | 19 23 | 0 5 | 4 24 | 12 48 | 24 22 | 28 52 | 4 ♓ 58'20" |
| 17 MO | 21:43:20 | 26 53 | 16 15 | 29 32 | 20 1 | 0 10 | 4 26 | 12 49 | 24 22 | 28 52 | 4 ♓ 58'20" |
| 18 TU | 21:47:17 | 2 ♌ 2 | 17 51 | 0 ♒ 30 | 20 39 | 0 15 | 4 28 | 12 50 | 24 22 | 28 52 | 4 ♓ 58'20" |
| 19 WE | 21:51:14 | 7 1 | 19 26 | 1 28 | 21 17 | 0 20 | 4 30 | 12 50 | 24 23 | 28 53 | 4 ♓ 58'20" |
| 20 TH | 21:55:10 | 11 50 | 21 2 | 2 25 | 21 55 | 0 25 | 4 32 | 12 51 | 24 23 | 28 53 | 4 ♓ 58'19" |
| 21 FR | 21:59: 7 | 16 30 | 22 38 | 3 23 | 22 33 | 0 30 | 4 34 | 12 52 | 24 23 | 28 53 | 4 ♓ 58'19" |
| 22 SA | 22: 3: 3 | 21 1 | 24 13 | 4 21 | 23 11 | 0 35 | 4 35 | 12 52 | 24 24 | 28 54 | 4 ♓ 58'19" |
| 23 SU | 22: 7: 0 | 25 24 | 25 49 | 5 19 | 23 49 | 0 40 | 4 37 | 12 53 | 24 24 | 28 54 | 4 ♓ 58'19" |
| 24 MO | 22:10:56 | 29 38 | 27 25 | 6 17 | 24 27 | 0 46 | 4 39 | 12 54 | 24 25 | 28 54 | 4 ♓ 58'19" |
| 25 TU | 22:14:53 | 3 ♍ 44 | 29 1 | 7 15 | 25 5 | 0 51 | 4 41 | 12 54 | 24 25 | 28 54 | 4 ♓ 58'19" |
| 26 WE | 22:18:49 | 7 43 | 0 ♈ 36 | 8 12 | 25 43 | 0 56 | 4 43 | 12 55 | 24 25 | 28 55 | 4 ♓ 58'19" |
| 27 TH | 22:22:46 | 11 35 | 2 12 | 9 10 | 26 20 | 1 1 | 4 44 | 12 56 | 24 26 | 28 55 | 4 ♓ 58'18" |
| 28 FR | 22:26:43 | 15 20 | 3 48 | 10 8 | 26 58 | 1 6 | 4 46 | 12 56 | 24 26 | 28 55 | 4 ♓ 58'18" |
| 29 SA | 22:30:39 | 19 0 | 5 24 | 11 6 | 27 36 | 1 11 | 4 48 | 12 57 | 24 26 | 28 56 | 4 ♓ 58'18" |
| 30 SU | 22:34:36 | 22 33 | 7 0 | 12 4 | 28 14 | 1 16 | 4 50 | 12 58 | 24 27 | 28 56 | 4 ♓ 58'18" |
| 31 MO | 22:38:32 | 26 1 | 8 36 | 13 2 | 28 52 | 1 21 | 4 52 | 12 58 | 24 27 | 28 56 | 4 ♓ 58'18" |

INGRESSES :

| | |
|---|---|
| 2 | ☿ → ♉ 13: 8 |
| 6 | ♀ → ♓ 18:48 |
| 7 | ☿ → ♊ 7:59 |
| 12 | ☿ → ♋ 4:41 |
| 15 | ♃ → ♑ 1:26 |
| 17 | ⊕ → ♒ 11:33 |
| | ☿ → ♌ 14:26 |
| 24 | ☿ → ♍ 2: 6 |
| 25 | ♀ → ♈ 14:53 |

ASPECTS (HELIOCENTRIC +MOON(TYCHONIC)) :

| | | | | | | | | | | | |
|---|---|---|---|---|---|---|---|---|---|---|---|
| 1 | ☿ ☌ ☊ 11:40 | | ☿ □ ♆ 10:20 | | ☿ ☍ ♄ 22:15 | 19 | ☽ ☌ ☿ 17:28 | 24 | ♀ □ ♇ 22:27 | 31 | ☿ □ ♇ 20:40 |
| | ♀ ⊓S ☊ 15:27 | | ☽ ☌ ♆ 15:57 | 13 | ☽ □ ♂ 15: 2 | 20 | ☽ ☍ ♂ 12:35 | 26 | ♀ □ ♃ 5: 7 | | |
| 2 | ☽ ☌ ♇ 6:50 | | ☽ □ ☿ 21:59 | 14 | ☽ □ ♆ 3:29 | | ☽ ☍ ♆ 16: 4 | | ☽ □ ♆ 22:46 | | |
| | ☽ ☌ ♃ 7: 4 | 7 | ☽ ☌ ♀ 4:27 | | ☿ □ ♅ 9:42 | 22 | ☿ ☍ ♂ 13:43 | 27 | ☽ □ ♂ 2:16 | | |
| | ☽ ☌ ♄ 16:22 | | ☿ □ ♀ 12:25 | 15 | ☽ □ ♀ 16:33 | | ☿ ☍ ♆ 18:28 | 28 | ♀ □ ♄ 14:52 | | |
| 3 | ♀ ☌ ♆ 4:25 | 9 | ☽ □ ♇ 13: 0 | 16 | ☿ N⊓ ☊ 8:48 | | ☽ ☍ ♀ 18:35 | | ☽ □ ☿ 17: 9 | | |
| | ☽ □ ♅ 8:23 | | ☽ □ ♃ 14:26 | | ☽ ☍ ♇ 18:55 | 23 | ☽ □ ♇ 0:14 | 29 | ☽ ☌ ♇ 13:21 | | |
| | ♂ ☌ P 10:42 | | ☽ □ ♄ 23:55 | | ☽ ☍ ♃ 21:11 | | ☽ □ ♃ 3:10 | | ☽ ☌ ♃ 17:39 | | |
| 4 | ☿ □ ♂ 11:48 | 10 | ☽ ☌ ♅ 17:11 | 17 | ☽ ☍ ♄ 4:42 | | ☽ □ ♄ 9:41 | 30 | ☽ ☌ ♄ 0:20 | | |
| 5 | ☽ ☌ ♂ 17:38 | 12 | ☿ ☍ ♇ 0: 1 | | ☿ ☍ ⊕ 15: 6 | | ♂ ☌ ♆ 22:37 | | ☽ □ ♀ 5: 0 | | |
| 6 | ☿ ☌ P 4:27 | | ☿ ☍ ♃ 3:41 | | ☽ □ ♅ 19:10 | | ☽ ☍ ♅ 23:24 | | ☽ □ ♅ 15:35 | | |

this region there was a whole mountain formed of salt.

In that basin, which had previously been drained and cleansed, the baptism of about thirty persons took place…The pagans were the last to be baptized. They had to prepare themselves for the ceremony by certain purifications. Jesus poured from a flask into the baptismal basin some of the Jordan water, which the disciples always carried with them, and then he blessed it. The trench around the basin was filled high enough for the neophytes to stand in it up to the knees in water.

Before administering baptism, Jesus prepared the aspirants by a long instruction. These latter wore long, gray mantles with hoods over the head, something like the mantles worn in prayer. When about to step into the trench around the basin, they laid aside the mantle. Their loins were covered, as also the back and breast, while from the shoulders fell a little open mantle like a scapular. A disciple laid one hand upon the shoulder of the neophyte, the other upon his head. The baptizer, in the name of the Most High, poured over his head several times from a flat shell water dipped from the basin.[71]

The mysteries of the Full Moon in Capricorn are intimately tied to the mysteries of stagnant vs pure and flowing water, and of the preserving and purifying power of salt. Images and questions upon which to meditate: How does the psyche experience, in an archetypal sense: Water? Salt? Stagnation? Cleansing flow?

For essentially the entire month of July, Mercury was square Mars, recalling the events of March 5–6 AD 30 (see commentary at the start of July). Between July 31 and August 15, Mars is now square Jupiter. This alignment is exact on **August 4, Mars 24°47' Pisces square Jupiter 24°47' Sagittarius.** These two planets were square, albeit with Mars in Sagittarius and Jupiter in Pisces, on March 5 AD 30. Again we return to the events of this time. Mars is related to the force of will; traditionally, Jupiter has been related to the tempest, to Zeus or Thor, or even

Jehovah, gods of thunder and lightning. On the evening of March 4 AD 30, Anne Catherine Emmerich witnessed the following:

That night I saw something else that appeared to me surprising and inexpressibly affecting. There happened on that night a great windstorm in the Holy Land, and I saw Jesus with many others in prayer. He prayed with outstretched hands that danger might be averted. Then I had a glance at the Sea of Galilee, which was lashed by the tempest, the ships of Peter, Andrew, and Zebedee being in distress. The apostles were, as I saw, asleep in Bethany, their servants alone being on the ships. And lo! As Jesus stood now on one, now on the other, and then again upon the raging billows. It was as if he were laboring among them, holding back the vessels, warding off the danger. He was not there in person, for I did not see him going, but he stood above the sufferers, he hovered on the waves. The sailors did not see him, for it was his spirit assisting them in prayer. Nobody knew anything about his being there, though he was really helping them. Perhaps the sailors believed in him and called on him for help.[72]

Again we return to the wild energies referred to in the commentaries at the start of the month. We may be facing serious challenges and upheavals right now. More or less simultaneously with Mercury opposite Pluto, Sun square Uranus, and Mars square Jupiter, Mercury also comes into opposition with Saturn between August 1 and 6; this alignment is exact on **August 4, Mercury 2°35' Cancer opposite Saturn 2°35' Capricorn.** At the same time, we see Venus approaching the Node between July 31 and August 10. The alignment is exact on **August 5: Venus conjunct Node 3°17' Gemini.** What an intense combination of alignments and aspects!

Mercury was opposite Saturn when Christ was in heated exchange with the Pharisees (June 9 AD 32 as well as January 5–6 AD 31). The two were also aligned during the temptation in the wilderness. The events of December 1 AD 31, however, best bear witness to the might of this combination. Saturn has to do with rigidity and death; Mercury

---

71 Ibid., p. 465.

72 Ibid., p. 412.

with quicksilver, movement. On December 1 AD 30, Anne Catherine witnessed the following occurring:

> Just at this moment a loud noise arose on the roof of the hall, and through the usual opening in the ceiling a paralytic on his bed was lowered by four men, who cried out: "Lord, have pity upon a poor sick man!"
>
> He was let down by two cords into the midst of the assembly before Jesus. The friends of the sick man had tried in vain to carry him through the crowd into the courtyard, and had at last mounted the outside steps to the roof of the hall, whose trap door they opened. All eyes were fixed upon the invalid, and the Pharisees were vexed at what appeared to them a great misdemeanor, a piece of unheard-of impertinence. But Jesus, who was pleased at the faith of the poor people, stepped forward and addressed the paralytic, who lay there motionless: "Be of good heart, son, thy sins are forgiven thee," words that were, as usual, particularly distasteful to the Pharisees. They thought within themselves: "This is blasphemy! Who but God can forgive sins?" Jesus saw their thoughts and said: "Wherefore have ye such thoughts of bitterness in your heart? Which is easier to say to the paralytic: Thy sins are forgiven thee, or to say: Arise, take up thy bed, and walk? But that you may know that the Son of Man has power on Earth to forgive sins, I say to thee" (here Jesus turned to the paralytic): "Arise! Take up thy bed, and go into thy house!" And immediately the man arose cured, rolled up the coverlets of his bed, laid the laths of the frame together, took them under his arm and upon his shoulder, and accompanied by those that had brought him and some other friends, went off singing canticles of praise while the whole multitude shouted for joy. The Pharisees, full of rage, slipped away, one by one.[73]

Here we see the good humor of Mercury (impudently entering through the roof), playfully upending the self-serious and oppressive Saturnine nature of the Pharisees. However, later in the day the opposite dynamic is emphasized: Jesus raises the young girl Salome, daughter of Jairus, from the dead for the second time. After her first raising, she and her parents took the event too lightly, with levity and frivolity. They did not heed his advice and entered immediately back into their vainglorious life of style, fashion, and frivolous expenditure. After this second raising they took Christ's words and deeds to heart, and truly changed and simplified their lives. Here we see Saturn giving necessary form to the wasteful Mercury. This was a busy day for Christ: in addition to the above two miracles, he healed a widow with an issue of blood named Enue, restored the sight of two blind men, and exorcised a possessed Pharisee.

Meanwhile, the Venus–Node conjunction brings us more into the mood of the Sagittarius Full Moon from August 3. These two were conjunct on June 24–25 AD 30:

> The disciples traveled in separate bands, and met Jesus in the Jewish meeting house, situated in another quarter of Tyre, to which led a broad canal bordered with trees.
>
> To this house, with which the school was connected, belonged a large bathing garden, which ran down even to the water that cut off this quarter of the city from the mainland. The bathing garden was surrounded by a wall, inside of which was a quickset hedge of bushes cut in figures. In the middle of the garden was an open portico containing numerous passages and little apartments, and around it was the spacious bathing cistern full of flowing water. There was in the middle of it a pillar with steps and hand supports, by means of which one could descend into the water to any depth....
>
> [Christ] spoke also of water and of purification, healed many of the sick, and directed them to receive the baptism of John. He cured many boys who had been brought to him on beds. He plunged several of them, holding them by the arms, into the water, Saturnin having poured into it from a bottle some other water that Jesus had blessed. The two disciples baptized these children. There were other boys approaching manhood who went down into the cistern and, holding to the column, plunged themselves under the water, and in this way were baptized.[74]

The mood of this month is an alternation between intense outer activity and tumult and the

---

73 Ibid., vol. 2, p. 162.

74 Ibid., vol. 1, pp. 460, 462.

soothing relief of Venusian healing through water. We are being baptized by both water and fire at this time! An intense mood may continue, with these flashes of relief, up through the end of the year. January saw an emphasis on the dialogue between Higher and Lower Self (Sun and Mercury) in the realm of thinking; February, a descent into feeling and community life (Venus); March a further descent into action (Mars). April saw a return from action back into the self-consciousness of thinking; in May, this thinking united with feeling, becoming "heart thinking." In June, we saw aspects involving the Sun and Mars—the Self was finding its sense of realization in performing deeds rather than thinking thoughts. And in July, Mars and Mercury dominated: a powerful and practical union of thinking and willing.

As the rest of the year moves on, Mars aspects are dominant. Our will is being called on ever more intensively, as Mars follows the path that was laid out by Sun, Mercury and Venus earlier in the year. Mars is now on the cusp of Pisces and Aries, coming into square alignment with Jupiter, Saturn and Pluto. Between August 1 and 28, Mars is square Pluto. This alignment is exact on **August 13: Mars 28°4' Pisces square Pluto 28°4' Sagittarius.** This aspect was active on December 7 AD 30:

> It was already quite dark when I saw Jesus walking straight over the waves. It was almost opposite Tiberius, a little eastward of the middle of the lake. He appeared as if intending to pass within a little distance of the disciples' boat. The high wind was contrary, and the disciples weary of rowing. When they saw the figure on the waves, they were affrighted, for they knew not whether it was Jesus or his spirit, and they cried aloud from fear. But Jesus called out: "Fear not! It is I!" Then Peter cried: "Lord, if it be thou, bid me come to thee upon the waters." And Jesus said: "Come!"
>
> Peter, in his ardor, leaped on the little ladder and out of the boat. He hurried along for a short distance on the troubled waters toward Jesus, as if on level ground. It seemed to me that he hovered over the surface, for the inequality of the waves appeared to be no obstacle to his progress. But when he began to wonder, and to think more of the sea, its winds and its waves, than of the words of Jesus, he grew frightened and commenced to sink. Crying out, "Lord, save me!" He sank up to the breast and stretched out his hand. Instantly Jesus was at his side. He seized his hand and said: "O thou of little faith, why didst thou doubt?" Then they entered the boat, and Jesus reproached Peter and the others for their fear. The wind lulled immediately and they steered toward Bethsaida.[75]

A powerful force is lent to us if we can properly absorb the Martian–Plutonian energy. Mars and Pluto will be aspecting on and off through the remainder of the year. At the same time that this aspect is unfolding, Mercury and Uranus come into square alignment between August 8 and 12. This alignment is exact on **August 10, Mercury 15°39' Cancer square Uranus 15°39' Aries.** When the Sun was square Uranus earlier this month it recalled the temptation in the wilderness; Mercury square Uranus recalls Christ's visit to Iscariot to meet Judas's uncle Simon the Tanner on October 27 AD 30:

> The tanner's trade, on account of the odors attending it, was held in detestation by the Jews.... In Iscariot, no calling was carried on but tanning.... Judas was very dear and quite useful to his old uncle in his leather trade. Sometimes he dispatched him with asses to purchase raw hides, sometimes with prepared leather to the seaport towns, for he was a clever and cunning broker and commission merchant. Still he was not at this time a villain, and had he overcome himself in little things, he would not have fallen so low. The blessed Virgin very often warned him, but he was extremely vacillating. He was susceptible of very vehement, though not lasting repentance. His head was always running on the establishment of an earthly kingdom, and when he found that not likely to be fulfilled, he began to appropriate the money entrusted to his care.[76]

**August 15: Uranus stations retrograde, 15°40' Aries;** Christian Celebration of the Assumption of the Virgin Mary.

---

75 Ibid., vol. 2, p. 173.
76 Ibid., pp. 89–90.

Uranus was retrograde at this degree in August, 1936. This was the time of: the Berlin Summer Olympics; the height of the Spanish Civil War and the rise of fascism throughout Europe; the first of the Moscow Trials in the Soviet Union; and the first BBC television broadcast. As Uranus returns to this degree, are we redeeming ourselves from the mass-media manipulation and central-state control that blossomed in 1936?

For guidance, we turn our gaze to the triumph of purity and innocence—Mary as Regina, crowned the Queen of Heaven—on this glorious Assumption Feast.

Between August 12 and 22, the Sun and Mercury once again achieve Superior Conjunction; Mercury seeks council from the stars on behalf of the Sun and Earth. This alignment is exact on **August 17: Superior Conjunction Sun and Mercury, 0°8' Leo.** These two planets have both just ingressed into Leo:

> Irradiate with senses' might
> Existing ground of worlds,
> The essence of feeling beings
> Toward firmly willed existence.
> In stream of life flowing,
> In weaving pain of growing,
> With senses' might, arise!

May our inner core, our essence, become so tangible to us that it becomes as clear and palpable as our sense impressions. A conjunction of Mercury and Sun occurred close to this degree on July 20 AD 32. Lazarus had just died; Mary and Martha had sent multiple entreaties to Christ to hasten to Bethany to help, yet he seemed to them to be traveling all too slowly. All seemed lost. If we can irradiate our core as described above, we can hold on to hope and certainty when outer events seem hopeless and chaotic.

**August 19: Mars enters Aries; New Moon 1°33' Leo. "Ray out awakening life."** (See February 29 for the full verse.)

Today's New Moon remembers the fulfillment of the star memory of the 17th: the Raising of Lazarus from the dead on July 26 AD 32, the culmination of the seven archetypal healing miracles of Christ. On that day, the New Moon was exact around 2:30 AM, actually just before the raising from the dead which Emmerich saw occur early in the morning. Over the course of the year, we have been keeping in mind that the New Moon represents to us something unique in the course of the month. While the other phases of the Moon are reflections of or portals for different spiritual planetary spheres (Mercury, Venus, Sun, etc.), the New Moon is a monthly Sabbath, an opening in the spiral. The forces of the Father, of future Vulcan are able to flow in at this time. At no other moment is the potency of the New Moon better shown to us than on the event of Lazarus's resurrection, which occurred just hours after the New Moon portal was opened, and the influx from the Father God and Daughter Sophia at the Heart of the Galaxy was received. The mantra of Mars in Aries, to "ray out awakening life," requires no further elaboration! Indeed, Mars was in Aries during this event as well.

While Mars and Pluto are square for essentially the entire month of August, another overarching aspect involving Mars begins to unfold, which covers an even longer period. Between August 10 and October 15, Mars and Saturn are in square alignment. This alignment is exact twice due to Mars's retrograde movement: once in September, and once on **August 24, Mars 1°20' Aries square Saturn 1°20' Capricorn.** This alignment occurred, with Saturn in Cancer rather than Capricorn, on May 29–30 AD 32:

Just outside the city, which was surrounded by gardens, pleasure grounds, and villas, Jesus and his followers encountered a dense crowd composed of people from all parts of the country around. They had assembled with their sick, who were lying on litters under sheds and tents. They had been waiting for Jesus, and now they beset him and his disciples on all sides. Zacchaeus, one of the chief publicans, who dwelt outside the city, had stationed himself on the road by which Jesus had to pass. As he was short in stature, he climbed a fig tree in order to be able to see Jesus better in the crowd. Jesus looked up into the tree and said: "Zacchaeus, make haste and come down, for this day I must abide in thy house." Zacchaeus hurried down, bowed humbly to Jesus and, very much touched, returned home to make preparations for receiving his honored guest.[77]

It took a real boldness and presumption for the small Zacchaeus (out little personality) to climb the tree (rise into the Tree of Life, the spiritual world) in order to be able to witness Christ in the midst of the masses (the being of Love as the Self of Humanity). After doing this, the being of Love requests to "enter the house of Zacchaeus," i.e., to enter into the heart of hearts of the little personality! This can be our meditation for the coming month and a half.

Simultaneously with the unfolding of this aspect, Venus and Jupiter come into opposition between August 21 and 30; this alignment is exact on **August 25, Venus 22°57' Gemini opposite Jupiter 22°57' Sagittarius.** This aspect occurred on May 24 AD 32, just five days prior to the events recounted above. The potency of the Zacchaeus story is heightened on August 24–25.

Then, between August 25 and September 5, Venus is opposite Pluto. We can see that, in addition to the overarching emphasis on Martian action, the Venusian feeling life comes to the fore as Venus follows the path laid out by Sun and Mercury on the Gemini–Cancer cusp. The alignment is exact on **August 30: Venus 27°45' Gemini opposite Pluto 27°57' Sagittarius.** This aspect occurred on both April 21 AD 31, as well as June 5 AD 32. On both of these occasions, Jesus taught the parables in Luke 15:3–10, on the Lost Sheep and the Lost Coin. It is the bold desire of Christ— and of the Christian Hermeticist—that *all* should be saved, and *nothing* should be lost. This aspect also occurred on July 1 AD 30:

He directed some of the cured to bathe in the water that he had blessed; these were the children and the leprous. Jesus went to a well near the synagogue and blessed it, casting in at the same time salt that he had previously blessed.

This well was very deep; a flight of steps led down to it. He taught on this occasion of Elisha, who with salt had rectified water near Jericho; then he explained the signification of salt. He furthermore commanded that the people, when sick, should use the water of the well for bathing purposes. He always blessed in the form of a cross. While he was thus engaged, the disciples held his mantle, which he sometimes laid off, and handed him the salt that he thew into the water. He performed all these ceremonies with great gravity and recollection.[78]

We are again brought to the healing power of water and salt, just as Venus and Node revealed to us on the 5th, and the Full Moon on the 3rd. We end the month with the opposition of Mercury and Neptune, which lasts from August 28 through September 2. The alignment is exact on **August 30: Mercury 24°52' Taurus opposite Neptune 24°52' Aquarius.** Venus has a special relationship to water in terms of the feeling life, the soul of the human being; the Moon has a relationship to salt, that which preserves and purifies. Neptune is like the ocean; she is the soul of the entire cosmos, beyond the individual human, while Mercury is himself quicksilver, the fluidity of thought and action. These two were also opposed on July 3 AD 30, during the Full Moon in Sagittarius recalled at the beginning of the month—we start and end this month with a reminder to immerse and purify.

# SEPTEMBER 2020

## STARGAZING PREVIEW

As the month begins, Venus will be moving into Cancer; you'll have four hours before dawn to observe her rise. As the Sun sets on the 2nd, the Moon, Full later in the day at 15° Aquarius, will crest the horizon; you'll find the Scorpion overhead, high in the southern sky. Also on the 2nd is an opposition between Venus and Saturn: watch Saturn set as Venus rises at 0300. The square between Venus and Mars on the 4th will be observable

---

77 Ibid., p. 471.

78 Ibid., vol. 1, p. 464.

before dawn. You might be able to sleep in until 0500 and still catch a glimpse of them—Venus low in the east and Mars high in the southwest.

The Moon will pass Mars from below on the 6th, so when the waning Moon rises at 2130, Mars will already be above the horizon. Mars stations retrograde on the 10th, at 3° Aries. Additionally on this day, the Moon will reach its Last Quarter in the last decan of the Bull.

There will be a Moon–Venus conjunction on Monday the 14th at 14° Cancer; at 0600 they'll be in the southeastern sky, as the Bull and Orion watch over them from the top of the ecliptic. From below the horizon, Jupiter will station direct as it makes it final direct approach to Saturn ahead of their December conjunction. The New Moon on the 17th (29° Leo) will be remarkable in that both the Sun and Moon will move into Virgo before the day's end.

The waxing First Quarter Moon at 6° Sagittarius will happen on the 23rd, two days ahead of the Moon's conjunction to both Jupiter and Saturn. This will be worth checking out, as the Moon will be about 20° above the ecliptic, while Jupiter and Saturn will be 20° below it. All three will be high in the southeast at sunset. On the 29th, Mars, at 0° Aries, will rise at 1920, exactly square to Saturn.

Orion tops the eastern horizon about an hour before midnight; look to the southwest to see him before dawn.

## September Commentaries

**September 1: Venus enters Cancer. "Create life warmth."** (See July 18 for the full verse.)

**September 2: Mercury enters Virgo.**

> Behold worlds, O soul!
> May the soul fathom worlds,
> May the spirit penetrate being,
> Work with powers of life,
> Build upon experiences undergone,
> Trust in blossoming worlds to come.
> O soul, know thou beings!

We begin the month of September with the following mantra: "Create life warmth. May the spirit penetrate being." We are reminded that creating life warmth—that is, cultivating the life of soul—is necessary if the spirit is to penetrate into being in a positive way. If the seed of the spirit is scattered on ground that is still cold, it will be of no effect. Similarly, if we are too absorbed in our own development to cultivate relationships with those around us, we may grow in our spiritual capacities, but to what good? Virgo is one of the two domiciles of Mercury (the other is Gemini).

**Full Moon 15°10' Aquarius.** There was a Full Moon in Aquarius on August 2 AD 30. This was the first time that Christ met Maroni of Nain, the widow who was the mother of Martialis, the Youth of Nain who Christ later raised from the dead. The next day, Christ performed the second of the seven healing miracles, the Healing of the Nobleman's Son. The Aquarius Full Moon also rose on August 9 AD 32. Christ was traveling during this period of his life with three young shepherds, making a pilgrimage to visit the two Magi who were still living (Mensor and Theokeno). On August 9, they had just arrived in Kedar, one of the last towns east of Palestine where there was a Jewish settlement:

> Kedar was situated at the foot of a mountain, in a valley through which flowed a river. It consisted of an old and a new city separated by the little river, which flowed from the east and off toward Palestine. The shore was very steep, and the river was spanned by two arches very solidly built. On this side the place was poor and insignificant, and inhabited principally by Jewish shepherds who likewise engaged in the manufacture of light huts, and shepherd and stable utensils. On the opposite side Kedar presented a more opulent appearance. There were no Jews there, but only pagans. The Jewish costume was somewhat modified here, for some of the people wore a pointed cap. In the city this side of the river, there was a synagogue, and upon a square surrounded by grass plots and walks of clean white sand, played a fountain. This was the most beautiful spot in the city.[79]

Christ shared with the people here the parable of the Prodigal Son, and of Zacchaeus climbing

---

79 Ibid., vol. 2, p. 485.

SIDEREAL GEOCENTRIC LONGITUDES :    SEPTEMBER 2020 Gregorian at 0 hours UT

| DAY | ☉ | ☽ | ☊ | ☿ | ♀ | ♂ | ♃ | ♄ | ♅ | Ψ | ♇ |
|---|---|---|---|---|---|---|---|---|---|---|---|
| 1 TU | 14 ♌ 0 | 0 ♒ 0 | 1 ♊ 25R | 26 ♌ 57 | 29 ♊ 16 | 2 ♈ 32 | 22 ♐ 37R | 0 ♑ 57R | 15 ♈ 33R | 24 ♒ 49R | 27 ♐ 43R |
| 2 WE | 14 58 | 12 26 | 1 13 | 28 39 | 0 ♋ 20 | 2 40 | 22 34 | 0 54 | 15 32 | 24 48 | 27 42 |
| 3 TH | 15 56 | 24 42 | 1 0 | 0 ♍ 20 | 1 24 | 2 46 | 22 32 | 0 52 | 15 31 | 24 46 | 27 41 |
| 4 FR | 16 54 | 6 ♓ 48 | 0 47 | 2 0 | 2 29 | 2 51 | 22 31 | 0 49 | 15 31 | 24 44 | 27 40 |
| 5 SA | 17 52 | 18 47 | 0 35 | 3 38 | 3 33 | 2 56 | 22 29 | 0 47 | 15 30 | 24 43 | 27 40 |
| 6 SU | 18 50 | 0 ♈ 41 | 0 24 | 5 15 | 4 38 | 3 0 | 22 27 | 0 45 | 15 29 | 24 41 | 27 39 |
| 7 MO | 19 48 | 12 30 | 0 17 | 6 51 | 5 44 | 3 3 | 22 26 | 0 42 | 15 27 | 24 39 | 27 38 |
| 8 TU | 20 47 | 24 20 | 0 12 | 8 26 | 6 49 | 3 5 | 22 25 | 0 40 | 15 26 | 24 38 | 27 37 |
| 9 WE | 21 45 | 6 ♉ 15 | 0 9 | 10 0 | 7 55 | 3 6 | 22 24 | 0 38 | 15 25 | 24 36 | 27 37 |
| 10 TH | 22 43 | 18 18 | 0 8 | 11 33 | 9 1 | 3 7R | 22 24 | 0 37 | 15 24 | 24 34 | 27 36 |
| 11 FR | 23 41 | 0 ♊ 37 | 0 8 | 13 4 | 10 7 | 3 6 | 22 23 | 0 35 | 15 23 | 24 33 | 27 35 |
| 12 SA | 24 40 | 13 15 | 0 8 | 14 34 | 11 13 | 3 5 | 22 23 | 0 33 | 15 22 | 24 31 | 27 35 |
| 13 SU | 25 38 | 26 17 | 0 6 | 16 3 | 12 20 | 3 3 | 22 23 | 0 31 | 15 20 | 24 30 | 27 34 |
| 14 MO | 26 37 | 9 ♋ 48 | 0 2 | 17 31 | 13 26 | 2 59 | 22 23D | 0 30 | 15 19 | 24 28 | 27 33 |
| 15 TU | 27 35 | 23 48 | 29 ♉ 55 | 18 58 | 14 33 | 2 55 | 22 23 | 0 28 | 15 17 | 24 26 | 27 33 |
| 16 WE | 28 34 | 8 ♌ 16 | 29 46 | 20 23 | 15 41 | 2 50 | 22 24 | 0 27 | 15 16 | 24 25 | 27 32 |
| 17 TH | 29 32 | 23 6 | 29 35 | 21 48 | 16 48 | 2 45 | 22 24 | 0 26 | 15 15 | 24 23 | 27 32 |
| 18 FR | 0 ♍ 31 | 8 ♍ 11 | 29 24 | 23 11 | 17 55 | 2 38 | 22 25 | 0 25 | 15 13 | 24 21 | 27 31 |
| 19 SA | 1 29 | 23 20 | 29 13 | 24 33 | 19 3 | 2 30 | 22 26 | 0 24 | 15 11 | 24 20 | 27 31 |
| 20 SU | 2 28 | 8 ♎ 23 | 29 4 | 25 53 | 20 11 | 2 22 | 22 27 | 0 23 | 15 10 | 24 18 | 27 30 |
| 21 MO | 3 27 | 23 11 | 28 58 | 27 13 | 21 19 | 2 13 | 22 29 | 0 22 | 15 8 | 24 16 | 27 30 |
| 22 TU | 4 25 | 7 ♏ 39 | 28 55 | 28 30 | 22 27 | 2 3 | 22 30 | 0 21 | 15 7 | 24 15 | 27 30 |
| 23 WE | 5 24 | 21 43 | 28 54 | 29 47 | 23 35 | 1 52 | 22 32 | 0 20 | 15 5 | 24 13 | 27 29 |
| 24 TH | 6 23 | 5 ♐ 23 | 28 54 | 1 ♎ 2 | 24 44 | 1 40 | 22 34 | 0 20 | 15 3 | 24 11 | 27 29 |
| 25 FR | 7 21 | 18 42 | 28 54 | 2 15 | 25 53 | 1 28 | 22 36 | 0 19 | 15 1 | 24 10 | 27 29 |
| 26 SA | 8 20 | 1 ♑ 42 | 28 52 | 3 27 | 27 2 | 1 15 | 22 39 | 0 19 | 15 0 | 24 8 | 27 28 |
| 27 SU | 9 19 | 14 26 | 28 48 | 4 36 | 28 11 | 1 2 | 22 41 | 0 19 | 14 58 | 24 7 | 27 28 |
| 28 MO | 10 18 | 26 57 | 28 41 | 5 44 | 29 20 | 0 47 | 22 44 | 0 19 | 14 56 | 24 5 | 27 28 |
| 29 TU | 11 17 | 9 ♒ 18 | 28 31 | 6 50 | 0 ♌ 29 | 0 33 | 22 47 | 0 18 | 14 54 | 24 4 | 27 28 |
| 30 WE | 12 16 | 21 30 | 28 19 | 7 54 | 1 38 | 0 17 | 22 50 | 0 19D | 14 52 | 24 2 | 27 28 |

INGRESSES :

| | | | |
|---|---|---|---|
| 1 ♀ → ♋ 16:32 | 19 ☽ → ♎ 10:35 | | |
| 2 ☿ → ♍ 19:11 | 21 ☽ → ♏ 11:13 | | |
| 3 ☽ → ♓ 10:28 | 23 ☿ → ♎ 4:11 | | |
| 5 ☽ → ♈ 22:37 | 25 ☽ → ♑ 20:49 | | |
| 8 ☽ → ♉ 11:26 | 28 ☽ → ♒ 5:53 | | |
| 10 ☽ → ♊ 22:49 | ♀ → ♌ 13:58 | | |
| 13 ☽ → ♋ 6:40 | 30 ☽ → ♓ 16:51 | | |
| 14 ☊ → ♉ 6:54 | | | |
| 15 ☽ → ♌ 10:22 | | | |
| 17 ☽ → ♍ 11: 0 | | | |
| ☉ → ♍ 11:25 | | | |

ASPECTS & ECLIPSES :

| | | | |
|---|---|---|---|
| 2 ☉ ☍ ☽ 5:21 | ☽ ☌ ☊ 23: 4 | ☉ ☌ ☽ 10:59 | ☽ ☌ ♇ 16: 7 |
| ♀ ☍ ♄ 12:16 | 11 ☉ ☍ Ψ 20:34 | 18 ☽ ☌ P 13:39 | ☽ ☌ ♄ 21:24 |
| 3 ☽ ☌ Ψ 0: 8 | 12 ☽ ☍ ♃ 16:53 | 19 ☽ ☌ ☿ 2: 6 | 28 ☽ ☍ ♀ 5: 3 |
| ☿ ☍ Ψ 8:28 | 13 ☽ ☍ ♇ 2:18 | ☽ ☍ ♂ 14:27 | 29 ♂ □ ♄ 21:47 |
| ☽ ⚼ ☊ 12:14 | ☽ ☍ ♄ 7:36 | 20 ☽ ☍ ♅ 10:54 | 30 ☽ ☌ Ψ 4:59 |
| ☽ ☍ ☿ 12:55 | 14 ☽ ☌ ♀ 6:52 | 21 ☿ □ ♇ 5:16 | ☽ ⚼ ☊ 13:16 |
| 4 ♀ □ ♂ 9:10 | 15 ♀ □ ♅ 15:27 | 23 ☿ □ ♄ 10:37 | |
| 6 ☽ ☌ ♂ 4:43 | 17 ☉ □ ☊ 0:56 | ☽ ☌ ☋ 12:31 | |
| ☽ ☌ A 6:11 | ☽ ☍ Ψ 2: 3 | 24 ☉ □ ☽ 1:53 | |
| 7 ☽ ☌ ♅ 5:58 | ☽ ⚼ ☊ 10:13 | ☿ ☍ ♂ 10:51 | |
| 10 ☉ □ ☽ 9:24 | ☿ □ ♃ 10:33 | 25 ☽ ☌ ♃ 7:10 | |

SIDEREAL HELIOCENTRIC LONGITUDES :    SEPTEMBER 2020 Gregorian at 0 hours UT

| DAY | Sid. Time | ☿ | ♀ | ⊕ | ♂ | ♃ | ♄ | ♅ | Ψ | ♇ | Vernal Point |
|---|---|---|---|---|---|---|---|---|---|---|---|
| 1 TU | 22:42:29 | 29 ♍ 24 | 10 ♈ 12 | 14 ♒ 0 | 29 ♒ 30 | 1 ♑ 26 | 4 ♑ 54 | 12 ♈ 59 | 24 ♒ 27 | 28 ♐ 57 | 4 ♓ 58'18" |
| 2 WE | 22:46:25 | 2 ♎ 43 | 11 48 | 14 58 | 0 ♓ 7 | 1 31 | 4 55 | 13 0 | 24 28 | 28 57 | 4 ♓ 58'18" |
| 3 TH | 22:50:22 | 5 57 | 13 24 | 15 56 | 0 45 | 1 37 | 4 57 | 13 0 | 24 28 | 28 57 | 4 ♓ 58'18" |
| 4 FR | 22:54:18 | 9 8 | 15 0 | 16 54 | 1 23 | 1 42 | 4 59 | 13 1 | 24 29 | 28 57 | 4 ♓ 58'17" |
| 5 SA | 22:58:15 | 12 15 | 16 36 | 17 53 | 2 0 | 1 47 | 5 1 | 13 2 | 24 29 | 28 58 | 4 ♓ 58'17" |
| 6 SU | 23: 2:12 | 15 19 | 18 12 | 18 51 | 2 38 | 1 52 | 5 3 | 13 2 | 24 29 | 28 58 | 4 ♓ 58'17" |
| 7 MO | 23: 6: 8 | 18 19 | 19 48 | 19 49 | 3 16 | 1 57 | 5 5 | 13 3 | 24 30 | 28 58 | 4 ♓ 58'17" |
| 8 TU | 23:10: 5 | 21 17 | 21 24 | 20 47 | 3 53 | 2 2 | 5 6 | 13 4 | 24 30 | 28 59 | 4 ♓ 58'17" |
| 9 WE | 23:14: 1 | 24 13 | 23 0 | 21 45 | 4 31 | 2 7 | 5 8 | 13 4 | 24 30 | 28 59 | 4 ♓ 58'17" |
| 10 TH | 23:17:58 | 27 7 | 24 36 | 22 44 | 5 8 | 2 12 | 5 10 | 13 5 | 24 31 | 28 59 | 4 ♓ 58'17" |
| 11 FR | 23:21:54 | 29 58 | 26 13 | 23 42 | 5 46 | 2 17 | 5 12 | 13 5 | 24 31 | 28 59 | 4 ♓ 58'16" |
| 12 SA | 23:25:51 | 2 ♏ 48 | 27 49 | 24 40 | 6 24 | 2 23 | 5 14 | 13 6 | 24 31 | 29 0 | 4 ♓ 58'16" |
| 13 SU | 23:29:47 | 5 37 | 29 25 | 25 39 | 7 1 | 2 28 | 5 15 | 13 7 | 24 32 | 29 0 | 4 ♓ 58'16" |
| 14 MO | 23:33:44 | 8 24 | 1 ♉ 1 | 26 37 | 7 38 | 2 33 | 5 17 | 13 8 | 24 32 | 29 0 | 4 ♓ 58'16" |
| 15 TU | 23:37:41 | 11 11 | 2 38 | 27 36 | 8 16 | 2 38 | 5 19 | 13 8 | 24 33 | 29 1 | 4 ♓ 58'16" |
| 16 WE | 23:41:37 | 13 56 | 4 14 | 28 34 | 8 53 | 2 43 | 5 21 | 13 9 | 24 33 | 29 1 | 4 ♓ 58'16" |
| 17 TH | 23:45:34 | 16 41 | 5 50 | 29 33 | 9 31 | 2 48 | 5 23 | 13 10 | 24 33 | 29 1 | 4 ♓ 58'16" |
| 18 FR | 23:49:30 | 19 26 | 7 27 | 0 ♓ 31 | 10 8 | 2 53 | 5 25 | 13 10 | 24 34 | 29 2 | 4 ♓ 58'15" |
| 19 SA | 23:53:27 | 22 11 | 9 3 | 1 30 | 10 45 | 2 58 | 5 26 | 13 11 | 24 34 | 29 2 | 4 ♓ 58'15" |
| 20 SU | 23:57:23 | 24 56 | 10 40 | 2 29 | 11 22 | 3 3 | 5 28 | 13 12 | 24 34 | 29 2 | 4 ♓ 58'15" |
| 21 MO | 0: 1:20 | 27 41 | 12 16 | 3 27 | 12 0 | 3 9 | 5 30 | 13 12 | 24 35 | 29 2 | 4 ♓ 58'15" |
| 22 TU | 0: 5:16 | 0 ♐ 26 | 13 53 | 4 26 | 12 37 | 3 14 | 5 32 | 13 13 | 24 35 | 29 3 | 4 ♓ 58'15" |
| 23 WE | 0: 9:13 | 3 12 | 15 29 | 5 25 | 13 14 | 3 19 | 5 34 | 13 14 | 24 35 | 29 3 | 4 ♓ 58'15" |
| 24 TH | 0:13:10 | 5 59 | 17 6 | 6 23 | 13 51 | 3 24 | 5 36 | 13 14 | 24 36 | 29 3 | 4 ♓ 58'15" |
| 25 FR | 0:17: 6 | 8 47 | 18 43 | 7 22 | 14 28 | 3 29 | 5 37 | 13 15 | 24 36 | 29 4 | 4 ♓ 58'15" |
| 26 SA | 0:21: 3 | 11 37 | 20 19 | 8 21 | 15 5 | 3 34 | 5 39 | 13 16 | 24 37 | 29 4 | 4 ♓ 58'14" |
| 27 SU | 0:24:59 | 14 28 | 21 56 | 9 20 | 15 42 | 3 39 | 5 41 | 13 16 | 24 37 | 29 4 | 4 ♓ 58'14" |
| 28 MO | 0:28:56 | 17 21 | 23 33 | 10 19 | 16 19 | 3 44 | 5 43 | 13 17 | 24 37 | 29 5 | 4 ♓ 58'14" |
| 29 TU | 0:32:52 | 20 15 | 25 10 | 11 17 | 16 56 | 3 50 | 5 45 | 13 18 | 24 38 | 29 5 | 4 ♓ 58'14" |
| 30 WE | 0:36:49 | 23 12 | 26 46 | 12 16 | 17 33 | 3 55 | 5 47 | 13 18 | 24 38 | 29 5 | 4 ♓ 58'14" |

INGRESSES :

| | |
|---|---|
| 1 ☿ → ♎ 4:15 | |
| ♂ → ♓ 19:21 | |
| 11 ☿ → ♏ 0:15 | |
| 13 ♀ → ♉ 8:42 | |
| 17 ⊕ → ♓ 11:10 | |
| 21 ☿ → ♐ 20:13 | |

ASPECTS (HELIOCENTRIC +MOON(TYCHONIC)) :

| | | | | | |
|---|---|---|---|---|---|
| 1 ☿ □ ♃ 15: 3 | ☽ ☌ ♀ 17: 6 | 16 ☽ □ ☿ 11:21 | 24 ☽ ☌ ☿ 1:20 | ☽ □ ♀ 12: 3 | |
| 2 ☿ □ ♄ 16:26 | 8 ☿ ☍ ♀ 1:59 | 17 ☽ ☍ Ψ 2:19 | ☿ □ ⊕ 5:17 | | |
| ♀ ☌ ♅ 18: 8 | ☿ ☌ ☋ 18:29 | 18 ☽ ☍ ♂ 3:13 | ☽ □ ♂ 15:55 | | |
| ☽ ☌ Ψ 23:33 | 10 ☽ □ Ψ 12:10 | 19 ☿ ☌ A 4:58 | 25 ☽ ☌ ♇ 19: 5 | | |
| 3 ☽ ☌ ♂ 12:37 | 11 ☽ □ ♂ 10:23 | ☽ □ ♇ 9: 3 | 26 ☽ ☌ ♃ 3:30 | | |
| 5 ☿ ☍ ♅ 6: 6 | ⊕ ☌ Ψ 20:17 | ☽ □ ♃ 15:25 | ☽ ☌ ♄ 7:24 | | |
| ☽ □ ♇ 20:32 | 13 ☽ ☍ ♇ 4:53 | ☽ □ ♄ 19:19 | ☽ □ ♅ 21:46 | | |
| 6 ☽ □ ♃ 2:25 | ☽ ☍ ♃ 11: 8 | ☿ □ Ψ 20:53 | ♀ ☌ ☊ 22:33 | | |
| ☽ □ ♄ 8:52 | ☽ ☍ ♄ 16: 3 | 20 ☽ ☍ ♅ 7:44 | 27 ☿ □ ♂ 13: 7 | | |
| 7 ☽ ☌ ♅ 1: 6 | 14 ☽ □ ♅ 5:47 | 22 ☽ ☍ ♀ 11:54 | 28 ♀ □ Ψ 16: 2 | | |
| ☽ ☍ ☿ 15:45 | 15 ☽ □ ♀ 16:34 | 23 ☽ □ Ψ 4:59 | 30 ☽ ☌ Ψ 6:12 | | |

up the fig tree. The inhabitants of Kedar listened attentively and were very fond of Jesus, but did not recognize who he was. With the recollections of Maroni and Martialis, the prodigal, and the nobleman's son, the focus of this Full Moon is the redemption of the son. Even Zacchaeus, in his small stature, might make us think of a lost child, climbing up a tree in order to find his way back home. Today is a good day to consider our children, literally and metaphorically: the successors of our endeavors, our artistic and academic creations, our work in the world. Are our children alive and well?

Throughout the year, we have been focusing on the Sun as the (Higher) Self, Mercury as the Lower Self expressed in Thinking, Venus as Feeling, and Mars as Action. During July, the focus was on the coming together of thought and action, with the Mercury–Mars square dominating the whole month. As of August, Mars aspects dominate the remaining five months of the year—it is time for action! Mars square Pluto lasted from August 1 through September 2; Mars square Saturn began on August 10 and will carry on through October 15. While these Martian aspects carry the overall mood, the last third of August also started a sequence of Venusian aspects: Venus opposite both Jupiter and Pluto between August 21 and September 5.

This journey through the feeling life continues through the first half of September. Venus is opposite Saturn between August 28 and September 6; this alignment is exact on **September 2, Venus 0°34' Cancer opposite Saturn 0°34' Capricorn.** At the same time, Venus comes into square alignment with Mars between August 30 and September 9; this alignment is exact on **September 4, Venus 2°51' Cancer square Mars 2°51' Aries.** Along with these two Venusian aspects, Mercury comes into square alignment with the Node between August 31 and September 6. The square is exact on **September 3, Mercury 1° Virgo square Node 1° Gemini.**

The first alignment, that of Venus opposite Saturn, occurred December 5 AD 30. During these days Christ was healing many who were possessed:

On the following day Jesus climbed the mountain, and encountered two Jewish youths who had come from Gorges to meet him. They were possessed by the devil. They were not furious, though the attacks of the evil one were frequent, and they roved restlessly about. When Jesus some time before had crossed the Jordan from Trachea and passed Gerasa, these young men were not yet possessed. They had then come out to meet him and begged to be received among his disciples, but Jesus had sent them away. Now again, after Jesus had delivered them, they desired to be received by him. They told him that the misfortune from which he had just freed them never would have overtaken them if he had yielded to their first request. Jesus exhorted them to amendment of life, and bade them return home and announce by what means their deliverance had been effected. The youths sobered. As Jesus went along, pausing here and there to teach before the huts and homes of the shepherds, many possessed and simpletons ran hiding behind the hedges and hills, crying after him and making signs for him to keep off and not disturb their peace. But Jesus called them to him, and delivered them. Many of those thus freed cried out, imploring him not to drive them into the abyss![80]

The alignment of Mercury and Node recalls the events of September 10–11 AD 29, almost two weeks prior to the Baptism in the Jordan. At this time, Jesus of Nazareth was spending many days traveling and teaching with the elderly Eliud the Essene. On September 10–11, they were in the somewhat dilapidated city of Endor:

Around the inns lay masses of broken walls all the way along the mountain, so broad that a wagon could pass over them. Endor was full of ruins interspersed with gardens. On one side were large, magnificent buildings like palaces, while in other quarters of the city the desolation of war was visible. It seemed to me that the inhabitants were a race apart from the Jews. There was no synagogue in Endor, so Jesus went with Eliud to a large square in which three side buildings containing small chambers were built around a pond. The pond was in the center of a green lawn, and on its

---

80 Ibid., p. 169.

waters little barks were sailing. There was a pump nearby, and the place bore the appearance of a health-giving resort. The little chambers around the pond were occupied by invalids....These people were not orthodox Jews. They were more like slaves, cast out and oppressed, who had to pay tribute of all that they earned. They were very compassionate and stood by one another under all circumstances. They wore long coats and girdles. Their pointed caps covered their ears like those of the ancient hermits.[81]

The description of Endor hearkens back to that of Kendar from the Full Moon: a city half dilapidated, half opulent; a central fountain around which the rabble gather; a mix of pagan and Jewish, with pointed caps like the "ancient hermits." What do these arcana offer to our meditations for the month? Anne Catherine Emmerich goes on:

The inhabitants were Canaanites...They had an idol hidden away in a subterranean cavern. By some kind of mechanism on springs it could be made to rise suddenly out of the earth and seat itself on an altar beautifully ornamented and prepared to receive it. They had procured this idol from Egypt, and it was named Astarte, which I understood yesterday to be the same as Esther. The idol had a face round like the Moon. On its outstretched arms it held something long and swathed, like the chrysalis of a butterfly, large in the middle and tapering at either end. It may have been a fish. On the back of the idol was a pedestal upon which stood a high pail, or a small half tub, which extended over the head. In it was something like ears in green husks, also fruits and green leaves. The idol stood in a cask that reached up to the lower part of the body, and all around it were pots of growing plants. These people worshipped their idol in secret, and Jesus in his instructions to them reprehended them for it. They had been accustomed to sacrifice deformed children to the goddess. There was a companion idol belonging to this goddess, the god Adonis, who I think was Astarte's husband.[82]

Finally, Venus was square Mars during the Temptation in the Wilderness, during Christ's

pilgrimage to Egypt, and in May AD 33, during the Ascension and Whitsuntide. The theme of these three aspects together is one of confronting the demonic and casting it out (temptation in the wilderness) amongst outcast and poverty stricken people (journeys to Egypt) in order to bring about renewal (Ascension and Whitsuntide).

**September 10: Mars stations retrograde, 3°7' Aries.** Mars was retrograde, close to this degree, on September 25, 805. This was the day that the young Parzival (not yet 17 years old) came heedlessly across the Fisher King Anfortas and Munsalvaeche, the Grail Castle. He witnessed the intensity of the Grail Rite on behalf of the wounded king, and remained stricken dumb during the entire event. Mars is related to the larynx chakra; perhaps its retrograde movement affects our ability to be tactful? We must remember that tact is the art of speaking at the right time, not simply being silent or secretive. Speak at the right time; be silent at the right time—this is the tightrope of tactfulness.

Between September 6 and 17, the Sun comes into opposition with Neptune. This alignment is exact on **September 11, Sun 24°33' Leo opposite Neptune 24°33' Aquarius.** Once again, we are reminded of the Assumption of the Holy Virgin Mary, when she became the Queen of Heaven. See the commentary for March 8.

**September 12–13: Jupiter stations direct, 22°23' Sagittarius.** Jupiter was close to this degree in April–May, 810, as Parzival rode from Trevrizent's hut with newfound courage and understanding, ultimately to resolve his failures of four and a half years prior. Jupiter was also here in April of 1830, when the young Kaspar Hauser (just barely 17 years old) was almost assassinated by gunshot. The last time that Jupiter was at this degree near conjunction with Saturn was in January 1961. President Eisenhower delivered his final speech as sitting President, his famous warning against the might of the military–industrial complex. Shortly after this, John F. Kennedy was sworn in as President of the United States—a role that would tragically be cut short by a gunshot wound. How is our time continuing the interwoven karma of Parzival and Kaspar Hauser?

---

81 Ibid., vol. 1, p. 317.
82 Ibid., pp. 317–318.

Are we exposing the apparatus that was responsible for the death of JFK—the same apparatus that has subsequently attempted to subject all of our children to the fate of Kaspar Hauser?

Between September 11 and 19, Venus comes into square alignment with Uranus. This alignment is exact on **September 15, Venus 15°17' Cancer square Uranus 15°17' Aries.** Simultaneously, the Sun comes into square alignment with the Node, exact on **September 17, Sun 29°35' Leo square Node 29°35' Taurus.** Finally, Mercury reaches square alignment with Jupiter between September 14 and 21, exact on **September 17, Mercury 22°24' Virgo square Jupiter 22°24' Sagittarius.**

Venus was square Uranus on October 11 AD 32. During this time, Christ was traveling through Ur, the birthplace of Abraham, on his way to Egypt. His teaching revolved around warnings against idolatry. The next day, October 12, Anne Catherine witnessed the following:

> Here Jesus strongly inveighed against the people's worship. The chief of the settlement was deaf to Jesus's teaching and became enraged, even contradicting him. The chief lived in a house full of idols. Jesus said that on the anniversary of the night on which the star had appeared to the three kings, the idols would all break, the oxen idols would bellow, the dog idols would bark, and the bird idols would squawk. This would be proof of the truth of his words. The people listened to him in disbelief. Jesus told them that this would take place throughout Chaldea in the places that he had visited.[83]

The Sun was square Node in the same signs of the Zodiac on August 21 AD 30. Here Christ taught in Bethulia:

> From Jotopata also there were visitors at the baths. They did not wait to hear Jesus's instruction but, returning to Jotopata, spread the news of his presence in Bethulia. Jotopoata was situated about an hour and a half to the southeast, but in the bosom of the mountains as in an immense cave.... It was a region full of wonderful

hiding places. There were numerous Herodians in Jotopata. In a wall of the fortifications they had a secret meeting place. The sect was composed of shrewd, intelligent people ranged under a secret superior. They had signs whereby they recognized one another, and the chiefs could also tell (how, I do not now know) if a member had betrayed anything. Secret enemies of the Romans, they were plotting a revolution in favor of Herod....Exteriorly and through motives of cunning, they were very bland and tolerant, though really treacherous sneaks. They had, properly speaking, no religion at all; but under the cloak of piety they labored at the founding of an independent kingdom of this world, and Herod supported them in their intrigues.[84]

Mercury was square to Jupiter (with Jupiter in Gemini rather than Sagittarius) on September 7–8. This was the end of Christ's time with the people in Kedar, after which on his travels he came across a nocturnal celebration of star worshippers:

> The light inside the temple was very extraordinary. It was like twilight, or rather moonlight. One seemed to be gazing up into a sky full of stars. The Moon likewise could be seen, and far up in the very center of all blazed the Sun. It was a most skillfully executed arrangement, and so natural that it produced upon the beholder an impression of awe, especially when he beheld by the dim light of the lower part of the temple the three idols that were placed around that central column. One was like a human being with a bird's head and a great, crooked beard. I saw the people offering to it in sacrifice all kinds of foods. They crammed into its enormous bill birds and similar things which fell down into its body and out again. Another of these idols had a head almost like that of an ox, and was seated like a human being in a squatting posture. They laid birds in its arms, which were outstretched as if to receive an infant. In it was a fire into which, through the holes made for that purpose, the worshippers cast the flesh of animals that had been slaughtered and cut up on the sacrificial table in front of it. The smoke escaped through a pipe sunk in the earth and communicating with the outer air. No flames

---

83 Ibid., vol. 2, p. 516.

84 Ibid., pp. 25–26.

were to be seen in the temple, but the horrible idols shone with a reddish glare in the dim light. During the ceremony, the multitude around the pyramid chanted in a very remarkable manner. Sometimes a single voice was heard, and then again a powerful chorus, the strains suddenly changing from plaintive to exultant; and when the Moon and different stars shone out, they sent up shouts of enthusiastic welcome. I think this idolatrous celebration lasted till sunrise.[85]

Perhaps some of the imagery from these three memories sounds familiar to our time. Who are the "bland and tolerant…treacherous sneaks" of our time? How have they contributed to the debasing of the archetypal, distorting it and literalizing it into the idol? Perhaps the Mars aspects of these months have something to do with turning the gaze of recognition to subversive and incredibly damaging activities that have been going on for far too long.

**September 17: New Moon 29°59' Leo.** A Leo New Moon occurred close to this degree on August 17 AD 30. On the days surrounding, Christ had journeyed to Peter's house in Bethsaida. He healed many people on his way to Bethsaida and in the town itself:

> The whole road was full of sick…. There were blind, lame, mute, deaf, paralytic, and an exceedingly large number of dropsical Jews. The ceremony of curing was performed with the greatest order and solemnity. The people had already been two days here, and the disciples of the place…had arranged them comfortably in the nooks, retired and shady, and the little gardens on the road…. Band after band passed before him, and the disciples preserved order.

> I saw again that Jesus exercised many different manners of curing, and that probably he did so in order to instruct the disciples as to how they should act, also the ministers of the church till the end of time…. There were no sudden, no magical transformations in the cures he wrought….They were like drooping plants regaining freshness in the rain…All was conducted quietly and methodically.[86]

**Sun enters Virgo. "Behold worlds, O soul!** (See September 2 for the full verse.)

Rudolf Steiner, as always, chooses his words carefully here: notice that the soul is to behold *worlds* and not "the world." The secret of the human soul is her unique ability to perceive in many—potentially all—worlds. She receives sense impressions from the physical world, thoughts from the cosmos, depth of feeling from within herself and the souls of others. She beholds memories of all of these, and each of them can become an impulse to action within her. And when she has passed through adequate training, she becomes receptive to the supersensible—the trans-subjective realm of the spirit. In truth, each being is an entire world unto itself—and there are infinite beings. Perhaps this was the lesson Christ showed his disciples with his many different manners of curing—that each person we meet is an entire world, and must be approached as such for any kind of healing to occur.

Between September 17 and 25, Mercury comes into square alignment with Pluto. This alignment is exact on **September 21, Mercury 27°30' Virgo square Pluto 27°30' Sagittarius.** In the meantime, Neptune slowly comes into square alignment with the Node—a powerful source of inspiration for the soul. They will come within 5° of square alignment as of September 18, and will continue to draw closer as the year ends; they will not achieve an exact alignment until next January. Also on September 18, Mars and Pluto once again approach square alignment due to the retrograde movement of Mars. This will last for over a month, until October 26— the exact alignment will not be until October 9 (see next month's commentary).

On September 20, Mercury begins to come into square alignment with Saturn, which will last until the 27th. The alignment is exact on **September 23, Mercury 0°20' Libra square Saturn 0°20' Capricorn.** Meanwhile, between September 21 and 29, Mercury comes into opposition with Mars, exact on **September 24, Mercury 1°40' Libra opposite Mars 1°40' Aries.** Finally, Jupiter and Pluto begin to come into conjunction once again on September

---

85 Ibid., p. 496.
86 Ibid., p. 19.

22. This alignment is exact on November 12, and lasts until December 13.

Mercury and Pluto were square on September 3 AD 32, as Christ and the three shepherd youths were staying in the town of Sichar on their way to the tent city of the Gold King, Mensor (also known as Melchior). This was two days after the raising of Nazor from the dead. He counseled a newly married couple: "Thou hast allowed thy heart to be moved by the beauty of thy wife! But think how great the beauty of the soul must be, since God sends his Son upon Earth to save souls by the sacrifice of his body! Whoever serves the body, serves not the soul. Beauty inflames selfish desire, and such desire corrupts the soul. Incontinence is like a creeping plant that chokes and destroys the wheat and the vines."[87]

Mercury was square Saturn a few weeks later, on September 29; Mercury was opposite Mars on September 20. This was exactly the time period (September 20–29 AD 32) that Christ visited with the Gold King, Mensor, in his tent city. On September 28, just prior to his departure, he healed the ailing "Frankincense King," Theokeno (also known as Caspar). It was during this time that Christ planted the seed for the reclamation of the debauchery of idol worship and fallen star lore that was remembered just a few days ago when Mercury was square Jupiter. This is the remedy for what has fallen, not to fight and eradicate it, but to absorb and resurrect it.

All of this stands as a portent, directing our gaze to the year's end, when Jupiter and Saturn will come together in Capricorn. For this was the Star followed by the Magi: a Great Conjunction of Saturn with Jupiter, although at that time it was in the constellation Pisces.

**September 23:** Mercury enters Libra.

> Worlds sustain worlds;
> In being experience being;
> In existing, embrace existence.
> And being effects being
> To pour forth deeds unfolding,
> In world enjoyment reposing.
> O worlds, uphold worlds!

**September 28: Venus enters Leo. "Existing ground of worlds."** (See August 17 the for full verse)

The combination of Mercury in Libra and Venus in Leo yields: "Existing ground of worlds: In existing, embrace existence." There is something here that calls to mind the process of individuation. Much of our malaise comes from the fact that the "ground of worlds" (i.e., our subconscious) does *not* embrace its own existence. It is kept in the cellar, like Kaspar Hauser, and our daytime awareness doesn't wish to be disturbed by it. But this is unsustainable—that which is unconscious in us is a driving force that *must* be consciously integrated, otherwise it will continue to operate as a destructive and disturbing force in our lives. To truly *exist*, we must also *embrace* existence!

**September 29: Michaelmas. Saturn stations direct 0°18' Capricorn.** Saturn was opposite this degree on June 14 AD 31. Christ visited his mother's house with some newly converted young disciples:

> Jesus, according to his custom, presented the newly converted to his mother. There was a tacit understanding, an interior agreement between Jesus and Mary, that she should take the disciples into her heart, into her prayers, into her benedictions and, to a certain degree, into her very being, as her own children and the brothers of Jesus, that she should be their spiritual mother as she was his mother by nature. Mary did this with singular earnestness, while Jesus on such occasions treated her with great solemnity. There was in this ceremony of adoption something so holy, something so interior, that I am unable to express it. Mary was the vine, the ear, the flowering source of Jesus's flesh and blood.[88]

Remember that the highest aspect of Saturn *is* the Virgin Mary, and that she is the spiritual mother of all of us! As Saturn stations direct, Mars is once again square Saturn, as it was on August 24 (see commentary on Zacchaeus): **Mars 0°18' Aries square Saturn 0°18' Capricorn.** While the highest aspect of Saturn is the Virgin Mary, the highest aspect of Mars is the Archangel Michael. Today we

---

87 Ibid., p. 494.

88 Ibid., p. 400.

set aside time to celebrate the season of Michael as the slayer of the dragon. Since August, the Perseid meteor showers have been raining down heavenly iron—strength for the will. These meteors originate in the constellation of Perseus. Perseus used the shield of Athena as a mirror to slay the Medusa. He then kept the head of Medusa as a weapon, using it to turn to stone Cetus, the Sea Serpent, who was keeping Andromeda chained to the rock in the midst of the ocean.

We (Perseus) are unable to take a direct look at our shadow, at the massive debt we owe our neighbors. It would make us swoon; therefore the Guardian of the Threshold keeps it concealed from our direct consciousness. However, we can use the reflective power of Wisdom (Athena's shield) in order to approach our shadow indirectly. Through this, that which was fallen, when redeemed, becomes a powerful new faculty. The subjective shadow within ourselves that we have overcome (Medusa) can now be used to overcome the objective shadow in the outer world (Cetus) that keeps the Divine Feminine—Purity, Innocence, the Soul of the World—chained to dead matter. Let this be our Michael Imagination for today, as Michael (Mars) squares the Divine Feminine (Saturn)!

# OCTOBER 2020

## STARGAZING PREVIEW

October begins and ends with a Full Moon! On the 1st, the Moon will be in full radiance as it reaches 14° Pisces: at moonrise, Jupiter and Saturn will be at culmination. In the last moments of the following day, the Moon will meet Mars in the last degree of Pisces. At that time, you'll be able to see them overhead, due south—the Moon will be below and to the right of Mars. The 9th brings us the Last Quarter Moon at 22° Gemini; before sunrise on the 10th, you'll see Venus low in the east, the Moon above her in the southeast, and Mars low in the west as it approaches setting.

On the 13th, Mars will be "Full," as it is opposed by the Sun, and the Moon and Venus will occupy 18° Leo together. On the following morning before sunrise, watch as Venus rises just ahead of the Moon.

October's New Moon will take place on the 16th at Spica (29° Virgo)! As the Sun and Moon set at 1800, you'll find Mars rising while Jupiter and Saturn are high in the south. (Mars and Jupiter will form a square aspect on the 19th—they'll both be visible between sunset and sunrise). On the 22nd and 23rd, the Moon will pass Jupiter and Saturn, respectively; they'll move from culmination to setting between sunset and midnight. The 23rd will also bring us the First Quarter Moon, at 6° Capricorn, just a degree from where it was at the birth of Valentin Tomberg.

The Moon laps Mars on the 29th—they'll be low in the east at sunset—and the last day of the month, as promised, will bestow another Full Moon, this time at 14° Aries, the zodiacal degree occupied by the Sun at the death of the Redeemer.

By now, Orion will be visible between 2000 and dawn.

## OCTOBER COMMENTARIES

**October 1: Mars enters Pisces. "And maintain in maintaining."** (For full verse, see February 3.)

**Full Moon 14°6' Pisces.** The Pisces Full Moon calls up the memory of Christ's relationship with children. The first memory is of Jesus of Nazareth traveling with the elderly mystic Eliud, prior to the Baptism in the Jordan, on September 12 AD 29:

> While Jesus dwelt at Nazareth, he had always much to do with children, who became still and quiet near him. No matter how passionately they cried, his blessing had power to calm them. The mothers, remembering this, now brought their little ones to him to see whether he had become too proud to notice them. There were some among them who kicked violently, rolling over and over on the floor, as if they had cramps, screaming loudly all the while. But Jesus's blessing stilled them instantly. I saw something like a dark vapor going out from some of them. Jesus laid his hand on the heads of the boys and gave them the patriarch's blessing in three lines, one from the head and one from either shoulder

down to the heart where all three united. He blessed the girls in the same way, but without laying his hand on them, though he made a sign on their lips. I thought as I saw him do it that it meant that they should not prattle so much; still, however, it was significant of something else.[89]

And again, during the Pisces Full Moon on August 31 AD 30:

Next morning found Jesus still at the school of Abel–Mehola. He was quite surrounded by the little girls who crowded close upon him, holding on to his garments and clasping his hand. He was unspeakably kind to them, and exhorted them to obedience and the fear of God. The larger ones stood back. The disciples present were somewhat annoyed and uneasy. They were anxious for their Master to take his departure. According to their Jewish notions, such familiarity with children was not becoming in a prophet, and they feared it would injure his reputation.

Jesus did not trouble himself about their thoughts. After he had instructed all the children, addressed some exhortations to the larger ones, and encouraged their teachers in their good resolutions, he directed one of the disciples to give the little girls a present, and each in effect received two coins fastened together. I think they were two drachmas. Then Jesus blessed them all in general and left the place with the disciples, starting eastward toward the Jordan.[90]

Both Mars and the Full Moon are in Pisces. This yields: "And maintain in maintaining   May loss be gain in itself!" While the disciples see only loss, both of reputation and of time, in Christ's ministrations to the children, his love of the children is a true foot washing, where the higher bows down to the lower. In order to maintain the flow of the Perennial Tradition, we must be willing not only to honor our Father and Mother (the past, the origins of the Tradition), but also the children—the future that is the entire *raison d'etre* for any spiritual movement. Honor the young future!

**October 4: Pluto stations direct, 27°27' Sagittarius.** The last time Jupiter and Pluto were conjunct

in Sagittarius was in 1771; the last time Pluto was at today's degree was on October 27, 1772. A rich cultural period was just blossoming during these years: Haydn, Bach, and a very young Mozart were producing great musical works; French occultists such as Martinez de Pasqually, Louis-Claude de St. Martin, and Jean-Baptiste Willermoz were sowing the seeds of Martinism; Emanuel Swedenborg was publishing his visions. The great German figures of Lessing and Herder were active at this time; indeed, it was in 1772 that the young Goethe met Herder, a relationship that would transform his life and kick-start his career as a giant of German culture. Both Novalis, a guiding star of German Romanticism, and Samuel Taylor Coleridge, a guiding star of British Romanticism, were born in 1772. In North America, Samuel Adams organized the Committee of Correspondence, the first conclave of the thirteen colonies to dialogue concerning mutual problems with the U.K. Pluto on the Sagittarius–Capricorn cusp portends cultural renaissance.

In the September commentaries, we made note of the fact that Mars and Pluto are square from September 18 through October 26; this alignment is exact on **October 9, Mars 27°28' Pisces square Pluto 27°28' Sagittarius.** Once again, these two recall the events of December 7 AD 30, as Christ walked on the water (see commentary for August 13). At the same time that Mars and Pluto are coming into alignment, Mercury and Uranus come into opposition between October 1 and 24. This alignment is exact on **October 7, Mercury 14°37' Libra opposite Uranus 14°37' Aries.** This could be a month of extremes: Pluto carries a similar energy to Mars, only exponentially greater—an incredibly powerful force of will. Uranus, on the other hand, plays the same role in regard to Mercury—the light of thinking heightened to its absolute brilliance. This month offers incredible potential, but the psychic material is volatile and hazardous—take care!

Mercury opposed Uranus on February 7 AD 31:

On this journey Jesus further instructed the twelve and the disciples exactly how to proceed in the future when healing the sick and

---

89 Ibid., vol. 1, p. 319.
90 Ibid., vol. 2, p. 38.

SIDEREAL GEOCENTRIC LONGITUDES :     OCTOBER 2020 Gregorian at 0 hours UT

| DAY | ☉ | ☽ | ☊ | ☿ | ♀ | ♂ | ♃ | ♄ | ♅ | ♆ | ♇ |
|---|---|---|---|---|---|---|---|---|---|---|---|
| 1 TH | 13 ♍ 15 | 3 ♓ 35 | 28 ♉ 6R | 8 ♎ 55 | 2 ♌ 48 | 0 ♈ 1R | 22 ♐ 54 | 0 ♑ 19 | 14 ♈ 50R | 24 ♒ 0R | 27 ♐ 27R |
| 2 FR | 14 14 | 15 34 | 27 52 | 9 54 | 3 58 | 29 ♓ 45 | 22 57 | 0 19 | 14 48 | 23 59 | 27 27 |
| 3 SA | 15 13 | 27 28 | 27 40 | 10 50 | 5 8 | 29 29 | 23 1 | 0 19 | 14 46 | 23 57 | 27 27 |
| 4 SU | 16 12 | 9 ♈ 19 | 27 29 | 11 43 | 6 18 | 29 10 | 23 5 | 0 20 | 14 44 | 23 56 | 27 27 |
| 5 MO | 17 11 | 21 8 | 27 20 | 12 33 | 7 28 | 28 52 | 23 9 | 0 20 | 14 42 | 23 54 | 27 27D |
| 6 TU | 18 10 | 2 ♉ 59 | 27 15 | 13 19 | 8 38 | 28 34 | 23 13 | 0 21 | 14 40 | 23 53 | 27 27 |
| 7 WE | 19 9 | 14 54 | 27 12 | 14 2 | 9 48 | 28 16 | 23 17 | 0 21 | 14 37 | 23 51 | 27 27 |
| 8 TH | 20 8 | 26 57 | 27 12 | 14 40 | 10 59 | 27 57 | 23 22 | 0 22 | 14 35 | 23 50 | 27 27 |
| 9 FR | 21 8 | 9 ♊ 13 | 27 12D | 15 14 | 12 10 | 27 38 | 23 27 | 0 23 | 14 33 | 23 49 | 27 28 |
| 10 SA | 22 7 | 21 48 | 27 12R | 15 43 | 13 21 | 27 19 | 23 32 | 0 24 | 14 31 | 23 47 | 27 28 |
| 11 SU | 23 6 | 4 ♋ 45 | 27 12 | 16 6 | 14 31 | 27 0 | 23 37 | 0 25 | 14 29 | 23 46 | 27 28 |
| 12 MO | 24 6 | 18 10 | 27 9 | 16 23 | 15 42 | 26 41 | 23 42 | 0 27 | 14 26 | 23 44 | 27 28 |
| 13 TU | 25 5 | 2 ♌ 4 | 27 4 | 16 34 | 16 54 | 26 22 | 23 47 | 0 28 | 14 24 | 23 43 | 27 28 |
| 14 WE | 26 4 | 16 27 | 26 57 | 16 38 | 18 5 | 26 2 | 23 53 | 0 29 | 14 22 | 23 42 | 27 29 |
| 15 TH | 27 4 | 1 ♍ 17 | 26 49 | 16 35R | 19 16 | 25 43 | 23 59 | 0 31 | 14 20 | 23 40 | 27 29 |
| 16 FR | 28 3 | 16 26 | 26 40 | 16 24 | 20 28 | 25 24 | 24 5 | 0 32 | 14 17 | 23 39 | 27 29 |
| 17 SA | 29 3 | 1 ♎ 44 | 26 31 | 16 4 | 21 39 | 25 6 | 24 11 | 0 34 | 14 15 | 23 38 | 27 29 |
| 18 SU | 0 ♎ 2 | 17 0 | 26 24 | 15 36 | 22 51 | 24 47 | 24 17 | 0 36 | 14 12 | 23 36 | 27 30 |
| 19 MO | 1 2 | 2 ♏ 4 | 26 19 | 14 59 | 24 3 | 24 29 | 24 23 | 0 38 | 14 10 | 23 35 | 27 30 |
| 20 TU | 2 2 | 16 46 | 26 17 | 14 13 | 25 15 | 24 11 | 24 30 | 0 40 | 14 8 | 23 34 | 27 31 |
| 21 WE | 3 1 | 1 ♐ 3 | 26 16D | 13 20 | 26 27 | 23 54 | 24 37 | 0 42 | 14 5 | 23 33 | 27 31 |
| 22 TH | 4 1 | 14 53 | 26 17 | 12 19 | 27 39 | 23 37 | 24 44 | 0 44 | 14 3 | 23 32 | 27 32 |
| 23 FR | 5 1 | 28 17 | 26 18 | 11 12 | 28 51 | 23 21 | 24 51 | 0 46 | 14 0 | 23 31 | 27 32 |
| 24 SA | 6 0 | 11 ♑ 17 | 26 18R | 9 59 | 0 ♍ 3 | 23 5 | 24 58 | 0 49 | 13 58 | 23 29 | 27 33 |
| 25 SU | 7 0 | 23 57 | 26 17 | 8 44 | 1 16 | 22 50 | 25 5 | 0 51 | 13 56 | 23 28 | 27 33 |
| 26 MO | 8 0 | 6 ♒ 22 | 26 13 | 7 28 | 2 28 | 22 35 | 25 13 | 0 54 | 13 53 | 23 27 | 27 34 |
| 27 TU | 9 0 | 18 34 | 26 7 | 6 14 | 3 41 | 22 21 | 25 20 | 0 57 | 13 51 | 23 26 | 27 35 |
| 28 WE | 10 0 | 0 ♓ 37 | 26 0 | 5 3 | 4 53 | 22 7 | 25 28 | 0 59 | 13 48 | 23 25 | 27 35 |
| 29 TH | 11 0 | 12 34 | 25 51 | 3 57 | 6 6 | 21 54 | 25 36 | 1 2 | 13 46 | 23 24 | 27 36 |
| 30 FR | 12 0 | 24 27 | 25 43 | 3 0 | 7 19 | 21 42 | 25 44 | 1 5 | 13 43 | 23 23 | 27 37 |
| 31 SA | 13 0 | 6 ♈ 18 | 25 34 | 2 12 | 8 31 | 21 31 | 25 52 | 1 8 | 13 41 | 23 22 | 27 38 |

INGRESSES :

```
 1  ♂ → ♓   1:32      23  ☽ → ♑   3: 7
 3  ☽ → ♈   5: 7          ♀ → ♍  22:55
 5  ☽ → ♉  17:58      25  ☽ → ♒  11:38
 8  ☽ → ♊   6: 0      27  ☽ → ♓  22:46
10  ☽ → ♋  15:16      30  ☽ → ♈  11:13
12  ☽ → ♌  20:29
14  ☽ → ♍  21:56
16  ☽ → ♎  21:17
17  ☉ → ♎  23: 1
18  ☽ → ♏  20:41
20  ☽ → ♐  22:11
```

ASPECTS & ECLIPSES :

```
 1  ☉ ☍ ☽  21: 4        ☽ ☍ ♄  16: 2        ☽ ☌ ☿  21:51     25  ☉ ☌ ☿  18:22
 3  ☽ ☌ ♂   3:55    11  ☉ □ ♃  13:33    18  ☉ □ ♄  13:56     27  ☽ ☌ ♆   9:39
    ☽ ☌ A   17:18    13  ☉ ☍ ♂  23:25        ♀ ☍ ♆  14:55         ☽ ∥ ☊  14:52
 4  ☽ ☍ ☿   5:15    14  ☽ ☌ ♀   2:53    19  ♂ □ ♃   5:37     28  ☽ ☍ ♀   9:31
    ☽ ☌ ♅  10:57        ☽ ☍ ♆  11:46    20  ☿ ☍ ♅   2:54     29  ☽ ☌ ♆  18:32
 7  ☿ ☍ ♅  20:52        ☽ ∥ ☊  16:54        ☽ ☌ ☋  15:52     30  ☽ ☍ ☿  16:11
 8  ☽ ☌ ☊   0:28    15  ☉ □ ♇  10: 8        ♀ □ ☊  20:33         ☽ ☌ A   18:27
 9  ♂ □ ♇  13:24    16  ☽ ☍ ♂  13:48    22  ☽ ☌ ♃  17:42     31  ☉ ☍ ☽  14:48
10  ☉ □ ☽   0:38        ☉ ☌ ☽  19:30        ☽ ☌ ♇  22:38         ☽ ☌ ♅  14:53
    ☽ ☍ ♃   3:15        ☽ ☌ P  23:34    23  ☽ ☌ ♄   4:33         ☉ ☍ ♅  15:50
    ☽ ☍ ♆  10:35    17  ☽ ☍ ♅  19:36        ☉ □ ☽  13:21
```

SIDEREAL HELIOCENTRIC LONGITUDES :     OCTOBER 2020 Gregorian at 0 hours UT

| DAY | Sid. Time | ☿ | ♀ | ⊕ | ♂ | ♃ | ♄ | ♅ | ♆ | ♇ | Vernal Point |
|---|---|---|---|---|---|---|---|---|---|---|---|
| 1 TH | 0:40:45 | 26 ♐ 12 | 28 ♉ 23 | 13 ♓ 15 | 18 ♓ 10 | 4 ♑ 0 | 5 ♑ 48 | 13 ♈ 19 | 24 ♒ 38 | 29 ♐ 5 | 4 ♓ 58'14" |
| 2 FR | 0:44:42 | 29 14 | 0 ♊ 0 | 14 14 | 18 46 | 4 5 | 5 50 | 13 20 | 24 39 | 29 6 | 4 ♓ 58'14" |
| 3 SA | 0:48:39 | 2 ♑ 19 | 1 37 | 15 13 | 19 23 | 4 10 | 5 52 | 13 20 | 24 39 | 29 6 | 4 ♓ 58'13" |
| 4 SU | 0:52:35 | 5 27 | 3 14 | 16 12 | 20 0 | 4 15 | 5 54 | 13 21 | 24 39 | 29 6 | 4 ♓ 58'13" |
| 5 MO | 0:56:32 | 8 39 | 4 51 | 17 11 | 20 36 | 4 20 | 5 56 | 13 21 | 24 40 | 29 7 | 4 ♓ 58'13" |
| 6 TU | 1: 0:28 | 11 55 | 6 28 | 18 11 | 21 13 | 4 25 | 5 57 | 13 22 | 24 40 | 29 7 | 4 ♓ 58'13" |
| 7 WE | 1: 4:25 | 15 15 | 8 5 | 19 10 | 21 50 | 4 31 | 5 59 | 13 23 | 24 41 | 29 7 | 4 ♓ 58'13" |
| 8 TH | 1: 8:21 | 18 39 | 9 42 | 20 9 | 22 26 | 4 36 | 6 1 | 13 23 | 24 41 | 29 7 | 4 ♓ 58'13" |
| 9 FR | 1:12:18 | 22 8 | 11 19 | 21 8 | 23 3 | 4 41 | 6 3 | 13 24 | 24 41 | 29 8 | 4 ♓ 58'13" |
| 10 SA | 1:16:14 | 25 43 | 12 56 | 22 7 | 23 39 | 4 46 | 6 5 | 13 25 | 24 42 | 29 8 | 4 ♓ 58'12" |
| 11 SU | 1:20:11 | 29 22 | 14 33 | 23 7 | 24 15 | 4 51 | 6 7 | 13 25 | 24 42 | 29 8 | 4 ♓ 58'12" |
| 12 MO | 1:24: 8 | 3 ♒ 8 | 16 10 | 24 6 | 24 52 | 4 56 | 6 8 | 13 26 | 24 42 | 29 9 | 4 ♓ 58'12" |
| 13 TU | 1:28: 4 | 7 0 | 17 47 | 25 6 | 25 28 | 5 1 | 6 10 | 13 27 | 24 43 | 29 9 | 4 ♓ 58'12" |
| 14 WE | 1:32: 1 | 10 58 | 19 24 | 26 5 | 26 4 | 5 6 | 6 12 | 13 27 | 24 43 | 29 9 | 4 ♓ 58'12" |
| 15 TH | 1:35:57 | 15 3 | 21 2 | 27 4 | 26 40 | 5 12 | 6 14 | 13 28 | 24 43 | 29 10 | 4 ♓ 58'12" |
| 16 FR | 1:39:54 | 19 16 | 22 39 | 28 4 | 27 17 | 5 17 | 6 15 | 13 29 | 24 44 | 29 10 | 4 ♓ 58'12" |
| 17 SA | 1:43:50 | 23 36 | 24 16 | 29 3 | 27 53 | 5 22 | 6 17 | 13 29 | 24 44 | 29 10 | 4 ♓ 58'11" |
| 18 SU | 1:47:47 | 28 4 | 25 53 | 0 ♈ 3 | 28 29 | 5 27 | 6 19 | 13 30 | 24 45 | 29 11 | 4 ♓ 58'11" |
| 19 MO | 1:51:43 | 2 ♓ 41 | 27 31 | 1 2 | 29 5 | 5 32 | 6 21 | 13 31 | 24 45 | 29 11 | 4 ♓ 58'11" |
| 20 TU | 1:55:40 | 7 26 | 29 8 | 2 2 | 29 41 | 5 37 | 6 23 | 13 31 | 24 45 | 29 11 | 4 ♓ 58'11" |
| 21 WE | 1:59:37 | 12 20 | 0 ♋ 45 | 3 2 | 0 ♈ 17 | 5 42 | 6 25 | 13 32 | 24 46 | 29 11 | 4 ♓ 58'11" |
| 22 TH | 2: 3:33 | 17 24 | 2 23 | 4 2 | 0 52 | 5 48 | 6 27 | 13 33 | 24 46 | 29 12 | 4 ♓ 58'11" |
| 23 FR | 2: 7:30 | 22 36 | 4 0 | 5 1 | 1 28 | 5 53 | 6 29 | 13 33 | 24 46 | 29 12 | 4 ♓ 58'11" |
| 24 SA | 2:11:26 | 27 57 | 5 37 | 6 1 | 2 4 | 5 58 | 6 30 | 13 34 | 24 47 | 29 12 | 4 ♓ 58'11" |
| 25 SU | 2:15:23 | 3 ♈ 28 | 7 15 | 7 1 | 2 40 | 6 3 | 6 32 | 13 35 | 24 47 | 29 13 | 4 ♓ 58'10" |
| 26 MO | 2:19:19 | 9 7 | 8 52 | 8 1 | 3 15 | 6 8 | 6 34 | 13 35 | 24 47 | 29 13 | 4 ♓ 58'10" |
| 27 TU | 2:23:16 | 14 54 | 10 30 | 9 1 | 3 51 | 6 13 | 6 36 | 13 36 | 24 48 | 29 13 | 4 ♓ 58'10" |
| 28 WE | 2:27:12 | 20 49 | 12 7 | 10 0 | 4 26 | 6 18 | 6 38 | 13 37 | 24 48 | 29 13 | 4 ♓ 58'10" |
| 29 TH | 2:31: 9 | 26 51 | 13 45 | 11 0 | 5 2 | 6 24 | 6 39 | 13 37 | 24 49 | 29 14 | 4 ♓ 58'10" |
| 30 FR | 2:35: 6 | 2 ♉ 59 | 15 22 | 12 0 | 5 37 | 6 29 | 6 41 | 13 38 | 24 49 | 29 14 | 4 ♓ 58'10" |
| 31 SA | 2:39: 2 | 9 12 | 17 0 | 13 0 | 6 13 | 6 34 | 6 43 | 13 39 | 24 49 | 29 14 | 4 ♓ 58'10" |

INGRESSES :

```
 2  ♀ → ♊   0: 0
    ☿ → ♑   6: 0
11  ☿ → ♒   4: 3
17  ⊕ → ♈  22:46
18  ☿ → ♓  10: 7
20  ♀ → ♋  12:49
    ♂ → ♈  12:55
24  ☿ → ♈   8:58
29  ☿ → ♉  12:20
```

ASPECTS (HELIOCENTRIC +MOON(TYCHONIC)) :

```
 1  ☿ ☌ ♇  22:54     9  ☽ ☌ ♀   4:37        ☽ ☍ ♂  17:42    22  ☽ □ ☿   7:10         ♀ ☍ ♄  13:16    30  ☽ □ ♆   9:41
 2  ☽ ☌ ♂   6:47        ☿ ∥ ☊   9:31        ☽ □ ♇  19:58    23  ☽ ☌ ♆   1:40         ♀ □ ⊕  15: 4        ♀ ☌ P  21:29
 3  ☽ □ ♇   3:18    10  ☽ □ ♂   3:38    17  ⊕ □ ♆   2:42        ☽ □ ♂   6: 6         ☿ □ ♃  11:13        ☽ ☌ ♂  23:48
    ☽ □ ☿  13:20        ☽ ☍ ♆  13:41        ☽ □ ♃   5:43        ☽ ☍ ♀  11:58     25  ☿ □ ♄  13:11    31  ☽ □ ♃   0:32
    ☽ □ ♃  13:39    11  ☽ ☍ ♃   0:10        ☿ ☌ ♆   6:10        ☽ ☌ ♃  14: 2         ☿ ☌ ⊕  18:22        ☽ □ ♄   0:50
    ☿ ☌ ♃  14:34        ☽ ☍ ♄   2:28        ☽ □ ♄   7: 9        ☽ ☌ ♄  15: 4         ☿ □ ♀  22:33         ☽ ☌ ♅  14:53
    ☽ □ ♄  17: 2        ☽ □ ♅  15:37        ☽ ☍ ♅  18:28        ⊕ □ ♃  22:34    26  ☿ ☌ ♅  18:37         ⊕ ☌ ♅  15:34
 4  ☿ ☌ ♄   3:21    13  ☽ ☍ ☿  11:27    19  ♂ □ ♇   4: 4    24  ☽ □ ♅   4:17    27  ☽ ☌ ♆  12:23         ♂ □ ♃  16:46
    ☽ ☌ ♅   8:11        ⊕ ☌ ♂  23:12    20  ♀ ☍ ♇   0:45        ♀ ☍ ♃   5:18    28  ☿ ☌ ☊  10:53         ♂ □ ♄  21:44
 6  ☿ □ ♅  10:32    14  ☽ ☍ ♆  13:27        ♀ □ ♂  12:45        ☿ □ ♆   5:29         ♀ □ ♅  22:10
 7  ☽ □ ♆  19:30    16  ☽ □ ♀  10:55        ☽ □ ♆  13:19        ⊕ □ ♄  12: 6
```

exorcising the possessed, as he himself did in such cases. He imparted to them the power and the courage always to effect, by imposition of hands and anointing withal, what he himself could do. This communication of power took place without the imposition of hands, though not without a substantial transmission. They stood around Jesus, and I saw rays darting toward them of different colors, according to the nature of the gifts received and the peculiar disposition of each recipient. They exclaimed: "Lord, we feel ourselves endued with strength! Thy words are truth and life!" And now each knew just what he had to do in every case in order to effect a cure. There was no room left for either choice or reflection.[91]

In Dante's *Divine Comedy*, there are three realms beyond the sphere of Saturn: the Realm of Fixed Stars, the Primum Mobile (the "first moved"), and the Empyrean (the "Realm of Fire"). The Empyrean is related to Pluto, the Fire of Love that is the origin of all, the realm of the Luminous Holy Trinity in the form of a white rose. The Primum Mobile is expressed in our solar system via Neptune; this is the realm of the nine Angelic Hierarchies who bring into movement the rest of the planets.

Uranus, then, reflects the realm of the fixed stars, the twelve signs of the Zodiac. Dante refers to this as the realm of the "Church Triumphant," formed out of Faith, Hope, and Love. Mercury is related to healing; in this opposition of Uranus and Mercury from the time of Christ, we see the quality of healing divided and ennobled into a twelvefold spectrum. This twelvefold dividing, ennobling, and harmonizing is the action of the Uranus sphere. In this sphere, is it possible to achieve pure spontaneous certainty, with "no room left for either choice or reflection."

While these two aspects carry through the entire month, the Sun comes into square alignment with Jupiter, beginning on October 6 and lasting through October 17. This alignment is exact on **October 11, Sun 23°37' Virgo square Jupiter 23°37' Sagittarius.** At the same time, beginning on October 6, Mars comes into square alignment with Jupiter, lasting

for the entire month, until November 2. This alignment is exact on **October 19, Mars 24°23' square Jupiter 24°23' Sagittarius** (see commentaries for August 4, when Christ twice stilled the storms).

Mars is square to Jupiter directly across from the Sun—they come into opposition between October 10 and 17. This opposition is exact on **October 13, Sun 26°22' Virgo opposite Mars 26°22' Pisces.** Remember that since September 22, Jupiter and Pluto have been coming into conjunction; therefore, the Sun is also square Pluto, from October 10 to 20. This alignment is exact on **October 15, Sun 27°29' Virgo square Pluto 27°29' Sagittarius.** What a dynamic time period! We have Pluto conjunct Jupiter in Sagittarius, with Sun square the two of them in Virgo, opposite Mars in Pisces.

We have three guiding images that last us the entire month: Mars square Pluto with the walking on water; Mercury opposite Uranus with the twelvefold spectrum; and Mars square Jupiter with the stilling of storms. The October 11 square of Sun and Jupiter remembers the square of September 13–14 AD 32, as Christ was on his way with the young shepherds to visit the Magi:

Jesus taught the shepherds again today. He spoke of the creation of the world and of the Fall and of the promise of the restoration of all. During this discourse something wonderful took place. He appeared to catch a sunbeam with his right hand, and he made a luminous globe of light from it. It hung from the palm of his hand on a ray of light. While he was talking, the shepherds could see all the things he was describing in the globe of light. The Holy Trinity itself appeared there. At the end of this discourse, the globe of light disappeared, and the shepherds cast themselves down in sorrow. Jesus later taught them a wonderful prayer and how to worship God, the creator of all.[92]

The Sun was opposite Mars on October 1–2 AD 32, just after Christ and the three youths had left the encampment of Mensor, who "begged him to remain with them, and wept profusely at Jesus's departure."[93] The travelers then stayed with Azar-

---

91 Ibid., p. 307.

92 Ibid., p. 498.
93 Ibid., p. 509.

ias, the nephew of Mensor, in the settlement of Atom. Our gaze continues to be drawn to the Star of the Magi, the conjunction of Jupiter and Saturn coming to us in December.

The Sun and Pluto were square on September 1 AD 30, and once again our attention is drawn to the children:

> Jesus gave a very touching instruction to the boys and girls. He counseled the boys to bear with one another. If one should strike a companion or throw him down, the ill-treated party should bear it patiently and think not of retaliating. He should turn away in silence, forgiving his enemy, and his love should become twice as great as it was before, yes, for they should show affection even to enemies. They should not covet the goods of others. If a boy wanted the pen, the writing materials, the plaything, the fruit belonging to his neighbor, the latter should relinquish not only the object coveted, but give him still more if allowed to do so. They should fully satisfy their neighbor's cupidity if permitted to give the things away, for only the patient, the loving, and the generous should have a seat in his kingdom. This seat Jesus described to them in childlike terms as a beautiful throne.
>
> He spoke of earthly goods which man must give up in order to attain those of Heaven. Among other admonitions to the girls, he warned them not to seek to excel others, not to envy them for their fine clothes, but to be gentle and obedient, to love their parents and to fear God.[94]

Some of our star memories for this month thus far have to do with magnificent displays (walking on water, stilling the storm, the globe of light) or show special attention to the children and disciples. This follows on from the themes of September which revolved around redeeming the idolatrous and demonic. All of this seems to point to the event of the Three Magi following the Star in the East to the baby Jesus of Nazareth. The Magi represent the decadent pagan stream that seeks renewal and redemption, following the magnificent display of the Star to the future—the Child.

**October 14: Mercury stations retrograde 16°38' Libra.** Mercury was at this degree on September 24 AD 32. Christ had arrived at the camp of Mensor, the Gold King, only three days previously. On this day he had gone with Mensor to visit the ailing Frankincense King, Theokeno:

> Then they [the kings] told him that they knew something of Melchizedek and his sacrifice of bread and wine, and said that they too had a sacrifice of the same kind, namely, a sacrifice of little leaves and some kind of green liquor. When they offered it they spoke some words like these: "Whoever eats me and is devout, shall have all kinds of felicity." Jesus told them that Melchizedek's sacrifice was a type of the most holy Sacrifice, and that he himself was the Victim. Thus, though plunged in darkness, these pagans had preserved many forms of truth.
>
> Either the night that preceded Jesus's coming or that which followed, I cannot now say which, all the paths and avenues to a great distance around the tent castle were brilliantly illuminated. Transparent globes with lights in them were raised on poles, and every globe was surmounted by a little crown that glistened like a star.[95]

**October 16: New Moon 28°52' Virgo.** Today recalls the Virgo New Moon that occurred on September 16 AD 30, which fell on the first day of the month of Tishri, marking the start of the civil year (as opposed to the first day of the month of Nisan, marking the start of the religious year, some six months earlier). Christ celebrated with the Rechabites of Betharamphtha:

> On the first of the month of Tishri the new year was celebrated, which fact was announced from the roof of the synagogue by all kinds of musical instruments, among them harps and a number of large trumpets with several mouthpieces. I saw again one of those wonderful instruments I had formerly seen on the synagogue of Capernaum. It was filled with wind by means of a bellows. All the houses and public buildings were adorned on this feast day with flowers and fruit. The different classes of people had different customs. During the night many persons,

---

94 Ibid., pp. 39–40.

95 Ibid., p. 504.

most of them women clothed in long garments and holding lighted lanterns, prayed upon the tombs. I saw too that all the inhabitants bathed, the women in their houses and the men at public baths. The married men bathed separated from the youths, as also the elder women from the maidens. As bathing was very frequent among the Jews and water not abundant, they made use of it sparingly. They lay on their back in tubs and, scooping up the water in a shell, poured it over themselves; it was often more like a washing than a bath. They performed their ablutions today at the baths outside the city, in water perfectly cold. Mutual gifts were interchanged, the poor being largely remembered. They commenced by giving them a good entertainment, and on a long rampart were deposited numerous gifts for them, consisting of food, raiment, and covers. Every one that received presents from his friends bestowed a part of them upon the poor. The Rechabites present superintended and directed all things. They saw what each one gave to the poor and how it was distributed. They kept three lists, in which they secretly recorded the generosity of the donors. One of these lists was called the Book of Life; another, the Middle Way; and the third, the Book of Death. It was customary for the Rechabites to exercise all such offices, while in the temple they were gatekeepers, treasurers, and above all, chanters. This last office they fulfilled on today's feast. Jesus also received presents in Betharamphtha of clothing, covers, and money, all of which he caused to be distributed among the poor.[96]

With the blasting of trumpets, and three books of account being opened, this celebration is a ritual which looks forward to the Day of Judgment, to the collective and final Resurrection. See the 20th Letter Meditation of *Meditations on the Tarot*, "The Judgment," for a full explication. It is a mood that characterizes the combined force of Pluto, Jupiter, and Saturn, who are all so close to each other in the heavens at this time.

**October 18: Sun enters Libra. "Worlds sustain worlds."** (See September 23 for full verse.)

The Sun's ingress into the sign of Libra brings us back to the reality that each being we encounter is a world unto itself. Not only is each being a unique world, each is necessary for the whole to be sustained. Like an arch, the mutual tension created holds every piece in place; if even a single member is missing, the whole falls apart. This is the ideal, the collective Resurrection to which we aspire— harmony out of tension, unity out of diversity; and Christ is the keystone.

The Sun comes into square alignment with Saturn between October 13 and 23; this alignment is exact on **October 18, Sun 0°36' Libra square Saturn 0°36' Capricorn.** Simultaneously, between October 14 and 22, Venus comes into opposition with Neptune, also exact on **October 18: Venus 23°36' Leo opposite Neptune 23°36' Aquarius.** Venus also comes into square alignment with the Node during this time (remember that Neptune and Node draw ever closer to square alignment for the remainder of the year). This alignment is exact on **October 20, Venus 26°17' Leo square Node 26°17' Taurus.** Recall that Mercury and Uranus are close to opposition for the entire month due to Mercury's retrograde movement; they too are exactly opposite once again on **October 20: Mercury 14°8' Libra opposite Uranus 14°8' Aries.**

The Sun in Libra was square Saturn in Cancer on October 17 AD 32. Christ and the four young shepherds had just departed a few days prior from Ur, the land of Abraham. "…Jesus and the four youths set off on the long journey to Egypt, traveling westward through the Arabian desert. They traveled rapidly…the course of this journey…lasted some two and one-half months…"[97]

Venus opposite Neptune tells of the events of August 7 AD 30, when Christ was teaching in Bethsaida:

When Jesus had finished teaching and healing, he went with his disciples to Andrew's to get something to eat. But he did not go in—he said that he had another kind of hunger. Taking with him Saturnin and another of the disciples,

---

96 Ibid., p. 54.

97 Ibid., p. 517.

they went up the shores of the lake about seven minutes' walk from Andrew's. There in a lonely hospital were some poor lepers, simpletons, and other miserable, forlorn creatures languishing, quite forgotten by the rest of the world; some of them were entirely nude. No one from Bethsaida had followed Jesus, for fear of contracting impurity. The cells of these poor creatures were built around a court. They never left them, their food being given them through an aperture in the door. Jesus commanded the superintendent of the hospital to bring out the miserable patients. The disciples covered all in need with the clothing they had brought. Then Jesus instructed and consoled them, going from one to another around the circle, and healing many by the imposition of his sacred hands. He passed some in silence, others he commanded to bathe or fulfill different prescriptions. The cured sank on their knees before him, giving thanks with abundant tears. It was truly touching. These people were utterly neglected. Jesus took the superintendent back to Andrew's to dine with him. As they were leaving the hospital, the relatives of some of the cured presented themselves from Bethsaida bringing them clothes. They took them joyfully first to their homes and next to the synagogue, to give thanks to God.[98]

Christ journeys deliberately both into the literal and metaphorical wilderness, making sure that all are invited to the feast. Venus square Node recalls the events of June 20–21 AD 31:

In the house of the father of the bride of Cana, an entertainment was given, at which the poor of the place were fed and presents bestowed upon them. Jesus and the apostles served…. It was a kind of memorial feast of the marriage at Cana [which had taken place 18 months prior], for now as then all the apostles, disciples, and friends were again assembled together. The house was garlanded with flowers, and the water urns of the first miracle were again in use. Children, bearing wreaths and pyramids of flowers, entered the festive hall playing on musical instruments.

From Cana, Jesus went with all the apostles and disciples to the mount of instruction near Gabara…. He was very affectionate to them and often addressed them with the words: "My beloved children!" He commanded them to relate their experience, to tell how things had gone with them…each was to hear what the others had done and all that had happened. Thereupon they began to relate their experience…. Several times he addressed them kindly and lovingly in the words: "Beloved little children," and listened to the account given by many of them….

While standing on the hill, Jesus appeared to be penetrated with joy, grave, and celestial, and he held his hands raised to Heaven. I saw him surrounded with splendor that fell upon him like a transparent cloud of light. He was perfectly enraptured and, in a transport of joy, he exclaimed: "I confess to thee, O Father, Lord of Heaven and Earth, because thou hast hidden these things from the wise and prudent, and hast revealed them to little ones. Yea, Father, for so it hath seemed good in thy sight. All things are delivered to me by my Father, and no one knoweth who the Son is but the Father, and who the Father is but the Son, and to whom the Son will reveal it!" And then turning to the disciples, he said: "Blessed are the eyes that see the things which you see! For I say to you that many prophets and kings have desired to see the things that you see, and have not seen them; and to hear the things that you hear, and have not heard them."[99]

We come here to the counterbalance to the memory of Mercury opposite Uranus that dominates the month. Whereas Mercury opposite Uranus expresses the divvying up of powers of healing to the twelve in a spectrum of light, here we have the Venusian aspect of conversation and the Nodal aspect of reflection and insight. Each is asked to share what they have done with the unique ability they have been given. And supreme honor continues to be given to the Child and the Fool!

**October 23: Venus enters Virgo. "May the soul fathom worlds."** (See September 2 for the full verse)

This simple phrase strikes right to the heart of our theme for the past two months: the unique and

---

98 Ibid., pp. 7–8.

99 Ibid., pp. 403–404.

crucial role of the human soul is that it can fathom worlds. Worlds can only properly be fathomed as members of the whole. The soul can be the uniting center, the communal space in which worlds that otherwise would not interact have the opportunity to do so, and thereby be truly understood.

Between October 16 and 28, Sun comes into conjunction with Mercury. Mercury's travels between the Zodiac and the Sun have completed, and now he draws between the Sun and Earth to transmit to full waking consciousness what has only been intuitive ferment until now. **The Inferior Conjunction of Sun and Mercury is exact on October 25, 7°46' Libra.** Sun and Mercury were conjunct in Libra on October 11 AD 30:

> Jesus journeyed on through the valley between Alexandrium and Lebona to Salem…Gardens and beautiful walks lay around the outskirts of the city, which was most delightfully situated. It was not very large, but cleaner and more regular than many others in this region, laid out in the form of a star, the points radiating from a fountain in the center. All the streets ran toward the fountain, and were broken up by beautiful walks…The fountain was regarded as sacred. It was once tainted…but Elisha had…purified it by casting into it salt and water in which the holy mystery had been immersed. The little edifice erected over it was very beautiful. In the center of the city and not far from the fountain arose a lofty castle, then in ruins, the large window casements destitute of windows. Nearby stood a high, round tower. On its flat top, which was surrounded by a gallery, a flag was waving. At about two-thirds of the height of the tower projected four beams toward the four corners of the world, upon which hung large polished globes that glittered in the Sun. They faced four different cities, and were a sort of memorial of David's time. He had once…by means of these globes received information from Jonathan concerning Saul and his movements against himself. The globes, by previous agreement, were hung sometimes this way, sometimes that, thus indicating by signs what was transpiring in these parts…

During [Christ's] discourse [in the synagogue there] he spoke of Melchizedek, also of Malachi who had once sojourned here and who had prophesied the sacrifice according to the order of Melchizedek. Jesus told them that the time for that sacrifice was drawing near, and that those ancient prophets would have been happy to have seen and heard what they now saw and heard.[100]

After coming into conjunction with Mercury, the Sun is then opposite Uranus between October 26 and November 5. This alignment is exact on **October 31: Sun 13°41' Libra opposite Uranus 13°41' Aries.** These two were opposed on January 31 AD 31. It was on this day that Christ began to more thoroughly unfold the teaching of the "sacrifice according to the order of Melchizedek," as this was his first time teaching concerning the Bread of Life. Only two days before, on January 29, he had accomplished the central Healing Miracle, the Feeding of the Five Thousand. This miracle was the archetypal expression of the phrase "I AM the Bread of Life," as Christ took five loaves and two fishes and fed five thousand people, with twelve baskets of leftovers. On January 31, he first delivered the teaching concerning the Bread of Life; the next day, on February 1, he first used the phrase "I AM the Bread of Life" before a crowd of two thousand.

**October 31: Full Moon 10°37' Aries.** The Aries Full Moon corresponded with the 14th day of Tishri, on which the Feast of Tabernacles was celebrated:

> The Feast of Tabernacles was being celebrated.… By [the side of the houses] were erected the booths formed of green branches of trees and adorned with bushes, festoons, and clusters of grapes. On one side of the road were the tabernacles and the little tents of the women; on the other, the huts in which the animals were slaughtered. All the food was carried across the road. The children, adorned with garlands, went in bands from one tabernacle to another, singing and playing upon musical instruments. These last consisted of triangles furnished with rings that they tinkled, triangles spanned by cords, and a wind instrument from which arose spiral tubes.

---

100 Ibid., pp. 75–76.

Jesus paused here and there to teach. Refreshments were offered to him and his disciples, grapes on sticks, two clusters on each... (10/10/29)

On the next day Jesus taught in the synagogue, taking again the parable of the sower...There were many of the pagan merchants near Jesus when he spoke of the call of the Gentiles, of the star that had appeared in the land of the kings, and of their going to visit the child... (10/11/29)

Jesus next went to Succoth where he arrived toward evening. He taught in the synagogue and allowed Saturnin and four other disciples to administer baptism. It took place at a spring in a rocky grotto facing westward toward the Jordan which, however, could not be seen from it as a hill intervened. But the spring was fed from the deep waters of the river. The light fell into the grotto from apertures in the roof. In front of it was an extensive pleasure garden beautifully laid out with small trees, aromatic shrubs, and well-kept lawns. In it was an ancient memorial stone commemorative of an apparition of Melchizedek to Abraham...

Abraham had once dwelt at Succoth with his nurse Mahara, and had owned fields in three different localities. Even here he had begun to share with Lot. It was here that Melchizedek first appeared to Abraham in the same way as did the angels. Melchizedek commanded of him a threefold sacrifice of doves, long-beaked birds, and other animals, promising to come again and offer bread and wine in sacrifice.... Jacob also dwelt at Succoth. (10/12/29)[101]

The celebration that the stars have been leading us to this month is the fulfillment of the Agape Feast inaugurated by Melchizedek: communion with the Bread of Life.

_____________

101 Ibid., vol. 1, pp. 359–360.

# NOVEMBER 2020

## STARGAZING PREVIEW

Our first noteworthy visible event this month will be the Last Quarter Moon on the 8th, at 21° Cancer; it won't rise until about 2300. On the following day, Venus (20° Virgo) and Mars (20° Pisces) will be in opposition. Even though they are as far apart as they can be, their deep interest in each other is evident! On the 12th, the Moon will pass above Venus when they are both under the horizon; they'll rise before 0500, Venus leading the way into an otherwise unoccupied sky. Mars moves direct on the 13th and will get back to Aries by the end of the year.

Our November New Moon (28° Libra) will take place during the first minutes of the 15th. Venus at 28° Virgo will square Jupiter from Sagittarius on the 16th, the day before she moves home, into Libra. However, as Venus rises early and Jupiter sets late (around 2000), you won't be able to observe them together. The night of the 17th will also bless us with the peak of the Leonid meteor showers—and, as the crescent Moon will set early, viewing conditions should be terrific, weather permitting. Set your alarm for midnight if you're not still up, and look to the northeast, close to the horizon.

The 19th is another big day in the heavens, as the Moon will conjoin both Jupiter and Saturn. You'll have over three hours to see them approaching the western horizon after dusk—Jupiter sets first, followed by Saturn and the Moon. Also on this day, Venus at 2° Libra will square Saturn (2° Capricorn), but as was the case with the Venus–Jupiter square, you won't be able to observe these two planets at the same time. The last moments of the 21st will grace us with First Quarter Moon at 5° Aquarius. The waxing Moon will sail above Mars on the 25th; they'll be in the southeast when the Sun sets.

November ends with a bang. The Full Moon on the 30th at 14° Taurus will bring about another Penumbral Lunar Eclipse, and this one will be experienced for *over four hours* in the Hawaiian Islands, Pōmaika'i.

Orion, nearly opposite the Sun, will be visible all night.

## NOVEMBER COMMENTARIES

The month of November begins with Mercury and Saturn coming into square alignment, not once but twice, as Mercury begins the month retrograde and stations direct on the 3rd. The two are square between October 27 and November 11, exact first on **November 1: Mercury 1°11' Libra square Saturn 1°11' Capricorn** and again on **November 6: Mercury 1°28' Libra square Saturn 1°28' Capricorn.** These two were exactly square over a month ago, on September 23, and once again we recall the events of September 29 AD 32. This was Christ's last day in Mensor's tent city. The day before, September 28, he had restored to the aged Theokeno the use of his limbs; he was no longer bedridden. On his last day with them, Emmerich witnessed the following:

> Next day Jesus again taught in the temple wherein all were gathered. He went in and out, leaving one crowd to go to another. He allowed the women and children also to come and speak to him, and he instructed the mothers how to rear their children and teach them to pray. This was the first time that I saw many children gathered together here. The boys wore only a short tunic, and the little girls, mantles. The children of the converted lady were present. She was a person of distinction and her spouse, a tall man, was near King Mensor. She had fully ten children with her. Jesus blessed them, laying his hand not on the head as he did to the children of Judea, but on the shoulder....
>
> Jesus still taught after nightfall in and around the temple. The whole place was brilliantly illuminated, the temple itself a blaze of light. The inhabitants of the whole region were gathered together, young and old, men and women. Upon the first command of Jesus, they had removed the idols. But I now saw something in the temple that I had not before noticed. Up in the roof I saw a whole firmament of shining stars, and in between were reflected little gardens and brooks and bushes, which were placed up high in the temple and illumined with lights. It was a most

wonderful contrivance, and I cannot imagine how it was done.[102]

Our meditative content continues to focus on honoring children, festive gathering, and glorious displays of light. At the same time that Mercury and Saturn are in square alignment, the conjunction to which the entire year has been building begins to take shape: starting on November 3, and lasting all the way until February 2, 2021, geocentric Jupiter and Saturn are within 5° of each other. Their geocentric conjunction is exact on December 21; we will consider this conjunction at length in the December commentaries.

**November 2 is the exact heliocentric conjunction of Jupiter and Saturn at 6°48' Capricorn.** Heliocentrically, the two planets have already been within 5° of each other since August 3; they remain close to each other from the heliocentric perspective until January 31, 2021. The promise of the Star in the East is already being realized on a more subtle plane, and over the course of the next month and a half will come to full realization on the earthly level.

**November 3: Mercury stations direct, 0°52' Libra.** Mercury at this degree once again recalls Christ's instruction to the shepherds in which he created a globe of light (see commentary for October 11, Sun square Jupiter). It also brings us back to the Aries Full Moon, the celebration of the Feast of Tabernacles. This celebration took place on September 30 AD 30, just after Christ's soulful delivery of the parable of the prodigal son:

> The parable they had just heard, that of the prodigal son, formed the subject of conversation, and all were cheerful and happy, full of love toward one another....
>
> And now was celebrated a great feast. The tabernacles were arranged in three rows and adorned with flowers, green branches, all kinds of devices formed of fruit, streamers, and innumerable lamps. The middle row was occupied by Jesus, the disciples, the priests, and the chief men of the city disposed in numerous groups. In one of the side rows were the women, and in

---

102  Ibid., vol. 2, pp. 508–509.

SIDEREAL  GEOCENTRIC  LONGITUDES :     NOVEMBER  2020  Gregorian at 0 hours UT

| DAY | ☉ | ☽ | ☊ | ☿ | ♀ | ♂ | ♃ | ♄ | ♅ | ♆ | ♇ |
|---|---|---|---|---|---|---|---|---|---|---|---|
| 1 SU | 14 ♎ 0 | 18 ♈ 9 | 25 ♉ 27R | 1 ♎ 35R | 9 ♍ 44 | 21 ♓ 20R | 26 ♐ 1 | 1 ♑ 11 | 13 ♈ 38R | 23 ♒ 21R | 27 ♐ 38 |
| 2 MO | 15 0 | 0 ♉ 1 | 25 22 | 1 9 | 10 57 | 21 10 | 26 9 | 1 14 | 13 36 | 23 20 | 27 39 |
| 3 TU | 16 0 | 11 57 | 25 19 | 0 55 | 12 10 | 21 1 | 26 18 | 1 18 | 13 33 | 23 20 | 27 40 |
| 4 WE | 17 0 | 23 58 | 25 18 | 0 52D | 13 24 | 20 53 | 26 27 | 1 21 | 13 31 | 23 19 | 27 41 |
| 5 TH | 18 0 | 6 ♊ 7 | 25 18D | 1 1 | 14 37 | 20 45 | 26 35 | 1 25 | 13 28 | 23 18 | 27 42 |
| 6 FR | 19 0 | 18 28 | 25 20 | 1 20 | 15 50 | 20 38 | 26 44 | 1 28 | 13 26 | 23 17 | 27 43 |
| 7 SA | 20 0 | 1 ♋ 5 | 25 22 | 1 48 | 17 3 | 20 32 | 26 54 | 1 32 | 13 23 | 23 16 | 27 44 |
| 8 SU | 21 0 | 14 0 | 25 23 | 2 26 | 18 17 | 20 27 | 27 3 | 1 35 | 13 21 | 23 16 | 27 45 |
| 9 MO | 22 1 | 27 19 | 25 23R | 3 12 | 19 30 | 20 22 | 27 12 | 1 39 | 13 19 | 23 15 | 27 46 |
| 10 TU | 23 1 | 11 ♌ 2 | 25 21 | 4 4 | 20 44 | 20 19 | 27 22 | 1 43 | 13 16 | 23 14 | 27 47 |
| 11 WE | 24 1 | 25 12 | 25 19 | 5 4 | 21 58 | 20 16 | 27 31 | 1 47 | 13 14 | 23 14 | 27 48 |
| 12 TH | 25 2 | 9 ♍ 47 | 25 15 | 6 8 | 23 11 | 20 14 | 27 41 | 1 51 | 13 11 | 23 13 | 27 49 |
| 13 FR | 26 2 | 24 42 | 25 11 | 7 18 | 24 25 | 20 13 | 27 51 | 1 55 | 13 9 | 23 13 | 27 50 |
| 14 SA | 27 2 | 9 ♎ 51 | 25 7 | 8 31 | 25 39 | 20 12 | 28 1 | 2 0 | 13 7 | 23 12 | 27 51 |
| 15 SU | 28 3 | 25 2 | 25 4 | 9 48 | 26 53 | 20 13D | 28 11 | 2 4 | 13 4 | 23 12 | 27 52 |
| 16 MO | 29 3 | 10 ♏ 8 | 25 2 | 11 8 | 28 7 | 20 14 | 28 21 | 2 8 | 13 2 | 23 11 | 27 53 |
| 17 TU | 0 ♏ 4 | 24 57 | 25 1 | 12 30 | 29 21 | 20 16 | 28 32 | 2 13 | 12 59 | 23 11 | 27 55 |
| 18 WE | 1 4 | 9 ♐ 24 | 25 1D | 13 55 | 0 ♎ 35 | 20 18 | 28 42 | 2 17 | 12 57 | 23 10 | 27 56 |
| 19 TH | 2 5 | 23 25 | 25 3 | 15 21 | 1 49 | 20 22 | 28 53 | 2 22 | 12 55 | 23 10 | 27 57 |
| 20 FR | 3 5 | 6 ♑ 59 | 25 4 | 16 49 | 3 3 | 20 26 | 29 3 | 2 26 | 12 53 | 23 10 | 27 58 |
| 21 SA | 4 6 | 20 6 | 25 5 | 18 18 | 4 17 | 20 31 | 29 14 | 2 31 | 12 50 | 23 9 | 28 0 |
| 22 SU | 5 7 | 2 ♒ 50 | 25 6 | 19 48 | 5 31 | 20 37 | 29 25 | 2 36 | 12 48 | 23 9 | 28 1 |
| 23 MO | 6 7 | 15 15 | 25 6R | 21 19 | 6 45 | 20 44 | 29 36 | 2 41 | 12 46 | 23 9 | 28 2 |
| 24 TU | 7 8 | 27 26 | 25 5 | 22 50 | 8 0 | 20 51 | 29 47 | 2 46 | 12 44 | 23 9 | 28 4 |
| 25 WE | 8 9 | 9 ♓ 25 | 25 3 | 24 23 | 9 14 | 20 59 | 29 58 | 2 51 | 12 41 | 23 9 | 28 5 |
| 26 TH | 9 9 | 21 18 | 25 0 | 25 55 | 10 28 | 21 8 | 0 ♑ 9 | 2 56 | 12 39 | 23 8 | 28 7 |
| 27 FR | 10 10 | 3 ♈ 9 | 24 58 | 27 28 | 11 43 | 21 17 | 0 21 | 3 1 | 12 37 | 23 8 | 28 8 |
| 28 SA | 11 11 | 14 59 | 24 56 | 29 1 | 12 57 | 21 27 | 0 32 | 3 6 | 12 35 | 23 8 | 28 9 |
| 29 SU | 12 11 | 26 52 | 24 54 | 0 ♏ 34 | 14 11 | 21 38 | 0 44 | 3 12 | 12 33 | 23 8 | 28 11 |
| 30 MO | 13 12 | 8 ♉ 51 | 24 52 | 2 7 | 15 26 | 21 49 | 0 55 | 3 17 | 12 31 | 23 8D | 28 12 |

INGRESSES :

```
 1  ☽ → ♉  23:57      21  ☽ → ♒  18:35
 4  ☽ → ♊  11:57      24  ☽ → ♓   5: 7
 6  ☽ → ♋  21:57      25  ♃ → ♑   4:12
 9  ☽ → ♌   4:45      26  ☽ → ♈  17:37
11  ☽ → ♍   7:57      28  ☿ → ♏  15:16
13  ☽ → ♎   8:25      29  ☽ → ♉   6:17
15  ☽ → ♏   7:51
16  ☉ → ♏  22:30
17  ☽ → ♐   8:18
    ♀ → ♎  12:47
19  ☽ → ♑  11:33
```

ASPECTS & ECLIPSES :

```
 1  ☿ □ ♄  19: 4      ♃ ☌ ♇  21: 3      ☽ ☌ ♃   9:41     29  ☽ ☍ ☿   8:31
 4  ☽ ☌ ☊   2:39      ☽ ☌ ♀  23:29      ♀ □ ♄  11:27     30  ☉ ☍ ☽   9:28
 6  ☿ □ ♄   9:11  13  ☽ ☌ ☿  21:43      ☽ ☌ ♄  15:50         ☽ ⚹ PN  9:44
    ☽ ☍ ♃  15:59  14  ☽ ☍ ♅   5: 8  22  ☉ □ ☽   4:43
    ☽ ☍ P  17:39  15  ☉ ☌ ♂   5: 6  23  ☽ ☌ ♆  15:30
 7  ☽ ☍ ♄   0:50      ♀ □ ♆  19:38      ☽ ⚺ ☊  19:20
 8  ☉ □ ☽  13:45  16  ♀ □ ♃   5:31  25  ☽ ☌ ♂  23:38
 9  ♀ ☍ ♂  16: 7  17  ☽ ☌ ♅   0: 6  27  ☽ ☌ A   0: 7
10  ☽ ☍ ♆  20:41      ♅ ☍ ♅   8: 5      ♀ ☍ ♅  17: 8
11  ☽ ⚻ ☊   0:10  19  ☽ ☌ ♆   7:56      ☽ ☌ ♅  19: 9
12  ☽ ☍ ♂  16:49                        ☽ ☍ ♀  19:23
```

SIDEREAL  HELIOCENTRIC  LONGITUDES :     NOVEMBER  2020  Gregorian at 0 hours UT

| DAY | Sid. Time | ☿ | ♀ | ⊕ | ♂ | ♃ | ♄ | ♅ | ♆ | ♇ | Vernal Point |
|---|---|---|---|---|---|---|---|---|---|---|---|
| 1 SU | 2:42:59 | 15 ♉ 29 | 18 ♋ 37 | 14 ♈ 0 | 6 ♈ 48 | 6 ♑ 39 | 6 ♑ 45 | 13 ♈ 39 | 24 ♒ 50 | 29 ♐ 15 | 4 ♓ 58' 9" |
| 2 MO | 2:46:55 | 21 47 | 20 15 | 15 0 | 7 23 | 6 44 | 6 47 | 13 40 | 24 50 | 29 15 | 4 ♓ 58' 9" |
| 3 TU | 2:50:52 | 28 6 | 21 52 | 16 0 | 7 59 | 6 49 | 6 49 | 13 41 | 24 50 | 29 15 | 4 ♓ 58' 9" |
| 4 WE | 2:54:48 | 4 ♊ 25 | 23 30 | 17 0 | 8 34 | 6 54 | 6 50 | 13 41 | 24 51 | 29 15 | 4 ♓ 58' 9" |
| 5 TH | 2:58:45 | 10 41 | 25 7 | 18 0 | 9 9 | 7 0 | 6 52 | 13 42 | 24 51 | 29 16 | 4 ♓ 58' 9" |
| 6 FR | 3: 2:41 | 16 54 | 26 45 | 19 1 | 9 44 | 7 5 | 6 54 | 13 43 | 24 51 | 29 16 | 4 ♓ 58' 9" |
| 7 SA | 3: 6:38 | 23 1 | 28 22 | 20 1 | 10 19 | 7 10 | 6 56 | 13 43 | 24 52 | 29 16 | 4 ♓ 58' 9" |
| 8 SU | 3:10:35 | 29 2 | 0 ♌ 0 | 21 1 | 10 54 | 7 15 | 6 58 | 13 44 | 24 52 | 29 17 | 4 ♓ 58' 8" |
| 9 MO | 3:14:31 | 4 ♋ 56 | 1 37 | 22 1 | 11 29 | 7 20 | 7 0 | 13 45 | 24 52 | 29 17 | 4 ♓ 58' 8" |
| 10 TU | 3:18:28 | 10 41 | 3 15 | 23 2 | 12 4 | 7 25 | 7 1 | 13 45 | 24 53 | 29 17 | 4 ♓ 58' 8" |
| 11 WE | 3:22:24 | 16 18 | 4 52 | 24 2 | 12 39 | 7 31 | 7 3 | 13 46 | 24 53 | 29 18 | 4 ♓ 58' 8" |
| 12 TH | 3:26:21 | 21 45 | 6 30 | 25 2 | 13 14 | 7 36 | 7 5 | 13 47 | 24 54 | 29 18 | 4 ♓ 58' 8" |
| 13 FR | 3:30:17 | 27 3 | 8 8 | 26 3 | 13 48 | 7 41 | 7 7 | 13 47 | 24 54 | 29 18 | 4 ♓ 58' 8" |
| 14 SA | 3:34:14 | 2 ♌ 12 | 9 45 | 27 3 | 14 23 | 7 46 | 7 9 | 13 48 | 24 54 | 29 18 | 4 ♓ 58' 8" |
| 15 SU | 3:38:10 | 7 10 | 11 23 | 28 3 | 14 57 | 7 51 | 7 11 | 13 49 | 24 55 | 29 19 | 4 ♓ 58' 7" |
| 16 MO | 3:42: 7 | 11 59 | 13 0 | 29 4 | 15 32 | 7 56 | 7 12 | 13 49 | 24 55 | 29 19 | 4 ♓ 58' 7" |
| 17 TU | 3:46: 4 | 16 39 | 14 37 | 0 ♉ 4 | 16 6 | 8 1 | 7 14 | 13 50 | 24 55 | 29 19 | 4 ♓ 58' 7" |
| 18 WE | 3:50: 0 | 21 10 | 16 15 | 1 5 | 16 41 | 8 6 | 7 16 | 13 51 | 24 56 | 29 20 | 4 ♓ 58' 7" |
| 19 TH | 3:53:57 | 25 32 | 17 52 | 2 5 | 17 15 | 8 12 | 7 18 | 13 51 | 24 56 | 29 20 | 4 ♓ 58' 7" |
| 20 FR | 3:57:53 | 29 46 | 19 30 | 3 6 | 17 49 | 8 17 | 7 20 | 13 52 | 24 56 | 29 20 | 4 ♓ 58' 7" |
| 21 SA | 4: 1:50 | 3 ♍ 52 | 21 7 | 4 7 | 18 23 | 8 22 | 7 22 | 13 53 | 24 57 | 29 21 | 4 ♓ 58' 7" |
| 22 SU | 4: 5:46 | 7 51 | 22 45 | 5 7 | 18 58 | 8 27 | 7 23 | 13 53 | 24 57 | 29 21 | 4 ♓ 58' 7" |
| 23 MO | 4: 9:43 | 11 42 | 24 22 | 6 8 | 19 32 | 8 32 | 7 25 | 13 54 | 24 58 | 29 21 | 4 ♓ 58' 6" |
| 24 TU | 4:13:39 | 15 27 | 25 59 | 7 8 | 20 6 | 8 38 | 7 27 | 13 55 | 24 58 | 29 21 | 4 ♓ 58' 6" |
| 25 WE | 4:17:36 | 19 6 | 27 37 | 8 9 | 20 40 | 8 43 | 7 29 | 13 55 | 24 58 | 29 22 | 4 ♓ 58' 6" |
| 26 TH | 4:21:33 | 22 40 | 29 14 | 9 10 | 21 14 | 8 48 | 7 31 | 13 56 | 24 59 | 29 22 | 4 ♓ 58' 6" |
| 27 FR | 4:25:29 | 26 8 | 0 ♍ 51 | 10 11 | 21 48 | 8 53 | 7 33 | 13 57 | 24 59 | 29 22 | 4 ♓ 58' 6" |
| 28 SA | 4:29:26 | 29 31 | 2 28 | 11 11 | 22 21 | 8 58 | 7 34 | 13 57 | 24 59 | 29 23 | 4 ♓ 58' 6" |
| 29 SU | 4:33:22 | 2 ♎ 49 | 4 5 | 12 12 | 22 55 | 9 3 | 7 36 | 13 58 | 25 0 | 29 23 | 4 ♓ 58' 6" |
| 30 MO | 4:37:19 | 6 3 | 5 43 | 13 13 | 23 29 | 9 7 | 7 38 | 13 59 | 25 0 | 29 23 | 4 ♓ 58' 5" |

INGRESSES :

```
 3  ☿ → ♊   7:11
 8  ♀ → ♌   0: 1
    ☿ → ♋   3:54
13  ☿ → ♌  13:39
16  ⊕ → ♉  22:15
20  ☿ → ♍   1:21
26  ♀ → ♍  11:24
28  ☿ → ♎   3:31
```

ASPECTS (HELIOCENTRIC +MOON(TYCHONIC)) :

```
 1  ☽ □ ♀   1: 6   8  ☿ ☍ ♆   0:59      ☽ □ ♄  19:43      ☽ ☌ ♃   2:22      ☽ ☌ ♅  21:54
 2  ☿ ☌ P   3:39   9  ☿ ☍ ♄   8:35      ☽ □ ♃  20:42      ☽ ☌ ♅  12:31      ☿ □ ♆  23: 2
    ☿ □ ♆  11:34      ☿ ☌ ♀   8:38  14  ☽ ☍ ♂   7:26      ☽ ☌ ♂  20:41
    ♃ ☌ ♀  18:51      ♅ ☌ ♃  10: 7      ☽ ☌ ♂   7:26
 4  ☽ □ ♆   1:44  10  ☿ □ ♂   6:29  16  ☽ □ ☿   4:22  23  ♀ ☍ ♆   8:50
 5  ☽ ☌ ☿  17:56      ☿ □ ♅  13: 4      ☽ □ ♀   5:10      ☽ ☌ ♆  19: 6
 6  ☽ ☍ ♇  20:35      ☽ ☍ ♆  23:27      ♃ ☌ ♀   7:51      ☽ ☍ ♀  20:41
 7  ☽ ☍ ♄  10:58  12  ☿ ⚻ ☊   8: 1      ☽ □ ♀  23:57  26  ☽ ☍ ☿   3:53
    ☽ ☌ ♃  11:27      ☽ □ ♇  23:57      ☽ ☌ ♆  16:20
    ☽ ☌ ♂  18: 1  13  ☽ □ ♇   7:18  19  ☽ ☌ ♆  10:22  27  ☽ □ ♄   8:56
    ☽ □ ♅  23:29      ♂ ☌ ♅  23:33  20  ☽ ☌ ♄   0:38      ☽ □ ♃  11:43
```

the other the school children, the youths, and the maidens forming three distinct bands. The teachers sat with their pupils, and every class had its own chanters. Soon the children, crowned with flowers, surrounded the tables with flutes and chimes and harps, playing and singing. I saw also that the men held in one hand palm branches on which were little tinkling balls, and branches of willow with fine, narrow leaves, also the branches of a kind of bush such as we cultivate in pots. It was myrtle. In the other they held the beautiful yellow Etrog apple....

The pagans also took part in this feast. They, too, had their tabernacles of green branches, and those that had received baptism took their places next to the Jews, by whom they were cordially and hospitably entertained. All were still influenced by the impressions received at the instruction upon the prodigal son. The meal lasted until late into the night. Jesus went up and down along the tables instructing the guests, and wherever anything was needed supplying the want through one of the disciples. Joyous sounds of conversation and merriment arose from all sides, occasionally interrupted by prayer and canticles. The whole place was ablaze with lights.[103]

Between November 5 and 13, Venus and Mars come into opposition. This alignment is exact on **November 9, Venus 20°19' Virgo opposite Mars 20°19' Pisces.** Venus and Mars were close to opposition on September 10, as Christ was about to take leave of a group of star worshippers while on his way to Mensor's tent city:

Before taking leave of these people on the following morning, Jesus gave them a few words of instruction...During this instruction, Jesus appeared to them so lovable, so much like a supernatural being, that they implored him to remain with them. They wanted to bring a wise, old priest to converse with him, but Jesus would not allow it. Then they produced some ancient manuscripts which they consulted. They were not rolls of parchment, but thick leaves, which looked as if made of bark, and upon which the

writing was deeply imprinted. These leaves were very like thick leather. The pagans insisted upon the Lord's remaining and instructing them, but he refused, saying that they should follow him when he had returned to his Father, and that he would not neglect to call them at the right time.

When about to leave, Jesus wrote for them with a sharp metallic rod on the stone floor of their tent the initials of five members of his race. It looked to me like only the letters, four or five of them, entwined together, and among them I recognized an *M*. They were deeply engraved on the stone. The pagans gazed in wonder at the inscription, for which they at once conceived great reverence. Later on they converted the stone upon which it was traced into an altar. I see it now at Rome enclosed in one of the corners of St. Peter's church, nor will the enemies of the church be able to carry it off![104]

Today Mars, the Word of Truth, is carved into Venus, the Foundation Stone of Love. While Mars aspects, related to our life of will and action, have held sway for months, in the month of November we have the sublimation of the will, as it unites with the realm of feeling, of love and devotion, of the social will of the community. May our hearts become like unto the Foundation Stone of Love, carved with the eternal name of Truth!

**November 12: Jupiter conjunct Pluto 27°49' Sagittarius.** Today we come to the third and final geocentric conjunction of Jupiter and Pluto (the first was April 5, the second June 30; the heliocentric conjunction occurred on July 31). Jupiter and Pluto were exactly opposed, with Pluto in Sagittarius and Jupiter in Gemini, three times during the last year of Christ's ministry. The first time was on July 18 AD 32. The second time was at the end of the year AD 32, while he was traveling through the desert to visit childhood acquaintances in Egypt. And the final time was in the early hours of the morning on April 4 AD 33, about 12 hours after Christ's death on the cross, during the Harrowing of Hell.

Of course, Jupiter and Pluto were close to opposition during this entire time period in Christ's life. Notice, however, that on July 18, Lazarus had

---

103 Ibid., pp. 67–68.

104 Ibid., p. 497.

already died three days previously, and would not be resurrected until eight days later, on July 26. From the visions of Estelle Isaacson we know that during this time that he was dead, Lazarus was journeying into the depths of the Earth, through layers of lost souls to the golden heart of the Earth, the realm of the Mother. This realm of innocence—Paradise— sank down beneath layers of trauma after Cain (the first incarnation of the individuality who became Lazarus) slew his brother Abel (who later incarnated as Mary Magdalene) in jealousy. Magdalene was the officiant of an Egyptian-style initiation rite through which Lazarus wished to pass. In undergoing this rite, Lazarus cleared the path for Christ to take during the Harrowing of Hell, making possible the resurrection of the paradisiacal realm of the Mother—in other words, redeeming his karma as Cain.

Lazarus's prescribed role was to traverse the spheres of trauma without succumbing to the temptation to attempt to help the fallen souls—this would be the task of Christ during the Harrowing. Lazarus's initiation took a dire turn when he could not help but turn aside from the path, attempting to help the fallen souls. It was this deeper form of death from which he was rescued by Christ on July 26 AD 32—one might consider him the first harvest of the Harrowing of Hell, some eight and a half months prior to the full event.

The conjunction of Saturn and Pluto began, and thereby set the tone for this year. These two were opposed at the beginning of Christ's ministry, centering around the Temptation in the Wilderness. We might say that the meeting of these two has to do with the confrontation with and overcoming of the Shadow, both in oneself and in the world. In the middle of the year, the Jupiter–Pluto alignment took the fore; this has more to do with the *redemption* of the Shadow, with the liberation of the Good, and the return to innocence after traveling the hard road of experience. Now we look forward to the Star of the Magi that awaits us at the year's end.

**November 14: Mars stations direct 20°12' Pisces.** Mars was at this degree on December 22 AD 30. The festive celebration that has been our guiding image for some time becomes a wedding feast:

Jesus assisted with two of the disciples at the marriage ceremony of the young couples. He even acted as witness. They were married facing the chest that contained the Law and under the open heavens, for they had opened the cupola of the synagogue. I saw that both parties allowed some drops of blood from the ring finger to fall into a glass of wine, which they then drank. They exchanged rings and went through other ceremonies. After the religious rites came the celebration of the nuptials, beginning with dance and banquet and merry-making, to all of which Jesus and the disciples were invited. The festivities took place in the beautiful public hall, which was supported by a colonnade.... The people of this region were particularly good-natured and sociable. The weddings of the poorer were now celebrated with those of the rich, greatly to the advantage of the former....

The feast began by a bridal dance in slow and measured step. The brides were veiled. The couples stood facing one another, and each bridegroom danced once with each bride. They never touched one another, but grasped the ends of the scarf that they held in their hands. The dance lasted one hour, because each groom danced once with all the brides separately, and then all danced together. Besides this, the step was very slow.

Then followed the banquet, at which the men and women were, as usual, separated. The musicians were children, little boys and girls, with crowns of wool on their heads and wreaths of the same on their arms. They played on flutes, little twisted horns, and other instruments.[105]

**November 14–15: New Moon 28°16' Libra.** The day after the Libra New Moon on September 26 AD 29, Christ was retracing the steps of his parents Mary and Joseph on their way to Bethlehem almost 30 years prior. This was the path he took from the time of his Baptism on September 23, up through the start of the Temptation in the Wilderness on October 21:

This region was that through which Joseph and Mary had journeyed to Bethlehem. Joseph was familiar with it, for his father owned meadows

---

105 Ibid., p. 186.

in the country around. Joseph had indeed kept clear of Jerusalem by a day and a half's journey, and had shunned the other cities. As the shepherd's houses were to be met all along the road, he made only a few hours a day, for the blessed Virgin found both sitting on the cross-saddle and continual walking very painful.

The chief places to which Jesus went were the houses of two shepherds at which during their journey his parents had asked admission. He went first to the one by whom Mary had been badly received. The master of the house was a rough, old man, and he refused hospitality to Jesus also...Then Jesus spoke of the mercy and hospitality exercised by all the holy patriarchs, for where would the Blessing and the Law then be had Abraham repulsed the angels that brought the former? The Lord spoke to them a parable: "He that had refused shelter when she knocked at his door to the travel-wearied virgin, so soon to become a mother, and had scorned the companion of her journey when so meekly seeking admission to the inn, had repulsed the son also along with the salvation that he brought with him." Jesus uttered these words so significantly that I saw them fall like a thunderbolt upon the heart of one present, for this was the house from which Mary and Joseph had been contemptuously repulsed when on their journey to Bethlehem. I recognized it at once. The most aged of the occupants became greatly distressed, for without naming himself, Mary, or Joseph, Jesus had in this parable related what they had done.

Hereupon one of them cast himself at Jesus's feet, begging him to tarry with them and accept refreshment, for, as he said, Jesus must surely be a prophet, since he knew all that had happened here thirty years ago. But Jesus would accept nothing from them. He taught the shepherds who had assembled around him, saying that one action is the type, the kernel of that which follows, that the roots of sin are destroyed by contrition and penance, and that by conversion man would be born anew in the baptism of the Holy Spirit and bring forth fruits of eternal life.[106]

Between November 11 and 19, Venus comes into square alignment with Pluto; this alignment is exact on **November 15: Venus 27°52' Virgo square Pluto 27°52' Sagittarius.** Since Jupiter and Pluto are still very close to conjunct, Venus comes into square alignment with Jupiter at the same time, between November 11 and 20. This alignment is exact on **November 16: Venus 28°21' Virgo square Jupiter 28°21' Sagittarius.** While Venus is coming into alignment with Jupiter and Pluto, Mercury is once again opposite Uranus, just as it was for much of October (the opposition was exact on both October 7 and 20). This time they are in alignment from November 13 to 20, exact on **November 17: Mercury 12°59' Libra opposite Uranus 12°59' Aries.**

The Mercury–Uranus opposition once again recalls the events of February 7 AD 31, when Christ rayed out healing power to the twelve disciples, creating a twelvefold spectrum of light as each received a unique knowledge and ability in healing.

The Venus aspects continue to bring us into the heartfelt celebration of marriage and the wedding feast. Venus was square Pluto on August 15 AD 32. This was the day after a wedding celebration attended by Christ and the three shepherd youths in Edon:

Jesus carried a shepherd's crook in his right hand. In the public feast house, on a large, open square to the left of the entrance to the city, a marriage was being celebrated. The house contained a large hall, at the end of which was the kitchen. All around it were sleeping apartments, in each of which there were three beds that could be separated from one another by an ornamented screen. Although it was clear daylight, a lamp was burning in the hall. The guests, male and female, as also the bride and bridegroom, adorned with flowery wreaths, were all assembled in the same apartment. Boys were singing and playing upon flutes and other instruments. These pious people were awaiting Jesus, whom they looked upon as a prophet...They received him joyfully and reverently, washed his feet and those of his young companions, and dried them with their own garments. They took from Jesus his staff, placed it in a corner, and prepared for him a table. On it were some little rolls, a

---

106 Ibid., vol. 1, p. 347.

honeycomb almost a foot in length, and some red berries from the top of which they detached before eating a little circle of black leaves tipped with white. . . .

During the meal, Jesus taught. He told the guests about that man in Judea who, at the marriage of Cana in Galilee, had changed water into wine . . . It was morning before the party retired to bed. . . . The Lord . . . went aside and, kneeling, prayed with uplifted hands to his heavenly Father. I saw streams of light issuing from his mouth, and another stream of light, or an angelic form, descending toward him. This often happened even in full daylight when at any time Jesus retired to a solitary place to pray. . . . I saw the blessed Virgin, up to the conception of the Savior, genially standing in prayer, her hands crossed on her breast, and her eyes lowered; but after the most holy Incarnation, she generally knelt, her face raised to Heaven, and her hands uplifted.[107]

Venus was square Jupiter just a few days later, on August 18. The theme of marriage continued throughout this time. Between August 13 and September 6 AD 32, his ministry was almost exclusively oriented to teaching on the topic of marriage, attending weddings, and healing couples who were either physically or emotionally unwell. The imagery of marriage is a potent ferment for inner transformation, e.g. the Alchemical Wedding. Inner resolution of polarities is required before outer resolution can occur.

**November 16: Sun enters Scorpio.**

> Existence consumes being;
> Yet, in being, existence endures.
> In activity, growth disappears;
> In growth, activity persists.
> In chastising world activation,
> In punishing self-formation,
> Being sustains beings.

**November 17: Venus enters Libra. "In being experience being."** (See September 23 for full verse.)

Scorpio is a sign of trade-offs, of sacrifice, of death that we hope leads to new life—but for the time being is only hope, not yet realized. Meanwhile, Libra is the Guardian of the Threshold, the weigher of debts. We might say Scorpio is the almost unbearable reality that lies beyond the Threshold—indeed, the experience of crossing the Threshold to the spiritual world can only be compared to death, as that which one holds dearest—the empirical personality—turns to water in one's hands in this sphere. Without due preparation, this is a shattering experience. It is the unconscious longing for this experience that draws so many to the realm of drug abuse, but the high produced by mind-altering drugs is exactly the dangerous scenario outlined above: crossing the threshold without due preparation, forcing one's way past the Guardian, and experiencing a shattering of the personality. The combined phrase: "Existence consumes being; in being experience being" more or less leads us to this inner death experience. Another way of phrasing this might be *"In Christo Morimur—In Christ, Death becomes Life."*

Between November 15 and 23, Venus comes into square alignment with Saturn. This alignment is exact on **November 19: Venus 2°26' Libra square Saturn 2°26' Capricorn.** Venus and Saturn were square on September 17 AD 32, as Christ was making his way to the tent city of Mensor. This aspect also appeared on May 30 AD 33, in the week after Whitsuntide. During this week, an old dilapidated synagogue close to the pool of Bethsaida was rehabilitated and became the first church. The first Holy Mass was held by Peter at this church on May 31 AD 33. The pool of Bethsaida was the same pool in which the paralyzed man waited for 38 years to be healed by Christ—the third of the archetypal healing miracles from the Gospel of St. John.

> . . . The whole of this quarter of Zion as far as the pool and across down into the valley of Jehoshaphat, presented an appearance of desolation. In the dilapidated buildings were formed dwellings for the poor, on the slopes grew groves of juniper trees, and the hollows were covered with high grass and reeds. The Jews shunned

---

107 Ibid., vol. 2, pp. 486–487.

this locality, so the new converts now began to settle in it.

The pool of Bethsaida was oval in form and surrounded by five terraces, like an amphitheater. Five flights of steps led down to the pool from these terraces to the little trough-like skiffs in which the sick who were seeking a cure were laid when waiting to be sprinkled by the bubbling waters. There was also in the pool a copper pump, which arose to nearly the height of a man above the surface of the water and was about as large around as a churn. A little wooden bridge with a railing led to it…The bottom of the pool was covered with shining white sand, through which three springs bubbled up and sometimes jetted above the surface of the water. The blood of the animals offered in sacrifice flowed through pipes under the altar in the temple down into the pool…on the northeast was a road conducting to the temple.

The old synagogue…was now erected into a church. I saw the apostles and disciples, after the Feast of Pentecost, working continually at the interior arrangements of the church.… Words cannot say what activity reigned throughout the whole community at all times. Weaving, plaiting, and every kind of work for the new church and the poor were carried on.

The church was a large, long, quadrangular edifice with real windows high up in the walls. By means of steps in the wall, one could mount up on the outside of the flat roof, which was surrounded by a gallery. On it were three little cupolas that could be opened like draught holes. The inside, on two lengths and one of the ends, was furnished with stone benches for the congregation, and the building was in all respects turned into a church. At one end was the altar, at such a distance from the wall that sufficient space was left behind for a sacristy, which was formed by wickerwork screens that reached from the altar to the side walls. On [the altar] was a bell-shaped tabernacle with a fine white cover closed in front by two little metallic shields.…

From the raised altar down to the pulpit was a space set aside [and] apart for the choir ceremonies of the apostles and disciples.… The apostles stood along either side of the hall facing the Holy of Holies.… The blessed Virgin usually stood under the middle entrance of the vestibule, her face turned toward the Holy of Holies. She wore the long white mantle and was veiled. Jesus had himself arranged the choral service, and about the time of the eating of the fish at Tiberius, or perhaps during the meal itself, explained to the apostles the mysterious signification of this religious ceremony. He had repeated the same on the occasion of Thomas's touching his sacred wounds and giving testimony of his faith…They daily assembled twice, in the evening till after dark, and before dawn in the morning.[108]

I have included only a small portion of the incredible and intimate details supplied by Anne Catherine Emmerich of this first church! See the third volume of *The Visions of Anne Catherine Emmerich* for the remainder of this description. Our wedding feast is becoming the musical celebration of the infant church.

**November 25: Jupiter enters Capricorn. "May world-beings' guard grow strong."** (See January 13 for the full verse.)

Jupiter's ingress into Capricorn is strongly related to the guardianship and protection of the flowing stream of Tradition. Jupiter is akin to the Emperor, the 4th of the Major Arcana—the unrecognized King, dedicated to his station of leaning (never sitting or standing) in support of the throne and the shield. He seems to be in the wilderness, suffering hunger and thirst for the sake of his dedication. Capricorn is akin to the 17th Arcanum, The Star. The star above the head of the woman in this image is of archetypal kinship to the shield of the Emperor; the woman herself is the throne re-enlivened, brought out of stillness and solidity into movement and fluidity. She quenches the perennial thirst of the Emperor—he who is the Guardian of the Tradition, of the Mysteries, grows strong through her ministration.

Between November 23 and December 1, Venus comes into opposition with Uranus. The two are exactly aligned on **November 27: Venus 12°37' Libra opposite Uranus 12°37' Aries.** These two

---

108 Ibid., vol. 3, pp. 414–416.

were opposed both at the death of Eliud on March 12 AD 30, as well as shortly after the death of John the Baptist, on January 12 AD 31. Christ announced John's death publicly on this day, building up to it with teaching of great depth and mystery:

> I remember that he said: "When the Sun and Moon are darkened, the mother brings the child to the temple to be redeemed." More than once he made use of the expression, "The obscuring of the Sun and of the Moon."
>
> He referred to conception, birth, circumcision, and presentation in the temple as connected with darkness and light. The departure from Egypt, so full of mystery, was applied to the birth of humankind. He spoke of circumcision as an external sign which, like the obligation to ransom the firstborn, would one day be abolished. No one gainsaid Jesus; all his hearers were very quiet and attentive. He spoke likewise of Hebron and of Abraham, and came at last to Zechariah and John. He alluded to John's high dignity in terms more detailed and intelligible than ever before, namely, his birth, his life in the desert, his preaching of penance, his baptism, his faithful discharge of his mission as precursor, and lastly of his imprisonment. Then he alluded to the fate of the prophets and of the high priest Zechariah, who had been murdered between the altar and the sanctuary, also the sufferings of Jeremiah in the dungeon at Jerusalem, and the persecutions endured by others....
>
> As Jesus was thus speaking in an impressive and very significant manner of John and the death of the prophets, the silence throughout the synagogue grew more profound. All were deeply affected, many were shedding tears, and even the Pharisees were very much moved. Several of John's relatives and friends at this moment received an interior illumination by which they understood that the Baptist himself was dead, and they fainted away from grief....
>
> To me there was something significant in the words, "Between the temple and the altar," as recorded of the murder of the first Zechariah. They might well be applied to John the Baptist's death since, in the life of Jesus, it also stood between the temple and the altar, for John died

between the birth of Jesus and his sacrifice upon the altar of the cross.[109]

**November 28: Mercury enters Scorpio. "In activity, growth disappears."** (See November 16 for full verse.)

We remain in the Scorpion's realm of acknowledging trade-offs, the necessity of sacrifice in world evolution. We see this phrase exemplified best of all in the transition from the plant realm to the animal realm. A tree will grow indefinitely, due to its complete lack of activity. It is in a perpetual state of sleep, especially in the dream world of the summertime. Animals, on the other hand, grow to a definite size and specific form, and then growth is sacrificed for the sake of *activity* in the world. We can consider how this might apply on a more sublime level to the guardianship and transmission of the Living Tradition; for example, consider the death of John the Baptist as a sacrifice of "growth" for the sake of the "activity" of Christ. The transmission moves in a spiral, never in a straight line.

**November 29: First Sunday of Advent.** During the first week of Advent, we bow down in appreciation to the mineral realm, the skeletal and crystalline— all that has sacrificed its life in order to establish structural foundations in the world. We struggle with the temptation to "turn stones into bread," while striving to cultivate the Platonic virtue of Justice. May we become as reliable as the solid stone in our righteousness.

In the Catholic tradition, one cultivates the virtue of Hope during this week, meditating on the *Parousia* (which is the literal meaning of the word Advent), the hoped-for Second Coming of Christ. Indeed, for many centuries the focus of this time of year was not as much on the past, the birth of Christ, as on the future—his promised return and "presence" or *Parousia*.

**November 30: Full Moon 13°36' Taurus (Lunar Eclipse); Neptune stations direct 23°8' Aquarius.** The Taurus Full Moon shone on October 30 AD 30. On this day, a group of about fifteen elderly friends and relatives came to meet with Christ at an inn on

---

109 Ibid., vol. 2, pp. 209–210.

the side of Mount Gilboa. They were full of concern for him, and pleaded with him to stop wandering the countryside and infuriating the authorities. They feared for his life and offered to establish a safe residence for him from where he could teach in peace and security.

These pious, simple-hearted people made this proposal to Jesus out of their great love for him. The bitter taunts uttered in their hearing against him by the evil-minded gave them pain. Jesus replied in affectionate, but vigorous terms, very different from those he was accustomed to use when addressing the multitude or the disciples. He spoke in plain words, explained the Promise, and showed them that it was his part to fulfill the will of his Father in Heaven. He told them moreover that he had not come for rest, not for any particular persons, nor for his own relatives, but for all humankind. All indiscriminately were his brethren, all were his relatives. Love rests not. Whoever dreams of succoring misery, must seek out the poor. After the comforts of this life he did not aim, for his kingdom was not of this world. Jesus took a great deal of trouble with these good old people, who listened with ever increasing astonishment to his words, whose deep significance gradually unfolded to their understanding. Their earnestness and their love for Jesus grew at each moment. He took them separately for a walk on the shady part of the mountain, where he instructed and comforted them, each according to his or her special needs, and after that he spoke to them again all together. And so the day closed, and they took together a simple repast of bread, honey, and dried fruits which they had brought with them.[110]

# DECEMBER 2020

## STARGAZING PREVIEW

On the 7th, the Moon will reach its Last Quarter in the last decan of Leo. As it continues to wane, Venus moves into Scorpio on the 11th, the day before she and the Moon find each other together in the first degree of the Scorpion. They rise two hours ahead of the Sun.

The following night, the 13th, marks the peak of the Geminid meteor showers. Look to the east and southeast for your best chance of seeing them. As it's so close to the day of the New Moon, the stars are in alignment for a great show! On the 14th, we'll experience the year's only Total Solar Eclipse, with the Sun and Moon at 28° Scorpio. The eclipse will last a maximum of over two minutes, and will be centered over northern Argentina, though all of the Andes will be affected.

The Moon conjoins Jupiter and Saturn, now less than a degree apart, on the 17th; you'll only have a couple of hours after sunset to see them together. The long-anticipated Great Conjunction, which happens (on average) once in twenty years, occurs on the 21st at 5° Capricorn! You won't have much time after dusk to see them, so be sure to be available for stargazing at 1630, when the Sun sets. Jupiter and Saturn will follow at 1850. At this time, you'll also be able to see the First Quarter Moon and Mars, both in Pisces, high in the southwest.

By the time the Sun sets on the 23rd, the Moon will have passed below Mars; you'll be able to find them high in the southeast at that time. Mars then moves into Aries on the 26th.

Late on the 29th, the Full Moon shines from 14° Gemini. Orion will be with us for most of the night.

## DECEMBER COMMENTARIES

**December 6: Second Sunday of Advent.**

We come one step closer to the Presence to whom we are being led by following the Star. The second Sunday of Advent honors all that lives, grows, and dies. It is to this abundance of living material that all sentient and conscious beings owe their existence. The temptation we face during this week is the temptation to cast ourselves down from the tower, to submerge ourselves in our instinctual life. Often we face the onset of illness this week. The Platonic virtue to be cultivated is Temperance. The plant world teaches us Temperance constantly—measured, consistent growth; neither

---

110 Ibid., p. 95.

over-extending nor holding back; constantly at peace and equanimity.

In the Catholic tradition, we consider during this time period the teachings and activities of the prophets and leaders of the Hebrew people leading up to the time of Christ's physical incarnation—in particular John the Baptist. The virtue exemplified by these ancients is that of Faith—operating like the Hanged Man, the 12th of the Major Arcana, through the dark certainty of the will, even when the clarity of the intellect has no certainty at all.

Underneath the overarching influence of the aspects involving Mars (which is square Pluto for most of the month, and Saturn at the very end), the month of December begins with a return to where the year began: aspects involving the Sun and Mercury with the Node. But seasonally, we are not in the midst of the Holy Nights between Christmas and Epiphany. Rather we are in the time of Advent, of expectation of the Presence of Christ. Traditionally this was also referred to as the "Fast of St. Martin," the forty-three days after Martinmas (Nov. 11) and before Christmas Eve (Dec. 24).

Between December 4 and 14, Sun is square Neptune, with an exact alignment on **December 9: Sun 23°10' Scorpio square Neptune 23°10' Aquarius.** At the same time, since Neptune and Node are also quite close to square alignment, the Sun comes into opposition with the Node between December 6 and 16. This alignment is exact on **December 11: Sun 24°54' Scorpio opposite Node 24°54' Taurus.** The Sun was square Neptune on October 16 AD 30:

> That evening Jesus taught in the synagogue. It was the Feast of the New Moon, consequently the synagogue and other public buildings were hung with wreaths of fruit.
>
> A great many sick had assembled in front of the synagogue. They were mostly afflicted with paralysis, gout, or issue of blood, and some were possessed. Jesus blessed numbers of children, both sick and well. Many of those that were paralyzed in their hands and on one side owed their sickness in most cases to their labors in the field and to lying on the damp earth at night or in the daytime when in a profuse perspiration. I

saw such cases in the fields outside of Gennabris, in Galilee.

> Jesus went next day into the harvest field and cured many whom he found there. Some people brought out from the city baskets of provisions, and a great entertainment was spread in one of the tabernacles that still remained standing. Jesus afterward delivered a long discourse, in which he spoke against unnecessary and extravagant care for the preservation of life. He brought forward the example of the lilies. They do not spin, and yet they are clothed more beautifully than Solomon in all his glory. Jesus said many beautiful things to the same effect of the different animals and objects around.[111]

An excellent reminder as we attempt to practice Temperance in this second week of Advent! The Sun and Node were opposed during the time of Christ on November 15 AD 31, just after the raising of Martialis, the son of the widow of Nain. On this day, it is the role of John the Baptist as ultimate prophet that is brought to mind:

> John always had trouble with his disciples, for they would not separate from him. It was for that reason that he sent them so often to Jesus, that they might learn to know him and eventually follow him. But they were so prejudiced in favor of John that what they saw and heard made little impression upon them. It was his desire that his disciples should follow Jesus that led John to urge him so frequently to manifest himself; he hoped that his followers would yield to the movement that converted the other Jews. He thought that, seeing them come again and again with their doubts, Jesus would be, as it were, necessitated to proclaim aloud that he was the Messiah, the Son of God; therefore it was that he sent those two with their usual questions to him....
>
> They could not understand his words relative to his kingdom. They saw no kingdom and no preparations for one. As John had been honored by so many and now lay proscribed in prison, they thought, among other things, that Jesus did not help him, that he allowed him to languish in captivity, in order to increase his own popularity. They were scandalized also

---

111 Ibid., pp. 78–79.

# SIDEREAL GEOCENTRIC LONGITUDES : DECEMBER 2020 Gregorian at 0 hours UT

| DAY | ☉ | ☽ | ☊ | ☿ | ♀ | ♂ | ♃ | ♄ | ♅ | ♆ | ♇ |
|---|---|---|---|---|---|---|---|---|---|---|---|
| 1 TU | 14 ♏ 13 | 20 ♉ 56 | 24 ♉ 52R | 3 ♏ 41 | 16 ♎ 40 | 22 ♓ 1 | 1 ♑ 7 | 3 ♑ 22 | 12 ♈ 29R | 23 ♒ 8 | 28 ♐ 14 |
| 2 WE | 15 14 | 3 ♊ 9 | 24 52D | 5 14 | 17 55 | 22 14 | 1 19 | 3 28 | 12 27 | 23 8 | 28 16 |
| 3 TH | 16 15 | 15 33 | 24 52 | 6 48 | 19 10 | 22 27 | 1 31 | 3 33 | 12 25 | 23 8 | 28 17 |
| 4 FR | 17 15 | 28 8 | 24 53 | 8 22 | 20 24 | 22 41 | 1 43 | 3 39 | 12 23 | 23 9 | 28 19 |
| 5 SA | 18 16 | 10 ♋ 57 | 24 54 | 9 55 | 21 39 | 22 55 | 1 55 | 3 45 | 12 21 | 23 9 | 28 20 |
| 6 SU | 19 17 | 24 0 | 24 54 | 11 29 | 22 54 | 23 10 | 2 7 | 3 50 | 12 19 | 23 9 | 28 22 |
| 7 MO | 20 18 | 7 ♌ 21 | 24 55 | 13 3 | 24 8 | 23 26 | 2 19 | 3 56 | 12 18 | 23 9 | 28 24 |
| 8 TU | 21 19 | 21 0 | 24 55R | 14 37 | 25 23 | 23 42 | 2 31 | 4 2 | 12 16 | 23 10 | 28 25 |
| 9 WE | 22 20 | 4 ♍ 58 | 24 55 | 16 10 | 26 38 | 23 58 | 2 44 | 4 8 | 12 14 | 23 10 | 28 27 |
| 10 TH | 23 21 | 19 14 | 24 55 | 17 44 | 27 53 | 24 15 | 2 56 | 4 14 | 12 12 | 23 10 | 28 29 |
| 11 FR | 24 22 | 3 ♎ 46 | 24 54 | 19 18 | 29 7 | 24 33 | 3 8 | 4 20 | 12 11 | 23 11 | 28 30 |
| 12 SA | 25 23 | 18 30 | 24 54D | 20 52 | 0 ♏ 22 | 24 51 | 3 21 | 4 26 | 12 9 | 23 11 | 28 32 |
| 13 SU | 26 24 | 3 ♏ 20 | 24 55 | 22 26 | 1 37 | 25 9 | 3 34 | 4 32 | 12 8 | 23 12 | 28 34 |
| 14 MO | 27 25 | 18 8 | 24 55 | 24 0 | 2 52 | 25 28 | 3 46 | 4 38 | 12 6 | 23 12 | 28 35 |
| 15 TU | 28 26 | 2 ♐ 49 | 24 55R | 25 34 | 4 7 | 25 48 | 3 59 | 4 44 | 12 5 | 23 13 | 28 37 |
| 16 WE | 29 27 | 17 13 | 24 54 | 27 8 | 5 22 | 26 8 | 4 12 | 4 50 | 12 3 | 23 13 | 28 39 |
| 17 TH | 0 ♐ 28 | 1 ♑ 16 | 24 54 | 28 43 | 6 37 | 26 28 | 4 25 | 4 57 | 12 2 | 23 14 | 28 41 |
| 18 FR | 1 29 | 14 55 | 24 53 | 0 ♐ 17 | 7 52 | 26 49 | 4 38 | 5 3 | 12 0 | 23 14 | 28 43 |
| 19 SA | 2 30 | 28 10 | 24 52 | 1 52 | 9 7 | 27 10 | 4 51 | 5 9 | 11 59 | 23 15 | 28 44 |
| 20 SU | 3 31 | 11 ♒ 0 | 24 52 | 3 27 | 10 22 | 27 32 | 5 4 | 5 16 | 11 58 | 23 16 | 28 46 |
| 21 MO | 4 33 | 23 30 | 24 51 | 5 2 | 11 37 | 27 54 | 5 17 | 5 22 | 11 56 | 23 17 | 28 48 |
| 22 TU | 5 34 | 5 ♓ 43 | 24 51D | 6 37 | 12 52 | 28 16 | 5 30 | 5 29 | 11 55 | 23 17 | 28 50 |
| 23 WE | 6 35 | 17 43 | 24 51 | 8 12 | 14 7 | 28 39 | 5 44 | 5 35 | 11 54 | 23 18 | 28 52 |
| 24 TH | 7 36 | 29 36 | 24 52 | 9 48 | 15 22 | 29 2 | 5 57 | 5 42 | 11 53 | 23 19 | 28 54 |
| 25 FR | 8 37 | 11 ♈ 25 | 24 53 | 11 23 | 16 37 | 29 26 | 6 10 | 5 48 | 11 52 | 23 20 | 28 56 |
| 26 SA | 9 38 | 23 16 | 24 55 | 12 59 | 17 52 | 29 49 | 6 24 | 5 55 | 11 51 | 23 21 | 28 58 |
| 27 SU | 10 39 | 5 ♉ 12 | 24 56 | 14 36 | 19 7 | 0 ♈ 14 | 6 37 | 6 2 | 11 50 | 23 22 | 28 59 |
| 28 MO | 11 40 | 17 17 | 24 57 | 16 12 | 20 22 | 0 38 | 6 51 | 6 8 | 11 49 | 23 23 | 29 1 |
| 29 TU | 12 41 | 29 33 | 24 57R | 17 49 | 21 37 | 1 3 | 7 4 | 6 15 | 11 48 | 23 24 | 29 3 |
| 30 WE | 13 43 | 12 ♊ 2 | 24 56 | 19 26 | 22 52 | 1 28 | 7 18 | 6 22 | 11 47 | 23 25 | 29 5 |
| 31 TH | 14 44 | 24 46 | 24 54 | 21 3 | 24 8 | 1 54 | 7 31 | 6 29 | 11 47 | 23 26 | 29 7 |

## INGRESSES :

| | | | |
|---|---|---|---|
| 1 ☽→♊ 17:50 | | 19 ☽→♒ 3:23 | |
| 4 ☽→♋ 3:31 | | 21 ☽→♓ 12:42 | |
| 6 ☽→♌ 10:50 | | 24 ☽→♈ 0:49 | |
| 8 ☽→♍ 15:31 | | 26 ♂→♈ 10:27 | |
| 10 ☽→♎ 17:48 | | ☽→♉ 13:34 | |
| 11 ♀→♏ 16:50 | | 29 ☽→♊ 0:51 | |
| 12 ☽→♏ 18:36 | | 31 ☽→♋ 9:45 | |
| 14 ☽→♐ 19:22 | | | |
| 16 ☉→♐ 12:56 | | | |
| ☽→♑ 21:48 | | | |
| 17 ☿→♐ 19:38 | | | |

## ASPECTS & ECLIPSES :

| | | | |
|---|---|---|---|
| 1 ☽☌☊ 7:45 | 12 ☽☌♇ 20:37 | 20 ☉∥☿ 3:24 | 30 ☉☍☽ 3:27 |
| 4 ☽☍♆ 0:20 | ☽☌♀ 20:58 | ☽☌♆ 23:33 | ♀□♆ 10:25 |
| ☽☍♃ 6:51 | 13 ☿□♆ 11:43 | 21 ☽∥☊ 2:37 | ☽☍☿ 16:2 |
| ☽☍♄ 10:28 | 14 ☽☌☿ 10:40 | ♃☌♄ 18:20 | 31 ☽☍♇ 8:8 |
| 8 ☉□☽ 0:35 | ☽☌☋ 11:1 | ☉□☽ 23:40 | ♀☍☊ 14:23 |
| ☽☍♆ 3:44 | ☿☍☊ 13:57 | 23 ♂□♇ 14:38 | ☽☍♄ 21:55 |
| ☽∥☊ 6:46 | ☉●T 16:13 | ☽☌♂ 22:49 | |
| 9 ☉□♆ 19:48 | 16 ☽☌♇ 19:31 | 24 ☽☌A 16:15 | |
| 10 ☽☍♂ 8:29 | 17 ☽☌♃ 5:33 | 25 ☽☌♅ 0:54 | |
| 11 ☉☍☊ 12:48 | ☽☌♄ 6:26 | 28 ☽☍♀ 6:45 | |
| ☽☍♅ 13:42 | | ☽☌☊ 15:2 | |

# SIDEREAL HELIOCENTRIC LONGITUDES : DECEMBER 2020 Gregorian at 0 hours UT

| DAY | Sid. Time | ☿ | ♀ | ⊕ | ♂ | ♃ | ♄ | ♅ | ♆ | ♇ | Vernal Point |
|---|---|---|---|---|---|---|---|---|---|---|---|
| 1 TU | 4:41:15 | 9 ♎ 14 | 7 ♍ 20 | 14 ♉ 14 | 24 ♈ 3 | 9 ♑ 14 | 7 ♑ 40 | 13 ♈ 59 | 25 ♒ 0 | 29 ♐ 23 | 4 ♓ 58' 5" |
| 2 WE | 4:45:12 | 12 20 | 8 57 | 15 14 | 24 36 | 9 19 | 7 42 | 14 0 | 25 1 | 29 24 | 4 ♓ 58' 5" |
| 3 TH | 4:49: 8 | 15 24 | 10 34 | 16 15 | 25 10 | 9 24 | 7 43 | 14 1 | 25 1 | 29 24 | 4 ♓ 58' 5" |
| 4 FR | 4:53: 5 | 18 25 | 12 11 | 17 16 | 25 43 | 9 29 | 7 45 | 14 1 | 25 2 | 29 24 | 4 ♓ 58' 5" |
| 5 SA | 4:57: 2 | 21 23 | 13 48 | 18 17 | 26 17 | 9 34 | 7 47 | 14 2 | 25 2 | 29 25 | 4 ♓ 58' 5" |
| 6 SU | 5: 0:58 | 24 18 | 15 25 | 19 18 | 26 50 | 9 40 | 7 49 | 14 3 | 25 2 | 29 25 | 4 ♓ 58' 5" |
| 7 MO | 5: 4:55 | 27 12 | 17 2 | 20 19 | 27 23 | 9 45 | 7 51 | 14 3 | 25 3 | 29 25 | 4 ♓ 58' 4" |
| 8 TU | 5: 8:51 | 0 ♏ 3 | 18 39 | 21 20 | 27 57 | 9 50 | 7 53 | 14 4 | 25 3 | 29 26 | 4 ♓ 58' 4" |
| 9 WE | 5:12:48 | 2 53 | 20 16 | 21 52 | 28 30 | 9 55 | 7 54 | 14 5 | 25 3 | 29 26 | 4 ♓ 58' 4" |
| 10 TH | 5:16:44 | 5 42 | 21 52 | 23 22 | 29 3 | 10 0 | 7 56 | 14 5 | 25 4 | 29 26 | 4 ♓ 58' 4" |
| 11 FR | 5:20:41 | [illegible] | [illegible] | 24 22 | 29 36 | 10 6 | 7 58 | 14 6 | 25 4 | 29 26 | 4 ♓ 58' 4" |
| 12 SA | 5:24:37 | 11 15 | 25 6 | 25 24 | 0 ♉ 9 | 10 11 | 8 0 | 14 6 | 25 4 | 29 27 | 4 ♓ 58' 4" |
| 13 SU | 5:28:34 | 14 1 | 26 42 | 26 25 | 0 42 | 10 16 | 8 2 | 14 7 | 25 5 | 29 27 | 4 ♓ 58' 4" |
| 14 MO | 5:32:31 | 16 46 | 28 19 | 27 26 | 1 15 | 10 21 | 8 4 | 14 8 | 25 5 | 29 28 | 4 ♓ 58' 3" |
| 15 TU | 5:36:27 | 19 31 | 29 56 | 28 27 | 1 48 | 10 26 | 8 5 | 14 9 | 25 6 | 29 28 | 4 ♓ 58' 3" |
| 16 WE | 5:40:24 | 22 16 | 1 ♎ 32 | 29 28 | 2 21 | 10 31 | 8 7 | 14 9 | 25 6 | 29 28 | 4 ♓ 58' 3" |
| 17 TH | 5:44:20 | 25 0 | 3 9 | 0 ♊ 29 | 2 53 | 10 37 | 8 9 | 14 10 | 25 6 | 29 29 | 4 ♓ 58' 3" |
| 18 FR | 5:48:17 | 27 45 | 4 45 | 1 30 | 3 26 | 10 42 | 8 11 | 14 10 | 25 7 | 29 29 | 4 ♓ 58' 3" |
| 19 SA | 5:52:13 | 0 ♐ 31 | 6 22 | 2 31 | 3 59 | 10 47 | 8 13 | 14 11 | 25 7 | 29 29 | 4 ♓ 58' 3" |
| 20 SU | 5:56:10 | 3 17 | 7 58 | 3 32 | 4 31 | 10 52 | 8 15 | 14 12 | 25 7 | 29 29 | 4 ♓ 58' 3" |
| 21 MO | 6: 0: 6 | 6 4 | 9 34 | 4 33 | 5 4 | 10 57 | 8 16 | 14 12 | 25 8 | 29 29 | 4 ♓ 58' 3" |
| 22 TU | 6: 4: 3 | 8 52 | 11 10 | 5 34 | 5 36 | 11 2 | 8 18 | 14 13 | 25 8 | 29 30 | 4 ♓ 58' 2" |
| 23 WE | 6: 8: 0 | 11 42 | 12 47 | 6 35 | 6 9 | 11 8 | 8 20 | 14 14 | 25 8 | 29 30 | 4 ♓ 58' 2" |
| 24 TH | 6:11:56 | 14 33 | 14 23 | 7 36 | 6 41 | 11 13 | 8 22 | 14 14 | 25 9 | 29 30 | 4 ♓ 58' 2" |
| 25 FR | 6:15:53 | 17 26 | 15 59 | 8 38 | 7 13 | 11 18 | 8 24 | 14 15 | 25 9 | 29 31 | 4 ♓ 58' 2" |
| 26 SA | 6:19:49 | 20 20 | 17 35 | 9 39 | 7 46 | 11 23 | 8 26 | 14 16 | 25 10 | 29 31 | 4 ♓ 58' 2" |
| 27 SU | 6:23:46 | 23 17 | 19 11 | 10 40 | 8 18 | 11 28 | 8 27 | 14 16 | 25 10 | 29 31 | 4 ♓ 58' 2" |
| 28 MO | 6:27:42 | 26 17 | 20 47 | 11 41 | 8 50 | 11 34 | 8 29 | 14 17 | 25 10 | 29 31 | 4 ♓ 58' 2" |
| 29 TU | 6:31:39 | 29 19 | 22 23 | 12 42 | 9 22 | 11 39 | 8 31 | 14 18 | 25 11 | 29 32 | 4 ♓ 58' 1" |
| 30 WE | 6:35:35 | 2 ♑ 24 | 23 59 | 13 43 | 9 54 | 11 44 | 8 33 | 14 18 | 25 11 | 29 32 | 4 ♓ 58' 1" |
| 31 TH | 6:39:32 | 5 33 | 25 35 | 14 44 | 10 26 | 11 49 | 8 35 | 14 19 | 25 11 | 29 32 | 4 ♓ 58' 1" |

## INGRESSES :

| | |
|---|---|
| 7 ☿ → ♏ 23:32 | |
| 11 ♂ → ♉ 17:20 | |
| 15 ♀ → ♎ 1: 4 | |
| 16 ⊕ → ♊ 12:41 | |
| 18 ☿ → ♐ 19:31 | |
| 29 ☿ → ♑ 5:19 | |

## ASPECTS (HELIOCENTRIC +MOON(TYCHONIC)) :

| | | | | |
|---|---|---|---|---|
| 1 ☿□♃ 0: 1 | ☽□♂ 5:21 | 14 ☽□♆ 11:19 | ♀□♄ 4:14 | 28 ☽□♆ 15:28 |
| ☽□♆ 8: 2 | 7 ☿☍♂ 2: 1 | ♀□♇ 17: 0 | 21 ☽☌♆ 3:10 | 29 ☿☌♆ 1:38 |
| 2 ♂☌☊ 3:36 | 8 ☽☍♆ 7: 1 | 16 ☿☌A 4:16 | ♀□♃ 21:53 | 31 ☽☍♆ 8:54 |
| ☽□♀ 12:57 | 10 ☽☌♀ 4:56 | ☽☌♇ 20:53 | 22 ☽□☿ 8:12 | ☿☌♄ 22:58 |
| ☿☍♅ 12:59 | ☽□♇ 16:53 | 17 ☿□♆ 0:51 | 23 ♀☍♅ 21:53 | |
| 4 ☽☍♇ 2:24 | 11 ☽□♄ 6:52 | ☽□♀ 3:41 | ☽□♆ 23:49 | |
| ☽☍♄ 18: 6 | ☽□♃ 10:23 | ☽☌♄ 12: 2 | 24 ☽□♄ 17:51 | |
| ☽☍♃ 21:26 | ⊕□♆ 16:28 | ☽☌♃ 16:26 | ☽□♃ 23:45 | |
| 5 ☽□♅ 5:43 | ☽☍♇ 16:51 | ☽□♇ 22:39 | 25 ☽☌♇ 5:45 | |
| ☿☌☋ 17:46 | 12 ☽☍♂ 19:34 | 19 ☽□♂ 11:15 | ☽☍♀ 10:42 | |
| 6 ☽□☿ 0:41 | 13 ☽☍☿ 21:14 | 20 ☿☍⊕ 3:24 | 27 ☽☌♂ 6:27 | |

at the liberty of his disciples. They esteemed it excessive humility in John to prize Jesus so highly and that he was constantly sending to implore him to manifest himself, to make an open declaration of who he was. As Jesus always spoke evasively on that point and as they had no idea that John sent them to him in order that they might know him, this knowledge was to them at the time, on account of their preconceived ideas, more difficult than it might have been to the most simple child....

Why, [Christ] asked, were they always doubting? What did they expect from John? He said: "What went ye out to see when ye went to John? Did ye go to see a reed shaken in the wind? Or a man effeminately and magnificently clothed? Listen! They that are clothed sumptuously and who live delicately are in the palaces of kings. But what did ye desire to see when ye went in quest of him? Was it to see a prophet? Yea, I tell ye, ye saw more than a prophet when ye saw him. This is he of whom it is written: 'Behold, I send my angel before thy face, who shall prepare thy way before thee. Amen, I say to you there hath not risen among them that are born of women a greater prophet than John the Baptist, and yet he that is least in the Kingdom of Heaven is greater than he. And from the days of John the Baptist until now the Kingdom of Heaven suffereth violence, and the violent bear it away. For all the prophets and the Law prophesied of it until John; and if ye will receive it, he is Elijah that is to come again. He that hath ears to hear, let him hear!"[112]

**December 11: Venus enters Scorpio. "Yet, in being, existence endures."** (See November 16 for full verse)

Venus in Scorpio is pointing to a paradox: being, i.e., the transcendent state of the I AM, existing outside of time, is consumed by coming into existence, i.e., development in the course of time through life, growth, and death (see Sun in Scorpio, November 16). On the other hand, the *process* of existence, is retained in the eternal memory of the I AM; and the I AM itself forms the foundation for the process of existence to unfold. The one is destroyed at the expense of the other. It is this self-sacrificial

---

112 Ibid., pp. 145–146.

gesture, a gesture of foot washing, that we honor during the Advent season.

**December 13: Third Sunday of Advent.** During the third week of Advent, we acknowledge the whole world of sentient beings, the animal kingdom. Even for those of us who are vegan or vegetarian, our entire existence relies on the biodiversity of the animal kingdom. Pollinating plants cannot grow without pollinating birds and insects. These birds and insects in turn rely on a complex and cooperative network of other beings. This week we are confronted with the temptation to bow down before the "kingdom of this world"—the kingdom of "survival of the fittest"—with the promise of great material reward. We must cultivate the virtue of Courage, the fortitude of the lion, in order to be able to refuse the material promise of the struggle for power, instead working with the principal of cooperation rather than competitive struggle (see the 19th Letter Meditation on The Sun from *Meditations on the Tarot*).

In the Catholic tradition, this week is seen as a "break" in the fast leading up to Christmas. We are reminded to rejoice in remembering the proclamation of the host of Angels to the shepherds: "Glory to God in the highest! And on Earth, Peace to those of Goodwill!" It is the virtue—or rather, the concrete experience—of Joy, of Beatitude, for which we strive this week.

Mercury continues along the path laid out by the Sun, racing to catch up. Between December 10 and 16, Mercury is square to Neptune; the alignment is exact on **December 13: Mercury 23°12' Scorpio square Neptune 23°12' Aquarius.** Around the same time, between December 11 and 17, Mercury is opposite the Node, exact on **December 14: Mercury 24°55' Scorpio opposite Node 24°55' Taurus.**

Mercury was square Neptune on October 20 AD 29; at sunset on the next day, October 21, Christ climbed Mount Quarantania and began his forty-day fast in the wilderness:

In obedience to Jesus's direction, Lazarus brought his silent sister Mary and left her alone with the Lord, the other women retiring in the meantime to the antechamber.

Silent Mary's bearing toward Jesus was somewhat different from that of the last interview, for she cast herself down before him and kissed his feet. Jesus made no attempt to prevent her, and raised her up by the hand. With her eyes turned heavenward, she, as once before, uttered the most sublime and wonderful things, though in the most simple and natural manner. She spoke of God, of his Son, and of his kingdom just as a peasant girl might talk of the father of the village lord and his inheritance. Her words were a prophecy, and the things of which she spoke she saw before her . . . She spoke of the resurrection. The Son, she said, would go to the servants in the subterranean prisons also. He would console them and set them free, because he had purchased their redemption. He would return with them to his Father. But at his second advent, when he would come again to judge, all those that had abused the satisfaction he had made and who would not turn from their evil ways, should be cast into the fire. She then spoke of Lazarus's death and resurrection: "He goes forth from this world," she said, "and gazes upon the things of the other life. His friends weep around him as if he were never to return. But the Son calls him back to Earth, and he labors in the vineyard." Of Magdalene, too, she spoke: "The maiden is in the frightful desert where once were the children of Israel. She wanders in accursed places where all is dark, where never human foot has trod. But she will come forth, and in another desert make amends for the past."

Mary the Silent spoke of herself as of a captive, for her body appeared to her a prison, and she longed to go home. She was so straitened on all sides; not one around her understood her and they were, as it seemed to her, all blind. But, she said, she was willing to wait, she would bear her captivity submissively, for she deserved nothing better. Jesus spoke to her lovingly, consoling her and saying: "After Passover, when I again come here, thou shalt indeed go home." Then as she knelt before him, he raised his hands over her and blessed her. It seemed to me that at the same time he poured over her something from a flask, but I cannot say whether it was oil or water.

Mary the Silent was a very holy person, but none knew or understood her. Her whole life was one uninterrupted vision of the work of redemption, of which she spoke like an innocent child. No one guessed her interior life, and she was regarded as a simpleton. When Jesus signified to her the time of her death, that is, that she should, freed from captivity, at last go home, he anointed her for death.

From this we may conclude that anointing is more necessary for the body than some people generally think. Jesus pitied Silent Mary who, as a reputed simpleton, would have received no embalming. Her holiness was hidden. Jesus dismissed her, and she returned to her abode.[113]

Silent Mary was a personality of incredible purity, a wondrous ideal to place before the eyes of the soul during the third week of Advent. Mercury was opposite the Node around the time of the healing of Anfortas and Parzival's coronation as Grail King. They were also opposed on September 24 AD 32, during Christ's visit to Mensor's tent city. The next day, September 25, Christ visited the temple of the kings:

In the center of the temple rose a pillar from which chevrons extended to the four walls, and from the highest point was suspended a wheel covered with stars and globes, which was used during the religious ceremonies.

The priests showed Jesus a representation of the crib, which, after their return from Bethlehem, they had caused to be made. It was exactly like that which they had seen in the star, entirely of gold, and surrounded by a plate of the same metal in the form of a star. The little child, likewise of gold, was sitting in the crib like that of Bethlehem, on a red cover. Its hands were crossed on its breast, up to which from the feet it was swathed. Even the straw of the manger was represented. Behind the child's head was a little white crown, but I do not now know of what it was made. Besides this crib there was no other image in the temple. A long roll, or tablet, was hanging on the wall. It was the sacred writings, and the letters were principally formed of symbolical figures. Between the pillar and the crib stood a little altar with openings in the sides, and

---

113 Ibid., vol. 1, pp. 363–364.

they sprinkled water around with a little brush, as we do holy water. I saw also a consecrated branch with which they performed all kinds of ceremonies, some little round loaves, a chalice, and a plate of the flesh of victims sacrificed. As they were showing all these things to Jesus, he enlightened them on the truth and refuted the reasons they advanced for their use....

Jesus drew for them on a plate the figure of the lamb resting on the Book with the Seven Seals, a little standard over its shoulder, and he bade them make one on that model and place it on the column opposite the crib.[114]

**December 14: New Moon 28°6' Scorpio—Total Solar Eclipse.** The Scorpio New Moon occurred at the start of the Temptation in the Wilderness, as well as Christ's journey into Egypt with the shepherd youths. It also occurred on November 14 AD 30, the day after he raised Martialis, the Youth of Nain, from the dead.

Friends came crowding from all corridors, all pressing eagerly to see the youth. The attendants gave him a bath, and clothed him in a white tunic and girdle....

Martialis, in his white tunic, was radiant with joy. He ran here and there, showing himself to the eager throng, and helping in the distribution of gifts. He was full of childish gaiety. It was amusing to see school children brought by their teachers into the courtyard and approaching him. Many of them hung back quite timidly as if they thought Martialis a spirit. He ran after them and they retreated before him. But others played the valiant and laughed at their companions' fears. They looked with disdain upon the cowardly and gave Martialis their hand, just as a large boy touches with the tips of his fingers a horse or other animal of which the little ones are afraid.[115]

Martialis later incarnated as the Iranian prophet Mani, and subsequently Parzival. The Grail Knighthood of which Parzival is the patron figure would then have been carried on in the life of Kaspar Hauser, had he lived. In all of these figures, the childlike joy and purity is accompanied by something beyond courage—one might consider it to be related to the presumptuous boldness of a child, yet fully permeated with the Good. It is the art of Play.

During a solar eclipse, incredibly powerful forces involving the darkest aspects of our subconscious can arise; we are called to be on guard. With the highest possible degree of vigilance, strive for right action and right speech today. Meditate on the following:

It was remarkable that [at the raising of Martialis] Jesus blessed [the entire crowd] with holy water, in order to drive out the evil spirits that held sway over several of the bystanders. Some of the latter were scandalized, others were envious, and some again were full of a certain malicious joy at the thought that Jesus would certainly be unable to raise the youth from the dead. When Jesus blessed with the water, I saw a little cloud, composed of the figures or shadows of noxious vermin, arise from the youth's body and disappear in the earth. At the raising of others from the dead, Jesus called back the soul of the deceased, which was separated from the body and in the abode assigned it according to its deeds. It came at the call of Jesus, hovered over the dead body, finally sank into it, and the dead arose. But with the youth of Nain, it was as if death—like a suffocating weight—had been taken away from his body.[116]

**December 16: Sun enters Sagittarius.**

**December 17: Mercury enters Sagittarius.**

> Growth attains power of existence;
> In existence, growth's power dies.
> Attainment concludes joyful striving
> In life's active force of will.
> World activity matures in dying;
> Forms vanish in re-forming.
> May existence feel existence!"

There is a feeling of triumph, exaltation, of crescendo accompanying the ingress of these two stellar bodies into the constellation of the Archer. One can truly feel that we are only days away from the conjunction of Jupiter and Saturn in Capricorn—our journey to joy is nearly complete.

---

114 Ibid., vol. 2, p. 505.
115 Ibid., p. 142.

116 Ibid., p. 143.

✳

Mercury and the Sun have been within 5° of each other since December 11; they will continue to be so through December 28. Their alignment is exact on **December 20: Superior Conjunction of Sun and Mercury, 3°31' Sagittarius. December 20 is also the fourth Sunday of Advent, during which we honor the human being.**

The human being is the Word composed of each letter of the cosmos; not only are we membered together from stone, plant, and animal, in that we are corporeal; we live and grow; and we sense the world around us—we contain within us all other members of the cosmos, woven into a seamless and harmonious whole. The beings of the planetary spheres, the angelic hierarchies, are membered into our souls; their activity is the very substance of our psychic makeup. Every thought, feeling, and impulse to activity is woven from their substance. Beyond that, the realm of the fixed stars, the Zodiac, as the body of the Holy Trinity and Trinosophia, is the body from which our very individualities, our Selves, are born. The human being is the "crown of Creation," in that we are the *only* being containing a piece of each part of the whole. Yet in the very center of this contrapuntal symphony is a silence, an open space—a realm of freedom. We are like newborn babies, beautiful in every detail but completely ignorant of what we are to do with this magnificent body–soul–spirit amalgam. And so we must learn to bow in return to that which bows to us—in order to come to self-knowledge, we must come to know ever more intimately the stone, the plant, the animal, the beings of the cosmos—and most of all, each other. For what Christ has come to show us is that, as Goethe averred, the highest treasure is the human personality. We must learn to worship at the altar of each other's biographies; the highest marriage of wisdom and freedom is expressed therein.

The Sun and Mercury are conjunct today 1° shy of the Galactic Center (2° Sagittarius); since this is a Superior Conjunction, this means Mercury is drawing inspirations directly from the heart of the galaxy and streaming them toward the Sun, who then sends them to Earth, where they arise as intuitions (i.e., not fully conscious). Beethoven was born with the Sun conjunct the Galactic Center; Whitsun occurred with the Sun opposite. Both Sun and Mercury were conjunct at the Center on November 23, 31 AD, when, according to the research of Robert Powell, the sixth archetypal healing miracle occurred: the Healing of the Man Born Blind.[117] In this healing, the mantra "My God, my God, why hast thou forsaken me?" is transformed into "My God, my God, how thou hast glorified me!" It is an aspect very much related to the awakening of the inner eye, of that moment when suddenly something "clicks," and we perceive or understand the unfamiliar correctly—and it becomes familiar. It portends a paradigm shift.

Appropriately enough, in honoring the human being, this week we cultivate the Platonic virtue of Wisdom. Justice (or Righteousness), Temperance (or Fidelity), and Courage—these are the three Knightly Vows. Wisdom is a harmonization of the three Priestly Vows: Obedience, Poverty, and Chastity. Wisdom, in this sense, is the protection against the fourth temptation—megalomania—but the concrete immunization from megalomania is the meeting in the spiritual world with a being greater than ourselves. This experience is unforgettable and eternally protective. In particular, it is the meeting with the Virgin Mary that can give us everlasting aid and comfort. It is to Mary that the Catholic tradition turns in celebrating the fourth Sunday of Advent—Mary, and the virtue of Love.

**December 21: Jupiter conjunct Saturn, 5°22' Capricorn.** Today concludes the journey of Saturn–Mary–Sophia and Jupiter–Holy Spirit over the course of 2020. We began with Saturn conjunct Pluto: the meeting of the Virgin Mary, the Mother, with the Divine Love of the Father. Often in human history, the meeting of these two is a difficult time for humanity as a whole. We come to realize how far we have abandoned the path laid out for us by the Wisdom of the Cosmos; we find out how little

---

117 Powell, "The Healing of the Man-Born-Blind and the Central Sun," *Journal for Star Wisdom*, 2016.

we have honored our Father and our Mother, and are induced to return to the path.

Jupiter and Pluto met in the middle of the year. This meeting of the joyous Holy Spirit with the Plutonic Fire of Love generally results in a celebratory time for humanity; sometimes this celebration can bleed over into a kind of mania. Finally, we come to the end of the year as Jupiter (the Holy Spirit) unites with Saturn (the Virgin Mary). The image that is created out of the meeting of these two is Whitsuntide, when the Virgin Mary became the vessel through which the Holy Spirit could descend in tongues of fire onto the circle of twelve apostles. In this event, the cosmic unity was divided into twelve. Each apostle contained within him and could bring to expression a completely personal, heartfelt iteration of what, up to that point, was a transpersonal, lofty spiritual reality.

Historically, the Jupiter–Saturn conjunctions—also known as Great Conjunctions—portend cultural shifts. These occur on a smaller scale, within the approximately 19.86-year rhythm of the conjunctions. More broadly, longer rhythms hold sway. The conjunctions take place for approximately 213.5 years in the Earth signs of Capricorn, Virgo, Taurus; then 213.5 years in the Air signs of Aquarius, Libra, Gemini; then Water, then Fire. After approximately 854 years, the cycle starts over again.

At the time of the Magi, and the birth of the Solomon Jesus, the Great Conjunction took place in the sign of Pisces. Due to retrograde movement of Jupiter and Saturn, three such conjunctions occurred over the course of the gestation of the Jesus child in 7 BC (he was born March 5, 6 BC). By the time the Magi actually arrived at the house of Mary and Joseph, the child was already over nine months old. The three Magi brought their gifts of gold, frankincense, and myrrh on December 26, 6 BC. While the Great Conjunction had occurred the previous year in Pisces, the Sun on the date of the Adoration of the Magi was at 6° Capricorn, very close to today's Great Conjunction.

At the time of Christ, the cycle of Great Conjunctions was shifting from Water signs to Fire signs. A kind of cosmic "Changing of Water to Wine" was taking place, as the clear Water of the old Law was transformed and fulfilled through the Fire of Love into New Wine. The same transition was taking place at the time of Parzival, who was very likely born close to the Great Conjunction in Pisces on February 15 AD 789, and whose redemption took place in the first half of 810, just after the Great Conjunction in Scorpio in 809.

In our time, however, it is a transition from Fire signs into Earth signs. All that has been inculcated into humanity from fiery spiritual realms can now begin to come into earthly manifestation. The twentieth century was the center of this vortex: heliocentrically, the conjunction of 1901 was in Sagittarius, a Fire sign, but then that of 1921 was in Virgo, an Earth sign. Subsequently, the conjunctions of 1940 and 1961 were in Aries and Sagittarius, respectively (again, heliocentrically). The 1981 conjunction was in Virgo (Earth), but the 2000 conjunction was in Aries (Fire). Thus the entire century wavered back and forth between Fire and Earth. Beginning with today's conjunction, we have ahead of us our first sequence entirely in Earth signs: Capricorn in 2020, Virgo in 2040, and Taurus in 2060. Today is not just a minor cultural shift within a 20-year rhythm; it marks a transition to a greater cycle of over 200 years.

The last time humanity stood at this threshold was in 1106, just prior to the magnificent time of the Knights Templar and the awesome Gothic Cathedrals, the Cathars, the School of Chartres, Aquinas and Francis, the troubadours and bards. The time before that was in AD 253, around the time of the rise of Coptic Christianity and the School of Alexandria, of the Neoplatonists such as Plotinus, Porphyry, and Iamblichus, and Manichaeism. Somewhat later came Emperor Constantine, and the concrete institution of Christianity in Constantinople. Prior to this were the Earth conjunctions of the sixth century BC, the peak of the Axial Age—Buddha, Pythagoras, and Confucius all taught during this century. This was the time of the Hebrew exile in Babylon, as well as their eventual return.

Prior to that we come to the conjunction of 1516 BC, marking the birth of Moses; before that, the twenty-fourth century BC, the height of ancient Egyptian culture and the construction of the pyramids. What we can conclude from this vast survey is that the transition out of the Fire signs into the Earth signs in terms of the cycle of Great Conjunctions marks an entry into a time of outer cultural flourishing, of renaissance and renewal. Under this sign, humanity has amazing prospects to fulfill the destiny laid out for them in the great age of Archangel Michael, which lasts until 2234. The first half of this age (which began in 1879) has been consumed with the struggle of transition from Fire to Earth; perhaps the second half will consist in humanity properly manifesting a truly Michaelic culture, the new culture of the Holy Grail: *Michael Sophia in Nomine Christi*!

**December 23: Mars 28°52' Pisces square Pluto 28°52' Sagittarius.** Mars and Pluto are within 5° of square alignment from December 6 through January 5. This is the third time this year: already on both August 13 and October 9 they were exactly square, close to the same degrees. We remember once again Christ walking on the water (see commentary for August 13).

**December 24–25: Christian celebration of Christmas; the start of the Twelve Holy Nights.** We finally achieve the great promise of Advent. While in modern times we celebrate the historical birth of Jesus on Christmas day, historically this time period was about the future Christ, the Parousia—the Christ who would appear in the clouds, as lightning flashing from east to west. This Christ must be born within our own souls, in the manger of our hearts. This is not a birth that occurs on just one day, but over the course of twelve nights. During this time of year, there is a thinning of the veil between the spiritual and material worlds, and during our sleep we receive a nourishing replenishment of our intuitive knowledge of our destiny. Each of these twelve nights moves us through the signs of the Zodiac of the coming year. The evening of December 24–25 is the Sagittarius time of the current year (December 16, 2020 through January 16, 2021). December 25–26 is Capricorn, 2021; December 26–27 is Aquarius, and so on, until we finally arrive at the evening of January 5–6. This is the evening that gives us a presentiment of the Christmas *in a year's time,* as it corresponds to December 16, 2021 through January 16, 2022.

Just as our biography is woven into us by the movement of the planets during our nine month gestation in the womb, each month corresponding to approximately eight years of earthly life,[118] so the Holy Nights are also a kind of gestation, ending in a birth—we are all born, or one might say Christ is born in each one of us, every year on January 6: Epiphany. Perhaps the movements of the planets during these days give us a picture of the coming year in miniature. We begin with Sun and Mercury still close to conjunction, remembering the Healing of the Man Born Blind; Jupiter and Saturn close to conjunction, the Star heralding the birth of a new era; and Mars and Pluto close to square, showing us the way to walk where we never thought we could before (e.g. on the water). Our eyes are opened so that we can see and follow the Star leading us into a new life in the fluid realm—the realm of the Etheric Christ.

**December 26: Mars enters Aries. "Ray out awakening life."** (See February 29 for full verse.)

Mars in Aries takes us on a journey. With Mars we can look to the 7th Major Arcanum, The Chariot, and Aries is The Fool, the 21st (or the numberless) Arcanum. Both of these individuals are on the move; both are grappling with the animal element below. We might see in them the Kings (Chariot) and Shepherds (Fool) who journeyed to see Christ. Both of them had an experience of the raying out of awakening life; the Kings with the Star, the Shepherds with the Angelic Host, and both with the child Jesus.

**December 29–30: Full Moon 13°51' Gemini.** The Gemini Full Moon occurred on November 28 AD 31:

> The son of the widow of Nain was here baptized [in the valley of Capernaum] and named Martialis, Saturnin imposing hands on him. The holy women did not follow Jesus to the instructions, but remained behind to celebrate with the widow of Nain the baptismal feast of her son....

---

118 See Powell, *Hermetic Astrology,* vol 2.

Jesus began by enumerating the [nine] beatitudes, and then went on to explain the first: "Blessed are the poor in spirit, for theirs is the Kingdom of Heaven"…Now was accomplished what the prophet foretold of the Desired of Nations: "And I will move all nations. And the Desired of all nations shall come, and I will fill this house with glory, saith the Lord of hosts."… Jesus devoted fourteen days to instructions on the [nine] beatitudes, and spent the intervening sabbath in Capernaum.[119]

Martialis is given his true Name on the same day that the epochal "Sermon on the Mount" began. Perhaps it would be a worthy exercise to take up each of the nine beatitudes in turn over the course of the next nine days (Dec. 29 through Jan. 6)?

We end our year with Love: Venus comes following along the trail blazed by the Sun and Mercury. Between December 26 and January 3, she is square to Neptune. This alignment is exact on **December 30: Venus 23°25' Scorpio square Neptune 23°25' Neptune.** Simultaneously, between December 27 and January 4, Venus and Node come into opposition, exact on **December 31: Venus 24°54' Scorpio opposite Node 24°54' Taurus.**

Venus was square Neptune on August 28 AD 32:

Today Jesus visited the house where the bride's parents lived. Then he went to the place where the vineyard was to be cultivated. A trellis had already been set up. A large bunch of grapes was brought to him, and he selected five grapes. He dug up the ground, planted the grapes at a certain distance from the trellis, and showed the people how the vine should be tied in a cross to the trellis. During this he taught concerning marriage, relating everything that takes place though nature and through cultivation of the vine to reproduction and spiritual fruit. Then they went to the synagogue and Jesus taught further about marriage. He talked of the dangers of intoxication.[120]

This story is ripe with nourishing Arcana. Five fruits are planted, tied in a cross to the trellis. This calls forth the five-pointed star upon the cross—the Rose Cross. We return to the mystery of nine, as the union of the five and the four. What is the occult nature of four? Of five? Of nine? What is the vine, and what is the trellis? What is being planted within us during these Holy Nights, and how must it be cared for?

Venus and Node were opposite one another on November 10 AD 31. This was midway between the first exorcism of Mary Magdalene and her subsequent anointing of Christ (November 8) and the raising of the Youth of Nain (November 13). It was on November 10 that the Widow Maroni, mother of Martialis, came to Christ requesting that he heal her son:

This morning, in Capernaum, Jesus was approached by the Roman centurion Cornelius, whose servant was desperately ill. Jesus praised Cornelius for his faith and healed the servant from afar (Matt. 8:5–13 and Luke 7:1–10). Next, Jesus went to a leper's hut and healed the leper, as described in Mark 1:40–45. Then, leaving the leper's hut, he went to an inn in the Valley of the Doves, south of Capernaum, where he met Maroni, the Widow of Nain, who begged him to come and heal her twelve-year-old son. In the afternoon he returned to Capernaum and taught in the synagogue as the sabbath began. Suddenly a man who was possessed ran in and caused a great commotion. Jesus healed him (Mark 1:21–28). Seeing this, the Pharisees—utterly astonished—gave up their plan to lay hands on Jesus.[121]

We continue to spend our time in the "Valley of the Doves," an adequate moniker for this special time of the Holy Nights. What requests do we have to bring into our sleep? What unresolved questions? This is the time of year to offer them up.

As the year comes to a close, already the form of next year's alignments is taking shape. Mars comes into square alignment with Saturn starting on December 29. Their alignment once again brings us to the memory of Zacchaeus climbing the fig tree

<hr>

119 Brentano, *The Visions of Anne Catherine Emmerich*, vol. 2, pp. 162–163.
120 Ibid., p. 491.

121 Ibid., p. 136.

(May 29–30 AD 32; see August 24's commentary). Jupiter begins to come into square alignment with Uranus on December 27; this aspect held sway around June of 804, when Parzival rescued Belrepeire and married Condwiramurs. It also occurred on July 7 AD 31:

> Today, in Thantia, Jesus healed several people in their homes, and the disciples baptized many converts. Jesus taught again concerning the star of Jacob, Micah's prophecy, and the journey of the three kings—all of this in relation to the coming of the Messiah.[122]

---

122 Ibid., p. 465.

And so we close the year continuing to follow the Star of the Magi, looking forward to the celebration of the Three Kings on Epiphany in six days' time. Many blessings on the New Year—welcome 2021!

> "The stars are the expression of love in the cosmic ether.... To see a star means to feel a caress that has been prompted by love.... To gaze at the stars is to become aware of the love proceeding from divine spiritual beings.... The stars are signs and tokens of the presence of gods in the universe." (*Karmic Relationships*, vol. 7, June 8, 1924)
>
> "We must see in the shining stars the outer signs of colonies of spirits in the cosmos. Wherever a star is seen in the heavens, there—in that direction—is a colony of spirits." (*Karmic Relationships*, vol. 6, June 1, 1924)
>
> "They looked up above all to what is represented by the zodiac. And they regarded what the human being bears within as the spirit in connection with the constellations, the glory of the fixed stars, the spiritual powers whom they knew to be there in the stars." (*Karmic Relationships*, vol. 4, Sept. 12, 1924)

# GLOSSARY

This glossary of entries relating to Esoteric Christianity lists only some of the specialized terms used in the articles and commentaries of *Star Wisdom*. Owing to limited space, the entries are very brief, and the reader is encouraged to study the foundational works of Rudolf Steiner for a more complete understanding of these terms.

**Ahriman:** An adversarial being identified by the great prophet Zarathustra during the ancient Persian cultural epoch (5067–2907 BC) as an opponent to the Sun God *Ahura Mazda* (obs.; "Aura of the Sun"). Also called Satan, Ahriman represents one aspect of the Dragon. Ahriman's influence leads to materialistic thinking devoid of feeling, empathy, and moral conscience. Ahriman helps inspire science and technology, and works through forces of sub-nature such as gravity, electricity, magnetism, radioactivity—forces that are antithetical to life. The influence of Ahriman's activity upon the human being limits human cognition to what is derived from sense perception, hardens thinking (materialistic thoughts), attacks the etheric body by way of modern technology (electromagnetic radiation, etc.), and hardens hearts (cold and calculating).

**ahrimanic beings:** Spiritual beings who have become agents of Ahriman's influences.

**Angel Jesus:** A pure immaculate Angelic being who sacrifices himself so that the Christ may work through him. This Angelic being is actually of the status of an Archangel, who has descended to work on the Angelic level to be closer to human beings and to assist them on the path of confrontation with evil.

**Ascension:** An unfathomable process at the start of which, on May 14 AD 33, Christ united with the etheric realm that surrounds and permeates the Earth with Cosmic Life. Thus began his cosmic ascent to the realm of the heavenly Father, with the goal of elevating the Earth spiritually and opening pathways between the Earth and the spiritual world for the future.

**astral body:** Part of the human being that is the bearer of consciousness, passion, and desires, as well as idealism and the longing for perfection.

**Asuras:** Fallen Archai (Time Spirits) from the time of Old Saturn, whose opposition to human evolution comes to expression through promoting debauched sexuality and senseless violence among human beings. So low is the regard that the Asuras have for the sacredness of human life, that as well as promoting extreme violence and debauchery (for example, through the film industry), they do not hold back from the destruction of the physical body of human beings. In particular, the activity of the Asuras retards the development of the consciousness soul.

**bodhisattva:** On the human level a bodhisattva is a human being far advanced on the spiritual path, a human being belonging to the circle of twelve great teachers surrounding the Cosmic Christ. One who incarnates periodically to further the evolution of the Earth and humanity, working on the level of an angelic, archangelic, or higher being in relation to the rest of humanity. Every 5,000 years, one of these great teachers from the circle of bodhisattvas takes on a special mission, incarnating repeatedly to awake a new human faculty and capacity. Once that capacity has been imparted through its human bearer, this bodhisattva then incarnates upon the Earth for the last time, ascending to the level of a Buddha to serve humankind from spirit realms. See also Maitreya Bodhisattva.

**Central Sun:** Heart of the Milky Way, also called the Galactic Center. Our Sun orbits this Central Sun over a period of approximately 225 million years.

**chakra:** One of seven astral organs of perception through which human beings develop higher levels of cognition such as clairvoyance, telepathy, and so on.

**Christ:** The eternal being who is the second member of the Trinity. Also called the "Divine 'I AM,'" the Son of God, the Cosmic Christ, and the Logoş–Word. Christ began to fully unite with the human vessel (Jesus) at the Baptism in the Jordan, and for 3½ years penetrated as the *Divine I AM* successively into the astral body, etheric body, and physical body of Jesus, spiritualizing each member. Through the Mystery of Golgotha Christ united with the Earth, kindling the spark of Christ consciousness (*Not I, but Christ in me*) in all human beings.

**consciousness soul:** The portion of the human soul in which "I" consciousness is awaking not only to its own sense of individuality and to the individualities of others, but also to its higher self—spirit self (Sanskrit: *manas*). Within the consciousness soul, the "I" perceives truth, beauty, and goodness; within the spirit self, the "I" becomes truth, beauty, and goodness.

**crossing the threshold:** a term applicable to our time, as human beings are increasingly encountering the spiritual world—in so doing, crossing the threshold between the sense-perceptible realm and non-physical realms of existence. To the extent that spiritual capacities have not been cultivated, this encounter with non-physical realms beyond the sense world signifies a descent into the subconscious (for example, through drugs) rather than an ascent to knowledge of higher worlds through the awaking of higher levels of consciousness.

**decan:** The zodiac of 360° is divided into twelve signs, each of 30°. A decan is 10°, thus one third of one sign or ¹/₃₆ of the zodiac.

**devil:** Another term for Lucifer.

**dragon:** As used in the Apocalypse of John, there are different appearances of the dragon, each one representing an adversarial being opposed to Michael, Christ, and Sophia. For example, the great red dragon of chapter 12 opposes Sophia, the woman clothed with the Sun (Sophia is the pure Divine-Cosmic Feminine Soul of the World). The imagery from chapter 12 of Revelation depicts the woman clothed with the Sun as pregnant and that the great red dragon attempts to devour her child as soon as it is born. The child coming to birth from the woman clothed with the Sun represents the Divine-Cosmic "I AM" born through the assistance of the pure Divine Feminine Soul of the World. The dragon is cast down from the heavenly realm by the mighty Archangel Michael. Cast down to the Earth, the dragon continues with attempts to devour the cosmic child (the Divine-Cosmic "I AM") coming to birth among humankind.

**ego:** The soul sheath through which the "I" begins to incarnate and to experience life on Earth (to be distinguished from the term *ego* used in Freudian and Jungian psychology). The terms *"I,"* and *soul* are sometimes used interchangeably in Spiritual Science. The ego maintains threads of integrity and continuity through memory, while experiencing new sensations and perceptions through observation and thinking, feeling, and willing. The ego is capable of moral discernment and also experiences temptation. Thus, it is often stated that the "I" comprises both a higher nature and the lower nature ("ego").

**Emmerich, Anne Catherine** (also "Sister Emmerich"): A Catholic stigmatist (1774–1824) whose visions depicted the daily life of Jesus, beginning some weeks before the event of the descent of Christ into the body of Jesus at the Baptism in the River Jordan and extending for a period of several weeks after the Crucifixion.

**Ephesus:** The area in Asia Minor (now Turkey) to which the Apostle John (also called John Zebedee, the brother of James the Greater) accompanied the Virgin Mary approximately three years after the death of Jesus Christ. Ephesus was a very significant ancient mystery center where cosmic mysteries of the East found their way into the West. Initiates at Ephesus were devoted to the goddess Artemis, known as "Artemis of Ephesus," whose qualities are more those of a Mother goddess than is the case with the Greek goddess Artemis, although there is a certain degree of overlap between Artemis and Artemis of Ephesus with regard to many of their respective characteristics. A magnificent Ionic mystery temple was built in honor of Artemis of Ephesus at a location close to the Aegean Sea. Mary's house, built by John, was located high up above, on the nearby hill known as Mount Nightingale, about six miles from the temple of Artemis at Ephesus.

**etheric body:** The body of life forces permeating and animating the physical body. The etheric body was formed during ancient Sun evolution. The etheric body's activity is expressed in the seven life processes permeating the seven vital organs. The etheric body is related to the movements of the seven visible planets.

**Fall, The:** A fall from oneness with spiritual worlds. The Fall, which took place during the Lemurian period of Earth evolution, was a time of dramatic transition in human evolution when the soul descended from "Paradise" into earthly existence. Through the Fall the human soul began to incarnate into a physical body upon the Earth and experience the world from "within" the body, perceiving through the senses.

**Fifth Gospel:** The writings and lectures of Rudolf Steiner based on new spiritual perceptions and insights into the mysteries of Christ's life on Earth, including the Second Coming of Christ— his appearance in the etheric realm in our time, beginning in the twentieth century.

**Golgotha, Mystery of:** Rudolf Steiner's designation for the entire mystery of the coming of Christ to the Earth. Sometimes this term is used more specifically to refer to the events surrounding the Crucifixion and Resurrection. In particular, the Crucifixion—the sacrifice on the cross— marked the birth of Christ's union with the Earth. Also referred to as the "Turning Point of Time," whereby at the Crucifixion Christ descended from the sphere of the Sun and became the "Spirit of the Earth."

**Grail:** An etheric chalice into which Christ can work to transform earthly substance into spiritual substance. The term *Grail* has many deep levels of meaning and refers on the one hand to a spiritual stream in service of Christ, and on the other hand to the means by which the human "I" penetrates and transforms evil into good. The power of transubstantiation expresses something of this process of transformation of evil into good.

**Grail Knights:** Those trained to confront evil and transform it into something good, in service of Christ. Members of a spiritual stream that existed in the past and continues to exist— albeit in metamorphosed form—in the present. Every human being striving for the good can potentially become a Grail Knight.

**I AM:** One's true individuality, that—with few exceptions—never fully incarnates but works into the developing "I" and its lower bodies (astral, etheric, and physical). The **Cosmic I AM** is the "I AM" of Christ, through which— on account of the Mystery of Golgotha—we are all graced with the possibility of receiving a divine spark therefrom.

**Jesus** (see Nathan Jesus and Solomon Jesus): The pure human being who received the Christ at the Baptism in the River Jordan.

**Jesus Christ:** The Divine-Human being; the God-Man; the union of the Divine with the Human. The presence of the Cosmic Christ in the physical body of the human being called the Nathan Jesus during the 3½ years of the ministry.

**Jesus of Nazareth:** The name of the human being whose birth is celebrated in the Gospel of Luke, also referred to as the Nathan Jesus. When Jesus of Nazareth reached the age of twelve, the spirit of the Solomon Jesus (Gospel of Matthew) united with the body and sheaths of the pure Nathan Jesus. This union lasted for about 18 years, until the Baptism in the River Jordan. During these eighteen years, Jesus of Nazareth was a composite being comprising the Nathan Jesus and the spirit ("I") of the Solomon Jesus. Just before the Baptism, the spirit of the Solomon Jesus withdrew, and at the Baptism Jesus became known as "Jesus Christ" through the union of Christ with the sheaths of Jesus.

**Jezebel:** Wife of King Ahab, approximately 900 BC, who worked through the powers of black magic against the prophet Elijah.

**Kali Yuga:** Yugas are ages of influence referred to in Hindu cosmography, each yuga lasting a certain numbers of years in length (always a multiple of 2,500). The Kali Yuga is also known as the Dark Age, which began with the death of Krishna in 3102 BC (-3101). Kali Yuga lasted 5,000 years and ended in AD 1899.

**Kingly Stream:** Biblically, the line of heredity from King David into which the Solomon Jesus (Gospel of Matthew) was born. The kings (the three magi) were initiates who sought to bring the cosmic will of the heavenly Father to expression on the Earth through spiritual forces working from spiritual beings dwelling in the stars. The minds of the wise kings were enlightened by the coming of Jesus Christ.

**Krishna:** A cosmic-human being, the sister soul of Adam that overlighted Arjuna as described in the Bhagavad Gita. The overlighting by Krishna of Arjuna could be described as an incorporation of Krishna into Arjuna. An incorporation is a partial incarnation. The cosmic-human being known as Krishna later fully incarnated as Jesus of Nazareth (Nathan Jesus—Gospel of Luke).

**Lazarus:** The elder brother of Mary Magdalene, Martha, and Silent Mary. At his raising from the dead, Lazarus became the first human being to be fully initiated by Christ (see Lazarus–John).

**Lazarus–John:** At the raising of Lazarus from the dead by Christ, the spiritual being of John the Baptist united with Lazarus. The higher spiritual members of John (spirit body, life spirit, spirit self) entered into the members of Lazarus, which were developed to the level of the consciousness soul.

**Lucifer:** The name of a fallen spiritual being, also called the Light-Bearer, who acts as a retarding force within the human astral body and also in the sentient soul. Lucifer inflames egoism and pride within the human being, often inspiring genius and supreme artistry. Arrogance and self-importance are stimulated, without humility or sacrificial love. Lucifer stirs up forces of rebellion, but cannot deliver true freedom—just its illusion.

**luciferic beings:** Spiritual beings who have become agents of Lucifer's influences.

**magi:** Initiates in the mystery school of Zarathustra, the Bodhisattva who incarnated as Zoroaster (Zaratas, Nazaratos) in the sixth century BC and who, after he came to Babylon, became a teacher of the Chaldean priesthood. At the time of Jesus, the magi were still continuing the star-gazing tradition of the school of Zoroaster. The task of the magi was to recognize when their master would reincarnate. With their visit to the newborn Jesus child in Bethlehem (Gospel of Matthew), to this child who was the reincarnated Zarathustra–Zoroaster, they fulfilled their mission. The three magi are the "priest kings from the East" referred to in the Gospel of Matthew.

**Maitreya Bodhisattva:** The bodhisattva individuality that is preparing to become the successor of Gautama Buddha and will be known as the Bringer of the Good. This bodhisattva was incarnated in the second century BC as Jeshu ben Pandira, the teacher of the Essenes, who died about 100 BC. Rudolf Steiner indicated that Jeshu ben Pandira reincarnated at the beginning of the twentieth century as a great bodhisattva individuality to fulfill the lofty mission of proclaiming Christ's coming in the etheric realm, beginning around 1933: "He will be the actual herald of Christ in his etheric form" (lecture about Jeshu ben Pandira held in Leipzig on November 4, 1911). There are differing points of view as to who this individuality actually was in his twentieth century incarnation.

**manas:** Also called the spirit self; the purified astral body, lifted into full communion with truth and goodness by becoming the true and the good within the essence of the higher self of the human being. Manas is the spiritual source of the "I," and as it is the eternal part of the human being that goes from life to life, manas bears the human being's true "eternal name" through its union with the Holy Spirit. The "eternal name" expresses the human being's true mission from life to life.

**Mani:** The name of a lofty initiate who lived in Babylon in the third century AD. The founder of the Manichean stream, whose mission is the transformation of evil into goodness through compassion and love. Mani reincarnated as Parzival in the ninth century AD. Mani–Parzival is one of the leading initiates of our present age—the age of the consciousness soul (AD 1414–3574). One of the highest beings ever to incarnate upon the Earth, he will become the future Manu beginning in the astrological age of Sagittarius. This future Manu will oversee the spiritual evolution of a sequence of seven ages, comprising the seven cultural epochs of the Sixth Great Age of Earth evolution from the Age of Sagittarius to the Age of Gemini—lasting a total of 7 x 2,160 years (15,120 years), since each zodiacal age lasts 2,160 years.

**Manu:** Like the word Buddha, the word Manu is a title. A Manu has the task of spiritually overseeing one Great Age of Earth evolution, comprising seven astrological ages (seven cultural epochs)—lasting a total of 7 x 2,160 years (15,120 years), since each zodiacal age lasts 2,160 years. The present Age of Pisces (AD 215–2375)—with its corresponding cultural epoch (AD 1414–3574)—is the fifth epoch during the Fifth Great Age of Earth evolution. (Lemuria was the Third Great Age, Atlantis the Fourth Great Age, and since the great flood that destroyed Atlantis, we are now in the Fifth Great Age.) The present Manu is the exalted Sun-initiate who guided humanity out of Atlantis during the ancient flooding that destroyed the continent of Atlantis formerly in the region of the Atlantic Ocean—the Flood referred to in the Bible in connection with Noah. He is the overseer of the seven cultural epochs corresponding to the seven astrological ages from the Age of Cancer to the Age of Capricorn, following the sequence: Cancer, Gemini, Taurus, Aries, Pisces, Aquarius, Capricorn. The present Manu was the teacher of the Seven Holy Rishis who were the founders of the ancient Indian cultural epoch (7227–5067 BC) during the Age of Cancer. He is known in the Bible as Noah, and in the Flood story belonging to the Gilgamesh epic he is called Utnapishtim. Subsequently this Manu appeared to Abraham as Melchizedek and offered Abraham an agape ("love feast") of bread and wine. Jesus "was designated by God to be high priest in the order of Melchizedek" (Heb. 5:10).

**Mary:** Rudolf Steiner distinguishes between the Nathan Mary and the Solomon Mary (see corresponding entries). The expression "Virgin Mary" refers to the Solomon Mary, the mother of the child Jesus whose birth is described in the Gospel of Matthew.

**Mary Magdalene:** Sister of Lazarus, whose soul was transformed and purified as Christ cast out seven demons who had taken possession of her. Christ thus initiated Mary Magdalene. Later, she anointed Jesus Christ. And she was the first to behold the Risen Christ in the Garden of the Holy Sepulcher on the morning of his resurrection.

**megastar:** Stars with a luminosity greater than 10,000 times that of our Sun.

**Nain, Youth of:** Referred to in the Gospel of Luke as the son of the widow of Nain. The Youth of Nain—at the time he was twelve years old—was raised from the dead by Jesus. The Youth of Nain later reincarnated as the Prophet Mani (third century AD) and subsequently as the Grail King Parzival (ninth century AD).

**Nathan Jesus:** From the priestly line of David, as described in the Gospel of Luke. An immaculate and pure soul whose one and only physical incarnation was as Jesus of Nazareth (Nathan Jesus).

**Nathan Mary:** A pure being who was the mother of the Nathan Jesus. The Nathan Mary died in AD 12, but her spirit united with the Solomon Mary at the time of the Baptism of Jesus in the River Jordan. From this time on, the Solomon Mary—spiritually united with the Nathan Mary—was known as the Virgin Mary.

**New Jerusalem:** A spiritual condition denoting humanity's future existence that will come into being as human beings free themselves from the *maya* of the material world and work together to bring about a spiritualized Earth.

**Osiris:** *Osiris* and *Isis* are names given by the Egyptians to the preincarnatory forms of the spiritual beings who are now known as Christ and Sophia.

**Parzival:** Son of Gahmuret and Herzeloyde in the epic *Parzival* by Wolfram von Eschenbach. Although written in the thirteenth century, this work refers to actual people and events in the ninth century AD, one of whom (the central figure) bore the name Parzival. After living a life of dullness and doubt, Parzival's mission was to seek the Castle of the Grail and to ask the question "What ails thee?" of the Grail King, Anfortas—moreover, to ask the question without being bidden to do so. Parzival eventually became the new Grail King, the successor of Anfortas. Parzival was the reincarnated prophet Mani. In the incarnation preceding that of Mani, he was incarnated as the Youth of Nain (Luke 7:11–15). Parzival is a great initiate responsible for guiding humanity during the Age of Pisces, which has given birth to the cultural epoch of the development of the consciousness soul (AD 1414–3574).

**Pentecost:** Descent of the Holy Spirit fifty days after Easter, whereby the cosmic "I AM" was birthed among the disciples and those individuals close to Christ. They received the capacity to develop manas, or spirit self, within the community of striving human individuals, whereby the birth of the spirit self is facilitated through the soul of the Virgin Mary. See also World Pentecost.

**phantom body:** The pure spiritual form of the human physical body, unhindered by matter.

The far-distant future state of the human physical body when it has become purified and spiritualized into a body of transformed divine will.

**Presbyter John:** Refers to Lazarus–John who moved to Ephesus about twenty years after the Virgin Mary had died there. In Ephesus he became a bishop. He is the author of the book of Revelation, the Gospel of St. John, and the Letters of John.

**Risen One:** The initial appearance of Christ in his phantom body (resurrection body), beginning with his appearance to Mary Magdalene on Easter Sunday morning. Christ frequently appeared to the disciples in his phantom body during the forty days leading from Easter to Ascension.

**Satan:** The traditional Christian name for Ahriman.

**Serpent:** Another name for Lucifer, but sometimes naming a combination of Lucifer and Ahriman: "The great dragon was hurled down—that ancient serpent called the devil, or Satan, who leads the whole world astray" (Rev. 12:9).

**Shepherd Stream:** Biblically, the genealogical line from David the shepherd through his son Nathan. It was into this line that the Nathan Jesus was born, whose birth is described in the Gospel of Luke. Rudolf Steiner describes the shepherds, who—according to Luke—came to pay homage to the newborn child, as those servants of pure heart who perceive the goodwill streaming up from Mother Earth. The hearts of the shepherds were kindled with the fire of Divine Love by the coming of the Christ. The shepherds can be regarded as precursors of the heart stream of humanity that now intuits the being of Christ as the spirit of the Earth.

**Solomon Jesus:** Descended from the genealogical line from David through his son Solomon. This line of descent is described in the Gospel of Matthew. The Solomon Jesus was a reincarnation of Zoroaster (sixth century BC). In turn, Zoroaster was a reincarnation of Zarathustra (6000 BC), the great prophet and founder of the ancient Persian religion of Zoroastrianism. He was a bodhisattva who, as the founder of this new religion that focused on the Sun Spirit Ahura Mazda, helped prepare humanity for the subsequent descent into incarnation of Ahura Mazda, the cosmic Sun Spirit, as Christ.

**Solomon Mary:** The wise mother of the Solomon Jesus, who adopted the Nathan Jesus after the death of the Nathan Mary. At the time of the Baptism of Jesus in the River Jordan, the spirit of the Nathan Mary united with the Solomon Mary. Usually referred to as the Virgin Mary or Mother Mary, the Solomon Mary bore witness at the foot of the cross to the Mystery of Golgotha. She died in Ephesus eleven years after Christ's Ascension.

**Sophia:** Part of the Divine Feminine Trinity comprising the Mother (counterpart of the Father), the Daughter (counterpart of the Son), and the Holy Soul (counterpart of the Holy Spirit). Sophia, also known as the Bride of the Lamb, is the Daughter aspect of the threefold Divine Feminine Trinity. To the Egyptians Sophia was known as Isis, who was seen as belonging to the starry realm surrounding the Earth. In the Book of Proverbs, attributed to King Solomon, Sophia's temple has seven pillars (Proverbs 9:1). The seven pillars in Sophia's temple represent the seven great stages of Earth evolution (from ancient Saturn to future Vulcan).

**Sorath:** The great enemy of Christ who works against the "I" in the human being. Sorath is identified with the two-horned beast that rises up from the depths of Earth, as described in the book of Revelation. Sorath is the Sun Demon, and is identified by Rudolf Steiner as the Antichrist. According to the book of Revelation, his number is 666.

**Sun Demon:** Another name for Sorath.

**Transfiguration:** The event on Mt. Tabor where Jesus Christ was illumined with Divine Light raying forth from the purified etheric body of Jesus, which the Divine "I AM" of Christ had penetrated. The Gospels of Matthew and Luke describe the Transfiguration. The sun-like radiance that shone forth from Jesus Christ on Mt. Tabor was an expression of the purified etheric body that had its origin during the Old Sun period of Earth evolution.

**Transubstantiation:** Sacramental transformation of physical substance—for example, the transubstantiation of bread and wine during the Mass to become the body and blood of Christ. During the Holy Eucharist the bread and wine are transformed in such a way that the substances of bread and wine are infused with the life force (body) and light (blood) of Christ. Thereby the bread and wine are reunited with their divine archetypes and are no longer "merely" physical substances, but are bearers on the physical level of a spiritual reality.

**Turning Point of Time:** Transition between involution and evolution, as marked by the Mystery of Golgotha. The descending stream of involution culminated with the Mystery of Golgotha. With the descent of the Cosmic Christ into earthly evolution, through his sacrifice on Golgotha an ascending stream of evolution began. This sacrifice of Christ was followed by the events of his Resurrection and Ascension, which were followed in turn by Whitsun (Pentecost)—all expressing the ascending stream of evolution. This path of ascent was also opened up to all human beings by way of the power of the divine "I AM" bestowed—at least, potentially—on all humanity by Christ through his sacrifice on the cross.

**Union in the Temple:** The event of the union of the spirit of the Solomon Jesus with the twelve-year-old Nathan Jesus. This union of the two Jesus children signified the uniting of the priestly (Nathan) line and the kingly (Solomon) line—both lines descended from King David.

**Whitsun:** "White Sunday"; Pentecost.

**World Pentecost** is the gradual event of cosmic revelation becoming human revelation as a signature of the end of the Dark Age (Kali Yuga). Anthroposophy (Spiritual Science) is a language of spiritual truth that could awake a community of striving human beings to the presence of the Holy Spirit and the founding of the New Jerusalem.

**Zarathustra:** The great teacher of the ancient Persians in the sixth millennium BC (around 6000 BC). In the sixth century BC, Zarathustra reincarnated as Zoroaster. He then reincarnated as the Solomon Jesus (6 BC–AD 12), whose birth is described in the Gospel of Matthew.

**Zoroaster:** An incarnation of Zarathustra. Zarathustra–Zoroaster was a Bodhisattva. Zoroaster lived in the sixth century BC. He was a master of wisdom. Among his communications as a teacher of wisdom was his specification as to how the zodiac of living beings in the heavens comes to expression in relation to the stars comprising the twelve zodiacal constellations. Zoroaster subsequently incarnated as the Solomon Jesus, whose birth is described in the Gospel of Matthew, to whom the three magi came from the East bearing gifts of gold, frankincense, and myrrh.

"It became clearer and clearer to me—as the outcome of many years of research—that in our epoch there is really something like a resurrection of the Astrology of the third epoch [the Egyptian–Babylonian period], but permeated now with the Christ Impulse. Today, we must search among the stars in a way different from the old ways. The stellar script must once more become something that speaks to us."

—RUDOLF STEINER (*Christ and the Spiritual World
and the Search for the Holy Grail,* p. 106)

"In Palestine during the time that Jesus of Nazareth walked on Earth as Jesus Christ—during the three years of his life, from his thirtieth to his thirty-third year—the entire being of the cosmic Christ was acting uninterruptedly upon him, and was working into him. The Christ stood always under the influence of the entire cosmos; he made no step without this working of the cosmic forces into and in him....It was always in accordance with the collective being of the whole universe with whom the Earth is in harmony, that all which Jesus Christ did took place."

—RUDOLF STEINER (*Spiritual Guidance of Man and Humanity,* p. 66)

# BIBLIOGRAPHY AND RELATED READING

*See "Literature" on page 10 for an annotated list of books on Astrosophy.*


Andreev, Daniel. *The Rose of the World.* Grt. Barrington, MA: Lindisfarne Books, 1997.

Anklesaria, Ervad Tahmras Dinshaji. *The Bundahisn.* Bombay, 1908.

Anonymous. *The Glories of the Virgin Mother, and Channel of Divine Grace.* Boston: Donahoe, 1867.

Anonymous. *Meditations on the Tarot: A Journey into Christian Hermeticism.* New York: Putman, 2002.

Anonymous. *The Wandering Fool: Love and Its Symbols.* San Rafael, CA: LogoSophia, 2009.

Apian, Peter. *Cosmographia,* Antwerp, 1524.

Augustine, *Enchiridion.*

Bamford, Christopher. *Healing Madonnas: Exploring the Sequence of Madonna Images Created by Rudolf Steiner and Felix Peipers for Use in Therapy and Meditation.* Grt. Barrington, MA: Lindisfarne Books, 2017.

Barfield, Owen. *Poetic Diction: A Study in Meaning.* Oxford, UK: Barfield Press, 2010.

———. *Saving the Appearances: A Study in Idolatry.* Middletown, CT: Wesleyan University Press, 1988.

Bock, Emil. *Threefold Mary.* Grt. Barrington, MA: SteinerBooks, 2003.

Bosse, Dankmar. *The Mutual Evolution of Earth and Humanity: Sketch of a Geology and Paleontology of the Living Earth.* Hudson, NY: Lindisfarne Books, 2019.

Bulgakov, Sergei. *Sophia: The Wisdom of God: An Outline of Sophiology.* Hudson, NY: Lindisfarne Books, 1993.

Campbell, Joseph (ed.). *Man and Time: Papers from the Eranos Yearbooks.* Princeton, NJ: Princeton University, 1983.

de Lille, Alain (Alanus ab Insulis). *The Complaint of Nature.* New Haven CT: Yale University, 1972.

Dorsan, Jacques. *The Clockwise House System: A True Foundation for Sidereal and Tropical Astrology.* Grt. Barrington, MA: Lindisfarne Books, 2011.

Douglass, James W. *JFK and the Unspeakable: Why He Died and Why It Matters.* New York: Touchstone, 2008.

Emberson, Paul. *From Gondishapur to Silicon Valley.* Edinburgh, UK: Etheric Dimensions Press, 2009.

Emmerich, Anne Catherine. *Visions of the Life of Christ* (3 vols.). Kettering, OH: Angelico Press, 2015.

Gray, Brian. *Discovering the Zodiac in the Raphael Madonna Series.* Stourbridge, UK: Wynstones Press, 2017.

Greub, Werner. *How the Grail Sites Were Found.* Amsterdam: Willehalm Institute, 2013.

Griffin, David Ray (ed.). *Archetypal Process: Self and Divine in Whitehead, Jung, and Hillman.* Evanston, IL: Northwestern University, 1989.

Hauschka, Rudolf. *The Nature of Substance: Spirit and Matter.* Forest Row, UK: Rudolf Steiner Press, 2003.

Hillman, James. *Re-Visioning Psychology.* New York: Harper Perennial, 1992.

Isaacson, Estelle. *Through the Eyes of Mary Magdalene,* 3 vols. Taos, NM: LogoSophia, 2012–2015.

Jung, Carl Gustav. "The Psychology of the Child Archetype." In *The Archetypes and the Collective Unconscious: Collected Works of Carl Gustav Jung* (tr. by R. F. C. Hull). Princeton, NJ: Princeton University, 1940.

Kennedy, E. S., and David Pingree (eds.). *The Astrological History of Masha'allah.* Cambridge, MA: Harvard University, 1971.

Krisciunas, Kevin, and Bill Yenne. *The Pictorial Atlas of the Universe.* New York: BDD, 1989.

Manilius. *Astronomica.* Cambridge, MA: Harvard University, 1977.

Maxwell, Grant. "Archetype and Eternal Object: Jung, Whitehead, and the Return of Formal Causation." *Archai: The Journal of Archetypal Cosmology* 3 (2011): 51–71.

McAllen, Audrey. *The Listening Ear: The Development of Speech as a Creative Influence in Education.* Fair Oaks, CA: Rudolf Steiner College Press, 1990.

McLaren Lainson, Claudia. *The Circle of Twelve and the Legacy of Valentin Tomberg.* Boulder: Windrose Academy, 2015.

Poppelbaum, Hermann. *A New Zoology.* Dornach, Switzerland: Philosophic–Anthroposophic Press, 1961.

Powell, Robert. *The Christ Mystery.* Fair Oaks, CA: Rudolf Steiner College, 1999.

———. *Christian Hermetic Astrology: The Star of the Magi and the Life of Christ.* Grt. Barrington, MA: Lindisfarne Books, 2009.

———. *Chronicle of the Living Christ: The Life and Ministry of Jesus Christ: Foundations of Cosmic Christianity.* Hudson, NY: Anthroposophic Press, 1996.

———. *Cultivating Inner Radiance and the Body of Immortality: Awakening the Soul through Modern Etheric Movement.* Grt. Barrington, MA: Lindisfarne Books, 2012.

———. *Elijah Come Again: A Prophet for Our Time: A Scientific Approach to Reincarnation.* Grt. Barrington, MA: Lindisfarne Books, 2009.

———. *Hermetic Astrology,* vols. 1 and 2. San Rafael, CA: Sophia Foundation Press, 2006.

———. *History of the Zodiac.* San Rafael, CA: Sophia Academic Press, 2007.

———. *The Most Holy Trinosophia: The New Revelation of the Divine Feminine.* Grt. Barrington, MA: SteinerBooks, 2000.

———. *The Mystery, Biography, and Destiny of Mary Magdalene: Sister of Lazarus–John and Spiritual Sister of Jesus.* Grt. Barrington, MA: Lindisfarne Books, 2008.

———. *Prophecy-Phenomena-Hope: The Real Meaning of the year 2012.* Grt. Barrington, MA: SteinerBooks, 2011.

———. *The Sign of the Son of Man in Heaven.* San Rafael, CA: Sophia Foundation, 2007.

———. *The Sophia Teachings: The Emergence of the Divine Feminine in Our Time.* Grt. Barrington, MA: Lindisfarne Books, 2007.

Powell, Robert, and David Bowden. *Astrogeographia: Correspondences between the Stars and Earthly Locations: Earth Chakras and the Bible of Astrology.* Grt. Barrington, MA: SteinerBooks, 2012.

Powell, Robert, and Kevin Dann. *The Astrological Revolution: Unveiling the Science of the Stars as a Science of Reincarnation and Karma.* Grt. Barrington, MA: SteinerBooks, 2010.

———. *Christ and the Maya Calendar: 2012 and the Coming of the Antichrist.* Grt. Barrington, MA. SteinerBooks, 2009.

Powell, Robert, and Estelle Isaacson. *Gautama Buddha's Successor: A Force for Good in our Time.* Grt. Barrington, MA: SteinerBooks, 2013.

———. *The Mystery of Sophia: Bearer of the New Culture: The Rose of the World.* Grt. Barrington, MA: SteinerBooks, 2014.

Powell, Robert, and Lacquanna Paul. *Cosmic Dances of the Planets.* San Rafael, CA: Sophia Foundation Press, 2006.

Powell, Robert, and Peter Treadgold. *The Sidereal Zodiac.* Tempe, AZ: AFA, 1985.

Querido, René. *The Golden Age of Chartres: The Teachings of a Mystery School and the Eternal Feminine.* Edinburgh, UK: Floris Books, 2008.

Richey, Margaret Fitzgerald. *Studies of Wolfram von Eschenbach.* London: Oliver and Boyd, 1957.

Schilpp, Paul Arthur (ed.). *The Philosophy of Alfred North Whitehead.* La Salle, IL: Open Court, 1951.

Solovyov, Vladimir. *War, Progress, and the End of History: Three Conversations, Including a Short Tale of the Antichrist.* Hudson, NY: Anthroposophic Press, 1990.

Steiner, Rudolf. *The Ahrimanic Deception.* Forest Row, UK: Rudolf Steiner Press, 1985.

———. *Ancient Myths and the New Isis Mystery* (rev. 2nd ed.). Grt. Barrington, MA: SteinerBooks, 2018.

———. *Anthroposophy in Everyday Life: Practical Training in Thought – Overcoming Nervousness – Facing Karma – The Four Temperaments.* Hudson, NY: Anthroposophic Press, 1995.

———. *The Apocalypse of St. John: Lectures on the Book of Revelation.* Hudson, NY: Anthroposophic Press, 1985.

———. *Astronomy and Astrology: Finding a Relationship to the Cosmos.* Forest Row, UK: Rudolf Steiner Press, 2009.

———. *Autobiography: Chapters in the Course of My Life, 1861–1907.* Grt. Barrington, MA: SteinerBooks, 2000,

———. *The Book of Revelation: And the Work of the Priest.* Forest Row, UK: Rudolf Steiner Press, 2008.

———. *Calendar 1912–1913: Facsimile Edition of the Original Book Containing the Calendar Created by Rudolf Steiner for the Year 1912–1913.* Grt. Barrington, MA: SteinerBooks, 2004.

———. *The Challenge of the Times.* Spring Valley, NY: Anthroposophic Press, 1941.

———. *Christ and the Spiritual World and the Search for the Holy Grail.* Forest Row, UK: Rudolf Steiner Press, 1963.

———. *Esoteric Christianity and the Mission of Christian Rosenkreutz.* Forest Row, UK: Rudolf Steiner Press, 2001.

———. *An Esoteric Cosmology: Evolution, Christ, and Modern Spirituality.* Grt. Barrington, MA: SteinerBooks, 2008.

———. *Esoteric Lessons, 1913–1923: From the Esoteric School,* vol. 3. Grt. Barrington, MA: SteinerBooks, 2008.

———. *The Fifth Gospel: From the Akashic Record.* Forest Row, UK: Rudolf Steiner Press, 1993.

———. *The Four Seasons and the Archangels: Experience of the Course of the Year in Four Cosmic Imaginations.* Forest Row, UK: Rudolf Steiner Press, 2002.

———. *From Crystals to Crocodiles…: Answers to Questions.* Forest Row, UK: Rudolf Steiner Press, 2002.

———. *From Elephants to Einstein...: Answers to Questions.* Forest Row, UK: Rudolf Steiner Press, 1998.

———. *How to Know Higher Worlds: A Modern Path of Initiation.* Hudson, NY: Anthroposophic Press, 1994.

———. *Human and Cosmic Thought.* Forest Row, UK: Rudolf Steiner Press, 2015.

———. *The Incarnation of Ahriman: The Embodiment of Evil on Earth.* Forest Row, UK: Rudolf Steiner Press, 2009.

———. *Isis Mary Sophia: Her Mission and Ours* (Selected Lectures and Writings). Grt. Barrington, MA: Rudolf Steiner Press, 2003.

———. *Karmic Relationships: Esoteric Studies,* 8 vols. Forest Row, UK: Rudolf Steiner Press, 1972–2017.

———. *The Knights Templar: Influences from the Past and Impulses for the Future.* Forest Row, UK: Rudolf Steiner Press, 2007.

———. *Materialism and the Task of Anthroposophy.* Hudson, NY: Anthroposophic Press, 1987.

———. *Life between Death and Rebirth.* Hudson, NY: Anthroposophic Press, 1975.

———. *The Mysteries of the East and of Christianity.* Blauvelt, NY: Garber, 1989.

———. *Mystery of the Universe: The Human Being, Model of Creation.* Forest Row, UK: Rudolf Steiner Press, 2001.

———. *Occult Physiology.* Forest Row, UK: Rudolf Steiner Press, 1983.

———. *An Outline of Esoteric Science.* Hudson, NY: Anthroposophic Press, 1997.

———. *The Search for the New Isis.* Spring Valley, NY: Mercury Press, 1983.

———. *The Spiritual Foundation of Morality: Francis of Assisi and the Christ Impulse.* Hudson, NY: Anthroposophic Press, 1995.

———. *Spiritual Guidance of the Individual and Humanity: Some Results of Spiritual-Scientific Research into Human History and Development.* Hudson, NY: Anthroposophic Press, 1991.

———. *The Sun Mystery and the Mystery of Death and Resurrection: Exoteric and Esoteric Christianity.* Grt. Barrington, MA: SteinerBooks, 2006.

———. *True and False Paths in Spiritual Investigation.* London: Rudolf Steiner Press, 1969.

———. *The True Nature of the Second Coming.* Forest Row, UK: Rudolf Steiner Press, 1971.

———. *Twelve Moods.* Spring Valley, NY: Mercury Press, 1984.

———. *Universal Spirituality and Human Physicality: Bridging the Divide: The Search for the New Isis and the Divine Sophia.* Forest Row, UK: Rudolf Steiner Press, 2014.

Sucher, Willi. *The Drama of the Universe.* Larkfield, UK: Landvidi Research Centre, 1958.

———. *Isis Sophia I: Introducing Astrosophy.* Meadow Vista, CA: Astrosophy Research Center, 1999.

———. *Isis Sophia II: An Outline of a New Star Wisdom.* Meadow Vista, CA: Astrosophy Research Center, 1985.

Tarnas, Richard. *Cosmos and Psyche: Intimations of a New World View.* New York: Plume, 2007.

Tomberg, Valentin. *Christ and Sophia: Anthroposophic Meditations on the Old Testament, New Testament, and Apocalypse.* Grt. Barrington, MA: SteinerBooks, 2006.

———. *Studies on the Foundation Stone Meditation.* San Rafael, CA: LogoSophia, 2010.

Upton-Ward, J. M. *The Rule of the Templars.* London: Boydell, 1992.

von Eschenbach, Wolfram. *Parzival: A Romance of the Middle Ages* (tr. by H. M. Mustard and C. E. Passage). New York: Vintage, 1961.

von Halle, Judith. *Descent into the Depths of the Earth on the Anthroposophic Path of Schooling.* Forest Row, UK: Temple Lodge Press, 2011.

———. *Secrets of the Stations of the Cross and the Grail Blood: The Mystery of Transformation.* Forest Row, UK: Temple Lodge Press, 2007.

von Eschenbach, Wolfram. *Parzival.* London; David Nutt, 1894.

———. *Parzival.* London; Penguin Classics, 1980.

Vreede, Elisabeth. *Astronomy and Spiritual Science: The Astronomical Letters of Elisabeth Vreede.* Grt. Barrington, MA: SteinerBooks, 2007.

Whitehead, Alfred North. "Autobiographical Notes," in Paul Arthur Schilpp (ed.). *The Philosophy of Alfred North Whitehead.* La Salle, IL: Open Court, 1951.

———. *Process and Reality.* New York: Free Press, 1985.

Yenne, Bill, and Kevin Krisciunas. *The Pictorial Atlas of the Universe.* New York: BDD, 1989.

# ABOUT THE CONTRIBUTORS

**DAVID BOWDEN** is a teacher of phenomenological physics and projective geometry and has taught at Orana School for Rudolf Steiner Education in Canberra, and the Mount Barker Waldorf School in Adelaide, Australia. He originally trained in electronics and telecommunications and is currently a researcher and a teacher of projective geometry and the new Goethean physics.

**KEVIN DANN**, PhD, has taught history at SUNY Plattsburgh, the University of Vermont, and Rutgers University. His books include *Bright Colors Falsely Seen* (1998); *Across the Great Border Fault* (2000); *Lewis Creek Lost and Found* (2001); *A Short Story of American Destiny, 1909–2009* (2008); and (with Robert Powell) *Christ & the Maya Calendar: 2012 & the Coming of the Antichrist* (2009) and *The Astrological Revolution: Unveiling the Science of the Stars as a Science of Reincarnation and Karma* (2010).

**JULIE HUMPHREYS** is a graduate of Stanford and a former pediatric nurse and Waldorf mom. An early interest in astrology lay dormant for more than three decades until she was introduced to the sidereal system, the works of Robert Powell, and the visions of Anne Catherine Emmerich. She has taken great joy in researching astrological phenomena for the *Journal for Star Wisdom*. Julie lives in Carmel, California, where shooting stars and the Milky Way are often visible.

**CLAUDIA MCLAREN LAINSON** is a teacher and Therapeutic Educator. She has been working in the field of Anthroposophy since 1982, when she founded her first Waldorf program in Boulder, Colorado. She lectures nationally on various topics related to Spiritual Science, human development, the evolution of consciousness and the emerging Christ and Sophia mysteries of the twenty-first century. Claudia is the founder of Windrose Farm and Academy near Boulder. Windrose is a biodynamic farm and academy for collaborative work in anthroposophic courses, therapeutic education, cosmic and sacred dance, and nature-based educational programs. Claudia most recently founded the School for the Sophia Mysteries at Windrose. She is the author of *The Circle of Twelve and the Legacy of Valentin Tomberg* (windroseacademypress.com).

**PHILLIP MALONE** practices Structural Integration in Peterborough, New Hampshire. He has been a student of Christian Hermeticism since 2001, with Rudolf Steiner and Valentin Tomberg being his primary influences. Currently he is engaged in a long-term meditative study of the *Tarot de Marseille*. He also enjoys singing in choirs, prayer eurythmy, basketball, and exploring cosmology.

**JOEL MATTHEW PARK** is a Hermeticist based in Copake, New York. From 2011 to 2019, he was a life-sharing coworker at Plowshare Farm (a Camphill affiliate), farming and candlemaking with people from a variety of countries, ages, and developmental backgrounds. During this time he earned a certification in Social Therapy from the School of Spiritual Science through the Camphill Academy. He is now, along with his wife Molly, householding in Ita Wegman, an elder-care house in Camphill Village Copake. Joel has been a student of Anthroposophy since 2008 and a Christian Hermeticist since 2010. In 2015, he joined the Grail Knighthood, a group spiritual practice offered through the Sophia Foundation. Through this, he met Robert Powell, whose work he had been studying since 2009. Since then, Joel has been actively working with him to continue the karma research Robert began in 1977, and exemplified in works such as *Hermetic Astrology,* volumes 1 and 2, and *Elijah, Come Again*. Joel has led two retreats on "Tarot and the Art of Hermetic Conversation" (2017 and 2019), and given talks on the karmic biography of Anfortas, the three essentials of Camphill," and the ideal social organism. Most recently he led courses on Astrological Biography and an exploration of Dieter Brull's "Creating Social Sacraments." His first contribution was to the *Journal for Star Wisdom* 2018, after which he became editor of the continuation of the journal, the *Star Wisdom* series. The first volume of this series was published in November 2018. A selection of his writings can be found on his website, "TreeHouse": www.treehouse.live.

**ROBERT POWELL**, PhD, is an internationally known lecturer, author, eurythmist, and movement therapist. He is founder of the Choreocosmos School of Cosmic and Sacred Dance, and cofounder of the Sophia Foundation of North America. He received his doctorate for his thesis *The History of the Zodiac,* available as a book from Sophia Academic Press. His published works include *The Sophia Teachings,* a six-tape series (Sounds True Recordings), as well as *Elijah Come Again: A Prophet for Our Time; The Mystery, Biography, and Destiny of Mary Madgalene; Divine Sophia—Holy Wisdom; The Most Holy Trinosophia and the New Revelation of the Divine Feminine; Chronicle of the Living Christ; Christian Hermetic Astrology; The Christ Mystery; The Sign of the Son of Man in the Heavens; Cultivating Inner Radiance and the Body of Immortality;* and the yearly *Journal for Star Wisdom* (previously *Christian Star Calendar*). He translated the spiritual classic *Meditations on the Tarot* and co-translated Valentin Tomberg's *Lazarus, Come Forth!* Robert is coauthor with David Bowden of *Astrogeographia: Correspondences between the Stars and Earthly Locations* and coauthor with Estelle Isaacson of *Gautama Buddha's Successor* and *The Mystery of Sophia.* Robert is also coauthor with Kevin Dann of *The Astrological Revolution: Unveiling the Science of the Stars as a Science of Reincarnation and Karma* and *Christ and the Maya Calendar: 2012 and the Coming of the Antichrist;* and coauthor with Lacquanna Paul of *Cosmic Dances of the Zodiac* and *Cosmic Dances of the Planets.* He teaches a gentle form of healing movement: the

sacred dance of eurythmy, as well as the Cosmic Dances of the Planets and signs of the zodiac. Through the Sophia Grail Circle, Robert facilitates sacred celebrations dedicated to the Divine Feminine. He offers workshops in Europe and Australia, and with Karen Rivers, cofounder of the Sophia Foundation, leads pilgrimages to the world's sacred sites: Turkey, 1996; the Holy Land, 1997; France, 1998; Britain, 2000; Italy, 2002; Greece, 2004; Egypt, 2006; India, 2008; Turkey, 2009; the Grand Canyon, 2010; South Africa, 2012; Peru, 2014; the Holy Land, 2016; and Bali, 2018. Visit www.sophiafoundation.org and www.astrogeographia.org.

**LUCIAN SCHLOSS** is a psychotherapist, astrologer and family constellation facilitator living in Oregon's Willamette Valley with his wife and three kids. He is a Waldorf graduate and has been studying Anthroposophy for the past 18 years. If you want to learn more about his work you can visit his website at www.lucianschlosscounseling.com or email him at lucianschloss@gmail.com.

**BECCA S. TARNAS**, PhD, is a scholar, artist, and editor of *Archai: The Journal of Archetypal Cosmology.* She received her doctorate in Philosophy and Religion from the California Institute of Integral Studies with her dissertation, *The Back of Beyond: The Red Books of C. G. Jung and J. R. R. Tolkien.* Becca received her BA from Mount Holyoke College in Environmental Studies and Theater Arts, and an MA in Philosophy, Cosmology, and Consciousness at CIIS. Her research interests include depth psychology, literature, philosophy, and the ecological imagination. She teaches in the Jungian Psychology and Archetypal Studies program at Pacifica Graduate Institute, and online for Nura Learning and PsicoCymática. Becca lives in Nevada City, California, where she has a private astrological counseling practice.

# *Exploring New Forms of Astrology*

## *Using the StarHouse as a training vessel for Astrosophy*

*Astrology is a tool that can reveal the wisdom in one's biography—the mystery of the triumphs and tragedies that belong to each individual.*

**WHEN**: Beginning Friday evening, **June 12, 2020**, and for succeeding days (different Parts A, B, and C explained at INFORMATION)

**WHERE: The StarHouse, Boulder**, Colorado (www.TheStarHouse.org)

## FOR WHOM: *Everyone seeking to understand one's personal biography and world events through anthroposophical astrology.*

## PRESENTERS:
- **Brian Gray,** teacher at Rudolf Steiner College for thirty-eight years, author of star wisdom articles (*Journal for Star Wisdom*) and presenter via internet videos (WiseCosmos.org)
- **Robert Schiappacasse,** for many years involved with the Waldorf school movement, author in star wisdom (*Journal for Star Wisdom*) and co-author of *Star Wisdom & Rudolf Steiner*
- **David Tresemer,** Ph.D., founder of StarHouse, author in star wisdom (*Journal for Star Wisdom* and other books), co-author of *Star Wisdom & Rudolf Steiner*

## MORE INFORMATION & Registration: *https://thestarhouse.net/star-wisdom/*

## You will learn:
- About the **foundations of western anthroposophical sidereal astrology**—*why* celestial events are important to human beings
- **Life stages**—the 7-year periods of a human biography and their relation to celestial events. Life stages are a good way into astrology, as you have very personal experiences of them!
- New and traditional **methods for interpreting birthcharts** and life events
- **Learning about yourself** by learning to read your own chart